SHAKESPEARE

THE CRITICAL HERITAGE

VOLUME 2 1693–1733

Edited by
BRIAN VICKERS
Professor of English, University of Zürich

ROUTLEDGE & KEGAN PAUL: LONDON AND BOSTON

First published in 1974
by Routledge & Kegan Paul Ltd
Broadway House, 68–74 Carter Lane
London EC4V 5EL and
9 Park Street
Boston, Mass. 02108, U.S.A.
© Brian Vickers 1974
No part of this book may be reproduced in
any form without permission from the
publisher, except for the quotation of brief
passages in criticism
ISBN 0 7100 7807 2
Library of Congress Catalog Card No. 73–85430

Printed in Great Britain by
Richard Clay (The Chaucer Press) Ltd
Bungay, Suffolk

FOR
PAT ROGERS

General Editor's Preface

The reception given to a writer by his contemporaries and near-contemporaries is evidence of considerable value to the student of literature. On one side we learn a great deal about the state of criticism at large and in particular about the development of critical attitudes towards a single writer; at the same time, through private comments in letters, journals or marginalia, we gain an insight upon the tastes and literary thought of individual readers of the period. Evidence of this kind helps us to understand the writer's historical situation, the nature of his immediate reading-public, and his response to these pressures.

The separate volumes in the *Critical Heritage Series* present a record of this early criticism. Clearly, for many of the highly productive and lengthily reviewed nineteenth- and twentieth-century writers, there exists an enormous body of material; and in these cases the volume editors have made a selection of the most important views, significant for their intrinsic critical worth or for their representative quality—perhaps even registering incomprehension!

For earlier writers, notably pre-eighteenth century, the materials are much scarcer and the historical period has been extended, sometimes far beyond the writer's lifetime, in order to show the inception and growth of critical views which were initially slow to appear.

Shakespeare is, in every sense, a special case, and Professor Vickers is presenting the course of his reception and reputation extensively over a span of three centuries, in a sequence of six volumes, each of which will document a specific period.

In each volume the documents are headed by an Introduction, discussing the material assembled and relating the early stages of the author's reception to what we have come to identify as the critical tradition. The volumes will make available much material which would otherwise be difficult of access and it is hoped that the modern reader will be thereby helped towards an informed understanding of the ways in which literature has been read and judged.

B.C.S.

Contents

CONTENTS

Preface

This collection includes material in four categories: literary criticism of Shakespeare; adaptations of his plays; theatrical criticism (both of the original texts and of the adaptations); textual criticism (the explanatory notes either appended to editions of his plays or issued separately).

Under the first heading there is little overall development in this period, while under the second there seems to have been a recession. The third is only just beginning to get under way, in the form of short appreciations of individual actors such as Betterton and Wilks and their roles: see, for instance, Nos 47, 48. Only in the fourth category, that of the editions, is there any notable move forward.

In preparing this volume I have been indebted, as ever, to the collections of the British Museum, the Bodleian, the Cambridge University Library, and the Birmingham Shakespeare Library. For the efficient and friendly help of the staff in all these institutions I am exceedingly grateful. I owe a special thanks to the Master and Fellows of Trinity College, Cambridge, for giving me permission to reprint Warburton's annotations in his copy of Theobald's edition, from the Capell library.

I am grateful to Mr Ian Thomson for verifying references in English libraries, and to Dr Willy Schmid for his timely help with the proofs and index.

B.W.V.

Introduction

The period from the 1690s to the 1730s is one in which the theoretical system of Neo-classicism was applied with energy and with few reservations. It is entirely fitting that the span of this volume coincides with the writing career of Charles Gildon, whom we might take as its representative critic, since he expresses the same attitudes as Dryden, Rymer and Dennis, while also (if more in his earlier than later work) showing some of the independent spirit which characterises the minority view, and of which Farquhar, Rowe and Addison are occasional exemplars. If the work of Gildon seems a limited attraction, the other writer whose career coincides with the time-span of this volume, Lewis Theobald, is of another magnitude. For long derided by Pope and his coterie—an adverse judgment that extended, alas, as far as Dr Johnson and Malone—Theobald deserves finally to be recognised as the best all-round editor of Shakespeare in this period or any other. While Johnson and Malone have their own special claims on our attention neither of them excelled in the whole range of scholarship, as Theobald did, nor applied their knowledge in such an imaginative way to the clarification of Shakespeare's text. If an editor may be allowed to express a hope, it is that this volume should permit the reinstatement of Theobald as one of the three or four major figures in the development of our understanding and appreciation of Shakespeare.

I

For the critics of this period, whether in separate literary essays or in the increasing number of journals,[1] Shakespeare was a dramatist who had to be attacked more often than praised. The canons of criticism were tested against him, and he was found wanting. It may seem clear to us that in fact their critical categories were wanting, but we must think ourselves back into the freshness of this phase of English criticism if we are to understand the fascination of testing out a critical system against the acknowledged 'greatest writer of this or any other age'. At times the excitement of discovering that by using this system one could demonstrate the presence of faults in Shakespeare seems to have gone to the heads of some critics. It is difficult otherwise to explain the demonic energy of Rymer's attack on *Othello* (No. 29), the way in which he construes Shakespeare's failure to conform to the tenets of neo-Aristotelianism as a provocative act, almost as a personal insult. We might well feel that Rymer's emotion, as T. S. Eliot said of Hamlet's (rightly or wrongly), is in excess of the facts, yet we must not allow our resentment at his crudest sarcasms to cloud the fact that he writes in perfect consistency with the dominant critical principles of this period. (The motives for Rymer's special animus might repay further enquiry.)

Taken at a lower level of intensity, the specific objections by Rymer were such as could have been made by any educated man of his time: Shakespeare had offended against the concept of imitation (what might be more helpful to think of as 'selective mimesis'): he had represented men as they were, not as they ought to be. He should have remembered the Horatian–Aristotelian concept of characters being good of their kind, or 'better than us': what was to be imitated was not life in the raw, which could be sordid and thus not 'instructive', but *'la belle nature'*, a world of types and ideals. He broke the unities of time and place; the language given to his characters was excessive, redundant, suffering from the two extreme vices of bombast and quibbles. (These were criticisms already made by Dryden: see Nos 10, 12 and 19 in Vol. 1.) Rymer works through the neo-Aristotelian categories (Fable, Characters, Thoughts, Manners, Words) and attacks *Othello* under each head. His most bitter criticisms are that the characters are unnatural (given the special sense of 'nature' outlined above), therefore improbable and inconsistent; therefore all the other 'parts' are necessarily flawed. An additional weakness is that Shakespeare has neglected morality. Iago's villainy is too shocking to be represented in the theatre; and poetic justice is not observed, for Desdemona is killed, yet innocent:

> What instruction can we make out of this Catastrophe? Or whither must our reflection lead us? Is not this to envenome and sour our spirits, to make us repine and grumble at Providence; and the government of the World?

> Shakespeare allows characters to be killed 'in a barbarous arbitrary way ... *Hab-nab*, ... against all Justice and Reason, against all Law, Humanity and Nature ...'.

2

To Neo-classics who took their critical system seriously, yet admired Shakespeare, Rymer was an embarrassment. The results of his analysis were extremely adverse, yet the evaluation had been carried out strictly according to the book. We meet a number of protests, but they are more or less inarticulate. In 1696 John Oldmixon complains that 'If Mr. Rymer had thus consider'd his Duty to *Shakespeare*, as he was the Father of our Stage, he would have sav'd himself and the World, a great deal of Trouble and Scandal'.[2] In other words, Rymer has committed a nuisance. Another typical reaction is this piece of journalistic fence-sitting by Peter Anthony Motteux in the *Gentleman's Journal* for December 1692 (cited in the *Shakespeare Allusion-Book*, II, 386):

Mr. *Rymer's* Book, which the Ingenious expected with so much Impatience, is publish'd and is call'd, *A Short View of Tragedy*. . . . Mr. *Rymer*, like some of the French that follow *Aristotle's* Precepts, declares for Chorus's, and takes an occasion to examin some plays of *Shakespeare's*, principally *Othello*, with the same severity and judgment with which he criticized some of *Beaumont* and *Fletcher's* in his Book called, *The Tragedies of the last Age.* . . . The Ingenious are somewhat divided about some Remarks in it, though they concur with Mr. *Rymer* in many things, and generally acknowledge that he discovers a great deal of Learning through the whole. For these Reasons I must forbear saying any more of it, and refer you to the Book it self.

'The Ingenious are somewhat divided': so we see from the attempts at refutation made here by Dryden (Nos 31, 33) and Dennis (No. 30). The only successful attack is that of Gildon (No. 32) who takes issue not so much with the Neo-classic principles as with Rymer's application of them, above all his appeal to the higher authority of the classics. Gildon's demonstration of the role of 'the marvellous' in Aeneas' tale to Dido is particularly effective. Yet Rymer continued to be an issue for many years, as we see from Rowe in 1709 (No. 47), Gildon in 1710 (No. 50), Theobald in 1733 (No. 82). An indication of a reaction against him is the tone of Thomas Brereton's denunciation of Rymer in the first number of his *Critic* (1718), for 'waging against all mankind that were eminent for their genius, only because they were so. . . . His witticisms upon Desdemona's handkerchief . . . are enough to make a wise man sick'.[3] Yet the orthodox Augustans continued to respect Rymer, as we shall see from Pope and indeed Dr Johnson.

Rymer not only produced the most unfavourable account of Shakespeare and Elizabethan drama yet written, he became the inspiration for another violent attack, that made by Jeremy Collier (No. 34). As

C. A. Zimansky noted in his useful edition of Rymer's criticism (which is, however, not without some special pleading)—'be it said with regret—Jeremy Collier was Rymer's most influential follower'. Mr Zimansky saw in this relationship 'a narrow moralist taking over the ideas of an outstanding critic',[4] although one may question whether Rymer was a less narrow moralist. Collier's attack on the 'immorality and profaneness' of the English stage was focused mainly on the Restoration dramatists, and provoked a flood of defence.[5] Shakespeare only figures incidentally, but, as we see from the examples reprinted here (Nos 35–7), Collier's criticisms were rejected with more vigour and more confidence than were those of Rymer. Collier was so evidently a lesser figure. Yet the refutations themselves stay within Neo-classical principles: all three defenders of Shakespeare assert that he has, in fact, kept to the principle of poetic justice.

The relationship between Shakespeare, the rules, and contemporary approval was in essence a simple one: when he kept to the rules he pleased. Thus the author (probably Charles Gildon)[6] of *Cato Examined* (1713, p. 4): 'Our *Shakespeare* . . . is exactly conformable to the Rules in all that pleases the Judicious, and never disgusts but for want of his knowledge of them.' Lest this simple comparison-process seem mechanical or trivial we might remember (if the example of Rymer were not already before us) the seriousness with which the rules were taken as a manifestation in the literary sphere of the principles of cosmological and social order. Thus Dennis argues that the rules give harmony, proportion, symmetry, indeed merely to observe them is to guarantee oneself success: 'writing Regularly is writing Morally, Decently, Justly, Naturally, Reasonably. . . .'[7] Shakespeare's failure to keep this index of competence is deplored by Gildon (Nos 50, 62) and Dennis (No. 67), just as his occasional observations of it are applauded by the orthodox.

The two plays most often praised in this period are *The Merry Wives of Windsor* and *The Tempest*, because they came closest to meeting the critical requirements of an integrated plot which observed the unities of place, time and action. In the totally representative formulation of *Cato Examined* (p. 7):

There must be a *Unity* of the *Dramatic Action*; that is, it must be but one Action, not many, of one Man; for that breaks the *Unity*. In which Point all our Old Authors are generally faulty, and *Shakespeare* might as well have brought his Play of *Julius Caesar* down to Nero's Time, as to the Death of *Brutus* and *Cassius*.

4

In his two extended essays (No. 50a, b) Gildon demonstrates Shakespeare's failings on this head, treating the apologies of the Chorus in *Henry V*, *Pericles* and *A Winter's Tale* as proof of Shakespeare's own sense of guilt for having violated order, singling out the fables of a number of comedies for their 'absurdities', and dismissing the histories *en bloc*: 'when they exceed the Unities I see no Reason why they may not as well, and with as good Reason, stretch the Time to 5000 Years, and the Actions to all the Nations and People of the Universe, and as there has been a Puppet Show of the Creation of the World, so there may be a Play call'd the History of the World.'

Given this yes/no model of critical argument, it is not surprising that Shakespeare's 'faults' were identified with the confidence of general agreement. In one of his more blatant pieces of book-making, the so-called *Life of Mr. Thomas Betterton* (1710), Gildon defended the absurdities of opera on the grounds that 'if All that is absurd and irrational should be excluded the Theatre, you must banish a great many of the most celebrated Pieces of the Stage; as, *Othello*, which is compos'd of Parts shocking to Reason, and full of Absurdities' (pp. 171–2). Dennis's *Essay on the Genius and Writings of Shakespeare* (No. 56) spends, despite its title, quite some time itemising Shakespeare's faults. E. N. Hooker, in his magnificent edition of that critic's works, has written that 'the valid objection to Dennis's essay is not that it criticises by observing faults, but that the "faults" observed are either trivial or, as in the case of the violation of poetic justice, perceptible only to a vision restricted by certain unfortunate prejudices of its age' (II, p. 422). But if the 'prejudices' form the consensus opinion, then Shakespeare's plots must come under attack. A writer in the *Universal Spectator* on 9 December 1732 pronounced that[8]

Our Writers who have of late attempted *Tragedy* want both *Art* and *Genius*, since either of these would make a tolerable Play. As for Example . . . most of *Shakespeare's* without a *Plot*. I mean by *Art* in a Play, all that Disposition of the Parts in respect of *Plotting*, which makes the Whole clear, natural, and uniform, which must be the Result of close Studying the Cricks ancient and modern.

Dennis criticised *The Merry Wives of Windsor* because 'there are no less than three Actions in it that are independant one of another, which divide and distract the minds of an Audience' (No. 44), and Addison echoed that objection, particularly against tragi-comedy (No. 55: *Spectator* 40), as, predictably enough, did Gildon (No. 50). Dennis, too, attacked Shakespeare's 'apparent Duplicity in some of his Plays, or

Triplicity of Action, and the frequent breaking of the Continuity of the Scenes' (No. 65). Dennis (No. 44) and Gildon (Nos 50, 68) are in agreement that soliloquies are 'unnatural' in drama.

All the examples which I have so far discussed of Shakespeare's failure to satisfy those New Critics who began their careers in the 1690s have been 'technical' in nature, concerned with such things as plot, structure, the unities. The modern reader might be tempted to dismiss them as relatively unimportant; if so, he will certainly not have that detachment (a rather irresponsible detachment, as it would appear to a Neo-classic critic) when confronted with their attacks on Shakespeare's morality. Gildon disposes of *Macbeth* brusquely: 'the character of Macbeth and his Lady are too monstrous for the Stage' (No. 50). A few years later he becomes still more adamant:[9]

> There are two Crimes which are never to be admitted in Tragedy, Cowardice in the Man, and want of Chastity in the Woman; in the last of which many of our Play-writers are abandonly guilty. Nor must there be any *Iagos*, *Villains*; they shock us too much, and seem really out of the character of Humankind. But the Success of *Iago* in *Shakespeare* has made our other Writers run mad after such-like characters. . . .

This reaction, disapproval–prohibition, echoes Rymer, yet is echoed in turn by Theobald's disgust with the character of Richard III (No. 78). Dennis finds Shakespeare at fault for showing the horrible murder of Julius Caesar on stage, and for presenting the punishment of Brutus and Cassius but not that of the other conspirators (No. 42), and later delivers a full-scale attack on Shakespeare's neglect of poetic justice in so many of the tragedies (No. 56). (We note silently that elsewhere Dennis praised *Macbeth* and *Coriolanus* for having a proper moral: Nos 36, 65.) In the orthodox Neo-classicism of his youth Lewis Theobald found the deaths of Lear, Cordelia and Hamlet instances of Shakespeare's failure to reward virtue (No. 59: *Censor* 7), and his preference for Tate's revised *Lear* is shared by Thomas Cooke in 1731 (No. 79).

Finally, Shakespeare's language came in for dispraise. Criticism in the later part of this period was less savage than the attacks of Dryden and Rymer, perhaps because a more detached historical sense prevailed. That is, whereas the post-Restoration critics were offended by 'bombast', now we find the more neutral recognition that his style was simply 'out of date'. So Edward Bysshe, in his compilation *The Art of English Poetry* (1702)—which consisted of three parts, 'Rules for Making

Verse', a 'Dictionary of Rhymes' and a 'Collection of Beauties'—wrote
that he had included in the third section[10]

not only Similes, Allusions, Characters, and Descriptions, but also the most
Natural and Noble Thoughts on all Subjects of our modern Poets; I say, of
our Modern: for though the Ancient, as *Chaucer*, *Spenser*, and others, have not
been excell'd, perhaps not equall'd by any that have succeeded them, either in
Justness of Description, or in Propriety and Greatness of Thought, yet the
Garb in which they are Cloath'd, tho' then Alamode, is now become so out
of Fashion, that the Readers of our Age have no Ear for them: And this is the
Reason that the Good *Shakespeare* himself is not so frequently Cited in the
following Pages, as he would otherwise deserve to be.

For the compiler of florilegia Shakespeare was to be avoided with the
minimum of fuss; for the educated general reader, though, the problem
could not be side-stepped, and gave rise to some irritation. This we can
observe in Addison (No. 55: *Spectator* 39 and 61), or in the learned
Francis Atterbury, who wrote to Pope (then beginning his edition of
Shakespeare):[11]

I have found time to read some parts of Shakespeare which I was least acquainted with. I protest to you, in an hundred places I cannot construe him,
I don't understand him. The hardest part of Chaucer is more intelligible to me
than some of those Scenes, not merely thro the faults of the Edition, but the
Obscurity of the Writer: for Obscure he is, & a little (not a little) enclin'd now
& then to Bombast, whatever Apology you may have contriv'd on that head
for him.

A writer in *Applebee's Journal* on 3 June 1732 explained that the style of
Shakespeare 'is indeed sometimes uncouth, owing to [his] too great
Heat, and to the vast Change of Language intervening since [he]
wrote'.[12]

This brief summary of the Neo-classics' quarrel with Shakespeare
cannot, of course, represent either the ubiquity or the density of the
general disapproval of this irregular, unlearned dramatist, who violated
every critical principle. Perhaps the texts collected in this volume will
give a more accurate impression. But already the reader may be
wondering why, if Shakespeare failed all the tests, he was still read,
acted and discussed. One reason is clear, that his prestige was already so
great that the unanimous objections of a generation of critics could not
damage it. Equally, although the majority of critics, and those the most
influential, found more to blame than to praise, there were certain
escape clauses. Although Rymer had found Shakespeare worthless in

every neo-Aristotelian category, a number of critics working within the system conceded that Shakespeare showed some ability in the category of 'manners', that is, in the representation of human behaviour, especially the passions. So the archetypal Gildon, in *Cato Examined* (p. 11):

The *Manners*, therefore, of the Principal Persons at least, ought to be so clearly and fully mark'd, as to distinguish them from all other Men. In this *Shakespeare* has excell'd; . . .

Several of the critics collected here would agree. Or again, one could accept the theory of poetic justice and argue that Shakespeare had, in fact, observed it. As we have seen, this was the tactic of the controversialists against Collier (Nos 35 to 37), and it was also used by Shaftesbury (No. 51), Hughes (No. 58) and others.

For critics who kept within the Neo-classic system two other strategies were available. The most popular was to accept the denunciation of all of Shakespeare's faults, but then to excuse them as being simply vices of the age. Dryden had begun this form of apologia in his *Essay on the Dramatique Poetry of the Last Age* (No. 12 in Vol. I), and it became increasingly used. In 1694 Charles Gildon applied it in his attack on Rymer (No. 32), while in the same year Laurence Echard, in the preface to his translation of Plautus' comedies, described the fidelity with which he had worked (Sig. ᵦ^v):

But I have not only been so scrupulous in this Case, but I have likewise imitated all his Faults and Imperfections, whenever I cou'd do it without extream Injury to the Translation; I speak of his *Puns, Quibbles, Rhimes, Gingles,* and his several ways of playing upon words; which indeed were the faults of his Age, as it was of ours in *Shakespeare's* and *Jonson's* days. . . .

In 1703 Charles Gildon used it again, in the preface to one of a number of plays by other men which he touched up and published under his own name (this time *The Patriot,* an adaptation of Lee's *Lucius Junius Brutus*) (cited in Branam, p. 4):

It is but a poor Defence, to shelter our Errors under the Failings of Great Men, or to imitate their Defects, when we can't arrive at their Perfections, for no Name is sufficient to justifie an Absurdity. But if they wou'd study Nature as much as *Shakespeare* did, their Errors would be less visible, and more supportable. But there is nothing more familiar with the ignorant Decryers of the Rules, than to instance *Shakespeare's* pleasing without them, never remembring that *Shakespeare* never pleases but when he has observed them, as in his Characters, Passions &c.—the Rules being only Nature Methodiz'd—for sure

8

no body (I mean of Sense) ever admir'd his Conduct; the Rules of which not being known in his Time is his best Plea for his Offences against them.

In the selections below we find the historical apologia coming from Nicholas Rowe in 1709 (No. 47), from Gildon and Shaftesbury in 1710 (Nos 50, 51), from Elijah Fenton in 1711 (No. 52) and from Addison in that year (No. 55: *Spectator* 61), from Dennis in 1719 (No. 65), from William Levin in 1731 (No. 80). The most important of these is Nicholas Rowe, whose preface was reprinted in almost every edition of Shakespeare's works up to the Variorum of 1821, and can thus be claimed as the most disseminated Shakespeare critic before Johnson. His extremely liberal views may have seemed strange in 1709, but as the century advanced the norm adjusted itself to Rowe.

The other strategy for the orthodox was to concede Shakespeare's faults but assert that he was great notwithstanding them. In the typical formulation of Gildon (*The Laws of Poetry*, 1721, p. 33), Shakespeare was a 'great, but very irregular genius', a judgment which can be found elsewhere in Gildon (No. 50), Hughes (No. 58) and Theobald (No. 59). It was possible to agree with Rymer yet disagree: 'Our best Poets of the last Age have been justly censur'd, *Shakespeare* by *Rymer* . . . yet [Shakespeare's] *Tragedies* . . ., however irregular in Form and Conduct, boast the noblest Sentiments, and best adapted to the Speakers. . . .' (*op. cit.* in n. 11). This defensive reaction had in fact been made by the first confuters of Rymer, Gildon (No. 32) and Dryden (No. 33). A further development of this position, which in fact carries the critic outside the orthodox camp altogether, is to argue that Shakespeare was great *because* he broke the rules, since genius and the laws of poetry are not compatible. Rowe set the key on this point too: Shakespeare's ignorance of the classics is proved by his unique quality, since their regularity—had he been familiar with it—might have restricted his 'Fire, Impetuosity, and even beautiful Extravagance' (No. 47). A genius unrestricted by rules is the picture presented by Henry Felton (No. 49), Leonard Welsted (No. 57), Addison (No. 55: *Spectator* 161) and—in part—by Dennis (No. 56). As early as 1694 a 'Mr G' could write a poem for the *Gentleman's Journal* (October–November, p. 275)[13] which begins:

> Shakespeare, the Prop and Glory of the Stage,
> Adorn'd a rough and charms a polish'd Age;
> True as the Life the vocal Painter Drew,
> Yet the nice Paths of Learning never knew.

His matchless works proceeded from his Wit,
The learned proud to read, and copy what he writ.
Each line the force of manly Sence displays,
In equal Words he mighty Thoughts arrays,
And, taught by Nature above Art to write,
Scorns his dull Critics and their feeble spight.

By 1730 Walter Harte could refer to this attitude as if it were a commonplace:[14]

We grant, that *Butler* ravishes the Heart,
As *Shakespeare* soar'd beyond the reach of Art;
(For Nature form'd those Poets without Rules,
To fill the world with *imitating Fools.*)

Among the recurrent topics in Steele's Shakespeare criticism is the praise of his author's ability to get inside human feeling (No. 48: *Tatler* 47), or to create 'strong Impressions of Honour and Humanity' (*ibid.* 8), or his power in arousing our sympathy: 'The Strings of the Heart, which are to be touch'd on to give us Compassion, are not so play'd on but by the finest Hand' (*ibid.* 68).

The creators of a warmer sensibility, as seen in the 'sentimental drama' and the cult of benevolence, appropriated Shakespeare to it (indeed Thomas Purney, in praising Shakespeare's use of 'the *Gloomy*' (No. 61) in 1717 seems fifty years ahead of his time). One example which predicts a later attitude is provided by Rowe again, this time in the prologue to his tragedy *Jane Shore, Written in Imitation of Shakespeare's Style* (1714):

In such an Age, Immortal *Shakespeare* wrote,
By no quaint Rules, nor hampering Criticks taught;
With rough, majestick Force, he mov'd the Heart,
And Strength and Nature made Amends for Art.
Our humble Author does his Steps pursue,
He owns he had the mighty Bard in view;
And in these Scenes has made it more his Care
To rouse the Passions, than to charm the Ear.

When Rowe's friend James Welwood prepared his translation of Lucan for posthumous publication he recorded how Rowe 'took all occasions to express the vast Esteem he had for that Wonderful Man . . .'. Welwood quoted those lines from Rowe's prologue 'because I believe there is no Man of Taste but pays to *Shakespeare*'s Memory the Homage that's due to one of the greatest Genius's that ever appear'd in

Dramatick Poetry'.[15] As throughout this tradition the spectator's ability to respond to the expression of emotion becomes a test of his warmth of feeling, indeed of his moral sense. A writer in the *Universal Journal* for 4 July 1724 asked

Who can see the filial Piety of *Hamlet* without partaking of his sorrows, and with equal Ardour in his Heart, pursuing the good old King's Murderer? . . . What Zealot can forbear embracing the Part of the Good *Humphrey* of *Gloucester*, against the Priestcraft and Persecutions of a haughty Cardinal? I could instance Numbers of such Examples, by which our Hearts are moved, and our Souls instructed.

We can already see that a climate of feeling was developing in which the rules, and the denigration of Shakespeare which their application would result in, could be played down or even ignored. It seems to me that critics escaped from the constraints of Art more by avoiding than confronting them, but occasional confrontations did occur. Thus Gildon rejected Bysshe's estimate of the 'obsolescence' of Shakespeare when he came to issue his own collection of beauties:[16]

Finding the Inimitable *Shakespeare* rejected by some Modern Collectors for his Obsolete Language, and having lately run over this great Poet, I could not but present the Reader with a Specimen of his Descriptions, and Moral Reflections, to shew the Injustice of Such an Obloquy. I might have been more large, for he abounds in Beauties; but these are sufficient to evince the Falsehood of their Imputation.

The orthodox Neo-classics could take it for granted that Shakespeare had no knowledge of the ancients—as did John Dennis (No. 56), or Jeremy Collier, mingling criticism and apologia:[17]

Shakespeare—a fam'd Poet, but of no great Learning, which made him so much admired; his Genius was jocular, but when disposed he could be very serious, and did so excel both in Tragedies and Comedies, that he was able to make *Heraclitus* laugh, and *Democritus* weep.

Yet Gildon could reject the charge of Shakespeare's small learning with vigour, and indeed cogency (No. 50).

If, as this last example shows, it is not always easy to discover the motives which prompted some critics to refute orthodoxy, on two issues at least there are clear-cut and genuine grounds for disagreement. The restrictions of the rules hampered practising dramatists most of all, and it is from them that the few objections come. In his *Short Vindication of the Relapse* (1698) Vanbrugh attacked the rules, especially those stating that action was more important than character, and that a double plot was a weakness (pp. 57, 60), while Congreve, also defending himself from Collier, hit out at those critics who talked 'in all the Pedantical Cant of Fable, Intrigue, Discovery, of Unities of Time, Place, and Action'.[18] A few years later Farquhar wrote a remarkable refutation of the doctrine of the unities (No. 45), a piece which, had it been better known and its argument properly appreciated, would have made the repetition of some of the more unthinking parts of the canon over the next decades unnecessary. Similarly one of the opponents of Collier argued that the greatest English tragedies (five of the seven cited are by Shakespeare) 'are so far from pent up in *Corneille*'s narrower *Unity Rules* . . . that nothing is so ridiculous as to pretend to it' (No. 35). It is equally refreshing to read Addison's attack on that 'ridiculous Doctrine in modern Criticism . . . the chymerical Notion of Poetical Justice' (No. 55: *Spectator* 40), or Thomas Purney's rejection of the French reverence for 'the common known mechanick Rules of Poetry' (No. 61). Yet, heartening as these reactions may be to the modern opponents of Neo-classicism, they are few and rare: Farquhar's case was not taken up for many years, while Addison stands completely alone.[19] Dennis's attack on him (No. 56) represents the general belief. The minority view, however attractive it may be, must not be exaggerated.

II

In the world of the theatre, criticism[20] of acting and production shows a move away from the self-confidence of the period covered in the previous volume. Diatribes against contemporary theatrical taste become more frequent. In the collection here we find such pieces from Steele in 1711 (No. 54: *Spectator* 208) and William Levin in 1731 (No. 80). In all such complaints one of the points is that Shakespeare's plays, especially the tragedies, are not properly appreciated: in the words of an anonymous writer, 'Farce and Pantomimes have taken place of *Shakespeare* and *Otway*; and the *Players* have destroy'd that Taste they did not understand.'[21] Be that as it may, there is no denying the remarkable surge in the performance of Shakespeare's plays and his popularity in the theatre, long before Garrick.[22] We find some signs of a reaction against the Restoration adaptations, stated in general terms

by Oldmixon (No. 41) and Sewell (No. 63), applied to the Dryden and
D'Avenant *Tempest* by Gildon (No. 50) and to Tate's *Lear* by Addison
(No. 55: *Spectator* 40). Yet Gildon praises Tate's version in the same
work (No. 50), as do Theobald in 1715 (No. 59) and Cooke in 1731
(No. 79).

As to the adaptations,[23] there are less of them in this period and they
are less good—that is, they are not carried out with that conviction of
need and justification which marked the work of the 1670s and 1680s.
Of the adaptations included here only one, Cibber's *Richard III* (No.
38) achieved any lasting success in the theatre, although Granville's *Jew*
(No. 43) held the stage until Macklin's revival of the original. I do not
suggest that opinion was turning against the adapters, but rather that
because the excitement of pioneering had died down, and because the
best 'vehicles' had already been claimed by the previous generation, the
assumptions behind the adapting process continued but without much
new impetus. Certainly the successful versions of the last age—the
Dryden–D'Avenant *Tempest* (sometimes with Shadwell's added attrac-
tions), Tate's *Lear*, Shadwell's *Timon*, Otway's *Romeo and Juliet*—all
continued to please.

It is equally the case that the adaptations show a continuity in principle and execution with their predecessors. 'Entertainments' continue
to be added. Gildon's *Measure for Measure* (No. 40) has a masque of
Dido and Aeneas, ostensibly presented by Escalus to celebrate Angelo's
birthday. Granville's *Jew of Venice* (No. 43) adds a supper and a show
(the masque of Peleus and Thetis), and in its epilogue points out that
Shadwell's *Timon of Athens* had not been a success until music was
added to it:

> How was the Scene forlorn, and how despis'd,
> When *Timon*, without Musick, moraliz'd?
> *Shakespeare's* sublime in vain entic'd the Throng,
> Without the Charm of *Purcell's* Syren Song.

'The throng' were doubtless pleased by the 'terrible Symphony' of
music accompanying the fairies' tormenting of Falstaff in Dennis's
Merry Wives (No. 44).

The attitudes of the age take other forms. To justify the intrigues
in *Measure for Measure* Gildon adds to his list of *dramatis personae* brief
glosses intended to make the characters socially more respectable, suggest-
ing that they were driven to perform these unusual deeds by the pressure
of reduced fortunes. In the finale to Dennis's *Merry Wives* Fenton does

not marry Anne secretly but asks her parents' consent, who duly promise a settlement on him. To move from social to political attitudes, Aaron Hill's *Henry V* (No. 69) is a fine example of the chauvinism which was regularly ascribed to Shakespeare in periods of xenophobia. Anti-French feeling is expressed in the prologue, in the martial song by the 'Genius of England' (which unites patriotism and entertainment at one go), and in the flag-waving conclusion. How much more intelligent is the use of Shakespeare (by Nicholas Amhurst?)[24] in the pages of the *Craftsman* (e.g. No. 75) to attack the corruption of Walpole's administration.

As to the critical principles governing their work, they also represent attitudes which we have already met. Dennis altered *The Merry Wives of Windsor* (No. 44) to give it a unified plot, with Fenton as the common centre, but even the excerpts here may be enough to show the excessive amount of explanation which he found necessary to add. For *Coriolanus* Dennis invoked another critical canon, poetic justice, to protest against what is evidently a deliberately unjust and ironic ending by Shakespeare. By making Coriolanus himself kill his crooked adversary Aufidius (together with three tribunes) Dennis gives Shakespeare's most complex character a simple, heroic status. Lewis Theobald's *Richard II* (No. 66) likewise takes exception to Shakespeare's evil king and substitutes a one-dimensional hero, and a 'more regular Fable'. The difficulties which the Neo-classics experienced with Shakespeare's subtle mixtures of sympathy and antipathy are very clearly seen in Thomas Killigrew Junior's[25] sketch at a revision of *Julius Caesar* (No. 60), which would make Brutus an unambiguously attractive character.

In the detail of language and feeling we can also trace a continuity between these adaptations and their predecessors. Cibber and Granville seem to show more self-consciousness about which lines are genuine Shakespeare and which imitation, since they use typographical means to distinguish the two categories (albeit not accurately). Yet when it came to altering neither showed any compunction. Cibber's version is a more streamlined vehicle, retaining only about half of Shakespeare's play, yet adding—as the reader will be surprised to find—many familiar speeches from the other histories, resulting in a type of Shakespeare anthology. Cibber also intensifies the feeling, giving more violence and brutality with one hand and more pathos (as in the princes' murder) with the other—although for some reason he deleted that scene for the 1718 reprint of the play and added a rather weak soliloquy for Richard. Violent feelings, verging on rant and posture-striking, can be found in Dennis's *Coriolanus* and Theobald's *Richard II*: indeed, a very instructive comparison could be made with Tate's version of both plays. It would show, I believe, that although historians of the drama in this period can speak of a move from heroic tragedy to the sentimental drama, in terms of the adaptations there had not been much change.

III

In the sphere of editing,[26] finally, we see a much more dynamic development. The beginning was not auspicious, since Rowe's edition of 1709 (for which Tonson, who owned the copyright of Shakespeare, paid him a mere £36 10*s.*) based its text on that of the Fourth Folio of 1685,[27] and thus inherited a multitude of misprints, for the original Folio edition had been progressively degenerating in its reprints. Rowe consulted the Quartos (the original printings of about half the plays, which appeared in Shakespeare's lifetime but not always from author-ised sources) for *Hamlet* and *Romeo and Juliet* and restored a few passages that had been omitted from the Folio text. Rowe, it might be said, provided the shape of a modern edition—he added lists of *dramatis personae*, corrected stage-directions, made exits and entrances con-sistent, divided the text into acts and scenes, adding localities—but not its substance. He made no fresh scrutiny of the text.

In Pope's edition we find similar anomalies. Pope was certainly more enterprising in locating Shakespearian Quartos, and knew of one such issue of all the Quarto editions bar one, but the use he made of them was mixed. To his credit he restored passages in plays for which the Folio text gives heavily-cut versions (*Hamlet, King Lear, Romeo and Juliet*), but the principle on which he restored lines seems to have been the quite arbitrary workings of his own taste. By assuming in some places that the variations between the texts meant that the longer version consisted of interpolations by the actors he was able to reject what he called 'trash', such as puns and word-play (including Othello's demented fixation on the word 'handkerchief'), as un-Shakespearian. Passages which Pope did not approve of were either 'degraded', that is printed in smaller type at the foot of the page (over 1,500 lines of Shakespeare suffered this ignominy) or else were omitted altogether, often without notice to the reader, as Theobald showed time and again in his edition. If we divide the activities of an editor, loosely enough, into questions of fact and questions of taste (though—of course—the latter constantly influences the former), under the first head we would have to say that Pope's statements about the text or the theatre are more often than not wildly erroneous. As for his taste, demonstrated both in the preface and the notes which follow, I never cease to be surprised by the arrogance with which Pope treats Shakespeare—despite his effusive panegyrics—and rejects lines or whole scenes that offend him. Sometimes he attempts to minimise the criticism by holding the players—those vulgar, unlearned, irresponsible people (nowhere is Pope's superiority more misplaced)—to blame for corrupting the text.

Yet even bad scholarship can be beneficial, if it provokes others to do better. Spurred by Pope, an anonymous work (No. 77) vigorously refuted Pope's false account of the actors' social status and went on to make the first accurate classification of the various categories of text which lie behind the printed editions of Shakespeare. More important still, Pope has to be given credit for arousing Lewis Theobald, a scholar whose classical labours had been interrupted by Shakespearian criticism and adaptation, to devote the best part of his life to editing Shakespeare. In his *Shakespeare Restored* (No. 74) Theobald made some enormous developments in the theory and practice of what I should like to call 'total editing' (in the face of our contemporaries' increasingly rigorous specialism into the text 'pure and simple'—as if a concern with the transmission of words through print were a sufficient basis to produce a complete text). What Theobald saw in this pioneer work, and expanded in his own edition of 1733 (No. 82), was that a text does not need to be emended if it can be satisfactorily explained: if we can establish the sense adequately we do not have to alter the reading so as to give some other sense. In order to establish meaning he saw that it was necessary to explain an author partly from himself (by indicating a continuity of style and thought which can justify an apparently unusual usage) and partly from the history and social experience of his age. By his own researches, in a period in which historical awareness of Elizabethan literature was not high,[28] Theobald was able to show the meaning of many words or phrases which would have otherwise been rejected or emended into some more commonplace construct. He also showed some of the workings of Shakespeare's style, his use of rhetoric, his freedom within metrical conventions, his characteristic practices in metaphor and word-play. Theobald was also aware of the nature of the copy from which the plays were printed; he showed what can happen to the transmission of a word due to possible errors in deciphering handwriting, or a scribe's abbreviations.

Theobald made intelligent use of the sources both for textual purposes (to emend a reading or add a stage-direction) and for criticism: his notes on the ending of *Lear*, the plot of *Measure for Measure*, or the difference between Giraldi's 'moral' for *Othello* and Shakespeare's, show a judgment superior to almost all critics this side of Dr Johnson. He saw, too, that an editor has to be able to reconstruct the flow of a scene, the conflict of personality and motive, if he is to discover what an individual character would want to say, and what Shakespeare is trying to do. Theobald showed that the Shakespearian editor must be simultaneously scholar and critic. One of his greatest successes as a scholar was his recognition that although the taste of a subsequent age might not approve of a metaphor or pun, say, the editor has no authority to alter it. To revive my simple distinction between matters of fact and matters of taste, Theobald is remarkably advanced on the first head—there are few errors, and his historical sense was not to be equalled before Malone—while on the second head one looks in vain for the kind of disabling contemporary attitudes expressed in the high-handed decisions of a Pope or Warburton. Whereas in the *Censor* essays, or in his correspondence with Warburton (No. 78) there are signs of period taste, these are left behind in the work of his maturity, as Theobald illuminated Shakespeare with objective and sympathetic insights that are extremely rare in this period.

On only one count can Theobald be faulted, and that is a judgment from biography rather than criticism: he had too much respect for William Warburton. That learned but perverse mind, that dogmatic, bullying controversialist, utterly sure of his judgments even at their most ridiculous, impressed many experienced writers and critics of his age, including Ralph Allen, Pope and Dr Johnson. His manner was so assured, the parade of learning so insistent, that it took an extremely acute and critical mind to see through him. Conyers Middleton did so, as did Thomas Edwards (see Vol. 3, No. 126), but Theobald, like Johnson, only did so intermittently. The nature of his acquaintance with Warburton can be seen from the letters below (No. 78), first printed by John Nichols in 1817, and which can be supplemented by those published by R. F. Jones in his biography of Theobald in 1919. Theobald was too deferential. He allowed his own judgment to be imposed upon by Warburton's superior strength, and although in this correspondence as in his edition we often find him politely rejecting many of Warburton's wilder conjectures he agreed with a few of them, and it remains puzzling why he thought well enough of others to want to include them among his own notes.

Further, Theobald's respect for Warburton caused him to ask his help in composing the preface to his edition. As we can see from the letters reprinted here Theobald sent drafts to Warburton, received suggestions and drafts in return, and wove the whole into one sequence under his own name. From Nichols's *Illustrations* we can see the ambivalence with which Warburton was clearly glad to have his work used by other people anonymously (as with Birch's biography of Shakespeare in 1739, and with Sir Thomas Hanmer's edition in the 1740s), but reserved the right subsequently to announce what his own part had been. Thus in the Capell library at Trinity College, Cambridge, there exists Warburton's copy of Theobald's edition, in which Warburton marked all the passages in the preface and notes which he claimed to have written. One might be tempted to doubt his word, but we have the evidence of the request by Theobald and, as David Nichol Smith was the first to point out,[29] some of the passages claimed by Warburton do in fact coincide with letters or other works by him. So I have decided to reconstruct here the process of collaboration between the two men, taking Warburton's word for it and giving (*a*) the preface, with their contributions separately distinguished (No. 82), (*b*) the most valuable of Theobald's notes, with the few which Warburton claimed (No. 82) and (*c*) those notes by Warburton which were declared to be such by Theobald in his edition (No. 83).

This whole affair is not flattering to Theobald's judgment, but neither is it to Warburton's. In his notes Warburton shows at times some sound scholarship in explaining social customs or historical allusions, but already we find the weakness that was to make his edition of 1747 the laughing-stock of the following hundred years, a totally arbitrary rage for emendation. In this Warburton reveals his disability in questions both of fact and taste: he emends because he does not understand the sense or else disapproves of the style, and he replaces the offending word or phrase either with blatant coinages of his own (as we will see more frequently in the 1747 edition) or with some commonplace more acceptable to Augustan taste—as in his attempts to 'restore' (*i.e.* 'create') the 'integrity of a metaphor'. In effect Warburton represents a regression to the methods of Pope, with their completely arbitrary elevation of taste over judgment. The saddest fact about Warburton's relationship with Theobald is that Warburton learned nothing from it. Happily, and for reasons which I hope will be apparent even from the small selection of notes which I have been able to reprint here, the rest of the eighteenth century profited a good deal from Theobald's pioneer work.

NOTES

1 On the periodicals in this period see W. Graham, *English Literary Periodicals* (New York, 1930); R. S. Crane and F. B. Kaye, *A Census of British Newspapers and Periodicals* (Chapel Hill, N.C., 1927) and K. K. Weed, R. P. Bond and M. E. Prior, *Studies of British Newspapers and Periodicals from the Beginning to 1800* (Chapel Hill, N.C., 1946)—both being 'extra series' issues of *Studies in Philology*; R. J. Mitford and D. M. Sutherland, 'Catalogue of English Newspapers and Periodicals in the Bodleian Library 1622–1800', *Publications of the Oxford Bibliographical Society*, IV, 2 (1935)—an interleaved copy exists in the Bodleian recording some valuable recent accessions; R. P. Bond (ed.), *Studies in the Early English Periodical* (Chapel Hill, N.C., 1957); G. W. Stone, 'Shakespeare in the Periodicals, 1700–40', (1) *Shakespeare Quarterly*, II (1951), 221–31; (2) *ibid.*, III (1952), 313–28; C. J. Stratman, *A Bibliography of British Dramatic Periodicals 1720–1960* (New York, 1962).

2 Oldmixon, letter dated 13 December 1695, in his *Poems on Several Occasions* (1696), p. 118; *Shakespeare Allusion-Book*, II, 404.

3 Brereton, quoted by Stone, *op. cit.* (1), p. 230.

4 Zimansky, *The Critical Works of Thomas Rymer* (New Haven, 1956), p. xlv. Mr Zimansky observes that Collier's critique of *The Relapse* follows the model of Rymer on *Othello* 'with remarkable fidelity' (p. xlvi).

5 See J. W. Krutch, *Comedy and Conscience after the Restoration* (New York, 1924, 1949); Sister Rose Anthony, *The Jeremy Collier Controversy 1698–1726* (Milwaukee, 1937; New York, 1966).

6 See G. L. Anderson, 'The Authorship of *Cato Examin'd* (1713)', *Publications of the Bibliographical Society of America*, LI (1957), 84–90, listing numerous self-plagiarisms; my own reading of Gildon's corpus supports this ascription.

7 See *The Critical Works of John Dennis*, ed. E. N. Hooker, 2 vols (Baltimore, 1939), I, 200–1.

8 My quotation is taken from the excerpt reprinted in the *Gentleman's Magazine*, II (1732), 1104.

9 *The Post-Man Robb'd of his Mail . . . A Collection of Miscellaneous Letters* (1719), pp. 244–5. This is one of a number of such compilations issued by Gildon (others appeared in 1692, 1693, 1706).

10 Bysshe, *The Art of English Poetry* (1702), part iii, Sig. $*2^v - *3^r$. In the 1720 edition the metaphor of 'Garb—cloath'd—Alamode—out of fashion' is replaced by more sober terms: 'yet their Language is now become so antiquated and obsolete . . .'.

11 Atterbury, letter of 2 August 1721, in *The Correspondence of Alexander Pope*, ed. G. Sherburn, 5 vols (Oxford, 1956), II, 78–9.

12 Quoted from the excerpt reprinted in the *Gentleman's Magazine*, II (1732), 786.

13 Cited by J. Munro, 'More Shakespeare Allusions', *Modern Philology*, XIII (1916), pp. 497–544, at pp. 538–9.

14 Harte, *An Essay on Satire, Particularly on the Dunciad* (1730), p. 12; cited by R. P. Bond, *English Burlesque Poetry, 1700–1750* (Cambridge, Mass., 1932), p. 47.

15 *Lucan's Pharsalia, Translated into English Verse by Nicholas Rowe, Esq.* (1718), p. xxi; cited by Bonamy Dobrée, *English Literature in the Early Eighteenth Century 1700–1740* (Oxford, 1959).

16 Gildon, *The Complete Art of Poetry* (1718), p. 304.

17 Collier, *Historical and Poetical Dictionary* (1701); cited by H. S. Robinson, *English Shakespearian Criticism in the Eighteenth Century* (New York, 1932), p. 14 n.

18 Congreve, *Amendments of Mr. Collier's False and Imperfect Citations* (1698), p. 82; this and the Vanbrugh quotation cited by E. N. Hooker, *The Critical Works of John Dennis*, I, pp. lxxx f.

19 For other writers, in addition to those represented in these pages, who supported the concept of poetic justice, see E. N. Hooker, *op. cit.*, I, p. 437, and J. Spingarn (ed.), *Critical Essays of the Seventeenth Century* (Oxford, 1908, 1957), III, pp. 89 f. (Sir William Temple) and p. 228 (Blackmore).

20 See the admirable survey by C. H. Gray, *Theatrical Criticism in London to 1795* (New York, 1931, 1969); also D. F. Smith, *The Critics in the Audience of the London Theatres from Buckingham to Sheridan, 1671–1779* (Albuquerque, 1953); A. C. Sprague, *Shakespeare and the Actors* (Cambridge, Mass., 1940); J. F. Arnott and J. W. Robinson, *English Theatrical Literature 1559–1900. A Bibliography* (1970).

21 *A Proposal for the Better Regulation of the Stage*, excerpted in the *Gentleman's Magazine*, II (1732), 566.

22 See A. H. Scouten, 'Shakespeare's Plays in the Theatrical Repertory When Garrick Came to London', *Studies in English* (Austin, Texas, 1945), 257–68; 'The Increase in Popularity of Shakespeare's Plays in the Eighteenth Century: A Caveat', *Shakespeare Quarterly*, VII (1956), 189–202; and 'The Shakespearean Revival', in *The London Stage 1660–1800. Part III, 1729–1747* (Carbondale, Ill., 1961), I, cxlix ff: where the following estimate is given of the proportion of Shakespeare's plays (taking both adaptations and original versions together) in the repertory between 1703 and 1741:

1703–10: *c.* 11 per cent
1710–17: *c.* 14 per cent
1717–23: *c.* 17 per cent
1723–34: *c.* 12 per cent
1740–1: *c.* 25 per cent

See also C. B. Hogan, *Shakespeare in the Theatre, 1701–1800* (Oxford, 1952–6), and M. Goldstein, *Pope and the Augustan Stage* (Stanford, Calif., 1958).

23 On the adaptations see the works by Odell, H. Spencer and C. Spencer, cited in the previous volume, also G. C. Branam, *Eighteenth Century Adaptations of Shakespearian Tragedy* (Berkeley, Calif., 1956).

24 No detailed study of the authorship of the *Craftsman* exists, but in his B. Litt. thesis (Oxford, 1963) Giles Barber ascribes over fifty papers to Bolingbroke: none of them is among the group that draws so frequently on Shakespeare. See also H. T. Dickinson, *Bolingbroke* (1970), p. 343.

25 For the ascription to the younger Killigrew, and for the date of about 1715 (which my examination of the manuscript hand would support) see G. B. Evans, 'The Problem of Brutus: an Eighteenth Century Solution', in *Studies in Honor of T. W. Baldwin*, ed. D. C. Allen (Urbana, Ill., 1958).

26 The best introduction is R. B. McKerrow, 'The Treatment of Shakespeare's Text by his Earlier Editors, 1706–1768', British Academy Shakespeare lecture for 1933, repr. in *Studies in Shakespeare*, ed. P. Alexander (London, 1964), pp. 103–31; see also H. L. Ford, *Shakespeare, 1700–1740. A Collation, of the Editions and Separate Plays with Some Account of T. Johnson and P. Walker* (Oxford, 1935); J. Isaacs, 'Shakespearian Scholarship', in *A Companion to Shakespeare Studies*, ed. H. Granville-Barker and G. B. Harrison (Cambridge, 1934), pp. 305–24. D. N. Smith gives a too favourable account of Pope as an editor, and a biased view of Theobald, in *Shakespeare in the Eighteenth Century* (Oxford, 1928); a more accurate assessment of both is that by T. R. Lounsbury, *The First Editors of Shakespeare (Pope and Theobald)* (1906). Useful studies include J. Butt, *Pope's Taste in Shakespeare* (1936)—a lecture read to the Shakespeare Association in 1935; P. Dixon, 'Pope's Shakespeare', *Journal of English and Germanic Philology*, LXIII (1964), 191–203; R. F. Jones, *Lewis Theobald. His Contribution to English Scholarship With Some Unpublished Letters* (New York, 1919).

27 The British Museum has acquired some trial pages from Rowe's edition of *The Tempest* which had been based on the Second Folio. See S. Schoenbaum, *Shakespeare's Lives* (1970), p. 130n.

28 See E. R. Wasserman, *Elizabethan Poetry in the Eighteenth Century* (Urbana, Ill., 1947).

29 Smith, *Eighteenth Century Essays on Shakespeare* (Glasgow, 1903), pp. xlvi ff.

Note on the Text

The texts in this collection are taken from the first printed edition, unless otherwise stated. The date under which a piece is filed is that of the first edition, with two exceptions: plays, for which the first performance is used (for such information I have relied on *The London Stage* for the period 1660 to 1800); and those works for which the author gives a date of composition substantially earlier than its first printing. The place of publication is London, unless otherwise indicated.

Spelling and punctuation are those of the original editions except where they seemed likely to create ambiguities for the modern reader. Spelling has, however, been standardised for writers' names (Jonson not Johnson, Rymer not Rhimer), for play titles, and for Shakespearian characters.

Small omissions in the text are indicated by three dots: [. . .]; larger ones by three asterisks.

Footnotes intended by the original authors are distinguished with an asterisk, dagger, and so on; those added by the editor are numbered. Editorial notes within the text are placed within square brackets.

Act, scene and line-numbers have been supplied in all quotations from Shakespeare, in the form 2.1.85 (Act 2, scene 1, line 85). The text used for this purpose was the 'Tudor Shakespeare', ed. P. Alexander (Collins, 1951).

Classical quotations have been identified, and translations added, usually those in the Loeb library.

29. Thomas Rymer, from *A Short View of Tragedy*

1693

From *A Short View of Tragedy, It's Original Excellency, and Corruption. With Some Reflections on Shakespeare, and other Practitioners for the Stage* (1693).

For contemporary reactions, in addition to the next four items, see the edition of *The Critical Works of Thomas Rymer* by C. A. Zimansky (New Haven, 1956). See also the head-note to No. 15 in Volume 1.

*   *   *

[Chapter I] This thing of *Action* finds the blindside of humane kind an hundred ways. We laugh and weep with those that laugh or weep; we gape, stretch, and are very *dotterels* by example.

Action is speaking to the Eyes, and all *Europe* over Plays have been represented with great applause in a Tongue unknown, and sometimes without any Language at all.

Many, peradventure, of the Tragical Scenes in *Shakespeare*, cry'd up for the *Action*, might do yet better without words. Words are a sort of heavy baggage, that were better out of the way at the push of Action; especially in his *bombast Circumstance*, where the Words and Action are seldom akin, generally are inconsistent, at cross purposes, embarrass or destroy each other. Yet to those who take not the words distinctly there may be something in the buz and sound that, like a drone to a Bagpipe, may serve to set off the *Action*. For an instance of the former, would not a rap at the door better express *Iago*'s meaning than

> —*Call aloud.*
> Iago. *Do with like timerous accent, and dire yel,*
> *As when by night and negligence the fire*
> *Is spied in populous Cities.*   [1.1.75 ff]

For, what Ship? Who is Arrived? The Answer is,

> [2 *Gent.*] *'Tis one* Iago, *Auncient to the General,*
> [*Cas.*] *He has had most Favourable and Happy speed;*
> *Tempests themselves, high Seas, and houling Winds,*
> *The guttered Rocks, and congregated Sands,*
> *Traytors ensteep'd, to clog the guiltless Keel,*
> *As having sense of Beauty, do omit*
> *Their common Natures, letting go safely by*
> *The divine Desdemona.* [2.1.66 ff]

Is this the Language of the Exchange, or the Insuring-Office? Once in a man's life he might be content at *Bedlam* to hear such a rapture. In a Play one should speak like a man of business, his speech must be Πολιτικός, which the *French* render *Agissante*, the *Italians Negotiosa*, and *Operativa*; but by this Gentleman's talk one may well guess he has nothing to do. [4–5]

*   *   *

[Chapter VII] Othello: *More of a piece. In Tragedy, four parts. Fable, the Poets part. Cinthio's Novels. Othello altered for the worse. Marriage, absurd, forbidden by Horace. Fable of Othello; Use and Application. Othello's Love powder. High-German Doctor. Venetians' odd taste of things; Their Women fools; Employ Strangers; Hate the Moors. Characters: Nothing of the Moor in Othello, of a Venetian in Desdemona, of a Souldier in Iago. The Souldiers Character, by Horace; What by Shakespeare. Agamemnon. Venetians no sense of Jealousie. Thoughts, in Othello: in a Horse, or Mastiff, more sensibly exprest. Ill Manners, Outragious to a Nobleman, to Humanity. Address, in telling bad news; In Princes' Courts; In Aristophanes; In Rabelais. Venetian Senate: Their Wisdom.*

From all the Tragedies acted on our English Stage, *Othello* is said to bear the Bell away. The *Subject* is more of a piece, and there is indeed something like—there is, as it were, some phantom of—a *Fable*. The *Fable* is always accounted the *Soul* of Tragedy, and it is the *Fable* which is properly the *Poets* part, because the other three parts of Tragedy, to wit, the *Characters* are taken from the Moral Philosopher, the *thoughts* or sence from them that teach *Rhetorick*, and the last part, which is the *expression*, we learn from the Grammarians.

This Fable is drawn from a Novel compos'd in Italian by *Giraldi*

Cinthio, who also was a Writer of Tragedies, and to that use employ'd such of his Tales, as he judged proper for the Stage. But with this of the *Moor*, he meddl'd no farther.

Shakespeare alters it from the Original in several particulars, but always, unfortunately, for the worse. He bestows a name on his *Moor*, and styles him *the Moor of Venice*: a Note of pre-eminence which neither History nor Heraldry can allow him. *Cinthio*, who knew him best, and whose creature he was, calls him simply a *Moor*. We say *the Piper of Strasburgh*; *the Jew of Florence*; and, if you please, *the Pindar of Wakefield*: all upon Record, and memorable in their Places. But we see no such Cause for the *Moor*'s preferment to that dignity. And it is an affront to all Chroniclers and Antiquaries to top upon 'em a *Moor* with that mark of renown who yet had never faln within the Sphere of their Cognisance.

Then is the *Moor*'s *Wife*, from a simple Citizen in *Cinthio*, dress'd up with her Top knots and rais'd to be *Desdemona*, a Senators Daughter. All this is very strange, and therefore pleases such as reflect not on the improbability. This match might well be without the Parents' Consent. Old *Horace* long ago forbad the banns:

> *Sed non ut placidis Coeant immitia, non ut*
> *Serpentes avibus geminentur, tigribus agni.*[1]

The Fable.

Othello, *a Blackamoor Captain, by talking of his Prowess and Feats of War makes* Desdemona, *a Senators Daughter, to be in love with him and to be married to him, without her Parents' knowledge. And having preferred* Cassio *to be his Lieutenant* (*a place which his Ensign* Iago *sued for*) Iago, *in revenge, works the* Moor *into a Jealousy that* Cassio *Cuckolds him: which he effects by stealing and conveying a certain Handkerchief, which had at the Wedding been by the* Moor *presented to his Bride. Hereupon* Othello *and* Iago *plot the Deaths of* Desdemona *and* Cassio. Othello *Murders her, and soon after is convinced of her Innocence. And as he is about to be carried to Prison, in order to be punish'd for the Murder He kills himself.*

What ever rubs or difficulty may stick on the Bark, the Moral, sure, of this Fable is very instructive.

1. First, This may be a caution to all Maidens of Quality how, without their Parents consent, they run away with *Blackamoors*.

---

[1] Horace, *Ars Poetica* (*A.P.*), 12 f: 'This licence we poets claim and in our turn we grant the like; but not so far that savage should mate with tame, or serpents couple with birds, lambs with tigers.'

Di non si accompagnare con huomo, cui la natura & il cielo, & il modo della vita, disgiunge da noi. Cinthio.

Secondly, This may be a warning to all good Wives that they look well to their Linnen.

Thirdly, This may be a lesson to Husbands, that before their Jealousie be Tragical the proofs may be Mathematical.

Cinthio affirms that *She was not overcome by a Womanish Appetite but by the Vertue of the Moor*. It must be a good-natur'd Reader that takes *Cinthio's* word in this case, tho' in a Novel. *Shakespeare*, who is accountable both to the *Eyes* and to the *Ears*, and to convince the very heart of an Audience, shews that *Desdemona* was won by hearing *Othello* talk.

> Othello.——*I spake of most disastrous chances,*
> *Of Moving accidents, by flood and field;* ...   [1.3.134 ff]

This was the Charm, this was the philtre, the love-powder that took the Daughter of this Noble Venetian. This was sufficient to make the *Black-amoor* White and reconcile all, tho' there had been a Cloven-foot into the bargain.

A meaner woman might be as soon taken by *Aqua Tetrachymagogon*. *Nodes, Cataracts, Tumours, Chilblains, Carnosity, Shankers*, or any *Cant* in the Bill of an High-German Doctor is as good *fustian Circumstance*, and as likely to charm a Senators Daughter. But it seems the noble Venetians have an other sence of things. The *Doge* himself tells us:

> Doge. *I think this Tale wou'd win my Daughter too.*   [1.3.171]

Horace tells us:

> *Intererit Multum—*
> *Colchus an Assyrius, Thebis nutritus, an Argis.*[1]

Shakespeare in this Play calls 'em the *supersubtle Venetians*, yet examine throughout the Tragedy, there is nothing in the noble *Desdemona* that is not below any Countrey Chamber-maid with us.

And the account he gives of their Noblemen and Senate can only be calculated for the latitude of *Gotham*.

The Character of that State is to employ strangers in their Wars. But shall a Poet thence fancy that they will set a Negro to be their General,

---

[1] *Ibid.*, 114 ff: 'Vast difference will it make, [whether a god be speaking or a hero] ... a Colchian or an Assyrian, one bred at Thebes or at Argos' [*i.e.*, the Assyrian would be effeminate, the Colchian not, but both would be barbarians].

or trust a *Moor* to defend them against the *Turk*? With us a *Black-amoor* might rise to be a Trumpeter: but *Shakespeare* would not have him less than a Lieutenant-General. With us a *Moor* might marry some little drab, or Small-coal Wench: *Shakespeare* would provide him the Daughter and Heir of some great Lord or Privy-Councellor, and all the Town should reckon it a very suitable match. Yet the English are not bred up with that hatred and aversion to the *Moors* as are the Venetians, who suffer by a perpetual Hostility from them.

Littora littoribus contraria—[1]

Nothing is more odious in Nature than an improbable lye; and certainly never was any Play fraught like this of *Othello* with improbabilities.

The *Characters* or Manners, which are the second part in a Tragedy, are not less unnatural and improper than the Fable was improbable and absurd.

Othello is made a Venetian General. We see nothing done by him nor related concerning him that comports with the condition of a General—or, indeed, of a Man—unless the killing himself to avoid a death the Law was about to inflict upon him. When his Jealousy had wrought him up to a resolution of's taking revenge for the suppos'd injury, he sets *Iago* to the fighting part to kill *Cassio*, and chuses himself to murder the silly Woman his Wife, that was like to make no resistance.

His Love and his Jealousie are no part of a Souldiers Character, unless for Comedy.

But what is most intolerable is *Iago*. He is no *Black-amoor* Souldier, so we may be sure he should be like other Souldiers of our acquaintance. Yet never in Tragedy nor in Comedy nor in Nature was a Souldier with his Character; take it in the Authors own words:

> Emilia.   —*some Eternal Villain,*
> *Some busie, and insinuating Rogue,*
> *Some cogging, couzening Slave, to get some Office.*   [4.2.131 ff]

Horace Describes a Souldier otherwise:

> *Impiger, iracundus, inexorabilis, acer.*[2]

[1] Virgil, *Aeneid*, 4.628: 'Shore clash with shore.'
[2] Horace, *A.P.*, 121: 'impatient, passionate, ruthless, fierce'.

Shakespeare knew his Character of *Iago* was inconsistent. In this very Play he pronounces,

> If thou dost deliver more or less than Truth,
> Thou are no Souldier.— [2.3.210 ff]

This he knew, but to entertain the Audience with something new and surprising, against common sense and Nature, he would pass upon us a close, dissembling, false, insinuating rascal instead of an open-hearted, frank, plain-dealing Souldier, a character constantly worn by them for some thousands of years in the World.

Tiberius Cæsar had a Poet Arraign'd for his Life because *Agamemnon* was brought on the Stage by him with a character unbecoming a Souldier.

Our *Ensigns* and Subalterns, when disgusted by the Captain, throw up their Commissions, bluster, and are bare-fac'd. *Iago*, I hope, is not brought on the Stage in a Red Coat. I know not what Livery the Venetians wear, but am sure they hold not these conditions to be *alla soldatesca.* . . .

Nor is our Poet more discreet in his *Desdemona*. He had chosen a Souldier for his Knave, and a Venetian Lady is to be the Fool. This Senator's Daughter runs away to (a Carriers Inn) the *Sagittary*, with a *Black-amoor*; is no sooner wedded to him but the very night she Beds him is importuning and teizing him for a young smock-fac'd Lieutenant, *Cassio*; and tho' she perceives the *Moor* Jealous of *Cassio*, yet will she not forbear, but still rings *Cassio*, *Cassio* in both his Ears.

Roderigo is the Cully of *Iago*, brought in to be murder'd by *Iago*, that *Iago*'s hands might be the more in Blood, and be yet the more abominable Villain—who without that was too wicked on all Conscience, and had more to answer for than any Tragedy, or Furies, could inflict upon him. So there can be nothing in the *characters* either for the profit, or to delight an Audience.

The third thing to be consider'd is the *Thoughts*. But from such *Characters* we need not expect many that are either true, or fine, or noble.

And without these—that is, without sense or meaning—the fourth part of Tragedy, which is the *expression*, can hardly deserve to be treated on distinctly. The verse rumbling in our Ears are of good use to help off the action. In the *Neighing* of an Horse or in the *growling* of a Mastiff there is a meaning, there is as lively expression and, may I say, more humanity than many times in the Tragical flights of *Shakespeare*.

Step then amongst the Scenes to observe the Conduct in this Tragedy.

The first we see are *Iago* and *Roderigo*, by Night in the Streets of *Venice*. After growling a long time together they resolve to tell *Brabantio* that his Daughter is run away with the *Black-a-moor*. *Iago* and *Roderigo* were not of quality to be familiar with *Brabantio*, nor had any provocation from him to deserve a rude thing at their hands. *Brabantio* was a Noble Venetian, one of the Sovereign Lords and principal persons in the Government, Peer to the most Serene *Doge*, one attended with more state, ceremony and punctillio than any English Duke or Nobleman in the Government will pretend to. This misfortune in his Daughter is so prodigious, so tender a point, as might puzzle the finest Wit of the most *supersubtle* Venetian to touch upon it, or break the discovery to her Father. See then how delicately *Shakespeare* minces the matter:

> Rod. *What ho*, Brabantio, *Signior* Brabantio, *ho.*
> Iago. *Awake, what ho*, Brabantio,
> *Thieves, thieves, thieves:*
> *Look to your House, your Daughter, and your Bags*
> *Thieves, thieves.*
>   [*Brabantio at a Window.*
> Bra. *What is the reason of this terrible summons?*
> *What is the matter there?*
> Rod. *Signior, is all your Family within?*
> Iago. *Are your Doors lockt?*
> Bra. *Why, wherefore ask you this?*
> Iago. *Sir, you are robb'd, for shame put on your Gown,*
> *Your Heart is burst, you have lost half your Soul,*
> *Even now, very now, an old black Ram*
> *Is tupping your white Ewe: arise, arise,*
> *Awake the snorting Citizens with the Bell,*
> *Or else the Devil will make a Grandsire of you, arise I say.*
>
> [1.1.79 ff]

Nor have they yet done; amongst other ribaldry they tell him:

> Iago. *Sir, you are one of those that will not serve God, if the Devil bid you; because we come to do you service, you think us Ruffians, you'le have your Daughter covered with a Barbary Stallion. You'le have your*

Nephews neigh to you; you'le have Coursers for Cousins, and Gennets for Germans.
Bra. *What prophane wretch art thou?*
Iago. *I am one, Sir, that come to tell you, your Daughter and the Moor, are now making the Beast with two backs.* [1.1.109 ff]

In former days there wont to be kept at the Courts of Princes some body in a Fools Coat, that in pure simplicity might let slip something which made way for the ill news and blunted the shock, which otherwise might have come too violent upon the party. *Aristophanes* puts *Nicias* and *Demosthenes* into the disguise of Servants, that they might, without indecency, be Drunk; and Drunk he must make them that they might without reserve lay open the *Arcana* of State, and the Knavery of their *Ministers*. After King *Francis* had been taken Prisoner at *Pavia*, *Rabelais* tells of a Drunken bout between *Gargantua* and Fryer *John*, where the valiant Fryer, bragging over his Cups, amongst his other flights says he, *Had I liv'd in the days of Jesus Christ, I would ha' guarded* Mount Olivet *that the Jews should never ha' tane him. The Devil fetch me, if I would not have ham string'd those Mr. Apostles, that after their good Supper, ran away so scurvily and left their Master to shift for himself. I hate a Man should run away, when he should play at sharps. Pox on't, that I shou'd not be King of France for an hundred years or two. I wou'd curtail all our French Dogs that ran away at* Pavia. This is address, this is truly Satyr, where the preparation is such that the thing principally design'd falls in, as it only were of course.

But *Shakespeare* shews us another sort of address, his manners and good breeding must not be like the rest of the Civil World. *Brabantio* was not in Masquerade, was not *incognito*; *Iago* well knew his rank and dignity.

Iago. *The Magnifico is much beloved,*
And hath in his effect, a voice potential
As double as the Duke— [1.2.12 ff]

But besides the Manners to a *Magnifico*, humanity cannot bear that an old Gentleman in his misfortune should be insulted over with such a rabble of Skoundrel language, when no cause or provocation. Yet thus it is on our Stage, this is our School of good manners, and the *Speculum Vitæ*.

But our *Magnifico* is here in the dark, nor are yet his Robes on: attend him to the Senate house and there see the difference, see the effects of Purple.

So, by and by, we find the Duke of *Venice* with his Senators in Councel at Midnight, upon advice that the Turks, or Ottamites, or both together were ready in transport Ships put to Sea in order to make a Descent upon *Cyprus*. This is the posture when we see *Brabantio* and *Othello* join them. By their Conduct and manner of talk a body must strain hard to fancy the Scene at *Venice*, and not rather in some of our Cinq-ports, where the Baily and his Fisher-men are knocking their heads together on account of some Whale or some terrible broil upon the Coast. But to shew them true Venetians the Maritime affairs stick not long on their hand; the publick may sink or swim. They will sit up all night to hear a Doctors Commons Matrimonial Cause, and have the Merits of the Cause at large laid open to 'em, that they may decide it before they Stir. What can be pleaded to keep awake their attention so wonderfully?

Never, sure, was *form* of *pleading* so tedious and so heavy as this whole Scene, and midnight entertainment. Take his own words: says the *Respondent*,

> Oth. *Most potent, grave, and reverend Signiors,*
> *My very noble, and approv'd good Masters:*
> *That I have tane away this old mans Daughter;*
> *It is most true: true, I have Married her,*
> *The very front and head of my offending*
> *Hath this extent, no more. Rude I am in my speech.*
> *And little blest with the set phrase of peace,*
> *For since these Arms of mine had seven years pith,*
> *Till now some nine Moons wasted, they have us'd*
> *Their dearest action in the Tented Field:*
> *And little of this great World can I speak,*
> *More than pertains to Broils and Battail,*
> *And therefore little shall I grace my Cause,*
> *In speaking of my self; yet by your gracious patience*
> *I would a round unvarnish'd Tale deliver,*
> *Of my whole course of love, what drugs, what charms*
> *What Conjuration, and what mighty Magick,*
> *(For such proceedings am I charg'd withal)*
> *I won his Daughter.*   [1.3.76 ff]

All this is but *Preamble*, to tell the Court that He wants words. This was the Eloquence which kept them up all Night, and drew their attention in the midst of their alarms.

One might rather think the novelty and strangeness of the case prevail'd upon them: no, the Senators do not reckon it strange at all. Instead of starting at the Prodigy every one is familiar with *Desdemona* as he were her own natural Father, rejoice in her good fortune and wish their own several Daughters as hopefully married. Should the Poet have provided such a Husband for an only Daughter of any noble Peer in *England* the *Black-amoor* must have chang'd his Skin to look our House of Lords in the Face.

Æschylus is noted in *Aristophanes* for letting *Niobe* be two or three *Acts* on the Stage before she speaks. Our Noble Venetian, sure, is in the other more unnatural extreme. His words flow in abundance, no Butter-Quean can be more lavish. Nay, he is for talking of State-Affairs too, above any body:

> Bra. *Please it your Grace, on to the State Affairs—* [1.3.190]

Yet is this *Brabantio* sensible of his affliction; before the end of the Play his Heart breaks, he dies.

> Gra. *Poor* Desdemona, *I am glad thy Father's dead,*
> *Thy match was mortal to him, and pure grief*
> *Shore his old thread in twain—* [5.2.207-9]

A third part in a Tragedy is the *Thoughts*. From Venetians, Noblemen, and Senators we may expect fine *Thoughts*. Here is a tryal of skill: for a parting blow the *Duke* and *Brabantio* Cap *sentences*. Where then shall we seek for the *Thoughts*, if we let slip this occasion? Says the Duke:

> Duk. *Let me speak like your self and lay a* Sentence,
> *Which like a greese or step, may help these lovers*
> *Into your favour.*
> *When remedies are past the grief is ended,*
> *By seeing the worst which late on hopes depended....*
> Bra. *So let the Turk of* Cyprus *us beguile*
> *We lose it not so long as we can smile;*
> *He bears the sentence well, that nothing bears*
> *But the free comfort which from thence he hears....* [1.3.199 ff]

How far wou'd the Queen of *Sheba* have travell'd to hear the Wisdom of our Noble Venetians? or is not our *Brentford* a *Venetian* Colony, for methinks their talk is the very same? ...

What provocation or cause of malice our Poet might have to Libel the most *Serene Republick* I cannot tell; but certainly there can be no wit in this representation.

For the *Second Act* our Poet, having dispatcht his affairs at *Venice*, shews the Action next (I know not how many leagues off) in the Island of *Cyprus*. The Audience must be there too: and yet our *Bays* had it never in his head to make any provision of Transport Ships for them. In the days that the *Old Testament* was Acted in *Clerkenwell* by the *Parish Clerks* of *London* the Israelites might pass through the *Red sea*: but alass, at this time, we have no *Moses* to bid the Waters *make way*, and to Usher us along. Well, the absurdities of this kind break no Bones. They make Fools of us but do not hurt our Morals.

Come a-shoar then, and observe the Countenance of the People after the dreadful Storm, and their apprehensions from an Invasion by the Ottomites, their succour and friends scatter'd and tost no body knew whither. The first that came to Land was *Cassio*. His first Salutation to the Governour, *Montano*, is:

> Cas. *Thanks to the valiant of this Isle:*
> *That so approve the Moor, and let the Heavens*
> *Give him defence against their Elements,*
> *For I have lost him on the dangerous Sea.*   [2.1.43 ff]

To him the Governour speaks, indeed, like a Man in his wits.

> Mont. *Is he well Shipt?*

The Lieutenant answers thus:

> Cas. *His Bark is stoutly Tymber'd, and his Pilot*
> *Of very expert, and approv'd allowance,*
> *Therefore my hopes (not surfeited to death)*
> *Stand in bold care.*   [2.1.47 ff]

The Governour's first question was very proper; his next question, in this posture of affairs, is:

> Mont. *But, good Lieutenant, is our general Wiv'd?*   [2.1.60]

A question so remote, so impertinent and absurd, so odd and surprising never entered *Bayes*'s *Pericranium*. Only the answer may Tally with it.

> Cas. *Most fortunately; he hath atcheiv'd a Maid,*
> *That Parragons description, and wild fame:*
> *One that excels the quirks of blasoning Pens:*
> *And in the essential vesture of Creation,*
> *Does bear an excellency—*   [2.1.61 ff]

They who like this Author's writing will not be offended to find so much repeated from him. I pretend not here to tax either the *Sense* or the *Language*; those *Circumstances* had their proper place in the Venetian Senate. What I now cite is to shew how probable, how natural, how reasonable the Conduct is, all along.

I thought it enough that *Cassio* should be acquainted with a Virgin of that rank and consideration in *Venice* as *Desdemona*. I wondred that in the Senate-house every one should know her so familiarly. Yet here also at *Cyprus* every body is in a rapture at the name of *Desdemona*: except only *Montano*, who must be ignorant that *Cassio*, who has an excellent cut in shaping an Answer, may give him the satisfaction:

> Mont. *What is she?*
> Cas. *She that I spoke of: our Captains Captain,*
> *Left in the Conduct of the bold* Iago,
> *Whose footing here anticipates our thoughts*
> *A Sennets speed: great* Jove Othello *guard,*
> *And swell his Sail with thine own powerful breath,*
> *That he may bless this Bay with his Tall Ship,*
> *And swiftly come to* Desdemona's *Arms,*
> *Give renewed fire to our extincted Spirits,*
> *And bring all* Cyprus *comfort:*
>
> Enter Desdemona, &c.
> —O behold,
>
> *The riches of the Ship is come on shoar.*
> *Ye men of* Cyprus, *let her have your Knees:*
> *Hail to the Lady: and the Grace of Heaven*
> *Before, behind thee, and on every hand.*
> *Enwheel thee round—* [2.1.73 ff]

In the name of phrenzy, what means this Souldier? or would he talk thus if he meant any thing at all? Who can say *Shakespeare* is to blame in his *Character* of a Souldier? Has he not here done him reason? When cou'd our *Tramontains* talk at this rate? But our *Jarsey* and *Garnsey* Captains must not speak so fine things, nor compare with the Mediterranean, or Garrisons in *Rhodes* and *Cyprus*.

The next thing our Officer does is to salute *Iago's* Wife, with this *Congee* to the Husband:

> Cas. *Good Ancient, you are welcome, welcome Mistriss,*
> *Let it not Gall your Patience, good* Iago,
> *That I extend my Manners, 'tis my Breeding,*

That gives me this bold shew of Curtesy.
Iago. *Sir, would she give you so much of her lips,*
As of her tongue she has bestow'd on me,
You'd have enough.
Desd. *Alass! she has no speech.*   [2.1.96 ff]

Now follows a long rabble of Jack-pudden farce betwixt *Iago* and
Desdemona, that runs on with all the little plays, jingle, and trash below
the patience of any Countrey Kitchin-maid with her Sweet-heart. The
Venetian *Donna* is hard put to't for pastime! And this is all, when they
are newly got on shoar from a dismal Tempest, and when every
moment she might expect to hear her Lord (as she calls him), that she
runs so mad after, is arriv'd or lost. And moreover,

— *In a Town of War,*
— *The peoples Hearts brimful of fear.*   [2.3.205 f]

Never in the World had any Pagan Poet his Brains turn'd at this
Monstrous rate. But the ground of all this Bedlam-Buffoonry we
saw [in Chapter V], in the case of the French *Strolers*: the Company for
Acting *Christs Passion* or the *Old Testament* were Carpenters, Coblers,
and illiterate fellows, who found that the Drolls and Fooleries inter-
larded by them brought in the rabble and lengthened their time, so
they got Money by the bargain. Our *Shakespeare*, doubtless, was a great
Master in this craft. These Carpenters and Coblers were the guides he
followed. And it is then no wonder that we find so much farce and
Apocryphal Matter in his Tragedies. Thereby un-hallowing the Theatre,
profaning the name of Tragedy, and instead of representing Men and
Manners turning all Morality, good sence, and humanity into mockery
and derision.

But pass we to something of a more serious air and Complexion.
Othello and his Bride are the first Night no sooner warm in Bed
together but a Drunken Quarrel happening in the Garison two
Souldiers Fight, and the General rises to part the Fray. He swears,

Othel. *Now by Heaven,*
My blood begins my safer guides to rule,
And passion, having my best judgment cool'd,
Assays to lead the way: if once I stir,
Or do but lift this arm, the best of you
Shall sink in my rebuke: give me to know
How this foul rout began; who set it on,
And he that is approv'd in this offence,

Tho' he had twin'd with me both at a birth,
Should lose me: what, in a Town of War,
Yet wild, the peoples Hearts brimful of fear,
To manage private, and domestick quarrels,
In Night, and on the Court, and guard of safety,
'Tis Monstrous. Iago, *who began?*   [2.3.196 ff]

In the days of yore, Souldiers did not swear in this fashion. What should a Souldier say farther when he swears, unless he blaspheme? Action shou'd speak the rest: what follows must be *ex ore gladii.* He is to rap out an Oath, not Wire-draw and Spin it out. By the style one might judge that *Shakespeare's* Souldiers were never bred in a Camp but rather had belong'd to some Affidavit-Office. Consider also throughout this whole Scene how the *Moorish* General proceeds in examining into this *Rout:* no Justice *Clod-pate* could go on with more Phlegm and deliberation. The very first night that he lyes with the *Divine Desdemona* to be thus interrupted might provoke a Mans Christian Patience to swear in another style. But a Negro General is a Man of strange Mettle: only his Venetian Bride is a match for him. She understands that the Souldiers in the Garison are by th' ears together, and presently she at midnight is in amongst them.

Desd. *What's the matter there?*
Othel. *All's well now Sweeting—*
Come away to Bed—   [2.3.243 ff]

In the beginning of this *second Act,* before they had lain together, *Desdemona* was said to be *our Captains Captain.* Now they are no sooner in Bed together but *Iago* is advising *Cassio* in these words:

Iago.—*Our Generals Wife is now the General, I may say so in this respect, for that he hath devoted, and given up himself to the contemplation, mark, and devotement of her parts and graces. Confess your self freely to her, importune her; she'll help to put you in your place again: she is so free, so kind, so apt, so blessed a disposition, that she holds it a vice in her goodness, not to do more than she is requested. This broken joint between you and her Husband, intreat her to splinter—* [2.3.304 ff]

And he says afterwards:

Iago.—*'Tis most easie*
The inclining Desdemona *to subdue,*
In any honest suit. She's fram'd as fruitful,
As the free Elements: And then for her

To win the Moor, were't to renounce his Baptism,
All seals and symbols of redeemed sin,
His soul is so enfetter'd to her love,
That she may make, unmake, do what she list:
Even as her appetite shall play the God
With his weak function—   [2.3.328 ff]

This kind of discourse implies an experience and long conversation, the Honey-Moon over, and a Marriage of some standing. Would any man in his wits talk thus of a Bridegroom and Bride the first night of their coming together? Yet this is necessary for our Poet; it would not otherwise serve his turn. This is the source, the foundation of his Plot; hence is the spring and occasion for all the Jealousie and bluster that ensues.

Nor are we in better circumstances for *Roderigo*. The last thing said by him in the former *Act* was,

> Rod.—*I'll go sell all my Land.*   [1.3.377]

A fair Estate is sold to *put money in his Purse* for this adventure. And lo here, the next day:

> Rod. *I do follow here in the Chace, not like a Hound that hunts, but one that fills up the cry: My Money is almost spent. I have been tonight exceedingly well cudgell'd. I think the issue will be, I shall have so much experience for my pains, and so no Money at all, and with a little more wit return to* Venice.   [2.3.352 ff]

The Venetian squire had a good riddance for his Acres. The Poet allows him just time to be once drunk, a very conscionable reckoning!

In this *Second Act* the face of affairs could in truth be no other than

> *—In a Town of War,*
> *Yet wild, the peoples Hearts brim-ful of fear.*   [2.3.205 f]

But nothing either in this *Act* or in the rest that follow shew any colour or complexion, any resemblance or proportion to that face and posture it ought to bear. Should a Painter draw any one *Scene* of this Play, and write over it *This is a Town of War*, would any body believe that the Man were in his senses? Would not a *Goose* or *Dromedary* for it be a name as just and suitable? And what in Painting would be absurd can never pass upon the World for Poetry.

Cassio, having escaped the Storm, comes on shoar at *Cyprus*; that night gets Drunk, Fights; is turn'd out from his Command; grows sober again, takes advice how to be restor'd, is all Repentance and Mortification; yet before he sleeps is in the Morning at his Generals door, with a noise of Fiddles and a Droll to introduce him to a little Mouth-speech with the Bride.

> Cassio. *Give me advantage of some brief discourse*
> *With* Desdemona *alone.*
> Em. *Pray you come in,*
> *I will bestow you, where you shall have time*
> *To speak your bosom freely.*   [3.1.52 ff]

So, they are put together. And when he had gone on a good while *speaking his bosom, Desdemona* answers him.

> Des. *Do not doubt that, before* Emilia *here,*
> *I give thee warrant of thy place; assure thee,*
> *If I do vow a friendship, I'll perform it,*
> *To the last article—*   [3.3.19 ff]

Then, after a ribble rabble of fulsome impertinence, she is at her Husband slap dash:

> Desd.—*Good love, call him back.*
> Othel. *Not now, sweet* Desdemona, *some other time.*
> Desd. *But shall't shortly?*
> Othel. *The sooner, sweet, for you.*
> Desd. *Shall't be to-night at Supper?*
> Othel. *No, not tonight.*
> Desd. *To-morrow Dinner then?*
> Othel. *I shall not dine at home,*
> *I meet the Captains at the Citadel.*
> Desd. *Why then to morrow night, or Tuesday morn,*
> *Or night, or Wednesday morn?*   [3.3.55 ff]

After forty lines more at this rate they part, and then comes the wonderful Scene where *Iago*, by shrugs, half-words, and ambiguous reflections works *Othello* up to be Jealous. One might think, after what we have seen, that there needs no great cunning, no great poetry and address to make the *Moor* Jealous. Such impatience, such a rout for a handsome young fellow the very morning after her Marriage must make him either to be jealous or to take her for a *Changeling*, below his Jealousie. After this *Scene* it might strain the Poet's skill to reconcile the couple and allay the Jealousie. *Iago* now can only *actum agere*, and vex the audience with a nauseous repetition.

Whence comes it then, that this is the top scene, the Scene that raises *Othello* above all other Tragedies on our Theatres? It is purely from the *Action*; from the Mops and the Mows, the Grimace, the Grins and Gesticulation. Such scenes as this have made all the World run after *Harlequin* and *Scaramuccio*.

The several degrees of *Action* were amongst the Ancients distinguish'd by the *Cothurnus*, the *Soccus*, and by the *Planipes*. Had this scene been represented at old *Rome Othello* and *Iago* must have quitted their Buskins. They must have played *bare-foot*: the spectators would not have been content without seeing their Podometry, and the Jealousie work at the very Toes of 'em. Words—be they Spanish, or Polish, or any inarticulate sound—have the same effect, they can only serve to distinguish and, as it were, beat time to the *Action*. But here we see a known Language does wofully encumber and clog the operation: as either forc'd, or heavy, or trifling, or incoherent, or improper, or most-what improbable. When no words interpose to spoil the conceipt every one interprets as he likes best. So in that memorable dispute betwixt *Panurge* and our English Philosopher in *Rabelais*, perform'd without a word speaking: the Theologians, Physicians, and Surgeons made one inference; the Lawyers, Civilians, and Canonists drew another conclusion more to their mind.

Othello, the night of his arrival at *Cyprus*, is to consummate with *Desdemona*: they go to Bed. Both are rais'd, and run into the Town amidst the Souldiers that were a fighting: then go to Bed again. That morning he sees *Cassio* with her; she importunes him to restore *Cassio*. *Othello* shews nothing of the Souldiers Mettle, but like a tedious, drawling, tame Goose, is gaping after any paultrey insinuation, labouring to be jealous, and catching at every blown surmize.

> Iago. *My Lord, I see you are moved.*
> Oth. *No, not much moved.*
> *Do not think but* Desdemona *is honest.*
> Iago. *Long live she so, and long live you to think so.*
> Oth. *And yet how Nature erring from it self,*
> Iago. *Aye, There's the point: as to be bold with you,*
> *Not to affect many proposed Matches*
> *Of her own clime, complexion, and degree,*
> *Wherein we see, in all things, Nature tends,*
> *Fye, we may smell in such a will most rank,*
> *Foul disproportion, thoughts unnatural—* [3.3.228 ff]

The Poet here is certainly in the right, and by consequence the foundation of the Play must be concluded to be Monstrous, and the constitution, all over, to be *most rank,*

> *Foul disproportion, thoughts unnatural.*

Which, instead of moving pity or any passion Tragical and Reasonable,
can produce nothing but horror and aversion, and what is odious and
grievous to an Audience. After this fair Morning's work the Bride
enters, drops a Curtsey.

> Desd. *How now, my dear* Othello,
> *Your Dinner, and the generous Islanders*
> *By you invited, do attend your presence.*
> Oth. *I am to blame.*
> Desd. *Why is your speech so faint? Are you not well?*
> Oth. *I have a pain upon my Fore-head, dear.*   [3.3.283 ff]

Michael Cassio came not from *Venice* in the Ship with *Desdemona,* nor
till this Morning could be suspected of an opportunity with her. And
'tis now but Dinner time; yet the *Moor* complains of his Fore-head. He
might have set a Guard on *Cassio,* or have lockt up *Desdemona,* or have
observ'd their carriage a day or two longer. He is on other occasions
phlegmatick enough: this is very hasty. But after Dinner we have
a wonderful flight:

> Othel. *What sense had I of her stoln hours of lust?*
> *I saw't not, thought it not, it harm'd not me:*
> *I slept the next night well, was free and merry,*
> *I found not Cassio's kisses on her lips—*   [3.3.342 ff]

A little after this says he:

> Oth. *Give me a living reason that she's disloyal.*
> Iago.—*I lay with* Cassio *lately.*
> *And being troubled with a raging Tooth, I could not sleep;*
> *There are a kind of men so loose of Soul,*
> *That in their sleeps will mutter their affairs,*
> *One of this kind is* Cassio:
> *In sleep I heard him say: sweet* Desdemona,
> *Let us be wary, let us hide our loves:*
> *And then, Sir, wou'd he gripe, and wring my hand,*
> *Cry out, sweet Creature; and then kiss me hard,*

As if he pluckt up kisses by the roots,
That grew upon my Lips, then laid his Leg
Over my Thigh, and sigh'd, and then
Cry'd, cursed fate, that gave thee to the Moor.   [3.3.413 ff]

By the Rapture of *Othello* one might think that he raves, is not of sound
Memory, forgets that he has not yet been two nights in the Matrimonial Bed with his *Desdemona*. But we find *Iago*, who should have
a better memory, forging his lies after the very same Model. The very
night of their Marriage at *Venice* the *Moor*, and also *Cassio*, were sent
away to *Cyprus*. In the *Second Act, Othello* and his Bride go the first
time to Bed; the *Third Act* opens the next morning. The parties have
been in view to this moment. We saw the opportunity which was given
for *Cassio* to *speak his bosom* to her; *once*, indeed, might go a great way
with a Venetian. But *once* will not do the Poets business: the *Audience*
must suppose a great many bouts, to make the plot operate. They must
deny their senses, to reconcile it to common sense, or make it any way
consistent, and hang together.

Nor, for the most part, are the single thoughts more consistent than
is the œconomy. The Indians do as they ought in painting the Devil
White: but, says *Othello*,

Oth.—*Her name that was as fresh*
As Dian's Visage, is now begrim'd and black,
As mine own face—   [3.3.389 ff]

There is not a Monky but understands Nature better; not a Pug in
Barbary that has not a truer taste of things.

Othel.   —*O now for ever*
Farewel the tranquil mind, farewell content;
Farewel the plumed troop, and the big Wars,
That make Ambition Vertue: O farewel,
Farewel the neighing Steed, and the shrill Trump,
The spirit stirring Drum, th' ear-piercing Fife,
The royal Banner, and all quality,
Pride, Pomp, and Circumstance of glorious War,
And O ye Mortal Engines, whose wide throats
Th' immortal Joves great clamours counterfeit,
Farewel, Othello's occupation's gone.   [3.3.351 ff]

These lines are recited here not for any thing Poetical in them, besides

43

the sound, that pleases. Yet this sort of imagery and amplification is
extreamly taking where it is just and natural. As in *Gorboduc*, when a
young Princess on whose fancy the personal gallantry of the King's
Son, then slain, had made a strong impression, thus, out of the abundance of her imagination, pours forth her grief:

> Marcella.—*Ah noble Prince! how oft have I beheld*
> *Thee mounted on thy fierce, and trampling Steed,*
> *Shining in Armour bright before the Tilt,*
> *Wearing thy Mistress sleeve ty'd on thy helm.*
> *Then charge thy staff, to please thy Ladies Eye,*
> *That bow'd the head piece of thy friendly Foe?*
> *How oft in arms, on Horse to bend the Mace,*
> *How oft in arms, on foot, to break the Spear;*
> *Which never now these Eyes may see agen?*

Notwithstanding that this Scene had proceeded with fury and bluster
sufficient to make the whole Isle ring of his Jealousy yet is *Desdemona*
diverting her self with a paultry buffoon, and only solicitous in quest
of *Cassio*.

> Desd. *Seek him, bid him come hither, tell him—*
> *Where shou'd I lose that Handkerchief,* Emilia?
> *Believe me I had rather lose my Purse,*
> *Full of Crusado's: And but my noble Moor*
> *Is true of mind, and made of no such baseness*
> *As Jealous Creatures are it were enough*
> *To put him to ill thinking.*
> Em. *Is he not Jealous?*
> Desd. *Who he? I think the Sun, where he was born,*
> *Drew all such humours from him.*   [3.4.16, 20 ff]

By this manner of speech one wou'd gather the couple had been
yoak'd together a competent while; what might she say more had
they cohabited and had been Man and Wife seven years?

She spies the *Moor*.

> Desd. *I will not leave him now,*
> *Till* Cassio *is recall'd.*   [3.4.29 f]
> *I have sent to bid* Cassio *come speak with you.*   [3.4.47]
> Othel.—*Lend me thy Handkerchief.*   [3.4.49]
> Desd.—*This is a trick to put me from my suit.*
> *I pray let* Cassio *be receiv'd agen.*   [3.4.88 f]

44

Em.—*Is not this man Jealous?* [3.4.100]
—*'Tis not a year or two shews us a man—* [3.4.104]

As if for the first year or two *Othello* had not been jealous! The *third Act* begins in the morning, at noon she drops the Handkerchief, after dinner she misses it, and then follows all this outrage and horrible clutter about it. If we believe a small Damosel in the last *Scene* of this *Act* this day is effectually seven days.

> Bianca.—*What keep a week away! seven days, seven nights,*
> *Eightscore eight hours, and lovers absent hours,*
> *More tedious than the Dial eightscore times.*
> *O weary reckoning!* [3.4.174 ff]

Our Poet is at this plunge that whether this *Act* contains the compass of one day, of seven days, or of seven years, or of all together the repugnance and absurdity would be the same. For *Othello*, all the while, has nothing to say or to do but what loudly proclaim him jealous; her friend and confidante *Emilia* again and again rounds her in the Ear that *the Man* is Jealous; yet this Venetian dame is neither to see, nor to hear, nor to have any sense or understanding, nor to strike any other note but *Cassio, Cassio*.

The Scotchman hearing *trut Scot, trut Scot*, when he saw it came from a Bird checkt his Choler, and put up his *Swerd* again, with a *Braad O God, God, if th'adst ben a Maan, as th' art ane Green Geuse, I sud ha stuck tha' to thin heart. Desdemona* and that Parrot might pass for Birds of a Feather; and if *Sauney* had not been more generous than *Othello*, but continued to insult the poor Creature after this beastly example, he would have given our Poet as good stuff to work upon, and his *Tragedy of the Green Geuse* might have deserv'd a better audience than this of *Desdemona*, or *The Moor of Venice*.

ACT IV.
Enter Iago *and* Othello

Iago. *Will you think so?*
Othel. *Think so*, Iago.
Iago. *What, to kiss in private?*
Othel. *An unauthorised kiss.*
Iago. *Or to be naked with her friend a-bed,*
An hour or more, not meaning any harm?
Othel. *Naked a-bed*, Iago, *and not mean harm?—* [4.1.1 ff]

At this gross rate of trifling our General and his Auncient March on most heroically, till the Jealous Booby has his Brains turn'd, and falls in a Trance. Would any imagine this to be the Language of Venetians, of Souldiers and mighty Captains? No *Bartholomew* Droll cou'd subsist upon such trash. But lo, a Stratagem never presented in Tragedy:

> Iago. *Stand you a while a part—*
> *—Incave your self;*
> *And mark the Jeers, the Gibes, and notable scorns,*
> *That dwell in every region of his face,*
> *For I will make him tell the tale a new,*
> *Where, how, how oft, how long ago, and when*
> *He has, and is again to Cope your Wife:*
> *I say, but mark his gesture—* [4.1.74 ff]

With this device *Othello* withdraws. Says *Iago* aside,

> Iago. *Now will I question* Cassio *of* Bianca,
> *A Huswife—*
> *That doats on* Cassio—
> *He when he hears of her cannot refrain*
> *From the excess of Laughter—*
> *As he shall smile, Othello shall go mad,*
> *And his unbookish jealousy must conster*
> *Poor Cassio's smiles, gesture, and light behaviour*
> *Quite in the wrong—* [4.1.93 ff]

So to work they go: and *Othello* is as wise a commentator, and makes his applications pat as heart cou'd wish—but I wou'd not expect to find this Scene acted nearer than in *Southwark* Fair. But the *Handkerchief* is brought in at last, to stop all holes and close the evidence. So now being satisfied with the proof, they come to a resolution that the offenders shall be murdered.

> Othel.—*But yet the pity of it,* Iago, *ah the pity.*
> Iago. *If you be so fond over her iniquity give her Patent to offend.*
> *For if it touches not you, it comes near no Body.*
> *Do it not with poison, strangle her in her Bed; Even the Bed she has contaminated.*
> Oth. *Good, good, the Justice of it pleases, very good.*
> Iago. *And for Cassio, let me be his undertaker—* [4.1.191 ff]

Iago had some pretence to be discontent with *Othello* and *Cassio*; and what passed hitherto was the operation of revenge. *Desdemona* had never done him harm, always kind to him and to his Wife; was his Country-woman, a Dame of quality. For him to abet her Murder shews nothing of a Souldier, nothing of a Man, nothing of Nature in it. The *Ordinary* of *Newgate* never had the like Monster to pass under his examination. Can it be any diversion to see a Rogue beyond what the Devil ever finish'd? Or wou'd it be any instruction to an Audience? *Iago* cou'd desire no better than to set *Cassio* and *Othello*, his two Enemies, by the Ears together: so he might have been reveng'd on them both at once. And chusing for his own share the Murder of *Desdemona* he had the opportunity to play booty, and save the poor harmless wretch. But the Poet must do every thing by contraries, to surprize the Audience still with something horrible and prodigious beyond any human imagination. At this rate he must out-do the Devil, to be a Poet in the rank with *Shakespeare*.

Soon after this arrives from *Venice Lodovico*, a noble Cousin of *Desdemona*; presently she is at him also, on the behalf of *Cassio*.

> Desd. *Cousin there's fallen between him and my Lord*
> *An unkind breach, but you shall make all well.* . . .
> Lod. *Is there division 'twixt my Lord and* Cassio?
> Desd. *A most unhappy one, I wou'd do much*
> *To attone them, for the love I bear to* Cassio.   [4.1.219 ff]

By this time, we are to believe the couple have been a week or two Married, and *Othello*'s Jealousie, that had rag'd so loudly and had been so uneasie to himself, must have reach'd her knowledge. The *Audience* have all heard him more plain with her than was needful to a Venetian capacity: and yet she must still be impertinent in her suit for *Cassio*. Well, this *Magnifico* comes from the *Doge* and Senators to displace *Othello*,

> Lod.—*Deputing* Cassio *in his Government.*
> Desd. *Trust me, I am glad on't.*
> Oth. *Indeed.*
> Desd. *My Lord.*
> Oth. *I am glad to see you mad.*
> Desd. *How, sweet* Othello?
> Oth. *Devil.*
> Desd. *I have not deserved this.*

Oth. O Devil, Devil—
Out of my sight.
Desd. I will not stay to offend you.
Lod. Truly, an obedient Lady.
I do beseech your Lordship call her back.
Oth. Mistress.
Desd. My Lord.
Oth. What would you with her, Sir?
Lod. Who, I, my Lord?
Oth. Aye, you did wish that I wou'd make her turn.
Sir, she can turn, and turn, and yet go on,
And turn agen, and she can weep, Sir, weep.
And she is obedient, as you say, obedient:
Very obedient—
Lod. What, strike your Wife?   [4.1.233 ff]

Of what flesh and blood does our Poet make these noble Venetians?
—the men without Gall; the Women without either Brains or Sense!
A Senator's Daughter runs away with this *Black-amoor*; the Government employs this *Moor* to defend them against the Turks, so resent
not the *Moor*'s Marriage at present; but, the danger over, her Father
gets the *Moor* Cashier'd, sends his Kinsman Seignior *Lodovico* to *Cyprus*
with the Commission for a new General; who, at his arrival, finds the
Moor calling the Lady his Kinswoman, Whore and Strumpet, and
kicking her. What says the *Magnifico?*

Lod. My Lord this would not be believ'd in Venice,
Tho' I shou'd swear I saw't, 'tis very much;
Make her amends: she weeps.   [4.1.238 ff]

The *Moor* has nobody to take his part, nobody of his Colour:
Lodovico has the new Governour *Cassio*, and all his Countrymen
Venetians about him. What Poet wou'd give a villanous *Black-amoor*
this Ascendant? What Tramontain could fancy the Venetians so low,
so despicable, or so patient? This outrage to an injur'd Lady, the *Divine
Desdemona*, might in a colder Climate have provoked some body to
be her Champion: but the Italians may well conclude we have a
strange Genius for Poetry. In the next Scene *Othello* is examining the
supposed Bawd. Then follows another storm of horrour and outrage
against the poor Chicken, his Wife. Some Drayman or drunken
Tinker might possibly treat his drab at this sort of rate, and mean no

harm by it; but for his excellency, a My lord General, to Serenade a Senator's Daughter with such a volly of scoundrel filthy Language, is sure the most absurd Maggot that ever bred from any Poets addle Brain. And she is in the right, who tells us,

> Emil.—*A Beggar in his Drink,*
> *Cou'd not have laid such terms upon his Callet.*   [4.2.121 f]

This is not to describe passion. *Seneca* had another notion in the Case:

> *Parvæ loquuntur curæ, ingentes stupent.*[1]

And so had the Painter, who drew *Agamemnon* with his Face covered. Yet to make all worse her Murder, and the manner of it, had before been resolv'd upon and concerted. But nothing is to provoke a Venetian: she takes all in good part. Had the Scene lain in *Russia* what cou'd we have expected more? With us a Tinker's Trull wou'd be Nettled, wou'd repartee with more spirit, and not appear so void of spleen.

> Desd. *O good* Iago,
> *What shall I do to win my Lord agen?*   [4.2.149 f]

No Woman bred out of a Pig-stye, cou'd talk so meanly. After this she is call'd to Supper with *Othello*, *Lodovico*, &c. After that comes a filthy sort of Pastoral Scene, where the *Wedding Sheets*, and Song of *Willow*, and her Mothers Maid, poor *Barbara*, are not the least moving things in this entertainment. But that we may not be kept too long in the dumps, nor the melancholy Scenes lye too heavy, undigested on our Stomach, this *Act* gives us for a farewell the *salsa, O picante*, some quibbles and smart touches, as *Ovid* had Prophecied:

> *Est & in obscœnos deflexa Tragœdia risus.*[2]

The last *Act* begins with *Iago* and *Roderigo*, who a little before had been upon the huff:

> Rod. *I say it is not very well: I will make my self known to Des-*
> *demona; if she will return me my Jewels, I will give over my suit, and*
> *repent my unlawful sollicitation, if not, assure your self, I'll seek*
> *satisfaction of you.*   [4.2.197 ff]

---

[1] Seneca, *Hippolytus*, 607: 'Light troubles speak; the weighty are struck dumb.'
[2] Ovid, *Tristia*, 2.409: 'There is too a tragedy involved in coarse laughter.'

Roderigo, a Noble Venetian, had sought *Desdemona* in Marriage, is troubled to find the *Moor* had got her from him, advises with *Iago*, who wheadles him to sell his Estate and go over the Sea to *Cyprus*, in expectation to Cuckold *Othello*, there having cheated *Roderigo* of all his Money and Jewels on pretence of presenting them to *Desdemona*. Our Gallant grows angry, and would have satisfaction from *Iago*; who sets all right by telling him *Cassio* is to be Governour, *Othello* is going with *Desdemona* into *Mauritania*. To prevent this you are to murder *Cassio* and then all may be well.

> Iago. *He goes into* Mauritania, *and takes with him the fair* Desdemona, *unless his abode be lingered here by some accident, wherein none can be so determinate, as the removing of* Cassio. [4.2.222 ff]

Had *Roderigo* been one of the *Banditi* he might not much stick at the Murder. But why *Roderigo* should take this for payment, and risque his person where the prospect of advantage is so very uncertain and remote no body can imagine. It had need to be a *supersubtle* Venetian that this Plot will pass upon. Then after a little spurt of villany and Murder we are brought to the most lamentable that ever appear'd on any Stage. A noble Venetian Lady is to be murdered by our Poet; in sober sadness, purely for being a Fool. No Pagan Poet but wou'd have found some *Machine* for her deliverance. *Pegasus* wou'd have strain'd hard to have brought old *Perseus* on his back, time enough, to rescue this *Andromeda* from so foul a Monster. Has our Christian Poetry no generosity, nor bowels? Ha, Sir *Lancelot*! ha St. *George*! will no Ghost leave the shades for us in extremity to save a distressed Damosel?

But for our comfort, however felonious is the Heart, hear with what soft language he does approach her, with a Candle in his Hand:

> Oth. *Put out the light and then put out the light;*
> *If I quench thee, thou flaming Minister,*
> *I can again thy former light restore—* [5.2.7 ff]

Who would call him a Barbarian, Monster, Savage? Is this a *Black-amoor*?

> *Soles occidere & redire possunt—*[1]

The very Soul and Quintessence of Sir *George Etheridge*.

One might think the General should not glory much in this action, but make an hasty work on't, and have turn'd his Eyes away from so

---

[1] Catullus, 5.4: 'Suns may set and rise again.'

unsouldierly an Execution. Yet is he all pause and deliberation, handles her as calmly, and is as careful of her Souls health, as it had been her *Father Confessor*: 'Have you prayed to Night, *Desdemona*?' But the suspence is necessary, that he might have a convenient while so to *roul his Eyes*, and so to *gnaw* his *nether lip* to the spectators. Besides the greater cruelty—*sub tam lentis maxillis.*[1]

But hark, a most tragical thing laid to her charge.

> Oth. *That Handkerchief, that I so lov'd, and gave thee,*
> *Thou gav'st to* Cassio.
> Desd. *No by my Life and Soul;*
> *Send for the man and ask him.*
> Oth.—*By Heaven, I saw my Handkerchief in his hand—*
> —*I saw the Handkerchief.*   [5.2.51 ff]

So much ado, so much stress, so much passion and repetition about an Handkerchief! Why was not this call'd the *Tragedy of the Handkerchief?* What can be more absurd than (as *Quintilian* expresses it) *in parvis litibus has Tragœdias movere?*[2] We have heard of *Fortunatus his Purse*, and of the *Invisible Cloak*, long ago worn thread-bare and stow'd up in the Wardrobe of obsolete Romances: one might think that were a fitter place for this Handkerchief than that it, at this time of day, be worn on the Stage, to raise every where all this clutter and turmoil. Had it been *Desdemona*'s Garter the Sagacious *Moor* might have smelt a Rat: but the Handkerchief is so remote a trifle no Booby on this side *Mauritania* cou'd make any consequence from it.

We may learn here, that a Woman never loses her Tongue, even tho' after she is stifl'd.

> Desd. *O falsly, falsly murder'd.*
> Em. *Sweet* Desdemona, *O sweet Mistress, speak.*
> Desd. *A guiltless death I dye.*
> Em. *O who has done the deed?*
> Desd. *No body, I my self, farewel.*
> *Commend me to my kind Lord, O farewel.*   [5.2.120 ff]

This *Desdemona* is a black swan; or an old *Black-amoor* is a bewitching Bed-fellow. If this be Nature, it is a *lascheté* below what the English Language can express.

For *Lardella*, to *make love, like an Humble Bee*, was, in *The Rehearsal*, thought a fancy odd enough. But hark what follows:

[1] Suetonius, *Tiberius*, 21.2: 'to be ground by jaws that crunch so slowly!'
[2] Quintilian, 6.1.36: 'to embark on such tragic methods in trivial cases.'

Oth.   —*O heavy hour!*
Methinks it shou'd be now a huge Eclipse
Of Sun and Moon, and that the affrighted globe
Shou'd yawn at Alteration.   [5.2.101 ff]

This is wonderful. Here is Poetry to *elevate* and *amuse*! Here is sound All-sufficient! It wou'd be uncivil to ask *Flamstead* if the Sun and Moon can both together be so hugely eclipsed, in any *heavy hour* whatsoever. Nor must the Spectators consult *Gresham* Colledge, whether a body is naturally *frighted* till he *Yawn* agen. The Fortune of *Greece* is not concern'd with these Matters. These are Physical circumstances a Poet may be ignorant in without any harm to the publick. These slips have no influence on our Manners and good Life, which are the Poets Province.

Rather may we ask here what unnatural crime *Desdemona*, or her Parents, had committed, to bring this Judgment down upon her?—to Wed a *Black-amoor*, and innocent to be thus cruelly murder'd by him. What instruction can we make out of this Catastrophe? Or whither must our reflection lead us? Is not this to envenome and sour our spirits, to make us repine and grumble at Providence and the government of the World? If this be our end, what boots it to be Vertuous?

Desdemona dropt the Handkerchief, and missed it that very day after her Marriage. It might have been rumpl'd up with her Wedding sheets, and this Night that she lay in her wedding sheets the *Fairey* Napkin (whilst *Othello* was stifling her) might have started up to disarm his fury, and stop his ungracious mouth. Then might she (in a Traunce for fear) have lain as dead. Then might he, believing her dead, touch'd with remorse, have honestly cut his own Throat, by the good leave and with the applause of all the Spectators. Who might thereupon have gone home with a quiet mind, admiring the beauty of Providence, fairly and truly represented on the Theatre.

Oth.—*Why, how shou'd she be murdered?*
Em. *Alas, who knows?*
Oth. *You heard her say her self it was not I.*
Em. *She did so, I must needs report a truth.*
Oth. *She's like a liar gone to burn in Hell.*
'*Twas I that did it.*
Em. *O, the more Angel she!*
And you the blacker Devil.

Oth. *She turn'd to folly, and she was an Whore.*
Em. *Thou dost belye her, and thou art a Devil.*
Oth. *She was false as Water.*
Em. *Thou art rash as Fire,*
To say that she was false: O she was heavenly true. [5.2.129 ff]

In this kind of Dialogue they continue for forty lines farther, before she bethinks her self to cry Murder.

Em.   —*Help, help, O help,*
The Moor has kill'd my Mistress, murder, Murder. [5.2.169 f]

But from this Scene to the end of the Play we meet with nothing but blood and butchery, described much-what to the style of *the last Speeches and Confessions of the persons executed at Tyburn.* With this difference, that there we have the *fact* and the due course of Justice, whereas our Poet, against all Justice and Reason, against all Law, Humanity and Nature, in a barbarous arbitrary way executes and makes havock of his subjects, *Hab-nab,* as they come to hand. *Desdemona* dropt her Handkerchief; therefore she must be stifl'd. *Othello,* by law to be broken on the Wheel, by the Poet's cunning escapes with cutting his own Throat. *Cassio,* for I know not what, comes off with a broken shin. *Iago* murders his Benefactor *Roderigo,* as this were poetical gratitude. *Iago* is not yet kill'd, because there never yet was such a villain alive. The Devil, if once he brings a man to be dipt in a deadly sin, lets him alone, to take his course: and now when the *Foul Fiend* has done with him, our wise Authors take the sinner into their poetical service there to accomplish him and do the Devils drudgery.

Philosophy tells us it is a principle in the Nature of Man *to be grateful*; *History* may tell us that *John an Oaks, John a Stiles,* or *Iago* were ungrateful. *Poetry* is to follow Nature. Philosophy must be his guide: history and *fact* in particular cases of *John an Oaks,* or *John of Styles* are no warrant or direction for a Poet. Therefore *Aristotle* is always telling us that Poetry is σπουδαιώτερον καὶ φιλοσοφώτερον, is more general and abstracted, is led more by the Philosophy, the reason and nature of things than History, which only records things higlety-piglety, right or wrong, as they happen. History might without any preamble or difficulty say that *Iago* was ungrateful; Philosophy then calls him unnatural. But the Poet is not without huge labour and preparation to expose the Monster; and, after, shew the Divine Vengeance executed upon him. The Poet is not to add wilful Murder to his ingratitude.

He has not antidote enough for the Poison: his Hell and Furies are not punishment sufficient for one single crime of that bulk and aggravation.

> Em. *O thou dull Moor, that Handkerchief thou speakest on,*
> *I found by Fortune, and did give my Husband:*
> *For often with a solemn earnestness,*
> *(More than indeed belong'd to such a trifle)*
> *He beg'd of me to steal it.*   [5.2.228 ff]

Here we see the meanest woman in the Play takes this *Handkerchief* for a *trifle* below her Husband to trouble his head about it. Yet we find it entered into our Poets head to make a Tragedy of this *Trifle.*

Then for the *unraveling of the Plot*, as they call it, never was old deputy Recorder in a Country Town, with his spectacles in summoning up the evidence, at such a puzzle so blunder'd and bedoultefied as is our Poet, to have a good riddance and get the *Catastrophe* off his hands.

What can remain with the Audience to carry home with them from this sort of Poetry for their use and edification? How can it work, unless, instead of settling the mind, and purging our passions, to delude our senses, disorder our thoughts, addle our brain, pervert our affections, hair our imaginations, corrupt our appetite, and fill our head with vanity, confusion, *Tintamarre* and Jingle-jangle beyond what all the Parish Clarks of *London*, with their *old Testament* farces and interludes in *Richard the Second*'s time, cou'd ever pretend to? Our only hopes for the good of their Souls can be, that these people go to the Playhouse as they do to Church, to sit still, look on one another, make no reflection, nor mind the Play more than they would a Sermon.

There is in this Play some burlesk, some humour, and ramble of Comical Wit; some shew, and some *Mimickry* to divert the spectators: but the tragical part is, plainly, none other than a Bloody Farce, without salt or savour.   (86–146)

[Chapter VIII] *Reflections on the* Julius Cæsar. *Men famous in History, to be rob'd of their good name, sacriledge.* Shakespeare, *abuse of History. Contradiction, in the character of* Brutus. . . . *Preparation in Poetry. Strong reasons in* Cassius. *Roman Senators impertinent as the Venetian,* Portia *as* Desdemona. *The same parts and good breeding. How talk of Business. Whispers.* Brutus's *Tinder-Box, Sleepy Boy, Fiddle.* Brutus *and* Cassius, *Flat-foot* Mimicks. *The Indignity.* . . . *Play of the Incarnation. The* Madonna's—*Shouting and Battel. Strollers in* Cornwal. *Rehearsal, law for acting it once a week.* . . .

In the former Play our Poet might be the bolder, the persons being all his own Creatures, and meer fiction. But here he sins not against Nature and Philosophy only but against the most known History and the memory of the Noblest Romans, that ought to be sacred to all Posterity. He might be familiar with *Othello* and *Iago*, as his own natural acquaintance: but *Cæsar* and *Brutus* were above his conversation. To put them in Fools Coats, and make them Jack-puddens in the *Shakespeare* dress, is a *Sacriledge* beyond any thing in *Spelman*. The Truth is, this authors head was full of villainous, unnatural images, and history has only furnish'd him with great names thereby to recommend them to the World, by writing over them *this is* Brutus, *this is* Cicero, *this is* Cæsar. But generally his History flies in his Face, and comes in flat contradiction to the Poets imagination. As for example: of *Brutus* says *Antony*, his Enemy,

> Ant.—*His life was gentle, and the Elements*
> *So mixt in him, that Nature might stand up,*
> *And say to all the World, this was a Man.*   [5.5.73 ff]

And when every body jug'd it necessary to kill *Antony*, our Author in his *Laconical* way, makes *Brutus* speak thus:

> Bru. *Our Course will seem too bloody,* Caius Cassius,
> *To cut the Head off, and then hack the Limbs,*
> *Like wrath in death, and envy afterwards;*
> *For* Antony *is but a Limb of* Cæsar:
> *Let's be Sacrificers, but not Butchers,* Caius.
> *We all stand up against the Spirit of* Cæsar,
> *And in the Spirit of man there is no blood;*
> *O that we then cou'd come by* Cæsars *Spirit,*
> *And not dismember* Cæsar; *but alas!*
> Cæsar *must bleed for it. And gentle friends,*
> *Let's kill him boldly, but not wrathfully;*
> *Let's carve him, as a dish fit for the Gods,*
> *Not hew him, as a Carkass fit for Hounds.*
> *And let our Hearts, as subtle Masters do,*
> *Stir up their Servants to an act of rage,*
> *And after seem to chide 'em. This shall make*
> *Our purpose necessary, and not envious:*
> *Which so appearing to the common eyes,*
> *We shall be call'd Purgers, not murderers.*

And for Mark Antony *think not of him:*
For he can do no more than Cæsars *arm,*
When Cæsars *head is off.*   [2.1.162 ff]

In these two speeches we have the true character of *Brutus*, according
to History. But when *Shakespeare*'s own blundering Maggot of self-
contradiction works, then must *Brutus* cry out:

Bru.—*Stoop*, Romans, *stoop,*
And let us bathe our hands in Cæsars *blood*
Up to the Elbows—   [3.1.106 ff]

... That Language which *Shakespeare* puts in the Mouth of *Brutus*
wou'd not suit, or be convenient, unless from some son of the Shambles,
or some natural offspring of the Butchery. But never any Poet so
boldly, and so barefac'd, flounced along from contradiction to contradiction. A little preparation and forecast might do well now and then.
For his *Desdemona*'s Marriage, he might have helped out the probability
by feigning how that some way or other a *Black-amoor* Woman had
been her Nurse, and suckl'd her, or that once upon a time some
Virtuoso had transfus'd into her Veins the Blood of a black Sheep:
after which she might never be at quiet till she is, as the Poet will have
it, *Tupt with an old black ram.*
But to match this pithy discourse of *Brutus* see the weighty argu-
mentative oration whereby *Cassius* draws him into the Conspiracy:

Cas.—Brutus, *and* Cæsar: *what shou'd be in that* Cæsar?
Why shou'd that name be sounded more than yours?
Write them together: yours is as fair a name:
Sound them, it doth become the mouth as well.
Weigh them, it is as heavy: conjure with them,
Brutus *will start a Spirit as soon as* Cæsar.
Now, in the names of all the Gods at once,
Upon what meat doth this our Cæsar *feed,*
That he is grown so great? Age, thou art sham'd;
Rome *thou hast lost the breed of noble bloods.*
When went there by an Age since the great flood,
But it was fam'd with more than with one man?
When could they say (till now) that talk'd of Rome,
That her wide Walls encompass'd but one man?
Now it is Rome *indeed, and room enough*
When there is in it but one only Man—   [1.2.142 ff]

One may Note that all our Author's Senators, and his Orators had their learning and education at the same school, be they *Venetians*, *Black-amoors*, *Ottamites*, or noble *Romans*. *Brutus* and *Cassius* here may *cap sentences* with *Brabantio* and the *Doge* of *Venice*, or any *Magnifico* of them all. We saw how the Venetian Senate spent their time when, amidst their alarms, call'd to Counsel at midnight. Here the *Roman* Senators, the midnight before *Cæsar's* death (met in the Garden of *Brutus* to settle the matter of their Conspiracy) are gazing up to the Stars, and have no more in their heads than to wrangle about which is the East and West.

> Decius. *Here lies the East, doth not the day break here?*
> Casca. *No.*
> Cinna. *O, pardon, Sir, it doth, and yon grey lines,*
> *That fret the Clouds, are Messengers of Day.*
> Casca. *You shall confess, that you are both deceiv'd:*
> *Here as I point my Sword, the Sun arises,*
> *Which is a great way growing in the South,*
> *Weighing the youthful season of the year.*
> *Some two months hence, up higher toward the North,*
> *He first presents his fire, and the high East*
> *Stands as the Capitol directly here.*   [2.1.101 ff]

This is directly, as *Bays* tells us, *to shew the World a Pattern here how men shou'd talk of Business.* But it wou'd be a wrong to the Poet not to inform the reader that on the Stage the Spectators see *Brutus* and *Cassius* all this while at *Whisper* together. That is the importance that deserves all the attention. But the *grand question* wou'd be: does the *Audience hear 'em Whisper?*

> Ush. *Why, truly I can't tell: there's much to be said upon the word Whisper—*

Another Poet wou'd have allow'd the noble *Brutus* a Watch-Candle in his Chamber this important night, rather than have puzzel'd his man *Lucius* to grope in the dark for a Flint and Tinder-box to get the Taper lighted. It wou'd have been no great charge to the Poet, however. Afterwards, another night, the Fiddle is in danger to be broken by this sleepy Boy:

> Bru. *If thou dost nod thou break'st thy Instrument.*   [4.3.269]

But pass we to the famous Scene where *Brutus* and *Cassius* are by the

Poet represented acting the parts of *Mimicks*: from the Nobility and Buskins they are made the *Planipedes*, are brought to daunce *barefoot* for a Spectacle to the people. Two Philosophers, two generals (*imperatores* was their title), the *ultimi Romanorum*, are to play the Bullies and Buffoon, to shew their Legerdemain, their *activity* of face, and divarication of Muscles. They are to play a prize, a tryal of skill in huffing and swaggering, like two drunken Hectors for a two-penny reckoning. . . . [Rymer is presumably referring to their quarrel, Act 4 scene 3.]

This may shew with what indignity our Poet treats the noblest *Romans*. But there is no other cloth in his Wardrobe. Every one must be content to wear a Fool's Coat who comes to be dressed by him. Nor is he more civil to the Ladies. *Portia* in good manners might have challeng'd more respect: she that shines, a glory of the first magnitude in the Gallery of Heroick Dames, is with our Poet scarce one remove from a Natural. She is the own Cousin-German, of one piece, the very same impertinent silly flesh and blood with *Desdemona*. *Shakespeare*'s genius lay for Comedy and Humour. In Tragedy he appears quite out of his Element; his Brains are turn'd, he raves and rambles, without any coherence, any spark of reason, or any rule to controul him or set bounds to his phrenzy. His imagination was still running after his Masters, the Coblers, and Parish Clerks, and *Old Testament Stroulers*. So he might make bold with *Portia* as they had done with the Virgin Mary, who, in a Church, Acting their Play call'd *The Incarnation*, had usually the *Ave Mary* mumbl'd over to a stradling wench for the blessed Virgin, straw-hatted, blew-apron'd, big-bellied, with her Immaculate Conception up to her chin.

The Italian Painters are noted for drawing the *Madonnas* by their own Wives or Mistresses; one might wonder what sort of *Betty Mackerel Shakespeare* found in his days to sit for his *Portia* and *Desdemona*, and Ladies of a rank and dignity for their place in Tragedy. But to him a Tragedy in *Burlesk*, a merry Tragedy, was no Monster, no absurdity, nor at all preposterous: all colours are the same to a Blind man. The Thunder and Lightning, the Shouting and Battel and alarms everywhere in this play, may well keep the Audience awake, otherwise no Sermon wou'd be so strong an Opiate. But since the memorable action by the *Putney Pikes*, the *Hammersmith Brigade*, and the *Chelsey Cuirassiers* one might think, in a modest Nation, no Battel wou'd ever presume to shew upon the Stage agen, unless it were at *Perin* in *Cornwal*, where the story goes that some time before the year 88 the *Spaniards* once were landing to burn the Town, just at the nick when a Company of *Stroulers* with their Drums and their shouting were setting *Sampson* upon the *Philistines*. Which so scar'd Mr. Spaniard that they Scampered back to their Galions, as apprehending our whole *Tilbury* Camp had lain in Ambush and were coming souse upon them.

At *Athens* (they tell us) the Tragedies of *Æschylus*, *Sophocles*, and *Euripides* were enroll'd with their Laws, and made part of their Statute-Book.

We want a law for Acting the *Rehearsal* once a week, to keep us in our senses, and secure us against the Noise and Nonsence, the Farce and Fustian which, in the name of Tragedy, have so long invaded, and usurp our Theater.

Tully defines an Orator to be, *Vir bonus dicendique peritus*.[1] Why must he be a *good Man*, as if a bad Man might not be a good Speaker? But what avails it to Speak well, unless a man is well heard? To gain attention, *Aristotle* told us, it was necessary that an Orator be a *good Man*; therefore he that writes Tragedy should be careful that the persons of his *Drama* be of consideration and importance, that the Audience may readily lend an Ear, and give attention to what they say, and act. Who would thrust into a crowd to hear what Mr. *Iago*, *Roderigo*, or *Cassio*, is like to say? From a Venetian Senate or a Roman Senate one might expect great matters. But their Poet was out of sorts; he had it not for them; the Senators must be no wiser than other folk. (147–59)

★   ★   ★

[Later in this chapter Rymer urges the value of the Chorus, which 'of necessity' ensures that the poet preserves the Unities of Time and Place.]

---

[1] Cato, cited by Quintilian, 12.1.1: 'A good man skilled in speaking.'

30. John Dennis on Rymer

1693

From *The Impartial Critick: Or, Some Observations Upon A Late Book, Entitled a Short View of Tragedy, Written by Mr. Rymer* (1693).

John Dennis (1657–1734), poet, essayist and dramatist, did not approve of Rymer but, like many of his contemporaries, did not know how to deal with him: much of this dialogue is shadow-boxing.

[Prefatory *Letter To A Friend*]

SIR,

Upon reading Mr. *Rymer's* late Book I soon found that its Design was to make several Alterations in the Art of the Stage, which instead of reforming would ruine the *English Drama*. For to set up the *Grecian* Method amongst us with success it is absolutely necessary to restore not only their Religion and their Polity but to transport us to the same Climate in which *Sophocles* and *Euripides* writ; or else, by reason of those different Circumstances, several things which were graceful and decent with them must seem ridiculous and absurd to us, as several things which would have appear'd highly extravagant to them must look proper and becoming with us.

For an Example of the first: the Chorus had a good effect with the *Athenians* because it was adapted to the Religion and Temper of that People, as I have observ'd more at large in the Fourth Dialogue. But we, having nothing in our Religion or Manners by which we may be able to defend it, it ought certainly to be banished from our Stage. For Poetry in general being an imitation of Nature, Tragedy must be so too. Now it is neither probable, nor natural, that the Chorus, who represent the Interested Spectators of a Tragical Action, should Sing and Dance upon such terrible or moving Events as necessarily arrive in every Tragedy. And I wonder that Mr. *Rymer* should cry up a Chorus in the very same Book in which he cries down the Opera: for no Man can give any Reason why an Opera is an extravagant thing; but I will, by retorting the same Reason, prove a Chorus extravagant too. (Sig. A²)

*   *   *

[Conclusion to the Fifth Dialogue]

Beaumont. But if your Musick does not make a part of the Modern Tragedy how can it be said to be one body, when the parts of it are not united?

Freeman. 'Tis not the tagging of the Acts with a Chorus that properly makes a Tragedy one Body, but the Unity of the Action; and for my part I cannot conceive but that the Parts are sufficiently united when the Action has a Beginning, a Middle, and an End, which have a mutual, necessary and immediate dependance. But if it should be granted to *Dacier* that the Fiddles between the Acts are absolutely destructive of the Unity of the Poem, he could never infer from it that there ought to be a Chorus, when the mischief may be prevented another way.

Beaumont. What way is that?

Freeman. Why, by not dividing Tragedy into Acts at all.

Beaumont. But several Inconveniences would follow from thence.

Freeman. I will easily grant it; but any inconvenience ought to be admitted rather than that grand absurdity, a Chorus. For Poetry being an imitation of Nature, any thing which is unnatural strikes at the very Root and Being of it and ought to be avoided like Ruine.

Beaumont. Well, thou hast here taken a great deal of pains to prove that we ought not to re-establish the Chorus; but you promis'd to shew me that we ought not to banish Love neither.

Freeman. I have now an appointment which I am oblig'd to keep touch with. But when we next meet I will not only engage to demonstrate that to you but to shew you that, contrary to Mr. *Rymer's* assertion, *Shakespeare* was a great Genius.

Beaumont. I shall be very glad if you perform what you say. But prithee tell me, before we part, your Opinion of Mr. *Rymer's* Judgment of our *English* Comedies.

Freeman. Never was there a more righteous Decree. We have particularly a Comedy which was writ by a Gentleman now living, that has more Wit and Spirit than *Plautus* without any of his little contemptible Affectations; and which, with the Urbanity of *Terence*, has the Comick force which the Great *Cæsar* requir'd in him.

Beaumont. What Comedy can that be?

Freeman. What indeed can it be, but the *Plain Dealer*?

Beaumont. I find, then, that you do not dissent from Mr. *R—* in every thing.

Freeman. No, I should be very sorry if I should do that; for his Censures of *Shakespeare* in most of the particulars are very sensible and very just. But it does not follow, because *Shakespeare* has Faults, that therefore he has no Beauties, as the next time we meet I shall shew you.

Beaumont. Well, till then, your Servant.

Freeman. Honest *Ned*, Adieu. (50–2)

31. John Dryden on Rymer

1693

From Epistle 'To the Right Honourable My Lord Radcliffe', prefixed to *Examen Poeticum: Being the Third Part of Miscellany Poems* (1693).

[On malicious critics] We have two sorts of those Gentlemen in our Nation. Some of them, proceeding with a seeming moderation and pretence of Respect to the Dramatick Writers of the last Age, only scorn and vilifie the present Poets to set up their Predecessours. But this is only in appearance; for their real design is nothing less than to do Honour to any Man beside themselves. . . . 'Tis not with an ultimate intention to pay Reverence to the Manes of *Shakespeare*, *Fletcher*, and *Ben Jonson* that they commend their Writings, but to throw Dirt on the Writers of this Age. . . . (Sig. A₅ᵛ–A₆ʳ)

[On Rymer] But there is another sort of Insects, more venomous than the former, those who manifestly aim at the destruction of our Poetical Church and State, who allow nothing to their Country-Men, either of this or of the former Age. These attack the Living by raking up the Ashes of the Dead, well knowing that if they can subvert their

Original Title to the Stage we who claim under them must fall of course. Peace be to the Venerable Shades of *Shakespeare,* and *Ben Jonson.* None of the Living will presume to have any competition with them: as they were our Predecessours so they were our Masters. We Trayl our Plays under them: but (as at the Funerals of a *Turkish* Emperour), our Ensigns are furl'd or dragg'd upon the ground, in Honour to the Dead. So we may lawfully advance our own afterwards to show that we succeed; if less in Dignity yet on the same Foot and Title, which we think, too, we can maintain against the Insolence of our own Janizaries. . . . (Sig. A$_6$^{r}–A$_6$^{v}) . . . in the *Drama* we have not arriv'd to the pitch of *Shakespeare* and *Ben Jonson.* (Sig. B$_6$^{v})

32. Charles Gildon on Rymer

1694

From 'Some Reflections on Mr. *Rymer's Short View of Tragedy* and an Attempt at a Vindication of *Shakespeare,* in an Essay directed to *John Dryden* Esq.', in Gildon's *Miscellaneous Letters and Essays on Several Subjects in Prose and Verse* (1694).

Charles Gildon (1665–1724) was an untiring editor of anthologies of poetry and essays, a dramatist and a critic. Although inarticulate on some points he gives the most thorough contemporary refutation, penetrating Rymer's speciousness and turning many of his weapons against him, notably the comparison with classical authors.

As soon as Mr. *Rymer's* Book came to my Hands I resolv'd to make some *Reflections* upon it, tho' more to shew my *Will* than my *Abilities.* But finding Mr. *Dennis* had almost promis'd the World a Vindication of the Incomparable *Shakespeare* I quitted the Design, since he had got a Champion more equal to his Worth; not doubting but Mr. *Dennis* wou'd as effectually confute our *Hypercritic* in this as all Men must grant he has in what he attempted in his *Impartial Critic.*

But expecting thus long, without hearing any farther of it, I concluded some other more *important* or at least more agreeable business had diverted him from it; or that he thought it an *unnecessary Undertaking* to perswade the *Town* of a Truth it already receiv'd, or to give any farther Answer to a Book that carry'd its own Condemnation in its self. However, since I find some build an Assurance on this *General Silence* of all the Friends of *Shakespeare* that Mr. *Rymer's* Objections are unanswerable I resolv'd to bestow two or three days on an Essay to prove the contrary. Which may at least bring this advantage to the *Cause*, to convince the World how very good it is when one of my *Inability*, in so little time, have so much to say for it, and that without going through the whole Defence.

I indeed, like the most *indifferent* Counsel, make the *Motion* but leave more able Heads to *Plead* the Cause. One great Satisfaction I have (however I succeed) is that I speak before a Judge that is the best Qualify'd to decide a Controversie of this Nature that ever *England* produc'd; for in you, Sir, [John Dryden] the *Poet* and the *Critic meet* in their highest Perfection; and if the *Critic* discover the Faults of *Shakespeare* the *Poet* will also see and admire his Beauties and Perfections. For as you have Learning and strong Judgment to discern his least Transgressions so have you a Genius that can reach his Noblest Flights, and a Justice that *will* acknowledge his Deserts. And were there no other Arguments to be brought in his Vindication it wou'd be more than sufficient to destroy all his weak Antagonist has huddl'd together against him, that you give him your Approbation. This, Sir, is *really* my Opinion, and I'm sure the most sensible Lovers of Poetry will side with me in it and secure me from the Imputation of being so foolishly vain to think I can flatter You when I speak of your POETRY, your JUDGMENT, and your CANDOR; since whatever can be said on that Subject by any one below Mr. DRYDEN's Abilities wou'd be but a very faint Shadow of the *Mighty Panegyric* of *your* NAME ALONE.

The Method I shall observe in these *Reflections* (for my time will not permit me to bring so confus'd a Chaos into a more regular Form) will be first to run over the Pages of his Book as they lye, and give you some Animadversions in part of those Absurdities they contain; for to examine all wou'd swell my Letter into a Volume and be five hundred times as big as the Text, like a certain Reverend Dr. on *Job*. Next, I shall attempt a Vindication of SHAKESPEARE where he more formally attaques him.

In the first, I hope you'll forgive me if I use him with no more Respect than he does SHAKESPEARE or YOU. And in the latter, I hope you will admit *Recriminations* on those Patterns he proposes to us for the Test of SHAKESPEARE's Faults as a sufficient Answer to what he Magisterially lays down as *Self-Evident* (with a Scornful tho' *Clumsy* Jest, without any other Reason to confirm it) if not as a *Demonstration* of that Injur'd Poet's Excellence. And that we may from thence conclude with Mr. *Rymer* (as he has it in his Preface to *Rapin*) since his *Standards* of Perfection are equally culpable, that *the greatest Wits, both Modern and Ancient, sometimes slip, and are liable to Cavils,* and by consequence that all his Pains were needless to bring SHAKESPEARE into that Number, since his greatest Admirers ever confess'd he had Faults (tho' no Man but himself, I believe, ever *Rob'd* him of *all* Excellence). And I must say that most that he produces are meer *Cavils,* and convict him of being one of those *Critics* that, *like Wasps, rather annoy the* Bees *than terrifie the* Drones.

But indeed the Lovers of SHAKESPEARE may well forgive the Author of *Edgar* and this *Short view of Tragedy* whatever he can say against his *Excellence* and *Genius*; since being his Opposite 'tis no wonder his Mind's not capacious enough to Comprehend, nor his Tast Poetical enough to relish, the Noble Thoughts which the Ingenious have admir'd in SHAKESPEARE ever since he Writ. (64–7)

*   *   *

[Modern critics are willing to explain the 'absurdities' in Homer] with the specious *Whim* of *Allegory,* never thought of by *Homer* himself. But he may thank his Fate for allotting him a time so much remote from ours, else they wou'd not be fond of him to so unreasonable an excess, since they can't allow no excuse for smaller Faults in their own Countrymen of a later date, such ill Patriots are these Partial Critics; for I defie Mr. *Rymer* and all of his Opinion to parallel in SHAKESPEARE the *Wounds,* the *Hatreds,* the *Battles,* and *Strifes* of the Gods. And he must confess, if he be not a sworn Enemy to all Reason, that *Homer's Juno* is a Character far beneath, and more disproportionable, than that of *Desdemona,* tho' the first be of the Queen of the Gods, *Jove's* Sister and his Wife, and the other a Senator's Daughter of *Venice,* Young, Innocent, and Tender. If *Desdemona* be too humble for

Tragedy, and discover not Elevation of Soul enough for her *Birth* and *Fortune*, *Homer*'s *Juno* must be much too low for an *Heroic* Poem, having no Parallel for Scolding but at *Billingsgate*. For the furious curtain Lectures of a City Wife who is supream Lady at home are nothing to hers. This *Jupiter* finds, when the only Remedy he has left to stop her Mouth is to threaten to thrash her *Divine Jacket*, which makes her Son *Vulcan* something concern'd about the Shame 'twill be to have his Goddess Mother suffer the *Bastinade* before the Heavenly Crew. Where is the Nature, where the Reason of this? If the Nobleness of *his* Thoughts, the Majesty of *his* Expression, and Variety of *his* Numbers made the succeeding Ages so fond of *Homer* as to find some Excuse for his failures in Conduct and Characters, is not *Shakespeare* more ungenerously dealt with, whose Faults are made a pretence to deny all his Beauties and Excellence?

But 'tis not these Instances in the Prince of the *Greek* Poets (with many more, both as to the Conduct and Characters) that influence me to incline to a better Opinion of the Moderns (I mean of my own Country) than Mr. *Rymer*, and some of the Graver *Pedants* of the Age. The Excellence I find in *Shakespeare* himself commands a juster Veneration, for in his Thoughts and Expressions he discovers himself Master of a very just Observation of things. So that if he had (which I deny) no Learning, his natural parts wou'd sufficiently have furnish'd him with better Ethics than our *Hypercritic* allows him. But that which aggravates his Malice is, he extends his censure to BEN [Jonson] himself, whose skill in *Moral Philosophy* we suppose at least equal to his. But to give the World some Satisfaction that SHAKESPEARE has had as great a Veneration paid his Excellence by Men of unquestion'd parts as this I now express for him, I shall give some Account of what I have heard from your Mouth, Sir, about the noble Triumph he gain'd over all the *Ancients* by the Judgment of the ablest *Critics* of that time.[1]

The Matter of Fact (if my Memory fail me not) was this: Mr. *Hales* of *Eaton* affirm'd that he wou'd shew all the Poets of Antiquity outdone by SHAKESPEARE in all the Topics and commonplaces made use of in Poetry. The Enemies of *Shakespeare* wou'd by no means yield him so much Excellence, so that it came to a Resolution of a trial of Skill

---

[1] This anecdote appeared for the first time in Dryden's *Essay of Dramatick Poesie* (Volume I above, p. 138), and is found in various forms throughout the eighteenth century, although there is no evidence that such a meeting ever took place. John Hales (1584–1656) was a respected scholar, and figures in Suckling's *Sessions of the Poets* (1637–8) and elsewhere as an arbiter of good taste. See J. Spingarn, *Critical Essays of the Seventeenth Century* (Oxford, 1908, 1957), i, pp. 193, 248–9; ii, pp. 320, 326.

upon that Subject. The place agreed on for the Dispute was Mr. *Hales*'s Chamber at *Eaton*; a great many Books were sent down by the Enemies of this Poet, and on the appointed day my Lord *Falkland*, Sir *John Suckling*, and all the Persons of Quality that had Wit and Learning and interested themselves in the Quarrel met there, and upon a thorough Disquisition of the point the Judges chosen by agreement out of this Learned and Ingenious Assembly unanimously gave the Preference to SHAKESPEARE. And the *Greek* and *Roman* Poets were adjudg'd to Vail at least their Glory in that to the English *Hero*. I cou'd wish, Sir, you wou'd give the Public a juster Account of this Affair, in Vindication of that Poet I know you extreamly esteem, and whom none but you excels.

Shall we therefore still admire *Shakespeare*, with these Learned and Ingenious Gentlemen, or put him in a Class below *Sternold* or *Flecknoe*, with Mr. *Rymer*, because he has not come close to the Rules *Aristotle* drew from the Practice of the *Greek* Poets (whom nothing it seems can please, but the Antic Forms and Methods of the *Athenian* Stage, or what comes up and sticks close to them in our Language)?

I can see no Reason why we shou'd be so very fond of imitating them here without better proofs than the Critical Historiographer has produc'd. 'Tis certain, the *Grecians* had not the advantage of us in *Physics* or any other part of Philosophy, which with them chiefly consisted in words. They were a Talkative People, and being fond of the Opinion of Learning more than the thing itself, as the most speedy way to gain that stop'd their Enquiries on Terms, as is evident from their *Sophistry* and *Dialectics*. There can be no dispute among the Learned but that we excel them in these Points. Since the time of *Des Cartes*, when the Dictates of *Greece* began to be laid aside, what a Progress has been made in the discovery of Nature, and what Absurdities laid open in the School Precepts, and Terms of *Aristotle*!

But Ethics is a Study not so abstruse as the search of Natural Causes and Effects: a nice Observation of Mankind will furnish a sensible Man with them. Which makes me unable to guess how the *Greeks* should have so monstrous an advantage over us in this particular as some wou'd give them, who are so far behind us in things of greater difficulty. But it can't be otherways whilst we make that Age and Nation the Standard of Excellence without regard to the difference of Custom, Age, Climate, &c. But I question not to make it appear hereafter that we much surpass the Greeks and Latins, at least in Dramatick Poetry. As for *Expression* (the difference of Language consider'd) the Merits of which is proportion'd to the Idea it presents to the Mind, and for *Thought* as well as for Design. And had you, Sir, but given us an *Heroic Poem* you had put the Controversie out of doubt as to the *Epic* too, as your *Oedipus* (for all the *Quantum mutatus*, of which another time), your *All for Love*, and some other of your Plays have in the *Dramatic*, in the esteem of impartial Judges.

Had our *Critic* entertain'd but common Justice for the *Heroes* of his *Own Country* he wou'd have set *Shakespeare*'s Faults in their true Light, and distinguish'd betwixt his and the Vices of the Age. For as *Rapin* (a much *juster* and more Candid *Critic*) observes, the Poet often falls into Vices by complying with the Palate of the Age he lives in, and to this may we truly and justly refer a great many of these Faults SHAKESPEARE is guilty of. For, he not having that advantage the *Greek* Poets had of a proper Subsistence, or to be provided for at the Public Charge, what Fruit he was to expect of his Labors was from the Applause of the Audience, so that his chief aim was to please them— who, not being so Skilful in *Criticisms* as Mr. *Rymer*, wou'd not be pleas'd without some Extravagances mingl'd in, tho' contrary to the Characters such-and-such a Player was to Act. This is the Reason that most of his *Tragedies* have a mixture of something Comical; the *Dalilah* of the Age must be brought in—the Clown and the Valet jesting with their Betters—if he resolv'd not to disoblige the Auditors. And I'm assur'd from very good hands that the Person that Acted *Iago* was in much esteem for a Comœdian, which made *Shakespeare* put several words and expressions into his part (perhaps not so agreeable to his Character) to make the Audience laugh, who had not yet learnt to endure to be serious a whole Play. This was the occasion of that particular place so much shouted at by our *Historiographer Royal*:

> *Awake, what ho*, Brabantio, *&c.*
> *An old black Ram is tupping your white Ewe, &c.*   [1.1.89 f]

This Vice of the Age it was that perverted many of his Characters in his other Plays. Nor cou'd it be avoided if he wou'd have his Audience sit the Play out, and receive that Profit that is the chief End of all Poets. To this same Cause may be attributed all those Quibbles and playing upon words, so frequent in some part of him, as well as that Language that may seem too rough and forc'd to the Ear, up and down in some of the best of his Plays.

After all, the Head of his Accusation is, that 'tis not improbable that *Shakespeare* was ignorant of the Rules of *Aristotle's Poetics* and was imperfect in the three Unities of Time, Place, and Action, which *Horace* in his *Art of Poetry* gives no Rules about. For that which I have heard quoted from him, has no relation to the *Dramatic Unities*—

> *Denique sit quod vis, simplex dumtaxat & unum.*[1]

—as is evident from what goes before, but to the Coherence, Uniformity, and Equality of any Poem in general—

> —*Amphora cœpit*
> *Institui, currente Rota cur urceus exit?*[2]

'Tis only the Conclusion of what he proposes about Seven Verses before,

> *Inceptis gravibus . . . & magna Professis, &c.,*[3]

and this of *Petronius* is a just Interpretation of it in my opinion: *Præterea ne sententiæ emineant extra corpus orationis expresse sed intecto vestibus colore niteant.*[4] That is, it gives only a Rule that all Poems be of a Piece and Equal.

So that, since he cou'd gather no instructions in this Point from *Horace* we may excuse him for transgressing against them: and this defect his greatest Admirers confess'd before his Useless piece of ill-natur'd censure, and cou'd have Pardon'd Mr. *Rymer* had he gone no farther. But when he Robs him of all *Genius*, and denies him the Elevation of a *Shirley*, a *Flecknoe*, or a *Jordan*, we must modestly return his Compliment, and tell him that never a *Blackamoor* (as he learnedly terms a *Negro*) in the Western Plantations but must have a better tast of Poetry than himself; and that 'tis evident from the Woman Judges— whose Judgment, he assures us, seldom errs—by their continual Approbation of *Othello*, *Hamlet*, &c. he is in the Wrong.

But shou'd we grant him that *Shakespeare* wanted *Art* (tho' *Ben Jonson* denies it) can he from thence infer he was no Poet? The dispute of which confers most to the forming a Poet (I mean, a Compleat one) *Art*, or *Nature*, was never yet agreed on. *Horace* joyns them, *Quintilian*

---

[1] Horace, *A.P.*, 23: 'In short, be the work what you will, let it at least be simple and uniform.'

[2] Horace, *A.P.*, 21 f: 'That was a wine-jar, when the moulding began: why, as the wheel runs round, does it turn out to be a pitcher?'

[3] *Ibid.*, 14 ff: 'Works with noble beginnings and grand promises often have one or two purple patches so stitched on. . . .'

[4] Petronius, *Satyricon*, 118: 'Besides, one must take care that the thoughts do not stand out from the body of the speech: they must shine with a brilliancy that is woven into the material.'

and some others give it to *Nature*: but till this Gentleman never did any Man yield it wholly to *Art*—for that all his Arguments both in this or his former Book seem to drive at.

A nice Observation of Rules is a Confinement a great *Genius* cannot bear, which naturally covets Liberty. And tho' the *French*, whose *Genius* as well as Language is not strong enough to rise to the Majesty of Poetry, are easier reduc'd within the Discipline of Rules, and have perhaps of late Years more exactly observ'd 'em, yet I never yet met with any Englishman who wou'd prefer their Poetry to ours. All that is great of Humane things makes a nearer approach to the *Eternal Perfection* of Greatness, and extends as much as possible its limits toward being Boundless. 'Tis not govern'd by Common Rules and Methods but Glories in a *Noble Irregularity*; and this not only in Writings but Actions of some Men. *Alexander, Cæsar, Alcibiades*, &c. seem'd actuated by other Principles than the common Maxims that govern the *Rest* of Humane Kind, and in them the greatest Virtues have been mixt with great Vices, as well as the Writings of *Shakespeare*. Yet are they granted *Heroes*, and so must He be confess'd a Poet. The *Heroes'* Race are all like *Achilles*: *Jura negunt, sibi nata.*[1]

But as I do not think that to be a *Great Man* one must necessarily be wholly exempt from Rules, so I must grant that *Virgil, Sophocles*, and *Your Self* are very *Great*, tho' generally very Regular. But these are Rarities so uncommon that Nature has produc'd very few of them, and like the Phœnixes of Honesty that live up to the Precepts of Morality, ought to have public Statues erected to them. But yet the less perfect ought not to be Rob'd of their Merits because they have defects, especially when the Number of those exceed these, as in *Shakespeare*, all whose Faults have not been able to frustrate his obtaining the end of all just Poems, *Pleasure* and *Profit*. To deny this wou'd be to fly in the Face of the known experience of so many Years. He has (I say) in most, if not all of his Plays attain'd the full end of Poetry, *Delight* and *Profit*, by moving Terror and Pity for the Changes of Fortune which Humane Life is subject to, by giving us a lively and just Image of them (the best Definition of a Play); for the Motion of these Passions afford us *Pleasure*, and their Purgation *Profit*. Besides, there are few or none of those many he has writ but have their Just Moral, not only of more general Use and Advantage, but also more naturally the Effect of them than that of the *Oedipus* of *Sophocles*, as may be soon perceiv'd by any one that will give himself the trouble of a little Thought, and which will

[1] Horace, *A.P.*, 122: 'Let him claim that laws are not for him.'

in some measure appear from what I have to say in the particular Defence I shall now make of

OTHELLO.

To begin with the *Fable* (as our Critic has done) I must tell him he has as falsly as ridiculously represented it, which I shall endeavour to put in a Juster light.

Othello a Noble *Moor*, or *Negro*, that had by long Services and brave Acts establish'd himself in the Opinion of the *Senate* of VENICE, wins the Affections of *Desdemona*, Daughter to *Brabantio* (one of the *Senators*), by the moving account he gives of the imminent Dangers he had passed and hazards he had ventur'd through, a belief of which his known Virtue confirm'd; and unknown to her Father Marries her, and carries her (with the leave of the Senate) with him to *Cyprus*, his Province. He makes *Cassio* his Lieutenant, tho' *Iago* had sollicited it by his Friends for himself; which Refusal, joyn'd with a jealousie that *Othello* had had to do with his Wife, makes him contrive the destruction of *Cassio* and the *Moor*, to gratifie his Revenge and Ambition. But having no way to revenge himself sufficiently on the *Moor* (from whom he suppos'd he had receiv'd a double *Wrong*) proportionable to the injury but this, he draws him with a great deal of Cunning into a Jealousie of his Wife, and that by a chain of Circumstances contriv'd to that purpose, and urg'd with all the taking insinuations imaginable; particularly by a Handkerchief he had convey'd to *Cassio* (which *Iago*'s Wife stole from *Desdemona*) to convince the *Moor* his Wife was too familiar with him, having parted with such a favour to him (which she had on her Marriage receiv'd from *Othello* with the strictest charge of preserving, it being a Gift of his Mother, of Curious Work and secret Virtue). *Othello*, by these means won to a belief of his own Infamy, resolves the Murder of those he concluded guilty, *viz. Cassio* and his Wife. *Iago* officiously undertakes the dispatching of *Cassio*, having got his Commission already, but is disappointed of his design, employing one *Roderigo* to that purpose, who had follow'd him from *Venice* in hopes by his means to enjoy *Desdemona*, as *Iago* had promis'd him. But the *Moor* effectually puts his Revenge in Execution on his Wife, which is no sooner done but he's convinc'd of his Error, and in remorse kills himself, whilst *Iago*, the Cause of all this Villany, having slain his Wife for discovering it, is borne away to a more ignominious Punishment, as more proportion'd to his *Villanies*.

The *Fable* to be perfect must be *Admirable* and *Probable*, and as it approaches those two 'tis more or less perfect in its kind. *Admirable* is what is *uncommon* and *extraordinary*. *Probable* is what is agreeable to common Opinion. This must be the Test of this *Fable* of *Othello*; but then we must not take it as given us by our Drolling Critic (who very truely confesseth in his former Book—and in that he is no Changeling— he must be merry out of Season, as he always is) but as I have laid it down, else we shou'd do *Shakespeare* a great deal of Injustice.

I suppose none will deny that it is *Admirable*: that is, compos'd of Incidents that happen not e'ery day. His Antagonist confesses as much; there is therefore nothing but the *Probability* of it attaqu'd by him, which I question not either wholly to prove, or at least to set it on the same bottom with the best of *Sophocles*, that of his *Oedipus*.

First, to see whether he have sinn'd against Probability, let us con- sider what our Caviller objects, all which may be reduc'd to two Points. First, that 'tis not probable that the Senate of *Venice* (tho' it usually employ Strangers) should employ a *Moor* against the *Turk*; neither is it in the next place *probable* that *Desdemona* shou'd be in Love with him. On this turns all the Accusation, this is the very Head of his offending.

All the Reason he gives, or rather implies, for the first Improbability is that 'tis not likely the State of *Venice* wou'd employ a *Moor* (taking him for a *Mahometan*) against the *Turk*, because of the mutual Bond of Religion. He indeed says not so, but takes it for granted that *Othello* must be rather for the *Turkish* interest than the *Venetian*, because a *Moor*. But, I think (nor does he oppose it with any reason), the Character of the *Venetian State* being to employ Strangers in their Wars, it gives sufficient ground to our Poet to suppose a *Moor* employ'd by 'em as well as a *German*; that is, a *Christian Moor*, as *Othello* is represented by our Poet, for from such a *Moor* there cou'd be no just fear of treachery in favour of the *Mahometans*. He tells us—

I fetch my Life and Being from Men of Royal Siege.   [1.2.21 f]

Supposing him therefore the Son or Nephew of the Emperor of *Monomotopa*, *Æthiopia* or *Congo*, forc'd to leave his Country for Religion (or any other occasion), coming to *Europe* by the convenience of the *Portugueze* Ships, might after several Fortunes serve first as a Voluntier till he had signaliz'd himself and prov'd himself worthy of Command; part of this may very reasonably be drawn from what the Poet makes him say. Now upon this Supposition it appears more rational and probable the *Venetians* shou'd employ a Stranger who wholly depended on themselves, and whose Country was too remote to influence him to their prejudice, than other Strangers whose Princes may in some measure direct their Actions for their own Advantage. But that *Othello* is suppos'd to be a Christian is evident from the Second Act, and from these words of *Iago*:

—And then for her
To Win the *Moor, were't to renounce his* Baptism, &c. [2.3.331 ff]

Why therefore an *African* Christian may not by the *Venetians* be suppos'd to be as zealous against the *Turks* as an *European* Christian, I cannot imagine. So that this Bustle of *Littora littoribus Contraria*,[1] &c. is only an inconsiderate Amusement to shew how little the Gentleman was troubled with thought when he wrote it.

No more to the purpose is that Heat he expresses against *Shakespeare's* giving a Name to his *Moor*, though *Cinthio* did not, though History did not warrant it. For this can be no more objected to our Poet, than the perverting the Character of *Dido*, and confounding the Chronology to bring her to the time of *Æneas*, is to *Virgil*; the first as 'tis not mention'd in History, so it does not contradict it; but the last is a plain opposition to express History and Chronology. If *Virgil* be allow'd his Reason for doing that, *Shakespeare* is not to seek for one for what he has done. 'Twas necessary to give his *Moor* a place of some Figure in the World to give him the greater Authority and to make his Actions the more Considerable, and what place more likely to fix on than *Venice*, where Strangers are admitted to the highest Commands in Military Affairs?

'Tis granted, a *Negro* here does seldom rise above a Trumpeter, nor often perhaps higher at *Venice*. But then that proceeds from the Vice of Mankind, which is the Poet's Duty, as he informs us, to correct, and to represent things as they should be, not as they are. Now 'tis certain, there is no reason in the nature of things why a *Negro* of equal Birth and Merit should not be on an equal bottom with a *German, Hollander, French-man*, &c. The Poet, therefore, ought to show justice to Nations as well as Persons, and set them to rights, which the common course of things confounds. The same reason stands in force for this as for punishing the Wicked and making the Virtuous fortunate, which as *Rapin* and all the Critics agree, the Poet ought to do though it generally happens otherways. The Poet has therefore well chosen a polite People

[1] 'Shore clash with shore.'

to cast off this customary Barbarity of confining Nations, without regard to their Virtue and Merits, to slavery and contempt for the meer Accident of their Complexion.

I hope I have brought by this time as convincing proofs for the probability in this particular as Mr. *Rymer* has against it, if I have not wholly gain'd my Point. Now therefore I shall proceed to the probability of *Desdemona*'s Love for the *Moor*, which I think is something more evident against him.

Whatever he aims at in his inconsistent Ramble against this may be reduc'd to the *Person* and the *Manner*. Against the *Person* he quotes you two Verses out of *Horace* that have no more reference to this than— *in the Beginning God made the Heaven and the Earth* has to the proof of the *Jus Divinum* of lay Bishops. The Verses are these:

> *Sed non ut placidis coeant immitia, non ut*
> *Serpentes avibus geminentur, tigribus agni.*[1]

Unless he can prove that the Colour of a Man alters his Species and turns him into a *Beast* or *Devil* 'tis such a vulgar Error, so criminal a fondness of our Selves, to allow nothing of Humanity to any but our own Acquaintance of the fairer hew that I wonder a Man that pretends to be at all remov'd from the very Dreggs of the thoughtless Mob should espouse it in so public a manner! A Critic, too, who puts the Poet in mind of correcting the common corruptions of Custom. Any Man that has convers'd with the best Travels, or read any thing of the History of those parts on the continent of *Africa* discover'd by the *Portugueze*, must be so far from robbing the *Negroes* of some Countrys there of *Humanity* that they must grant them not only greater Heroes, nicer observers of Honour and all the Moral Virtues that distinguish'd the old *Romans*, but also much better Christians (where Christianity is profess'd) than we of *Europe* generally are. They move by a nobler Principle, more open, free and generous, and not such slaves to sordid Interest.

After all this, *Othello* being of *Royal Blood*, and a Christian, where is the disparity of the Match? If either side is advanc'd, 'tis *Desdemona*. And why must this Prince, though a Christian and of known and experienc'd *Virtue*, *Courage*, and *Conduct*, be made such a Monster that the *Venetian* Lady can't love him without perverting Nature? Experience tells us that there's nothing more common than Matches of this

---

[1] Horace, *A.P.*, 12 f: 'This licence we poets claim and in our turn we grant the like; but not so far that savage should mate with tame, or serpents couple with birds, lambs with tigers.'

kind where the Whites and Blacks cohabit, as in both the *Indies*. And Even here at home Ladys that have not wanted white Adorers have indulg'd their Amorous Dalliances with their Sable Lovers, without any of *Othello*'s Qualifications, which is proof enough that Nature and Custom have not put any such unpassable bar betwixt Creatures of the same kind because of different colors; which I hope will remove the improbability of the Person, especially when the powerful Auxilarys of extraordinary Merit and Vertues come to plead with a generous Mind.

The probability of the *Person* being thus confirmed, I shall now consider that of the *Manner* of his obtaining her *Love*. To this end we must still keep in mind the known and experienc'd Virtue of the *Moor*, which gave Credit and Authority to what he said; and then we may easily suppose the story of his Fortunes and Dangers would make an impression of Pity and admiration, at least on the bosom of a Woman of a noble and generous Nature. No *Man* of any generous Principle but must be touch'd at suff'ring Virtue, and value the noble sufferer whose Courage and Bravery bears him through uncommon Trials and extraordinary Dangers. Nor would it have less force on a Woman of any principle of Honour and tenderness. She must be mov'd and pleas'd with the Narration, she must admire his constant Virtue; and Admiration is the first step to Love, which will easily gain upon those who have once entertain'd it.

Dido in *Virgil* was won by the *Trojan* stranger she never saw before by the relation of his fortunes and Escapes; and some particulars of the Narration of *Æneas* carry full as ridiculous and absurd a Face as any thing *Othello* says; the most trifling of which is,

> And of the Cannibals that each other eat,
> The Anthropophagi, and Men whose Heads
> Do grow beneath their Shoulders.　　　　　　[1.3.144 ff]

for all the rest is admirably fine, though our wonderful Critic can't relish it. There is a moving Beauty in each Line, the words are well chosen, and the Image they give great and Poetical; what an Image does *Desarts* IDLE give? That very Epithet is a perfect *Hypotyposis*, and seems to place me in the midst of one where all the active hurry of the World is lost; but all that I can say will not reach the excellence of that Epithet, so many properties of such a place meet in it. But as for the *Cannibals*, &c. *and the Men whose Heads grow beneath their Shoulders*, I have heard it condemn'd by Men whose tast I generally approve; yet must they give me leave to dissent from them here and permit me either wholly to justifie *Shakespeare*, even here, or at least to put him on an equal bottom with *Virgil* in his most beautiful part. For the fault lyes either in the *Improbability* of those things, or their *Impertinence* to the business in Hand. First, Probability we know is built on common Opinion; but 'tis certain the *Cannibals* have been generally believed, and that with very good grounds of Truth; so that there can be no doubt of the probability of that. Next for the *Men whose Heads grow beneath their Shoulders*: though that is not establish'd on so good a Foundation as Truth yet the general Traditionary belief of it in those days is sufficient to give it a poetical probability. As this was not *Improbable*, so neither was it *Impertinent*, for 'tis certain that whatever contributed to the raising her Idea of his Dangers and Escapes must conduce to his aim. But to fall into the Hands of those whom not only the fury of War but that of Custom makes Cruel, heightens the danger and by consequence the Concern, especially in a young Lady possess'd with the legend of the Nursery, whence she must have amazing Ideas of the Danger of the brave *Moor* from them.

But at worst, *Shakespeare* is on as good a bottom as *Virgil* in this particular. The Narrative of *Æneas* that won the Heart of *Dido* has many things full as trifling and absurd as this, if not far more! For is there not as much likelyhood that there shou'd be a People that have their Heads grow beneath their Shoulders as the Race of the *Cyclops*, that have but one Eye, just beneath their Forheads; and that *Polyphemus* his Eye was as big as a *Grecian* Shield or the Sun; or that he cou'd wade through the Sea without being up to his middle? Can there be invented any thing so unnatural as the Harpys in the third Book, who had the Faces of Virgins, Wings, Feathers, &c. of Birds, and a human Voice?— as is evident from the *infælix vates*, that foretold 'em they shou'd not build their destin'd City till they had eaten their Tables or Trenchers (which by the way was a trivial and ridiculous sort of a pun, as the event shew'd, when *Iulus* found out the Jest); nor is *Scylla* a more natural mixture. But let's hear the description of all three from *Virgil* himself, least I be thought to injure his Memory; first of the Harpys in the Strophades.

> *Virginei volucrum vultus, fædissima ventris,*
> *Proluvies, uncæque Manus, & pallida semper*
> *Ora fame.*—[1]

---

[1] Virgil, *Aeneid*, 3.216 ff: 'Maiden faces have these birds, foulest filth they drop, clawed hands are theirs, and faces ever gaunt with hunger.'

The beginning of *Horace's* Art of Poetry, *Humano Capiti, &c.*[1] seems a Copy of this; nor is *Scylla* a more *Homogeneous* Composition.—

> *At Scyllam cæcis cohibet spelunca latebris*
> *Ora exsertantem, & navis in saxa trahentem:*
> *Prima hominis facies, & pulchro pectore virgo*
> *Pube tenus, postrema immani Corpore pistrix*
> *Delphinum Caudas utero commissa luporum.*[2]

Then for the Cyclop *Polyphemus*, the *Grecian* he takes aboard tells him his Eye is

> *Argolici clypei, aut Phæbeæ lampadis Instar.*[3]

and a little after, lest this shou'd be taken as an hyperbolical magnifying it by the terror of the fearful *Greek*, in his own Person he says of him

> *—Graditurque per æquor.*
> *Jam medium, necdum fluctus latera ardua tinxit.*[4]

The Absurdities in *Homer* are much more numerous than those in *Virgil* (I mean those that must pass for such if this in *Shakespeare* is so), but because they relate not to this particular I shall say nothing of them here. All these I have remark'd in the Narration of *Æneas* hinder'd not but that it won the Heart of *Dido*, though firmly bent against a second Amour:

> *Ille meos primus, qui me sibi junxit amores*
> *Abstulit: ille habeat secum, servetque sepulchro.*[5]

especially one that was not like to be so very Honorable. *Desdemona* had no such tye to steel her Heart against *Othello's* Tongue, no reason to curb that Passion she ne'er felt before when the prevailing Virtue of the *Moor* attaqu'd her Heart; well may we therefore believe *Desdemona* shou'd yield to the same force that conquer'd *Dido*, with all her

[1] Horace, *A.P.*, 1 ff: 'If a painter chose to join a human head to the neck of a horse. . . .

[2] Virgil, *Aeneid*, 3.424 ff: 'But a cavern confines Scylla in blind recesses, whence she thrusts forth her mouths and draws ships within her rocks. Above she is of human form, down to the waist a fair-bosomed maiden; below, she is a sea-dragon of monstrous frame, with dolphins' tails joined to a belly of wolves.'

[3] *Ibid.*, 3.637: 'like unto an Argive shield or the lamp of Phoebus.'

[4] *Ibid.*, 3.664 f: 'then strides through the open sea; nor has the wave yet wetted his towering sides'.

[5] *Ibid.*, 4.28 f: 'He, who first linked me to himself, has taken away my heart; may he keep it with him, and guard it in the grave!'

Resolutions and Engagements to the memory of *Sychaeus*. Hear how she cries out to her Sister *Ann*,

> *Quis novus hic nostris successit sedibus hospes*
> *Quem sese ore ferens? Quam forti pectore & Armis?*
> *Credo equidem, nec vana fides, genus esse deorum.*
> *Degeneres animos timor arguit, heu quibus ille*
> *Jactatur fatis*, quæ bella exhausta canebat.¹

and at the beginning of this fourth Book,

> — *Hærent infixi pectore Vultus*
> Verbaque—²

and the latter end of the first Book confirms this

> *Multa super* Priamo *Rogitans super Hectore multa.*³

Cou'd *Æneas's* Story, not one jot more moving or probable, make a meer stranger pass for a God with the Carthaginian Queen at first hearing; and must it be incredible that the same shall not make *Othello* pass for so much as a Man? The Parallel is so exact that I am apt to think *Shakespeare* took the Copy from *Virgil*. Nor can it justly be urg'd that these things were believ'd by the *Romans*, since they were so far from believing these trifles that *Seneca* in his Epistles laughs at those Fables that constituted their Hell, which was of much greater consequence. But supposing they were believ'd, the same will hold good for *Shakespeare* in this particular I vindicate him in: for 'tis built on as vulgar and general a tradition as these Fables of old were, so that the advantage is equal betwixt these two great Poets in this particular.

By this time, I hope, our *Drolling Caviller* will grant it no such monstrous absurdity for the *Doge* to say:

> *I think this Tale wou'd win my Daughter too.*   [1.3.171]

since without doubt that short summing-up of what was only the subject of his tale to *Desdemona*, with only the supposition of the particulars, must move any generous Brest.

But should all I have said fail of clearing the *Probability* of the *Fable*

---

¹ *Ibid.*, 4.10 ff: 'Who is this stranger guest that hath entered our home? How noble his mien! how brave in heart and feats of arms! I believe it well—nor in assurance vain—that he is sprung from gods. 'Tis fear that proves souls base-born. Alas! by what fates is he vexed! What wars, long endured, did he recount!'

² *Ibid.*, 4.4 f: 'His looks and words cling fast within her bosom.'

³ *Ibid.*, 1.750: 'asking much of Priam, of Hector much'.

from Mr. *Rymer's* Objections, yet ought not that to rob *Shakespeare* of his due Character of being a *Poet*, and a great *Genius*: unless he will for the same reason deny those prerogatives to *Homer* and *Sophocles*. The former has often lost the *Probable* in the *Admirable*, as any Book of the *Iliads* and *Odysses* will prove; and the latter, as *Rapin* justly observes, has not kept to probability ev'n in his best performance, I mean in his *Oedipus Tyrannus*. For (as *Rapin* has it) Oedipus *ought not to have been ignorant of the assassinate of Laius; the ignorance he's in of the Murder, which makes all the Beauty of the intrigue, is not probable*; and if a Man wou'd play the Droll with this *Fable* of *Oedipus* it would furnish full as ridiculous a Comment as witty Mr. *Rymer* has done from this of *Othello*; and sure I can't err in imitating so great a Critic.

First, then, let all Men before they defend themselves on the Highway think well of what they do, lest, not being Mathematically sure he's at home, he kill his own Father. (Which perhaps is something dangerous in this Age, where such boon Blades frequent the Road and such good-natur'd Ladies have the disposing of our fate.)

Next, let e'ry Younger Brother that ventures to ride in another Man's Boots be very circumspect, lest he marries his own Mother.

Thirdly and Lastly, this may be a caution to the few Fools that doat on Virtue, that they trust to a rotten Reed that will be of little use to 'em, since all is whirl'd about by an unavoidable necessity.

These are much more the consequence of this *Fable* of *Oedipus* than those wond'rous Truths he draws from that of *Othello*. Nay, the moral *Sophocles* concludes his *Oedipus* with will serve as justly for *Othello*, viz. *That no Man can be call'd happy before his Death*. But the whole *Fable* of *Oedipus*, tho' so much admir'd, is so very *singular* and *improbable* that 'tis scarce possible it ever cou'd have happen'd. On the other hand, the fatal Jealousie of *Othello* and the Revenge of *Iago* are the natural Consequences of our ungovern'd Passions, which by a prospect of such Tragical effects of their being indulg'd may be the better regulated and govern'd by us. So that tho' *Othello* ends not so formally with a moral Sentence as *Oedipus* does yet it sets out one of much greater Value. If it be a fault in *Shakespeare* that it end not with such a sentence, *Sophocles* is guilty of no less in his *Philoctetes*, which not only concludes without any Moral but is also incapable of being reduc'd to any, at least of any moment. Whereas the Morals of *Hamlet*, *Macbeth*, and most of *Shakespeare's* Plays prove a lesson of mightier consequence than any in *Sophocles* except the *Electra*, *viz.* that Usurpation, tho' it thrive a while, will at last be punish'd, *&c.*

Besides, the worst and most irregular of *Shakespeare*'s Plays contains two or three such Fables as that of *Philoctetes*, which answers not one of the ends of Poetry. For it neither pleases or profits, it moves neither Terror nor Compassion, containing only a dry account, without any variety, of the perswasions of [Neoptolemus] to get *Philoctetes* to go with him to *Troy* with the Arrows of *Hercules*; who, after he had by Treachery gain'd 'em as foolishly restores 'em to him again. And *Troy* might have stood long enough if *Hercules* had not come from the Gods to bend the stubborn Fool, that rather chose to be miserable himself with his endless πάπα, πάπα, πάπα'ς and his Complaints of his Foot, something like the *Tumors*, *Chilblains*, *Carnosities*, *&c.* rak'd together by Mr. *Rymer*. And all that can be learnt from this Play of *Sophocles* is,

First, that we never send Boys of our Errand unless we have a God at command to make up the business he has spoil'd; if we mean our business shall be thoroughly done, and not the fate of a Nation sacrific'd to a pain in the Foot.

Secondly, Not to trust Strangers we never saw before, for a fair Tale, with our Safety and Treasure, without a Mathematical Demonstration of their Fidelity and Trust.

Lastly, That all Men with sore Feet shou'd not despair of a Cure.

But I have dwelt so long on the Fable that I have not time enough to discuss the other parts, as the *Characters*, *Thoughts*, and *Expressions*, so fully as I ought; especially the *Thought* and *Expression*, for 'twou'd require a Volumn near as big as *Shakespeare* to set them off according to their worth, with all the proofs from Grammar or Rhetoric of their Truth and Justness. The Fable is look'd upon by *Rapin*, and after him by our *Gleaner of Criticisms*, as the Soul of the Play, and therefore I may be excus'd for my prolixity in its defence, and allow'd a little more time for a full Justification of the other parts of *Shakespeare*, attaqu'd with less Reason and Justice. Mr. *Rymer* has taken above ten Year to digest his Accusations, and therefore it can't in reason be thought I shou'd not in half so many days be able to perform all the work he has cut out. Nor can I proceed to a particular consideration of all the Characters of this Play at this time. *Desdemona* I think is the most faulty; but since our *Antagonist* will have *Iago* the most *intollerable*, I shall confine my self to that.

What I have said in the beginning of my Vindication of *Shakespeare* must here be recollected on *Iago*'s behalf; besides which I have some other considerations to offer, which I hope will lighten the insupportable load of Contempt and Ridicule cast on him by our Caviller.

First, therefore, in our Judgment of *Iago*, we must follow the Rule of *Horace*, so much stood upon by Mr. *Rymer*.

> *Intererit multum*
> *Cholcus an Assyrius, Thebis nutritus, an Argis.*[1]

We are not only to respect the profession of the Man in our Judgment of the Character but we must also have an Eye to his Nation, the Country he was born in, and the prevailing temper of the People, with their National Vices. By this Rule we shall find *Iago* an *Italian*, by Nature *Selfish, Jealous, Reserv'd, Revengeful* and *Proud*, nor can I see any reason to suppose his Military Profession shou'd too powerfully influence him to purge away all these Qualities and establish contrary in their room. Nor can I believe the quotation from *Horace* which our Caviller produces can justly be extended to all degrees of Soldiers. It runs thus in *Horace*:

> —*Honoratum si forte reponis Achillem*
> *Impiger, Iracundus, Inexorabilis, Acer,*
> *Jura neget sibi Nata, nihil non arroget armis.*[2]

'Tis plain from what goes before and what follows after that *Horace* meant not this at least for a general Character of all Soldiers, but only as a direction for the drawing *Achilles* or such a Hero. For he's enumerating the *Manners* of those public Characters that were generally made use of by the *Romans* in their Tragedies, for this follows

> *Sit Medea ferox invictaque Flebilis* Ino,
> *Perfidus* Ixion, Io *vaga, tristis* Orestes.[3]

And a few Lines before he is giving the Characters of several Professions and Ages, from whence he proceeds to these particular Characters of *Achilles, Ino, Medea, &c.* drawn from the known Stories of them; and this is confirm'd by what he joyns to this:

> *Siquid inexpertum scenæ committis, &c.*[4]

---

[1] Horace, *A.P.*, 114 ff: 'Vast difference will it make, whether a god be speaking or a hero, . . . a Colchian or an Assyrian, one bred at Thebes or at Argos.'

[2] *Ibid.*, 120 ff: 'If haply, when you write, you bring back to the stage the honouring of Achilles, let him be impatient, passionate, ruthless, fierce; let him claim that laws are not for him, let him ever make appeal to the sword.'

[3] *Ibid.*, 123 f: 'Let Medea be fierce and unyielding, Ino tearful, Ixion forsworn, Io a wanderer, Orestes sorrowful.'

[4] *Ibid.*, 125: 'If it is an untried theme you entrust to the stage . . .'

That is, if you take known Persons that have for so many Ages trod the Stage this must be their Character; but if you bring some new person on it that was never there before then take care that your Persons preserve that Character you give 'em at first, &c.

I know *Rapin* gives a Soldier these qualities: *Fierce, Insolent, Surly, Inconstant,* which partly are the effects of their manner of Life, but I can't conceive these to be opposite to those other in *Iago.* The *Characters* or *Manners,* as the same *Rapin* observes, are to be drawn from Experience; and that tells us that they differ in Soldiers according to their Nature and Discipline. That also tells us that the Camp is not free from Designs, Supplantings, and all the effects of the most criminal of Passions; and this indeed is evident from the Draught *Homer* gives us of the Grecian Camp, where *Love* was not judg'd so contrary to the Character of a General as Mr. *Rymer* wou'd have it thought: *Achilles* and *Agamemnon* having both their admir'd Captives. And let Mr. *Rymer* say what he please, I can prove that 'twas the Love of *Briseis* that troubl'd *Achilles* and confirm'd his anger, as well as the meer affront of having his prize taken from him—but of that in another place. In short, the *Thersites* of *Homer* differs as much from the Soldiers of Mr. *Rymer*'s acquaintance as *Iago* does; nor is he the only Soldier that cou'd dissemble. *Sinon* in *Virgil,* and *Neoptolemus* in *Sophocles,* are as guilty of it as he.

But granting that *Iago*'s Character is defective something in the Manners, *Homer* and *Sophocles* have been guilty (the first much more, the other not much less) of the same. What are the Wounds, Scuffles, Passions, Adulteries, &c. of the Gods and Goddesses, obvious to the meanest Capacity, and beyond all dispute? Is not the Character of *Oedipus Coloneus* of *Sophocles,* as *Rapin* remarks, extreamly unproportionable to *Oedipus Tyrannus?* And tho' Mr. *Rymer* is so severe to deny that the Character of *Iago* is that of a Soldier, because so different from his Military Acquaintance, yet I'm confident he wou'd take it extreamly amiss if I shou'd deny him to be a Critic because so contrary to all the Critics that I have met with, playing the merry Droll instead of giving serious and solid Reasons for what he advances.

The other Characters of this Play I must defer till another time, as well as a thorough defence of his Thoughts and Expression, both which he wholly denies him, and with an extravagantly wonderful Assurance publicly tells us that the Neighing of a Horse has more *Humanity* (for that is his Wittycism) than the Tragical Flights of *Shakespeare.*

Mr. *Rymer*'s Friend *Rapin* tells us that the Thoughts are the expression of the Manners, as Words are of Thoughts—that is, the natural result of the Manners; which, being already clear'd from his Accusations, the vindication of the Thoughts are included in them as well as their Condemnation in his Charge against the other, for he disdains to be particular in his proof. Then for the Expressions of *Shakespeare*, none but Mr. *Rymer* can find fault with 'em. The excellence of expression consists in this, that it bear a proportion to the Things—that is, that it give us a full Idea of 'em, that it be *apt, clear, natural, splendid,* and *numerous.* There is scarce a serious part of *Shakespeare* but has all these qualities in the Expression.

To omit several Scenes in *Hamlet,* particularly that betwixt him and his Fathers Ghost, I'll only instance in two or three Speeches that are and have been on the Stage in our Memory, which may give some sample of the Poetry, Thought, and Expression of *Shakespeare.* The first is in the *Midsummer Nights Dream,* now acted under the name of the *Fairy Queen.* Act the Third, *Titania* speaks thus,

> Titania. *Be kind and courteous to this Gentleman.*
> *Hop in his Walks, and Gambol in his Eyes,*
> *Feed him with Apricocks and Dewberrys,*
> *With purple Grapes, green Figgs and Mulberrys,*
> *The Hony Baggs steal from the Humble Bees;*
> *And for Night Tapers crop their waxen Thighs,*
> *And light them at the fiery Glow-worms Eyes;*
> *To have my Love to Bed and to Arise.*
> *And pluck the Wings from painted Butter-flyes,*
> *To fan the Moon Beams from his sleeping Eyes.*
> *Nod to him Elves, and do him Courtesies.*   [3.1.150 ff]

Is not this extreamly poetical and fine? The next I shall take from the 2d. Scene of *Richard II,* [Act 5]:

> York. *Then as I said the Duke* (*great* BOLINGBROKE)
> *Mounted upon a hot and fiery Steed,*
> *Which his aspiring Rider seem'd to know,*
> *With slow but stately Grace kept on his course*
> *While all Tongues cry'd God save thee* BOLINGBROKE.
> *You wou'd have thought the very Windows spoke,*
> *So many greedy looks of Young and old,*
> *Through Casements darted their desiring Eyes*

Upon his Visage, and that all the Walls
With painted Imag'ry had said at once,
JESU *preserve thee, welcome* BOLINGBROKE
Whilst He, from one side to the other turning,
Bare headed, lower than his proud Steeds Neck,
Bespeak them thus; I thank ye Countrymen.
And thus still doing thus he pass'd along.
Duchess. *Alass! Poor Richard where rides he the while?*
York. *As in a Theatre the Eyes of Men,*
After a well grac'd Actor leaves the Stage
Are idly bent on him that enters next
Thinking his prattle to be tedious
Even so, or with much more contempt Mens Eyes,
Did scowl on Richard: *No Man cry'd God save him.*
No joyful Tongue gave Him his welcome home.
But Dust was thrown upon his Sacred Head
Which with such gentle sorrow he shook off
His Face still combating with Tears and Smiles,
(The Badges of Grief and Patience)
That had not God (for some strong purpose) steel'd
The Hearts of Men, they must perforce have melted,
And Barbarism itself have pitty'd him.   [5.2.7 ff]

Are not here all the Beautys of Thought joyn'd with all those of expression? Is it possible any thing that has but the least Humanity shou'd be dull enough not to relish, not to be mov'd, nay transported with this? I must confess it has fir'd me, so that I think our Critic better deserves the Arraignment *Tiberius* gave the Poet for ill representing *Agamemnon*, whose Character at best was but a Child of Fancy and therefore subject to the Poet's Will. But to Blaspheme such a visible Excellence Merits the highest contempt, if not a greater Punishment.

Shakespeare's Numbers carry such an Harmonious Majesty that what *Rapin* and some other Critics say of *Homer* is justly his due: they give a noble Beauty to the meanest things. 'Tis true, the Words he sometimes uses by their obsoleteness renders some of his Expressions a little dark, but then we must remember the great alteration our Language has undergone since his time. But examine well the sense of his Words you'l seldom find him guilty of Bombast (tho' laid to his charge by Mr. *Rymer*), that is, Words and Thoughts ill match'd. On the contrary, they are generally so well sorted that they present us with so lively and sensible an Image of what they import that it fixes itself in our Minds with an extream satisfaction; and the more we view it, the more it gains upon us.

I shall hereafter step into the Scenes with Mr. *Rymer* and also examine his [Shakespeare's] Narrations, Deliberations, Didactic and Pathetic Discourses, which are all that are made use of in Tragedy. In which, if he sometimes err, he has yet perform'd well; and amidst his faults you shall find some thoughts of a great Genius. I shall only now observe *en passant*, in defence of that Scene betwixt *Iago* and *Othello*, that we ought not to be imposed on by positive assertions, or think—because Mr. *Rymer* tells us so—that half-words and ambiguous Reflexions do not naturally work up Jealousie, or that 'tis not natural for *Othello to catch at every blown surmise*. These Assertions of our Critic shew him to be very ignorant of the very nature of this Passion, for as 'tis reduc'd to the primitive *Desire* by the Moralists, so 'tis thus by them defin'd:

> *Jealousie is a fear of loosing a good we very much value and esteem, arising from the* least *causes of Suspicion.*

Now 'tis evident even from the trifling and false Objections of his enemies that *Shakespeare* had this very notion of this passion. For this reason 'tis, he makes *Othello* swallow the very first bait laid by *Iago* for him. *Cassio* is found with *Desdemona*, and on *Othello's* approach consciously retires, which tho' he did to avoid his Anger, not Jealousie, yet *Iago* improves the opportunity to his purpose with an *I like not that*. [3.3.35] Then, to awake the *Moor's* Jealousie by degrees, he takes occasion from *Cassio's* departure to question him—*did* CASSIO *when you woo'd my Lady know of your Love?* Which he pursues with *half-words* and ambiguous *Reflexions*, that plainly imply more than they barely express, in which he discover'd fear to speak out what he desir'd *Othello* shou'd know. The natural consequence of which is the touching a jealous Nature with curiosity in a thing that so nearly related to his Happiness. Evry word rous'd some surmize; and as *Ovid* observes, *cuncta timemus Amantes,*[1] Lovers fear any Appearance. But more of this hereafter. In the mean while I'm pretty confident every Mans own Sence will supply my defect of a particular defence of the working up of *Othello's* passion of Jealousie. (84–117)

[1] Ovid, *Metamorphoses*, 7.719: 'we lovers fear everything'.

33. John Dryden on Rymer

March 1694

From a letter to Dennis, 3 March 1694, printed in *Letters Upon Several Occasions: Written by and between Mr. Dryden . . . and Mr. Dennis* (1696); this text from *Original Letters* in Vol. II of *The Select Works of Mr. John Dennis* (1718).

After I have confess'd thus much of our modern Heroick Poetry, I cannot but conclude with Mr. *Rymer* that our *English* Comedy is far beyond any thing of the Antients. And notwithstanding our Irregularities, so is our Tragedy. *Shakespeare* had a Genius for it; and we know, in spite of Mr. *Rymer*, that Genius alone is a greater Virtue (if I may so call it) than all other Qualifications put together. You see what success this Learned Critick has found in the World, after his Blaspheming *Shakespeare*. Almost all the Faults which he has discover'd are truly there; yet who will read Mr. *Rymer*, or not read *Shakespeare*? For my own part, I reverence Mr. *Rymer*'s Learning, but I detest his Ill-Nature and his Arrogance. I indeed, and such as I, have reason to be afraid of him, but *Shakespeare* has not. (504)

34. Jeremy Collier, from *A Short View of the Immorality, and Profaneness of the English Stage*

1698

Jeremy Collier (1650–1726), clergyman and controversialist, attacked the immorality of the contemporary theatre with such polemic that his book went through three editions in 1698 and produced a rage of pamphlets in the next decade. Although the controversy was mainly about Restoration drama, Shakespeare was dragged in as well, for both praise and rebuke.

[Chapter I. 'The Immodesty of the Stage']

*　　*　　*

For Modesty, as Mr. *Rapin* observes, is the *Character* of Women. To represent them without this Quality is to make Monsters of them, and throw them out of their Kind. *Euripides*, who was no negligent Observer of Humane Nature, is always careful of this Decorum. Thus *Phædra*, when possess'd with an infamous Passion, takes all imaginable Pains to conceal it. She is as regular and reserv'd in her Language as the most virtuous Matron. 'Tis true, the force of Shame and Desire, the Scandal of Satisfying, and the Difficulty of Parting with her Inclinations, disorder her to Distraction. However, her Frensy is not Lewd; She keeps her Modesty even after She has lost her Wits. Had *Shakespeare* secur'd this point for his young Virgin *Ophelia* the *Play* had been better contriv'd. Since he was resolv'd to drown the Lady like a Kitten he should have set her a swimming a little sooner. To keep her alive only to sully her Reputation, and discover the Rankness of her Breath, was very cruel. But it may be said the Freedoms of Distraction go for nothing, a Fever has no Faults, and a Man *non Compos* may kill without Murther. It may be so: but then such People ought to be kept in dark Rooms and without Company. To shew them, or let them loose, is somewhat unreasonable. (9–10)

*　　*　　*

87

[Chapter IV. 'The Stage-Poets make their Principal Persons Vitious, and reward them at the End of the Play']

*   *   *

Ben Jonson's Fox is clearly against Mr. *Dryden,* and here I have his own Confession for Proof. He declares the *Poet's end in this Play was the Punishment of Vice, and the Reward of Virtue. Ben* was forced to strain for this piece of Justice, and break through the *Unity of Design.* This Mr. *Dryden* remarks upon him: however he is pleased to commend the Performance, and calls it an excellent *Fifth Act.*

Ben Jonson shall speak for himself afterwards in the Character of a Critick, in the mean time I shall take a Testimony or two from *Shakespeare.* And here we may observe the admir'd *Falstaff* goes off in Disappointment. He is thrown out of Favour as being a *Rake,* and dies like a Rat behind the Hangings. The Pleasure he had given would not excuse him. The *Poet* was not so partial as to let his Humour compound for his Lewdness. If 'tis objected that this remark is wide of the Point because *Falstaff* is represented in Tragedy, where the Laws of Justice are more strictly observ'd: to this I answer, that you may call *Henry the Fourth* and *Fifth* Tragedies if you please, but for all that *Falstaff* wears no *Buskins,* his Character is perfectly comical from end to end. (153-4)

35. Unsigned work, Shakespeare defended from Collier

1698

From *A Defence of Dramatick Poetry: Being a Review of Mr. Collier's View of the Immorality and Profaneness of the Stage* (1698); and *A Farther Defence of Dramatick Poetry. Being the Second Part of the Review* (1698).

The authorship of these two pamphlets is sometimes ascribed, on no good grounds, to Edward Filmer (*fl.* 1707), who produced a rather different work, *A Defence of the Plays*, in 1707.

Next let us examine one of the most Capital Offences of Dramatick Poetry arraign'd both by the Philosophers, Fathers of the Church, and the Son of the Church, Mr. *Collier*, viz. *The Raising the Passions*, &c.

Here we'll begin with *Tragedy*. *Tragedy* indeed does raise the Passions; and its chief work is to raise *Compassion*. For the great Entertainment of Tragedy is the moving that tenderest and noblest Humane Passion, *Pity*. And what is it we pity there but the Distresses, Calamities and Ruins of *Honour*, *Loyalty*, *Fidelity* or *Love*, &c. represented in some True or Fictitious, Historick or Romantick Subject of the Play? Thus *Virtue*, like *Religion* by its *Martyrdom*, is rendred more shining by its *Sufferings*, and the Impression we receive from *Tragedy* is only making us in Love with *Virtue* (for Pity is a little Kin to Love), and out of Love with Vice. For at the same time we pity the suffering Virtue it raises our Aversions and Hate to the Treachery or Tyranny in the *Tragedy*, from whence and by whom that Virtue suffers. How often is the good Actor (as for Instance, the *Iago* in the *Moor of Venice*, or the Countess of *Nottingham* in the *Earl of Essex*) little less than Curst for Acting an Ill Part? Such a Natural Affection and Commiseration of *Innocence* does Tragedy raise, and such an Abhorrence of *Villany*.

And that this is truly the Entertainment of Tragedy, we come on purpose to see *Virtue* made Lovely, and *Vice* made Odious. That

Expectation brings us to the Play; and if we find not that very Expectation answer'd instead of any satisfactory Delight we receive or any Applause we return we Explode and Hiss our Entertaiment. The Play sinks, and the Performance is lost, and we come away with this Disrelish as to think both our Money and Time ill spent.

'Tis true a Character that has not all the perfections of true Honour or Innocence, nay a Vicious one sometimes, may move Compassion. But then 'tis not the Vice or Blemishes in the Character that moves that Pity. For Instance in the *Orphan*, we pity the Vicious and Libertine *Polydore* that lyes with his Brother's Wife. But when do we pity him? When he's touch'd with that sense and horror of his Guilt that he gives up his Life (picks a feign'd Quarrel with the Injur'd *Castalio*, and runs upon his Sword) to Expiate. 'Tis not the *Criminal* but the *Penitent*, the *Virtue* not *Vice* in the Character moves the Compassion.

Thus we pity *Timon of Athens*, not as the Libertine nor Prodigal, but the *Misanthropos*: when his Manly and Generous Indignation against the Universal *Ingratitude* of Mankind makes him leave the World and fly the Society of Man; when his open'd Eyes and recollected Virtue can stand the Temptation of a Treasure he found in the Woods enough to purchase his own Estate again; when all this glittering Mine of Gold has not Charm to bribe him back into a hated World, to the Society of *Villains*, *Hypocrites* and *Flatterers*. We pity *Evandra* too, his Mistress,[1] not for the Vice and Frailty in her Character but for that Generous Gratitude to the Founder of her Fortunes, that she sells all she has in the World, and brings it all in Jewels to relieve the Distresses of *Timon*; and what heightens our Pity is that she follows him not for a Criminal or wanton Conversation with him. Nay, what's yet greater, she can quit all the Vanities and Temptations of Life, and with an equal Contempt of Jewels and Gold can embrace his voluntary Poverty, eat Roots, drink Water, and dye with him. (part 1, 71-4)

*　　*　　*

Here the shortest way to tell you what *will* please an *English* Audience, I think, is to look back and see what *has* pleased them. And here let us first take a view of our best English Tragedies, as our *Hamlet*, *Macbeth*, *Julius Cæsar*, *Oedipus*, *Alexander*, *Timon of Athens*, *Moor of Venice*, and all the rest of our most shining Pieces. All these, and the Rest of their Honourable Brethren, are so far from pent up in *Corneille's*

[1] The reference is to Shadwell's adaptation of the play: see Volume 1, No. 17.

narrower *Unity Rules*—viz. the Business of the Play confined to no longer Time than it takes up in the Playing, or his largest Compass of 24 Hours—that nothing is so ridiculous as to pretend to it. The Subjects of our English *Tragedies* are generally the whole Revolutions of Governments, States or Families, or those great Transactions, that our *Genius* of Stage-poetry can no more reach the Heights that can please our Audience under his Unity Shackles than an Eagle can soar in a Hen-coop. If the *French* can content themselves with the sweets of a single Rose-bed nothing less than the whole Garden, and the Field round it, will satisfie the *English*. Every Man as he likes. *Corneille* may reign Master of his own Revels but he is neither a Rule-maker nor a Play-maker for our Stage. And the Reason is plain. For as Delight is the great End of Playing, and those narrow Stage-restrictions of *Corneille* destroy that Delight by curtailing that Variety that should give it us, every such Rule therefore is Nonsense and Contradiction in its very Foundation. Even an Establish'd *Law*, when it destroys its own *Preamble* and the *Benefits* design'd by it, becomes void and null in it self.

'Tis true, I allow thus far, that it ought to be the chief care of the Poet to confine himself into as narrow a Compass as he can, without any particular stint, in the two First Unities of *Time* and *Place*; for which end he must observe two Things. First, upon occasion (suppose in such a Subject as *Macbeth*) he ought to falsifie even History it self. For the Foundation of that Play in the *Chronicles* was the Action of 25 Years: but in the Play we may suppose it begun and finish'd in one third of so many Months. Young *Malcom* and *Donalbain*, the Sons of *Duncan*, are but Children at the Murder of their Father, and such they return with the Forces from *England* to revenge his Death: whereas in the true Historick Length they must have set out Children and return'd Men. Secondly, the length of Time and distance of Place required in the Action ought to be never pointed at, nor hinted in the Play. For example, neither *Malcom* nor *Donalbain* must tell us how long they have been in *England* to raise those Forces, nor how long those Forces have been Marching into *Scotland*; nor *Macbeth* how far *Scone* and *Dunsinane* lay asunder, &c. By this means the Audience, who come both willing and prepar'd to be deceiv'd (*populus vult decipi, &c.*[1]), and indulge their own Delusion, can pass over a considerable

[1] 'Populus vult decipi: decipiatur': 'the people wish to be deceived: let them be deceived'; Cardinal Caraffa's comment on the Parisians, *c.* 1560. Cf. De Thou, *Historia sui temporis*, i.17.

distance both of *Time* and *Place* unheeded and unminded if they are not purposely thrown too openly in their way to stumble at. Thus *Hamlet, Julius Cæsar* and those Historick Plays shall pass glibly, when the Audience shall be almost quite shockt at such a Play as *Henry VIII* or the *Duchess of Malfi*. And why, because here's a Marriage and the Birth of a Child, possibly in two Acts, which points so directly to Ten Months length of time that the Play has very little Air of Reality, and appears too much unnatural. In this case therefore 'tis the Art of the Poet to shew all the Peacocks Train, but as little as possible of her Foot.

And as to the second Unity of Place, here our Audience expect a little Variety, *viz.* some change of Scene. To continue it all on one spot of Ground, in one Chamber or Room, would rather disgust than please: And an Author that toyls for any such *difficiles Nugæ,*[1] such an over-curious Unity, only labours to be dull; and deserves a success accordingly. (Part 2, 32-5)

36. John Dennis, Shakespeare defended

1698

From *The Usefulness of the Stage, To the Happiness of Mankind, To Government, and To Religion. Occasioned by a Late Book, written by Jeremy Collier, M.A.* (1698).

The second part of natural Religion contains the things which are to be done, which include

1. Our duty to God.
2. Our duty to our Neighbour.
3. Our duty to ourselves.

[1] Martial, *Ep.* 2.86: 'turpe est difficiles habere nugas':' 'Tis degrading to undertake difficult trifles'.

And all these it is the Business of Tragedy to teach; . . . to exhort men to Piety and the worship of the Gods; to perswade them to Justice, to Humility, and to Fidelity, and to incline them to moderation and temperance. And 'tis for the omission of one of these duties that the persons of the modern Tragedy are shewn unfortunate in their Catastrophes.

Thus *Don John*[1] is destroy'd for his libertinism and his impiety; *Timon* for his profusion and his intemperance; *Macbeth* for his lawless ambition and cruelty . . . (115–17)

37. James Drake, Shakespeare defended

1699

From *The Antient and Modern Stages survey'd. Or, Mr. Collier's View of the Immorality and Profaneness of the English Stage Set in a True Light. Wherein some of Mr. Collier's Mistakes are rectified, and the comparative Morality of the English Stage is asserted upon the Parallel* (1699).

James Drake (1667–1707) was a Tory pamphleteer and author of one play. As with Gildon's refutation of Rymer (No. 32) the argument is at its most convincing here when it deals with the detractor's faults of logic, such as the confusion of general and particular.

The *Modern* Tragedy is a Field large enough for us to lose our selves in, and therefore I shall not take the Liberty of ranging thro 'em at large, but for the most part confine myself to such as Mr *Collier* has already attackt. Upon presumption therefore that these are the weakest, if these can be defended the rest I suppose may hold out of themselves.

---

[1] This is not the Don John in *Much Ado*.

I shall begin with *Shakespeare*, whom notwithstanding the severity of Mr *Rymer* and the hard usage of Mr *Collier*, I must still think the *Proto-Dramatist* of *England*, tho he fell short of the Art of *Jonson* and the Conversation of *Beaumont* and *Fletcher*. Upon that account he wants many of their Graces, yet his Beauties make large amends for his Defects, and Nature has richly provided him with the materials, tho his unkind Fortune denied him the Art of managing them to the best Advantage.

His *Hamlet*, a Play of the first rate, has the misfortune to fall under Mr *Collier*'s displeasure, and *Ophelia*, who has had the luck hitherto to keep her reputation, is at last censur'd for Lightness in her Frenzy. Nay, Mr *Collier* is so familiar with her as to make an unkind discovery of the unsavouriness of her Breath, which no Body suspected before. But it may be this is a groundless surmise, and Mr *Collier* is deceived by a bad Nose, or a rotten Tooth of his own; and then he is obliged to beg the Poet's and the Lady's pardon for the wrong he has done 'em. But that will fall more naturally under our consideration in another place.

Hamlet, King of *Denmark*, was privately murther'd by his Brother, who immediately thereupon marry'd the Dowager and supplanted his Nephew in the Succession to the Crown. Thus far before the proper action of the Play.

The late King's Ghost appears to his Son, young *Hamlet*, and declares how and by whom he was murther'd, and engages him to revenge it. *Hamlet* hereupon grows very much discontented, and the King very jealous of him. Hereupon he is dispatched with Ambassadors to *England*, then supposed Tributary to *Denmark*, whither a secret Commission to put him to Death is sent by 'em, which *Hamlet*, discovering, writes a new Commission in which he inserts the names of the Ambassadors instead of his own. After this a Pirate engaging their Vessel, and *Hamlet* too eagerly boarding her, is carried off and set ashore in *Denmark* again. The Ambassadors, not suspecting *Hamlet*'s Trick, pursue their Voyage and are caught in their own Trap. *Polonius*, a Councellour to the King, conveying himself as a Spy behind the Hangings at an interview between *Hamlet* and his Mother, is mistaken for the King and killed by him. *Laertes* his Son, together with the King, contrive the Death of *Hamlet* by a sham Match at Foyls, wherein *Laertes* uses a poyson'd unrebated Weapon. The King, not trusting to this single Treachery, prepares a poysoned Bowl for *Hamlet*, which the Queen ignorantly drinks. *Hamlet* is too hard for *Laertes* and closes with him, and recovers the envenom'd weapon from him; but in so doing, he is hurt by and hurts him with it. *Laertes* perceiving himself wounded and knowing it to be mortal, confesses that it was a train laid by the King for *Hamlet's* Life, and that the foul Practice is justly turn'd upon himself. The Queen at the same times cries out, that she is poysoned, whereupon *Hamlet* wounds the King with the envenom'd weapon. They all die.

Whatever defects the Criticks may find in this Fable, the Moral of it is excellent. Here was a Murther privately committed, strangely discover'd, and wonderfully punish'd. Nothing in Antiquity can rival this Plot for the admirable distribution of Poetick Justice. The Criminals are not only brought to execution, but they are taken in their own Toyls, their own Stratagems recoyl upon 'em, and they are involv'd themselves in that mischief and ruine which they had projected for *Hamlet*. *Polonius* by playing the Spy meets a Fate which was neither expected by nor intended for him. *Guildenstern* and *Rosencrantz*, the King's Decoys, are counterplotted and sent to meet that fate to which they were trepanning the Prince. The Tyrant himself falls by his own Plot, and by the hand of the Son of that Brother whom he had murther'd. *Laertes* suffers by his own Treachery, and dies by a Weapon of his own preparing. Thus every one's crime naturally produces his Punishment, and every one (the Tyrant excepted) commences a Wretch almost as soon as a Villain.

The Moral of all this is very obvious. It shews us *That the Greatness of the Offender does not qualifie the Offence, and that no Humane Power or Policy are a sufficient Guard against the Impartial Hand and Eye of Providence, which defeats their wicked purposes and turns their dangerous Machinations upon their own heads.* This Moral *Hamlet* himself insinuates to us when he tells *Horatio* that he ow'd the Discovery of the Design against his Life in *England* to a rash indiscreet curiosity, and thence makes this Inference:

> *Our Indiscretion sometimes serves as well,*
> *When our dear Plots do fail, and this shou'd teach us,*
> *There's a Divinity, that shapes our ends,*
> *Rough hew 'em how we will.*   [5.2.8 ff]

The Tragedies of this Author in general are Moral and Instructive, and many of 'em such as the best of Antiquity can't equal in that respect. His *King Lear, Timon of Athens, Macbeth*, and some others are so remarkable upon that score that 'twou'd be impertinent to trouble the Reader with a minute examination of Plays so generally known and approved. (201–6)

★ ★ ★

To digress no farther, I think we are obliged to the *Modern* Tragick Poets for the introduction of Poetick Justice upon the Stage, and must own that they were the first that made it their constant aim to instruct as well as please by the Fable. The *Antients* brought indifferently all sorts of subjects upon the Stage, which they took from History or Tradition, and were therefore more solicitous to make their stories conform to the relation or to the publick Opinion than to Poetick Justice or the Propriety of Tragick Action. By this means all hopes of a *Moral* was cut off, or if by chance the story afforded any we are more obliged to the Poets luck for it than to his Skill or Care. Thus the Moral, the highest and most serviceable improvement that ever was or ever can be made of the *Drama*, is of *Modern* Extraction, and may very well be pleaded in bar to all claim laid in behalf of the Antients to preference in point of Morality and service to Virtue, as likewise in answer to all Objections made to the Manners and Conduct of the *Modern* Stage in general.

Thus the *Modern* Stage, against which Mr *Collier* maliciously declaims with so much bitterness, is upon this account infinitely preferable to the *Athenians'*, which he commends and admires. And that which he rails at as the bane of Sobriety and the Pest of Good Manners is prov'd the most commodious instrument to propagate Morality, and the easiest and most palatable Vehicle to make Instruction go down with effect. (229–30)

★ ★ ★

The Poets (says Mr *Collier*) *make* Women *speak smuttily. They bring 'em under such misbehaviour, as is violence to their Native Modesty, and a misrepresentation of their Sex. For Modesty, as Mr* Rapin *observes, is the Character of Women. They represent their single Ladies, and persons of Condition, under these disorders of Liberty. This makes the Irregularity still more monstrous, and a greater Contradiction to Nature and Probability.*

Here again, according to his usual method, Mr *Collier* mistakes his point and runs away with a wrong scent. However, he opens, and cries it lustily away, that the Musick may atone for the mistake, and draw all those that are not stanch in Partners to his Error. Mr *Rapin* observes that the Character of Women is Modesty, and therefore Mr *Collier* thinks

96

that no *Woman* must be shewn without it. *Aristotle* has given *Courage* or *Valour* as the *Characteristick* or Mark of distinction proper to the other *Sex*, which was a notion so *Antient* and so universally receiv'd that most Nations have given it a denomination from the Sex as if peculiar to it. The *Greeks* call'd it 'Aνδρεία, we *Manhood*. Yet 'tis no Solecism in *Poetical Manners* to represent Men sometimes upon the Stage as Cowards; nor did any man ever think the whole Sex affronted by it, how near soever it might touch some individuals.

If the *Poets* set up these Women of Liberty for the Representatives of their whole Sex, or pretended to make them the Standards to measure all the rest by, the Sex wou'd have just reason to complain of so abusive a Misrepresentation. But 'tis just the contrary: the Sex has no Interest in the Virtues or Vices of any Individual, either on the Stage, or off of it. They reflect no honour or disgrace on the Collective Body, any more than the Neatness and good Breeding of the *Court* affect the Nastiness and ill Manners of *Billingsgate*, or are affected by 'em.

In Plays the *Characters* are neither *Universal* nor *General*. Marks so comprehensive are the Impresses and Signatures of Nature, which are not to be corrected or improv'd by us, and therefore not to be meddled with. Besides, they give us no Idea of the person characteriz'd but what is common to the rest of the species, and do not sufficiently distinguish him. Neither are they so *Singular* as to extend no farther than single *Individuals*. *Characters* of so narrow a Compass wou'd be of very little use, or diversion, because they wou'd not appear natural, the Originals being probably unknown to the greatest part, if not the whole Audience. Nor cou'd any of the Audience find any thing to correct in themselves by seeing the Infirmity peculiar to a particular man expos'd. This was indeed the method of the *Old Greek Comedy*; but then they pick'd out publick persons, whom they dress'd in Fool's Coats and expos'd upon the Stage not in their own Shapes but those of the Poet's Fancy; an Insolence that never would have been endur'd in any but a Popular Government, where the best of Men are sometimes sacrificed to the Humours and Caprices of a giddy multitude. Yet even by them it was at last suppressed.

The *Characters* therefore must neither be too general nor too singular; one loses the distinction, the other makes it monstrous; we are too familiar with that to take notice of it, and too unacquainted with this to acknowledge it to be real. But betwixt these there is an almost infinite variety; some natural and approaching to Generals, as the several *Ages* of the World, and of *Life*, *Sexes* and *Tempers*; some Artificial and more particular, as the vast Varieties and Shapes of *Villany*, *Knavery*, *Folly*, *Affectation* and *Humour*, &c. All these are within the *Poet*'s Royalty, and he may summon 'em to attend him whenever he has occasion for their service. Yet tho these make up perhaps the greatest part of Mankind he is not fondly to imagine that he has any Authority over the whole, or to expect homage from any of 'em as the Publick Representatives of their Sex.

Yet even granting to the *Poets* such an unlimited Authority (which I shall not do) Mr *Collier*'s Argument falls to the Ground nevertheless. For as in *Painting*, so in *Poetry*, 'tis a Maxim as true as common that there are two sorts of Resemblances, one handsome, t'other homely. Now *Comedy*, whose Duty 'tis not to flatter, like Droll Painting gives the Features true, tho the Air be ridiculous. The Sex has its *Characteristick* Blemishes as well as Ornaments; and those are to be copied when a Defective Character is intended, as the others are for a perfect one. And yet, for the reasons already given, when the Virtues or Vices of any particular Women are represented the Sex in general have no share either in the Compliment or the Affront. Because, any particular Instances to the contrary notwithstanding, the Sex may be in the main either good or bad. So that Mr *Collier*'s charge of misrepresenting the Sex in general is groundless.

But he pursues his Argument to particulars, and takes notice that even Quality it self is not excepted from these Mismanagements.

If Dignities conferr'd true Merit and Titles took away all Blemishes, the *Poets* were certainly very much in the wrong to represent any Person of Quality with failings about her. But if Birth or Preferment be no sufficient Guard to a weakly Virtue or Understanding; if Title be no security against the usual Humane Infirmities; I see no reason why they mayn't as well appear together upon the lesser Stage of the Theatre as upon the grand one of the World. But this will be more properly consider'd in another place.

From these more general exceptions he descends to particular *Expressions*. Which, that he may render the more inexcusable, he flies out into extravagant Commendations of the *Antients* upon the score of their Mòdesty and the Cleanness of their *Expressions*. In this employment he bestirs himself notably, and pretends not to leave one exceptionable Passage unremarked. But either he has had a Prodigious Crop or is a very ill Husband; for he leaves very large gleanings behind him. We shall make bold to walk over the same ground and pick up some of his leavings (for all wou'd be too bulky to find room in this place), and restore 'em to their Owners, whether left by him out of negligence or design.

One thing I must desire the Reader to take notice of, which is that I don't charge these passages as faults or immoralities upon the *Antients*, but only instance in 'em to shew the partiality of Mr *Collier*, who violently wrests the Words and Sense of the Moderns only to make that monstrous and unsufferable in them which he either excuses or defends in the others. Nor do I here pretend to present the Reader with a compleat Collection of the kind. I assure him that I shall leave un-touch'd some hundreds of those instances which I have actually observ'd amongst the *Greek* and *Latin Dramatists*, and only give him so many as are indispensably necessary to shew how unjustly Mr *Collier* has drawn his parallel. For *since* both *Antients* and *Moderns*, as *Poets*, are submitted to and ought to be govern'd by the same Laws, 'tis but rea-son that one as well as t'other shou'd be allow'd the benefit of 'em.

Shakespeare's *Ophelia* comes first under his Lash for not keeping her mouth clean under her distraction. He is so very nice that her breath, which for so many years has stood the test of the most critical Noses, smells rank to him. It may therefore be worth while to enquire whether the fault lies in her Mouth, or his Nose.

Ophelia was a modest young Virgin, beloved by *Hamlet*, and in Love with him. Her Passion was approv'd and directed by her Father, and her Pretensions to a match with *Hamlet*, the heir apparent to the Crown of *Denmark*, encouraged and supported by the Countenance and Assistance of the *King* and *Queen*. A warrantable Love, so naturally planted in so tender a Breast, so carefully nursed, so artfully manured, and so strongly forced up, must needs take very deep Root and bear a very great Head. Love, even in the most difficult Circumstances, is the Passion naturally most predominant in young Breasts, but when it is encouraged and cherish'd by those of whom they stand in awe it grows Masterly and Tyrannical, and will admit of no Check. This was poor *Ophelia*'s case. *Hamlet* had sworn, her *Father* had approved, the *King* and *Queen* consented to, nay desired the Consummation of her Wishes. Her hopes were full blown when they were miserably blasted. *Hamlet* by mistake kills her Father and runs mad; or, which is all one to her, counterfeits madness so well that she is cheated into a belief of the reality of it. Here Piety and Love concur to make her Affliction piercing and to impress her Sorrow more deep and lasting. To tear up two such passions violently by the roots must needs make horrible Convulsions in a Mind so tender and a Sex so weak. These Calamities distract her and she talks incoherently; at which Mr *Collier* is amaz'd, he is downright stupified; and thinks the Woman's mad to run out of her wits. But tho she talks a little light-headed, and seems to want sleep, I don't find she needed any *Cashew* in her Mouth to correct her Breath. That's a discovery of Mr *Collier*'s (like some other of his), who perhaps is of Opinion that the Breath and the Understanding have the same Lodging and must needs be vitiated together. However, *Shakespeare* has drown'd her at last, and Mr *Collier* is angry that he did it no sooner. He is for having Execution done upon her seriously, and in sober sadness, without the excuse of madness for Self-murther. To kill her is not sufficient with him unless she be damn'd into the bargain. Allowing the Cause of her madness to be *Partie per Pale*, the death of her Father and the loss of her Love—which is the utmost we can give to the latter—yet her passion is as innocent and inoffensive in her distraction as before, tho not so reasonable and well govern'd. Mr *Collier* has not told us what he grounds his hard censure upon, but we may guess that if he be really so angry as he pretends 'tis at the mad Song which *Ophelia* sings to the Queen, which I shall venture to transcribe without fear of offending the modesty of the most chaste Ear.

> *To morrow is St* Valentine'*s day,*
> *All in the morn betimes,*
> *And I a Maid at your Window,*
> *To be your Valentine.*
> *Then up he rose, and don'd his Cloaths,*
> *And dupt the Chamber door,*
> *Let in a Maid that out a Maid*
> *Never departed more.*
> *By Gis, and by St* Charity:
> *Alack, and fie for shame!*
> *Young men will do't, if they come to't,*
> *By Cock they are to blame.*
> *Quoth she, 'before you tumbled me,*
> *You promis'd me to wed':*
> '*So had I done, by yonder Sun,*
> *And thou hadst not come to bed.'*   [4.5.46 ff]

'Tis strange this stuff shou'd wamble so in Mr *Collier*'s Stomach and put him into such an Uproar. 'Tis silly, indeed, but very harmless and inoffensive; and 'tis no great Miracle that a Woman out of her Wits shou'd talk Nonsense, who at the soundest of her Intellects had no extraordinary Talent at Speech-making. Sure Mr *Collier's* concoctive Faculty's extreamly deprav'd, that meer Water-Pap turns to such virulent Corruption with him.

But Children and Mad Folks tell truth, they say, and he seems to discover thro her Frenzy what she wou'd be at. She was troubled for the loss of a Sweet-heart and the breaking off her Match, Poor Soul. Not unlikely. Yet this was no Novelty in the days of our Fore-fathers; if he pleases to consult the Records, he will find even in the days of *Sophocles* Maids had an itching the same way, and longed to know what was what before they died.[1] (286–97)

38. Colley Cibber, from his adaptation of *Richard III*

1700

From *The Tragical History of King Richard III* [1700].

Colley Cibber (1671–1757), dramatist, actor, theatre manager and poet laureate, had his adaptation performed probably in January/ February 1700 (although December 1699 has also been suggested). It became the most popular of all adaptations, holding the stage (and more recently the screen) well into this century.

THE
PREFACE.

This Play came upon the Stage with a very Unusual disadvantage, the whole first Act being Intirely left out in the Presentation; and tho' it had been read by several persons of the first Rank and Integrity, some of which were pleas'd to honour me with an offer of giving it under

[1] Perhaps a reference to Sophocles' *Antigone*, 808–920.

their hands that the whole was an Inoffensive piece and free from any bold Paralel or ill manner'd reflection, yet this was no satisfaction to him who had the Relentless power of licensing it for the Stage. I did not spare for intreaties; but all the reason I could get for its being refus'd was that *Henry VI* being a Character Unfortunate and Pitied, wou'd put the Audience in mind of the late *King James.* Now I confess I never thought of him in the Writing it, which possibly might proceed from there not being any likeness between 'em. But, however, there was no hazard of offending the Government though the whole Play had been refus'd, and a man is not obliged to be Just when he can get as much by doing an Injury. I am only sorry it hapned to be the best Act in the Whole, and leave it to the Impartial Reader how far it is offensive, and whether its being Acted would have been as injurious to good Manners as the omission of it was to the rest of the Play.

Tho' there was no great danger of the Reader's mistaking any of my lines for *Shakespeare*'s; yet, to satisfie the curious, and unwilling to assume more praise than is really my due, I have caus'd those that are intirely *Shakespeare*'s to be Printed in this *Italick Character*; and those lines with this mark (') before 'em are generally his thoughts, in the best dress I could afford 'em. What is not so mark'd, or in a different Character, is intirely my own. I have done my best to imitate his Style and manner of thinking. If I have fail'd I have still this comfort, that our best living Author in his imitation of *Shakespeare*'s Style only writ Great and Masterly.

[Act I, Scene i.] London.
The Scene, A Garden within the Tower.

Enter the Lieutenant with a Servant.

Lieu. Has King *Henry* walk'd forth this Morning?
Ser. No, Sir, but 'tis near his Hour.
Lieu. At any time when you see him here,
Let no Stranger into the Garden:
I wou'd not have him star'd at—See! Who's that
Now entring at the Gate?
Ser. Sir, the Lord *Stanley.*
Lieu. Leave me.—

[*Exit Servant.*

Enter Lord Stanley.

My Noble Lord, you're welcome to the Tower.
I heard last Night you late arriv'd with News
Of *Edward*'s Victory to his joyful Queen.

   Ld. Sta. Yes, Sir; and I am proud to be the Man
That first brought home the last of Civil Broils.
The Houses now of *York* and *Lancaster*,
Like Bloody Brothers fighting for Birth-right,
No more shall wound the Parent that wou'd part 'em.
Edward now sits secure on *England*'s Throne.

   Lieu. Near *Tewkesbury*, my Lord, I think they fought:
Has the Enemy lost any Men of Note?

   Ld. Sta. Sir, I was Posted Home
Ere an Account was taken of the Slain.
But as I left the Field a Proclamation
From the King was made in Search of *Edward*,
Son to your Prisoner, King *Henry* the Sixth,
Which gave Reward to those Discover'd him,
And him his Life if he'd surrender.

   Lieu. That Brave Young Prince, I fear's unlike his Father,
Too high of Heart to brook submissive Life.
This will be heavy News to *Henry*'s Ear:
For on this Battle's cast his All was set.

   Ld. Sta. King *Henry* and ill Fortune are familiar.
He ever threw with an indifferent Hand,
But never yet was known to lose his Patience.
How does he pass the Time in his Confinement?

   Lieu. As one whose Wishes never reacht a Crown.
The King seems Dead in him: But as a Man
He sighs sometimes in want of Liberty.
Sometimes he Reads, and Walks, wishes
That Fate had blest him with an humbler Birth,
Not to have felt the falling from a Throne.

   Ld. Sta. Were it not possible to see this King?
They say he'll freely talk with *Edward*'s Friends,
And ever treats him with Respect and Honour.

   Lieu. This is his usual Time of walking forth,
(For he's allow'd the freedom of the Garden)
After his Morning-Prayer: he seldom fails.
Behind this Arbor we unseen may stand
A while t'observe him.   *[They retire.*

Enter King Henry *VI in Mourning.*

K. Hen. By this time the Decisive Blow is struck,
Either my Queen and Son are blest with Victory,
Or I'm the cause no more of Civil Broils.
Wou'd I were Dead if Heavens good Will were so,
'For what is in this World but Grief and Care?
What Noise and Bustle do Kings make to find it?
When Life's but a short Chace, our Game's Content,
Which most pursued is most compell'd to fly;
And he that mounts him on the swiftest Hope
Shall often Run his Courser to a stand,
While the poor Peasant from some distant Hill
Undanger'd and at Ease views all the Sport,
And sees Content take shelter in his Cottage.

Ld. Sta. He seems Extreamly mov'd. ⎫
Lieu. Does he know you?   ⎪
Ld. Sta. No! nor wou'd I have him. ⎬ *Aside.*
Lieu. We'll show our selves.   ⎭ [*They come forward.*

K. Hen. Why, there's another Check to Proud Ambition.
That Man receiv'd his Charge from me, and now
I'm his Prisoner, he lock's me to my Rest:
Such an unlook'd for Change who cou'd suppose
That saw him kneel to Kiss the Hand that rais'd him?
But that I shou'd not now complain of,
Since I from thence may happily derive
His Civil Treatment of me.—'Morrow, Lieutenant,
Is any News arriv'd?—Who's that with you?

Lieu. A Gentleman that came last Night Express
From *Tewkesbury.* We've had a Battle, Sir.

K. Hen. Comes he to me with Letters or Advice?

Lieu. Sir, he's King *Edward's* Officer, your Foe.

K. Hen. Then he won't flatter me. You're welcome, Sir;
Not less because you are King *Edward's* Friend,
For I have almost learn'd my self to be so.
Cou'd I but once forget I was a King
I might be truly Happy, and his Subject.
You've gain'd a Battle: Is't not so?

Ld. Sta. We have, Sir; How, will reach your Ear too soon.

K. Hen. If to my Loss, it can't too soon. Pray speak,

For Fear makes Mischief greater than it is.
My Queen! my Son! say, Sir, are they living?

 Ld. Sta. Since my Arrival, Sir, another Post
Came in, who brought us word your Queen and Son
Were Prisoners now at *Tewkesbury.*

 K. Hen. Heav'ns Will be done! the Hunters have 'em now—
And I have only Sighs and Prayers to help 'em!

 Ld. Sta. King *Edward*, Sir, depends upon his Sword,
Yet prays heartily when the Battle's won.
And Soldiers love a Bold and Active Leader:
Fortune like Women will be close pursu'd.
The *English* are high Mettl'd, Sir, and 'tis
No easie part to Sit 'em well. King *Edward*
Feels their Temper and 'twill be hard to throw him.

 K. Hen. Alas, I thought 'em Men, and rather hop'd
To win their Hearts by Mildness than Severity.
My Soul was never form'd for Cruelty:
In my Eye Justice has seem'd bloody.
When on the City Gates I have beheld
A Traytor's Quarters parching in the Sun
My Blood has turn'd with Horror of the Sight.
I took 'em down, and Buried with his Limbs
The Memory of the Dead Man's Deeds. Perhaps
That Pity made me look less Terrible,
Giving the mind of weak Rebellion Spirit.
For Kings are put in Trust for all Mankind,
And when themselves take Injuries, who is safe?
If so, I have deserv'd these frowns of Fortune.

Enter a Servant to the Lieutenant.

 Ser. Sir, here's a Gentleman brings a Warrant
For his Access to King *Henry's* Presence.

 Lieu. I come to him.

 Ld. Sta. His Business may require your Privacy,
I'll leave you, Sir, wishing you all the Good
That can be wish'd, not wronging him I serve.   [*Exit Lord* Stan.

 K. Hen. Farewell. Who can this be? A sudden Coldness,
Like the Damp Hand of Death, has seiz'd my Limbs:
I fear some heavy News!—

Enter Lieutenant.

Who is it, good Lieutenant?
  Lieu. A Gentleman, Sir, from *Tewkesbury*. He seems
A melancholly Messenger, for when I ask'd
What News? His Answer was a deep-fraught Sigh.
I wou'd not urge him, but I fear 'tis fatal.

Enter Tressel in Mourning.

  K. Hen. Fatal indeed! His Brow's the Title Page
That speaks the Nature of a Tragick Volume;
'Say, Friend, how does my Queen, my Son?
Thou tremblest, and the whiteness of thy Cheek
Is apter than thy Tongue to tell the Errand,
Ev'n such a Man, so Faint, so Spiritless,
So Dull, so Dead in Look, so Woe-begone,
Drew Priam's Curtain in the Dead of Night,
And wou'd have told him half his Troy was burn'd,
But Priam found the Fire, ere he his Tongue,
And I my poor Son's Death ere thou relatest it;
Now wou'd'st thou say: Your Son did thus and thus,
'And thus your Queen; So fought the Valiant *Oxford*,
Stopping my greedy Ear with their bold Deeds,
But in the End (to stop my Ear indeed)
Thou hast a Sigh to blow away this Praise,
'Ending with Queen, and Son, and all are Dead.
  Tress. 'Your Queen yet Lives, and many of your Friends,
'But for my Lord your Son—
  K. Hen. Why, he is Dead;—yet speak, I charge thee!
'Tell thou thy Master his Suspicion lies,
And I will take it as a kind Disgrace,
'And thank thee well for doing me such wrong.
  Tress. Wou'd it were wrong to say, but Sir, your Fears are true.
  K. Hen. Yet for all this say not my Son is Dead!
  Tress. Sir, I am sorry I must force you to
Believe what wou'd to Heav'n I had not seen!
But in this last Battle near *Tewkesbury*
'Your Son, whose Active Spirit lent a Fire
'Ev'n to the dullest Peasant in our Camp,
Still made his way where Danger stood t'oppose him.

A braver Youth of more Couragious Heat,
'Ne'er spurr'd his Courser at the Trumpets sound.
But who can Rule th' uncertain Chance of War?
In Fine, King *Edward* won the Bloody Field,
Where both your Queen and Son were made his Prisoners.
   K. Hen. 'Yet, hold! for oh! this Prologue lets me in
'*To a most fatal Tragedy to come.*—
Dy'd he Prisoner, say'st thou? How? By Grief,
Or by the bloody Hands of those that caught him?
   Tress. After the Fight *Edward* in Triumph ask'd
To see the Captive Prince. The Prince was brought,
Whom *Edward* roughly Chid for bearing Arms,
Asking what Reparation he cou'd make
For having stirr'd his Subjects to Rebellion?
Your Son, impatient of such Taunts, reply'd:
'Bow like a Subject, Proud Ambitious *York!*
'While I now speaking with my Father's Mouth
'Propose the self-same Rebel Words to thee
'Which, Traytor, thou wou'dst have me answer to'.
From these more Words arose, till in the End
King *Edward*, swell'd with what th'unhappy Prince
At such a time too freely spoke, his Gauntlet
In his young Face with Indignation struck.
At which Crook'd *Richard*, *Clarence*, and the rest
Buried their fatal Daggers in his Heart.
In Bloody State I saw him on the Earth,
From whence with Life he never more sprung up.
   K. Hen. 'O had'st thou stabb'd, at every Word's deliverance,
'Sharp Ponyards in my Flesh while this were told
'Thy Wounds had giv'n less Anguish than thy Words.—
O Heav'ns! methinks I see my tender Lamb
Gasping beneath the Ravenous Wolves' fell gripe!
But say, did all? Did they all strike him, say'st thou?
   Tress. All, Sir: But the first Wound Duke *Richard* gave.
   K. Hen. There let him stop! be that his last of Ills!
O barbarous Act! Unhospitable Men!
Against the rigid Laws of Arms to kill him!
Was't not enough his hope of Birth-right gone,
But must your Hate be levell'd at his Life?
Nor cou'd his Father's Wrongs content you?

Nor cou'd a Father's Grief disswade the Deed?
'You have no Children (Butchers if you had),
'The thought of them wou'd sure have stirr'd Remorse.
   Tress. Take Comfort, Sir; and hope a better Day.
   K. Hen. O! who can hold a Fire in his Hand,
By thinking on the Frosty Caucasus?
Or wallow Naked in December's *Snow,*
'By the remembrance of the Summer's Heat?
Away! by Heav'n, I shall abhor his Sight
'Whoever bids me be of Comfort more.
If thou wilt sooth my Sorrows, then I'll thank thee.
Ay! now thou'rt kind indeed! these Tears oblige me.
   Tress. Alas, my Lord! I fear more Evils toward you.
   K. Hen. Why, let it come! I scarce shall feel it now.
My present Woes have beat me to the Ground
And my hard Fate can make me fall no lower.
What can it be? Give it its ugliest Shape,—O my poor Boy!—
   Tress. A word does that it comes in *Gloucester's* Form.
   K. Hen. Frightful indeed! give me the worst that threatens.
   Tress. After the Murther of your Son stern *Richard,*
As if unsated with the Wounds he had giv'n,
With unwash'd Hands went from his Friends in hast,
And being ask'd by *Clarence* of the Cause,
He low'ring cry'd, 'Brother, I must to the Tower!
I've Business there, excuse me to the King;
Before you reach the Town expect some News'.
This said, he vanish'd, and I hear's arriv'd.
   K. Hen. Why, then the Period of my Woes is set;
For Ills but thought by him are half perform'd.

Enter Lieutenant with a Paper.

   Lieu. Forgive me, Sir; what, I'm compell'd t'obey
An Order for your close Confinement.
   K. Hen. Whence comes it, good Lieutenant?
   Lieu. Sir, from the Duke of *Gloucester.*
   K. Hen. Good Night to all then: I obey it—
And now good Friend suppose me on my Death-bed,
And take of me, thy last, short Living leave:—
Nay, keep thy Tears till thou hast seen me Dead.
And when in tedious Winter Nights, with Good

Old Folks, thou sit'st up late
To hear 'em tell thee Dismal Tales
'Of times long past, even now with Woe remember'd;
Before thou bidst good night, to quit their Grief,
Tell thou the lamentable fall of me,
And send thy hearers weeping to their Beds.　　　　　　　[Exeunt.

[Act I, Scene ii.]

Enter Richard *Duke of* Gloucester, *Solus.*

　　Rich. Now are our Brows bound with Victorious wreaths,
Our stern allarms are changed to Merry meetings,
Our dreadfull marches to delightful measures.
Grim-visaged War has smoothed his wrinkled Front,
And now instead of mounting Barbed Steeds
To fright the Souls of fearful Adversaries,
He Capers nimbly in a Ladies Chamber
To the Lascivious Pleasing of a Lute.
But I that am not shaped for sportive tricks,
I that am curtailed of Man's fair proportion,
Deform'd, Unfinish'd, sent before my time
Into this breathing World, scarce half made up,
And that so lamely and unfashionable
That Dogs bark at me as I halt by 'em;
Why I, in this weak, this piping time of Peace,
Have no delight to pass away my hours,
Unless to see my shadow in the Sun,
And descant on my own deformity:
—Then since this Earth affords no joy to me,
But to Command, to Check, and to Orebear such,
'As are of Happier Person than my self,
'Why then to me this restless World's but Hell,
Till this mishapen trunk's aspiring head
'Be circled in a glorious Diadem.
But then 'tis fixt on such an heighth, O! I
Must stretch the utmost reaching of my Soul.
　　　I'll climb betimes without Remorse or Dread,
　　　And my first steps shall be on *Henry's* Head.　　　　[*Exit.*

★　　　★　　　★

[Act II, Scene i.]

The SCENE, *St.* Pauls.

Enter Tressel *meeting Lord* Stanley.

Tress. My Lord, your Servant. Pray what brought you to *Paul*'s?

Ld. Stan. I came amongst the Crowd to see the Corps
Of poor King *Henry.* 'Tis a dismal sight.
But yesterday I saw him in the Tower;
His talk is still so fresh within my memory
That I could weep to think how Fate has us'd him.
I wonder where's Duke *Richard*'s policy
In suffering him to lie exposed to view?
Can he believe that Men will love him for't?

Tress. O yes, Sir, love him as he loves his Brothers.
When was you with King *Edward*, pray, my Lord?
I hear he leaves his Food, is Melancholy,
And his Physicians fear him mightily.

Ld. Stan. 'Tis thought he'll scarce recover:
Shall we to Court, and hear more News of him?

Tress. I am oblig'd to pay Attendance here,
The Lady *Ann* has license to remove
King *Henry*'s Corps to be Interr'd at *Chertsey*,
And I am engag'd to follow her.

Ld. Stan. Mean you King *Henry*'s Daughter-in-Law?

Tress. The same, Sir, Widow to the late Prince *Edward*
Whom *Gloucester* kill'd at *Tewkesbury.*

Ld. Stan. Alas, poor Lady, she's severely used.
And yet I hear *Richard* attempts her Love:
Methinks the wrongs he's done her should discourage him.

Tress. Neither those wrongs nor his own shape can fright him;
He sent for leave to visit her this morning,
And she was forc'd to keep her Bed to avoid him.
But see, she is arriv'd: Will you along
To see this doleful Ceremony?

Ld. Stan. I'll wait on you.   [*Exeunt.*

Enter Richard, *solus.*

Rich. 'Twas her excuse t'avoid me—Alas!
She keeps no Bed—
She has health enough to progress far as *Chertsey*,

Tho' not to bear the sight of me;
—I cannot blame her—
Why Love forswore me in my Mothers Womb,
And for I should not deal in his soft Laws,
He did corrupt frail Nature with some Bribe
To shrink my Arm up like a wither'd Shrub,
To make an envious Mountain on my back,
Where sits Deformity to mock my Body,
To shape my Legs of an unequal size,
To disproportion me in every part:
And am I then a man to be belov'd?
O monstrous Thought! more vain my Ambition.

Enter a Gentleman hastily.

    Gent. My Lord, I beg your Grace—
    Rich. Be gone, Fellow—I'm not at leisure—
    Gent. My Lord, the King your Brother's taken ill.
    Rich. I'll wait on him. Leave me, Friend—
Ha! *Edward* ta'en ill!—
Wou'd he were wasted, Marrow-bones and all,
'That from his loins no more young Brats may rise
'To cross me in the golden time I look for.—
But see, my Love appears! Look where she shines,
Darting pale Lustre like the Silver Moon
Through her dark Veil of Rainy sorrow.
So mourn'd the Dame of *Ephesus* her Love,
And thus the Soldier arm'd with Resolution
Told his soft tale, and was a thriving Wooer.
'Tis true, my Form perhaps will little move her,
But I've a Tongue shall wheadle with the Devil.
Yet hold; She mourns the Man whom I have kill'd.
First, let her sorrows take some vent.—Stand here;
I'll take her passion in its wain, and turn
This storm of grief to gentle drops of pity
For his Repentant Murderer.—   *[He retires.*

Enter Bearers with King Henry's *Body, the Lady* Ann *in Mourning,*
Lord Stanley, Tressel, *and Guards, who all advance from the middle of the*
Church.

    Lady A. 'Hung be the Heavens with black, yield day to night,

'Comets importing change of Times and States,
'Brandish your fiery Tresses in the Sky,
'And with 'em scourge the bad revolting Stars
'That have consented to King *Henry*'s death.
O be Accurst the Hand that shed this Blood;
Accurst the Head that had the Heart to do it.
More direful hap betide that hated Wretch
Than I can wish to Wolves, to Spiders, Toads,
Or any creeping venom'd thing that lives:
If ever he have Wife, let her be made
'More miserable by the Life of him,
'Than I am now by *Edward*'s death and thine.

 Rich. Poor Girl! What pains she takes to curse her self! [*Aside.*
 Lady A. If ever he have Child, Abortive be it,
Prodigious and Untimely brought to Light,
'Whose hideous Form, whose most unnatural Aspect
May fright the hopeful Mother at the view,
And that be Heir to his unhappiness.
'Now on, to *Chertsey* with your sacred Load.

Richard comes forward.

 Rich. Stay, you that bear the Coarse, and set it down.
 Lady A. What black Magician Conjures up this Fiend
To stop devoted charitable deeds?
 Rich. Villains, set down the Coarse, or, by St. Paul,
I'll make a Coarse of him that disobeys.

* * *

[Act II, Scene ii.] The Presence.

* * *

 Queen. May Heav'n prosper all your good intents.

[*Exeunt all but* Buck. *and* Richard.

 Rich. Amen, with all my Heart. For mine's the Crown.
And is not that a good one? ha! Pray'd she not well, Cousin?
 D. Buck. I hope she prophesied.—You now stand Fair.
 Rich. Now by St. *Paul,* I feel it here! Methinks
The massy weight on't galls my laden Brow.

112

What think'st thou, Cousin, wer't not an easie matter
To get Lord *Stanley*'s hand to help it on?

D. Buck. 'My Lord, I doubt that for his Fathers sake,
'He loves the Prince too well, he'll scarce be won
'To any thing against him.

Rich. Poverty, the reward of Honest Fools,
O'retake him for't! what thinkst thou then of *Hastings*?

D. Buck. He shall be tri'd, my Lord: I'll find out *Catesby*,
Who shall at subtle distance sound his thoughts;
But we must still suppose the worst may happen.
What if we find him cold in our design?

Rich. Chop off his head.—Something we'll soon determine.
But haste, and find out *Catesby*,
That done, follow me to the Counsel Chamber;
We'll not be seen together much, nor have
It known that we confer in Private.—Therefore
Away good Cousin.

D. Buck. I am gone, My Lord.   [*Exit* Buck.

Rich. Thus far we run before the wind—Let me see,
The Prince will soon be here—let him—the Crown!
O yes! he shall have twenty, Globes and Scepters too,
New ones made to play withall—But no Coronation!
No! nor no Court flies about him, no Kinsmen—
—Hold ye!—Where shall he keep his Court!—
—Ay!—the *Tower*.   [*Exit.*

[Act III, Scene i.]

*   *   *

D. Buc. 'Doubt not, my Lord, I'll play the Orator
'As if my self might wear the Golden Fee,
'For which I Plead.

Rich. If you thrive well, bring 'em to see me here,
'Where you shall find me seriously employ'd
'With the most Learned Fathers of the Church.

D. Buc. I fly, my Lord, to serve you.

Rich. To serve thy self, my Cousin;
*For look when I am King claim thou of me
The Earldom of Hereford and all those Moveables*

Whereof the King my Brother stood possest.

   D. Buc. *I shall remember that your Grace was Bountiful.*

   Rich. Cousin, I have said it.

   D. Buc. I am gone, my Lord.   [*Exit* Buc.

   Rich. So—I've secur'd my Cousin here: These Moveables

Will never let his Brains have rest till I am King. *Catesby,*

Go thou with speed to Doctor Shaw, *and thence*

'To Fryar *Beuker*: Haste, and bid 'em both

'Attend me here, within an hour at farthest.   [*Exit* Catesby.

Mean while my private orders shall be given

To lock up all admittance to the Princes.

Now, by St. *Paul,* the work goes bravely on.—

How many frightful stops wou'd Conscience make

In some soft heads to undertake like me.

—Come; this Conscience is a convenient Scarecrow,

It Guards the fruit which Priests and Wisemen tast,

Who never set it up to fright themselves:

They know 'tis rags, and gather in the face on't,

While half-starv'd shallow Daws thro Fear are honest.

Why were Laws made, but that we're Rogues by Nature?

Conscience! 'tis our Coin, we live by parting with it,

And he thrives best that has the most to spare.

The protesting Lover buys hope with it,

And the deluded Virgin short-liv'd pleasure.

Old gray-beards cram their Avarice with it,

Your Lank-jaw'd hungry Judge will dine upon't,

And hang the Guiltless rather than eat his Mutton cold.

The Crown'd Head quits it for Despotick sway,

The stubborn People for unaw'd Rebellion.

There's not a Slave but has his share of Villain;

Why then shall after Ages think my deeds

Inhumane? Since my worst are but Ambition:

     Ev'n all Mankind to some lov'd Ills incline,

     Great Men chuse Greater Sins—Ambition's mine.   [*Exit.*

[Act III, Scene ii.]

Enter Lady Ann, *sola.*

   Lady A. When, when shall I have rest? Was Marriage made

To be the Scourge of our Offences here?

Ah no! 'Twas meant a Blessing to the Vertuous.
It once was so to me, tho' now my Curse.
The fruit of *Edward*'s Love was sweet and pleasing:
But oh! Untimely cropt by cruel *Richard*,
Who rudely having grafted on his stock
Now makes my Life yield only sorrow.
Let me have Musick to compose my thoughts.

                                    [*Song here.*

It will not be: Nought but the grave can close my Eyes.
—How many labouring Wretches take their rest,
While I, night after night, with cares lie waking,
As if the gentle Nurse of Nature, Sleep,
Had vow'd to rock my peevish sense no more.
'O partial sleep! Canst thou in smoaky Cottages
'Stretch out the Peasant's Limbs on Beds of Straw,
'And lay him fast, cram'd with distressful Bread?
Yet in the softest breeze of Peaceful Night
'Under the Canopies of costly State,
'Tho' lull'd with sounds of sweetest melody,
Refuse one moment's slumber to a Princess?
O mockery of Greatness! But see,
He comes! The rude disturber of my Pillow.

Enter Richard, *Aloof.*

  Rich. Ha! still in tears? let 'em flow on; they're signs   [*Aside.*
Of a substantial grief.—Why don't she die?
She must: My Interest will not let her live.
The fair *Elizabeth* has caught my Eye,
My Heart's vacant, and she shall fill her place.
They say that Women have but tender hearts—
'Tis a mistake, I doubt, I've found 'em tough.
They'll bend, indeed: But he must strain that cracks 'em.
All I can hope's to throw her into sickness:
Then I may send her a Physician's help.
—So, Madam. What, you still take care, I see,
To let the World believe I love you not.
This outward Mourning now, has malice in't,
So have these sullen disobedient tears.
I'll have you tell the World I doat on you.

Lady A. I wish I could, but 'twill not be believ'd.
Have I deserv'd this usage?
   Rich. You have: You do not please me as at first.
   Lady A. What have I done? What horrid Crime committed?
   Rich. To me the worst of Crimes, out-liv'd my liking.
   Lady A. If that be Criminal, Just Heaven be kind,
And take me while my Penitence is warm.
O Sir, forgive, and kill me!
   Rich. Umh! No.—The medling World will call it murder,
And I wou'd have 'em think me pitifull.
Now, wert thou not afraid of self-Destruction,
Thou hast a fair excuse for't.
   Lady A. How fain wou'd I be Friends with Death! O name it.
   Rich. Thy Husband's hate. Nor do I hate thee only
From the dull'd edge of sated Appetite,
But from the eager Love I bear another.
Some call me Hypocrite: What think'st thou now,
Do I dissemble?
   Lady A. Thy Vows of Love to me were all dissembled.
   Rich. Not one: For when I told thee so, I lov'd.
Thou art the only Soul I never yet deceiv'd.
And 'tis my honesty that tells thee now
With all my heart, I hate thee.—
If this have no Effect, she is immortal.   [*Aside.*
   Lady A. Forgive me, Heaven, that I forgave this Man.
O may my story, told in after Ages,
Give warning to our easie Sexes ears.
May it Unveil the hearts of Men, and strike
Them deaf to their dissimulated Love.

Enter Catesby.

   Cat. My Lord, his Grace of *Buckingham* attends
Your Highness' Pleasure.
   Rich. Wait on him; I'll expect him here.   [*Exit* Cat.
Your Absence, Madam, will be necessary.
   Lady A. Wou'd my death were so.   [*Exit.*
   Rich. It may be shortly.

      ★   ★   ★

[Act IV, Scene i.] The Tower.

Enter the two Princes with the Queen, the Duchess of York, and Lady Ann in tears.

Pr. Ed. Pray, Madam, do not leave me yet,
For I have many more complaints to tell you.
Queen. And I unable to redress the least.
What wou'dst thou say, my Child?
Pr. Ed. O Mother! Since I first have lain i'th' Tower
My rest has still been broke with frightful Dreams,
Or shocking News has wak'd me into tears.
I'm scarce allow'd a Friend to visit me.
All my old honest Servants are turn'd off,
And in their rooms are strange ill-natur'd fellows,
Who look so bold, as they were all my Masters;
And, I'm afraid, they'll shortly take you from me.
Duch. Y. O mournful hearing!
Lady A. O unhappy Prince!
D. York. Dear Brother, why do you weep so?
You make me cry too.
Queen. Alas, poor Innocence!
Pr. Ed. Wou'd I but knew at what my Uncle aims.
If 'twere my Crown, I'd freely give it him,
So he'd but let me 'joy my life in quiet.
D. York. Why! will my Uncle kill us, Brother?
Pr. Ed. I hope he won't: We never injur'd him.
Queen. I cannot bear to see 'em thus.—   [*Weeping.*

Enter to them Lord Stanley.

Ld. Stan. Madam, I hope your Majesty will pardon
What I am griev'd to tell, Unwelcome News.
Queen. Ah me! more sorrow yet! My Lord, we've long
Despair'd of happy Tydings, pray what is't?
Ld. Stan. On *Tuesday* last, your noble Kinsmen *Rivers*,
Grey, and Sir *Thomas Vaughan* at *Pomfret*
Were Executed on a publick Scaffold.
Duch. Y. O dismal Tydings.
Pr. Ed. O poor Uncles! I doubt my turn is next.
Lady A. Nor mine, I fear, far off.
Queen. Why, then, let's welcome Blood and Massacre,

117

Yield all our Throats to the fierce Tyger's rage,
And die lamenting one another's wrongs.
O! I foresaw this ruin of our House.   [*Weeps.*

Enter Catesby *to Lady* Ann.

   Cat. Madam, the King
Has sent me to inform your Majesty
That you prepare (as is advis'd from Council)
To morrow for your Royal Coronation.
   Queen. What do I hear? Support me, Heaven!
   Lady A. Despightful Tydings! O unpleasing News!
Alas, I heard of this before, but cou'd not
For my soul take heart to tell you of it.
   Cat. The King does further wish your Majesty
Wou'd less employ your visits at the Tower.
He gives me leave t'attend you to the Court,
And is impatient, Madam, till he sees you.
   Lady A. Farewel to all, and thou, poor injur'd Queen:
Forgive the unfriendly duty I must pay.
   Queen. Alas, kind Soul, I envy not thy Glory,
Nor think I'm pleas'd thou'rt partner in our sorrows.
   Cat. Madam.—
   Lady A. I come—
   Queen. Farewel, thou woeful welcomer of Glory.
   Cat. Shall I attend your Majesty?
   Lady A. Attend me! Whither, to be Crown'd?
Let me with deadly Venome be Anointed,
And die eer Men can say, Long live the Queen.
   Queen. Poor grieving heart, I pity thy complaining.
   Lady A. No more than with my Soul I mourn for yours:
A long farewel to all.—   [*Exit* Lady A. *and* Cat.

*   *   *

[Act IV, Scene iii.] The Tower.

Enter Tirrell, Dighton, *and* Forrest.

   Tir. Come, Gentlemen:
Have you concluded on the means?
   Digh. Smothering will make no noise, Sir.
   Tir. Let it be done i'th' dark. For shou'd you see

Their young faces, who knows how far their looks
Of Innocence may tempt you into pity.
    For. 'Tis ease and living well makes Innocence:
I hate a face less guilty than my own.
Were all that now seem Honest deep as we
In trouble and in want they'd all be Rogues.
    Tir. Stand back—Lieutenant, have you brought the Keys?

Enter Lieutenant.

    Lieu. I have 'em, Sir.
    Tir. Then here's your warrant to deliver 'em.   *[Gives a Ring.*
    Lieu. Your Servant, Sir.—
What can this mean? Why, at this dead of night to
Give 'em too?—'Tis not for me t'enquire.   *[Exit Lieu.*
    Tir. There, Gentlemen: *[Giving them the Keys.*
That way! You have no farther need of me.   *[Exeunt severally.*

[Act IV, Scene iv.]

SCENE *a Chamber, the Princes in Bed. The Stage darkned.*

    Pr. Ed. Why do you startle, Brother?
    D. York. O! I have been so frighted in my sleep!
Pray turn this way!
    Pr. Ed. Alas, I fain wou'd sleep but cannot,
Tho' 'tis the stillest night I ever knew.
Not the least breath has stir'd these four hours.
Sure all the World's asleep but we.
    D. York. Hark! Pray Brother count the Clock!   *[Clock strikes.*
—But two! O tedious night: I've slept an Age.
Wou'd it were day, I am so melancholy.
    Pr. Ed. Hark! What noise is that?
I thought I heard some one upon the stairs!
Hark! Again!
    D. York. O dear, I hear 'em too! Who is it, Brother?
    Pr. Ed. Bless me! a light too, thro' the door! look there!
    D. York. Who is it? Hark! it unlocks! O! I am so afraid!

Enter Dighton *and* Forrest *with dark lanthorns.*

    Pr. Ed. Bless me! What frightful men are these?

Both. Who's there?   *Pr. Ed.* Who's there?

Digh. Hist, we've wak'd 'em! What shall we say?

For. Nothing. We come to do.

Digh. I'll see their Faces—

D. York. Won't they speak to us?

[*Dighton looks in with his Lanthorn.*

O save me! Hide me! Save me, Brother!

Pr. Ed. O mercy Heaven! Who are you, Sirs,

That look so ghastly pale and terrible?

Digh. I am a Fool.—I cannot answer 'em.

For. You must die, my Lord, so must your Brother.

Pr. Ed. O stay, for pity sake! What is our Crime, Sir?

Why must we die?

Digh. The King, your Uncle, loves you not.

Pr. Ed. O Cruel man!

Tell him we'll live in Prison all our days,

And, when we give occasion of offence,

Then let us die. H'as yet no cause to kill us.

For. Pray.

Pr. Ed. We do, Sir, to you. O spare us, Gentlemen!

I was some time your King, and might have shown

You mercy. For your dear Souls sake pity us.

For. We'll hear no more.

Both Pr. O Mercy, Mercy!

For. Down, down with 'em.

[*They smother them, and the Scene shuts on them.*

Enter Tyrrell, *Solus.*

Tyr. ' 'Tis done: The barbarous bloody act is done:

'O the most Arch-deed of pitious Massacre

'That ever yet this Land was guilty of.

Ha! the King: His coming hither at this

Late hour, speaks him impatient for the welcome News.

Enter Richard.

Rich. Now my *Tyrrell*, how are the Brats dispos'd?

Say: am I happy? Hast thou dealt upon 'em?

Tyr. 'If to have done the thing you gave in charge

'Beget your happiness, then, Sir, be happy;

For it is done.

Rich. *But didst thou see 'em dead?*

Tyr. *I did, my Lord.*

Rich. *And buried, my good* Tyrrell?

Tyr. In that I thought to ask your Grace's Pleasure.

Rich. I have't—I'll have 'em sure.—Get me a Coffin
Full of holes, let 'em be both cram'd into't;
And, hark thee, in the night-tide throw 'em down
The *Thames*; once in, they'll find the way to th' bottom.
Meantime but think how I may do thee good,
And be Inheritor of thy desire.

Tyr. I humbly thank your Highness.

*   *   *

[Act IV, Scene iv.]

*   *   *

Enter a Messenger.

Mes. *My Lord, the Army of Great* Buckingham
By sudden Floods, and fall of Waters,
Is half lost and scatter'd,
And he himself wander'd away alone;
No man knows whither.

Rich. 'Has any careful Officer proclaim'd
Reward to him that brings the Traytor in?

Mes. *Such Proclamation has been made, my Lord.*

Enter Catesby.

Cat. *My Liege, the Duke of* Buckingham *is taken.*

Rich. *Off with his head. So much for* Buckingham.

Cat. My Lord, I'm sorry I must tell more News.

Rich. Out with it.

Cat. *The Earl of* Richmond *with a mighty power*
Is Landed, Sir, at Milford:
And, to confirm the News, Lord Marquess Dorset,
And Sir Thomas Lovel *are up in* Yorkshire.

Rich. Why ay, this looks Rebellion. Ho! my Horse!
By Heaven the News allarms my stirring Soul.

'And as the Wretch, whose favour-weakned joynts,
'Like strengthless hinges buckle under Life;
'Impatient of his fit, breaks like a fire
'From his fond Keeper's Arms, and starts away:
'Even so these War-worn Limbs grown weak
'From Wars disuse, being now inrag'd with War,
'Feel a new Fury, and are thrice themselves.
Come forth my Honest Sword, which here I vow,
By my Souls hope, shall ne'er again be sheath'd,
Ne'er shall these watching Eyes have needful rest,
Till Death has clos'd 'em in a glorious Grave,
Or Fortune given me Measure of Revenge.   [*Exeunt.*

★   ★   ★

[Act V, Scene v.] Bosworth Field.

Enter Richard *from his Tent, solus.*

   Rich. 'Tis now the dead of Night, and half the World
Is with a lonely solemn darkness hung.
Yet I (so coy a dame is sleep to me)
With all the weary Courtship of
My Care-tir'd thoughts can't win her to my Bed;
Tho' ev'n the Stars do wink as 'twere, with over watching.
I'll forth, and walk a while.—The Air's refreshing,
And the ripe Harvest of the new-mown Hay
Gives it a sweet and wholesome Odour.
'How awful is this gloom—and hark from Camp to Camp
'The humm of either Army stilly sounds,
That the fixt Centinels almost receive
The secret whispers of each other's watch.
'Steed threatens Steed in high and boastful neighings,
'Piercing the nights dull Ear. Hark from the Tents,
The Armourers accomplishing the Knights,
'With clink of hammers closing rivets up,
Give Dreadful note of Preparation; while some
'Like sacrifices by their fires of watch,
'With patience sit, and inly ruminate
'The morning's danger. By yon Heav'n my stern
'Impatience chides this tardy-gaited night,

122

'Who, like a foul and ugly Witch, does limp
So tediously away: I'll to my Couch,
And once more try to sleep her into morning.

[*Lies down.*

[*A Groan is heard.*

Ha! What means that dismal voice? Sure 'tis
The Eccho of some yawning Grave,
That teems with an untimely Ghost.—'Tis gone.
Twas but my Fancy, or perhaps the Wind
Forcing his entrance thro' some hollow Cavern;
No matter what—I feel my eyes grow heavy.

[*Sleeps.*

The Ghost of Henry *VI rises.*

K. H. Gh. O thou, whose unrelenting thoughts not all
The hideous Terrours of thy Guilt can shake,
Whose Conscience with thy Body ever sleeps:
Sleep on, while I by Heavens high Ordinance
In dreams of horror wake thy frighted Soul.
Now give thy thoughts to me, let 'em behold
These gaping Wounds, which thy Death-dealing hand
Within the Tower gave my Anointed Body,
Now shall thy own devouring Conscience gnaw
Thy heart, and terribly revenge my Murder.

The Ghosts of the young Princes rise.

Pr. Gh. Richard, dream on; and see the wandring spirits
Of thy young Nephews, murder'd in the Tower.
Cou'd not our Youth, our Innocence perswade
Thy cruel heart to spare our harmless lives?
Who, but for thee, alas, might have enjoy'd
Our many promis'd years of Happiness.
No Soul save thine but pitties our misusage:
O! 'twas a cruel deed! therefore alone,
Unpittying, unpittied shalt thou fall.

[*Vanish.*

The Ghost of Ann *his Wife rises.*

A. Gh. Think on the wrongs of wretched *Ann* thy Wife,
Ev'n in the Battle's heat remember me,
And edgeless fall thy Sword. Despair, and Die.
K. H. Gh. The mornings dawn has summon'd me away:

Now *Richard* wake in all the Hells of Guilt,
And let that wild despair which now does prey
Upon thy mangled thoughts, allarm the World.
Awake *Richard*, awake! To guilty minds
A terrible Example.—   [*Sinks. Rich. starts out of his sleep.*
    Rich. *Give me another Horse: Bind up my wounds!*
'Have mercy, Heaven. Ha!—soft!—'Twas but a dream:
But then so terrible, it shakes my Soul.
Cold drops of sweat hang on my trembling Flesh,
My blood grows chilly, and I freeze with horror.
O Tyrant Conscience! how dost thou aflict me!
When I look back, 'tis terrible Retreating.
I cannot bear the thought, nor dare repent:
I am but Man, and Fate, do thou dispose me.
Who's there?

Enter Catesby.

    Cat. *'Tis I, my Lord. The Village Cock*
Has thrice done salutation to the morn:
Your Friends are up, and buckle on their Armour.
    Rich. 'O *Catesby*! I have had such horrid dreams.—
    Cat. 'Shadows, my Lord, below the Soldier's heeding.
    Rich. Now, by my this days hopes, shadows to night
'*Have struck more terror to the Soul of* Richard,
Than can the substance of ten Thousand Soldiers
Arm'd all in Proof, and led by shallow Richmond.
    Cat. 'Be more your self, my Lord. Consider, Sir,
'Were it but known a dream had frighted you,
'How wou'd your animated Foes presume on't.
    Rich. Perish that thought. No, never be it said,
That Fate it self could awe the Soul of *Richard*.
Hence, Babling dreams, you threaten here in vain:
Conscience avant; *Richard*'s himself again.
        Hark! the shrill Trumpet sounds, to Horse: Away!
        My Soul's in Arms, and eager for the Fray.   [*Exeunt*

[Act V, Scene vi.]

Enter Richmond, Oxford, *&c. Marching.*

    Richm. Halt!— [*Soldiers:* Halt, Halt, *&c.*

How far is it into the morning, Friends?

   Oxf. Near four, my Lord.

   Richm. 'Tis well: I'm glad to find we are such early stirrers.

   Oxf. Methinks the Foe's less forward than we thought 'em:

Worn as we are, we brave the Field before 'em.

   Richm. Come, there looks life in such a cheerful haste.

'If dreams should animate a Soul resolv'd,

'I'm more than pleas'd with those I've had to night.

'Methought that all the Ghosts of them whose Bodies

'*Richard* murther'd came mourning to my Tent,

'And rous'd me to revenge 'em.

   Oxf. A good Omen, Sir: Hark! the Trumpet of

The Enemy. It speaks them on the march.

   Richm. 'Why, then let's on, my Friends, to face 'em:

'In Peace there's nothing so becomes a Man

'As mild behaviour and humility:

'But when the blast of War blows in our ears,

'Let us be Tygers in our fierce deportment.

'*For me, the ransome of my bold attempt*

'Shall be this Body, on the Earth's cold Face:

But, if we thrive, the Glory of the Action

The meanest here shall share his part of.

'Advance your Standards, draw your willing Swords:

'Sound, Drums and Trumpets, boldly and cheerfully.

The Word's Saint *George, Richmond,* and Victory!   [*Exeunt.*

[Act V, Scene vii.]

Enter Richard, Catesby, *marching.*

   Rich. *Who saw the Sun today?*

   Cat. He has not yet broke forth, my Lord.

   Rich. *Then he disdains to shine; For by the Clock*

He should have brav'd the East an hour ago.

Not shine to day?—Why, what is that to me,

'More than to *Richmond*? For the self-same Heaven

'That frowns on me, looks lowring upon him.

Enter Norfolk.

   Nor. *Prepare, my Lord, the Foe is in the Field.*

   Rich. *Come, bustle, bustle! Caparison my Horse:*

Call forth Lord Stanley; *bid him bring his Power.*
My self will lead the Soldiers to the Plain.   [Exit *Catesby.*
Well, *Norfolk,* what thinkst thou now?
    Nor. That we shall Conquer, Sir; but on my Tent
This morning early was this Paper found.
    Rich. [*reads.*] Jockey *of* Norfolk *be not too bold,*
                    For Dickon *thy Master is bought and sold.*
'A weak invention of the Enemy.
'Come, Gentlemen, now each man to his Charge.
What shall I say more than I have infer'd:
Remember whom you are to Cope withal,
A scum of Britains, *Rascals, Run-aways;*
Whom their o'er-cloy'd Country vomits forth
To desperate adventures and assur'd destruction.
If we be Conquer'd, let Men Conquer us,
And not these Bastard Britains, *whom our Fathers*
'Have in their own Land beaten, spurn'd, and trod on,
And left 'em on Record, the Heirs of shame.
Are these Men fit to be the Heirs of England?

Enter Catesby.

What says Lord Stanley: *Will he bring his Power?*
    Cat. He does refuse, my Lord: He will not, Sir.
    Rich. Off with his Son George's head.   [*Trumpet sounds.*
    Nor. My Lord, the Foe's already past the Marsh:
After the Battle let young *Stanley* die.
    Rich. Why, after be it then—
A thousand hearts are swelling in my bosom.
'Draw Archers, draw your Arrows to the head,
'Spur your proud Horses hard, and ride in blood.
And thou, our Warlike Champion, thrice Renown'd
St. *George,* inspire us with the Rage of Lyons!—
Upon 'em! Charge!—Follow me!—   [*Exeunt.*

[Act V, Scene viii.]

An Allarm is heard: Richard *re-enters alone.*

    Rich. What, ho! young *Richmond,* ho! 'tis *Richard* calls.
I hate thee, *Harry,* for thy blood of *Lancaster;*
'Now if thou dost not hide thee from my Sword,

'Now while the angry Trumpet sounds Allarm,
'And dead mens' groans transpierce the wounded Air,
'*Richmond*, I say, come forth, and single face me:
'*Richard* is Hoarse with Daring thee to Arms.

The Allarm continues: Enter Catesby, *and the Duke of* Nor. *in disorder.*

Cat. Rescue! rescue! my Lord of *Norfolk*, haste.
The King Enacts more wonders than a Man,
Daring an opposite to every danger.
His Horse is slain, and all on foot he fights,
Seeking for Richmond *in the throat of Death.*
'Nay, haste my Lord: the day's against us.   [*Exeunt.*

Enter Richard *and* Ratcliff *in disorder.*

Rich. A Horse! a Horse! my Kingdom for an Horse!
Rat. 'This way, this way, my Lord; below yon thicket
'Stands a swift Horse. Away, ruin pursues us.
'Withdraw, my Lord, for only flight can save you.
Rich. Slave, I have set my Life upon a Cast,
And I will stand the hazard of the Dye.
I think there be six Richmonds *in the Field;*
Five have I slain to day, instead of him.
An Horse! an Horse! my Kingdom for an Horse.   [*Exit.*

[Act V, Scene ix.]

Re-enter Richard *and* Richmond, *meeting.*

Rich. 'Of one, or both of us the time is come.
Richm. Kind Heaven I thank thee, for my Cause is thine;
If *Richard*'s fit to live let *Richmond* fall.
Rich. Thy Gallant bearing, *Harry*, I cou'd plaud,
But that the spotted Rebel stains the Soldier.
Richm. Nor shou'd thy Prowess, *Richard*, want my praise,
But that thy cruel deeds have stampt thee Tyrant.
So thrive my Sword as Heaven's high Vengeance draws it.
Rich. 'My Soul and Body on the Action both.
Richm. A dreadful lay: Here's to decide it.   [*Allarm, fight.*
Rich. Perdition catch thy Arm. The chance is thine:
                            [Richard *is wounded.*
But oh! the vast Renown thou hast acquired
In Conquering *Richard*, does afflict him more

Than ever his Bodies parting with its Soul.
'Now let the World no longer be a Stage
'To feed contention in a lingring Act:
'But let one spirit of the First-born *Cain*
'Reign in all bosoms, that each heart being set
'On bloody Actions, the rude Scene may end,
'And darkness be the Burier of the Dead.   [*Dies.*

    Richm. Farewel, *Richard*, and from thy dreadful end
May future Kings from Tyranny be warn'd;
Had thy aspiring Soul but stir'd in Vertue
With half the Spirit it has dar'd in Evil,
How might thy Fame have grac'd our *English* Annals:
But as thou art, how fair a Page thou'st blotted.
Hark! the glad Trumpets speak the Field our own.

Enter Oxford *and Lord* Stanley: *Soldiers follow with* Richard's *Crown.*

    Richm. O welcome Friends: My Noble Father welcome.
Heaven and our Arms be prais'd the day is ours.
See there, my Lords, stern *Richard* is no more. . . .

39. Samuel Cobb, Shakespeare's artless tragedies

1700

From *Poetae Britannici. A Poem, Satyrical and Panegyrical* (1700).

Samuel Cobb (1675–1713), translator and poet, was a pupil, and subsequently a master, at Christ's Hospital.

Ev'n *Shakespeare* sweated in his narrow Isle,
And Subject *Italy* obey'd his Style.
Boccace and *Cynthio* must a Tribute pay
T'inrich his Scenes, and furnish out a Play.
Tho' Art ne'er taught him how to write by Rules,
Or borrow Learning from *Athenian* Schools:
Yet He with *Plautus* could instruct and please,
And what requir'd long toil, perform with ease. . . .
Tho' sometimes Rude, Unpolish'd and Undress'd,
His Sentence flows more careless than the rest.
But when his Muse complying with his Will,
Deigns with informing heat his Breast to fill,
Then hear him Thunder in the pompous strain
Of *Aeschylus*, or sooth in *Ovid*'s Vein.
Then in his Artless Tragedies I see,
What Nature seldom gives, Propriety.
I feel a Pity working in my Eyes
When *Desdemona* by her Husband dies.
When I view *Brutus* in his Dress appear,
I know not how to call him too severe.
His rigid Vertue there atones for all,
And makes a Sacrifice of *Caesar*'s Fall. . . .

40. Charles Gildon, from his adaptation of *Measure for Measure*

1700

From *Measure for Measure, or Beauty the Best Advocate. . . . Written originally by Mr. Shakespeare: And now very much alter'd; With additions of several Entertainments of Musick* (1700).

Gildon's adaptation, performed between January and March 1700, resembles *The Fairy Queen* in that its operatic element, the masque of *Dido and Aeneas*, is performed at the end of each act. Gildon follows D'Avenant (No. 5 in Volume 1) in omitting the comic characters, and also borrows much of his language from that version. Gildon's major changes are to restore Mariana, who has been married secretly by Angelo before he deserts her, and to make Claudio and Juliet also man and wife.

Purcell's *Dido and Aeneas* (the text by Nahum Tate) was performed in 1689/90 for Josias Priest's school in Chelsea. Apart from its inclusion in Gildon's play it seems not to have been performed in public again for another two hundred years.

The Persons' NAMES.

MEN.

The Duke of *Savoy*
Angelo his Deputy (Privately Marry'd to *Mariana*).
Escalus. Chief Minister under *Angelo*.
Claudio (A Young Nobleman, of an Ancient Family, but Decay'd Fortune; one that Behav'd himself well in the War, privately Marry'd to *Juliet*).
Lucio }
Balthazar } Two Courtiers.
Fryer *Thomas*.
Provost.

WOMEN.

Isabella (Sister to *Claudio*, a Young Votary, design'd, for want of
Fortune, to a Nunnery).

Juliet (A Lady of Considerable Fortune; but left in the hands of a
Covetous Uncle, who is a Hypocrite, and will give Consent to none,
that he may not part with it).

Mariana (A Lady of no Fortune, secretly Marry'd to *Angelo*).

SCENE: Turin.

[Act I, Scene i.] A Large Hall in the Palace.

*   *   *

Isa. You shou'd instruct the Law: Oh! shew some Pity.

Ang. I shew it most of all when I shew Justice;
For then I pity those I do not know,
When Pardon'd Crimes might teach 'em to offend.
Be satisfy'd your Brother dyes to morrow.

Isa. So you must be the first that gives this Sentence,
And he the first that suffers.

Esca. That's well urg'd.

Isa. If Men cou'd Thunder
As great *Jove* does, we ne'er shou'd be at quiet,
For every Cholerik petty Officer
Wou'd use the Magazeen of Heaven for Thunder,
Nothing but Thunder. Oh! Merciful Heav'n!
Thou rather, with thy sharp and Sulphurous Bolt,
Dost split the Knotty and Obdurat *Oak*
Than the soft *Mirtle*. Oh! but Man, Proud Man,
(Dress'd in a little *Breef* Authority,
Most ignorant of what he thinks himself
Assur'd) In his frail Glassy Essence, like
An Angry *Ape*, plays such Fantastick Tricks
Before High Heav'n as wou'd make Angels laugh,
If they were Mortal and had Spleens like us.

Esca. To him, he will relent, I find him coming.　　　　　　[*Aside.*

Ang. Why shew you all this Passion before me?

Isa. Authority, tho' it may err like others,
Yet has a kind of Medicine in it's self
That skins the top of Vice. Knock at your Bosom,

And ask your Heart, Sir, if it knows no Crime
That's like my Brothers. If it does, then let it
Ne'er give Sentence from your Tongue against his Life.

    Ang. Ha! She speaks such pointed Truths, that wounds   [*Aside.*
My guilty Soul.—Farewell.   [*Going.*

    Isa. Ha, my Lord, turn back!

    Ang. I will consider—come again anon.

    Esca. Away, enough.   [*Aside.*

    Isa. All Blessings on your Excellence.
At what hour shall I attend you, Sir?

    Ang. Soon as the Opera is over.

    Isa. Angels Preserve you.   [*Exit.*

    Ang. From thee—ev'n from thy Virtue.   [*Aside.*
What's this I feel? Is it her fault or mine?
The Tempter or the Tempted, who sins most? Ha!
Not She; nor does She Tempt, but it is I
That, lying by the Violet in the Sun,
Corrupt like Carrion by his friendly Beams,
But Ripen not like the Flower into Sweets.

    Esca. He's grown Thoughtful, I hope he's won.

    Ang. Can Virtue win us more to Vice, than Vice?   [*Aside.*
Oh! fie! fie! fie! What dost thou *Angelo*?
Is it her Virtue, that thou lov'st? oh, no!
Thou false and deluding Guide who in Disguise
Of Virtues shape leadst us thro' Heav'n to Hell!
No Vicious Beauty cou'd with Practis'd Art
Subdue my Heart like Virgin Innocence.
I'll think no more on't, but with Musick chase
Away the Guilty Image.
Musick they say can Calm the ruffled Soul,
I'm sure a mighty Tempest ruffles mine.
[*Aloud.*] My Lord, if your Diversions now are ready
I am dispos'd to see 'em.

    Esc. Please you to sit, they wait but your Command.

    Luc. Begin the *Opera*, the Deputy attends.   [*They all sit.*

The LOVES of *Dido* and *Æneas*, a MASK, in Four MUSICAL
ENTERTAINMENTS.
The First Entertainment.

*   *   *

[Act II, Scene i.] A Room in the Palace.

* * *

Isa. I understand you not.

Ang. Know then, I Love you.

Isa. My Brother Lov'd *Juliet*,
And you've just told me he must dye for it.

Ang. No: he shall live, if you'l reward my Love.

Isa. Securely from your Power you take a License
To seem what you are not, to fathom others.

Ang. Believe me on my Honour I do Love thee;
Nor can I Live unless thou make me happy.

Isa. My Lord, this is too Palpable.

Ang. By Heaven!
By what I most Desire, thy Charming Self,
Thy Words express my Purpose.

Isa. If, my Lord, you Love with Honour, you will not deny
That I with Honour Ask.

Ang. Our Contest is
On Empty Names, Grim Justice and Stern Honour.
Drive thou that Fantome from thy Downy Breast,
And give a loose to more Substantial Joys.
And I will Shackle up Destroying Justice
And give thy Brother his Requested Life.

Isa. I am Amaz'd.

Ang. How can'st thou doubt thy Eyes,
Whose warmth can melt Proud Virtue into Lust,
Fire Age's Icy Winter with Desires
As Fierce and Uncontroulable as Youth?
Behold me, Maid! 'Spight of my Rigid Nature
And the Acquir'd Severity of Custom,
Before thy Eyes grown soft as Luxury;
Intemperate as thoughtless *Libertines*;
And Rash and Unadvised as Youthful Love.
Yes, *Isabella*, I, that have Condemn'd thy Brother,
I, whom Law binds to see him Suffer Death,
Sell for a Smile my Fame, my Honour, Justice.

Isa. I will Proclaim thee, *Angelo*, look for't.
Sign me a present Pardon for my Brother

133

Or I will tell the World Aloud what Man
Thou art.

Ang. Who will believe you, *Isabella*?
My Name Unsully'd, and my Life Austere,
My Word against you, and my Place i'th' State,
Will stifle all your single Voice can Publish.
And thus secure, I give Desire the Reins:
Yield to my Passion or your Brother shall
Not only Dye but Dye in Burning Torments.

Isa. To whom shall I Complain? If I tell this
Who will believe me?

Ang. You have Consider'd right.
This is a Day of Joy, our Good Duke's Birth-Day,
And in Complyance with Lord *Escalus*
I have Devoted it to Mirth and Pastime;
And Love has given a tast of Harmony,
Till now I knew not. If you will partake
Go with me to the Hall, where now they wait me.
It may disarm you of your froward Virtue
And make you relish Pleasure.

Isa. How ill Men
Pervert most Heav'nly things! No; I'll away,
And bid my Brother for his Death Prepare.

Ang. Consider on it, and at Ten this Evening,
If you'll comply, you'll meet me at the *Opera*.   [*Exit.*

Isa. Oh! let me fly from this deceitful World
To Virgin Cloisters, the Retreat of Truth,
Where Arts of Men are banish'd from our Ears;
Remov'd from all the Anxious Roads of Fears.
But to m'expecting Brother first I'll go
And end his hopes on this false *Angelo*.   [*Exit.*

[Act II, Scene ii.] *Changes to the great* Hall.

Enter Angelo, Escalus, Lucio, *&c.*

Esc. My Lord, I hope your Fair Petitioner
At length prevails.

Ang. What, am I so ill known
To think I'd barter Justice for weak Pray'rs,
Or sell the Laws for a fond Woman's Tears?

I fear, my Lord, because I thus comply
To wear the Gaiety this day requires,
Attend your Sports, and listen to your *Musick*,
You think my Soul Enervate, without force,
That I am grown a Boy!
　Esc. No, my good Lord,
I have no cause to Censure what I seek,
These shows my Loyal Love prepar'd, and that
You please to share 'em gives me double Joy;
The Pleasure's Noble, as 'tis Innocent.
　Ang. I do allow it—come, let 'em begin.

The Second Entertainment.

*　　*　　*

Eccho Dance of Furies.

At the end of the Dance Six Furies *Sink. The four open the Cave, fly up.*

　Ang. All will not do, All won't divert my Pain;　　　[*Aside.*
The Wound enlarges by these Medicines:
'Tis She alone can yield the Healing Balm.
This Scene just hits my case; her Brother's danger
Is here the storm must furnish Blest Occasion.
And when, my Dido, I've Possess'd thy Charms,　⎱
I then will throw thee from my glutted Arms　　⎬
And think no more on all thy Soothing Harms.　⎰　　[*Exit.*

[Act II, Scene iii.]

SCENE *Changes to the* Prison.

Enter Duke, *dress'd like a* Fryer, *and with him* Fryer Thomas.

　Duke. Think not I've chang'd my Ducal Robes for these
Because I Love.—No, 'tis a cause more wrinkl'd
Has made me assume this Habit, tho' your Duke.
We have strict Statutes and sharp Penal Laws
Which I have suffer'd Nineteen years to sleep,
Ev'n like an over-grown Lion in a Cave
That goes not out to Prey. But as fond Fathers
So long stick up the Rod for Terror that
The bold Child contemns it, so our Decrees

135

Dead to Infliction to themselves are dead,
And forward Liberty does Justice strike
As Infants do the Nurse. Wherefore I have
Fixt all my Pow'r in *Angelo*, that he
May wake these drowsie Laws to Execution.

    Fryer. Ty'd-up Justice, Sir, you soon might loose;
And 'twou'd more dreadful seem in you than *Angelo.*

    Duke. Too dreadful, Sir, in me:—for since it was
My fault to give the People so much Hope
It may seem Tyranny to punish them
For what my own Permission bid them act:
For Pow'r that hinders not ill Deeds commands them.

    Fryer. I am convinc'd.

    Duke. I have on *Angelo* impos'd
Th' unpleasant Pow'r of punishing, while I
In this Disguise may visit Prince and People
And hear how both approve this means I've taken.

    Fryer. You find already how you've been mistaken
In *Angelo*, you so long thought a Saint;
And I am glad I've found this way to help
The injur'd *Mariana.*

    Duke. But that she told it
In her Confession, I should yet doubt the Truth
That *Angelo* is her true married Husband,
While he has made his false severity
Bawd to his Fame and Broaker to his Vice
Of Avarice. This makes me, Father,
By your Assistance try to speak with *Claudio,*
To sift and know if what Report has spread
Be true, of his being married to *Juliet.*

    Fryer. 'Twill not be difficult, because we always
Go forth in Pairs, ev'n to these Deeds of Goodness.
—But see the Provost.

Enter Provost.

    Duke. Hail to thee, Provost, so I think you are.

    Prov. I am the Provost: What's your Will, good Fathers?

    Fryer. Bound by our Charity and holy Orders
We come to visit the afflicted Minds
In Prison here. Do us the common Right

To let us see 'em and to tell their Crimes,
That we may minister according to their nature.
　Prov. I wou'd do more than that if more were needful.

Enter Claudio.

This, Sir, is *Claudio*,
Who dies tomorrow for uncertain Crimes,
For Innocence that wants a Proof is Guilt.
　Duke. Must he then die?
　Prov. I think, tomorrow.
I'll leave him to your pious Exhortations.　　　　　　　[*Exit.*
　Claud. There is no Rack so painful in this Prison
As that which stretches me 'twixt Hope and Doubt.
　Duke. Blessings on you, Son, I've heard your Fortune;
And as the Duty of my Orders bid me
I wou'd exhort you to a true Repentance.
　Claud. O Fathers, I rejoice at your Arrival,
For it will ease me of my greatest Pain.
　Duke. This pious Disposition's a good Sign
That you repent the Sin that brought you hither.
　Claud. 'Twas not my Sin but Folly brought me hither;
And yet it was a Sin to wish for ought
Beyond Possession of so pure a Virtue.
You say you are no Stranger to my Story:
You then have heard too of a Lady's Suff'rings
Which I thro' Avarice, alas, have caus'd.
That, that, my Fathers, is the Sin that racks me;
That haunts my Conscience; and that only you
Can e'er appease. For oh! a Lady's Honour,
And lost for me, is a more cruel Murther
Than if I'd ta'ne her Life.
　Duke. Have Comfort, Son, for Heav'n,
Indulgent to our Frailty, is content
To take our Penitence, if it be true,
For our Transgressions.
　Claud. Oh! Heaven is merciful;
Because 'tis wise and just, and knows our Sorrows.
But Man by Ignorance, jealous of our Hearts,
Or else by his own Passions led from Goodness,
Still deviates from the beauteous Paths of Mercy

And seldom keeps the noble Tracks of Justice.
Oh, hear me then: I look on you as Heaven:—   *[Kneels.*
(For we are taught you represent high Heaven;
By Delegation, too, possess its Power of Mercy)
My Birth was Noble tho' my Fortune small,
Which is a Clog upon a generous Soul.
That might excuse the Caution that I us'd,
When to secure the mighty Dowr of *Juliet*
I married her in private.

   Duke. Then are you married?

   Claud. I call all Heav'n to witness that we are.
A Father of your Order joyn'd our Hands.

   Fryer. His Name, my Son.

   Claud. 'Twas Father *Pierre*, not long
Return'd to *France* to his own Monastery.
I've writ to him; but the too cruel Deputy,
Press'd by the barb'rous Avarice of *Pedro*,
Will not expect his Answer.

   Duke. Rise up, my Son.

   Claud. No, my good Father, till I have your Promise
To justifie immediately *Juliet's* Honour.

   Duke. We promise our Endeavour, Sir, to do it.

   Claud. Avouch it as my dying Oath, by all
My Hopes of Happiness hereafter,   *[Rises.*
She is my Wife. There being a doubtful Clause
In her Father's Will in favour of this *Pedro*,
Her Guardian, we conceal'd our Wedding
Till being out of his Wardship and possess'd
Of all her Fortune she might own it
Without so great a Hazard. But oh! that
He had taken all, had she but escap'd
This hateful Scandal; that I'm sure must torture
Her nice and vertuous Soul.

   Duke. Who is this *Pedro*?

   Claud. The Deputy's *Privado*, his Right-hand;
One that by well-acted Piety has gain'd
Trusts from believing Friends that think him honest,
To ruin their Children and enrich himself.
And thus he hopes by pushing on my Death
To have her too, on the same Law, confin'd

Within a Cloyster's Walls during her Life,
And so secure himself her wealthy Dowr.
   Duke. Son, Put your trust in Heav'n, that can relieve
When least you hope it. I'll do my endeavour
To help your Fortune; but if my Pow'r's too small
T'assist in that, I will still help your Soul.
   Claud. I thank you, Fathers, and desire your Prayrs.   [*Exit.*
   Duke. I am confirm'd he's innocent of this,
Tho' his most watchful Foe has taken this time
To make him suffer.

Enter Provost and Juliet.

But who is this?
   Prov. The Lady, Sir, with Child by *Claudio,*
But by strict Order of the Deputy confin'd
From farther Commerce with him. Your Advice
May steed her much, good Fathers.
   Duke. Repent you, Fair One, of the Sin you carry?
   Jul. I do repent me of my Sins, good Father:
But sure the Blessings of the Marriage-bed
Can be no Sin.
   Duke. You may amuse your self
With the firm Vows of him you call your Husband,
His secret Contracts and his plighted Faith:
But these, my Daughter, will not salve the Sin.
They're oft the giddy Rashness of hot Youth,
Which it repents and breaks without a Pang.
   Jul. 'Tis true, I am a Woman frail and ignorant:
But yet my Honour and Religion joyn'd
Have taught me the full Knowledge of this Point;
And we are marry'd with all those holy Rites
The Church ordains. The pious Father *Pierre*
Of your good Order joyn'd our Hands in private.
'Tis true, for worldly Cause, and for that Fault
I take this Shame most patiently.
   Duke. Can you forgive the Cause of this your Infamy?
Can you love still the Man that seems to've wrong'd you?
   Jul. Yes, as I love the Woman that wrong'd him,
That has undone him, taken away his Life.
O Heav'n! prevent his Fate, or take me too.

Duke. Resign your self to Heav'n. If you're Innocent,
Be sure of Help. We'll to your Partner. Benedicite.

[Exit with the Fryer.

Jul. Must die to morrow! Oh, injurious Love,
That dost the Life of my sad Life remove,
Yet doom'st me still to agonizing Breath
And barr'st me from the sweet Retreat of Death!
O, Heav'n! my *Claudio* to these Arms restore;
Or, when he dies, O let me be no more!

*   *   *

[Act III, Scene i.] The Prison.

*   *   *

Isa. There is a devilish mercy in the Judge,
That will if you'l implore it, free your Life,
But fetter you till Death.

Claud. Perpetual durance?

Isa. 'Tis worse, more painful too, than Racks and Tortures
For 'tis a rack of Mind.

Clau. But of what Nature?

Isa. 'Tis such as shou'd you give it your consent
Wou'd leave you stript of all your wreaths of War
And shew you naked to the scornful World.

Clau. Let me know my Doom.

Isa. If I cou'd fear thee *Claudio*, I should weep,
Lest thou a shameful life should'st now prefer,
And six or seven short Winters more respect
Than a perpetual Honour. Dar'st thou dye?
The sense of Death is most in Apprehension;
And the small Beetle when we tread on it
In corporal Sufferance finds a pang as great
As when a Gyant dyes.

Clau. Why give you me this shame?
Think you I can Resolution fetch
From flowing tenderness? If I must dye,
I'll welcome Darkness as a shining Bride
And hug it in my Arms.

Isa. There spoke my Brother; there my Fathers Grave

Sent forth a chearful Voice. Yes, you must dye:
Thou art too Noble to preserve thy Life
By such base means. This outward rigid Saint
Does in his gracious Looks disguise the Devil.
His filth within being cast, he wou'd appear
A pond as foul as Hell.
    Clau. What, *Angelo*?
    Isa. Oh! he is uglier than a Fiend confess'd.
Speak, *Claudio,* cou'd you think it, you may live
If to his Lust I'd Sacrifice my Honour?
    Clau. Impossible! it cannot be!—Hypocrite!
    Isa. Yes, he that wou'd not hear your Innocence
Would quit you now of the most horrid Guilt,
Give you a Licence to Sin on securely
Wou'd I consent to be more black than he is.
This Night's the time that he would have me do
What I abhor to name, or else you dye
To Morrow.
    Clau. By Heav'n thou shalt not do it.
    Isa. Oh! were it but my Life, dear *Claudio,*
I'd throw it down for your Deliverance
Without the least delay.
    Clau. Thanks my Dear Sister.
    Isa. Since nothing but my Honour can Redeem you
Prepare to dye to Morrow.
    Clau. Hah!—to Morrow?
But *Isabella*!
    Isa. What says my Brother?
    Clau. Death is a fearful thing!
    Isa. But Infamy more hateful.
Sure you have study'd what it is to dye.
    Clau. Oh! Sister, 'tis to go we know not whither;
To lye a kneaded Clod in the dark Grave,
And have this sensible warm motion end.
Or rotting get another of crawling Worms;
That springs from every part of our Corruption.
The Spirit perhaps must bathe in fiery Floods,
Or shiver in shrilling Regions of rib'd Ice;
Or be imprison'd in the viewless Winds,
And blown with restless Violence round about

This pendant World; or if condemn'd, like those
Whom our uncertain Thoughts imagine howling.
Oh! 'tis too horrible, and the most loath'd Life
That Age or Ache, or Want, or Imprisonment,
Can lay on Nature is a Paradise
To what we fear of Death.

 Isa. Alass! alass!

 Clau. Ah! My Dear Sister, I would live!

 Isa. Ha! Live d'ye say? O you base one!
O faithless Coward! O dishonest Wretch!
Wilt thou be made a Man out of my Vice?
Is't not a kind of Incest to take Life
From thy own Sisters shame? But sure thou art not
My Brother! Dye, Perish! If but my word
Would save thy loathsom Life, I wou'd not speak it.
I'll pray a thousand Prayers for thy Death,
But not a word to save thee.

 Clau. But hear me.

 Isa. Oh! Fie! fie! fie! how can I think thou art Innocent?

 Clau. Your over-nicety of Honour feeds
Your fancy with strange ugly forms
That have no real Existence;
But by excess of Vertue you offend.
I said indeed that I wou'd Live: what then?
Is't not the Voice of Nature that abhors
The fatal Separation? Then where's the Crime?

 Isa. None but in living by a Crime.

 Claud. You're right; but eagerly you cut off half my Words,
Which had imply'd that Truth. No,—my Sister,—
I have no thoughts of living on your Ruin.
My Honour's not so shrunk with my low Fortune;
And what I had to add was for my *Juliet,*
That if you e'er did love your hapless Brother,
Have any share in our dead Mother's Pity,
You'd take the tender Mourner to your Bosome
And comfort her sad Soul for my Misfortunes.

 Isa. First I must ask your Pardon, injur'd *Claudio,*
For this Offence of Jealousie of Honour.
And now I do most solemnly assure thee,
I will invite her to my Breast within

A Cloyster'd Shade, where we with mutual Grief
Will mourn in sad Rememberance your Loss.
   Claud. O! rather teach her to forget that Loss:
Rememberance will keep her Griefs still waking.
Bear her this fatal Pledge of our first Vows.   [*Gives a Ring.*
Tell her how hard I think the Tyrant's Will
That will not let us take our last Farewel.
Tell her I have no Pang to leave this World
But that of leaving her; That fond Desire
Of her so heavy sits upon my Soul
It cloggs its Pinions and retards its Flight.
Tell her—But oh! I never shou'd have done
Shou'd I pursue the Dictates of my Heart,
Which, oh! is full of tender faithful Love.
Farewel—to happy Cloysters both retire;
And there—O, may you ever live above
The Rage of Pow'r and Injuries of Love.   [*Exit.*

Enter Duke and Frier.

   Isa. Farewel, my Brother; noble Youth, farewel!
And with thee all my Cares of earthly Things.   [*She is going.*
   Duke. Vouchsafe a Word with you, good Sister, but one Word.
   Isa. What is your Will?
   Duke. What I hope will be yours too.
   Isa. My Sorrows, Father, hasten me from hence.
I beg you wou'd be brief.
   Duke. The Hand that made you fair, has made you good.
Th' Assault that *Angelo* has giv'n your Vertue
Chance to my Knowledge brings. I have o'er-heard you,
And am amaz'd at *Angelo*'s Hypocrisie.
   Isa. How is the noble Duke deceiv'd in him!
If he return my Injuries shall speak:
To him I will discover the Impostor.
   Duke. That may do well, but he'll evade the Charge
By vouching it a Trial, or denying all.
But hearken to me, I will propose a way
Shall save your Brother and not injure you,
And get a Proof that will confound his Cunning,
If you will join and do what I propose.
   Isa. O, let me hear you speak, I will do all

143

That Virtue will permit. Good Father, speak.

Duke. Vertue is bold, and Goodness never fearful.
You've heard of *Mariana, Frederick's* Sister,
Who, with her Brother, lost her Hopes and Fortune?

Isa. Both sunk at Sea, or I mistake.

Duke. Ev'n so.—This *Angelo,* then but low in Fortune,
In *Frederick's* Absence won this Maid to love him;
And fearing *Frederick's* Aversion to the Match
Shou'd hinder him from doing what he'd promis'd,
Marry'd her in private, none being by
But his own Creatures. But that same Day
News came of *Frederick's* Ship being cast away,
And with it him and all her Hopes of Wealth.

Isa. Thus far how like my Brother's State!

Duke. But no farther. This sordid Man convey'd
Away all proof of what was done
And thus has left her a poor mournful Widow,
Maid and Wife.

Isa. O, base ungrateful Villain!

Duke. She loves him still, ungrateful as he is.
Go you again then to Lord *Angelo:*
Seem as if won, and make the dark Appointment.
She shall supply your Place: the Act is just
And innocent, and must save your Brother.

Isa. But is she marry'd?

Fryer. We both assure you that. You sure may trust us.

Isa. I dare not doubt you. It grows near the time
That he appointed me to come again.

Duke. Haste you to him; and from him to us.
You'll find us at St. *Luke's,* at th' *Moated Grange,*
With poor dejected *Mariana.*

Isa. Your Blessings, and I'm gone.   [*Exit.*

Duke. I have not patience of Concealment longer,
Yet I must stay to see the black Event.
But I have sent him Letters of my coming,
And that at Noon to morrow I reach *Turin.*
Now, my Good Father, let us haste to *Mariana.*   [*Exeunt ambo.*

*   *   *

41. John Oldmixon on the mangling of Shakespeare's plays

1700

The Epilogue to Gildon's *Measure for Measure*.

John Oldmixon (1673–1742), poet, dramatist, translator, historian, journalist, gives in this epilogue one of the first reactions against the stage's handling of Shakespeare, albeit in the context of the rivalry between the theatres.

The Epilogue.
Spoken by *Shakespeare*'s Ghost.

Enough! Your Cruelty Alive I knew,
And must I Dead be Persecuted too?
Injur'd so much of late upon the *Stage*,
My *Ghost* can bear no more, but comes to Rage.
My *Plays* by *Scriblers* Mangl'd I have seen;
By Lifeless *Actors* Murder'd on the *Scene*.
Fat *Falstaff* here with Pleasure I beheld,
Toss off his Bottle and his *Truncheon* weild:
Such as I meant him, such the *Knight* appear'd;
He Bragg'd like *Falstaff*, and like *Falstaff* fear'd.
But when, on yonder *Stage*[1], the Knave was shewn
Ev'n by my Self the Picture scarce was known.
Themselves, and not the Man I drew, they *Play'd*;
And Five *Dull Sots* of One poor Coxcomb made.
Hell! that on you such Tricks as these shou'd pass,
Or I be made the Burden of an *Ass*!
Oh! if *Macbeth* or *Hamlet* ever pleas'd,

---

[1] Gildon's play was performed at Lincoln's Inn Fields, where *I Henry IV* was currently enjoying a revival with Betterton as Falstaff; 'yonder Stage' is presumably Drury Lane, the home (together with Dorset Garden) of the 'United Company' from which Betterton and others had withdrawn in 1694–5.

Or *Desdemona* e'er your Passions rais'd;
If *Brutus* or the Bleeding *Cæsar* e'er
Inspir'd your Pity or provok'd your Fear,
Let me no more endure such Mighty Wrongs,
By *Scriblers* Folly or by *Actors* Lungs.
So, late may *Betterton* forsake the *Stage*,
And long may *Barry* Live to Charm the *Age*.
May a New *Otway* Rise and Learn to Move
The *Men* with *Terror*, and the *Fair* with *Love*!
Again may *Congreve* try the *Commic* Strain;
And *Wycherley* Revive his Ancient *Vein*:
Else may your Pleasure prove your greatest Curse;
And those who now *Write dully* still *Write worse*.

42. John Dennis on Shakespeare's morals

1701

From *The Advancement and Reformation of Modern Poetry* (1701);
'The Epistle Dedicatory To ... John, Lord Marquess of Normanby,
Earl of Mulgrave, &c.'

The Design of all Poetical Criticism must be, if it is just and good, to advance so useful and so noble an Art as Poetry. And the design of the following Treatise is no less than to set the Moderns upon an equal foot with even admir'd Antiquity. In order to the doing which I humbly desire leave of your Lordship, that I may make an enquiry in what the pre-heminence of the Ancient Poets consists; and why I prefer one of the *Grecian* Tragedies as, for Example, the *Oedipus* of *Sophocles*, to one of our celebrated *English* Tragedies; as, for instance, the *Julius Cæsar* of *Shakespeare*.

Upon reflection I find that the reason is, because I am more delighted and more instructed by the former; and that for this very reason, because I am more mov'd by it. For I find by experience that I am no further pleas'd nor instructed by any Tragedy than as it excites Passion in me. But in order to the discovering why I am more mov'd by the former than the latter of those Tragedies, I desire Leave to make an enquiry into the principal differences between them, and that in all probability will determine the matter. I find then, my Lord, that there are two very signal differences between the *Oedipus* and the *Julius Cæsar*. First, the *Oedipus* is exactly Just and Regular and the *Julius Cæsar* is very Extravagant and Irregular. Secondly, the *Oedipus* is very Religious, and the *Julius Cæsar* is Irreligious. For, with submission to your Lordship's Judgment, I conceive that every Tragedy ought to be a very solemn Lecture, inculcating a particular Providence and showing it plainly protecting the good and chastizing the bad, or at least the violent; and that if it is otherwise, it is either an empty amusement or a scandalous and pernicious Libel upon the government of the world. The killing of *Julius Cæsar* in *Shakespeare* is either a Murder or a Lawful Action; if the killing *Cæsar* is a Lawful Action, then the killing of *Brutus* and *Cassius* is downright Murder; and the Poet has been guilty of polluting the Scene with the blood of the very best and last of the *Romans*. But if the killing of *Cæsar* is Murder, and *Brutus* and *Cassius* are very justly punish'd for it, then *Shakespeare* is on the other side answerable for introducing so many Noble *Romans* committing in the open face of an Audience a very horrible Murder, and only punishing two of them; which proceeding gives an occasion to the people to draw a dangerous inference from it, which may be Destructive to Government, and to Human Society.

Thus, my Lord, I have a great deal of reason to suspect that the *Oedipus* derives its advantage from its Regularity, and its Religion; and the presumption grows still more strong, when upon enquiry I find that the foremention'd Regularity is nothing but the bringing some Rules into practice, which Observation and Philosophy have found requisite for the surer exciting of Passion. For as this, I think, cannot be contested, that of two Combatants who have equal Strength and equal Courage, he is most likely to have the better who has the most address; so in a contention and prize of Poetry, between persons who have equal force of mind, he will be certain to have the advantage who is the best instructed to use his strength.

If any of the enemies to Regularity will give themselves the trouble to peruse the *Oedipus* of *Sophocles* with an impartial eye he will easily discern how instrumental the Poetical Art is in leading him from

Surprize to Surprize, from Compassion to Terror, and from Terror to Compassion again, without giving him so much as a Time to breathe; and he will as easily discover how the Religion that is every where inter-mix'd with the Play shews all the Surprizes, even when he least expects this, as so many immediate successive effects of a particular Dreadful Providence, which make them come like so many Thunder-claps from a serene Heaven, to confound and astonish him. (Sig. A$_6$^{r}–A$_7$^{v})

*   *   *

Your Lordship knows that it was towards the beginning of the last Century that the *French*, a subtle and discerning Nation, began to be sensible of this, and upon it several of their extraordinary men, both Poets and Philosophers, began to cultivate Criticism. Upon which there follow'd two very remarkable things. For first, the cultivating of the Poetical Art advanc'd their Genius's to such a height, as was unknown to *France* before; and secondly, the appearing of those great Genius's was very instrumental in spreading their language thro' all the Christian World; and in raising the esteem of their Nation to that degree that it naturally prepar'd the way for their Intrigues of State, and facilitated the execution of their vast Designs.

My Lord, these Alterations happen'd in *France*, while the *French* reform'd the structure of their Poems by the noble models of ancient Architects; and your Lordship knows very well that the very contrary fell out among us; while, notwithstanding your generous attempt to reform us, we resolv'd with an injudicious obstinacy to adhere to our *Gothick* and Barbarous Manner. For in the first place, our Stage has degenerated not only from the taste of Nature, but from the Greatness it had in the Time of *Shakespeare*, in whose *Coriolanus* and *Cassius* we see something of the Invincible Spirit of the *Romans*; but in most of our Heroes which have lately appear'd on the Stage, Love has been still the predominant passion, whether they have been *Grecian* or *Roman* Heroes; which is false in Morality, and of scandalous Instruction, and as false and absurd in Physics. (Sig. a$_2$^{v}–a$_3$^{r})

43. George Granville, from his adaptation of *The Merchant of Venice*

1701

From *The Jew of Venice* (1701).

George Granville, Baron Lansdowne (1667–1735), was a poet and dramatist. In his adaptation many characters are omitted, there are various cuts, prose is transformed into verse, and the obligatory entertainment is inserted.

ADVERTISEMENT TO THE READER.

The Foundation of the following Comedy being liable to some Objections, it may be wonder'd that any one should make Choice of it to bestow so much Labour upon. But the judicious Reader will observe so many Manly and Moral Graces in the Characters and Sentiments that he may excuse the Story for the Sake of the Ornamental Parts. Undertakings of this kind are justify'd by the Examples of those Great Men who have employ'd their Endeavours the same Way. The only Dramatique Attempt of Mr. *Waller* was of this Nature, in his Alterations of the *Maid's Tragedy*. To the Earl of *Rochester* we owe *Valentinian*; to the Duke of *Buckingham, The Chances*; Sir *William D'Avenant* and Mr. *Dryden* united in restoring the *Tempest*. *Troilus and Cressida, Timon*, and *King Lear*, were the Works of three succeeding Laureats: besides many others, too many to mention. The Reader may please moreover to take Notice (that nothing may be imputed to *Shakespeare* which may seem unworthy of him), that such Lines as appear to be markt, are Lines added to make good the Connexion where there was a necessity to leave out; in which all imaginable Care has been taken to imitate the same fashion of Period and turn of Stile and Thought with the Original. What other Alterations have been requisite as to the change of Words or single Lines, the Conduct of Incidents, and Method of Action throughout the whole Piece, to bring it into the Form and Compass of a Play would be superfluous to examin, every Reader being able to satisfy himself, if he thinks fit, by comparing.

PROLOGUE
Written by Bevill Higgons, Esq;

The Ghosts of *Shakespeare* and *Dryden* arise
Crown'd with Lawrel.

Dryden. This radiant Circle, reverend *Shakespeare*, view;
An Audience only to thy Buskin due.
Shakespeare. A Scene so noble antient *Greece* ne'er saw,
Nor *Pompey*'s Dome when *Rome* the World gave Law.
I feel at once both Wonder and Delight,
By Beauty warm'd, transcendently so bright.
Well, *Dryden*, might'st thou sing; well may these Hero's fight.
Dryden. With all the outward Lustre which you find,
They want the nobler Beauties of the Mind.
Their sickly Judgments what is just, refuse,
And French Grimace, Buffoons, and Mimicks choose.
Our Scenes desert some wretched Farce to see;
They know not Nature for they tast not Thee.
Shakespeare. Whose stupid Souls thy Passion cannot move,
Are deaf indeed to Nature and to Love.
When thy *Ægyptian* weeps, what Eyes are dry?
Or who can live to see thy *Roman* dye?
Dryden. Thro' Perspectives revers'd they Nature view,
Which give the Passions Images not true.
Strephon for *Strephon* sighs; and *Sapho* dies,
Shot to the Soul by brighter *Sapho's* Eyes.
No Wonder then their wand'ring Passions roam,
And feel not Nature, whom th' have overcome.
For shame let genial Love prevail agen,
You Beaux Love Ladies, and you Ladies Men.
Shakespeare. These Crimes, unknown in our less polisht Age,
Now seem above Correction of the Stage.
Less Heinous Faults our Justice does pursue:
To day we punish a *Stock-jobbing Jew*.
A piece of Justice terrible and strange;
Which, if pursu'd, would make a thin Exchange.
The Law's Defect the juster Muse supplies,
Tis only we can make you Good or Wise,
Whom Heav'n spares the Poet will Chastise.

These Scenes in their rough Native Dress were mine,
But now improv'd with nobler Lustre shine;
The first rude Sketches *Shakespeare*'s Pencil drew,
But all the shining Master stroaks are new.
This Play, ye Criticks, shall your Fury 'stand,
Adorn'd and rescu'd by a faultless Hand.

   Dryden. I long endeavour'd to support thy Stage ⎫
With the faint Copies of thy Nobler Rage,   ⎬
But toyl'd in vain for an Ungenerous Age.   ⎭
They starv'd me living; nay, deny'd me Fame,
And scarce now dead do Justice to my Name.
Wou'd you repent? Be to my Ashes kind,
Indulge the Pledges I have left behind.

★   ★   ★

[Act II, Scene ii.] Antonio's House.

SCENE *opens, and discovers* Bassanio, Antonio, Shylock, *and others,
sitting as at an Entertainment. Musick playing. During the Musick* Gratiano
enters, and takes his Place.

   Anto. 'This to immortal Friendship; fill it up—
'Be thou to me, and I to my *Bassanio*,
'Like *Venice* and her *Adriatick* Bride,
'For ever link'd in Love.
   Bass. 'Thou joynst us well: And rightly hast compar'd.
'Like *Venice* on a Rock my Friendship stands,
'Constant and fix'd. But 'tis a barren Spot,
'Whilst like the liberal *Adriatick* thou
'With Plenty bath'st my Shoars.—
'My Fortunes are the Bounty of my Friend.
   Anto. 'My Friend's the noblest Bounty of my Fortune.
'Sound every Instrument of Musick there
'To our immortal Friendship.

[All drink. Loud Musick.

   Bass. 'Let Love be next—what else should
'Follow Friendship?
'To Love, and to Love's Queen, my charming *Portia*,
'Fill till the rosy Brim reflects her Lips

151

'Then kiss the Symbol round.
'Oh, in this Lottery of Love where Chance,
'Not Choice, presides, Give, give, ye Powers, the Lot,
'Where she her self would place it. Crown her wish,
'Tho' Ruine and Perdition catch *Bassanio*.
'Let me be wretched, but let her be blest.

[Drink and Musick again.

    Grat. 'Mine's a short Health. Here's to the Sex in general!
'To Woman, be she black, or brown, or fair,
'Plump, slender, tall, or middle-statur'd—
'Let it be Woman, and 'tis all I ask.

[Drink again. Musick as before.

    Shyl. 'I have a Mistress, that outshines 'em all—
'Commanding yours—and yours, tho' the whole Sex.
'O may her Charms encrease and multiply:
'My Money is my Mistress! Here's to
'Interest upon Interest.   *[Drinks.*
    Anto. 'Let Birds and Beasts of Prey howl to such Vows,
'All generous Notes be hushed. Pledge thy self, Jew:
'None here will stir the Glass—   *[All Rise.*
'Nor shall the Musick sound: O *Bassanio*!
'There sits a Heaviness upon my Heart
'Which Wine cannot remove: I know not
But Musick ever makes me thus.
    Bassanio. The Reason is, your Spirits are attentive.
For do but note, a wild and wanton Herd
Or Race of skittish and unhandled Colts
Fetching mad Bounds, bellowing and neighing loud,
If they but hear by Chance some Trumpet sound
Or any Aire of Musick touch their Ears
You strait perceive 'em make a mutual stand,
Their savage Eyes turn'd to attentive Gaze
By the soft Power of Musick. Therefore the Poet
Did feign That *Orpheus* melted Stones and Rocks;
For what so hard, so stubborn, or so fierce,
But Musick for the Time will change its Nature.
The Man who has not Musick in his Soul,
Or is not touch'd with Concord of sweet Sounds,

Is fit for Treasons, Stratagems and Spoils,
The Motions of his Mind are dull as Night,
And his Affections dark as *Erebus*;
Let no such Man be trusted.—Mark the Musick.

Peleus & Thetis.

A

MASQUE

The ARGUMENT.

Peleus *in Love with* Thetis, *by the Assurance of* Proteus *obtains her Favor.
But* Jupiter, *also in Love with her, interposing,* Peleus *in Despair consults*
Prometheus, *famous for his Skill in Astrology, upon whose Prophesie, that
the Son born of* Thetis *should prove greater than his Father,* Jupiter *desists.
The Prophesie was afterwards verefy'd in the Birth of* Achilles, *the Son of*
Thetis *by* Peleus.

Persons in the Masque.

JUPITER. ⎱ ⎰ PROMETHEUS.
PELEUS. ⎰ ⎱ THETIS.

Prometheus *is seen upon Mount* Caucasus, *chain'd to a Rock with the
Vulture at his Breast. A Flourish of all the Instruments. Then plaintive
Musick.*

Peleus *Enters to* Prometheus.

> *Pel.* Condemn'd on *Caucasus* to lie,
> Still to be dying, not to dye,
> With certain Pain uncertain of relief,
> True Emblem of a wretched Lover's Grief!
>   To whose inspecting Eye 'tis given
>   To view the Planetary Way,
>   To penetrate eternal Day,
> And to revolve the starry Heaven.
> To thee, *Prometheus*, I complain,
> And bring a Heart as full of Pain.
>
> *Pro.* From *Jupiter* spring all our Woes,
>   *Thetis* is *Jove's*, who once was thine.

153

'Tis vain, O *Peleus*! to oppose
    Thy Torturer and mine.
  Contented with Despair
    You must, you must resign,
    Or wretched Man prepare
For change of Torments, great as mine.

Pel. In change of Torment would be ease.
    Could you divine what Lovers bear,
Even you, *Prometheus*, would confess
    There is no Vulture like Despair.
Pro. Cease, cruel Vulture, to devour.
Pel. Cease, cruel *Thetis*, to disdain.
If for the Pleasures of an Hour
    We must endure an Age of Pain,
Love give me back my Heart again.

          Both together.

Pro. ⎱ Cease cruel Vulture to devour;
Pel. ⎰   Cease cruel *Thetis* to disdain.

Enter Thetis.

    The. Peleus, unjustly you complain.
    Pel. Give, give me back my Heart again.
    The. Peleus, unjustly you complain.
      The Gods, alas! no Refuge find
From Ill's resistless Fates ordain:
      I still am True—And would be kind.

    Pel. Despair tormented first my Heart,
Now Falshood a more cruel Smart!
    O for the Peace of Human-kind,
Make Women longer true, or sooner kind!
    With Justice, or with Mercy reign:
Or give me, give me back my Heart again.

          Both together.

The. ⎱ *Peleus* unjustly you complain.
Pel. ⎰ Give, give me back my Heart again.
    The. Accursed Jealousie!
Thou Jaundice in the Lover's Eye,

Thro' which all Objects false we see;
    Accursed Jealousy!
Pro. Love is by Fancy led about,
From Hope to Fear, from Joy to Doubt.
    Whom we now a Goddess call,
    Divinely grac'd in every Feature,
    Strait's a deform'd, a perjur'd Creature.
    Love and Hate, are fancy all:
    'Tis but as fancy shall present
    Objects of Grief, or of Content,
        That the Lover's blest, or dyes.
    Visions of mighty Pains, or Pleasure,
    Imagin'd want, Imagin'd Treasure,
        All in powerful Fancy lyes.

CHORUS

Cho. Accursed Jealousy,
Thou Jaundice in the Lovers Eye,
Thro' which all Objects false we see;
    Accursed Jealousy.
The. Thy Rival, *Peleus*, rules the Sky,
    Yet I so prize thy Love,
With *Peleus* I would chuse to die,
    Rather than live with *Jove*.

                        [Jupiter *appears descending.*
But see! the mighty Thund'rer's here,
    Tremble *Peleus*, tremble, fly.
The Thunderer! the mighty Thunderer!
    Tremble *Peleus*, tremble, fly.

[*A full Chorus of all the Voices and Instruments while* Jupiter
    is descending. Thunder the while.

CHORUS.

Cho. But see! the mighty Thund'rer's here;
    Tremble Peleus, *tremble, fly.*
The Thunderer! the mighty Thunderer!
    Tremble Peleus, *tremble, fly.*

                        [Jupiter *being descended.*
Jup. Presumptuous Slave, Rival to *Jove*,
    How dar'st thou, Mortal, thus defy

155

A Goddess with audacious Love,
  And irritate a God with Jealousy?
    Presumptuous Mortal, hence,
    Tremble at Omnipotence.
Pel. Arm'd with Love, and *Thetis* by,
      I fear no Odds
      Of Men or Gods,
    But *Jove* himself defy.
  Jove lay thy Thunder down!
Arm'd with Love, and *Thetis* by,
  There is more Terrour in her Frown,
And fiercer Lightning in her Eye.
      I fear no Odds
      Of Men or Gods,
    But *Jove* himself defy.
Jup. Bring me Lightning, give me Thunder;
  Hast ye *Cyclops* with your forked Rods.
  This Rebel Love braves all the Gods,
  And every Hour by Love is made
  Some Heaven-defying *Encelade.*
Bring me Lightning, give me Thunder.
The. Jove may kill, but ne'er shall sunder.
          [Pel. *and* The. *holding by each other.*
      All three repeat.
Jup.   } Bring me Lightning, give me Thunder.
Pel. and The. } Jove may kill, but ne'er shall sunder.
    The. Thy Love, still arm'd with Fate,
  Is dreadful as thy Hate.
    O might it prove to me
  (So gentle *Peleus* were but free)
    O might it prove to me
As fatal as to lost, consuming *Semele!*
Pro. Son of *Saturn,* take advice
  From one whom thy severe decree
  Has furnisht leisure to grow wise.
    Thou rul'st the Gods, but Fate rules thee.

        The *PROPHESY.*
'Whoe'er th' immortal Maid compressing
'Shall tast the Joy and reap the Blessing,

'Thus th' unerring Stars advise,
'From that auspitious Night an Heir shall rise,
  'Paternal Glories to outshine,
  'And be the foremost of his Line.
     CHORUS Repeat.
Cho. *Son of* Saturn, *take Advice;*
From that auspitious Night an Heir shall rise,
  Paternal Glories to outshine,
  And be the foremost of his Line.

[Jupiter *during the* Chorus *seems to stand considering.*

Jup. Shall then the Son of *Saturn* be undone,
  As *Saturn* was, by an Aspiring Son?
    Justly th'impartial Fates conspire,
    Dooming that Son to be the Syre
      Of such another Son.
    Conscious of Ills that I have done,
  My Fears to Prudence shall advise
And Guilt that made me great shall make me wise.
            [*Turning to* Peleus.
    The Fatal Blessing I resign,
    Peleus take the Maid Divine;
    Jove consenting, she is thine.
            [Peleus *receiving* Thetis.

Pel. Heav'n had been lost, had I been *Jove*,
There is no Heav'n like Mutual Love.
            [Jupiter *turning to* Prometheus.
Jup. And thou, the Stars' Interpreter,
    'Tis just I set thee free
    Who giv'st me Liberty;
  Arise, arise, and be thy self a Star.

The Vulture drops dead at the Feet of Prometheus. *His Chains fall off, and he is borne up to Heaven with* Jupiter, *to a loud Flourish of all the Instruments.*

     Peleus *and* Thetis *together.*
Pel. &| Be true all ye Lovers, whate'er ye endure,
The. ⌡ Tho' cruel the Pain is how sweet is the Cure!
    So Divine is the Blessing
    In the Hour of possessing,
      That one Moment's obtaining
      Pays an Age of Complaining.

Be true, all ye Lovers, whate'er you endure,
Tho' cruel the Pain is, how sweet is the Cure!

Anto. 'With such an Air of true Magnificence
'My noble minded Brother treats his Friends
'As hardly has been known to *Italy*
'Since *Pompey* and *Lucullus* entertain'd.
'To frame thy Fortunes ample as thy Mind,
'New Worlds shou'd be created.

Enter Servant.

Ser. The Master of the Ship sends word the Wind is
Come about: and he desires you wou'd hast Aboard.
Bass. turning to Ant.] 'Oh my lov'd Friend! till now I never knew
'The pangs of parting Friendship.
'At distance I have tasted of the Pain
'When the rude Morn has sunder'd us away
'To our Repose. But by my Soul I swear
'Even then my Eyes would drop a silent Tear,
'Repugnant still to close and shut out Thee.
Ant. 'You go for your Advantage, and that Thought
'Shall keep *Antonio* comforted.
Bass. 'The Traject is from hence to *Belmont* short,
'And Letters may come dayly. Such Intercourse
'Is all the Cordial absent Friends enjoy:
'Fail not in that. Your Trouble shall be short,
'I will return with the best speed I can.
Ant. 'Be not too hasty, my *Bassanio*, neither.
'Slubber not Business for my Sake, my Friend,
'But stay the very ripening of thy Love.
'Be gay, assiduous, and imploy such Arts
'As best incline the Fair. Love is not seiz'd, but won.
'Hard is the Labour: you must plant and prune,
'And watch occasion just. This fruit is nice,
' 'T will promise Wonders and grow fairly up,
'Seem hopeful to the Eye, look ripe, and then
'A sudden Blast spoils all.

Enter another Servant.

Serv. 'The Master of the Ship has sent agen.
Bass. 'One more Embrace. To those who know not Friendship

'This may appear unmanly Tenderness;
'But 'tis the frailty of the bravest Minds.
   Ant. 'I ask but this, *Bassanio*,
'Give not your Heart so far away
'As to forget your Friend.
'Come, is all ready? I must hasten you.
   Grat. 'If you were ready to part
' 'Tis all we stay for now.
   Bass. Shylock, thy Hand. Be gentle to my Friend.
'Fear not thy Bond, it shall be justly paid.
'We soon shall meet agen,
'Always, I hope, good Friends.
'Oh my *Antonio*! 'tis hard, tho' for a Moment,
'To lose the Sight of what we Love.
   Shyl. aside.] 'These two Christian Fools put me in mind
'Of my Money: just so loath am I to part with that.
   Bass. '*Gratiano*, lead the way: *Shylock*, once more farewell.
'We must not part but at the Ship, *Antonio*.
'Lovers and Friends, should they for Ages stay,
'Would still find something left that they would say.   [*Exeunt.*

        *   *   *

EPILOGUE.

Each in his turn, the Poet* and the Priest,†
Have view'd the Stage, but like false Prophets guess'd.
The Man of Zeal in his Religious Rage
Would silence Poets, and reduce the Stage.
The Poet, rashly, to get clear retorts
On Kings the Scandal and bespatters Courts.
Both err; for without mincing, to be plain,
The Guilt is yours of every Odious Scene.
The present time still gives the Stage its Mode,
The Vices which you practice, we explode.
We hold the Glass, and but reflect your Shame,
Like *Spartans*, by exposing, to reclaim.
The Scribler, pinch'd with Hunger, writes to Dine,
And to your Genius must conform his Line,

   * Mr *Dryden*, in his *Prologue* to the *Pilgrim.*
   † Mr *Collier*, in his *View of the Stage.*

Not lewd by Choice, but meerly to submit.
Would you encourage Sense, Sense would be writ.
 Plain Beauties pleas'd your Sires an Age ago,
Without the Varnish and the Dawb of Show.
At vast Expence we labour to our Ruine,
And court your Favour with our own undoing.
A War of Profit mitigates the Evil,
But to be tax'd and beaten is the Devil.
How was the Scene forlorn, and how despis'd,
When *Timon*, without Musick, moraliz'd!
Shakespeare's sublime in vain entic'd the Throng,
Without the Charm of *Purcell*'s Syren Song.
 In the same Antique Loom these Scenes were wrought,
Embelish'd with good Morals and just Thought.
True Nature in her Noblest Light you see, ⎫
Ere yet debauch'd by modern Gallantry ⎬
To trifling Jest, and fulsom Ribaldry. ⎭
What Rust remains upon the shining Mass
Antiquity may privilege to pass.
'Tis *Shakespeare*'s Play, and if these Scenes miscarry,
Let *Gormon*★ take the Stage—or Lady *Mary*†.

★ A famous Prize-Fighter.
† A famous Rope-Dancer.

44. John Dennis, from his adaptation of *The Merry Wives of Windsor*

1702

From *The Comical Gallant: or the Amours of Sir John Falstaff. . . . To which is added, A large account of the taste in poetry, and the causes of the degeneracy of it* (1702).

Dennis's adaptation of *The Merry Wives of Windsor* was performed in the spring of 1702: it was a failure, and in his preface Dennis blames both the actor who played Falstaff and the taste of the age. Dennis has cut much of the subsidiary comedy, and focused more on the intrigue by Fenton and the deception of Ford; he has added a second Host, of the Bull inn.

[*From* The Epistle Dedicatory to the Honourable George Granville, Esq.: 'A large account of the Taste in Poetry, and the Causes of the Degeneracy of it.']

*   *   *

When I first communicated the design which I had of altering this Comedy of *Shakespeare* I found that I should have two sorts of People to deal with, who would equally endeavour to obstruct my success. The one believed it to be so admirable that nothing ought to be added to it; the others fancied it to be so despicable that any one's time would be lost upon it.

That this Comedy was not despicable, I guess'd for several Reasons. First, I knew very well that it had pleas'd one of the greatest Queens that ever was in the World, great not only for her Wisdom in the Arts of Government but for her knowledge of Polite Learning and her nice taste of the Drama (for such a taste we may be sure she had, by the relish which she had of the Ancients). This Comedy was written at her Command, and by her direction, and she was so eager to see it Acted that she commanded it to be finished in fourteen days; and was afterwards, as Tradition tells us, very well pleas'd at the Representation.

In the second place, in the Reign of King *Charles* the Second, when People had an admirable taste of Comedy, all those men of extraordinary parts who were the Ornaments of that Court—as the late Duke of *Buckingham*, my Lord *Normanby*, my Lord *Dorset*, my late Lord *Rochester*, Sir *Charles Sedley*, Dr *Frazer*, Mr *Savil*, Mr *Buckley*—were in Love with the Beauties of this Comedy. In the third place, I thought that after so long an acquaintance as I had with the best Comick Poets among the Antients and Moderns, I might depend in some measure upon my own Judgment, and I thought I found here three or four extraordinary Characters, that were exactly drawn and truly Comical; and that I saw besides in it some as happy touches as ever were in Comedy. Besides I had observed what success the Character of Falstaff had had, in the first part of *Henry IV*. And as the Falstaff in the *Merry Wives* is certainly superior to that of the second part of *Henry IV*, so it can hardly be said to be inferior to that of the first.

For in the second part of *Henry IV*, *Falstaff* does nothing but talk, as indeed he does nothing else in the third and fourth Acts of the first part. Whereas in the *Merry Wives* he everywhere Acts, and that action is more Regular and more in compass than it is in the first part of *Henry IV*. 'Tis true, what he says in *Henry IV* is admirable; but action at last is the business of the Stage. The Drama is action itself, and it is action alone that is able to excite in any extraordinary manner the curiosity of mankind. What News, is the Question nowadays ev'ry moment; but people by that question demand what is done and not what is said upon the Great Stage of the World. In short, I defie any man to name me a Play that has ever succeeded without some sort of action or another. But I could, if I pleased, mention more than one that has succeeded barely by the force of Action, without almost anything else.

It was for the above-named reasons that I thought this by no means a despicable Comedy. And it was for the Reasons which follow that I believed it not so admirable but that it might receive improvement. First, I knew very well that in so short a time as this Play was writ nothing could be done that is perfect. Secondly, I knew very well that this Comedy had never upon Revivals had any great success, and that particularly when it was Revived in King *Charles* the Second's time the only Character that pleased to a height was *Slender*, acted by *Wintershal*. And that tho something like this may very well happen to a living Author without any just Cause, yet that there must be reason for it when it happens to an Author who has a long time been dead, and whose Reputation has been long established. And indeed the *Merry Wives of Windsor*, as it has great Beauties, so it has strange Defects, which tho they past at first for the sake of the Beauties yet will come to be less endured as the Stage grows more Regular. For there are no less than three Actions in it that are independant one of another, which divide and distract the minds of an Audience; there is more than one insignificant Scene which has nothing to do with any other part of the Play, which is enough to obstruct and stifle the Action. The Style in some places is stiff and forced and affected, whereas the Dialogue in Comedy ought to be as free as the air. This affectation is particularly remarkable in some part of the first Scene between the Wives, and in all *Ford*'s part of the first Scene between him and *Falstaff*. This is not said in the least with a design to derogate from *Shakespeare*'s merit, who performed more than any one else could have done in so short a time. In the alteration I have endeavoured to Correct the foresaid Errours.

I have made every thing Instrumental to *Fenton*'s Marriage, and the whole to depend on one common Center, which I believe was hardly in the power of every Writer to perform. I have added to some of the parts in order to heighten the Characters and make them show the better. I have above all things endeavoured to make the Dialogue as easie and free as I could. For in Comedy, which is an Image of common Life, every thing which is forc'd is abominable. In short, I have alter'd every thing which I dislik'd and retain'd every thing which I or my Friends approved of, excepting something of Justice *Shallow* in the first Scene of the Play, which I omitted for two Reasons: the one was because I could not bring it into the same design with the rest, the second because I knew no body who would be capable of Acting that Character, unless those who would be otherwise employed.

*　　*　　*

... Sir, I who am resolved to have you fully informed before you come to give sentence, and who am ignorant whether you were in Town when this Play was Acted or no, think myself obliged to make you acquainted that *Falstaff*'s part, which you know to be the principal one of the Play, and that on which all the rest depends, was by no means acted to the satisfaction of the Audience. Upon which, several fell from disliking the Action to disapproving the Play (which will be always very natural upon such occasions, tho sometimes not very reasonable), and divers objections were immediately made, which if the Play had succeeded had perhaps never been thought of. I desire that you would give me leave to lay them and their answers before you, and so leave the whole to your impartial decision.

The first is, the Characters in this Comedy are very low, and that there is neither much Wit nor Love nor Gallantry in it. To which I answer, first, that tho the Characters are low they are true and good; that there is as perfect a Plot as I was able to build upon another man's Foundation; and that the lowness of the Characters derogates not a jot from the perfection of the Fable; that in all Fables all Characters are Universal and Allegorical, and that it signifies nothing to the Beauty of the Fiction or the importance of the Moral whether we bring in Kings or Shepherds, so they are introduced aptly. In the next place, there is Humour every where in this Comedy. And Humour, after the Plot, is what is most valuable in Comedy. I desire then, Sir, that I may have leave to prove two things: First, that Humour is more the business of Comedy than Wit; And secondly, that Humour is more to be found in low Characters than among Persons of a higher Rank; and consequently that low Characters are more proper for Comedy than high, and that low Comedy is to be preferred to the high. And when I have done this I desire to speak a word of Love and Gallantry, of the want of which this Play is accus'd.

* * *

Another Objection is that several Characters of this Comedy are obsolete and quite out of date. The matter of Fact indeed cannot be denied, and the Objection has some force. For if there is any thing resembling in Poetry and Painting, as the Sisters are certainly like, then Heroick and Tragick Poetry may be compar'd to History Painting, and Comedy to Drawing after the Life. Now the Pictures which are done after the Life, if they are drawn by Masters, will certainly please Masters and all who are able to judge of the boldness and the delicacy of the strokes: but the People who judge only of the resemblance are most delighted with the Pictures of their acquaintance. Thus any Characters in Comedy which are finely drawn will please those who can judge; but a Poet, to please the generality, must Copy the present Age. Thus, Sir, have I fairly stated the objection in its utmost force; and now I shall answer two things to it, first, that I never made it my chief aim to please the generality, and a little lower shall give my Reasons for it. Secondly, that supposing I had, tho several of the Characters of this Play are indeed obsolete, yet that of *Falstaff* will always be new, and whenever it comes to be Acted to the satisfaction of an Audience will infallibly fill the Stage better than a great many Characters.

These, Sir, are the two general Objections, but there are two particular ones. The first is, that I have introduc'd an unnecessary Character in the Host of the *Bull*. But I believe, Sir, that I have consider'd of this matter with a little more attention than they who made the Objection, and I know that that Character is absolutely necessary for the carrying on the Action probably, which in the original Play is by no means probable. For it is not likely, that *Falstaff* would suffer himself to be carried in the Basket as far as *Datchet Mead*, which is half a Mile from *Windsor*; and it is plain, that they could not carry him if he made any resistance. Nor is it likely that he would defer his reflections upon his adventure till he came back to *Windsor*. So that the Soliloquies which he makes in the fourth Act, before *Ford*'s entrance, are not design'd for himself but apparently address'd to the Audience, which is the greatest fault that can possibly be in the *Drama*.

The last Objection is that the forementioned Scene in the fourth Act, which is very long, is nothing but a discovery of what the Audience had been Eye-Witnesses of before. But this objection is unreasonable with Relation to the original Play, and more unreasonable with Relation to the altered one. For in the original Play *Falstaff* makes a Relation to *Ford* not so much of his being put into the Buck Basket as of the circumstances which attended it; of what he suffer'd while he was in it and upon his coming out of it. And in this lyes the excellency of that Scene, that it gives an occasion for a great Actor to shew himself. For all the while *Falstaff* is making this Relation *Ford*, at the same time that in dumb acting he shews a concern and a fellow-feeling to the Knight, shews a great deal of Joy and Satisfaction to the Audience.

Thus in the original Scene *Falstaff* makes a relation of what had happened to him since he left the Stage last, and that Relation must be Comical by Reason of the occasion that it gives for an excellent Actor to shew himself. But for the Alter'd Scene there is something more to be said. For after that *Falstaff* has rais'd *Ford*'s Joy for the other's disappointment, which yet he was forced to screen and shelter from the Knight with a dissembled sorrow, *Falstaff* by making a discovery of something which had not happened, and strangely altering the Adventure of Mrs *Page*—which he thought himself obliged to do for the sake of his Credit—gives his jealous Coxcomb a fresh alarm and throws him into real Convulsions.

Thus, Sir, have I laid before you the objections and the answers to

them, and leave it to you to judge whether the last are satisfactory, and
whether the first had ever been made if the Play had succeeded on the
Stage; for you know, Sir, that Plays are like Men, the successful are
sure to find Friends enough let them be never so worthless, while
ev'ry Maggot will be censuring the conduct of the deserving
unfortunate.

* * *

PROLOGUE

Whate'er the Title on our Bills may say,
The Merry Wives of *Shakespeare* is the Play.
But then a different intreague we have got,
And what makes a new Play but a new Plot?
As, in the mixture of the Humane frame,
'Tis not the Flesh, 'tis the Soul makes the Man,
So of Dramatick Poems we may say
'Tis not the Lines, 'tis the Plot makes the Play.
The Soul of every Poem's the design,
And words but serve to make that move and shine.
But *Shakespeare*'s Play in fourteen days was writ,
And in that space to make all just and fit
Was an attempt surpassing human Wit.
Yet our great *Shakespeare*'s matchless Muse was such
None e'er in so small time perform'd so much.
The Comick Muse herself inspir'd his vein,
And with herself brought all her sprightly Train.
When first he took his Pen the charming Maid
Laughing aloud, descended to his aid,
And all her secret Beauties she display'd.
His master touches, so exact, so true,
We thought it Sacriledge to change for new,
Except a very few which ne'er could joyn
In the same just and uniform design.
His haste some errors caus'd, and some neglect,
Which we with care have labour'd to correct.
Then since to please we have try'd our little Art,
We hope you'll pardon ours for *Shakespeare*'s part.

* * *

[Act II, Scene ii.] The Garter Inn.

*   *   *

Falstaff. Has my Discourse warm'd you so?

Ford. Set me all in a flame, Sir *John.*

Falst. Ay, for now you have gain'd your point.

Ford. I have, and therefore I'm grown impatient.

Falst. Ah ha, old Boy!

Ford. I cannot conceal the transport you have raised in me.

Falst. Go to, you're a wag, you're a wag.

Ford. 'Sheart, I believe I shall run distracted.

Falst. Ha! ha! Letchery! Letchery, my own case but now, my own case but now.

Ford. Adzounds, how I long for Night!

Falst. Ah Rogue, thou art of the game, e'faith, little *Broom*!

Ford. But Sir, one thing I had almost forgot: how long has *Ford* been a Cuckold?

Falst. Why, ever since the Knave his Father compounded him.

Ford. What do you mean, Sir *John*?

Falst. Why, he was got under *Aries*, and born under *Capricorn*, and the Rogue his Father made him a Cuckold, by lying with the Jade his Mother.

Ford. Oh, I understand you, then as yet he is not actually a Cuckold? [*Aside.*] Ha! I begin to recover a little.—Then as yet he is not actually a Cuckold?

Falst. Actually a Cuckold?

Ford. Ay.

Falst. Humph! Actually, do you say?

Ford. Ay! Answer me to that, Sir *John*.

Falst. Why then, I do positively avouch—

Ford. Ha!

Falst. That he is actually a Cuckold.

Ford. [*Aside.*] 'Sdeath! The old Dog has shot me quite thro the Head again.

Falst. For mind you me, Master *Broom*, since *Ford* is a Cuckold by Destiny, which no man you know can avoid, he is one, as it were, d'e see, actually.

Ford. You are so arch one knows not where to have you, Sir *John*.

Falst. You may find me about two hours hence between a pair of Sheets, at the *Bull*, Master *Broom*.

Ford. With *Ford*'s Wife? ha!

Falst. [*Aside.*] How eager this Fellow is: This is a very Goat. I will divert myself by raising his appetite.—Not actually with her in these two arms, Mr *Broom*, but stretching and panting in expectation of her, while she is stripping for the encounter. Now, Master *Broom*, do you fancy *Ford*'s Wife undressing herself . . .

Ford. To do that wou'd make me mad, Sir *John*.

Falst. Her Night Gown just slipping off . . .

Ford. Nay, Sir *John*.

Falst. Her under Petticoat falling about her Heels . . .

Ford. Nay, good Sir *John*!

Falst. Her Smock-sleeves loose about her Elbows . . .

Ford. Nay, dear Sir *John*.

Falst. And then her Lilly white Arm stretch'd out, and her milk white Bubbies display'd . . .

Ford. Nay, blood and fire, Sir *John*!

Falst. The Bed-cloaths just turning up . . .

Ford. Oh—oh—oh—

Falst. And one of the Buxome Legs advanc'd to the Bedstead . . .

Ford. Oh! Devil, Devil, Devil! [*Stops his mouth.*]

*   *   *

[Act IV, Scene i.] The Bull Inn.

*   *   *

Host. Who told you this?

Ford. Why, e'en Sir *John* himself, Sir.

Host. Good Heavens! And are you acquainted with the Character of Sir *John* no better? Is not all his conversation larded at this rate, with lyes as gross and palpable as their Inventer?

Ford. But for what Reason should he tell me such a lye as this is?

Host. Why if there has been so much as the likeness of a man in this part of the House today, excepting your self, my own Family, and Mrs *Page* in Breeches, I am the errantst Villain upon Earth.

Ford. But for what reason should he tell me this, and with so much concern too?

Host. I don't know. Mrs *Page* has us'd him like a Dog, and perhaps the care that he has of his Reputation has thrown him upon this invention.

Ford. Ha! That may be. [*Aside.*] Well, but Sir *John Falstaff* charg'd you to your face with pimping for him: And you were so modest as to be silent. I hope you will plead guilty at least to that.

Host. I must confess, Brother, I make Sir *John* believe some such thing in order to the entring into his Secrets, and to the gaining his Confidence, that I may prevent the Dishonour that is design'd to my Sister and the affront that is intended to you. But you will never know your Friends.

Ford. Humh! There is some colour of Truth in this. But how shall I know that it is not only colour?

Host. Why, you may be certain of my Sincerity by the Discovery I am going to make. Sir *John* and my Sister are to have another meeting to night; they are to meet in Masks.

Ford. Nay then, Brother, I beg your pardon. You are my friend, and give me your hand. *Falstaff* has already told me of this meeting, and I suppose the Messenger that is below with him is come to appoint the time and place.

Host. Those I am already acquainted with: The Time is midnight, the Place *Hern* the Hunters Oak in the Park.

Ford. Midnight? a very odd time! And *Hern*'s Oak in the Park? A very odd place!

Host. There is an old Tale goes that *Hern* the Hunter, sometime a Keeper here in *Windsor* Forest, does all the winter time, at dead of night, walk round about an Oak with huge Ragged Horns. And there he blasts the Trees, and smites the Cattel, and makes milch Kine yield Blood, and shakes a Chain in a most hideous and dreadful manner. You have heard of such a Spirit, and well you know the superstitious Blockheads, our Ancestors, receiv'd and deliver'd down to us this tale of *Hern* the Hunter for a truth.

Ford. Why there are several yet that are afraid to walk by this Tree in the dead of Night. But what of this?

Host. This Hunter *Falstaff* is to represent. Now Brother, I have had a lucky thought come into my Head for your advantage. The time of appointment is midnight: now will I send to your Wife a Messenger who shall pretend that he comes from *Falstaff*, and desire, for some important reasons, that the meeting may be precisely upon the stroak of twelve.

Ford. And what advantage shall I have from this?

Host. Why, you shall send home word to your Wife that upon receiving Letters of great importance you are obliged to take Post for

London this evening; and when that is done you shall lie conceal'd here till twelve, and then we will dress you in *Falstaff*'s shape, which is luckily drying below at the Fire, and putting a pair of Horns on your Head, send you to *Hern*'s Oak before *Falstaff*'s time is come, and there you may make a plain discovery whether you deservedly wear them or no.

Ford. Death! A very good contrivance! But you will be true to me in this business? Will you make no discovery to my Wife?

Host. No, upon my credit. No, you jealous Fool! [*Aside.*] She loves you too well, if she knows who you are, to take the Revenge of you that I design for you.

*   *   *

[Act V, Scene i.] Windsor Park.

*   *   *

Mrs Ford. Mrs *Page* is coming with me, Sweetheart.

Falst. Divide me like a Bribe Buck, each a Haunch! I will keep my sides to my self, my Shoulders for the Fellow of this walk, and my Horns I bequeath your Husbands. Am I a Woodman? Ha? speak I like *Hern* the Hunter? Why now is *Cupid* a Child of Conscience, he makes restitution. As I am a true Spirit, welcome!

[*Terrible Symphony.*

Mrs Page. Bless me, what noise is that?

Mr Ford. Heaven forgive our Sins!

Falst. What should this be?

Mrs Page. Mrs Ford. Away, away, away.

Falst. The Devil take the hindmost, I say! I'll into that Tuft of Trees, and sculk there till the Storm is over.

[*As they go out, Enter Maskers on the other side, crying* follow, follow, follow. *They go after* Falstaff. *Three or four of them come back.*

1 *Mask.* 'Slife, he'll make his escape.

2. *Mask.* Why, the Devil is good to his own. While we are playing the mock Spirits, the real Fiend is abroad. I was never so cudgelled in my Life.

3. *Mask.* For my part I am Stock-fish. Who should these be that charged us so fiercely? But see, our comrades are successful, and have retrieved *Falstaff*.

170

[*Symphony Recommences, and the Maskers bring in* Ford *in the shape of*
Falstaff.

1 *Fairy.* Mortal, it is in vain to struggle here.
2 *Fairy.* Bring him near, bring him near.
3 *Fairy.* With Fiery tryal touch his Fingers end.
If he be chast, the Flame will back descend,
And vex him with no pain. But if he start,
It is the Flesh of a corrupted Heart.
1 *Fairy.* A Tryal, come.
2 *Fairy.* Come, will this Wood take fire?
Ford. Oh—Oh—Oh—
2 *Fairy.* Corupt, corrupt and tainted in Desire,
About him Fairies sing a scornful Rhime,
And as you trip, still pinch him to your time.

[*Symphony.*

Spirit.   Ye Goblins and Fairies and Satyrs and Fawns,
        That merrily Revel o'er midnight Lawns,
            Come away, Come away,
            And make no delay,
        But our cheerful Gamesome Summons obey.
        Come away, Come away with your frolicksom train,
            And nimbly advance
            In a whimsical Dance,
            And prettily trip it,
            And merrily skip it,
            And wantonly leap it,
        Over the Skirts of the painted Plain,
        For this is the Time for us Goblins to Reign.
Chorus. See, see, we advance
            In a whimsical Dance,
            And prettily trip it,
            And prettily skip it,
            And wantonly leap it,
        Over the Skirts of the painted Plain,
        For this is the Time for us Goblins to Reign.
Spirit.   Ye Goblins and ev'ry Fairy Spright,
        Come about, about, about this unwieldy Wight,
            Who is a freakish frolicksom Elf,
            And a fantastick Goblin himself.

171

And as round him you go
In a Jovial Row,
To be reveng'd of his lustful Crime,
Merrily trowl out a scornful Rhime,
And cuff him in Cadence and kick him in Time.

Chorus. See round him we go
In a Jovial Row,
And merrily trowling a scornful Rhime,
We cuff him in Cadence and kick him in Time.

Ford. *Oh—Oh—Oh—*

Spirit. Now laugh at his Woe,
And as he cries Oh—
Reply with a He, Ho, Hi, Ho.

1 *Chorus.* Hi, Hi, Hi.

2 *Chorus.* Hi, Ho, Ho.

Ford. *Oh—Oh—Oh—*

1 *Chorus.* Hi, Hi, Hi.

2 *Chorus.* Ho, Ho, Ho.

Mrs *Page.* Come, come, let us carry on the jest no farther. Now, good Sir *John,* how like you *Windsor* Wives? How do you like Washing and Buck Baskets?

Mrs *Ford.* Sir *John,* we have had ill luck, we could never meet to any purpose. I will never take you for my Love again, but I will always count you my Dear.

Page. Come, pray Sir, be pleas'd to unmask.

Mrs *Page.* No, let us attend him as he is to *Windsor.*

Mrs *Ford.* And let the Children hollow to adorn our Triumph.

Enter Host of the Bull, *and* Falstaff *unmask'd.*

Falstaff (*entring*). Mine Honest Host of the Bull, I thank thee; thou has sav'd me from running the Gauntlet. I'faith, the Whoreson Villains had pepper'd me. Why, how now, my mad Wags! why, what have we here a-mummy?

Mrs *Page.* Defend me, ye pow'rs!

Mrs *Ford.* Have mercy upon me!

Page. May I believe my Eyes?

Falst. Those Eyes, Sweetheart, are worth but little that can take me for another. I was never mistaken, or so much as doubted before.

Page. But who the Devil is this then?

Falst. Nay, no Devil, for all his Horns.

Page. That's true, my Cudgel tells me that he is Flesh and Blood. But what is he then?

Falst. What is he? A Beast he is!

Mrs *Ford.* But what Beast?

Falst. Why, a Beast of Husband, as thou art a Devil of a Wife.

Mrs *Ford.* Bless me, whose Husband?

Falst. Why, whose Husband should a true Wife take pains to cudgel but her own?

Mr *Ford.* My husband!

Page. 'Sheart, I'll see who he is. By your leave, Sir.

[*They unmask him.*

Mrs *Ford.* Save me, and deliver me!

Ford. Oh—Oh—

Mrs *Page.* Bless my Eyes! what do I see?

Falst. Marry, and Amen. Why this is no *Ford*! This is no peaking Cornuto! This is that Bucksom Whoremaster *Broom*, that gave me 20 *l.* today to help him to *Ford*'s Wife.

Mrs *Ford.* Can it be possible that you are my Husband?

Falst. Thy Husband he was, but he's Stockfish now; these Spirits have metamorphos'd him.

Page. Why, this is wonderful! How do you find your self, Neighbour?

Ford. Oh—Oh—Oh—

Falst. Why, plaguy sore, damnable sore, sore with a vengeance.

Mrs *F.* Why Husband, dear Husband, now speak to us.

Ford. Oh, I am maim'd, I am crippled for ever.

Mrs *F.* Ah me, I have murder'd my Husband!

Ford. No, Wife, thou hast made me the happiest man. Within me, Oh, such ease, such Peace I find—

Falst. The Staff that broke his Bones has heal'd his mind.

Ford. Wife, I return thee ten thousand thanks.

Falst. By his taking a beating thus, this should be a *Muscovite.*

Ford. Thou hast made me wise.

Falst. A Cudgel with some I see has more vertue than *Seneca.*

Ford. Thou hast open'd my Eyes for ever.

Falst. A Crab Tree to this Fool has been the Tree of Knowledge!

Mrs *Ford.* But how came you here? You amaze me!

Host of the Bull. By my contrivance.

Mrs *Ford.* By your contrivance, Brother?

Host of the Bull. Yes, I acquainted him with this second apointment which you had made to *Falstaff*, and advis'd him to pretend a Journey to *London*, and so lie conceal'd in my House till midnight; and then to come thither in *Falstaff*'s shape to see whether his jealousie was well grounded, or no.

Mrs Ford. But why would you do that, when you knew how scurvily the Knight was design'd to be used?

Host of the Bull. Why, in return of some favours of which your Husband has been over liberal to day.

Mrs Ford. But still I am confounded, for we had *Falstaff* here just now with us in this very shape. We saw him, we talk'd to him, he answer'd us.

Host of the Bull. Yes, when your Mock Spirits first gave him the alarm, *Falstaff*, who flew more nimbly from them than one wou'd guess from his Bulk, gave time to me (who was waiting hard by with two of my Servants for the better conducting my design), to charge the foremost of your Friends with three lusty Cudgels; so that while that gave time to the Knight to make his escape the Maskers met with your Husband, who at that instant, upon a signal agreed on between us, began to move from the post where we had placed him and advanc'd to meet you.

Mrs Ford. But Husband, why would not you discover yourself when you saw that we took you for another?

Ford. Shame, shame would not suffer me, to think that I had been such an Ass and so vilely wrong'd the very best of Women.

Caius. Come, come, there is very good edifications, look you, that may be learnt from this. Mr *Ford*, leave you your Jealousies, look you, and you will be no more beaten, look you, and kick'd and cudgell'd and pinch'd and terrify'd.

Page. Well said, Fairy *Hugh*!

Ford. I will never mistrust my Wife again, till thou art able to make Love to her in good *English*.

Caius. And, Sir *John Falstaff*, leave you, I pray you, your wicked desires, and you shall be no more frightened and washed, and buck'd by the Maids, look you.

Mrs Page. There's a lesson for you, Sir *John*, let the washing of your outside make your inside clean. . . .

* * *

45. George Farquhar on the Three Unities

1702

From *A Discourse Upon Comedy, In Reference to the English Stage*, included in his *Love and Business in a Collection of Occasionary Verse and Epistolary Prose* (1702); this text from the *Works*, 2 vols (1711).

George Farquhar (1678–1707), comic dramatist and poet, appeals to the nature of dramatic illusion and the necessary co-operation of the imagination to counter the authority of the rules and the invocation of Aristotle. Farquhar's attack on conventional criticism is so cogent, and so witty, that I have included more excerpts than those of purely Shakespearian interest.

With Submission, Sir, my Performance in the practical Part of Poetry is no sufficient Warrant for your pressing me in the Speculative. I have no Foundation for a *Legislator*; and the two or three little *Plays* I have written are cast carelesly into the World without any Bulk of *Preface*, because I was not so learn'd in the Laws as to move in Defence of a bad Cause. Why then should a Compliment go farther with me than my own Interest? Don't mistake me, Sir, here is nothing that could make for my Advantage in either *Preface* or *Dedication*; no *Speculative Curiosities*, nor *Critical Remarks*, only some present Sentiments which Hazard, not Study, brings into my Head without any preliminary *Method* or *Cogitation*.

Among the many Disadvantages attending Poetry none seems to bear a greater Weight than that so many set up for Judges when so very few understand a tittle of the matter. Most of our other Arts and Sciences bear an awful Distance in their Prospect, or with a bold and glittering Varnish dazle the Eyes of the weak-sighted Vulgar. The *Divine* stands wrapt up in his Cloud of Mysteries, and the amus'd *Layety* must pay Tyths and Veneration to be kept in Obscurity, grounding their Hopes of future Knowledge on a competent Stock of present Ignorance. (In the greater part of the Christian World this is plain.) With what Deference and Resignation does the bubbled *Client* commit his Fees and Cause into the Clutches of the *Law*, where Assurance beards Justice by *Prescription*, and the wrong Side is never known to make its *Patron* blush! *Physick* and *Logick* are so strongly fortify'd by their impregnable Terms of Art, and the *Mathematician* lies so cunningly intrench'd within his *Lines* and *Circles*, that none but those of their Party dare peep into their puzzling Designs.

Thus the Generality of Mankind is held at a gazing Distance, whose Ignorance, not presuming perhaps to an open Applause, is yet satisfy'd to pay a blind Veneration to the very Faults of what they don't understand.

Poetry alone, and chiefly the *Drama*, lies open to the Insults of all Pretenders. She was one of Nature's eldest Offsprings, whence, by her Birthright and plain Simplicity she pleads a genuine Likeness to her Mother. Born in the Innocence of Time, she provided not against the Assaults of succeeding Ages; and, depending altogether on the generous End of her Invention, neglected those secret Supports and serpentine Devices us'd by other Arts that wind themselves into Practice for more subtle and politick Designs. Naked she came into the World, and 'tis to be fear'd, like its Professors, will go naked out.

'Tis a wonderful thing that most Men seem to have a great Veneration for *Poetry* yet will hardly allow a favourable Word to any Piece of it that they meet; like your Virtuoso's in Friendship, that are so ravish'd with the notional Nicety of the Vertue that they can find no Person worth their intimate Acquaintance. The Favour of being whipt at School for *Martial's Epigrams* or *Ovid's Epistles* is sufficient Privilege for turning Pedagogue and lashing all their Successors, and it would seem by the Fury of their Correction that the Ends of the Rod were still in their Buttocks. The Scholar calls upon us for *Decorums* and *Oeconomy*; the Courtier cries out for *Wit* and *Purity of Stile*; the Citizen for *Humour* and *Ridicule*; the Divines threaten us for Immodesty, and the Ladies will have an Intrigue. Now here are a Multitude of Criticks, whereof the twentieth Person only has read *Quae Genus*, and yet every one is a Critick after his own way; that is, 'Such a Play is best, because I like it.' A very familiar Argument, methinks, to prove the Excellence of a Play, and to which an Author wou'd be very unwilling to appeal for his Success! Yet such is the unfortunate State of Dramatick Poetry that it must submit to such Judgments, and by the Censure of Approbation of such Variety it must either stand or fall. But what *Salvo*, what Redress for this Inconvenience? Why, without all Dispute, an Author must endeavour to pleasure that part of the Audience who can lay the best Claim to a judicious and impartial Reflection. But before he begins let him well consider to what Division that Claim does most properly belong. The Scholar will be very angry at me for making that the Subject of a Question which is self-evident without any Dispute; for, says he, who can pretend to understand Poetry better than we, who have read *Homer, Virgil, Horace, Ovid,* &c. at the University? What Knowledge can out-strip ours, that is founded upon the Criticisms of *Aristotle, Scaliger, Vossius* and the like? We are the better sort, and therefore may claim this as a due Compliment to our Learning; and if a Poet can please us, who are the nice and severe Criticks, he cannot fail to bring in the rest of an inferior Rank.

I should be very proud to own my Veneration for Learning and to acknowledge any Compliment due to the better sort upon that Foundation. But I'm afraid the Learning of the Better Sort is not confin'd to College Studies; for there is such a thing as Reason without Syllogism, Knowledge without *Aristotle,* and Languages besides *Greek* and *Latin.* We shall likewise find in the Court and City several Degrees superior to those at Commencements. From all which I must beg the Scholar's Pardon for not paying him the Compliment of the Better Sort (as he calls it); and in the next Place enquire into the Validity of his Title from his Knowledge of *Criticism* and the Course of his Studies.

I must first beg one Favour of the Graduate—Sir, here is a Pit full of *Covent-Garden* Gentlemen, a Gallery full of Cits, a hundred Ladies of Court-Education, and about two hundred Footmen of nice Morality, who, having been unmercifully teiz'd with a Parcel of foolish, impertinent, irregular Plays all this last Winter, make it their humble Request that you wou'd oblige them with a Comedy of your own making, which they don't question will give them Entertainment. O, Sir, replies the *Square-Cap,* I have long commiserated the Condition of the *English* Audience, that has been forc'd to take up with such wretched Stuff as lately has crouded the Stage; your *Jubilees* and your *Foppingtons* and such irregular Impertinence that no Man of Sense cou'd bear the Perusal of 'em. I have long intended, out of pure pity to the Stage, to write a perfect Piece of this Nature; and now since I am honour'd by the Commands of so many my Intentions shall immediately be put in Practice.

So to work he goes; old *Aristotle, Scaliger,* with their Commentators, are lugg'd down from the high Shelf, and the Moths are dislodged from their Tenement of Years. *Horace, Vossius, Heinsius, Hedelin, Rapin,* with some half a Dozen more, are thumb'd and toss'd about, to teach the Gentleman, forsooth, to write a Comedy; and here is he furnish'd with *Unity of Action, Continuity of Action, Extent of Time, Preparation of Incidents, Episodes, Narrations, Deliberations, Didacticks, Patheticks, Monologues, Figures, Intervals, Catastrophes, Chorus's, Scenes, Machines, Decorations*, &c. A Stock sufficient to set up any Mountebank in *Christendom*; and if our new Author would take an Opportunity of reading a Lecture upon his Play in these Terms, by the Help of a *Zany* and a Joint-stool, his Scenes might go off as well as the Doctor's Packets. But the Misfortune of it is, he scorns all Application to the Vulgar, and will please the better Sort, as he calls his own. Pursuant therefore to his Philosophical Dictates, he first chooses a single Plot, because most agreeable to the Regularity of Criticism, no matter whether it affords Business enough for Diversion or Surprize. He wou'd not for the World introduce a Song or Dance, because his Play must be one entire Action. We must expect no Variety of Incidents because the Exactness of his three Hours won't give him time for their Preparation. The Unity of Place admits no Variety of Painting and Prospect, by which mischance perhaps we shall lose the only good Scenes in the Play. But no matter for that; this Play is a regular Play; this Play has been examin'd and approv'd by such and such Gentlemen, who are staunch Criticks, and Masters of Art; and this Play I will have acted. Look'ee, Mr. *Rich*, you may venture to lay out a hundred and fifty Pound for dressing this Play, for it was written by a great Scholar, and Fellow of a College.

Then a grave dogmatical Prologue is spoken, to instruct the Audience what should please them; that this Play has a new and different Cut from the Farce they see every Day; that this Author writes after the manner of the *Ancients*, and here is a Piece according to the Model of the *Athenian Drama*. Very well! This goes off *Hum drum, So, so*. Then the Players go to work on a piece of hard knotty Stuff, where they can no more shew their Art than a Carpenter can upon a piece of Steel. Here is the Lamp and the Scholar in every Line, but not a Syllable of the Poet. Here is elaborate Language, sounding Epithets, Flights of Words that strike the Clouds, whilst the poor Sense lags after (like the Lanthorn in the Tail of the Kite, which appears only like a Star), while the Breath of the Player's Lungs has Strength to bear it up in the Air.

But the Audience, willing perhaps to discover his ancient Model and the *Athenian Drama*, are attentive to the first Act or two. But not finding a true Genius of Poetry nor the natural Air of free Conversation, without any Regard to his Regularity they betake themselves to other Work. Not meeting the Diversion they expected on the Stage, they shift for themselves in the Pit; every one turns about to his Neighbour in a Mask, and for default of Entertainment now they strike up for more diverting Scenes when the Play is done. And tho' the Play be regular as *Aristotle*, and modest as Mr. *Collier* cou'd wish, yet it promotes more Lewdness in the Consequence, and procures more effectually for Intriegue, than any *Rover*, *Libertine*, or *Old Batchelor* whatsoever. At last comes the Epilogue, which pleases the Audience very well, because it sends them away and terminates the Fate of the Poet. The *Patentees* rail at him, the Players curse him, the Town damns him, and he may bury his Copy in *Paul's*, for not a Bookseller about it will put it in Print.

This familiar Account, Sir, I would not have you charge to my Invention, for there are Precedents sufficient in the World to warrant it in every Particular. The Town has been often disappointed in those Critical Plays, and some Gentlemen that have been admir'd in their speculative Remarks have been ridiculed in the practick. All the Authorities, all the Rules of Antiquity have prov'd too weak to support the Theatre, whilst others who have dispenc'd with the Criticks, and taken a Latitude in the *Oeconomy* of their Plays, have been the chief Supporters of the Stage and the Ornament of the *Drama*. This is so visibly true that I need bring in no Instances to enforce it. But you say, Sir, 'tis a Paradox that has often puzzled your Understanding, and you lay your Commands upon me to solve it, if I can.

Look'ee, Sir, to add a Value to my Complaisance to you, I must tell you in the first Place that I run as great a hazard in nibling at this *Paradox* of *Poetry* as *Luther* did by touching *Transubstantiation*. 'Tis a Mystery that the World has sweetly slept in so long that they take it very ill to be waken'd, especially being disturb'd of their Rest when there is no Business to be done. But I think that *Bellarmine* was once as *Orthodox* as *Aristotle*; and since the *German Doctor* has made a shift to hew down the *Cardinal* I will have a tug with *ipse dixit*, tho' I dye for't.

But in the first Place I must beg you, Sir, to lay aside your superstitious Veneration for Antiquity, and the usual Expressions on that Score—that the present Age is illiterate, or their Taste is vitiated; that we live in the Decay of Time, and the Dotage of the World is fall'n to our Share.— 'Tis a Mistake, Sir; the World was never more active or youthful, and true downright Sense was never more universal than at this very Day. 'Tis neither confin'd to one Nation in the World, nor to one part of a City. 'Tis remarkable in *England* as well as *France*, and good genuine Reason is nourish'd by the Cold of *Swedeland* as by the Warmth of *Italy*. 'Tis neither abdicated the Court with the late Reigns, nor expell'd the City with the Play-house Bills. You may find it in the *Grand Jury* at *Hicks's Hall*, and upon the Bench sometimes among the Justices. Then why should we be hamper'd so in our Opinions as if all the Ruins of Antiquity lay so heavily on the Bones of us that we cou'd not stir Hand nor Foot? No, no, Sir, *ipse dixit* is remov'd long ago, and all the Rubbish of old Philosophy that in a manner bury'd the Judgment of Mankind for many Centuries is now carry'd off. The vast Tomes of *Aristotle* and his Commentators are all taken to pieces, and their Infallibility is lost with all Persons of a free and unprejudic'd Reason.

Then above all Men living why should the Poets be hoodwink'd at this rate, and by what Authority should *Aristotle*'s Rules of Poetry stand so fixt and immutable? Why, by the Authority of two thousand Years standing, because thro' this long Revolution of time the World has still continu'd the same.—By the Authority of their being receiv'd at *Athens*, a City the very same with *London* in every Particular, their Habits the same, their Humours alike, their publick Transactions and private Societies *Alamode France*; in short, so very much the same in every Circumstance that *Aristotle*'s Criticisms may give Rules to *Drury-Lane*, the *Areopagus* give Judgment upon a Case in the *King's Bench*, and old *Solon* shall give Laws to the *House of Commons*. (59–64)

★   ★   ★

I have talk'd so long to lay a Foundation for these following Conclusions: *Aristotle* was no Poet, and consequently not capable of giving Instructions in the Art of Poetry; his *Ars Poetica* are only some Observations drawn from the Works of *Homer* and *Euripides*, which may be meer Accidents resulting casually from the Composition of the Works and not any of the essential Principles on which they are Compil'd. That without giving himself the Trouble of searching into the Nature of Poetry he has only complimented the Heroes of Wit and Valour of his Age by joining with them in their Approbation; with this Difference, that their Applause was plain, and his more Scholastick.

But to leave these only as Suppositions to be relish'd by every Man at his Pleasure, I shall without Complimenting any Author, either Ancient or Modern, inquire into the first Invention of Comedy; what were the true Designs and honest Intentions of that Art; and from a

Knowledge of the *End* seek out the *Means*, without one Quotation of *Aristotle*, or Authority of *Euripides*.

In all Productions either Divine or Humane the final Cause is the first Mover, because the End or Intention of any rational Action must first be consider'd before the material or efficient Causes are put in Execution. Now to determine the final Cause of Comedy we must run back beyond the material and formal Agents and take it in its very Infancy, or rather in the very first Act of its Generation, when its primary Parent, by proposing such or such an End of his Labour, laid down the first Sketches or Shadows of the Piece. Now as all Arts and Sciences have their first rise from a final Cause, so 'tis certain that they have grown from very small beginnings, and that the current of time has swell'd 'em to such a Bulk that no Body can find the Fountain by any Proportion between the Head and the Body. This, with the Corruption of time, which has debauch'd things from their primitive Innocence to selfish Designs and Purposes, renders it difficult to find the Origin of any Offspring so very unlike its Parent.

This is not only the Case of Comedy as it stands at present but the Condition also of the ancient Theatres, when great Men made shows of this Nature a rising Step to their Ambition, mixing many lewd and lascivious Representations to gain the Favour of the Populace, to whose Taste and Entertainment the Plays were chiefly adapted. We must therefore go higher than either *Aristophanes* or *Menander* to discover Comedy in its primitive Institution, if we wou'd draw any moral Design of its Invention to warrant and authorise its Continuance.

I have already mention'd the difficulty of discovering the Invention of any Art in the different Figure it makes by Succession of Improvements. But there is something in the Nature of Comedy, even in its present Circumstances, that bears so great a Resemblance to the Philosophical *Mythology* of the Ancients that old *Æsop* must wear the Bays as the first and original Author; and whatever Alterations or Improvements farther Application may have subjoin'd his *Fables* gave the first Rise and Occasion.

Comedy is no more at present than a *well-fram'd Tale handsomly told, as an agreeable Vehicle for Counsel or Reproof*. This is all we can say for the Credit of its Institution, and is the Stress of its Charter for Liberty and Toleration. Then where shou'd we seek for a Foundation but in *Æsop*'s symbolical way of moralizing upon Tales and Fables?—with this difference, that his Stories were shorter than ours. He had his Tyrant *Lyon*, his Statesman *Fox*, his Beau *Magpy*, his coward *Hare*, his

Bravo *Ass*, and his Buffoon *Ape*, with all the Characters that crowd our Stages every Day—with this Distinction nevertheless, that *Æsop* made his Beasts speak good *Greek*, and our Heroes sometimes can't talk *English*.

But whatever difference time has produc'd in the Form, we must in our own Defence stick to the *End* and Intention of his *Fables*. *Utile Dulci* was his Motto and must be our Business. We have no other Defence against the Presentment of the *Grand Jury*, and for ought I know it might prove a good means to mollify the Rigour of that Persecution to inform the Inquisitors that the great *Æsop* was the first Inventor of these poor Comedies that they are prosecuting with so much Eagerness and Fury, that the first *Laureat* was as just, as prudent, as pious, as reforming, and as ugly as any of themselves. And that the Beasts which are lug'd upon the Stage by the Horns are not caught in the City, as they suppose, but brought out of *Æsop*'s own Forest. We shou'd inform them besides, that those very Tales and Fables which they apprehend as obstacles to Reformation were the main Instruments and Machines us'd by the wise *Æsop* for its Propagation; and as he would improve Men by the Policy of Beasts so we endeavour to reform Brutes with the Examples of Men. *Fondlewife* and his young Spouse are no more than the *Eagle* and *Cockle*; he wanted Teeth to break the Shell himself, so somebody else run away with the Meat.—The Fox in the Play, is the same with the Fox in the Fable, who stuft his Guts so full that he cou'd not get out at the same Hole he came in; so both *Reynards*, being Delinquents alike, come to be truss'd up together. Here are Precepts, Admonitions, and Salutary *Innuendos* for the ordering of our Lives and Conversations, couch'd in these *Allegories* and *Allusions*. The Wisdom of the Ancients was wrapt up in Veils and Figures; the *Ægyptian Hierogliphicks* and the History of the Heathen Gods are nothing else. But if these Pagan Authorities give Offence to their scrupulous Consciences let them but consult the Tales and Parables of our *Saviour* in holy Writ, and they may find this way of Instruction to be much more Christian than they imagine. *Nathan*'s Fable of the Poor Man's Lamb had more Influence on the Conscience of *David* than any force of downright Admonition. So that by ancient Practice and modern Example, by the Authority of Pagans, Jews, and Christians, the World is furnish'd with this so sure, so pleasant, and expedient an Art of schooling Mankind into better Manners. Now here is the primary Design of Comedy illustrated from its first Institution; and the same end is equally alledg'd for its daily Practice and Continuance.—

Then, without all Dispute, whatever means are most proper and expedient for compassing this End and Intention they must be the *just Rules of Comedy*, and the *true Art of the Stage*.

We must consider then, in the first place, that our Business lies not with a *French* or a *Spanish* Audience; that our Design is not to hold forth to ancient *Greece*, nor to moralize upon the Vices and Defaults of the *Roman* Commonwealth. No, no—an English Play is intended for the Use and Instruction of an English Audience, a People not only separated from the rest of the World by Situation but different also from other Nations as well in the Complexion and Temperament of the Natural Body as in the Constitution of our Body Politick. As we are a Mixture of many Nations, so we have the most unaccountable Medley of Humours among us of any People upon Earth. These Humours produce Variety of Follies, some of 'um unknown to former Ages. These new Distempers must have new Remedies, which are nothing but new Counsels and Instructions.

Now, Sir, if our *Utile*, which is the End, be different from the Ancients, pray let our *Dulce*, which is the Means, be so too. For you know that to different Towns there are different ways; or if you wou'd have it more Scholastically, *ad diversos fines non idem conducit medium*; or Mathematically, One and the same Line cannot terminate in two Centers. But, waiving this manner of concluding by Induction, I shall gain my Point a nearer way, and draw it immediately from the first Principle I set down, *That we have the most unaccountable Medley of Humours among us of any Nation upon Earth*. And this is demonstrable from common Experience: we shall find a *Wildair* in one Corner, and a *Morose* in another; nay, the space of an Hour or two shall create such Vicissitudes of Temper in the same Person that he can hardly be taken for the same Man. We shall have a Fellow bestir his Stumps from *Chocolate* to *Coffee-House* with all the Joy and Gayety imaginable, tho' he want a Shilling to pay for a Hack; whilst another, drawn about in a Coach and Six, is eaten up with the Spleen, and shall loll in State with as much Melancholy, Vexation, and Discontent as if he were making the *Tour* of *Tyburn*. Then what sort of a *Dulce* (which I take for the Pleasantry of the Tale, or the Plot of the Play) must a Man make use of to engage the Attention of so many different Humours and Inclinations? Will a single Plot satisfy every Body? Will the turns and Surprizes that may result naturally from the ancient Limits of Time be sufficient to rip open the Spleen of some, and Physick the Melancholy of others? screw up the Attention of a Rover and fix him to the Stage, in spight of his Volatile Temper and the Temptation of a Mask? To make the Moral Instructive, you must make the Story diverting. The Splenatick Wit, the Beau Courtier, the heavy Citizen, the fine Lady, and her fine Footman, come all to be instructed and therefore must all be diverted; and he that can do this best, and with most Applause, writes the best Comedy, let him do it by what Rules he pleases so they be not offensive to Religion and good Manners.

But *hic labor, hoc opus*.[1] How must this secret of pleasing so many different Tastes be discovered? Not by tumbling over Volumes of the Ancients but by studying the Humour of the Moderns. The Rules of English Comedy don't lie in the Compass of *Aristotle* or his followers but in the Pit, Box, and Galleries. And to examine into the Humour of an English Audience let us see by what means our own English Poets have succeeded in this Point. To determine a Suit at Law we don't look into the Archives of *Greece* or *Rome*, but inspect the Reports of our own Lawyers and the Acts and Statutes of our *Parliaments*; and by the same Rule we have nothing to do with the Models of *Menander* or *Plautus*, but must consult *Shakespeare*, *Jonson*, *Fletcher* and others, who by Methods much different from the Ancients have supported the English Stage and made themselves famous to Posterity. We shall find that these Gentlemen have fairly dispenc'd with the greatest part of Critical Formalities. The Decorums of Time and Place, so much cry'd up of late, had no force of Decorum with them; the Economy of their Plays was *ad libitum* and the extent of their Plots only limited by the Convenience of Action. I would willingly understand the Regularities of *Hamlet*, *Macbeth*, *Henry IV* and of *Fletcher*'s Plays: and yet these have long been the Darlings of the English Audience, and are like to continue with the same Applause in Defiance of all the Criticisms that ever were publish'd in *Greek* and *Latin*. (69-73)

* * *

Now these are the material Irregularities of a Play, and these are the Faults which down-right Mother-Sense can censure and be offended at as much as the most learn'd Critick in the Pit. And altho' the one cannot give me the Reasons of his Approbation or Dislike, yet I will take his Word for the Credit or Disrepute of a Comedy sooner perhaps than the Opinion of some *Virtuosos*. For there are some Gentlemen that have fortify'd their Spleen so impregnably with Criticism, and hold out so stiffly against all Attacks of Pleasantry, that the most

---

[1] Virgil, *Aeneid*, 6.129: 'this is the task, this the toil!'

powerful Efforts of Wit and Humour cannot make the least Impression. What a Misfortune is it to these Gentlemen to be Natives of such an ignorant, self-will'd, impertinent Island, where let a Critick and a Scholar find never so many Irregularities in a Play yet five hundred saucy People will give him the Lie to his Face and come to see this wicked Play forty or fifty times in a Year. But this *Vox Populi* is the Devil, tho' in a Place of more Authority than *Aristotle* it is call'd *Vox Dei*. Here is a Play with a Vengeance (says a Critick), to bring the Transaction of a Year's time into the Compass of three Hours; to carry the whole Audience with him from one Kingdom to another by the changing of a Scene. Where's the Probability, nay, the Possibility of all this? The Devil's in the Poet, sure, he don't think to put Contradictions upon us?

Look'ee, Sir, don't be in a Passion. The Poet does not impose Contradictions upon you, because he has told you no Lie; for that only is a Lie which is related with some fallacious Intention that you should believe it for a Truth. Now the Poet expects no more that you should believe the Plot of his Play than old *Æsop* design'd the World should think his *Eagle* and *Lyon* talk'd like you and I; which, I think, was every Jot as improbable as what you quarrel with—and yet the Fables took, and I'll be hang'd if you your self don't like 'em. But besides, Sir, if you are so inveterate against Improbabilities, you must never come near the Play-house at all; for there are several Improbabilities, nay Impossibilities, that all the Criticisms in Nature cannot correct. As, for Instance, in the part of *Alexander the Great*. To be affected with the Transactions of the Play we must suppose that we see that great Conqueror, after all his Triumphs, shunn'd by the Woman he loves and importun'd by her he hates; cross'd in his Cups and Jollity by his own Subjects; and at last miserably ending his Life in a raging Madness. We must suppose that we see the very *Alexander*, the Son of *Philip*, in all these unhappy Circumstances, else we are not touch'd by the Moral, which represents to us the Uneasiness of Humane Life in the greatest State and the Instability of Fortune in respect of Worldly Pomp. Yet the whole Audience at the same time knows that this is Mr. *Betterton* who is strutting upon the Stage and tearing his Lungs for a Livelihood. And that the same Person should be Mr. *Betterton* and *Alexander the Great* at the same time is somewhat like an Impossibility in my Mind. Yet you must grant this Impossibility in spight of your Teeth, if you han't Power to raise the old Hero from the Grave to act his own Part.

Now for another Impossibility. The less rigid Criticks allow to a

Comedy the Space of an artificial Day, or twenty-four Hours; but those of the thorough Reformation will confine it to the natural or Solar Day, which is but half the time. Now admitting this for a Decorum absolutely requisite, this Play begins when it is exactly Six by your Watch, and ends precisely at Nine, which is the usual time of the Representation. Now is it feasible in *rerum natura*, that the same Space or Extent of Time can be three Hours by your Watch, and twelve Hours upon the Stage, admitting the same Number of Minutes, or the same Measure of Sand to both? I'm afraid, Sir, you must allow this for an Impossibility too; and you may with as much Reason allow the Play the Extent of a whole Year. And if you grant me a Year, you may give me seven, and so to a thousand. For that a thousand Years should come within the Compass of three Hours is no more an Impossibility than that two Minutes should be contain'd in one. *Nullum minus continet in se majus* is equally applicable to both.

So much for the Decorum of *Time*; now for the Regularity of *Place*. I might make the one a Consequence of t'other, and alledge that by allowing me any Extent of Time you must grant me any Change of Place, for the one depends upon t'other. And having five or six Years for the Action of a Play I may travel from *Constantinople* to *Denmark*, so to *France*, and home to *England*, and rest long enough in each Country besides. But, you'll say, how can you carry us with you? Very easily Sir, if you be willing to go! As for Example: here is a new Play, the House is throng'd, the Prologue's spoken, and the Curtain drawn represents you the Scene of *Grand Cairo*. Whereabouts are you now, Sir? Were not you the very Minute before in the Pit in the *English* Playhouse, talking to a Wench, and now *presto pass* you are spirited away to the Banks of the River *Nile*. Surely, Sir, this is a most intolerable Improbability; yet this you must allow me, or else you destroy the very Constitution of Representation. Then in the second Act, with a Flourish of the Fiddles, I change the Scene to *Astrachan*. *O this is intolerable!* Look'ee, Sir, 'tis not a Jot more intolerable than the other; for you'll find that 'tis much about the same Distance between *Ægypt* and *Astrachan* as it is between *Drury-Lane* and *Grand Cairo*; and if you please to let your Fancy take Post it will perform the Journey in the same moment of Time, without any Disturbance in the World to your Person. You can follow *Quintus Curtius*[1] all over *Asia* in the Train of

---

[1] A historian who wrote (in the first century A.D.) a history of Alexander the Great in ten books, of which the first two are lost: it gives much space to the adventures on the Asiatic expedition.

Alexander, and trudge after *Hannibal*, like a *Cadet*, through all *Italy*, *Spain*, and *Africk*, in the Space of four or five Hours; yet the Devil a one of you will stir a Step over the Threshold for the best Poet in *Christendom*, tho' he make it his Business to make Heroes more amiable, and to surprize you with more wonderful Accidents and Events.

I am as little a Friend to those rambling Plays as any body, nor have I ever espous'd their Party by my own practice; yet I could not forbear saying something in Vindication of the great *Shakespeare*, whom every little Fellow that can form an *Aoristus primus* will presume to condemn for Indecorums and Absurdities. (Sparks that are so spruce upon their *Greek* and *Latin* that, like our Fops in Travel, they can relish nothing but what is foreign, to let the World know they have been abroad, forsooth). But it must be so, because *Aristotle* said it. Now I say it must be otherwise, because *Shakespeare* said it, and I'm sure that *Shakespeare* was the greater Poet of the two. But you'll say that *Aristotle* was the greater Critick.—That's a Mistake, Sir, for Criticism in Poetry is no more than Judgment in Poetry; which you will find in your Lexicon. Now if *Shakespeare* was the better Poet, he must have the most Judgment in his Art; for every body knows that Judgment is an essential part of Poetry, and without it no Writer is worth a Farthing. But to stoop to the Authority of either, without consulting the Reason of the Consequence, is an Abuse to a Man's Understanding; and neither the Precept of the Philosopher, nor Example of the Poet, should go down with me without examining the Weight of their Assertions. We can expect no more Decorum or Regularity in any Business than the Nature of the thing will bear. Now if the Stage cannot subsist without the Strength of Supposition and Force of Fancy in the Audience, why should a Poet fetter the Business of his Plot and starve his Action for the Nicety of an Hour, or the Change of a Scene?—since the Thought of Man can fly over a thousand Years with the same Ease and in the same Instant of Time that your Eye glances from the Figure of six to seven on the Dial-plate; and can glide from the *Cape of Good Hope* to the *Bay of St. Nicholas* (which is quite cross the World) with the same Quickness and Activity as between *Covent-Garden Church* and *Will's Coffee-House*. Then I must beg of these Gentlemen to let our old *English* Authors alone.—If they have left Vice unpunish'd, Vertue unrewarded, Folly unexpos'd, or Prudence unsuccessful—the contrary of which is the *Utile* of Comedy—let them be lashed to some purpose. If any part of their Plots have been independent of the rest or any of their Characters forc'd or unnatural—which destroys the *Dulce* of

Plays—let them be hiss'd off the Stage. But if, by a true Decorum in these material Points, they have writ successfully and answer'd the End of Dramatick Poetry in every Respect, let them rest in Peace and their Memories enjoy the Encomiums due to their Merit, without any Reflection for waiving those Niceties which are neither instructive to the World nor diverting to Mankind, but are like all the rest of Critical Learning, fit only to set People together by the Ears in ridiculous Controversies that are not one Jot material to the Good of the Publick, whether they be true or false. (76–9)

46. John Downes, Shakespeare on the Restoration stage

1708

From *Roscius Anglicanus, or an Historical Review of the Stage from 1660 to 1706* (1708).

John Downes (c. 1640–1710) was the prompter to D'Avenant's company for over forty years. His memoir has evident inaccuracies but is one of our main sources of information for the productions of this period and their reception.

[Downes records how, shortly after the Restoration, Killigrew's Company performed (unaltered versions of) *Othello*, *Henry IV*, *Julius Caesar*, *The Merry Wives of Windsor* and *Titus Andronicus*.] These being Old Plays, were Acted but now and then; yet being well Perform'd, were very Satisfactory to the Town.(9)

✳   ✳   ✳

[1663] The Tragedy of *Hamlet*, Hamlet being Perform'd by *Mr. Betterton*. . . . No succeeding Tragedy for several years got more Reputation or Money to the Company than this.(21).

✳   ✳   ✳

[Before 1665] This Tragedy of *Romeo and Juliet* was made some time after into a Tragi-comedy by Mr. *James Howard*, he preserving *Romeo and Juliet* alive; so that when the Tragedy was Reviv'd again 'twas Play'd Alternately, Tragical one Day, and Tragicomical another, for several Days together. (22)

*   *   *

[1664] The Tragedy of *Macbeth*, alter'd by Sir *William D'Avenant*; being drest in all its Finery, as new Cloath's, new Scenes, Machines (as flyings for the Witches), with all the Singing and Dancing in it, the first Compos'd by Mr. *Locke*, the other by Mr. *Channell* and Mr. *Joseph Priest*. It being all Excellently perform'd, being in the nature of an Opera, it Recompenc'd double the Expence; it proves still a lasting Play.

Note That this Tragedy, *King Lear* and *Tempest*, were *Acted* in *Lincolns-Inn-Fields*; Lear, being *Acted* exactly as *Mr. Shakespeare* Wrote it; as likewise the *Tempest*, alter'd by Sir *William D'Avenant* and Mr. *Dryden*, before 'twas made into an Opera. (33)

*   *   *

The Year after in 1673 [–74]: *The Tempest, or the Inchanted Island*, made into an Opera by Mr. *Shadwell*, having all New in it, as Scenes, machines —particularly, one Scene Painted with *Myriads* of aerial Spirits; and another flying away, with a Table Furnisht out with Fruits, Sweet meats, and all sorts of Viands, just when Duke *Trinculo* and his Companions were going to Dinner. All . . . things [were] perform'd in it so Admirably well that not any succeeding Opera got more Money. (34–5)

*   *   *

[1678] *Timon of Athens*, alter'd by Mr. *Shadwell*; 'twas very well *Acted*, and the Musick in't well Perform'd. It wonderfully pleas'd the Court and City; being an Excellent Moral. (37)

*   *   *

[1692] *The Fairy Queen*, made into an Opera, from a Comedy of Mr. *Shakespeare*'s. This in Ornaments was Superior to the other two, especially in Cloaths, for all the Singers and Dancers, Scenes, Machines and Decorations, all most profusely set off and excellently perform'd, chiefly the Instrumental and Vocal part Compos'd by the said Mr. *Purcell*, and Dances by Mr. *Priest*. The Court and Town were wonderfully satisfy'd with it; but the Expences in setting it out being so great, the Company got very little by it. (42–3)

47. Nicholas Rowe, Shakespeare's life and works

1709

From *Some Account of the Life, &c of Mr. William Shakespeare*, prefixed to Rowe's edition of Shakespeare, 6 vols (1709).

Nicholas Rowe (1674–1718) was a prolific poet and dramatist, and as the first editor of Shakespeare—however limited his grasp of textual criticism—deserves his status as pioneer for the first attempt to write a coherent biography of Shakespeare and for the first general survey of his works.

As for what relates to Men of Letters, the knowledge of an Author may sometimes conduce to the better understanding his Book. And tho' the Works of Mr. *Shakespeare* may seem to many not to want a Comment, yet I fancy some little Account of the Man himself may not be thought improper to go along with them.

He was the Son of Mr. *John Shakespeare*, and was Born at *Stratford* upon *Avon*, in *Warwickshire*, in *April* 1564. His Family, as appears by the Register and Publick Writings relating to that Town, were of good Figure and Fashion there, and are mention'd as Gentlemen. His Father, who was a considerable Dealer in Wool, had so large a Family, ten Children in all, that tho' he was his eldest Son he could give him no better Education than his own Employment. He had bred him, 'tis true, for some time at a Free-School, where 'tis probable he acquir'd that little *Latin* he was Master of. But the narrowness of his Circumstances, and the want of his assistance at Home, forc'd his Father to withdraw him from thence, and unhappily prevented his further Proficiency in that Language. It is without Controversie that he had no knowledge of the Writings of the Antient Poets, not only from this Reason, but from his Works themselves, where we find no traces of any thing that looks like an Imitation of 'em. The Delicacy of his Taste, and the natural Bent of his own Great *Genius*—equal, if not

superior to some of the best of theirs—would certainly have led him to
Read and Study 'em with so much Pleasure that some of their fine
Images would naturally have insinuated themselves into, and been
mix'd with his own Writings; so that his not copying at least something
from them may be an Argument of his never having read 'em. Whether
his Ignorance of the Antients were a disadvantage to him or no, may
admit of a Dispute. For tho' the knowledge of 'em might have made
him more Correct, yet it is not improbable but that the Regularity and
Deference for them which would have attended that Correctness
might have restrain'd some of that Fire, Impetuosity, and even beautiful Extravagance which we admire in *Shakespeare*. And I believe we are
better pleas'd with those Thoughts, altogether New and Uncommon,
which his own Imagination supply'd him so abundantly with than if
he had given us the most beautiful Passages out of the *Greek* and *Latin*
Poets, and that in the most agreeable manner that it was possible for
a Master of the *English* Language to deliver 'em. Some *Latin* without
question he did know, and one may see up and down in his Plays
how far his Reading that way went. In *Love's Labour's Lost* the Pedant
comes out with a Verse of *Mantuan*; and in *Titus Andronicus*, one of the
Gothick Princes, upon reading

> *Integer vitæ scelerisque purus*
> *Non eget Mauri jaculis nec arcu—*

says, ' *'Tis a Verse in* Horace', [*Titus Andronicus*, 4.2.22 ff] *but he remem-
bers it out of his* Grammar: which, I suppose, was the Author's Case.
Whatever *Latin* he had, 'tis certain he understood *French*, as may be
observ'd from many Words and Sentences scatter'd up and down his
Plays in that Language; and especially from one Scene in *Henry V*
written wholly in it. (ii–iv)

*   *   *

It is at this Time, and upon this Accident, that he is said to have made
his first Acquaintance in the Play-house. He was receiv'd into the
Company then in being, at first in a very mean Rank. But his admirable
Wit, and the natural Turn of it to the Stage, soon distinguish'd him,
if not as an extraordinary Actor, yet as an excellent Writer. His Name
is Printed, as the Custom was in those Times, amongst those of the
other Players before some old Plays, but without any particular
Account of what sort of Parts he us'd to play; and tho' I have inquir'd

I could never meet with any further Account of him this way than that the top of his Performance was the Ghost in his own *Hamlet*. I should have been much more pleas'd to have learn'd from some certain Authority which was the first Play he wrote; it would be without doubt a pleasure to any Man curious in Things of this Kind to see and know what was the first Essay of a Fancy like *Shakespeare*'s. Perhaps we are not to look for his Beginnings, like those of other Authors, among their least perfect Writings. Art had so little, and Nature so large a Share in what he did, that for ought I know the Performances of his Youth, as they were the most vigorous and had the most fire and strength of Imagination in 'em, were the best. I would not be thought by this to mean that his Fancy was so loose and extravagant as to be Independent on the Rule and Government of Judgment; but that what he thought was commonly so Great, so justly and rightly Conceiv'd in it self, that it wanted little or no Correction, and was immediately approv'd by an impartial Judgment at the first sight. Mr. *Dryden* seems to think that *Pericles* is one of his first Plays;[1] but there is no judgment to be form'd on that, since there is good Reason to believe that the greatest part of that Play was not written by him; tho' it is own'd some part of it certainly was, particularly the last Act. But tho' the order of Time in which the several Pieces were written be generally uncertain, yet there are Passages in some few of them which seem to fix their Dates. So the *Chorus* in the beginning of the fifth Act of *Henry V*, by a Compliment very handsomly turn'd to the Earl of *Essex*, shews the Play to have been written when that Lord was General for the Queen in *Ireland*. And his Elogy upon Q. *Elizabeth* and her Successor K. *James*, in the latter end of his *Henry VIII*, is a Proof of that Play's being written after the Accession of the latter of those two Princes to the Crown of *England*. Whatever the particular Times of his Writing were, the People of his Age, who began to grow wonderfully fond of Diversions of this kind, could not but be highly pleas'd to see a *Genius* arise amongst 'em of so pleasurable, so rich a Vein, and so plentifully capable of furnishing their favourite Entertainments. Besides the advantages of his Wit he was in himself a good-natur'd Man, of great sweetness in his Manners, and a most agreeable Companion; so that it is no wonder if with so many good Qualities he made himself acquainted with the best Conversations of those Times. Queen *Elizabeth* had several of his Plays Acted before her, and without doubt

[1] See Volume 1, p. 15.

gave him many gracious Marks of her Favour. It is that Maiden
Princess plainly, whom he intends by

>   —*A fair Vestal, Throned by the West.*
>   *Midsummer Night's Dream* [2.1.158]
>   (vi–viii)

⋆   ⋆   ⋆

Ben [*Jonson*] was naturally Proud and Insolent, and in the Days of his
Reputation did so far take upon him the Supremacy in Wit that he
could not but look with an evil Eye upon any one that seem'd to stand
in Competition with him. And if at times he has affected to commend
him it has always been with some Reserve, insinuating his Uncorrect-
ness, a careless manner of Writing, and want of Judgment. The Praise
of seldom altering or blotting out what he writ, which was given him
by the Players who were the first Publishers of his Works after his
Death,[1] was what *Jonson* could not bear. He thought it impossible,
perhaps, for another Man to strike out the greatest Thoughts in the
finest Expression and to reach those Excellencies of Poetry with the
Ease of a first Imagination which himself with infinite Labour and
Study could but hardly attain to. *Jonson* was certainly a very good
Scholar, and in that had the advantage of *Shakespeare*; tho' at the same
time I believe it must be allow'd that what Nature gave the latter was
more than a Balance for what Books had given the former; and the
Judgment of a great Man upon this occasion was, I think, very just and
proper.[2] In a Conversation between Sir *John Suckling*, Sir *William
D'Avenant, Endymion Porter*, Mr. *Hales* of Eton, and *Ben Jonson*, Sir *John
Suckling*, who was a profess'd Admirer of *Shakespeare*, had undertaken
his Defence against *Ben Jonson* with some warmth. Mr. *Hales*, who had
sat still for some time, hearing *Ben* frequently reproaching him with the
want of Learning and Ignorance of the Antients told him at last, *That if
Mr.* Shakespeare *had not read the Antients, he had likewise not stollen
any thing from 'em* (a Fault the other made no Conscience of); *and that
if he would produce any one Topick finely treated by any of them, he would
undertake to shew something upon the same Subject at least as well written by*
Shakespeare. *Jonson* did indeed take a large liberty, even to the
transcribing and translating of whole Scenes together; and sometimes,
with all Deference to so great a Name as his, not altogether for the

---

[1] See Volume I, p. I, and Jonson's comment, p. 26.
[2] For the first appearance of this anecdote see Volume I, p. 138; also p. 66 above.

advantage of the Authors of whom he borrow'd. And if *Augustus* and *Virgil* were really what he has made 'em in a Scene of his *Poetaster*, they are as odd an Emperor and a Poet as ever met. *Shakespeare*, on the other Hand, was beholding to nobody farther than the Foundation of the Tale, the Incidents were often his own, and the Writing intirely so. There is one Play of his indeed, *The Comedy of Errors*, in a great measure taken from the *Menæchmi* of *Plautus*. How that happen'd I cannot easily Divine, since, as I hinted before, I do not take him to have been Master of *Latin* enough to read it in the Original, and I know of no Translation of *Plautus* so Old as his Time.[1]

As I have not propos'd to my self to enter into a Large and Compleat Criticism upon Mr. *Shakespeare*'s Works, so I suppose it will neither be expected that I should take notice of the severe Remarks that have been formerly made upon him by Mr. *Rymer*. I must confess, I can't very well see what could be the Reason of his animadverting with so much Sharpness upon the Faults of a Man Excellent on most Occasions, and whom all the World ever was and will be inclin'd to have an Esteem and Veneration for. If it was to shew his own Knowledge in the Art of Poetry, besides that there is a Vanity in making that only his Design, I question if there be not many Imperfections as well in those Schemes and Precepts he has given for the Direction of others, as well as in that Sample of Tragedy which he has written to shew the Excellency of his own *Genius*. If he had a Pique against the Man, and wrote on purpose to ruin a Reputation so well establish'd, he has had the Mortification to fail altogether in his Attempt and to see the World at least as fond of *Shakespeare* as of his Critique. But I won't believe a Gentleman, and a good-natur'd Man, capable of the last Intention. Whatever may have been his Meaning finding fault is certainly the easiest Task of Knowledge, and commonly those Men of good Judgment, who are likewise of good and gentle Dispositions, abandon this ungrateful Province to the Tyranny of Pedants. If one would enter into the Beauties of *Shakespeare*, there is a much larger, as well as a more delightful Field; but as I won't prescribe to the Tastes of other People so I will only take the liberty, with all due Submission to the Judgment of others, to observe some of those Things I have been pleas'd with in looking him over.

His Plays are properly to be distinguish'd only into Comedies and Tragedies. Those which are called Histories, and even some of his Comedies, are really Tragedies with a run or mixture of Comedy

---

[1] But cf. Langbaine's statement, Volume I, p. 419.

amongst 'em. That way of Tragi-Comedy was the common Mistake of that Age, and is indeed become so agreeable to the *English* Tast that tho' the severer Critiques among us cannot bear it yet the generality of our Audiences seem to be better pleas'd with it than with an exact Tragedy. *The Merry Wives of Windsor, The Comedy of Errors*, and *The Taming of the Shrew*, are all pure Comedy; the rest, however they are call'd, have something of both Kinds. 'Tis not very easie to determine which way of Writing he was most Excellent in. There is certainly a great deal of Entertainment in his Comical Humours; and tho' they did not then strike at all Ranks of People, as the Satyr of the present Age has taken the Liberty to do, yet there is a pleasing and a well-distinguish'd Variety in those Characters which he thought fit to meddle with. *Falstaff* is allow'd by every body to be a Master-piece. The Character is always well-sustain'd, tho' drawn out into the length of three Plays, and even the Account of his Death, given by his Old Landlady Mrs. *Quickly* in the first Act of *Henry V*, tho' it be extremely Natural, is yet as diverting as any Part of his Life. If there be any Fault in the Draught he has made of this lewd old Fellow, it is that tho' he has made him a Thief, Lying, Cowardly, Vain-glorious, and in short every way Vicious, yet he has given him so much Wit as to make him almost too agreeable; and I don't know whether some People have not, in remembrance of the Diversion he had formerly afforded 'em, been sorry to see his Friend *Hal* use him so scurvily when he comes to the Crown in the End of the Second Part of *Henry IV*. Amongst other Extravagances, in *The Merry Wives of Windsor*, he has made him a Deer-stealer, that he might at the same time remember his *Warwickshire* Prosecutor, under the Name of Justice *Shallow*; he has given him very near the same Coat of Arms which *Dugdale*, in his Antiquities of that County, describes for a Family there, and makes the *Welsh* Parson descant very pleasantly upon 'em. That whole Play is admirable: the Humours are various and well oppos'd; the main Design, which is to cure *Ford* of his unreasonable Jealousie, is extremely well conducted. *Falstaff*'s *Billet-doux*, and Master *Slender*'s 'Ah! Sweet Ann Page!' [*Merry Wives of Windsor*, 3.1.65, 105] are very good Expressions of Love in their Way. In *Twelfth Night* there is something singularly Ridiculous and Pleasant in the fanatical Steward *Malvolio*. The Parasite and the Vain-glorious in *Parolles*, in *All's Well that ends Well*, is as good as any thing of that Kind in *Plautus* or *Terence*. *Petruchio*, in *The Taming of the Shrew*, is an uncommon Piece of Humour. The Conversation of *Benedick* and *Beatrice*, in *Much ado about Nothing*, and of *Rosalind* in

As you like it, have much Wit and Sprightliness all along. His Clowns, without which Character there was hardly any Play writ in that Time, are all very entertaining; and, I believe, *Thersites* in *Troilus and Cressida*, and *Apemantus* in *Timon* will be allow'd to be Master-Pieces of ill Nature and satyrical Snarling. To these I might add that incomparable Character of *Shylock* the *Jew*, in *The Merchant of Venice*; but tho' we have seen that Play Receiv'd and Acted as a Comedy,[1] and the Part of the *Jew* perform'd by an Excellent Comedian, yet I cannot but think it was design'd Tragically by the Author. There appears in it such a deadly Spirit of Revenge, such a savage Fierceness and Fellness, and such a bloody designation of Cruelty and Mischief, as cannot agree either with the Stile or Characters of Comedy. The Play it self, take it all together, seems to me to be one of the most finish'd of any of *Shakespeare*'s. The Tale, indeed, in that Part relating to the Caskets and the extravagant and unusual kind of Bond given by *Antonio*, is a little too much remov'd from the Rules of Probability. But taking the Fact for granted we must allow it to be very beautifully written. There is something in the Friendship of *Antonio* to *Bassanio* very Great, Generous and Tender. The whole fourth Act—supposing, as I said, the Fact to be probable—is extremely Fine. But there are two Passages that deserve a particular Notice. The first is, what *Portia* says in praise of Mercy; and the other on the Power of Musick. The Melancholy of *Jaques*, in *As you like it*, is as singular and odd as it is diverting. (xiii–xx)

*　　*　　*

His Images are indeed ev'ry where so lively that the Thing he would represent stands full before you, and you possess ev'ry Part of it. I will venture to point out one more, which is, I think, as strong and as uncommon as any thing I ever saw; 'tis an Image of Patience. Speaking of a Maid in Love, he says,

> —*She never told her Love,*
> *But let Concealment, like a Worm i'th' Bud*
> *Feed on her Damask Cheek: She pin'd in Thought,*
> *And sate like* Patience *on a Monument,*
> *Smiling at* Grief.
>
> [*Twelfth Night*, 2.4.109 ff]

What an Image is here given! and what a Task would it have been for the greatest Masters of *Greece* and *Rome* to have express'd the Passions

---

[1] Granville's adaptation, No. 43 above.

designed by this Sketch of Statuary! The Stile of his Comedy is, in general, Natural to the Characters, and easie in it self; and the Wit most commonly sprightly and pleasing, except in those places where he runs into Dogrel Rhymes, as in *The Comedy of Errors*, and a Passage or two in some other Plays. As for his Jingling sometimes, and playing upon Words, it was the common Vice of the Age he liv'd in. And if we find it in the Pulpit, made use of as an Ornament to the Sermons of some of the Gravest Divines of those Times, perhaps it may not be thought too light for the Stage.

But certainly the greatness of this Author's Genius do's nowhere so much appear as where he gives his Imagination an entire Loose, and raises his Fancy to a flight above Mankind and the Limits of the visible World. Such are his Attempts in *The Tempest, Midsummer-Night's Dream, Macbeth* and *Hamlet*. Of these *The Tempest*, however it comes to be plac'd the first by the former Publishers of his Works, can never have been the first written by him: it seems to me as perfect in its Kind as almost any thing we have of his. One may observe that the Unities are kept here with an Exactness uncommon to the Liberties of his Writing: Tho' that was what, I suppose, he valu'd himself least upon, since his Excellencies were all of another Kind. I am very sensible that he does, in this Play, depart too much from that likeness to Truth which ought to be observ'd in these sort of Writings; yet he does it so very finely that one is easily drawn in to have more Faith for his sake than Reason does well allow of. His Magick has something in it very Solemn and very Poetical, and that extravagant Character of *Caliban* is mighty well sustain'd, shews a wonderful Invention in the Author who could strike out such a particular wild Image, and is certainly one of the finest and most uncommon Grotesques that was ever seen. The Observation which, I have been inform'd,* three very great Men concurr'd in making upon this Part, was extremely just. *That* Shakespeare *had not only found out a new Character in his* Caliban, *but had also devis'd and adapted a new manner of Language for that Character.* Among the particular Beauties of this Piece I think one may be allow'd to point out the Tale of *Prospero* in the First Act; his Speech to *Ferdinand* in the Fourth, upon the breaking up the Masque of *Juno* and *Ceres*; and that in the Fifth, where he dissolves his Charms, and resolves to break his Magick Rod. This Play has been alter'd by Sir *William D'Avenant* and Mr. *Dryden*; and tho' I won't Arraign the Judgment of those two great Men, yet

---

* *Ld.* Falkland, *Ld. C. J.* Vaughan, *and Mr.* Selden.

I think I may be allow'd to say that there are some things left out by them that might, and even ought to have been kept in. (xxii–xxv)

★　　★　　★

It is the same Magick that raises the Fairies in *Midsummer Night's Dream*, the Witches in *Macbeth*, and the Ghost in *Hamlet*, with Thoughts and Languages so proper to the Parts they sustain and so peculiar to the Talent of this Writer. But of the two last of these Plays I shall have occasion to take notice among the Tragedies of Mr. *Shakespeare*.

If one undertook to examine the greatest part of these by those Rules which are establish'd by *Aristotle* and taken from the Model of the *Grecian* Stage, it would be no very hard Task to find a great many Faults. But as *Shakespeare* liv'd under a kind of mere Light of Nature, and had never been made acquainted with the Regularity of those written Precepts, so it would be hard to judge him by a Law he knew nothing of. We are to consider him as a Man that liv'd in a State of almost universal License and Ignorance. There was no establish'd Judge, but every one took the liberty to Write according to the Dictates of his own Fancy. When one considers that there is not one Play before him of a Reputation good enough to entitle it to an Appearance on the present Stage it cannot but be a Matter of great Wonder that he should advance Dramatick Poetry so far as he did. The Fable is what is generally plac'd the first among those that are reckon'd the constituent Parts of a Tragick or Heroick Poem; not, perhaps, as it is the most Difficult or Beautiful but as it is the first properly to be thought of in the Contrivance and Course of the whole; and with the Fable ought to be consider'd the fit Disposition, Order and Conduct of its several Parts. As it is not in this Province of the *Drama* that the Strength and Mastery of *Shakespeare* lay so I shall not undertake the tedious and ill-natur'd Trouble to point out the several Faults he was guilty of in it. His Tales were seldom invented, but rather taken either from true History or Novels and Romances, and he commonly made use of 'em in that Order, with those Incidents and that extent of Time in which he found 'em in the Authors from whence he borrow'd them. So *The Winter's Tale*, which is taken from an old Book call'd *The Delectable History of Dorastus and Faunia*, contains the space of sixteen or seventeen Years, and the Scene is sometimes laid in *Bohemia* and sometimes in *Sicily*, according to the original Order of the Story. Almost all his Historical Plays comprehend a great length of Time and very different and distinct Places, and in his *Antony and Cleopatra* the

Scene travels over the greatest Part of the *Roman* Empire. But in Recompence for his Carelessness in this Point, when he comes to another Part of the *Drama, The Manners of his Characters in Acting or Speaking what is proper for them, and fit to be shown by the Poet,* he may be generally justify'd and in very many places greatly commended. For those Plays which he has taken from the *English* or *Roman* History, let any Man compare 'em and he will find the Character as exact in the Poet as the Historian. He seems indeed so far from proposing to himself any one Action for a Subject that the Title very often tells you, 'tis *The Life of King John, King Richard, &c.* What can be more agreeable to the Idea our Historians give of *Henry VI*, than the Picture *Shakespeare* has drawn of him! His Manners are every where exactly the same with the Story; one finds him still describ'd with Simplicity, passive Sanctity, want of Courage, weakness of Mind, and easie Submission to the Governance of an imperious Wife or prevailing Faction. Tho' at the same time the Poet does Justice to his good Qualities, and moves the Pity of his Audience for him by showing him Pious, Disinterested, a Contemner of the Things of this World, and wholly resign'd to the severest Dispensations of God's Providence. There is a short Scene [3.3] in the *Second Part of Henry VI* which I cannot but think admirable in its Kind. Cardinal *Beaufort*, who had murder'd the Duke of *Gloucester*, is shewn in the last Agonies on his Death-Bed with the good King praying over him. There is so much Terror in one, so much Tenderness and moving Piety in the other as must touch any one who is capable either of Fear or Pity. In his *Henry VIII* that Prince is drawn with that Greatness of Mind and all those good Qualities which are attributed to him in any Account of his Reign. If his Faults are not shewn in an equal degree, and the Shades in this Picture do not bear a just Proportion to the Lights, it is not that the Artist wanted either Colours or Skill in the Disposition of 'em. But the truth, I believe, might be that he forbore doing it out of regard to Queen *Elizabeth*, since it could have been no very great Respect to the Memory of his Mistress to have expos'd some certain Parts of her Father's Life upon the Stage. He has dealt more freely with the Minister of that Great King, and certainly nothing was ever more justly written than the Character of Cardinal *Wolsey*. He has shewn him Tyrannical, Cruel, and Insolent in his Prosperity; and yet, by a wonderful Address, he makes his Fall and Ruin the Subject of general Compassion. The whole Man, with his Vices and Virtues, is finely and exactly described in the second Scene of the fourth Act. The Distresses likewise of Queen *Katherine* in this Play, are very movingly touch'd; and tho' the Art of the Poet has skreen'd King *Henry* from any gross Imputation of Injustice yet one is inclin'd to wish the Queen had met with a Fortune more worthy of her Birth and Virtue. Nor are the Manners proper to the Persons represented less justly observ'd in those Characters taken from the *Roman* History; and of this, the Fierceness and Impatience of *Coriolanus*, his Courage and Disdain of the common People, the Virtue and Philosophical Temper of *Brutus*, and the irregular Greatness of Mind in M. *Antony*, are beautiful Proofs. For the two last especially, you find 'em exactly as they are describ'd by *Plutarch*, from whom certainly *Shakespeare* copy'd 'em. He has indeed follow'd his Original pretty close, and taken in several little Incidents that might have been spar'd in a Play. But, as I hinted before, his Design seems most commonly rather to describe those great Men in the several Fortunes and Accidents of their Lives than to take any single great Action and form his Work simply upon that. However, there are some of his Pieces where the Fable is founded upon one Action only. Such are, more especially, *Romeo and Juliet, Hamlet,* and *Othello.* The Design in *Romeo and Juliet* is plainly the Punishment of their two Families for the unreasonable Feuds and Animosities that had been so long kept up between 'em, and occasion'd the Effusion of so much Blood. In the management of this Story he has shewn something wonderfully Tender and Passionate in the Love-part, and very Pitiful in the Distress. *Hamlet* is founded on much the same Tale with the *Electra* of *Sophocles.* In each of 'em a young Prince is engag'd to Revenge the Death of his Father; their Mothers are equally Guilty, are both concern'd in the Murder of their Husbands and are afterwards married to the Murderers. There is in the first Part of the *Greek* Tragedy something very moving in the Grief of *Electra*; but, as Mr. *D'Acier* has observ'd, there is something very unnatural and shocking in the Manners he has given that Princess and *Orestes* in the latter Part. *Orestes* embrues his Hands in the Blood of his own Mother; and that barbarous Action is perform'd, tho' not immediately upon the Stage, yet so near that the Audience hear *Clytemnestra* crying out to *Ægysthus* for Help, and to her Son for Mercy; while *Electra*, her Daughter, and a Princess—both of them Characters that ought to have appear'd with more Decency—stands upon the Stage and encourages her Brother in the Parricide. What Horror does this not raise! *Clytemnestra* was a wicked Woman, and had deserv'd to Die; nay, in the truth of the Story, she was kill'd by her own Son. But to represent an Action of this Kind on the Stage is certainly an Offence against those Rules of Manners proper to the Persons that ought to be observ'd there. On the contrary, let us only look a little on the Conduct of *Shakespeare*. *Hamlet* is represented with the same Piety towards his Father, and Resolution to Revenge his Death, as *Orestes*; he has the same Abhorrence for his Mother's Guilt, which, to provoke him the more, is heighten'd by Incest. But 'tis with wonderful Art and Justness of Judgment that the Poet restrains him from doing Violence to his Mother. To prevent any thing of that Kind, he makes his Father's Ghost forbid that part of his Vengeance.

> *But howsoever thou pursu'st this Act,*
> *Taint not thy Mind; nor let thy Soul contrive*
> *Against thy Mother ought; leave her to Heav'n,*
> *And to those Thorns that in her Bosom lodge,*
> *To prick and sting her.* [1.5.84 ff]

This is to distinguish rightly between *Horror* and *Terror*. The latter is a proper Passion of Tragedy, but the former ought always to be carefully avoided. And certainly no Dramatick Writer ever succeeded better in raising *Terror* in the Minds of an Audience than *Shakespeare* has done. The whole Tragedy of *Macbeth*, but more especially the Scene where the King is murder'd (in the second Act) as well as this Play, is a noble Proof of that manly Spirit with which he writ; and both shew how powerful he was in giving the strongest Motions to our Souls that they are capable of.

I cannot leave *Hamlet* without taking notice of the Advantage with which we have seen this Master-piece of *Shakespeare* distinguish itself upon the Stage by Mr. *Betterton*'s fine Performance of that Part. A Man who, tho' he had no other good Qualities, as he has a great many, must have made his way into the Esteem of all Men of Letters by this only Excellency. No Man is better acquainted with *Shakespeare*'s manner of Expression, and indeed he has study'd him so well and is so much a Master of him that whatever Part of his he performs he does it as if it had been written on purpose for him, and that the Author had exactly conceiv'd it as he plays it. I must own a particular Obligation to him for the most considerable part of the Passages relating to his Life which I have here transmitted to the Publick, his Veneration for the Memory of *Shakespeare* having engag'd him to make a Journey into *Warwickshire* on purpose to gather up what Remains he could of a Name for which he had so great a Value.

Since I had at first resolv'd not to enter into any Critical Controversie I won't pretend to enquire into the Justness of Mr. *Rymer*'s

Remarks on *Othello*. He has certainly pointed out some Faults very judiciously, and indeed they are such as most People will agree with him to be Faults. But I wish he would likewise have observed some of the Beauties too; as I think it became an Exact and Equal Critique to do. It seems strange that he should allow nothing Good in the whole. If the Fable and Incidents are not to his Taste yet the Thoughts are almost every where very Noble, and the Diction manly and proper. These last, indeed, are Parts of *Shakespeare*'s Praise which it would be very hard to Dispute with him. His Sentiments and Images of Things are Great and Natural; and his Expression (tho' perhaps in some Instances a little Irregular) just, and rais'd in Proportion to his Subject and Occasion. It would be even endless to mention the particular Instances that might be given of this Kind, but his Book is in the Possession of the Publick, and 'twill be hard to dip into any Part of it without finding what I have said of him made good.

The latter Part of his Life was spent, as all Men of good Sense will wish theirs may be, in Ease, Retirement, and the Conversation of his Friends. He had the good Fortune to gather an Estate equal to his Occasion, and in that to his Wish; and is said to have spent some Years before his Death at his native *Stratford*. His pleasurable Wit and good Nature engag'd him in the Acquaintance, and entitled him to the Friendship, of the Gentlemen of the Neighbourhood. . . . (xxvi–xxxvi)

48. Sir Richard Steele, from the *Tatler*

1709–10

Sir Richard Steele (1672–1729), poet, dramatist, essayist, shows in these essays a personal appropriation of Shakespeare to a new sentimental morality.

No. 8 (26 April 1709)

The Play of *The London Cuckolds* was acted this Evening before a suitable Audience, who were extremely well diverted with that Heap of Vice and Absurdity. The Indignation which *Eugenio*, who is a Gentleman of a just Tast, has upon Occasion of seeing Human Nature fall so low in their Delights, made him, I thought, expatiate upon the Mention of this Play very agreeably. 'Of all Men living', said he, 'I pity Players, (who must be Men of good Understanding to be capable of being such) that they are oblig'd to repeat and assume proper Gestures for representing Things of which their Reason must be asham'd and which they must disdain their Audience for approving. The amendment of these low Gratifications is only to be made by People of Condition, by encouraging the Presentation of the Noble Characters drawn by *Shakespeare* and others, from whence it is impossible to return without strong Impressions of Honour and Humanity. On these Occasions Distress is laid before us, with all its Causes and Consequences, and our Resentment plac'd according to the Merit of the Persons afflicted. Were *Drama's* of this Nature more acceptable to the Tast of the Town Men who have Genius would bend their Studies to excel in 'em.'

* * *

No. 47 (27 July 1709)

* * *

Tragical Passion was the subject of the Discourse where I last visited this Evening; and a Gentleman who knows that I am at present writing a very deep Tragedy directed his Discourse in a particular Manner to

me. 'It is the common Fault' (said he) 'of you Gentlemen who write in
the Buskin Style that you give us rather the Sentiments of such who
behold Tragical Events, than of such who bear a Part in 'em themselves. I would advise all who pretend this Way to read *Shakespeare*
with Care, and they will soon be deterr'd from putting forth what is
usually call'd Tragedy. The Way of common Writers in this Kind is
rather *the Description than the Expression of Sorrow*. There is no Medium
in these Attempts; and you must go to the very Bottom of the Heart,
or it is all mere Language; and the Writer of such Lines is no more a
Poet than a Man is a Physician for knowing the Names of Distempers
without the Causes of them. Men of Sense are profess'd Enemies to all
such empty Labours, for he who pretends to be sorrowful, and is not,
is a Wretch yet more contemptible than he who pretends to be merry,
and is not. Such a Tragedian is only maudlin drunk.' The Gentleman
went on with much Warmth, but all he could say had little Effect upon
me. But when I came higher I so far observ'd his Counsel that I look'd
into *Shakespeare*. The Tragedy I dipp'd into was *Henry IV*. In the
Scene where *Morton* is preparing to tell *Northumberland* of his Son's
Death, the old Man does not give him Time to speak but says:

> *The Whiteness of thy Cheeks*
> *Is apter than thy Tongue to tell thy Errand;*
> *Ev'n such a Man, so faint, so spiritless,*
> *So dull, so dead in Look, so woe-begone,*
> *Drew* Priam's *Curtain at the Dead of Night,*
> *And would have told him Half his* Troy *was burnt:*
> *But* Priam *found the Fire, ere he his Tongue,*
> *And I my* Percy's *Death ere thou report'st it.*
>
> [2 *Henry IV*, 1.1.68 ff]

The Image in this Place is wonderfully noble and great; yet this Man
in all this is but rising towards his great Affliction and is still enough
himself, as you see, to make a Simile. But when he is certain of his
Son's Death he is lost to all Patience, and gives up all the Regards of
this Life; and since the last of Evils is fall'n upon him he calls for it upon
all the World.

> *Now let not Nature's Hand*
> *Keep the wild Flood confin'd; let Order die,*
> *And let the World no longer be a Stage,*
> *To feed Contention in a lingring Act;*

But let one Spirit of the first-born Cain
Reign in all Bosoms, that each Heart being set
On bloody Courses, the wide Scene may end,
And Darkness be the Burier of the Dead.

[2 *Henry IV*, 1.1.153 ff]

Reading but this one Scene has convinc'd me that he who describes the Concern of great Men must have a Soul as noble, and as susceptible of high Thoughts, as they whom he represents. I shall therefore lay by my *Drama* for some Time, and turn my Thoughts to Cares and Griefs somewhat below that of Heroes, but no less moving.

*   *   *

No. 53 (10 August 1709)

*   *   *

Mr. *Truman*, who is a mighty Admirer of Dramatick Poetry, and knows I am about a Tragedy, never meets me but he is giving Admonitions and Hints for my Conduct. 'Mr. *Bickerstaff*' (said he) 'I was reading last Night your second Act you were so kind to lend me; but I find you depend mightily upon the Retinue of your Hero to make him magnificent. You make Guards, and Ushers, and Courtiers, and Commons, and Nobles march before, and then enters your Prince and says, they can't defend him from his Love. Why, prithee *Isaac*, who ever thought they could? Place me your loving Monarch in a Solitude; let him have no Sense at all of his Grandeur, but let it be eaten up with his Passion. He must value himself as the greatest of Lovers, not as the first of Princes. And then let him say a more tender Thing than ever Man said before—for his Feather and Eagle's Beak is nothing at all. The Man is to be express'd by his Sentiments and Affections, and not by his Fortune or Equipage. You are also to take Care that at his first Entrance he says something which may give us an Idea of what we are to expect in a Person of his Way of thinking. *Shakespeare* is your Pattern. In the Tragedy of *Julius Cæsar* he introduces his Hero in his Night-Gown. He had at that Time all the Power of *Rome*. Depos'd Consuls, subordinate Generals, and Captive Princes might have preceded him; but this Genius was above such Mechanick Methods of showing Greatness. Therefore he rather presents that great Soul debating upon the Subject of Life and Death with his intimate Friends, without endeavouring to prepossess his Audience with empty Show and Pomp. When those who

attend him talk of the many Omens which had appear'd that Day, he
answers:

> Cowards die many Times before their Deaths;
> The Valiant never talk of Death but once.
> Of all the Wonders that I yet have heard,
> It seems to me most strange that Men should fear;
> Seeing that Death, a necessary End,
> Will come, when it will come.   [Julius Cæsar, 2.2.32]

When the Hero has spoken this Sentiment there is nothing that is great
which cannot be expected from one whose first Position is the Contempt of Death to so high a Degree, as making his *Exit* a Thing wholly
indifferent, and not a Part of his Care, but that of Heav'n and Fate.'

*   *   *

No. 68 (14 September 1709)

*   *   *

The Strings of the Heart, which are to be touch'd to give us Compassion, are not so play'd on but by the finest Hand. We see in Tragical
Representations, it is not the Pomp of Language or Magnificence of
Dress in which the Passion is wrought that touches sensible Spirits,
but something of a plain and simple Nature which breaks in upon our
Souls by that Sympathy which is given us for our mutual Good-will
and Service. In the Tragedy of *Macbeth*, where *Wilks* acts the Part of
a Man whose Family has been murder'd in his Absence, the Wildness
of his Passion, which is run over in a Torrent of calamitous Circumstances, does but raise my Spirits and give me the Alarm; but when he
skilfully seems to be out of Breath and is brought too low to say more,
and upon a second Reflection cry, only wiping his Eyes, 'What, both
my Children! Both, both my Children gone—' there is no resisting
a Sorrow which seems to have cast about for all the Reasons possible
for its Consolation but has no Recourse. There is not one left, but both,
both are murder'd! Such sudden Starts from the Thread of the
Discourse, and a plain Sentiment express'd in an artless Way, are the
irresistible Strokes of Eloquence and Poetry.

The same great Master, *Shakespeare*, can afford us Instances of all the
Places where our Souls are accessible, and ever commands our Tears.
But it is to be observ'd that he draws 'em from some unexpected
Source which seems not wholly of a Piece with the Discourse. Thus

when *Brutus* and *Cassius* had a Debate in the Tragedy of *Cæsar* and rose
to warm Language against each other, insomuch that it had almost
come to something that might be fatal 'till they recollected themselves,
Brutus does more than make an Apology for the Heat he had been in,
by saying, '*Portia* is dead'. Here *Cassius* is all Tenderness, and ready to
dissolve, when he considers that the Mind of his Friend had been
employ'd on the greatest Affliction imaginable when he had been
adding to it by a Debate on Trifles; which makes him in the Anguish
of his Heart cry out 'How scap'd I killing when I thus provok'd you?'
[*Julius Cæsar*, 4.3.147] This is an Incident which moves the Soul in all
its Sentiments, and *Cassius*'s Heart was at once touch'd with all the soft
Pangs of Pity, Remorse, and Reconciliation.

It is said indeed by *Horace*, If you would have me weep you must
first weep your self.[1] This is not literally true for it would have been
as rightly said, if we observe Nature, that I shall certainly weep if you
do not. But what is intended by that Expression is that it is not possible
to give Passion except you show that you suffer your self. Therefore
the true Art seems to be that when you would have the Person you
represent pitied, you must show him at once, in the highest Grief and
Strugling, to bear it with Decency and Patience. In this Case, we sigh
for him, and give him every Groan he suppresses.

*   *   *

No. 71 (20 September 1709)

*   *   *

I was going on in reading my Letter, when I was interrupted by
Mr. *Greenhat*, who has been this Evening at the Play of *Hamlet*. 'Mr.
Bickerstaff,' said he, 'had you been to Night at the Play-house you had
seen the Force of Action in Perfection. Your admir'd Mr. *Betterton*
behav'd himself so well that tho' now about Seventy he acted Youth;
and by the prevalent Power of proper Manner, Gesture and Voice,
appear'd through the whole *Drama* a Youth of great Expectation,
Vivacity and Enterprize. The Soliloquy where he began the celebrated
Sentence of *To be, or not to be*; the Expostulation where he explains
with his Mother in her Closet; the noble Ardor after seeing his Father's
Ghost, and his generous Distress for the Death of *Ophelia*; are each of
them Circumstances which dwell strongly upon the Minds of the
Audience, and would certainly affect their Behaviour on any parallel

[1] *A.P.*, 102 f.

Occasions in their own Lives. Pray, Mr. *Bickerstaff*, let us have Virtue thus represented on the Stage with its proper Ornaments, or let these Ornaments be added to her in Places more sacred. As for my Part,' said he, 'I carry'd my Cousin *Jerry*, this little Boy, with me and shall always love the Child for his Partiality in all that concern'd the Fortune of *Hamlet*. This is entring Youth into the Affections and Passions of Manhood before-hand, and as it were antedating the Effects we hope from a long and liberal Education.'

★   ★   ★

No. 90 (4 November 1709)

★   ★   ★

I came home this Evening in a very pensive Mood; and to divert me took up a Volume of *Shakespeare*, where I chanc'd to cast my Eye upon a Part in the Tragedy of *Richard III* which fill'd my Mind with a very agreeable Horror. It was the Scene in which that bold but wicked Prince is represented as sleeping in his Tent, the Night before the Battle in which he fell. The Poet takes that Occasion to set before him in a Vision a terrible Assembly of Apparitions, the Ghosts of all those innocent Persons whom he is said to have murther'd. Prince *Edward*, *Henry VI*, the Duke of *Clarence*, *Rivers*, *Gray*, and *Vaughan*, Lord *Hastings*, the two young Princes, Sons to *Edward* the Fourth, his own Wife, and the Duke of *Buckingham*, rise up in their Blood before him, beginning their Speeches with that dreadful Salutation, *Let me sit heavy on thy Soul to Morrow*; and concluding with that dismal Sentence, *Despair and die*. This inspires the Tyrant with a Dream of his past Guilt and of the approaching Vengeance. He anticipates the fatal Day of *Bosworth*, fancies himself dismounted, weltring in his own Blood; and in the Agonies of Despair (before he is throughly awake) starts up with the following Speech:

> *Give me another Horse— Bind up my Wounds!*
> *Have Mercy Jesu— Soft, I did but dream.*
> *Oh Coward Conscience! How dost thou afflict me?*
> *The Lights burn blue! Is it not dead Midnight?*
> *Cold fearful Drops stand on my trembling Flesh;*
> *What do I fear? Myself! &c.*   [*Richard III*, 5.3.177 ff]

A Scene written with so great Strength of Imagination indispos'd me from further reading and threw me into a deep Contemplation.

I began to reflect upon the different Ends of good and bad Kings; and as this was the Birth-Day of our late Renown'd Monarch I could not forbear thinking on the Departure of that excellent Prince, whose Life was crown'd with Glory, and his Death with Peace. I let my Mind go so far into this Thought as to imagine to my self what might have been the Vision of his departing Slumbers. He might have seen Confederate Kings applauding him in different Languages, Slaves that had been bound in Fetters lifting up their Hands and blessing him, and the Persecuted in their several Forms of Worship imploring Comfort on his last Moments. The Reflection upon this excellent Prince's Mortality had been a very melancholy Entertainment to me had I not been re-liev'd by the Consideration of the glorious Reign which succeeds it.

We now see as great a Virtue as ever was on the *British* Throne, surrounded with all the Beauty of Success. Our Nation may not only boast of a long Series of great, regular, and well-laid Designs, but also of Triumphs and Victories; while we have the Happiness to see our Sovereign exercize that true Policy which tends to make a Kingdom great and happy, and at the same Time enjoy the good and glorious Effect of it.

No. 106 (12 December 1709)

*   *   *

We could not go on in our Treaty, by Reason of Two or Three Criticks that joined us. They had been talking, it seems, of the Two Letters which were found in the Coffin and mentioned in one of my late Lucubrations, and came with a Request to me that I would com-municate any others of them that were legible. One of the Gentlemen was pleased to say that it was a very proper Instance of a Widow's Constancy; and said he wished I had subjoined, as a Foil to it, the following Passage in *Hamlet*. The young Prince was not yet acquainted with all the Guilt of his Mother, but turns his Thoughts on her sudden Forgetfulness of his Father and the Indecency of her hasty Marriage.

> —*That it should come to this!*
> *But Two Months dead! Nay, not so much, not Two!*
> *So excellent a King! That was to this*
> *Hyperion to a Satyr! So loving to my Mother!*
> *That he permitted not the Winds of Heav'n*
> *To visit her Face too roughly! Heav'n and Earth!*
> *Must I remember? Why she would hang on him!*

As if Increase of Appetite had grown
By what it fed on! And yet, within a Month!
Let me not think on't— Frailty, thy Name is Woman!
A little Month! Or ere those Shoes were old,
With which she follow'd my poor Father's Body,
Like Niobe all Tears; Why she! ev'n she!
Oh Heav'n! a Brute, that wants Discourse of Reason,
Would have mourn'd longer!— Married with mine Uncle!
My Father's Brother! But no more like my Father,
Than I to Hercules! Within a Month!
Ere yet the Salt of most unrighteous Tears,
Had left the Flushing of her gauled Eyes,
She marry'd— O most wicked Speed! To post
With such Dexterity to incestuous Sheets!
It is not, nor it cannot come to Good!
But break, my Heart; for I must hold my Tongue!

[*Hamlet*, 1.2.137 ff]

The several Emotions of Mind and Breaks of Passion in this Speech are admirable. He has touched every Circumstance that aggravated the Fact and seemed capable of hurrying the Thoughts of a Son into Distraction. His Father's Tenderness for his Mother, expressed in so delicate a Particular; his Mother's Fondness for his Father no less exquisitely described; the great and amiable Figure of his dead Parent drawn by a true Filial Piety; his Disdain of so unworthy a Successor to his Bed; but above all the Shortness of the Time between his Father's Death and his Mother's Second Marriage, brought together with so much Disorder, make up as noble a Part as any in that celebrated Tragedy. The Circumstance of Time I never could enough admire. The Widowhood had lasted Two Months. This is his First Reflection. But as his Indignation rises, he sinks to 'scarce Two Months'; Afterwards into 'a Month'; and at last, into a 'Little Month'. But all this so naturally that the Reader accompanies him in the Violence of his Passion and finds the Time lessen insensibly, according to the different Workings of his Disdain. I have not mentioned the Incest of her Marriage, which is so obvious a Provocation, but can't forbear taking Notice that when his Fury is at it's Height he cries, *Frailty, thy Name is Woman!* As railing at the Sex in general, rather than giving himself Leave to think his Mother worse than others.— *Desiderantur multa.*

*   *   *

No. 111 (23 December 1709)

The Watchman, who does me particular Honours as being the chief Man in the Lane, gave so very great a Thump at my Door last Night that I awakened at the Knock and heard my self complimented with the usual Salutation of, *Good morrow Mr.* Bickerstaff, *Good morrow my Masters all.* The Silence and Darkness of the Night disposed me to be more than ordinarily serious; and as my Attention was not drawn out among exterior Objects by the Avocations of Sense my Thoughts naturally fell upon my self. I was considering, amidst the Stillness of the Night, what was the proper Employment of a thinking Being? What were the Perfections it should propose to it self? And, What the End it should aim at? My Mind is of such a particular Cast that the Falling of a Shower of Rain or the Whistling of Wind at such a Time is apt to fill my Thoughts with something awful and solemn. I was in this Disposition, when our Bellman began his Midnight Homily (which he has been repeating to us every Winter Night for these Twenty Years) with the usual Exordium.

> *Oh! mortal Man, thou that art born in Sin!*

Sentiments of this Nature, which are in themselves just and reasonable however debased by the Circumstances that accompany them, do not fail to produce their natural Effect in a Mind that is not perverted and depraved by wrong Notions of Gallantry, Politeness, and Ridicule.

The Temper which I now found my self in, as well as the Time of the Year, put me in Mind of those Lines in *Shakespeare* wherein, according to his agreeable Wildness of Imagination, he has wrought a Country Tradition into a beautiful Piece of Poetry. In the Tragedy of *Hamlet*, where the Ghost vanishes upon the Cock's Crowing, he takes Occasion to mention its Crowing all Hours of the Night about *Christmas* Time and to insinuate a Kind of religious Veneration for that Season.

> *It faded on the Crowing of the Cock.*
> *Some say, That ever 'gainst that Season comes*
> *Wherein our Saviour's Birth is celebrated,*
> *The Bird of Dawning singeth all Night long;*
> *And then, they say, no Spirit dares walk abroad:*
> *The Nights are wholesom then, no Planets strike,*
> *No Fairy takes, no Witch has Power to charm;*
> *So hallowed, and so gracious is the Time.*
>
> [*Hamlet*, 1.1.157 ff]

This admirable Author, as well as the best and greatest Men of all Ages and of all Nations, seems to have had his Mind throughly seasoned with Religion, as is evident by many Passages in his Plays that would not be suffered by a modern Audience; and are therefore certain Instances that the Age he lived in had a much greater Sense of Virtue than the present.

★ ★ ★

No. 167 (2 May 1710)

Having received Notice that the famous Actor Mr. *Betterton* was to be interred this Evening in the Cloysters near *Westminster Abbey*, I was resolved to walk thither and see the last Office done to a Man whom I had always very much admired, and from whose Action I had received more strong Impressions of what is great and noble in Human Nature than from the Arguments of the most solid Philosophers or the Descriptions of the most charming Poets I have ever read. As the rude and untaught Multitude are no Way wrought upon more effectually than by seeing publick Punishments and Executions, so Men of Letters and Education feel their Humanity most forcibly exercised when they attend the Obsequies of Men who had arrived at any Perfection in Liberal Accomplishments. Theatrical Action is to be esteemed as such, except it be objected that we cannot call that an Art which cannot be attained by Art. Voice, Stature, Motion, and other Gifts must be very bountifully bestowed by Nature, or Labour and Industry will but push the unhappy Endeavourer in that Way the further off his Wishes. . . .

I have hardly a Notion that any Performer of Antiquity could surpass the Action of Mr. *Betterton* in any of the Occasions in which he has appeared on our Stage. The wonderful Agony which he appeared in when he examined the Circumstance of the Handkerchief of *Othello*, the Mixture of Love that intruded upon his Mind upon the innocent Answers *Desdemona* makes, betrayed in his Gesture such a Variety and Vicissitude of Passions as would admonish a Man to be afraid of his own Heart, and perfectly convince him that it is to stab it to admit that worst of Daggers, Jealousy. Whoever reads in his Closet this admirable Scene will find that he cannot, except he has as warm an Imagination as *Shakespeare* himself, find any but dry, incoherent, and broken Sentences. But a Reader that has seen *Betterton* act it observes there could not be a Word added, that longer Speech had been unnatural, nay impossible to be uttered in *Othello*'s Circumstances. The charming

Passage in the same Tragedy where he tells the Manner of winning the Affection of his Mistress was urged with so moving and graceful an Energy that, while I walked in the Cloysters, I thought of him with the same Concern as if I waited for the Remains of a Person who had in real Life done all that I had seen him represent.

The Gloom of the Place, and faint Lights before the Ceremony appeared, contributed to the melancholy Disposition I was in; and I began to be extremely afflicted that *Brutus* and *Cassius* had any Difference; that *Hotspur*'s Gallantry was so unfortunate; and that the Mirth and good Humour of *Falstaff* could not exempt him from the Grave. Nay this Occasion in me, who look upon the Distinctions amongst Men to be meerly Scenical, raised Reflections upon the Emptiness of all Human Perfection and Greatness in general; and I could not but regret that the Sacred Heads which lie buried in the Neighbourhood of this little Portion of Earth in which my poor old Friend is deposited are returned to Dust as well as he, and that there is no Difference in the Grave between the Imaginary and the Real Monarch. This made me say of Human Life it self, with *Macbeth*,

> *To Morrow, to Morrow, and to Morrow,*
> *Creeps in a stealing Pace from Day to Day,*
> *To the last Moment of recorded Time!*
> *And all our Yesterdays have lighted Fools*
> *To their eternal Night! Out, out short Candle!*
> *Life's but a walking Shadow, a poor Player*
> *That struts and frets his Hour upon the Stage,*
> *And then is heard no more.* [5.5.19 ff]

* * *

No. 188 (21 June 1709)

* * *

This Letter is a natural Picture of ordinary Contracts, and of the Sentiments of those Minds that lie under a Kind of intellectual Rusticity. This trifling Occasion made me run over in my Imagination the many Scenes I have observed of the married Condition, wherein the Quintessence of Pleasure and Pain are represented as they accompany that State and no other. It is certain there are a Thousand Thousand like the above-mentioned Yeoman and his Wife, who are never highly pleased or distasted in their whole Lives. But when we consider the more informed Part of Mankind and look upon their Behaviour, it then appears that very little of their Time is indifferent, but generally spent in the most anxious Vexation or the highest Satisfaction.

Shakespeare has admirably represented both the Aspects of this State in the most excellent Tragedy of *Othello*. In the Character of *Desdemona* he runs through all the Sentiments of a virtuous Maid and a tender Wife. She is captivated by his Virtue, and faithful to him, as well from that Motive as Regard to her own Honour. *Othello* is a great and noble Spirit, misled by the Villany of a false Friend to suspect her Innocence and resents it accordingly. When after the many Instances of Passion the Wife is told her Husband is jealous, her Simplicity makes her incapable of believing it and say, after such Circumstances as would drive another Woman into Distraction,

> *I think the Sun where he was born,*
> *Drew all such Humours from him.*   [3.4.27 f]

This Opinion of him is so just that his noble and tender Heart beats it self to Pieces before he can affront her with the Mention of his Jealousy; and owns, this Suspicion has blotted out all the Sense of Glory and Happiness which before it was possessed with, when he laments himself in the warm Allusions of a Mind accustomed to Entertainments so very different from the Pangs of Jealousy and Revenge. How moving is his Sorrow! He cries out as follows:

> *I had been happy, if the general Camp,*
> *Pioneers and all, had tasted her sweet Body,*
> *So I had nothing known. Oh now! for ever*
> *Farewel the Tranquil Mind! Farewel Content,*
> *Farewel the plumed Troops, and the big Wars,*
> *That make Ambition Virtue! Oh Farewel!*
> *Farewel the neighing Steed and the shrill Trump,*
> *The Spirit-stirring Drum, th' Ear-piercing Fife,*
> *The Royal Banner, and all Quality,*
> *Pride, Pomp, and Circumstance, of glorious War!*
> *And Oh ye Mortal Engines! whose rude Throats*
> *Th' Immortal Jove's dead Clamours counterfeit,*
> *Farewel! Othello's Occupation's gone.*   [3.3.349 ff]

I believe I may venture to say there is not in any other Part of *Shakespeare*'s Works more strong and lively Pictures of Nature than in this. I shall therefore steal *incog.* to see it, out of Curiosity to observe how *Wilks* and *Cibber* touch those Places where *Betterton* and *Sandford* so very highly excelled. . . .

49. Henry Felton on Shakespeare's genius

1709

From *A Dissertation on Reading the Classics, And Forming a Just Style. Written in the Year 1709* . . . (1713).

Henry Felton (1679–1740), clergyman, became Master of St Edmund Hall, Oxford, in 1722, and published numerous theological works. This small handbook had reached its fifth edition by 1753.

Shakespeare is a wonderful Genius, a single Instance of the Force of Nature, and the Strength of Wit. Nothing can be greater and more lively than his Thoughts; nothing nobler and more forcible than his Expression. The Fire of his Fancy breaketh out into his Words and sets his Reader on a Flame. He maketh the Blood run cold or warm, and is so admirable a Master of the Passions that he raises Your Courage, Your Pity, and Your Fear, at his Pleasure; but he delighteth most in Terror. (212–13)

50. Charles Gildon, Shakespeare's life and works

1710

From (a) *An Essay on the Art, Rise and Progress of the Stage in Greece, Rome and England*, and (b) *Remarks on the Plays of Shakespeare*, both prefixed to *The Works of Mr. William Shakespeare. Volume the Seventh* (1710).

Rowe's edition of Shakespeare, in six volumes, was published in 1709 by Tonson; in the following year Curll brought out a spurious 'volume seven' which was designed to fill the gaps in Rowe's edition by including the poems and two long essays. Charles Gildon thus became the first critic to write an extended critical commentary on all the works of Shakespeare: see the account of it by George Sewell (No. 72 below).

[(a): From *An Essay on the Art . . . of the stage*]

. . . I shall here say a few Words of the Author, and then of his Works. I confess that I have nothing to add to his Life, written by Mr. *Rowe*, who has perfectly exhausted that Subject; yet he has, by declining a general and full Criticism, left me Room enough to discourse both of the Author's Genius and his Writings. As I shall give many more Examples of his Beauties than those few which his Editor has but very slightly glanc'd on in his Life, so shall I lay down such Rules of Art that the Reader may be able to distinguish his *Errors* from his *Perfections*, now too much and too unjustly confounded by the foolish Biggotry of his blind and partial Adorers. For there are a sort of Men who deal by him as some of our Modern Dedicators do by their Patrons, denying them all Defects and at the same Time dawbing them with shining Qualities which they do not only not possess but have no need of to compleat their Character; by so childish a Conduct not only bringing into Question those which are really their Due but making their Patrons as ridiculous as themselves. For an unjust or ill-grounded Praise of the *Living* is no better than fulsome Flattery, and of the *Dead* only a meer assuming Compliment to our selves as Men of greater Genius, Discernment, and Penetration than others in the Discovery of Beauties which they are not able to find out. This is the very Fault which those *Modernists* lay to the Charge of the Admirers of the *Antients*. For while they wou'd perswade us that these have given Beauties to *Homer*, *Virgil*, *Horace*, &c. which those Poets never thought of or design'd, they advanc'd so unreasonable a Biggotry to our Poet that if a Man by Art and Reason but question the greatest and most absurd of his Faults, with the *Romans* of old on the same Occasion —*Clamant periisse Pudorem.*[1]

'Tis my opinion that if *Shakespeare* had had those Advantages of Learning which the perfect Knowledge of the Ancients wou'd have given him, so great a *Genius* as his wou'd have made him a very dangerous Rival in Fame to the greatest Poets of Antiquity, so far am I from seeing how this Knowledge cou'd either have curb'd, confin'd, or spoil'd the natural Excellence of his Writings. For tho' I must always think our Author a Miracle for the Age he liv'd in yet I am oblig'd, in Justice to *Reason* and *Art*, to confess that he does not come up to the Ancients in all the Beauties of the *Drama*. But it is no small Honour to him that he has surpass'd them in the *Topics* or *Common Places*. And to confirm the Victory he obtain'd on that Head at Mr. *Hales*'s Chamber at *Eton* I shall, in this present Undertaking, not only transcribe the most shining but refer the Reader to the same Subjects in the *Latin* Authors.

This I do that I might omit nothing that cou'd do his Memory that Justice which he really deserves. But to put his Errors and his Excellencies on the same Bottom is to injure the Latter, and give the Enemies of our Poet an Advantage against him of doing the same; that is, of rejecting his Beauties as all of a Piece with his Faults. This unaccountable Biggotry of the Town to the very Errors of *Shakespeare* was the Occasion of Mr. *Rymer*'s Criticisms, and drove him as far into the contrary Extream. I am far from approving his Manner of treating our Poet, tho' Mr. *Dryden* owns that all or most of the Faults he has found are Just, but adds this odd Reflection: and yet, says he, who minds the Critick and who admires *Shakespeare* less? That was as much as to say, Mr. *Rymer* has indeed made good his Charge, and yet the Town admir'd his Errors still: which I take to be a greater Proof of the Folly and abandon'd Taste of the Town than of any Imperfections in the *Critic*. Which in my Opinion expos'd the Ignorance of the Age he

[1] Horace, *Epistles*, 2.1.80: 'nearly all our elders would cry out that modesty is dead'.

liv'd in, to which Mr. *Rowe* very justly ascribes most of his Faults. It must be own'd that Mr. *Rymer* carried the Matter too far, since no Man that has the least Relish of Poetry can question his *Genius*. For in spite of his known and visible Errors, when I read *Shakespeare*, even in some of his most irregular Plays, I am surpriz'd into a Pleasure so great that my Judgment is no longer free to see the Faults, tho' they are never so Gross and Evident. There is such a Witchery in him that all the Rules of Art which he does not observe, tho' built on an equally Solid and Infallible Reason, vanish away in the Transports of those that he does observe, so entirely as if I had never known any thing of the Matter. The Pleasure, I confess, is peculiar as strong, for it comes from the admirable Draughts of the Manners visible in the Distinction of his Characters, and his surprizing Reflections and Topics, which are often extreamly heightned by the Expression and Harmony of Numbers; for in these no Man ever excell'd him and very few ever came up to his Merit. Nor is his Nice touching the Passion of Joy the least Source of this Satisfaction, for he frequently moves this, in some of the most Indifferent of his Plays, so strongly that it is impossible to quell the Emotion. There is likewise ever a Sprightliness in his Dialogue and often a Genteelness, especially in his *Much ado about Nothing*, which is very surprizing for that Age, and what the Learned BEN [Jonson] cou'd not attain by all his Industry; and I confess, if we make some small Allowance for a few Words and Expressions, I question whether any one has since excell'd him in it.

Tho' all these Beauties were owing chiefly to a natural Strength of Genius in him yet I can never give up his Acquaintance with the Ancients so entirely as Mr. *Rowe* has done; because I think there are many Arguments to prove that he knew at least some of the *Latin* Poets, particularly *Ovid*, two of his Epistles[1] being here translated by him. His Motto to *Venus and Adonis* is another Proof; but that he had read *Plautus* himself is plain from his *Comedy of Errors*, which is taken visibly from the *Menachmi* of that Poet, as will be evident when we come to consider that Play. The Characters he has in his Plays drawn of the *Romans* is a Proof that he was acquainted with their Historians, and *Ben* himself, in his Commendatory Verses before the first Folio Edition of *Shakespeare*'s Works, allows him to have a little *Latin* and less *Greek*. That is, he wou'd not allow him to be as perfect a Critic in the

---

[1] Two poems printed in this 'seventh volume' of Shakespeare were the *Amorous Epistle of Paris to Helen* and *Helen to Paris*. In fact, they were written by Thomas Heywood, as Farmer showed in 1767.

Latin as he himself was, but yet that he was capable of reading at least the *Latin* Poets—as is, I think, plainly prov'd. For I can see no manner of Weight in that Conjecture which supposes that he never read the Ancients because he has not any where imitated them, so fertile a Genius as his having no need to borrow Images from others which had such plenty of his own. Besides, we find by Experience that some of our Modern Authors, nay those who have made great Figures in the University for their Wit and Learning, have so little follow'd the Ancients in their Performances that by them a Man cou'd never ghess that they had read a Word of them, and yet they wou'd take it amiss not to be allow'd to be very well read both in the *Latin* and *Greek* Poets. If they do this in their Writings out of Pride or want of Capacity, may we not as justly suppose that *Shakespeare* did it out of an Abundance in his own Natural Stock? I contend not here to prove that he was a perfect Master of either the *Latin* or *Greek* Authors, but all that I aim at is to shew that as he was capable of reading some of the *Romans* so he had actually read *Ovid* and *Plautus* without spoiling or Confining his *Fancy* or *Genius*.

Whether his Ignorance of the Ancients were a Disadvantage to him or no, may admit of a Dispute.[1] I am surpriz'd at the Assertion, unless he [Rowe] mean That all things may be argu'd upon and that the Problems of *Euclid*, so long admitted as indisputable, may by a New Sort of Scepticism be call'd in Question. The Reason he assigns for this, is thus—*For, tho' the Knowledge of them, might have made him more Correct; yet it is not improbable, but that the Regularity and Deference for them, which would have attended that Correctness, might have restrain'd some of that Fire, Impetuosity, and even Beautiful Extravagance, which we admire in* SHAKESPEARE. I must own that I am not capable of comprehending his [Rowe's] Proof, or that indeed it is any Proof at all, for if the Knowledge of the Ancients wou'd have made him *Correct* it wou'd have given him the only Perfection he wanted, and that is certainly an Advantage not to be disputed. But then this *Correctedness* MIGHT *have restrain'd some of that Fire, Impetuosity, and even* BEAUTIFUL EXTRAVAGANCE, &c. We do not find that *Correctness* in *Homer, Virgil, Sophocles, Euripides,* &c. restrain'd any Fire that was truly Celestial, and why we shou'd think that it wou'd have had a worse Effect on *Shakespeare* I cannot imagine; nor do I understand what is meant by *Beautiful Extravagance*. For if it be something beyond Nature it is so far from being admir'd by Men of *Sense* that it is contemn'd and laugh'd at.

[1] Cf. Rowe's *Preface*, above, p. 191.

For what there is in any Poem which is out of Nature, and contrary to *Verisimilitude* and *Probability*, can never be *Beautiful* but *Abominable*. For the Business of Poetry is to copy Nature truely and observe *Probability* and *Verisimilitude* justly, and the Rules of Art are to shew us what Nature is and how to distinguish its Lineaments from the unruly and presposterous Sallies and Flights of an irregular and uninstructed Fancy. So that, as I think it is plain that *Shakespeare* was not entirely ignorant of the Ancients so I believe it is as evident that he wou'd have been much more, not less, perfect than he is had his Ignorance of them been much less than it really was. A judicious Reader of our Author will easily discover those Defects, that his Beauties wou'd make him wish had been corrected by a Knowledge of the whole *Art* of the *Drama*. For it is evident that by the Force of his own Judgment or the Strength of his Imagination he has follow'd the *Rules* of Art in all those Particulars in which he pleases. I know that the *Rules of Art* have been sufficiently clamour'd against by an ignorant and thoughtless sort of Men of our Age, but it was because they knew nothing of them, and never consider'd that without some Standard of Excellence there cou'd be no Justice done to Merit to which Poetasters and Poets must else have an equal Claim, which is the highest Degree of Barbarism. Nay, without an Appeal to these very Rules *Shakespeare* himself is not to be distinguish'd from the most worthless Pretenders, who have often met with an undeserv'd Applause and challenge the Title of Great Poets from their Success.

Nature, Nature, is the great Cry against the Rules. We must be judg'd by *Nature*, say they, not at all considering that *Nature* is an equivocal Word, whose Sense is too various and Extensive ever to be able to appeal to since it leaves it to the Fancy and Capacity of every one to decide what is according to Nature and what not. Besides, there may be a great many things Natural which Dramatick Poetry has nothing to do with. To do the Needs of Life is as natural as any Action of it, but to bring such a thing into a Piece of History Painting or Dramatic Poetry wou'd be monstrous and absur'd, tho' natural; for there may be many things natural in their proper Places which are not so in others. It is therefore necessary that there shou'd be Rules to let the Poet know not only what is natural but when it is proper to be introduc'd and when not. The Droll Pieces of the Dutch are all very natural, yet I dare believe there is no Man so very ignorant of the Decorum of History Painting as to think that in the *Tent of Darius* of Monsieur *Le Brun* or the *Jephtha's Sacrifice* it wou'd be natural or proper to Introduce one of those Droll Pieces, either of Drinking, dancing, snick or snee, or the like. For tho' both the Painters have propos'd Nature for their Copy and have drawn her perfectly well, yet Grief and Laughter are so very incompatible that to join these two Copies of Nature together wou'd be monstrous and shocking to any Judicious Eye. And yet this Absurdity is what is done so commonly among us in our *Tragi-Comedies*; this is what our *Shakespeare* himself has frequently been guilty of, not only in those mixtures which he has given us of that kind but in many other Particulars for want of a thorough knowledge of the Art of the Stage. (ii–x)

* * *

[On the rules] The later end of this is perfectly prov'd by our *Shake-speare*, who in all that pleases is exactly conformable to the Rules, tho' 'tis evident by his Defects that he knew nothing of them. (xxv)

* * *

Nature enabl'd *Shakespeare* to succeed in the *Manners* and Diction often to Perfection, but he cou'd never by his Force of Genius or Nature vanquish the barbarous Mode of the Times and come to any Excellence in the *Fable*, except in the *Merry Wives of Windsor* and the *Tempest*.

Next to the Fable the *Manners* are the most considerable (and in these *Shakespeare* has generally excell'd, as will be seen when we come to his plays). For as *Tragedy* is the Imitation of an *Action* so there are no *Actions* without the *Manners*, since the *Manners* are the Cause of Actions. By the *Manners* we discover the Inclinations of the Speaker, what Part, Side, or Course he will take on any important and difficult Emergence, and know how he will behave himself before we see his Actions. Thus we know from the Manners of *Achilles* what Answer he will give the Ambassadors of *Agamemnon* by what the Poet has told us of his *Heroe*. And when *Mercury* brings *Jove*'s Orders to *Æneas* we know that the *Piety* of the Heroe will prevail over *Love*. And the Character of *Oedipus* makes us expect his extravagant Passions and the Excesses he will commit by his Obstinacy. Those Discourses therefore that do not do this are without the *Manners*. The Character of *Coriolanus* in *Shakespeare* prepares us to expect the Resolution he will take to disoblige the People, for Pride naturally contemns Inferiours and over-values it self. The same may be said of *Tybalt* in *Romeo and Juliet*, and most of the Characters of this Poet.

The *Sentiments* are the next in degree of Excellence to the *Fable* and the *Manners*, and justly demand the third place in our Care and Study, for those are for the *Manners* as the *Manners* for the *Subject Fable*. The Action can't be justly imitated without the *Manners*, nor the Manners express'd without the *Sentiments*. In these we must regard Truth and Verisimilitude, as when the Poet make a Madman speak exactly as a Madman does, or as 'tis probable he wou'd do. This *Shakespeare* has admirably perform'd in the Madness of King *Lear*, where the Cause of his Frenzy is ever uppermost and mingles with all he says or does. (xxxiii–xxxiv)

*   *   *

For to make a good *Tragedy*, that is, a *just Imitation*, the Action imitated ought not in reality to be longer than the Representation; for by that Means it has the more Likeness and by Consequence is the more perfect. But as there are Actions of ten or twelve Hours, and their Representations cannot possibly be so long, then must we bring in some of the Incidents in the Intervals of the Acts the better to deceive the Audience, who cannot be impos'd on with such tedious and long Actions as we have generally on the Stage, as whole Lives, and many Actions of the same Man, where the *Probable* is lost as well as the *Necessary*. And in this our *Shakespeare* is every where faulty through the Ignorant Mode of the Age in which he liv'd, and which I instance not as a Reproach to his Memory but only to warn the Reader or young Poet to avoid the same Error.

Having shewn what an *Action* is we now come more closely to the *Subject*, and first to the Unity of the Action, which can never be broke without destroying the Poem. This *Unity* is not preserv'd by the Representation of several Actions of *one* Man, as of *Julius Cæsar*, or *Antony* and *Brutus*. Thus in the *Julius Cæsar* of *Shakespeare* there is not only the Action of *Caesar*'s Death, where the Play ought to have ended, but many other Subsequent Actions of *Antony* and *Brutus* even to the Overthrow and Death of *Brutus* and *Cassius*. And the Poet might as well have carried it down to the Settling of the Empire in *Augustus*, or indeed to the fall of the *Roman* Empire in *Augustulus*, for there was no more Reason for the *Ending* it where he does than at the Establishment of *Augustus*. Natural Reason indeed show'd to *Shakespeare* the Absurdity of making the Representation longer than the *Time*, and the *Place* more extensive than the Place of acting, as is plain from his *Choruses* in his Historical Plays, in which he apologizes for the Absurdity, as in the Beginning of the fourth Act of *The Winter's Tale* among other things. *Time*, the *Chorus*, says

> —*Your Patience this allowing*
> *I turn my Glass, and give my Scene such growing*
> *As you had slept between, &c.* [4.1.15 ff]

And the [Third] Act of *Henry V* begins another *Chorus* excusing the variation of the Place.

> *Thus with imagin'd Wings our first Scene flies*
> *In motion of no less Celerity*
> *Than that of Thought. Suppose that you have seen*
> *The well appointed King at* Dover *Pier, &c.* [3.Prol.1 ff]

And so goes on to describe all his Passage &c., introducing a Narration to supply the Gap of the Action, or rather in the Actions. But that *Chorus* of the fifth Act is plainer on this Head.

> *Vouchsafe to those, that have not read the Story,*
> *That I may prompt them; and of such as have*
> *I humbly pray them to admit th' Excuse*
> *Of* TIME, *of Numbers, and true Course of things*
> *Which cannot in their Huge and proper Life*
> *Be here presented, &c.* [5.Prol.1 ff]

In *Pericles, Prince of Tyre*, the *Choruses* excuse the Rambling from Place to Place and the like. But 'tis pity that his Discovery of the Absurdity did not bring him to avoid it rather than make an Apology for it. But this is not the only Fault of the way of Writing in his Time which he did not correct, for in the *Chorus* of the [fourth] Act of *Henry V* he concludes in this Manner:

> *And so our Scene must to the Battle fly;*
> *Where O! for pity, we shall much disgrace*
> *With four or five most vile and ragged Foils*
> *(Right ill dispos'd, in Brawl ridiculous)*
> *The Name of* Agincourt. *Yet sit and see*
> *Minding true things by what their Mock'ries be.* [4.Prol.48 ff]

Hence it is plain that *Shakespeare*'s good Sense perceiv'd the ridiculous Absurdity of our fighting Scenes, our Drum and Trumpetting Scenes, but he chose to go on in the Way that he found beaten to his Hands because he unhappily knew no better Road.

But to return from this short Digression.— This *Unity of Action* does not exclude the *Episodes* or various under-Actions which are dependent on, and contribute to the chief, and which without it are nothing. Thus a Painter represents in a Battle Piece the Actions of every particular that makes up the Army, but all these compose that main Action of the Battle. But this does not excuse the faulty *Episodes* or *underplots* (as they call them) of our *English* Plays, which are distinct Actions and contribute nothing at all to the principal. Of this kind is *Creon* and *Eurydice*, and *Adrastus* in our lamentable *Oedipus*. But indeed we have few Plays free from this Absurdity, of which the *Orphan* is one where the Action is *one*, and every Episode, Part or under-Action carries on and contributes to the *Main Action* or *Subject*.

Thus the different Actions of different Men are not more distinctly different Actions than those of *One Man* at different Times. And we might as well make a *Unity* of all the Actions in the World as of those of *One Man*. No Action of the same Man can be brought into a Tragedy but that which necessarily or probably relates to that Action which the Tragedy imitates. The Wound of *Ulysses* which he receiv'd in *Parnassus* was necessary to his Discovery, but his Madness to avoid the War was not, and therefore *Homer* takes Notice of the former but not of the later. For as in all other *Imitations* so in *Tragedy*, the thing *imitated* must be but One. This *Action* with its *Episodes* or *under-Actions* ought to be so link'd together that to take any Part away or to endeavour to transpose them destroys the whole: for these *Episodes* or *under Actions* ought either Necessarily or probably to be produc'd by the main Action, as the Death of *Patroclus* by the Anger of *Achilles*. For whatever can be put in or left out without causing a sensible Change can never be part of the Action. This is a sure Rule to distinguish the true Episodes from the false. And this Rule will indeed condemn most of our *English Tragedies*, in some of which the very principal Character may be left out and the Play never the worse. But more of that hereafter. From what has been said of the *Action main* and *Episodic* it is plain that the Poet is not oblig'd to relate things just as they happen but as they might or ought to have happen'd, that is, the Action ought to be general and Allegoric, not particular, for Particular Actions can have no general Influence. (xxxviii–xlii)

*   *   *

The Manners therefore of the principal Persons, at least, ought to be so clearly and fully mark'd as to distinguish them from all other Men, for Nature has made as great a Distinction between every individual Man by the Turn of his Mind as by the Form of his Countenance. In this *Shakespeare* has excell'd all the Poets, for he has not only distinguish'd his principal Persons but there is scarce a Messenger comes in but is visibly different from all the Rest of the Persons in the Play. So that you need not to mention the Names of the Person that speaks when you read the Play, the Manners of the Persons will sufficiently inform you who it is speaks; whereas in our Modern Poets if the Name of the Person speaking be not read you can never by what he says distinguish one from the Other. (li)

* * *

[On the appropriate verse-forms for Tragedy]

. . . the first Verse of the earliest Tragedies were *Tetrameters* or a Sort of Burlesque, and fit for Country mens Songs, and not unlike our *Dogrel*. But on the Reforming the Stage it was turn'd into *Trimeter Iambics*, for as *Dacier* from *Aristotle* observes, those Numbers were fittest for *Tragedy* which were most like our common Discourse, and consequently it was *Trimeter Iambics*, for that was most us'd in familiar Conversation; and *Tragedy*, says he, being an Imitation ought to admit nothing but what is easy and Natural.

But as this seems to relate chiefly to the *Greek* and Latin Diction so it will not be amiss to give you something like it in the *English* at the Rise of the *Drama* here. I shall take the Examples of both from *Shakespeare* alone, to show this Error mended by himself and brought to such a Perfection that the highest praise is to imitate his Stile.

What they call'd their *Tetrameters* may be answer'd by the *Dogrel* in the *Comedy of Errors* and *Love's Labour's Lost*.

Bal. *Good Meat, Sir, is common, that every Churle affords.*
E. Ant. *And Welcome more common, for that's nothing but Words.*
S. Drom. *Either get thee from the Door, or sit down at the Hatch.*
Dost thou conjure for Wenches, that thou call'st for such Store
When One is one too many? go get thee from the Door.

[*Comedy of Errors*, 3.1.24 ff]

But lest this shou'd be thought passable in the Mouths of the *Dromios* and their Masters we shall see in those of Lords and Princes, in *Love's Labour's Lost*, first *Boyet* of the Retinue of the Princess of *France*, and the Princess her self:

Princess. *It was well done of you to take him at his Word.*
Boyet. *I was as willing to graple, as he was to board.*
Maria one of the ⎱ *Two hot Sheeps, Marry, and therefore not Ships.*
Ladies of Honour. ⎰
Boyet. *No Sheep, sweet Lamb, unless we feed on your Lips.*
Princess. *Good Wits will be jangling, but Genteels agree—*
The civil War of Wits were much better us'd
On NAVARRE, and his Book men, for here 'tis abus'd.

[*Love's Labour's Lost*, 2.1.217 ff]

In short, these false Numbers and Rhimes are almost through the whole Play, which must confirm any One that this was one of his first. But that Verse which answers both the *Latin* and the *Greek* is our *Blank Verse*, which generally consists of *Iambics*, and so fit for the *Drama* that tho' Mr. *Dryden* had once brought Rhiming on the Stage so much into Fashion that he told us plainly in one of his Prefaces that we shou'd scarce see a Play take in this Age without it, yet as soon as the *Rehearsal* was acted the violent and unnatural Mode vanish'd and *Blank Verse* resum'd its Place. A thousand beautiful Examples of this Verse might be taken out of *Shakespeare*, there scarce being a Play of his which will not furnish us with many. I shall satisfy my self here with an Instance or two out of the *Much Ado about Nothing*.

And bid her steal into the pleached Bower,
Where honeysuckles, ripened by the sun,
Forbid the sun to enter—like favourites,
Made proud by princes, that advance their pride
Against the power that bred it. . . . (lxii–lxiv)

[*Much Ado about Nothing*, 3.1.7 ff]

*　　*　　*

[(b) From *Remarks on the Plays of Shakespeare*]

Mr. *Rowe* has very well observ'd that the *Fable* is not the Province of the *Dramma* in which the Strength and Mastery of *Shakespeare* lies, yet I shall give a Scheme of all his Plots, that so we may the more easily see how far he has succeeded by the Force of Nature and where he has fail'd. I begin in the Order in which they are printed in this new Edition. And in the First we find his *Tempest*.

[The 'Argument or Fable' is summarised]

I can't find that this Plot was taken from any Novel, at least not from any that Mr. *Langbaine* had seen, who was very conversant with Books of that Nature. But it does not at all follow that there was no such Story in any of the Books of his Time which might never reach our Age, nor is it of much Importance.

Tho' the Fable of this Play must come short of Perfection in some Particulars yet I must say this, that we have few on the *English* Stage that can compare with it for Excellence. For first it is the Imitation of one Action, i.e. *The Restoration of* Prospero *to his Dutchy of* Milan. The Action is of a just Extent, for it has a *Beginning, Middle* and *End.* The casting away of the K. of *Naples, Antonio,* &c. on the Enchanted Island is plainly the Beginning, since to this there is nothing necessary to be before; it is the Sequel, indeed, of something else, but not the Effect. Thus their being cast on the Coast produces all that happens to them till the Discovery, which is the *Middle*; and when *Prospero* is reconcil'd by their Sufferings, and his Passions abated, the *Middle*—which is their Sufferings—produces the End in the Reconciliation of the Parties. Here is likewise in this Fable a *Peripetie* and *Discovery.* For the State, Condition, and Fortune of the King is chang'd from the extreamest Misery to Happiness by the *Discovery of* Prospero and *Ferdinand.* 'Tis true the Discovery of *Prospero* is not so fine as that of *Ulysses* by the Nurse, but it is e'ry whit as good as the *Discovery* that *Ulysses* makes of himself to the Shepherds. There is a perfect Unity in the Action and in the Time, which tho' a little confusedly express'd (which I attribute to the repeated Errors of the Editors, not to *Shakespeare*) yet it is concluded by *Alonso* and the Sailors to be but three Hours. . . . The whole Time from the raising the Storm to the End of the Play is but six Hours. The Play plainly opens at the very End of the Storm, so that we cannot suppose it more than three Hours and a half; which is far more Regular in that Particular than any that I know of on the Stage. The Unity of Place is not quite so regular, and yet we have few Plays that excell it even in this Particular. But if the Scene of the Storm were out, and which has very little to do there, the Place wou'd be brought into much a less Compass, and the several Scenes may very well be allow'd to be reasonably suppos'd pretty contiguous. At least when two Gentlemen set themselves to alter a Poet of *Shakespeare*'s Genius, one wou'd expect that they shou'd endeavour to correct his Errors, not to add more. It had been extreamly easy for Sir *William* and Mr. *Dryden* to have remedy'd this Particular, which they have not at all attempted, nay they have added nothing but what makes their

Composition not only much less perfect but infinitely more Extravagant than this Poem which they pretend to alter; as I shall show when I come to the Characters. *Shakespeare* had met with this Fortune in many of his Plays, while Mr. *D——y*, and Mr. *C——b——r*[1] have only given us their wise Whimseys for what they blotted out of the Poet. The Pretenders to alter this Poet shou'd never meddle with him unless they cou'd mend his Fable and Conduct, since they can never give us the *Manners*, *Sentiments*, *Passions*, and *Diction* finer and more perfect than they find them in the Original.

As the Fable has all these Advantages so is the Conduct of the Play very regular. *Aristotle* divides the Parts of Quantity of a Play into four Parts, which he call the *Prologue*, the *Episode*, the *Exode*, and the *Chorus*. By the *Prologue* he does not mean what is nowadays spoke before the Play and has seldom any Relation to the Play, and will therefore serve any other Play as well as that to which it is spoken; but by the *Prologue* here is understood all our *first Act*, and is to explain to the Audience not only what concerns the Subject of the Poem but what is proper and necessary, and makes a true Part of it. Thus *Prospero*, to satisfy his Daughter of the Cause of his raising the Storm, very artfully lets the Audience know the material part of his History which past before that Hour, and that necessarily: for it was not only natural for *Miranda* to enquire into the Cause of so terrible a Storm, the Effects of which had extreamly mov'd her Compassion, and the Work that was going to be done by *Prospero* seems to mark out that as the only proper time that he cou'd ever have related his Fortunes to her and inform her of her Condition, that he had now got all his Enemies into his Hands. 'Tis true this Narration may seem a little too calm and that it had been more Dramatic had it been told in a Passion, but if we consider it the Story as *Prospero* tells it is not without a *Pathos*. And if this first Narration cou'd be brought under this Censure yet the second is as far from it, being very artfully thrown into a sort of Passion or Anger against *Ariel*, and is therefore truly Dramatic, for in the *Drama* indeed there shou'd be very little that is not *Action* and *Passion*. It was very necessary likewise that when the Poet was giving the Audience a Creature of his own Formation he shou'd let them know whence he sprung, his very Origin preparing us for a Character so much out of the Way and makes us expect that Language from him which he utters. But there being still some things done which fell not into

---

[1] For D'Urfey's *Cymbeline* see Volume 1, pp. 407-13; for Cibber's *Richard III* above, pp. 101 ff.

the Knowledge of *Prospero* and yet were necessary to be known to the Audience, the Poet, in the first Scene of the second Act, makes the Shipwreck'd Princes discover it very Judiciously.

The next to the *Prologue* is the *Episode*, which was all that us'd formerly to go betwixt the four *Choruses*, which with us is the second, third, and fourth Act; that is, it contains all the *Subject* of the Play, or rather the Intrigues and *Plot* till the *Unravelling*. And the *Exode*, which was all that came after the last singing of the *Chorus*, contain'd the *Perepetie* and *Discovery* or the *unravelling* of the Plot, which answered our fifth Act and is the *Unravelling* or *Catastrophe* of the Piece. This division of *Aristotle* is perfectly observ'd by *Shakespeare* in the Conduct of this Play of the *Tempest*. For, as we have seen, the *first Act* Discovers all that was necessary for the Audience to know of the Story that happen'd before the Commencement of the Action of the Play, and that in an admirable and judicious Manner. Next, all the Intrigue of the Play, as the several Adventures and Torments of the King, the uniting the Hearts of *Miranda* and *Ferdinand,* and the Attempts of the Mob Characters, make up the second, third, and fourth Acts. The fifth is wholly employ'd in the *Discovery* and *Perepetie*, or in the *Unravelling* of the Plot, restoring Tranquility to all the *Dramatic* Persons. The Scene likewise is generally unbroken; especially in the first, fourth, and fifth, they are perfectly entire. The Manners are every way just; they are well-*Mark'd*, and *Convenient*, and *equal* (there is no room here for the *Likeness*, the Story being a Fiction). Thus we find every one perfectly distinct from the other. *Caliban*, as born of a Witch, shews his Original Malice, ill Nature, Sordidness, and Villany. *Antonio* is always Ambitious and Treacherous, and even there promoting and persuading *Sebastian* to the committing the same unnatural Act against his Brother that he had against *Prospero*, with his Aggravation of adding Fratricide to Usurpation.

The *Sentiments* are every where the just Effect of the *Manners*, and the *Diction* generally just and elegant, as we shall see in those beautiful Thoughts I shall add to my Remarks on this Play. But I can't leave my general Consideration of this Play till I have added a Word about the most questionable Part of it, and that is the *Magic* or *Sorcery*.

Those who make this a Fault in our Poet know little of the Matter, for it is sufficient for him to go upon received Notions, no Matter whether Philosophically or absolutely true or not. *Shakespeare* liv'd in an Age not so remote from a Time in which the Notion of Spirits and Conjurers and the strange and wonderful Power of Magic, but that it was almost an Article of Faith among the *Many*—I mean not the very Mob, but Men of Figure and true Learning. *Ariosto* is full of this, and instead of one enchanted Isle gives us many enchanted Castles. Nay *Lavater* and several others have wrote seriously upon this Head; *Mizaldus* gives us many Receipts for magical Operations; and the *Rosicrucians* and Cabalists profess a Conversation with Spirits of the Earth, the Air, Water, and Elemental Fire. Doctor *Beaumont* has even in our Time wrote a Book in English upon this Head, and has declared to many his frequent Conversations with these *Hobgoblins*; nor is there to this Day scarce a venerable Citizen or Country Squire but as firmly believes these Beings as they do their own. And tho' it is not our Business here to enter into the Examination of this Point Philosophically, common Opinion being sufficient to justify *Shakespeare*, yet perhaps the nicest Philosopher would be puzl'd to demonstrate the Falsehood of this Notion. At least we are sure that there are Spirits departed, since the Scripture it self assures us of it. The same wou'd hold against *Virgil* and *Homer* for their *Cyclops*, their *Harpeys*, their *Circes*, &c. if common Opinion could not clear them. Our Poet therefore is at least on as good a Bottom in this as those great Men of Antiquity, and has manag'd these Machines as well as either of them in this Play.

The Reader, having seen all the Beauties of the *Fable*, *Conduct* and *Manners* of this Play, may perhaps think it would not be from the Purpose if I should take some Notice of the Alteration made of it by Mr. *Dryden* and Sr. *William D'Avenant*, and since it seems a sort of Justice to *Shakespeare* I shall venture to show how far they have been from improving our Author. Mr. *Dryden* in his Preface, after he has told us that the Play it self had been acted with Success, and that *Fletcher* and Sr. *John Suckling* had made bold with our Poet in their *Sea-Voyage*, and the *Goblins*, adds: Sr. William D'Avenant, *as he was a Man of a quick and piercing Imagination soon found, that* somewhat *might be added to the Design of* Shakespeare, *of which neither* Fletcher *nor* Suckling *had ever thought* (something, I hope, to add to his Excellence, or else it had better never have been added) *and therefore to put the last Hand to it, he design'd the Counterpart to Shakespeare's Plot, namely that of a Man who had never seen a Woman, that by this Means these two Characters of Innocence and Love might the more illustrate and commend each other.*[1]

He further tells us his Approbation of Sr. *William's* Design, but with

---

[1] See Volume 1, p. 77.

Submission to so great a Man as Mr. *Dryden* must be allowed to be in his Way, I think he had very little Reason for his Approbation. For let us consider but the Rules of true Judgment and we shall find that what these Gentlemen have done could be only advantagious to our Author by improving the *Fable* and *Conduct*, the *Manners*, the *Sentiments*, the *Diction*, &c. But Mr. *Dryden* in what is quoted seems to place all the Benefit of the Alteration in the Counterpart of his Plot, i.e. *A Man that had never seen a Woman, that by this Means, those two Characters of* Innocence *and* Love *might the more illustrate and commend each other.* That is, by spoiling the natural Innocence and Character of *Miranda*, to foist in some Scenes betwixt a Company of unequal and inconsistent Characters, which are sometimes meer *Naturals* indeed and at other *Times* Proficients in Philosophy.

But what did these Characters or what do these Scenes towards the improving the Plot? It has every where broken the Scenes and embarrass'd the Conduct, but scarce any where added the least Beauty to make Amends unless, in *Prospero*'s separating *Ferdinand* and the Father in his Rage and his Threats of his Death, making the meeting of Father and Son the more distressful by so sudden a Calamity in their Joy [Vol. 1, pp. 122 ff]. Every where else the Alterations are monstruous, especially in the *Manners* and *Sentiments*, to shew which I shall give some Instances.

Dorinda says to her Father on his examining of her about seeing the Man—

> Dor. *No Sir, I am as well, as ever I was in all my Life,*
> *But that I cannot eat nor drink for Thought of him,* &c. [Vol. 1, p. 98]

She saw him but the last Scene of the second Act and this is the first Scene of the third Act, so what Time she had to try whether she cou'd eat or not I cannot tell, unless it was her Afternoons *Nuncion* (as the Children call it), for it was near four, as *Ariel* assured us. But all that Scene indeed [Vol. 1, pp. 97–9] between *Prospero* and *Dorinda* (a Creature of our Correctors' making, not of *Shakespeare*'s, but more out of Nature and more inconsistent than *Caliban*) has nothing at all *Dramatick* in it, nor any thing conducive to the Fable, Conduct or Plot. It discovers nothing of the least Use and only gives a very imperfect Sketch of the insensible Approaches of Love in Innocence and Ignorance, and may perhaps be worthy the Contemplation of the young Misses of the Nursery.

Enter eight fat Spirits with Cornucopias *in their Hands.* These fat

Spirits I confess are very surprising and merry, tho' never thought of by *Shakespeare*.

The Discourse in *Eccho* betwixt *Ferdinand* and *Ariel* [Vol. 1, pp. 101 f], if tolerable in Prose, is beyond Measure ridiculous and trifling in singing. *Ferdinand* seems too full of Despair and Concern to have that petty Whim of Curiosity to come into his Head, and therefore I presume no Body will think that any Improvement of *Shakespeare's* Play, unless it be in adding the Mode which was afterwards in the *Rehearsal*.

> *And then to serious Business we'll advance*
> *But first lets have a Dance.*

But our Improvers have never been eminent for their Imitations of Nature in the *Drama*; Mr. *Dryden* had wandred too far in *Romance* to relish Nature or know how to copy her. Tho' in his latter Plays Age had worn something of that away and he has given us some Scenes worthy his Greatness in other Parts of Poetry, in which lay his Excellence. But to go on.

Soon after this [Vol. 1, p. 103] *Miranda*, seeing *Ferdinand* by an odd Caprice (which we never cou'd expect from her Character as drawn in *Shakespeare*) she fancies him a Spirit, tho' she had before seen *Hippolito*, and had been told that he was a Man, and assur'd by her Father that she shou'd soon see another Man of riper Growth than him she had seen. But this artless trifling Ignorance of *Miranda* spoils that Character *Shakespeare* has given her, where she is Innocent indeed, but not a Fool: whereas this might be call'd as alter'd the *Comedy of Fools*.

But now for *Hippolito*, bred to Books and Philosophy under so wise a Master as *Prospero*.

> *Hippolito* and *Prospero*
> Hip. *Methinks I wish, and wish for what I know not;*
> *But still I wish:— yet if I had that Woman,*
> *She, I believe, cou'd tell me what I wish for.* [Vol. 1, p. 106]

This is indeed indulging Fancy with a Vengeance, and throwing all Art, Nature, and Judgment aside as useless. Certainly the first Wishes of Innocence in Love must be the Company of the Object belov'd, and that he might easily find and tell. But why shou'd he fancy (if it were not absurd to ask a Reason for any thing in such a Character) that the Woman cou'd tell him what he wish'd for, when he did not know himself?

Prosp. *What wou'd you do to make that Women yours?*
Hip. *I'd quit the rest of the World, that I might be alone with her; she never shou'd be from me, &c. [Ibid.]*

This is Nature indeed, and this is the real Effect of a real Passion; this is what *Tibullus*, that tender Lover, said about 1700 years ago—

> *Sic Ego secretis possum bene vivere silvis,*
> *Qua nulla humano sit via trita pede.*
> *Tu mihi Curarum Requies, in Nocte vel atra*
> *Lumen, & in solis tu mihi turba Locis, &c.*[1]

But then our young Lover, if he wou'd have maintained his Character of Innocence and Love, shou'd have kept to that Point and not immediately after—contrary to the Nature of Love and Innocence—run Mad for all the Women in the World, as if not bred in a Cave but a Brothel. This has neither Sense nor Reason in it but is perfectly Monstrous. In the beginning of this Scene betwixt him and *Ferdinand* [Vol. I, p. 107] he discovers all the Symptoms of a real Passion, which makes his after Extravagance impossible in Nature, even for a *Debauchee*, at least till Enjoyment was past.

Ferdinand's fighting him [Vol. 1, pp. 118 f] is a Monstrous Incident, and an intollerable Breach of his Charrecter and contrary to the *Manners*, he not being only a tender Stripling but as Ignorant of a Sword as a very Woman; as is plain in the Scene before the Duel, for *Hippolito* has desir'd his Friendship, and told him *that next a Women he found he cou'd Love him* [Vol. 1, p. 109].

This with his Ignorance and Innocence ought to have deter'd a Man of any Honour, especially a Prince of no ill Character, from committing so Barbarous and inhumane a Murder for a Childish Impertinence.

But here we must have a Nice touch at Jealousie. *Miranda* tells him,

> *That he is a Stranger,*
> *Wholly unacquainted with the World, &c.* [Vol. 1, p. 12]

But all this will not do, *Ferdinand* must be jealous without any Reason, to make him the more resolute in so scandalous an Attempt as the

---

[1] Tibullus, 3.19 (= 4.13), ascription uncertain: 'Thus shall I live happily in forest depths where foot of man has never worn a path. For me thou art repose from cares, light even in night's darkness, a throng amid the solitudes.'

Killing *Hippolito*, at least of Wounding him, so that nothing but *Moly* and the Influence of the Moon (forc'd down by his good Angel) cou'd recover him to Life again. 'Tis true, when *Ferdinand* proves such a Coxcomb to be jealous on what *Miranda* says of *Hippolito*—tho' she had assur'd him of her Love and, as far as appear'd to him, ventur'd her Father's Displeasure by coming to him—we may easily suspect he wou'd be guilty of any Folly, nay the Villany of fighting with *Hippolito*. Nay, it was a Mercy that he did not draw on *Miranda* too, for it had been fully as Heroic.

Dorinda is more sensible of Nature and Love than *Hippolito*. She can tell that he can truly love but one at a time, and naturally resents his professing that he will have all the Women. But he is more learn'd in the World in this fourth Act than in the Former. I suppose he had receiv'd some Intelligence of the Incontinence of the Men of this World from one of the Devils of *Sycorax*, for he says—

I've heard Men have Abundance of them there— [Vol. 1, p. 115]

Of whom could he hear this? Of *Prospero?* Impossible. His Business had all along been to fright him from the Conversation of *Women*, making them Enemies and noxious to Men and his Safety, which is directly contrary to the letting him know that other Men had convers'd with so many without Hurt. In this Place indeed a *Poeta loquitur* had not been amiss. He had convers'd with no Body else but *Ferdinand* once, who, tho' he told him that there were more Women in the World, yet was so far from letting him know that one had many, that he told him that one Man was to have but one Woman.

But as knowing as *Hippolito* is in some things and in some lucid Intervals, he knows not a Word of Death, tho' we must think he had read strange Books and heard odd Instructions that cou'd leave him so entirely ignorant of that Point. But were this just yet that very Ignorance makes *Ferdinand* still the more inexcusable, nay *Ferdinand* himself (at last in the Fourth Act) seems himself sensible of his Ignorance, for he says

> *He's so ignorant, that I pity him,*
> *And fain wou'd avoid Force—* [Vol. 1, p. 117]

And indeed a Man wou'd think that he might very easily avoid Force if he wou'd, at least till *Hippolito* had seiz'd his Mistress, which he had sufficient Reason to imagine that *Prospero* wou'd never permit. But he that, notwithstanding all that had past between them, cou'd not before this find out his Ignorance may do any thing.

But *Hippolito* in one Line says he does not know what *Right* is, and yet in the next tells us of Baseness and Honour [*Ibid.*]. His Lectures were very peculiar, that cou'd give him a Notion of one and not of the other.

The Terms of the Combat or Duel are as ridiculous as all the Rest;— that is, to fight till Blood is drawn from one of the two, or his Sword taken from him [Vol. 1, p. 118]. *Ferdinand* was resolv'd to be on the sure Side of the Hedge with him, but he is so dull of Apprehension that he may well be a Rascal, for as Monsieur *Rochefoucauld* says, *A Fool has not Matter enough to make an Honest Man of.* Tho' *Hippolito* had told him that they had no Swords growing in their World yet *Ferdinand* did not find it out, till he had wounded him, that he was unskilful in his Weapon.

I'm loath to kill you, Sir, you are unskilful. [Vol. 1, p. 119]

Risum teneatis?[1] was ever such Stuff wrote since the Time of *Gammer Gurton's Needle*? But it would be endless to observe all the Blunders of these added Scenes, they are all of a Piece and scarce guilty of a Thought which we could justly attribute to *Shakespeare*. I have given Instances enough, I hope, to show what I propos'd, that the Alteration has been no Benefit to the Original.

I shall only take notice of some fine things in this Play both as to Topicks and Descriptions and moral Reflections, and then pass to the next.

Ariel's Description of his managing the Storm is worth remarking, and *Ferdinand's* Speech, when *Prospero* is leading him away at the End of the first Act, is pathetic, and justly expresses the Nature of a true Lover.

> My Father's Loss, the Weakness that I feel
> The Wreck of all my Friends, and this Man's Threats,
> To whom I am subdu'd; are but light to me
> Might I but through my Prison once a Day
> Behold this Maid. All Corners else of the Earth
> Let Liberty make use of; Space enough
> Have I in such a Prison. [1.2.487]

I must not omit the Description that *Francisco* makes in the second Act, of *Ferdinand's* swimming ashore in the Storm.

[1] Horace, *A.P.*, 5: 'could you . . . refrain from laughing?'

I saw him beat the Surges under him,
And ride upon their Backs; he trod the Water,
Whose Enmity he threw aside; and breasted
The Surge most swoln, that met him. His bold Head
'Bove the contentious Waves he kept; and oared
Himself with his bold Arms in lusty Strokes
To th'Shoar; that o'er his wave-worn Backs bow'd
As stooping to relieve him.   [2.1.108 ff]

The Reader may compare this with *Otway*'s Description of *Jaffier*'s
Escape. His Reflections and Moralizing on the frail and transitory State
of Nature is wonderfully fine. (258–73)

*   *   *

[*The Two Gentlemen of Verona*] Tho' this Play be plac'd after the
Tempest 'tis evident from the Writing, and the Faults, and even
Absurdities that it was writ long before it, for I can by no means
think that *Shakespeare* wrote worse and worse. For if his Fire may
be suppos'd to abate in his Age yet certainly his Judgment increas'd,
but most of the Faults of this Play are Faults of Judgment more than
Fancy. . . . (274)

Besides the Defect of the *Plot*, which is too visible to criticise upon,
the *Manners* are nowhere agreeable or convenient. *Silvia* and the rest
not behaving themselves like Princes, Noblemen or the Sons and
Daughters of such. . . .

But how defective soever this Interlude may be in the *Plot*, *Conduct*,
Manners and *Sentiments*, we yet shall see that it is not destitute of Lines
that discover the Author to be *Shakespeare*. . . .

Oh! how this Spring of Love resembleth
The uncertain Glory of an *April* Day. . . . (275–6)   [1.3.84 f]

The fifth Act of this Play is much the best, but *Valentine* is too easily
reconciled to a Man whose Treachery and Villany deserv'd the stab,
especially when it is discovered at the very Time that he goes to ravish
his Friend's Betrothed. (278)

*   *   *

[On Aristotle's theory of comedy] In all these particulars *Shakespeare*
has come up to the Rules, and Definition of *Aristotle*, for he has in his
Characters chosen the Defects and Deformities which are without

Pain and which never Contribute to the Destruction of the Subject
in which it is. (281)

*   *   *

[*The Merry Wives of Windsor*] There are two *Walks* in this Play, but
much better join'd, connected and incorporated, than in any Play that
I remember, either in *Latin* or *English*. The chief *Plot* or *Walk* is that of
exposing the Character of Sir *John Falstaff* for his ridiculous Amours or
Attempts of two Women at once, when by Years and other Defects
he cou'd be agreeable to neither. . . . (285–6)

[In Act V] Mrs. *Ford* and Mrs. *Page* meet him first, and just as he is
rejoycing on his good Luck, and dividing himself and Favours betwixt
them, Sir *Hugh* with his Fairies start out of the *Saw-pit* where they were
hid for that Purpose and pinch and burn him with their Lights; from
whom endeavouring to run away they all come in, and the Discovery
is made and the Knight expos'd to publick Shame as he ought to be.
Here the *under-Plot* or second Walk is join'd in the Conclusion, for
Mrs. *Ann Page*, Mr. *Page*'s handsome Daughter, is in Love with Mr.
Fenton, a well-bred Gentleman, and of Quality superior to *Page*, tho'
he had been a little wild and a Companion of the Prince, by which he
had something run his Estate aground, and for that Reason rejected by
Page and his Wife. The Father is for *Slender*, a very silly Country Gent.
of 300 *l.* a Year; the Mother was for Dr. *Caius*, an impertinent old
French Physician, because he was rich and had Friends at Court. So
that the Wife taking this Opportunity of the nocturnal Mask to abuse
Sir *John Falstaff*, orders the Doctor to take her Daughter (who should
be dress'd in white) and so go off with her and marry her immediately
before the Father cou'd hinder it. The Father had order'd *Slender* to
take his Daughter (dress'd in Green) and lead her away to *Eton* and
there marry her without her Mother's Knowledge; but the young
Lady loving *Fenton* deceives both Father and Mother, to obey both
which she had promis'd, goes and is marry'd to her Beloved, which
Discovery coming on that of Sir *John*'s concludes the Play.

All the other Persons of the *Drama* are plainly join'd to and depending
on those two *Walks*, and their incorporating them into the Plot seems
very well contriv'd. The Quarrel betwixt Sir *John* and Justice *Shallow*
occasions Sir *Hugh*'s Proposal of a Mediation and the Match betwixt
Mr. *Slender* and Mrs. *Anne Page*. This brings Mr. *Page* and Sir *John*
out of Mr. *Page*'s House, where the Motion is made and approv'd, and
all invited in to Dinner, where all the Principal Characters of both

Walks are brought acquainted with each other. The Comical Duel is likewise to Effect the *Plot*, for Sir *Hugh* sends to the Doctor's House-keeper to assist his Friend *Slender* in his Amour, she being intimately acquainted with Mother and Daughter. This Messenger is intercepted by the Doctor, on which he sends the Priest a Challenge, which produces the Comical Scene of both their Passions and Preparations for Fighting. In short the least Incident of the Play, except Mrs. *Page*'s and her Son's Confabulation with Sir *Hugh* his Master, cannot well be left out without leaving a Gap in the Plot and Connection of the Play.

I Confess that the Unities of Time, Place, and Action are not exactly observ'd according to the Rule and Practice of the *Antients*, yet as they are now manag'd among us they may well pass. The Time is not above two Days and a half at most; the Place *Windsor* and the Adjacent Fields and Places. The Action is visibly double, but that it is in all the Comedies of *Terence*.

The first Act shows all the principal Characters except the two *Fords*; prepares all the Business of the Play and enters a little into the Action, in the two Letters sent by Sir *John*, and the Match Propos'd by Sir *Hugh*, and the Doctor's Challenge to the Welsh Levite. So that it is an exact *Protasis* or *Prologue*. The *Episode* begins with the second Act and carries on to the *fifth*; where the *Exode* is in the Discovery and punishment of the Old Letcher, and the disappointment of a forc'd Match in *Fenton*'s Marrying Mrs. *Anne Page*. Mrs. *Ford*'s Resentment of Sir *John*'s Letter puts her and Mrs. *Page* on the Revenge of the Affront, and that Revenge furnishes the Intrigue or Episodical Turns of the Play.

The Information of *Pistol* and *Nym* prepares and rouses *Ford*'s Jealousie admirably, and with a great deal of Art and Nature. Nor can any thing be more ridiculous and entertaining than the Scenes betwixt *Ford* under the Name of *Broom* and Sir *John*.

Upon the whole I think it is pretty plain that nothing can be more agreeable to *Aristotle*'s definition of *Comedy*, for he says 'tis an Imitation of the *Worst Sort*, and that in *Ridicule*, it having thus all the Parts both of Quality and Quantity.

But to make the Parts of Quality more plain it wou'd be necessary to speak of the *Humours*, yet that wou'd be too tedious as well as unnecessary, being so many and yet so various, and so plainly distinguish'd from each other that there is no need to point out Particulars. I shall only give you what Mr. *Dryden* says of the Character of *Falstaff* in his Essay on Dramatic Poetry.[1]—Falstaff *is the best of Comic Characters* —*there are* (says he) *many Men resembling him—old, fat, merry, cowardly, drunken, amorous, vain and lying;* and the Duke of *Buckingham* confirms it in this Verse

> *But* Falstaff *seems inimitable yet.*

Ford's is an excellent Character of a Politic, cautious, jealous Coxcomb; and all his Endeavours at the cautious and cunning Management of the Discovery of his Doubts and Fears involves him the more and makes him the more ridiculous, for the Conferences he has with Sir *John* confirm him in his Suspicions, and his Disappointments expose his Folly.

The *Fairys* in the fifth Act make a Handsome Compliment to the Queen in her Palace of *Windsor*, who had oblig'd him to write a Play of Sir *John Falstaff* in Love, and which I am very well assured he perform'd in a Fortnight; a prodigious Thing, when all is so well contriv'd, and carry'd on without the least Confusion. (288–91)

[*Measure for Measure*]

*   *   *

There are some little under Characters in this Play which are produced naturally enough by the Severity of the new Law, as that of the Bawd and the Pimp, as well as of *Lucio*, which Character is admirably maintain'd, as *Shakespeare* does every where his Comic Characters whatever he does his *Tragic*.

The Unities of Action and Place are pretty well observed in this Play, especially as they are in the Modern Acceptation. The Design of the Play carries an excellent Moral and a just Satire against our present Reformers, who wou'd alter their Course of Nature and bring us to a Perfection Mankind never knew since the World was half Peopled. But while they are so very severe against the Frailties of Men, they never think of their Villanies, Oppression, Extorsion, Cheating, Hypocrisie and the like, which are the Vices of Devils not of Men. Nay, which is extreamly merry, many of the foresaid Character are zealous Reformers; which proves thus much at least that the Kingdom of Hell cannot stand long when it is so divided in it self. But to return to this Play.

[1] See Volume I, pp. 139 f.

The Scene betwixt *Isabella* and *Angelo* in the second Act is very fine; and the not bringing the Yielding of *Isabella* to *Angelo* on the Stage is Artfully manag'd, for it wou'd have been a Difficult Matter to have contriv'd it so that it shou'd not have given a slur to her Modesty to the Audience, tho' they knew it Dissembled.

Allowing for some *Peccadillos* the last Act is wonderful and moving to such a Degree that he must have very little Sense of Things and Nature who finds himself Calm in the reading it.

The Main Story or Fable of the Play is truly *Tragical*, for it is Adapted to move Terror and Compassion, and the Action is one. Its having a Fortunate *Catastrophe* is nothing to the purpose, for that is in many of the Greek Tragedies, tho' *Aristotle* indeed makes the Unfortunate Ending the most beautiful and perfect. Leaving therefore a farther Examen of the Fable, Conduct, &c. to the Reader and the Rules which I have laid down, I shall proceed to the fine Moral Reflections and Topics of it. But it contains so many Beauties of this Kind that to transcribe them all I should leave very little untouch'd. . . . (292–4)

*   *   *

[*The Comedy of Errors*] This Play is exactly regular, as any one may see who will examine it by the Rules. The Place is part of one Town, the Time within the Artificial Day, and the Action the finding the lost Brother, &c. Allowing for the Puns, which were the Vice of the Age he liv'd in, it is extreamly diverting; the Incidents are wonderfully pleasant, and the *Catastrophe* very happy and strongly moving. . . . (299)

This Comedy is an undeniable Proof that *Shakespeare* was not so ignorant of the *Latin* Tongue as some wou'd fain make him . . . for as it is beyond Contradiction plain that this Comedy is taken from that of *Plautus* so I think it as obvious to conclude from that that *Shakespeare* did understand *Latin* enough to read him, and knew so much of him as to be able to form a Design out of that of the *Roman* Poet; and which he has improv'd very much in my Opinion. He has made two Servants as like as their Masters, who are not in *Plautus*. (300)

[*Much Ado About Nothing*]

*   *   *

This Fable is as full of Absurdities as the Writing is full of Beauties; the first I leave to the Reader to find out by the Rules I have laid down, the second I shall endeavour to shew, and point out some few of the many that are contain'd in the Play. *Shakespeare* indeed had the Misfortune which other of our Poets have since had of laying his Scene in a Warm Climate, where the Manners of the People are very different from ours, and yet he has made them talk and act generally like Men of a colder Country. *Marriage à la Mode* has the same Fault.

This Play we must call a *Comedy*, tho' some of the Incidents and Discourses too are more in a Tragic Strain, and that of the Accusation of *Hero* is too shocking for either Tragedy or Comedy; nor cou'd it have come off in Nature if we regard the Country without the Death of more than *Hero*. The Imposition on the Prince and *Claudio* seems very lame, and *Claudio*'s Conduct to the Woman he lov'd highly contrary to the very Nature of Love, to expose her in so barbarous a Manner and with so little Concern and struggle, and on such weak Grounds without a farther Examination into the Matter; yet the Passions this produces in the old Father make a wonderful amends for the Fault. Besides which there is such a pleasing Variety of Characters in the Play, and those perfectly maintain'd as well as distinguish'd, that you lose the Absurdities of the Conduct in the Excellence of the *Manners*, Sentiments, Diction and Topics. *Benedick* and *Beatrice* are two sprightly, witty, talkative Characters, and tho' of the same Nature yet perfectly distinguish'd, and you have no need to read the Names to know who speaks. As they differ from each other, tho' so near a Kin, so do they from that of *Lucio* in *Measure for Measure*, who is likewise a very talkative Person, but there is a gross Abusiveness, Calumny, Lying, and Lewdness in *Lucio* which *Benedick* is free from. One is a Rake's Mirth and Tattle; the other that of a Gentleman, and a Man of Spirit and Wit.

The Stratagem of the Prince on *Benedick* and *Beatrice* is manag'd with that Nicety and Address that we are very well pleas'd with the Success, and think it very resonable and just.

The Character of *Don John* the Bastard is admirably distinguish'd, his Manners are well mark'd and every where convenient, or agreeable. Being a sour, melancholly, saturnine, envious, selfish, malicious Temper, Manners *Necessary* to produce these villanous Events they did; these were productive of the *Catastrophe*, for he was not a Person brought in to fill up the Number only, because without him the Fable could not have gone on.

To quote all the comic Excellencies of this Play would be to transcribe three Parts of it. For all that passes betwixt *Benedick* and *Beatrice* is admirable. His Discourse against Love and Marriage in the later End of the second Act is very pleasant and witty, and that which *Beatrice* says of Wooing, Wedding and repenting. And the Aversion that the Poet gives *Benedick* and *Beatrice* for each other in their Discourse heightens the Jest of making them in Love with one another. Nay the Variety and natural Distinction of the vulgar Humours of this Play are remarkable.

The Scenes of this Play are something obscure, for you can scarce tell where the Place is in the two first Acts, tho' the Scenes in them seem pretty entire and unbroken. But those are things we ought not to look much for in *Shakespeare*. But whilst he is out in the dramatic Imitation of the Fable, he always draws Men and Women so perfectly that when we read we can scarce perswade our selves but that the Discourse is real and no Fiction. (304-6)

* * *

[*Love's Labour's Lost*] Tho' I can't well see why the Author gave this Play this Name yet since it has past thus long I shall say no more to it but this, that since it is one of the worst of *Shakespeare*'s Plays, nay I think I may say the very worst, I cannot but think that it is his first, notwithstanding those Arguments or that Opinion that has been brought to the contrary. . . . (308)

But tho' this Play be so bad yet there is here and there a Stroak that persuades us that *Shakespeare* wrote it. . . . (311)

The Discovery of the King's, *Longaville*'s, and *Dumaine*'s Love is very prettily manag'd, and that of *Biron* by *Costard*'s mistake is a well contriv'd Incident. (312)

* * *

[*A Midsummer Night's Dream* breaks the unity of time.] It is plain from the Argument that the Fable can never bear the Test of the Rules. . . . (315)

Tho' this cannot be call'd either Tragedy or Comedy, as wanting the Fable requir'd to either, yet it contains abundance of beautiful Reflections, Descriptions, Similes, and Topics. Much of it is in Rhime, in which the Author is generally very smooth and flowing. (316)

* * *

[*The Merchant of Venice*] The Ignorance that *Shakespeare* had of the *Greek Drama* threw him on such odd Stories as the Novels and Romances of his time cou'd afford, and which were so far from being natural that they wanted that Probability and Verisimilitude which is absolutely necessary to all the Representations of the Stage. The Plot of this Play is of that Number. But the Errors of the Fable and the Conduct are too visible to need Discovery. This Play has receiv'd considerable Advantages from the Pen of the honorable *George Granville*, Esq.

The Character of the *Jew* is very well distinguish'd by Avarice, Malice, implacable Revenge, &c. But the Incidents that necessarily shew these Qualitys are so very Romantic, so vastly out of Nature, that our Reason, our Understanding is every where shock'd; which abates extremely of the Pleasure the Pen of *Shakespeare* might give us. This is visible in his Speech to the Doge, for all the while that Distinction of Character, which is beautiful and otherwise pleases you, the Incredibility of such a Discourse to such a Prince and before such a Court of Judicature has so little of Nature in it that it is impossible to escape the Censure of a Man of common Sense.

The Character of *Portia* is not every where very well kept, that is, the Manners are not always *agreeable* or *convenient* to her Sex and Quality; particularly [3.4.63 ff] where she scarce preserves her Modesty in the Expression.

The Scene betwixt *Shylock* and *Tubal* in the third Act is artfully managed, and the Temper of the Jew excellently discover'd in its various Turns upon the different News of which *Tubal* gives him an Account.

This Play, as well as most of the rest, gives Instances that *Shakespeare* was perfectly acquainted with the fabulous Stories of the old Poets, which is to me a Confirmation that he was well acquainted with the Authors of the *Latin* Antiquity, whence only he cou'd learn them.

Tho' there are a great many Beauties in what our modern Gentlemen call the *Writing* in this Play yet it is almost every where calm, and touches not the Soul; there are no sinewy Passions, which ought every where to shine in a serious Dramatic Performance, such as most of this is. . . . (321–2)

He is generally excellent in his Choice of Epithets of a strong, proper, and natural Signification, and such as denote the Quality of the thing wonderfully. . . . (323)

*　　*　　*

[*As You Like It*] This Story has nothing Dramatic in it, yet *Shakespeare* has made as good use of it as possible. . . .

The old Duke's Speech preferring that Solitude to the World is full of moral Reflections. . . . The scene betwixt *Orlando* and *Adam* moving by the Gratitude of the old Servant. . . . And *Rosalinda*'s Character of a Man in Love is very pretty. (326)

* * *

[*The Taming of the Shrew*] This Play is indeed *Dramatic*, for it is all Action and there is little Room left for Reflections and fine Topics. Tho' it be far from Regular as to Time and Place, yet it is perfectly so in the Action, and some of the Irregularities of Time might easily have been prevented. . . . (328)

* * *

[*All's Well That Ends Well*] The Irregularity of the Plot is visible enough when we are in one Part of a Scene in *France*, in another in *Italy*, &c. The Story itself is out of a Possibility almost, at least so far out of the Way of Custom and Experience, that it can't be call'd natural. The Character of *Parolles* is taken Notice of by Mr. *Rowe* very justly for its Excellence, being, I think, preferable to all in that kind except his own *Falstaff*. . . . (330–1)

This Play is not destitute however of fine Reflections and instructive Sentences; the Speech of the Countess to her Son on his leaving her to go to Court is very good. (331)

* * *

[*Twelfth Night*] There is a sort of under-Plot of Sir *Toby*'s bubbling Sir *Andrew* in hopes of his having *Olivia*, of their imposing on *Olivia*'s Steward *Malvolio* as if his Lady was in Love with him, and the Quarrel promoted betwixt *Caesario* and Sir *Andrew*, which yet are so interwove that there is nothing that is not necessary to the main Plot but that Episode of the Steward. . . . (333)

The Captain's Description of *Sebastian*'s coming ashoar is fine, and if compar'd with that before of *Ferdinand*'s Escape (describ'd in the *Tempest*) wou'd show the Fertility of the Author in his Variety on the same Subject. . . .

Olivia's Declaration of Love to *Viola* is very fine and pathetick:

Caesario, by the Roses of the Spring, &c.
[*Twelfth Night*, 3.1.146] (334)

* * *

[*The Winter's Tale*] This Story needs no Critick, its Errors are visible enough. *Shakespeare* himself was sensible of this Grossness of making the Play above sixteen Years, and therefore brings in Time as a Chorus to the fourth Act to excuse the Absurdity. . . . (335)

The Narration of the Discovery in the last Act is not only entertaining but moving, and he seems accidentally to have hit on something like the Ancients, whose *Catastrophes* were generally in Narration. And is a Proof that if our Poets had the Genius of *Shakespeare* the shocking Representations of the Stage might easily and with Beauty be thrown into Narration and so leave Room for the Poet to shew his Eloquence and his *Imagery*.

This Tale is taken from an old story-Book of *Dorastus* and *Faunia*, whence I suppose the Absurdities are copyed and the making *Bohemia* of an Inland, a maritime Country. (336)

★   ★   ★

I come now to the Historical Plays of *Shakespeare*, which, with Submission to the *Writer* of his Life, cannot be placed under *Tragedy* because they contain no Tragic Imitation. They are Draughts of the Lives of Princes brought into *Dialogue*, and in Regard of their Mixture of serious and comical Characters may be compared to the Greek Pieces that were wrote before *Æschylus* and *Sophocles* had reformed the Stage of *Athens*, or the rambling unartful Pieces first represented in *Rome* after the calling in of the *Etrurian* Players, nay after the Time of *Livius Andronicus*. In their Extent they may be compar'd to the *Theseids*, the *Heracleids*, written by some Greek Poets and reflected on by *Aristotle* in his Art of Poetry for imagining that the Unity of the Hero made the Unity of the Action.

These Instances from this polite Nation will be a very good Plea for this Error of *Shakespeare*, who liv'd when the Stage was not regarded by the State as it was in *Athens*. For had a Reformation then begun he wou'd doubtless have done as Mr. *Corneille* did upon the studying the Art of the Stage, by which the Plays which he wrote afterwards excell'd those he wrote without any Knowledge of that Art.

I shall only add here that since these Plays are Histories there can be no Manner of Fable or Design in them. I shall not therefore give the Plot but refer the Reader to those Historians where he may find the Stories at large, and by them judge how near *Shakespeare* has kept to the Character History has given us of them.

[*King John*] He begins with King *John*, whose History you will find not only in the common English Chronicles, but also in Mr. *Daniel*, in Mr. *Tyrel*, Mr. *Echard*; especially in Mr. *Tyrel*, in all its Extent and Particularities. But it must be remark'd that he begins not the History with the Birth of King *John* or the Manner of his obtaining the Crown, but of the Breach betwixt him and *France* on the Behalf of *Arthur* the Son of *Geffry Plantagenet* the true Heir.

I had some Thoughts of placing an Abstract of the Reigns of the Kings before each of his history Plays, but considering farther I found that to make of it any Use they wou'd take up much more Room than I cou'd by any Means allow, and the Princes being all English I find it might seem a little superfluous, since that is what every Gentleman that is capable of reading this Poet is very well acquainted with.

As for the Characters of this History I think there are none of any Figure but the *Bastard* and *Constance*; they indeed engage your Attention.when ever they enter. There is Boldness, Courage, self-Assurance, Haughtiness, and Fidelity in what ever he says or does. But here is the Misfortune of all the Characters of Plays of this Nature, that they are directed to no End and therefore are of little Use, for the Manners cannot be necessary and by Consequence must lose more than half their Beauty. The Violence, Grief, Rage, and Motherly Love, and Despair of *Constance* produce not one Incident and are of no Manner of Use, whereas if there had been a just Design, a tragic Imitation of some one grave Action of just Extent, both these Characters being form'd by the Poet must have had their Manners directed to that certain End and the Production of those Incidents which must beget that End.

There are too many good Lines in this Play for me to take Notice or point to them all. . . . (337–9)

The Scolding betwixt *Elinor* and *Constance* is quite out of Character, and indeed 'tis a difficult Matter to represent a Quarrel betwixt two Women without falling into something indecent for their Degree to speak, as most of what is said in this Scene is. For what ever the Ladies of *Stocks Market* might do, Queens and Princesses can never be suppos'd to talk to one another at that rate. The Accounts which the *French* and *English* Heralds give of the Battle to the Town of *Angiers* is very well worded, and it had been better we had heard more of the Battles and seen less of those ridiculous Representations. The Citizens Proposal of the Lady *Blanch*, &c. to the King's contains many Lines worth reading and remarking from this Line—

If lusty Love shou'd go in Quest of Beauty, &c. [2.1.426]

There is a considerable Part of the second Act lost of this Piece, it containing only two Pages, which are so well adorn'd with the well-drawn Passion of *Constance* that we are oblig'd to Fortune that it is not lost with the rest. Her Passion in the first Scene of the third Act is likewise just and masterly, and well worthy our perusing with Care.

The Topic of Interest or Advantage is well handled in *Falconbridge*'s Speech beginning thus—

> *Rounded in the Ear,*
> *With that same Purpose-changer, that sly Devil,* &c. [2.1.567]

Whatever *Pandulph* might really have urg'd to make a Breach betwixt the Kings, what *Shakespeare* makes him speak is perfectly the natural Result of the Notions and biggotted Opinions of those Times: see [3.1.136 ff]. The Passion of *Constance* in the third Scene of Act 3 is extreamly touching; among the rest, this one Line is admirable,

> *He talks to me, that never had a Son.* [3.4.91].

The pleading of Prince *Arthur* with *Hubert* is very natural and moving, allowing for two or three Playing on Words which seems not so proper for that place (see Scene 1st Act 4). *Hubert*'s Description of the Peoples Confusion on the Prodigies is very well. *Old Men and Beldams in the Streets do Prophesy on it,* &c. [4.2.186] and King *John*'s Anger with *Hubert* in the next page is well drawn, as the King's Madness is [5.7.28 ff]. The Hearty *Englishman* appears so well in the last Speech of the Play that I must point it out for some of the Gentlemen of this Age to Study. (340–1)

Remarks on the *Life and Death of Richard II.*

Shakespeare has drawn *Richard*'s Character according to the best Accounts of History, that is, Insolent, Proud, and Thoughtless in Prosperity, and full of the Notion that he cou'd not any Way forfeit his Crown being the Lord's Anointed—the common Flattery by which Kings are perverted into Tyrants—but then Poor, Low, Dejected, Despairing on the Appearance of Danger. In Distress always dissembling Complyance in all things, but never sincere in Performance when the Danger is over. There are indeed several things that look something Whimsical and Extravagant which yet are agreeable to what History has said of his Actions and Temper, in which our Poet has ever observ'd the *Likeness.*

The Topics are not many in this Piece, but there are several Speeches which are worth remarking. . . . *Gaunt*'s Speeches to *York* and the King before he dies are Very Moral and Good. . . . (341-2)

*   *   *

[*1 & 2 Henry IV*] Tho' the Humour of *Falstaff* be what is most valuable in both these Parts yet that is far more excellent in the first, for Sir *John* is not near so Diverting in the second Part. *Hotspur* is the next in Goodness, but that wou'd have shew'd much more had it been in a regular Tragedy, where the Manners had not only been necessary but productive of Incidents Noble, and Charming. *Glendower* is fine for Comedy. (344)

*   *   *

[*Henry V*] [In the Chorus's appeals to our imagination Shakespeare] expresses how preposterous it seem'd to him and unnatural to huddle so many Actions, so many Places, and so many Years into one Play, one Stage, and two Hours. So that it is not to be doubted but that he wou'd have given us far more noble Plays if he had had the good Fortune to have seen but any one regular Performance of this Nature. The Beauty of Order wou'd have struck him immediately, and at once have made him more correct and more excellent; and I do not at all doubt but that he wou'd have been the *Sophocles* of *England*, as he is now but little more than the *Thespis*, or at most the *Aeschylus*. . . . [Yet] *Shakespeare* by his own Genius brought [the English stage] so far as to leave it some Beauties which have never since been equal'd. . . . (347)

The Character of *Fluellen* is extreamly comical, and yet so very happily touch'd that at the same time when he makes us laugh he makes us value his Character. The Scene of Love betwixt *Henry V* and *Katherine* is extravagantly silly and unnatural, for why he shou'd not allow her to speak in English as well as all the other *French* I cannot imagine, since it adds no Beauty but gives a patch'd and pyebald Dialogue of no Beauty or Force. (350)

*   *   *

[*3 Henry VI*] The long Soliloquy of *Richard* [3.3.124-95] is highly unnatural, for as the Duke of *Buckingham* justly has observ'd they ought to be few, and short. Nor wou'd this, which is so frequent in our Poet, be borne from the best Hand that cou'd now arise, but there is always by the Many biggotted Deference paid to our Predecessors, and Years add Authority to a Name. Our young Poets shou'd never imitate our *Shakespeare* in this, for tho' a Man may be suppos'd to speak a few Words to himself in the Vehemence of a Passion (as it do's happen in Nature, of which the Drama is in all its Parts an Imitation) yet to have near fourscore Lines of calm Reflections, nay Narrations to my self, by which the Hearer shou'd discover my Thoughts and my Person, as here (and before when *Henry VI* is discover'd and taken) is unpardon-able, because against Nature, and by Consequence not at all according to Art. There are several good Lines in this Speech of *Richard* but ill brought in. The Instances which *Shakespeare* makes him give of *Nestor*, *Ulysses*, and *Sinon* are a Proof still of his Knowledge at least in *Ovid*, and some other of the Latin *Classics*. The ill Omens given by *Henry VI* of *Richard*'s Death are Poetical enough. . . . (352–3)

Remarks on the *Life and Death of Richard III* and *Henry VIII*

The first of these Plays begins with a long Soliloquy of *Richard*'s of forty or fifty Lines to let the Audience know what Contrivances he had made for the Destruction of *Clarence*, and what a Villain he intended to be. But *Richard* as he is here drawn is not a fit Character for the Stage, being shocking in all he does, and we think (notwithstanding the hudling so much time into two Hours) that Providence is too slow and too mild in his Punishment. The Antients have indeed introduc'd an *Atreus* and *Thyestes*, a *Medea*, &c. but the Cruelties committed by them have been the suddain Effect of Anger and Revenge. But *Richard* is a calm Villain and does his Murders deliberately, wading through a Sea of his nearest Relations' Blood to the Crown. (353–4)

* * *

This concludes the English Historical plays; tho' the rest are indeed little better, yet they generally are within a narrower Compass of Time and take in fewer Actions. Tho' when they exceed the Unities I see no Reason why they may not as well and with as good Reason stretch the Time to 5000 Years, and the Actions to all the Nations and People of the Universe; and as there has been a Puppet Show of the Creation of the World, so there may be a Play call'd the History of the World. (357)

* * *

[*Troilus and Cressida*] This Play is alter'd by Mr. *Dryden*, and tho' clear'd of some Errors is far from a Play even according to the Rules laid down by Mr. *Dryden* before this very Play, as he indeed Confesses[1]; but to alter a play and leave the fundamental Errors of Plot and Manners is a very Whimsical undertaking. *Shakespeare* is to be Excus'd in his falsifying the Character of *Achilles*, making him and *Ajax* perfect Idiots, tho' sometimes *Achilles* talks like a nice Reasoner, as with *Ulysses* [3.3.75 ff], so making the Manners *unequal* as well as unlike. I say *Shakespeare* is excusable in this because he follow'd *Lollius*, or rather *Chaucer's* Translation of him. But Mr *Dryden*, who had *Homer* to guide him right in this particular, is unpardonable. Thus *Achilles* is made to absent himself from the Field for the sake of *Polyxena*, whereas the receiv'd Story is that it was upon the Quarrel betwixt *Agamemnon* and him for taking away *Briseis*. But I know not on what Account both the Poets seem fonder of the *Barbarians* than the *Greeks*, Arbitrary Power than Liberty, Ignorance than Learning. I know not but it may be that the Reason that gave *Virgil* the *Trojan* for his Hero is that which has made our Bards so indulgent to the same Side, *viz*, a Notion that the Trojans were the Source of our two Nations, tho' with much less Reason and probability on our side than in that of the *Romans*.

I wonder Mr. *Dryden* continued the Error of *Shakespeare* in making *Cressida* a Whore. Her Character is too scandalous to draw our Pity, and therefore he shou'd have made her virtuous and not of blasted Honour. Yet it must be acknowledg'd that Mr. *Dryden* has corrected the Diction, and added a considerable Beauty in that Scene betwixt *Hector* and *Troilus* upon the Surrender of *Cressida*, with whom he seems to part in the Original with too small Reluctance. Mr. *Dryden* himself tells us[2] that he took the Hint of that Scene from that in *Euripides* between *Agamemnon* and *Menelaus*, which I shall give the Reader in my Remarks on *Julius Cæsar* that he may compare it with that of *Shakespeare* and this of Mr. *Dryden*, from whom I must a little dissent in the Occasion, for the Ground of the Quarrel in the *Greek* is stronger than either Mr *Dryden's* or *Shakespeare's*. For the Glory and Honour of *Greece* depends on that of *Euripides*, but I can't find the Liberty of *Rome* much interested on that of *Brutus* and *Cassius*. But more of this when I come to that Play.

I am something of Mr. *Dryden's* Mind that this was one of his earliest Plays, both for the Manners and Diction, which are both more faulty than usually in any of his later Tragedies. There are, notwith-

[1] See Volume 1, pp. 250 ff.
[2] See Volume 1, p. 251.

standing what I have said, a great many fine Lines in this Piece worth the Remarking, as the very first Lines:

Call here my Varlet, I'll unarm again. (358–9)

★   ★   ★

[*Coriolanus*] The Character of *Martius* is truely Dramatic, for his Manners are not only equal but necessary to his Misfortunes. His Pride and Rashness are what History gives him, but his Modesty and Aversion to Praise I cannot find in *Plutarch*, who makes him very well satisfy'd with the Praise given by *Cominius*. And indeed it seems something opposite to his Pride, which both in the Play and History was so signal in him. Our Poet seems fond to lay the Blame on the People and every where is representing the Inconstancy of the People, but this is contrary to Truth, for the People have never discover'd that Changeableness which Princes have done. And *Plutarch* in the Life of *Pyrrhus* seems sensible of this when he says—*Thus Kings have no Reason to Condemn the People for changing for their Interest, who in that do but imitate them, as the* great Teachers of Unfaithfulness *and Treachery, holding him the Bravest, who makes the least Account of being an honest Man.* And any one that will look over the *Roman* History will find such Inconstancy and such a perpetual Changeableness in the Emperors as cannot be parallel'd in the People of any Time or Country. What the *Greeks* or *Romans* have ever done against any of their fortunate or great Generals is easily vindicated from a guilty Inconstancy and Ingratitude. For the fault has always been in the great Men, who, swelling in the Pride of their Success, have thought, in deference to that, that they might and ought to do whatever they pleas'd, and so often attempted the Ruin of that Liberty themselves for the Preservation of which their warlike Actions were only valuable. And so it was their changing their Manners, and not the People, that produc'd their Misfortunes. They lov'd them for Defending their Country and Liberties, but by the same Principle must hate them when they sought by their Ambition and Pride to subvert them, and this by a Constancy, not variableness, of Principle or Temper.

This is plain in the very Story of this Play, for their Anger was just against *Coriolanus*, who thought so well of his own Actions as to believe that ev'n the Rights, Customs, and Priviledges of his Country were his due for his Valour and Success. His turning a Traytor to his Country on his Disgrace is a Proof of his Principle. *Camillus* on the contrary, banish'd on far less Occasion or Ground, brought his Country in Distress Relief against the *Gauls*, so far was he from joining them.

This Contempt of the People often proceeds from an over Value of our selves, and that not for our superiour Knowledge, Virtue, Wisdom, &c. but for the good Fortune of our Birth, which is a Trifle no farther valuable in Truth than it is join'd to Courage, Wisdom or Honour; yet what, when blindly valu'd by the Possessor, sets aside all Thoughts and endeavour to obtain those nobler Advantages.

Our English Poets, indeed, to flatter Arbitrary Powers have too often imitated *Shakespeare* in this Particular and preposterously brought the Mob on the Stage, contrary to the Majesty of Tragedy and the Truth of the Fact. *Shakespeare* has here represented, as in *Julius Cæsar*, the Commons of *Rome* as if they were the Rabble of an *Irish* Village, as senseless, ignorant, silly and cowardly, not remembring that the Citizens of *Rome* were the Soldiers of the Common-wealth by whom they Conquer'd the World, and who in *Julius Cæsar's* time were at least as Polite as our Citizens of *London*. And yet, if he had but consulted them, he wou'd have found it a difficult Matter to have pick'd out such ignorant unlick'd Cubbs to have fill'd up his Rout.

It is no hard Matter to prove that the People were never in the Wrong but once, and then they were byass'd by the Priest to choose *Barabas* and cry out Crucify.

I have not room here to examine this Point with that Clearness that I might, nor is it so much to our present Purpose; and yet I presume the Digression is not so foreign to the Matter as to deserve a judicious Censure.

The Character of *Martius* is generaly preserv'd, and that Love of their Country which is almost peculiar to *Rome* and *Greece* shown in the principal Persons. The Scene of the Mother, Wife, and *Valeria*, is moving and noble. There are a great many fine Lines in this Play, tho' the Expression of Diction is sometimes obscure and puffy. That of 1 *Citiz.* is very just on all proud Men.

—And cou'd be content to give him good Report for't but that he pays himself with being proud. [1.1.30 ff]

The Fable that *Menenius* tells the People, tho' in History, is very well brought in here and express'd. [1.1.87 ff] The noble Spirit of *Volumnia* is well express'd in her Speech, [1.3.1 ff] and in all that Scene, where

the Character is admirably distinguish'd from *Virgilia* and *Valeria*.
The Speech of *Coriolanus* to the Soldiers is good.

—*If any such be here*
(*As it were Sin to doubt*) *that love this Painting*, &c. [1.6.67 ff]

In the Scene betwixt the *Tribunes* and *Martius* [3.1] the haughty
Pride and insolent and virulent Temper of *Coriolanus* is justly painted.
Menenius is drawn an old humorous Senator, and indeed he talks
like one in Defence of the Pride and Outrage of his Friend. [3.1.277 ff]
And the next page, when he asks what he has done against *Rome*, &c.,
when it is plain he was against the Rights of the Commons, as essential
to the Government as the Nobles, perhaps more if that State be thoroughly consider'd. (362–5)

        *   *   *

[*Titus Andronicus*] As this Play is not founded in any one Particular on
the *Roman* History, tho' palm'd upon *Rome*, so the whole is so very
shocking that if there be any Beauties in the Diction I cou'd not find
them, or at least they are very faint and very few. I can easily believe
what has been said, that this is none of *Shakespeare*'s Play, that he
only introduc'd it and gave it some few Touches. (367)

        *   *   *

[*Romeo and Juliet*] Tho' this Play have no less than five or six Murthers
yet they are nothing akin to those of the foregoing Piece [*Titus*];
these, for the most Part, are the Effect of Heat and Passion, and by Way
of Duels, which Custom has given a sort of Reputation to, as being
upon the Square. If therefore they are faulty, they yet are of that
Nature that we pity, because every Gentleman is liable to fall into that
by the Necessity of Custom. Tho' this Fable is far from Dramatic
Perfection yet it undeniably raises Compassion in the later scenes.
There are in it many Beauties of the Manners, and Sentiments, and
Diction. The Character of *Mercutio* is pleasant and uniform; that of
Tybalt always *equal*; as indeed they all are; the Nurse is a true Comic
Character, tho' some of our *Chit-chat* Poets wou'd look on it as Farce
or low Comedy. . . . (369–70)
What *Romeo* says on his first seeing *Juliet* is very pretty.

Her Beauty hangs upon the Cheek of Night,
Like a rich Jewel in an *Aethiop*'s Ear, &c. [1.5.43 f]

*   253

Whether Passion be so pregnant of Similes as *Romeo* and *Juliet* every-where give us I dare not determine, since to say that all they speak is not natural wou'd be to provoke too many that admire it as the Soul of Love.

Mercutio's conjuring for *Romeo* is pleasant, tho' it ends a little too smutty for an Audience. . . . [2.1.6 ff]

The Scene betwixt *Romeo* and *Juliet* when he is in the Garden and she at her Window [2.2], tho' it contain many things that will not join with Probability, and tho' perhaps *Shakespeare*, like *Cowley*, was a little corrupted by reading *Petrarch*, that modern Debaucher of Poetry into *Conceits* and *Conundrums*, yet the Fancy is every where so fine and Nature so agreeably painted that we are pleas'd with the very *Fucus* and per-swade our selves that it is pure unsophisticated Nature. . . . (371)

There are likewise a great many fine Lines in *Juliet*'s *Soliloquy*, but her Thought of cutting him out into little Stars, &c. [3.2.21 ff] is ridi-culous. The Parting of *Romeo* and *Juliet* is very pretty. The Fryar's Comfort to the Father and Lover in their clamorous Sorrow for the suppos'd Death of *Juliet* is not amiss.

Romeo's Description of the poor *Apothecary*, and his Shop is very good. This Story is taken out of *Bandello*'s *Novels*. (372)

★   ★   ★

[*Timon of Athens*] This Play is plainly taken from *Lucian*'s *Timon*, and I wonder that *Shakespeare* rather chose to give *Roman* Names to his Persons as *Lucius*, *Lucullus*, &c. than *Gnathonides*, *Philiades*, *Demeas* a flattering Orator, from whence our Author seems to have taken his Poet; *Thrasycles* a Philosopher but not of *Apemantus*'s kind, but a Lover of Money or rather a Hypocrite; *Blapsius*, *Laches*, *Gniphon*. *Apemantus* is indeed *Shakespeare*'s own, and much better for the End he introduces him than *Thrasycles* cou'd have been, tho' the later is better in *Lucian*. *Shakespeare* has thrown the Infamy on the Poet which *Lucian* threw on the Orator, not considering that Poets made another sort of Figure in *Athens* (where the Scene lies) than they do in *England*, the State thinking them so useful to the Public that on the Death of *Eupolis* in a Sea Fight all Poets were for the future forbid to go to the War. Yet a Poet methinks shou'd have more regard to his Art and himself than to bring in a Character of one mean or ridiculous. But Mr. *Shadwell*, who has pretended to alter this Play[1], has made him a very Scoundrel, and the Players always take Care in Dress and Action to make him more so.

But this is not the only thing in which Mr. *Shadwell* has made this Poem worse in the Copy or Amendments than it is in the Original: he has created two Ladies of his own with a very odd Design. *Melissa* he makes a Woman of Quality and Honour, but has given her Qualities more abandon'd than a Prostitute; and *Evandra* is a Whore profess'd, but to her he has given Gratitude, Love, and Fidelity even to the forsaking of the World to bear the Hardships of *Timon*'s Miseries, to perswade the Town that a Whore is a more eligible and excellent Creature than a Woman of Honour. Such Doctrines as these have rais'd so many Enemies to the Stage with too much Reason and Justice. For in them indeed the Stage has lost all its Beauty and Greatness, nay and all its Art and *Genius*, it being so easie a Matter to please at the Expence of Religion and Morality but so hard to do it on the solid Grounds of Art, which are subservient to Virtue, and I may say an Assistant of Religion in purging and reforming the Manners.

It is plain that the Plot is not regular as to Time or Place, but the Action may be look'd on as pretty uniform, unless we wou'd make the Banishment and Return of *Alcibiades* an under Plot, which yet seems to be born of the main Design.

The Play is full of Moral Reflections and useful Satire. The Characters are well mark'd and observ'd, and the Diction generally speaking expressive. . . .

The trying and Refusal of the Friends is very touching, and too natural and obvious to need a Comment; a Hint of this is in the latter End of *Lucian*'s Dialogue of *Timon*. . . . (373–4)

The false Supper *Timon* invites his false Friends to is all *Shakespeare*'s Contrivance. *Timon*'s Curses on *Athens* in the Beginning of the fourth Act is worthy his Rage and Passion.

—*O! thou Wall, that girdlest in those Wolves*, &c. [4.1.1 ff]

The parting of the Servants something touching [4.2.23 ff]. *Timon*'s Speech, tho' disguis'd too much in affected Words, contains good satirical Reflections.

On Gold.

—Thus much of this will make
Black White, Foul Fair; Wrong Right;

¹ See Volume 1, pp. 204–38.

Base Noble; Old Young; Cowards Valiant, &c. [4.3.1-47]

The Scene betwixt him, *Alcibiades, Timandra,* &c. is full of whole-some Satire against Whoring, &c. (375)

* * *

[*Julius Cæsar*] This Play or History is call'd *Julius Cæsar,* tho' it ought rather to be call'd *Marcus Brutus. Cæsar* is the shortest and most in-considerable Part in it, and he is kill'd in the beginning of the third Act. But *Brutus* is plainly the shining and darling Character of the Poet, and is to the End of the Play the most considerable Person. If it had been properly call'd *Julius Cæsar* it ought to have ended at his Death, and then it had been much more regular, natural and beautiful. But then the Moral must naturally have been the Punishment or ill Success of Tyranny.

I know that a noble Man of great Judgment in the *Drama* is and has been for some time altering this Play,[1] in which I believe *Shakespeare* will have a better Fate than in most of those which have been alter'd. For generally they who have undertaken this Province have been care-ful to leave all the Faults and to rob him of many of the Beauties. But this has been because few who have attempted it knew more of the Art of the Stage than our Author, and wanted his Genius to relish those things which were really good. But the principal Character *Cæsar,* that is left so little touch'd by *Shakespeare,* will merit his Regard, and the Regulation of the Design without Doubt will be Object of his Care and Study. . . . (377)

[The Orations of Brutus and Antony] are indeed the Beginning of a new Action, the Death of *Brutus* and *Cassius,* and have nothing (in a Dramatic Sense) to do with the Death of *Cæsar,* which is the first Action. But this is a Part of the *Drama* which our *Shakespeare* is not to be accountable for. We shall therefore proceed to those Beauties of which he is undoubtedly Master. The *Manners* first, and here I think he is generally wonderful, for there is the *Likeness* in all and a perfect *Con-venience* and *Equality.* . . . (378)

---

[1] John Sheffield, Duke of Buckingham (1647-1721). His version, which he was known to have worked on for many years before it was published in Vol. I of his *Works* in 1723—it was never acted—divided Shakespeare's play into two separate plays, *Julius Caesar* (based on Acts I-III) and *The Tragedy of Marcus Brutus* (Acts IV-V), in order to preserve the unity of time. Pope wrote 'Two Chorus's to the Tragedy of Brutus' which were published in his *Works,* 1717.

There is one thing in this Play which I remark for those judicious Gentlemen *who by a swelling gouty Style have set up for fine* Language *in the* Drama. The Stile of this Play is generally speaking plain, easie and natural. (393)

*　　*　　*

[*Macbeth*] To say much in the Praise of this Play I cannot, for the Plot is a sort of History and the Character of *Macbeth* and his Lady are too monstrous for the Stage. But it has obtained, and [is] in too much Esteem with the *Million* for any Man yet to say much against it.

The Topics and Lines of this Play are less in Number and Beauty than most of his. (394)

*　　*　　*

[*Hamlet*] Tho' I look upon this as the Master-Piece of *Shakespeare* according to our Way of Writing yet there are abundance of Errors in the Conduct and Design which will not suffer us in Justice to prefer it to the *Electra* of *Sophocles*, with the Author of his Life[1], who seems to mistake the Matter wide when he puts this on the same Foot with the *Electra*. *Hamlet*'s Mother has no Hand in the Death of her Husband, as far as we can discover in this Poem, but her fault was in yielding to the incestuous Amour with her Husband's Brother—that at least is all that the Ghost charges her with. Besides, *Shakespeare* was Master of this Story, but *Sophocles* was not. *Orestes*' father was commanded by the Oracle to kill his Mother, and therefore, all moral Duties yielding to the immediat Command of the Gods, his Action according to that System of Religion under which *Sophocles* wrote had nothing in it of Barbarity but was entirely pious, as *Agamemnon*'s Sacrificing his own Daughter *Iphigenia* on *Diana*'s Order.

This Play indeed is capable of being made more perfect than the *Electra* but then a great deal of it must be thrown away, and some of the darling Trifles of the Million, as all the comical Part entirely and many other things which relate not to the main Action, which seems here to be pretty entire, tho' not so artfully Conducted as it might be. But I wander from my Point. I propos'd not to show the Errors especially when this Play contains so many Beauties. *Hamlet* every-where almost gives us Speeches that are full of the Nature of his Passion, his Grief, &c. The Advice of *Laertes* to his Sister is very moral and just and full of prudential Caution. And that of *Polonius* to his

---

[1] Rowe: see above, pp. 200 f.

Son, and that of the same to his Daughter: *Ay Springes to catch Wood-cocks*, &c. [1.3] If the young Ladies wou'd Study these Pages they wou'd Guard their Vertues and Honors better than many of them do. All the Scene betwixt *Hamlet* and the Ghost is admirable, as the Ghost's Description of his Residence in the other World. . . . (397–8)

The Discourse betwixt *Hamlet* and the Grave-Maker is full of moral Reflections, and worthy minding—tho' that Discourse itself has nothing to do there where it is, nor of any use to the Design, and may be as well left out; and whatever can be left out has no Business in a Play, but this being low Comedy has still less to do here. The Character *Hamlet* gives of *Osrick* is very satirical and wou'd be good anywhere else. (404)

*   *   *

[*King Lear*] The King and *Cordelia* ought by no means to have dy'd, and therefore Mr *Tate* has very justly alter'd that particular which must disgust the Reader and Audience, to have Vertue and Piety meet so unjust a Reward[1]. So that this Plot, tho' of so celebrated a Play, has none of the Ends of Tragedy, moving neither Fear nor Pity. We rejoice at the Death of the *Bastard* and the two Sisters, as of Monsters in Nature under whom the very Earth must groan. And we see with horror and Indignation the Death of the King, *Cordelia* and *Kent*. Tho' of the Three the King only cou'd move pity, if that were not lost in the Indignation and Horror the Death of the other two produces, for he is a truly *Tragic* Character, not supremely Virtuous nor Scandalously vicious. He is made up of *Choler* and Obstinacy, Frailties pardonable enough in an Old Man, and yet what drew on him all the Misfortunes of his Life.

The Bastard's Speech of the Folly of laying our Fate and Follies on the Stars is worth reading—

This is the excellent Foppery of the World, that when we are sick in Fortune, &c. [1.2.128]

Lear's Passion on the Ingratitude of his Daughter *Gonerill* is very well, and his Curses on her very well and naturally chose. *Lear's* Speech to *Regan* is very well—

No Regan *thou shalt ne'er have my Curses*, &c.

and his Passion in the whole Scene agreeable to the Manners. . . . (406–7)

1 See Volume 1, pp. 344–85.

There is nothing more beautiful than *Lear*'s first Starts of Madness, when *Edgar* comes out in the Habit of a Madman—*Didst thou give all to thy Daughters? And art thou come to this?* And again—*Have his Daughters brought him to this pass, coud'st thou save nothing? Would'st thou give 'em all*—

—*Now all the Plagues, that in the pendulous Air*
Hang fated o'er Mens Faults, Light on thy Daughters.
    Kent. *He has no Daughters, Sir.*
    Lear. *Death, Traitor, nothing cou'd have subdued Nature*
To such a Lowness, but his unkind Daughters, &c. [3.4.48–70]

Edgar's Account of a Servingman is very pretty, as all that he says in the Play is according to the Character which his Affairs oblige him to assume. . . . (407–8)
    Edgar's Description of the Precipice of *Dover* Cliff is very good. . . .
Tho' all *Lear*'s Madness is good, yet [Act IV, Scene vi] is particularly remarkable for the satyrical Reflections:

    The Usurer hangs the Couzener,
    Through tatter'd Cloaks great Vices do appear, &c. (408)

★   ★   ★

[*Othello*] I have drawn the Fable with as much favour to the Author as I possibly cou'd, yet I must own that the Faults found in it by Mr *Rymer* are but too visible for the most Part. That of making a *Negro* of the Hero or chief Character of the Play wou'd shock any one, for it is not the Rationale of the thing, and the Deductions that may thence be brought to diminish the Opposition betwixt the different Colours of Mankind—that wou'd not be sufficient to take away that which is shocking in this Story, since this entirely depends on Custom which makes it so. And on common Women's admitting a *Negro* to a Commerce with her every one almost starts at the Choice. Much more in a Woman of Vertue; and indeed *Iago, Brabantio,* &c. have shewn such Reasons as make it monstrous. I wonder *Shakespeare* saw this in the Persons of his Play and not in his own Judgment. If *Othello* had been made deformed, and not over young, but no Black, it had removed most of the Absurdities; but now it pleases only by Prescription. 'Tis possible that an innocent tender young Woman who knew little of the World might be won by the brave Actions of a gallant Man not to regard his Age or Deformities, but Nature—or what is all one in this Case, Custom—having put such a Bar as so opposite a Colour it takes away our Pity from her, and only raises our Indignation against him. I shall pass over the other Observations founded on this Error since they have been sufficiently taken Notice of already. It must be own'd that *Shakespeare* drew Men better than Women, to whom indeed he has seldom given any considerable Place in his Plays. Here and in *Romeo and Juliet* he has done most in this matter, but here he has not given any graceful Touches to *Desdemona* in many places of her Part.

Whether the Motives of *Othello*'s Jealousie be strong enough to free him from the Imputation of Levity and Folly I will not determine, since Jealousie is born often of very slight Occasions, especially in the Breasts of Men of those warmer Climates. Yet this must be said: *Shakespeare* has manag'd the Scene so well that it is that alone which supports his Play, and imposes on the Audience so very successfully that till a Reformation of the Stage comes I believe it will always be kindly receiv'd.

Iago is a Character that can hardly be admitted into the *Tragic* Scene, tho' it is qualify'd by his being push'd on by *Revenge, Ambition* and *Jealousie,* because he seems to declare himself a settled Villain. But leaving these things to every Man's Humour, which is in our Age all the Rule of Judging, let us take a View of what we can find beautiful in the Reflections and Sentiments. . . . (410-1)

I do not think *Othello*'s Account to the Senate of the progress of his Love with *Desdemona* so ridiculous as Mr. *Rymer* makes it, for as for the *Canibals,* and Men whose Heads grew beneath their Shoulders, *&c.* being Objects of vulgar Credulity, they are as probable and as moving as the *Cyclops* and *Harpyes* of *Virgil*; and then—abating for the Colour of the *Moor,* and the improbability of his having that Post—the Tale has a great deal of the *Pathos. Iago* to insinuate into *Roderigo* that he may have hopes of *Desdemona,* says—*mark me with what violence she lov'd the* Moor *but for bragging, and telling her fantastical Lies,* &c. [2.1.220]

There are in this Play as well as in most of this Poet a great abundance of *Soliloquies* in which the *Dramatic* Person discourses with the Audience his Designs, his Temper, *&c.,* which are highly unnatural and not to be imitated by any one.

The *Moor* has not bedded his Lady till he came to *Cyprus,* nay it was not done [2.3.8 ff], and yet it is before and after urg'd that she was or might be sated with him. But those little Forgetfulnesses are not worth minding. (412)

★ ★ ★

[*Cymbeline*] Tho' the usual Absurdities of irregular Plots abound in this, yet there is something in the Discovery that is very touching. The Character of the King, Queen and *Cloten* do not seem extreamly agreeable to their Quality. (419)

★ ★ ★

[*Pericles*] It being certain that this Play was printed before *Shakespeare*'s Death and often acted then with Applause, I have taken the Pains to give you the Argument; in which there is nothing Dramatic but the Discovery, which, tho' built on the highest Improbability, is very moving. (423)

★ ★ ★

I have thus at last past through all *Shakespeare*'s Plays, in which if any good judge shall think me too partial to my Author they must give me the allowance of an Editor, who can seldom see a Fault in the Author that he publishes; nay if he publish two of the same kind, that which is then under Consideration has the Advantage and excells all others. Besides, if I have shown you all that was any way beautiful in him I have also been so just to the Art as often to point out his Errors in that particular. And having gone over this celebrated Author with so much Care, an Author asserted by the Number of his Admirers (whom to oppose is counted little less than Heresie in Poetry) to be the greatest *Genius* of the modern Times, especially of this Nation, I find my self confirm'd in the Opinion I have long had of the *Antients* in the *Drama*, I mean in *Tragedy*. For, having been so long conversant with the Confusions of want of Art in this Poet (tho' supported with all the Advantages of a great Genius) the Beauty of Order, Uniformity, and Harmony of Design appears infinitely more Charming, and that is only to be found in the *Greek Poets*. (Tho' *Otway* and a very few Plays wrote by some yet living are not without their just Praise; but those are not such as have been the longest lived on the Stage, tho' very well receiv'd, it being a difficult Matter to bring such a Town to judge of the Man by the Performance and not of the Performance by the Man.)

Shakespeare is indeed stor'd with a great many Beauties, but they are in a heap of Rubbish; and as in the Ruines of a magnificent Pile we are pleas'd with the Capitals of Pillars, the *Basso-relievos* and the like, as we meet with them, yet how infinitely more beautiful and charming must it be to behold them in their proper Places in the standing Building, where every thing answers the other, and one Harmony of all the Parts heightens the Excellence even of those Parts. And thus, if those partial Beauties of *Shakespeare* cou'd be or had been view'd in a true Position with their Correspondence to some perfect whole, they wou'd receive a Praise that they cannot, as they are come up to. (424-5)

★ ★ ★

Remarks on the poems

[Shakespeare's poems] are more perfect in their kind, than his Plays.... (444)

★ ★ ★

[*Venus and Adonis*] . . . it is but too visible that *Petrarch* had a little infected his way of thinking on . . . Love and its Effects. (450)
[*Ibid.*] . . . it wou'd be tedious to refer to all the *Similes*, since there is scarce a Page but has one or more very well adapted to the heightening of the Subject. (454)

★ ★ ★

[*Rape of Lucrece*] *Lucrece* is too talkative and of too wanton a Fancy for one in her Condition and of her Temper, yet there are many good Lines, some very good Topics, tho' a little too far spread: as those of *Night, Opportunity,* and *Time.* . . . (456)

★ ★ ★

How far *Shakespeare* has excell'd in this Way is plain from his Poems before us. But this must be allow'd him, that much of the Beauty and Sweetness of Expression, which is so much contended for, is lost by the Injury of Time and the great Change of our Language since his Time; and yet there is a wonderful Smoothness in many of them, that makes the Blood dance to its Numbers. (463)

51. The Earl of Shaftesbury on Shakespeare

1710

From *Characteristicks of Men, Manners, Opinions, Times . . . Vol. I . . . Soliloquy, or Advice to an Author* (1710); this selection from 'The Second Edition, Corrected' (1714).

Anthony Ashley Cooper, 3rd Earl of Shaftesbury (1671–1713), was a philosopher who had considerable influence on the discussions of ethics, aesthetics and literature over the next century or more.

[Before the Restoration England was in a state of 'precarious Liberty', war and violence.] THE BRITISH MUSES, in this Dinn of Arms, may well lie abject and obscure, especially being as yet in their mere Infant-State. They have hitherto scarce arriv'd to any-thing of Shapeliness or Person. They lisp as in their Cradles; and their stammering Tongues, which nothing beside their Youth and Rawness can excuse, have hitherto spoken in wretched Pun and Quibble. Our *Dramatick* Shakespeare, our Fletcher, Jonson, and our *Epick* Milton preserve this Stile. (217)

*   *   *

Besides some laudable Attempts which have been made with tolerable Success of late years towards a just manner of Writing, both in the heroick and familiar Stile; we have older Proofs of a right Disposition in our People towards the moral and instructive Way. Our old Dramatick Poet* may witness for our good Ear and manly Relish. Notwithstanding his natural Rudeness, his unpolish'd Stile, his antiquated Phrase and Wit, his want of Method and Coherence, and his Deficiency in almost all the Graces and Ornaments of this kind of Writing, yet by the Justness of his Moral, the Aptness of many of his *Descriptions*, and the plain and natural Turn of several of his *Characters* he pleases his Audience, and often gains their Ear without a single Bribe from Luxury

* SHAKESPEARE

263

or Vice. That piece of his* which appears to have most affected *English* Hearts, and has perhaps been oftenest acted of any which have come upon our Stage, is almost one continu'd *Moral*; a Series of deep Reflections, drawn from *one* Mouth, upon the Subject of *one* single Accident and Calamity, naturally fitted to move Horrour and Compassion. It may be properly said of this Play, if I mistake not, that it has only ONE *Character* or *principal Part*. It contains no Adoration or Flattery of *the Sex*; no ranting at *the Gods*; no blustring *Heroism*; nor any thing of that curious mixture of *the Fierce* and *Tender* which makes the hinge of modern Tragedy, and nicely varies it between the Points of *Love* and *Honour*. (275–6)

★ ★ ★

Thro a certain Surfeit taken in a wrong kind of *serious* Reading we apply our-selves, with full Content, to the most *ridiculous*. The more remote our Pattern is from any-thing moral or profitable the more Freedom and Satisfaction we find in it. We care not how *Gothick* or *Barbarous* our Models are, what ill-design'd or monstrous Figures we view, or what false Proportions we trace or see describ'd in History, Romance, or Fiction. And thus our *Eye* and *Ear* is lost. Our Relish or *Taste* must of necessity grow barbarous, whilst *Barbarian* Customs, *Savage* Manners, *Indian* Wares, and Wonders of the *Terra Incognita*, employ our leisure Hours, and are the chief Materials to furnish out a Library. . . . in this Race of Authors, *he* is ever compleatest, and of the first Rank, who is able to speak of Things the most *unnatural* and *monstrous*.

This Humour our old Tragick Poet† seems to have discover'd. He hit our Taste in giving us a *Moorish* Hero full fraught with Prodigy: a wondrous *Story-Teller*! But for the attentive Part, the Poet chose to give it to Woman-kind. What passionate Reader of *Travels*, or Student in the prodigious Sciences can refuse to pity that fair Lady, who fell in Love with the *miraculous* MOOR? especially considering with what suitable grace such a Lover cou'd relate the most monstrous Adventures and satisfy the wondring Appetite with the most wondrous Tales. *Wherein* (says the Hero-Traveller)

> *Of Antars vaste, and Desarts idle,*
> *It was my Hint to speak:*

★ The Tragedy of *Hamlet*.
† SHAKESPEARE

264

And of the Cannibals *that each other eat!*
The Anthropophagie*! and Men whose Heads*
Do grow beneath their Shoulders. These to hear
Wou'd DESDEMONA *seriously incline.* [*Oth.*, 1.3.140 ff]

Seriously, 'twas a woful Tale! unfit, one wou'd think, to win a tender Fair-one. It's true, the Poet sufficiently condemns her Fancy; and makes her (poor Lady!) pay dearly for it in the end. But why, amongst his *Greek* Names, he shou'd have chosen one which denoted the Lady *Superstitious,* I can't imagine. . . . (344–8)

*   *   *

52. Elijah Fenton on Shakespeare

January 1711

From *An Epistle to Mr. Southerne, From Kent, January 28, 1711* (1711), lines 29 ff.

Elijah Fenton (1638–1730), poet, critic and dramatist, translated books 1, 4, 19 and 20 of the *Odyssey* in Pope's edition, and edited Waller.

Shakespeare the Genius of our Isle, whose Mind—
The universal Mirror of Mankind—
Express'd all Images, enrich'd the Stage
But stoop'd too low to please a barb'rous Age.
When his Immortal Bays began to grow
Rude was the Language, and the Humour Low.
He, like the God of Day, was always bright,
But rolling in its Course, his Orb of Light
Was sully'd and obscur'd, tho' soaring high,
With Spots contracted from the nether Sky.

But whither is th'advent'rous Muse betray'd?
Forgive her Rashness, venerable Shade!
May Spring with Purple Flow'rs perfume thy Urn,
And *Avon* with his Greens thy Grave adorn.
Be all thy Faults, whatever Faults there be,
Imputed to the Times, and not to Thee.

Some *Cyons* shot from this immortal Root,
Their Tops much lower, and less fair the Fruit.
Jonson the Tribute of my Verse might claim,
Had he not strove to blemish *Shakespeare*'s Name.
But, like the radiant Twins that gild the Sphere,
Fletcher and *Beaumont* next in Pomp appear.
The first a fruitful Vine, in bloomy Pride
Had been by Superfluity destroy'd,
But that his Friend, judiciously severe,
Prun'd the luxuriant Boughs with artful Care.
On various sounding Harps the Muses play'd,
And sung, and quaff'd their *Nectar* in the Shade.

Few Moderns in the List with these may stand,
For in those Days were Giants in the Land.
Suffice it now by Lineal Right to claim,
And bow with Filial Awe to *Shakespeare*'s Fame,
The second Honours are a glorious Name.
Achilles dead, they found no equal Lord,
To wear his Armour, and to wield his Sword.

53. Joseph Trapp, Shakespeare and English drama

c. 1712

From *Lectures on Poetry* (1742), the English translation by William Bowyer and William Clarke of Trapp's *Praelectiones Poeticae: In Schola Naturalis Philosophiae Oxon. Habitae* (Oxford, 1711, 1715, 1719).

Joseph Trapp (1679–1747) was the first Professor of Poetry at Oxford (1708–18), a Tory churchman who wrote for the *Examiner*. He translated the *Aeneid* into English and *Paradise Lost* into Latin.

[From Lectures 19 and 20, 'Of the Drama in general']

The principal Species of the Drama are two, Comedy and Tragedy. Some others there are of less Note, as Pastoral and Satire, both which we have already spoke of. Tragi-Comedy I don't reckon one of them, because I think it the greatest Absurdity in Nature, and is not so properly a Species distinct from the other two I first mention'd as the Abuse and Corruption of them. For what can be more ridiculous than in the Compass of three Hours to distract the Mind with Joy and Grief in such a Manner that the two contrary Passions may debilitate, or totally extinguish each other? How ill are such incoherent Parts united! And what is it but a monstrous Production?

> —*Turpiter atrum*
> *Desinit in piscem mulier formosa superne.*[1]
> A handsome Woman with a Fish's Tail.   *Roscommon*

How irrational a Transition is it, from beholding the Conflicts of Kings and Heroes with Misfortunes, to descend on a sudden to low Scenes of Ribaldry, and to return again from these to so moving a Spectacle! A Poem, indeed, should be adorn'd with Variety but not

[1] *A.P.*, 3 f: 'what at the top is a lovely woman ends below in a black and ugly fish'.

with Inconsistencies. The Passions, likewise, and Affections of the Mind should be bent and bow'd down, but so bent that they may not grow languid but recover new Strength. This poetic Kind of Prodigy, I think, is altogether modern, and chiefly of *British* Extraction; for it was the last Age produc'd Multitudes of them in our own Tongue. . . . (239)

The subject-Matter of this Kind of Poem is call'd the *Fable*, tho' it is often grounded upon true History; because the greatest Part of it is fabulous, tho' the Fiction be intermix'd with Matter of Fact. When it is not so it ought to be styled rather a *Dramatical History* than *Drama*; of which Sort are many of the Plays of our celebrated Countryman Shakespeare, who has crowded together the Annals of some of our Kings without any Regard to the dramatical Rules of Time or Place. But in other Respects, he

—*Spirat tragicum satis, & feliciter audet.*[1]
With happy Boldness draws a tragic Scene.

Yes, extremely happy, and in these Works—but more especially in his truer Tragedies—has deserv'd well of Posterity. (250)

[1] Horace, *Ep.*, 2.1.166: 'he has some tragic inspiration, and is happy in his ventures'.

54. Sir Richard Steele on Shakespeare

1711

From the *Spectator*, 141, 208, 238 (Folio edition).

No. 141 (11 August 1711)

[On *The Lancashire Witches* by Shadwell]

★　　　★　　　★

The Gentleman who writ this Play, and has drawn some Characters in it very justly, appears to have been mis led in his Witchcraft by an unwary following the inimitable *Shakespeare*. The Incantations in *Macbeth* have a solemnity admirably adapted to the occasion of that Tragedy, and fill the Mind with a suitable Horror; besides that, the Witches are a part of the Story it self as we find it very particularly related in *Hector Boetius*, from whom he seems to have taken it. This therefore is a proper Machine where the Business is dark, horrid and bloody; but is extreamly foreign from the Affair of Comedy. Subjects of this kind, which are in themselves disagreeable, can at no time become entertaining but by passing thro' an Imagination like *Shakespeare's* to form them; for which Reason Mr. *Dryden* wou'd not allow even *Beaumont* and *Fletcher* capable of imitating him.

> *But* Shakespeare's *Magick cou'd not copy'd be,*
> *Within that Circle none durst Walk but He.*[1]

★　　　★　　　★

No. 208 (29 October 1711)

I have several Letters from People of good Sense who lament the Depravity or Poverty of Taste the Town is fallen into with Relation to Plays and publick Spectacles. A Lady in particular observes that there

---

[1] Prologue to *The Tempest* adaptation; cf. Vol. 1, pp. 78–9.

is such a Levity in the Minds of her own Sex that they seldom attend any thing but Impertinences. It is indeed prodigious to observe how little Notice is taken of the most exalted Parts of the best Tragedies in *Shakespeare*; nay it is not only visible that Sensuality has devoured all Greatness of Soul but the under Passion (as I may so call it) of a noble Spirit, Pity, seems to be a Stranger to the Generality of an Audience. The Minds of Men are indeed very differently disposed, and the Reliefs from Care and Attention are of one sort in a great Spirit and of another in an ordinary one. The Man of a great Heart and a serious Complexion is more pleased with Instances of Generosity and Pity than the light and ludicrous Spirit can possibly be with the highest Strains of Mirth and Laughter. It is therefore a melancholy Prospect when we see a numerous Assembly lost to all serious Entertainments, and such Incidents as should move one sort of Concern excite in them a quite contrary one. In the Tragedy of *Macbeth* the other Night, when the Lady who is conscious of the Crime of murdering the King seems utterly astonished at the News and makes an Exclamation at it, instead of the Indignation which is natural to the Occasion that Expression is received with a loud Laugh: they were as merry when a Criminal was stabbed. It is certainly an Occasion of rejoycing when the Wicked are seized in their Designs; but, I think, it is not such a Triumph as is exerted by Laughter.

★   ★   ★

<h2 style="text-align:center">No. 238 (3 December 1711)</h2>

Among all the Diseases of the Mind there is not one more epidemical or more pernicious than the Love of Flattery. For as where the Juices of the Body are prepared to receive a malignant Influence there the Disease rages with most Violence, so in this Distemper of the Mind where there is ever a Propensity and Inclination to suck in the Poison it cannot be but that the whole Order of reasonable Action must be overturn'd. For, like Musick, it

> —*So softens and disarms the Mind,*
> *That not one Arrow can Resistance find.*

First we flatter our selves, and then the Flattery of others is sure of Success. It awakens our Self-Love within, a Party which is ever ready to revolt from our better Judgment and joyn the Enemy without. Hence it is that the Profusion of Favours we so often see poured upon the Parasite are represented to us by our Self-Love, as Justice done to the Man so agreeably reconciles us to our selves. When we are overcome by such soft Insinuations and ensnaring Compliances we gladly recompence the Artifices are made Use of to blind our Reason, and which triumph over the Weaknesses of our Temper and Inclinations. ... It sometimes happens that even Enemies and envious Persons bestow the sincerest Marks of Esteem when they least design it. Such afford a greater Pleasure as extorted by Merit and freed from all Suspicion of Favour or Flattery. Thus it is with *Malvolio*. He has Wit, Learning, and Discernment, but temper'd with an Allay of Envy, Self-Love, and Detraction. *Malvolio* turns pale at the Mirth and good Humour of the Company if it center not in his Person; he grows jealous and displeased when he ceases to be the only Person admired, and looks upon the Commendations paid to another as a Detraction from his Merit and an Attempt to lessen the Superiority he affects; but by this very Method he bestows such Praise as can never be suspected of Flattery. His Uneasiness and Distastes are so many sure and certain Signs of another's Title to that Glory he desires and has the Mortification to find himself not possessed of.

*　　　*　　　*

55. Joseph Addison on Shakespeare

1711–14

From the *Spectator*, 39, 40, 42, 44, 61, 161, 279, 419, 592 (Folio edition).

Joseph Addison (1672–1719), poet, dramatist and essayist, was one of the few writers in this period to criticise some of the assumptions of Neo-classic doctrine. Even so he finds Shakespeare wanting on other heads.

No. 39 (14 April 1711)

*　　*　　*

... our *English* Poets have succeeded much better in the Stile than in the Sentiments of their Tragedies. Their Language is very often Noble and Sonorous, but the Sense either very trifling or very common. ... I must in the next place observe that when our Thoughts are great and just they are often obscured by the sounding Phrases, hard Metaphors, and forced Expressions in which they are cloathed. *Shakespeare* is often very Faulty in this Particular.

*　　*　　*

No. 40 (16 April 1711)

The *English* Writers of Tragedy are possessed with a Notion that when they represent a virtuous or innocent Person in Distress they ought not to leave him till they have delivered him out of his Troubles, or made him triumph over his Enemies. This Errour they have been led into by a ridiculous Doctrine in modern Criticism, that they are obliged to an equal Distribution of Rewards and Punishments and an impartial Execution of poetical Justice. Who were the first that established this Rule I know not; but I am sure it has no Foundation in Nature, in Reason, or in the Practice of the Ancients. We find that Good and Evil happen alike to all Men on this Side the Grave; and as the principal

Design of Tragedy is to raise Commiseration and Terrour in the Minds of the Audience we shall defeat this great End if we always make Virtue and Innocence happy and successful. Whatever Crosses and Disappointments a good Man suffers in the Body of the Tragedy, they will make but small Impression on our Minds when we know that in the last Act he is to arrive at the End of his Wishes and Desires. When we see him engaged in the Depth of his Afflictions we are apt to comfort ourselves because we are sure he will find his Way out of them, and that his Grief, how great soever it may be at present, will soon terminate in Gladness. For this Reason the ancient Writers of Tragedy treated Men in their Plays as they are dealt with in the World, by making Virtue sometimes happy and sometimes miserable, as they found it in the Fable which they made choice of, or as it might affect their Audience in the most agreeable Manner. *Aristotle* considers the Tragedies that were written in either of these Kinds, and observes That those which ended unhappily had always pleased the People and carried away the Prize in the publick Disputes of the Stage from those that ended happily. Terrour and Commiseration leave a pleasing Anguish in the Mind and fix the Audience in such a serious Composure of Thought as is much more lasting and delightful than any little transient Starts of Joy and Satisfaction. Accordingly we find that more of our *English* Tragedies have succeeded in which the Favourites of the Audience sink under their Calamities than those in which they recover themselves out of them. The best Plays of this Kind are the *Orphan*, *Venice Preserv'd*, *Alexander the Great*, *Theodosius*, *All for Love*, *Oedipus*, *Oroonoko*, *Othello*, &c. *King Lear* is an admirable Tragedy of the same Kind, as *Shakespeare* wrote it; but as it is reformed according to the chymerical Notion of poetical Justice in my humble Opinion it has lost half its Beauty. At the same time I must allow that there are very noble Tragedies which have been framed upon the other Plan and have ended happily; as indeed most of the good Tragedies which have been written since the starting of the above mentioned Criticism have taken this Turn. As, the *Mourning Bride*, *Tamerlane*, *Ulysses*, *Phædra and Hyppolitus*, with most of Mr. *Dryden*'s. I must also allow that many of *Shakespeare*'s, and several of the celebrated Tragedies of Antiquity, are cast in the same Form. I do not therefore dispute against this Way of writing Tragedies but against the Criticism that would establish this as the only Method, and by that Means would very much cramp the *English* Tragedy, and perhaps give a wrong Bent to the Genius of our Writers.

The Tragi-Comedy, which is the Product of the English Theatre, is one of the most monstrous Inventions that ever enter'd into a Poet's Thoughts. An Author might as well think of weaving the Adventures of *Æneas* and *Hudibras* into one Poem as of writing such a motly Piece of Mirth and Sorrow. But the Absurdity of these Performances is so very visible that I shall not insist upon it.

The same Objections which are made to Tragi-Comedy may in some Measure be apply'd to all Tragedies that have a double Plot in them, which are likewise more frequent upon the *English* Stage than upon any other. For tho' the Grief of the Audience in such Perform-ances be not chang'd into another Passion, as in Tragi-Comedies, it is diverted upon another Object, which weakens their Concern for the principal Action and breaks the Tide of Sorrow by throwing it into different Channels. This Inconvenience, however, may in a great Measure be cur'd, if not wholly remov'd, by the skilful Choice of an Under-Plot, which may bear such a near Relation to the principal Design as to contribute towards the Completion of it and be concluded by the same Catastrophe.

*   *   *

No. 42 (18 April 1711)

*   *   *

The Taylor and the Painter often contribute to the Success of a Tragedy more than the Poet. Scenes affect ordinary Minds as much as Speeches, and our Actors are very sensible that a well-dress'd Play has sometimes brought them as full Audiences as a well-written one. The *Italians* have a very good Phrase to express this Art of imposing upon the Spectators by Appearances: They call it the *Fourberia della Scena, The Knavery or trickish Part of the Drama.* But however the Show and Outside of the Tragedy may work upon the Vulgar, the more understanding Part of the Audience immediately see through it and despise it.

A good Poet will give the Reader a more lively Idea of an Army or a Battle in a Description than if he actually saw them drawn up in Squadrons and Battallions, or engaged in the Confusion of a Fight. Our Minds should be open'd to great Conceptions and inflamed with glorious Sentiments by what the Actor speaks more than by what he appears. Can all the Trappings or Equipage of a King or Hero give *Brutus* half that Pomp and Majesty which he receives from a few Lines in *Shakespeare?*

*   *   *

274

No. 44 (20 April 1711)

Among the several Artifices which are put in Practice by the Poets to fill the Minds of the Audience with Terrour, the first Place is due to Thunder and Lightning, which are often made use of at the Descending of a God or the Rising of a Ghost, at the Vanishing of a Devil or at the Death of a Tyrant. I have known a Bell introduced into several Tragedies with good Effect, and have seen the whole Assembly in a very great Alarm all the while it has been ringing. But there is nothing which delights and terrifies our *English* Theatre so much as a Ghost, especially when he appears in a bloody Shirt. A Spectre has very often saved a Play, though he has done nothing but stalked across the Stage, or rose through a Cleft of it, and sunk again without speaking one Word. There may be a proper Season for these several Terrours, and when they only come in as Aids and Assistances to the Poet they are not only to be excused but to be applauded. Thus the sounding of the Clock in *Venice preserv'd* makes the Hearts of the whole Audience quake, and conveys a stronger Terrour of the Mind than it is possible for Words to do. The Appearance of the Ghost in *Hamlet* is a Masterpiece in its kind, and wrought up with all the Circumstances that can create either Attention or Horrour. The Mind of the Reader is wonderfully prepared for his Reception by the Discourses that precede it. His dumb Behaviour at his first Entrance strikes the Imagination very strongly; but every Time he enters he is still more terrifying. Who can read the Speech with which young *Hamlet* accosts him, without trembling?

> Hor. *Look, my Lord, it comes.*
> Ham. *Angels and Ministers of Grace defend us.*
> *Be thou a Spirit of Health, or Goblin damn'd;*
> *Bring with thee Airs from Heav'n, or Blasts from Hell;*
> *Be thy Events wicked or charitable;*
> *Thou com'st in such a questionable Shape*
> *That I will speak to thee. I'll call thee* Hamlet,
> *King, Father, Royal* Dane: *Oh! Oh! Answer me,*
> *Let me not burst in Ignorance; but tell*
> *Why thy canoniz'd Bones, hearsed in Death,*
> *Have burst their Cearments? Why the Sepulchre*
> *Wherein we saw thee quietly inurn'd,*
> *Hath op'd his ponderous and marble Jaws*

To cast thee up again? What may this mean?
That thou dead Coarse again in compleat Steel,
Revisit'st thus the Glimpses of the Moon,
Making Night hideous? [1.4.38 ff]

I do not therefore find Fault with the Artifices abovementioned when they are introduced with Skill and accompanied by proportionable Sentiments and Expressions in the Writing.

For the moving of Pity our principal Machine is the Handkerchief, and indeed in our common Tragedies we should not know very often that the Persons are in Distress by any thing they say if they did not from time to time apply their Handkerchiefs to their Eyes. Far be it from me to think of banishing this Instrument of Sorrow from the Stage: I know a Tragedy could not subsist without it. All that I would contend for is to keep it from being misapplied. In a Word, I would have the Actor's Tongue sympathize with his Eyes. . . .

But among all our Methods of moving Pity or Terrour there is none so absurd and barbarous, and what more exposes us to the Contempt and Ridicule of our Neighbours, than that dreadful butchering of one another which is so very frequent upon the *English* Stage. To delight in seeing Men stabb'd, poyson'd, rack'd, or impaled, is certainly the Sign of a cruel Temper. And as this is often practis'd before the *British* Audience several *French* Criticks, who think these are grateful Spectacles to us, take Occasion from them to represent us as a People that delight in Blood. It is indeed very odd to see our Stage strow'd with Carcasses in the last Scene of a Tragedy, and to observe in the Ward-robe of the Play-house several Daggers, Poniards, Wheels, Bowls for Poison, and many other Instruments of Death. Murders and Executions are always transacted behind the Scenes in the *French* Theatre, which in general is very agreeable to the Manners of a polite and civiliz'd People. But as there are no Exceptions to this Rule on the *French* Stage it leads them into Absurdities almost as ridiculous as that which falls under our present Censure. I remember in the famous Play of *Corneille* written upon the Subject of the *Horatii* and *Curiatii*, the fierce young Heroe who had overcome the *Curiatii* one after another, instead of being congratulated by his Sister for his Victory, being upbraided by her for having slain her Lover, in the Height of his Passion and Resentment kills her. If any thing could extenuate so brutal an Action it would be the doing of it on a sudden, before the Sentiments of Nature, Reason, or Manhood could take Place in him. However, to avoid *publick*

Blood-shed, as soon as his Passion is wrought to its Height he follows his Sister the whole Length of the Stage, and forbears killing her till they are both withdrawn behind the Scenes. I must confess, had he murder'd her before the Audience the Indecency might have been greater, but as it is it appears very unnatural, and looks like killing in cold Blood. To give my Opinion upon this Case: the Fact ought not to have been represented but to have been told, if there was any Occasion for it.

It may not be unacceptable to the Reader to see how *Sophocles* has conducted a Tragedy under the like delicate Circumstances. *Orestes* was in the same Condition with *Hamlet* in *Shakespeare*, his Mother having murder'd his Father and taken Possession of his Kingdom in Conspiracy with her Adulterer. That young Prince therefore, being determin'd to revenge his Father's Death upon those who filled his Throne, conveys himself by a beautiful Stratagem into his Mother's Apartment with a Resolution to kill her. But because such a Spectacle would have been too shocking to the Audience this dreadful Resolution is executed behind the Scenes. The Mother is heard calling out to her Son for Mercy, and the Son answering her, that she shew'd no Mercy to his Father. After which she shrieks out that she is wounded, and by what follows we find that she is slain. I don't remember that in any of our Plays there are Speeches made behind the Scenes, tho' there are other Instances of this Nature to be met with in those of the Ancients. And I believe my Reader will agree with me that there is something infinitely more affecting in this dreadful Dialogue between the Mother and her Son behind the Scenes than cou'd have been in any thing transacted before the Audience. *Orestes* immediately after meets the Usurper at the Entrance of his Palace, and by a very happy Thought of the Poet avoids killing him before the Audience by telling him that he should live some Time in his present Bitterness of Soul before he would dispatch him, and ordering him to retire into that Part of the Palace where he had slain his Father, whose Murther he would revenge in the very same Place where it was committed. By this Means the Poet observes that Decency, which *Horace* afterwards establish'd by a Rule, of forbearing to commit Paracides or unnatural Murthers before the Audience.

Nec coram populo natos Medea *trucidet.*

Let not Medea *draw her murth'ring Knife.*
And spill her Childrens Blood upon the Stage;[1]

★   ★   ★

[1] Horace, *A.P.*, 185; trans. Roscommon.

No. 61 (10 May 1711)

There is no kind of false Wit which has been so recommended by the Practice of all Ages as that which consists in a Jingle of Words, and is comprehended under the general Name of *Punning*. It is indeed impossible to kill a Weed which the Soil has a natural Disposition to produce. The Seeds of Punning are in the Minds of all Men, and tho' they may be subdued by Reason, Reflection and good Sense, they will be very apt to shoot up in the greatest Genius that is not broken and cultivated by the Rules of Art. Imitation is natural to us, and when it does not raise the Mind to Poetry, Painting, Musick, or other more noble Arts, it often breaks out in Punns and Quibbles.

Aristotle, in the Eleventh Chapter of his Book of Rhetorick, describes two or three kinds of Punns (which he calls Paragrams) among the Beauties of good Writing, and produces Instances of them out of some of the greatest Authors in the *Greek* Tongue. *Cicero* has sprinkled several of his Works with Punns, and in his Book where he lays down the Rules of Oratory quotes abundance of Sayings as Pieces of Wit, which also upon Examination prove arrant Puns. But the Age in which *the Punn* chiefly flourished, was the Reign of King *James* the First. That learned Monarch was himself a tolerable Punnster, and made very few Bishops or Privy-Counsellors that had not some time or other signalized themselves by a Clinch or a *Conundrum*. It was therefore in this Age that the Punn appeared with Pomp and Dignity. It had before been admitted into merry Speeches and ludicrous Compositions but was now delivered with great Gravity from the Pulpit, or pronounced in the most solemn manner at the Council-Table. The greatest Authors, in their most serious Works, made frequent use of Punns. The Sermons of Bishop *Andrewes*, and the Tragedies of *Shakespeare*, are full of them. The Sinner was punned into Repentance by the former, as in the Latter nothing is more usual than to see a Hero weeping and quibbling for a dozen Lines together.

* * *

No. 161 (3 September 1711)

* * *

Among great Geniuses, those few draw the Admiration of all the World upon them and stand up as the Prodigies of Mankind who, by

the meer strength of natural Parts, and without any Assistance of Art
or Learning, have produced Works that were the Delight of their
own Times and the Wonder of Posterity. There appears something
nobly wild and extravagant in these great natural Geniuses that is
infinitely more beautiful than all the Turn and Polishing of what the
French call a *Bel Esprit* (by which they would express a Genius refined
by Conversation, Reflection, and the Reading of the most polite
Authors). The greatest Genius that runs through the Arts and
Sciences takes a kind of Tincture from them, and falls unavoidably
into limitation.

Many of these great natural Geniuses that were never disciplined
and broken by Rules of Art are to be found among the Ancients, and
in particular among those of the more Eastern Parts of the World.
Homer has innumerable Flights that *Virgil* was not able to reach, and
in the Old Testament we find several Passages more elevated and
sublime than any in *Homer*. At the same Time that we allow a greater
and more daring Genius to the Ancients we must own that the greatest
of them very much failed in, or, if you will, that they were very much
above the Nicety and Correctness of the Moderns. In their Similitudes
and Allusions, provided there was a Likeness, they did not much trouble
themselves about the Decency of the Comparison. Thus *Solomon* resembles the Nose of his Beloved to the Tower of *Libanon* which looketh
toward *Damascus*; as the Coming of a Thief in the Night is a Similitude
of the same Kind in the New Testament. It would be endless to make
Collections of this Nature. *Homer* illustrates one of his Heroes en-
compassed with the Enemy by an Ass in a Field of Corn that has his
Sides belaboured by all the Boys of the Village without stirring a Foot
for it; and another of them tossing to and fro in his Bed, and burning
with Resentment, to a Piece of Flesh broiling on the Coals. This
particular Failure in the Ancients opens a large Field of Raillery to the
little Wits, who can laugh at an Indecency but not relish the Sublime
in these Sorts of Writings. The present Emperor of *Persia*, comfortable
to this Eastern way of Thinking, amidst a great many pompous
Titles denominates himself the Sun of Glory and the Nutmeg of
Delight. In short, to cut off all Cavelling against the Ancients, and
particularly those of the warmer Climates who had most Heat and
Life in their Imaginations, we are to consider that the Rule of observing
what the *French* call the *Bien se'ance* in an Allusion has been found out
of latter Years and the colder Regions of the World; where we would
make some Amends for our want of Force and Spirit, by a scrupulous

Nicety and Exactness in our Compositions. Our Countryman *Shakespeare* was a remarkable Instance of this first kind of great Geniuses.

*   *   *

No. 279 (19 January 1712)

*   *   *

It shows a greater Genius in *Shakespeare* to have drawn his *Calyban* than his *Hotspur* or *Julius Caesar*: The one was to be supplied out of his own Imagination, whereas the other might have been formed upon Tradition, History and Observation.

*   *   *

No. 419 (1 July 1712)

*   *   *

[On the poetry of the supernatural] Amongst the *English Shakespeare* has incomparably excelled all others. That noble Extravagance of Fancy, which he had in so great Perfection, throughly qualified him to touch this weak superstitious Part of his Reader's Imagination, and made him capable of succeeding where he had nothing to support him besides the Strength of his own Genius. There is something so wild and yet so solemn in the speeches of his Ghosts, Fairies, Witches, and the like Imaginary Persons, that we cannot forbear thinking them natural tho' we have no Rule by which to judge of them, and must confess, if there are such Beings in the World, it looks highly probable they should talk and act as he has represented them.

*   *   *

No. 592 (10 September 1714)

*   *   *

In the next Place, our Criticks do not seem sensible that there is more Beauty in the Works of a great Genius who is ignorant of the Rules of Art than in those of a little Genius who knows and observes them. . . . Our inimitable *Shakespeare* is a Stumbling-block to the whole Tribe of these rigid Criticks. Who would not rather read one of his Plays, where there is not a single Rule of the Stage observed, than any Production of a modern Critick, where there is not one of them violated? *Shakespeare* was indeed born with all the Seeds of Poetry, and may be compared to the Stone in *Pyrrhus*'s Ring, which, as Pliny tells us, had the Figure of *Apollo* and the Nine Muses in the Veins of it, produced by the spontaneous Hand of Nature without any Help from Art.

56. John Dennis on Shakespeare's genius and morality

1711

From *An Essay upon the Genius and Writings of Shakespeare: with Some Letters of Criticism to the* SPECTATOR (1712); published 1712, the letters are dated between February and October 1711.

Dennis offers some conventional praise of Shakespeare in the first letter, but devotes most of his energy either to justifying the concept of poetic justice (in opposition to Addison) and attacking Shakespeare for not having observed it, or to proving (against Gildon) that Shakespeare did not know the classics. In his arguments, attitudes, and indeed even at times his phrasing Dennis echoes Rymer.

On the Genius and Writings of SHAKESPEARE

To Mr.—, LETTER I.

Feb. 1. 1711

SIR,

I here send you the Tragedy of *Coriolanus*, which I have alter'd from the Original of *Shakespeare*[1], and with it a short Account of the Genius and Writings of that Author, both which you desired me to send to

[1] Although apparently completed by 1711 Dennis's version was not performed until 1719; cf. No. 64 below.

you the last time I had the good Fortune to see you. But I send them both upon this condition, that you will with your usual Sincerity tell me your Sentiments both of the Poem and of the Criticism.

Shakespeare was one of the greatest Geniuses that the World e'er saw for the Tragick Stage. Tho' he lay under greater Disadvantages than any of his Successors, yet had he greater and more genuine Beauties than the best and greatest of them. And what makes the brightest Glory of his Character, those Beauties were entirely his own, and owing to the Force of his own Nature; whereas his Faults were owing to his Education and to the Age that he liv'd in. One may say of him as they did of *Homer*, that he had none to imitate, and is himself inimitable. His Imaginations were often as just as they were bold and strong. He had a natural Discretion, which never cou'd have been taught him, and his Judgment was strong and penetrating. He seems to have wanted nothing but Time, and Leisure for Thought, to have found out those Rules of which he appears so ignorant. His Characters are always drawn justly, exactly, graphically, except where he fail'd by not knowing History or the Poetical Art. He has for the most part more fairly distinguish'd them than any of his Successors have done, who have falsified them or confounded them by making Love the predominant Quality in all. He had so fine a Talent for touching the Passions, and they are so lively in him and so truly in Nature, that they often touch us more without their due Preparations than those of other Tragick Poets, who have all the Beauty of Design and all the Advantage of Incidents. His Master-Passion was Terror, which he has often mov'd so powerfully and so wonderfully that we may justly conclude that if he had had the Advantage of Art and Learning he wou'd have surpass'd the very best and strongest of the Ancients. His Paintings are often so beautiful and so lively, so graceful and so powerful, especially where he uses them in order to move Terror, that there is nothing perhaps more accomplish'd in our *English* Poetry. His Sentiments for the most part, in his best Tragedies, are noble, generous, easie and natural, and adapted to the Persons who use them. His Expression is in many Places good and pure after a hundred Years; simple tho' elevated, graceful tho' bold, and easie tho' strong. He seems to have been the very Original of our *English* Tragical Harmony: that is, the Harmony of Blank Verse, diversifyed often by Dissyllable and Trissyllable Terminations. For that Diversity distinguishes it from Heroick Harmony, and, bringing it nearer to common Use, makes it more proper to gain Attention and more fit for Action and Dialogue.

Such Verse we make when we are writing Prose; we make such Verse in common Conversation.

If *Shakespeare* had these great Qualities by Nature, what would he not have been if he had join'd to so happy a Genius Learning and the Poetical Art? For want of the latter our Author has sometimes made gross Mistakes in the Characters which he has drawn from History, against the Equality and Conveniency of Manners of his Dramatical Persons. Witness *Menenius* in the following Tragedy, whom he has made an errant Buffoon, which is a great Absurdity. For he might as well have imagin'd a grave majestick *Jack-Pudding* as a Buffoon in a *Roman* Senator. *Aufidius* the General of the *Volscians* is shewn a base and a profligate Villain. He has offended against the Equality of the Manners even in his Hero himself, for *Coriolanus* who in the first part of the Tragedy is shewn so open, so frank, so violent, and so magnanimous is represented in the latter part by *Aufidius*—which is contradicted by no one—a flattering, fawning, cringing, insinuating Traytor.

For want of this Poetical Art *Shakespeare* has introduced things into his Tragedies which are against the Dignity of that noble Poem, as the Rabble in *Julius Cæsar*, and that in *Coriolanus*; tho' that in *Coriolanus* offends not only against the Dignity of Tragedy but against the Truth of History likewise, and the Customs of Ancient *Rome*, and the Majesty of the *Roman* People, as we shall have occasion to shew anon.

For want of this Art he has made his Incidents less moving, less surprizing, and less wonderful. He has been so far from seeking those fine Occasions to move, with which an Action furnish'd according to Art would have furnish'd him, that he seems rather to have industriously avoided them. He makes *Coriolanus* upon his Sentence of Banishment take his leave of his Wife and his Mother out of sight of the Audience, and so has purposely, as it were, avoided a great occasion to move.

If we are willing to allow that *Shakespeare* by sticking to the bare Events of History has mov'd more than any of his Successors, yet his just Admirers must confess that if he had had the Poetical Art he would have mov'd ten times more. For 'tis impossible that by a bare Historical Play he could move so much as he would have done by a Fable. . . .
(1-5)

★   ★   ★

The second Reason why the Fiction of a Fable pleases us more than an Historical Relation can do is because in an Historical Relation we seldom are acquainted with the true Causes of Events, whereas in a feign'd Action which is duly constituted, that is, which has a just beginning, those Causes always appear. For 'tis observable that both in a Poetical Fiction and an Historical Relation those Events are the most entertaining, the most surprizing, and the most wonderful in which Providence most plainly appears. And 'tis for this Reason that the Author of a just Fable must please more than the Writer of an Historical Relation. The Good must never fail to prosper, and the Bad must be always punish'd. Otherwise the Incidents, and particularly the Catastrophe—which is the grand Incident—are liable to be imputed rather to Chance than to Almighty Conduct and to Sovereign Justice. The want of this impartial Distribution of Justice makes the *Coriolanus* of *Shakespeare* to be without Moral. 'Tis true, indeed, *Coriolanus* is kill'd by those Foreign Enemies with whom he had openly sided against his Country, which seems to be an Event worthy of Providence, and would look as if it were contriv'd by infinite Wisdom and executed by supreme Justice to make *Coriolanus* a dreadful Example to all who lead on Foreign Enemies to the Invasion of their native Country, if there were not something in the Fate of the other Characters which gives occasion to doubt of it, and which suggests to the Sceptical Reader that this might happen by accident. For *Aufidius*, the principal Murderer of *Coriolanus*, who in cold Blood gets him assassinated by Ruffians instead of leaving him to the Law of the Country and the Justice of the *Volscian* Senate, and who commits so black a Crime not by any erroneous Zeal or a mistaken Publick Spirit but thro' Jealousy, Envy, and inveterate Malice; this Assassinator not only survives, and survives unpunish'd, but seems to be rewarded for so detestable an Action by engrossing all those Honours to himself which *Coriolanus* before had shar'd with him. But not only *Aufidius* but the *Roman* Tribunes, *Sicinius* and *Brutus*, appear to me to cry aloud for Poetick Vengeance. For they are guilty of two Faults, neither of which ought to go unpunish'd, the first in procuring the Banishment of *Coriolanus*. If they were really jealous that *Coriolanus* had a Design on their Liberties when he stood for the Consulship it was but just that they should give him a Repulse; but to get the Champion and Defender of their Country banish'd upon a pretended Jealousy was a great deal too much, and could proceed from nothing but that Hatred and Malice which they had conceiv'd against him for opposing their Institution. Their second Fault lay in procuring this Sentence by indirect Methods, by exasperating and inflaming the People by Artifices and Insinuations, by taking a base Advantage of the Open-heartedness and Violence of *Coriolanus*, and by oppressing him with a Sophistical Argument—that he aim'd at Sovereignty because he had not delivered into the Publick Treasury the Spoils which he had taken from the *Antiates*. As if a Design of Sovereignty could be reasonably concluded from any one Act; or any one could think of bringing to pass such a Design by eternally favouring the Patricians and disobliging the Populace. For we need make no doubt but that it was among the young Patricians that *Coriolanus* distributed the Spoils which were taken from the *Antiates*; whereas nothing but caressing the Populace could enslave the *Roman* People, as *Cæsar* afterwards very well saw and experienc'd. So that this Injustice of the Tribunes was the original Cause of the Calamity which afterwards befel their Country by the Invasion of the *Volscians*, under the Conduct of *Coriolanus*. And yet these Tribunes at the end of the Play, like *Aufidius*, remain unpunish'd. But indeed *Shakespeare* has been wanting in the exact Distribution of Poetical Justice not only in his *Coriolanus* but in most of his best Tragedies, in which the Guilty and the Innocent perish promiscuously; as *Duncan* and *Banquo* in *Macbeth*, as likewise Lady *Macduff* and her Children; *Desdemona* in *Othello*; *Cordelia*, *Kent*, and King *Lear*, in the Tragedy that bears his Name; *Brutus* and *Portia* in *Julius Cæsar*, and young *Hamlet* in the Tragedy of *Hamlet*. For tho' it may be said in Defence of the last that *Hamlet* had a Design to kill his Uncle who then reign'd, yet this is justify'd by no less than a Call from Heaven, and raising up one from the Dead to urge him to it. The Good and the Bad then perishing promiscuously in the best of *Shakespeare*'s Tragedies there can be either none or very weak Instruction in them, for such promiscuous Events call the Government of Providence into Question, and by Scepticks and Libertines are resolv'd into Chance. I humbly conceive therefore that this want of Dramatical Justice in the Tragedy of *Coriolanus* gave occasion for a just Alteration, and that I was oblig'd to sacrifice to that Justice *Aufidius* and the Tribunes, as well as *Coriolanus*.

Thus have we endeavour'd to shew that for want of the Poetical Art *Shakespeare* lay under very great Disadvantages. At the same time we must own to his Honour, that he has often perform'd Wonders without it . . . *Shakespeare* would have wonderfully surpass'd himself, if Art had been join'd to Nature. (6–10)

*   *   *

LETTER II.

Feb. 6. 1711

SIR,

Upon the Encouragement I have receiv'd from you I shall proceed to shew under what Disadvantages *Shakespeare* lay for want of being conversant with the Ancients. But because I have lately been in some Conversation where they would not allow but that he was acquainted with the Ancients, I shall endeavour to make it appear that he was not; and the shewing that in the Method in which I pretend to convince the Reader of it will sufficiently prove what Inconveniencies he lay under, and what Errors he committed for want of being conversant with them. But here we must distinguish between the several kinds of Acquaintance. A Man may be said to be acquainted with another who never was but twice in his Company; but that is at the best a superficial Acquaintance, from which neither very great Pleasure nor Profit can be deriv'd. Our Business is here to shew that *Shakespeare* had no familiar Acquaintance with the *Græcian* and *Roman* Authors. For if he was familiarly conversant with them how comes it to pass that he wants Art? Is it that he studied to know them in other things, and neglected that only in them which chiefly tends to the Advancement of the Art of the Stage? Or is it that he wanted Discernment to see the Justness and the Greatness and the Harmony of their Designs, and the Reasonableness of those Rules upon which those Designs are founded? Or how come his Successors to have that Discernment which he wanted, when they fall so much below him in other things? How comes he to have been guilty of the grossest Faults in Chronology, and how come we to find out those Faults? In his Tragedy of *Troilus and Cressida* he introduces *Hector* speaking of *Aristotle*, who was born a thousand Years after the Death of *Hector*. In the same Play mention is made of *Milo*, which is another very great Fault in Chronology.[1] *Alexander* is mention'd in *Coriolanus* [5.4.21], tho' that Conqueror of the Orient liv'd above two hundred Years after him. In this last Tragedy he has mistaken the very Names of his Dramatick Persons, if we give Credit to *Livy*. For the Mother of *Coriolanus* in the *Roman* Historian is *Vetturia*, and the Wife is *Volumnia*. Whereas in *Shakespeare* the Wife is *Virgilia*, and the Mother *Volumnia*. And the *Volscian* General in *Shakespeare* is *Tullus Aufidius*, and *Tullus Attius* in *Livy*. How comes it that he takes *Plutarch*'s Word (who was by Birth a *Græcian*) for the Affairs of *Rome*

[1] Cf. *Troilus and Cressida*, 2.2.166 and 2.3.241.

rather than that of the *Roman* Historian, if so be that he had read the Latter? Or what Reason can be given for his not reading him, when he wrote upon a *Roman* Story, but that in *Shakespeare*'s time there was a Translation of *Plutarch* and there was none of *Livy*?[1] If *Shakespeare* was familiarly conversant with the *Roman* Authors, how came he to introduce a Rabble into *Coriolanus*, in which he offended not only against the Dignity of Tragedy but the Truth of Fact, the Authority of all the *Roman* Writers, the Customs of Ancient *Rome*, and the Majesty of the *Roman* People? By introducing a Rabble into *Julius Cæsar* he only offended against the Dignity of Tragedy. For that part of the People who ran about the Streets upon great Festivals, or publick Calamities, or publick Rejoicings, or Revolutions in Government are certainly the Scum of the Populace. But the Persons who in the Time of *Coriolanus* rose in Vindication of their just Rights and extorted from the Patricians the Institution of the Tribunes of the People, and the Persons by whom afterwards *Coriolanus* was tried, were the whole Body of the *Roman* People to the Reserve of the Patricians; which Body included the *Roman* Knights and the wealthy substantial Citizens, who were as different from the Rabble as the Patricians themselves, as qualify'd as the latter to form a right Judgment of Things, and to contemn the vain Opinions of the Rabble. . . .

If *Shakespeare* was so conversant with the Ancients how comes he to have introduc'd some Characters into his Plays so unlike what they are to be found in History? In the Character of *Menenius* in the following Tragedy he has doubly offended against that Historical Resemblance. For first, whereas *Menenius* was an eloquent Person *Shakespeare* has made him a downright Buffoon. And how is it possible for any Man to conceive a *Ciceronian Jack-pudding*? Never was any Buffoon eloquent, or wise, or witty, or vertuous. All the good and ill Qualities of a Buffoon are summ'd up in one Word, and that is a Buffoon. And secondly, whereas *Shakespeare* has made him a Hater and Contemner, and Vilifyer of the People, we are assur'd by the *Roman* Historian that *Menenius* was extremely popular. He was so very far from opposing the Institution of the Tribunes, as he is represented in *Shakespeare*, that he was chiefly instrumental in it. After the People had deserted the City and sat down upon the sacred Mountain he was the chief of the Delegates whom the Senate deputed to them, as being look'd upon to be the Person who would be most agreeable to them. In short, this very *Menenius* both liv'd and dy'd so very much their

[1] But Philemond Holland's translation of Livy appeared in 1600.

Favourite that dying poor he had pompous Funerals at the Expence of the *Roman* People.

Had *Shakespeare* read either *Sallust* or *Cicero* how could he have made so very little of the first and greatest of Men, as that *Cæsar* should be but a Fourth-rate Actor in his own Tragedy? How could it have been that seeing *Cæsar*, we should ask for *Cæsar*? That we should ask, where is his unequall'd Greatness of Mind, his unbounded Thirst of Glory, and that victorious Eloquence with which he triumph'd over the Souls of both Friends and Enemies, and with which he rivall'd *Cicero* in Genius as he did *Pompey* in Power? How fair an Occasion was there to open the Character of *Cæsar* in the first Scene between *Brutus* and *Cassius*! For when *Cassius* tells *Brutus* that *Cæsar* was but a Man like them, and had the same natural Imperfections which they had, how natural had it been for *Brutus* to reply that *Cæsar* indeed had their Imperfections of Nature but neither he nor *Cassius* had by any means the great Qualities of *Cæsar*: neither his Military Vertue nor Science, nor his matchless Renown, nor his unparallell'd Victories, his unwearied Bounty to his Friends nor his Godlike Clemency to his Foes, his Beneficence, his Munificence, his Easiness of Access to the meanest *Roman*, his indefatigable Labours, his incredible Celerity, the Plausibleness if not Justness of his Ambition, that knowing himself to be the greatest of Men he only sought occasion to make the World confess him such. In short, if *Brutus*, after enumerating all the wonderful Qualities of *Cæsar*, had resolv'd in spight of them all to sacrifice him to publick Liberty, how had such a Proceeding heighten'd the Vertue and the Character of *Brutus*! But then indeed it would have been requisite that *Cæsar* upon his Appearance should have made all this good. And as we know no Principle of human Action but human Sentiment only, *Cæsar* who did greater Things and had greater Designs than the rest of the *Romans* ought certainly to have outshin'd by many Degrees all the other Characters of his Tragedy. *Cæsar* ought particularly to have justified his Actions and to have heighten'd his Character by shewing that what he had done, he had done by Necessity; that the *Romans* had lost their *Agrarian*, lost their Rotation of Magistracy, and that consequently nothing but an empty Shadow of publick Liberty remain'd; that the *Gracchi* had made the last noble but unsuccessful Efforts for the restoring the Commonwealth; that they had fail'd for want of arbitrary irresistible Power, the Restoration of the *Agrarian* requiring too vast a Retrospect to be done without it; that the Government when *Cæsar* came to publick Affairs was got into the Hands of a few, and that those few were factious and were contending among themselves, and if you will pardon so mean an Expression, scrambling as it were for Power; that *Cæsar* was reduc'd to the Necessity of ruling or himself obeying a Master; and that, apprehending that another would exercise the supreme Command without that Clemency and Moderation which he did, he had rather chosen to rule than to obey. So that *Cæsar* was faulty not so much in seizing upon the Sovereignty, which was become in a manner necessary, as in not re-establishing the Commonwealth by restoring the *Agrarian* and the Rotation of Magistracies after he had got absolute and uncontroulable Power. And if *Cæsar* had seiz'd upon the Sovereignty only with a View of re-establishing Liberty he had surpass'd all Mortals in Godlike Goodness as much as he did in the rest of his astonishing Qualities. I must confess, I do not remember that we have any Authority from the *Roman* Historians which may induce us to believe that *Cæsar* had any such Design. Nor if he had had any such View could he, who was the most secret, the most prudent, and the most discerning of Men, have discover'd it before his *Parthian* Expedition was over for fear of utterly disobliging his Veterans. And *Cæsar* believ'd that Expedition necessary for the Honour and Interest of the State, and for his own Glory.

But of this we may be sure, that two of the most discerning of all the *Romans*, and who had the deepest Insight into the Soul of *Cæsar*, *Sallust* and *Cicero*, were not without Hopes that *Cæsar* would really re-establish Liberty. . . . (13–20)

★   ★   ★

I am apt to believe that if *Shakespeare* had been acquainted with all this we had had from him quite another Character of *Cæsar* than that which we now find in him. He might then have given us a Scene something like that which *Corneille* has so happily us'd in his *Cinna*; something like that which really happen'd between *Augustus*, *Mecænas* and *Agrippa*. He might then have introduc'd *Cæsar* consulting *Cicero* on the one side and on the other *Antony* whether he should retain that absolute Sovereignty which he had acquir'd by his Victory, or whether he should re-establish and immortalize Liberty. That would have been a Scene which might have employ'd the finest Art and the utmost force of a Writer. That had been a Scene in which all the great Qualities of *Cæsar* might have been display'd. I will not pretend to determine here how that Scene might have been turn'd, and what I have already said on this Subject has been spoke with the utmost Caution and Diffidence. But this I will venture to say, that if that Scene had been manag'd so as by the powerful Motives employ'd in it to have shaken the Soul of *Cæsar* and to have left room for the least Hope, for the least Doubt, that *Cæsar* would have re-establish'd Liberty after his *Parthian* Expedition; and if this Conversation had been kept secret till the Death of *Cæsar* and then had been discover'd by *Antony*, then had *Cæsar* fall'n so belov'd and lamented by the *Roman* People, so pitied and so bewail'd even by the Conspirators themselves, as never Man fell. Then there would have been a Catastrophe the most dreadful and the most deplorable that ever was beheld upon the Tragick Stage. Then had we seen the noblest of the Conspirators cursing their temerarious Act, and the most apprehensive of them in dreadful expectation of those horrible Calamities which fell upon the *Romans* after the Death of *Cæsar*. But, Sir, when I write this to you, I write it with the utmost Deference to the extraordinary Judgment of that great Man,[1] who some Years ago, I hear, alter'd the *Julius Cæsar*. And I make no doubt but that his fine Discernment and the rest of his great Qualities have amply supply'd the Defects which are found in the Character of *Shakespeare's Cæsar*. (22-4)

★   ★   ★

LETTER III.

Feb. 8

SIR,

I come now to the main Argument which some People urge to prove that *Shakespeare* was conversant with the Ancients. For there is, say they, among *Shakespeare's* Plays, one call'd *The Comedy of Errors* which is undeniably an Imitation of the *Menechmi* of *Plautus*. Now *Shakespeare*, say they, being conversant with *Plautus*, it undeniably follows that he was acquainted with the Ancients, because no *Roman* Author could be hard to him who had conquer'd *Plautus*. To which I answer that the Errors which we have mention'd above are to be accounted for no other way, but by the want of knowing the Ancients, or by downright want of Capacity. But nothing can be more absurd or more unjust than to impute it to want of Capacity. For the very Sentiments of *Shakespeare* alone are sufficient to shew that he had a great Understanding and therefore we must account some other way for his imitation of the *Menechmi*. . . .

---

[1] Buckingham: cf. note above, p. 256.

There are at this day several Translators who, as *Hudibras* has it,

> *Translate from Languages of which*
> *They understand no part of Speech.*

I will not affirm that of *Shakespeare*. I believe he was able to do what Pedants call construe, but that he was able to read *Plautus* without Pain and Difficulty I can never believe. Now I appeal to you, Sir, what time he had between his Writing and his Acting to read any thing that could not be read with Ease and Pleasure? We see that our Adversaries themselves acknowledge that if *Shakespeare* was able to read *Plautus* with Ease nothing in Latinity could be hard to him. How comes it to pass then that he has given us no Proofs of his familiar Acquaintance with the Ancients but this Imitation of the *Menechmi* and a Version of two Epistles of *Ovid*[1]? How comes it that he had never read *Horace*'s [works] of a superiour Merit to either, and particularly his Epistle to the *Piso's*, which so much concern'd his Art? Or if he had read that Epistle how comes it that in his *Troilus and Cressida* (we must observe, by the way, that when *Shakespeare* wrote that Play, *Ben Jonson* had not as yet translated that Epistle) he runs counter to the Instructions which *Horace* has given for the forming the Character of *Achilles*?

> *Scriptor: Honoratum si forte reponis Achillem,*
> *Impiger, Iracundus, Inexorabilis, Acer,*
> *Jura neget sibi nata.*[2]

Where is the *Impiger*, the *Iracundus*, or the *Acer*, in the Character of *Shakespeare*'s *Achilles*? who is nothing but a drolling, lazy, conceited, overlooking Coxcomb, so far from being the honour'd *Achilles*, the Epithet that *Homer*, and *Horace* after him give him, that he is deservedly the Scorn and the Jest of the rest of the Characters, even to that Buffoon *Thersites*.

Tho' *Shakespeare* succeeded very well in Comedy, yet his principal Talent and his chief Delight was Tragedy. If then *Shakespeare* was qualify'd to read *Plautus* with Ease he could read with a great deal more Ease the Translations of *Sophocles* and *Euripides*. And tho' by these Translations he would not have been able to have seen the charming colouring of those great Masters yet would he have seen all the

---

[1] But cf. note above, p. 218.

[2] *A.P.*, 120 ff: 'If haply, when you write, you bring back to the stage the honouring of Achilles, let him be impatient, passionate, ruthless, fierce; let him claim that laws are not for him. . . .'

Harmony and the Beauty of their great and their just Designs. He would have seen enough to have stirr'd up a noble Emulation in so exalted a Soul as his. How comes it then that we hear nothing from him of the *Oedipus*, the *Electra*, the *Antigone of Sophocles*, of the *Iphigenia's*, the *Orestes*, the *Medea*, the *Hecuba of Euripides*? How comes it that we see nothing in the Conduct of his Pieces that shews us that he had the least Acquaintance with any of these great Master-pieces? Did *Shakespeare* appear to be so nearly touch'd with the Affliction of *Hecuba* for the Death of *Priam*, which was but daub'd and bungled by one of his Countrymen, that he could not forebear introducing it as it were by Violence into his own *Hamlet*, and would he make no Imitation, no Commendation, not the least Mention of the unparallell'd and inimitable Grief of the *Hecuba of Euripides*? How comes it that we find no Imitation of any ancient Play in Him but the *Menechmi* of *Plautus*? How came he to chuse a Comick preferably to the Tragick Poets? Or how comes he to chuse *Plautus* preferably to *Terence*, who is so much more just, more graceful, more regular, and more natural? Or how comes he to chuse the *Menechmi* of *Plautus*, which is by no means his Master-piece, before all his other Comedies? I vehemently suspect that this Imitation of the *Menechmi* was either from a printed Translation of that Comedy which is lost, or some Version in Manuscript brought him by a Friend, or sent him perhaps by a Stranger, or from the original Play it self recommended to him and read to him by some learned Friend. In short, I had rather account for this by what is not absurd than by what is, or by a less Absurdity than by a greater. For nothing can be more wrong than to conclude from this that *Shakespeare* was conversant with the Ancients, which contradicts the Testimony of his Contemporary and his familiar Acquaintance *Ben Jonson*, and of his Successor *Milton*[1]:

> *Lo* Shakespeare, *Fancy's sweetest Child,*
> *Warbles his native Wood-notes wild.*

and of Mr. *Dryden*[2] after them both, and which destroys the most glorious Part of *Shakespeare*'s Merit immediately. For how can he be esteem'd equal by Nature or superior to the Ancients when he falls so far short of them in Art, tho' he had the Advantage of knowing all that they did before him? Nay it debases him below those of common

---

[1] Cf. Volume 1, pp. 2, 24.

[2] Cf. Volume 1, p. 138: 'Those who accuse him to have wanted learning, give him the greater commendation. . . .'

Capacity by reason of the Errors which we mention'd above. Therefore he who allows that *Shakespeare* had Learning and a familiar Acquaintance with the Ancients ought to be look'd upon as a Detractor from his extraordinary Merit and from the Glory of *Great Britain*. For whether is it more honourable for this Island to have produc'd a Man who, without having any Acquaintance with the Ancients or any but a slender and a superficial one, appears to be their Equal or their Superiour by the Force of Genius and Nature, or to have bred one who, knowing the Ancients, falls infinitely short of them in Art, and consequently in Nature it self? (25–30)

*　　*　　*

So that *Shakespeare* having neither had Time to correct, nor Friends to consult, must necessarily have frequently left such faults in his Writings, for the Correction of which either a great deal of Time or a judicious and a well-natur'd Friend is indispensably necessary. . . . There is more than one Example of every kind of these Faults in the Tragedies of *Shakespeare*, and even in the *Coriolanus*. There are Lines that are utterly void of that celestial Fire of which *Shakespeare* is sometimes Master in so great a Degree. And consequently there are Lines that are stiff, and forc'd, and harsh, and unmusical, tho' *Shakespeare* had naturally an admirable Ear for the Numbers. But no Man ever was very musical who did not write with Fire, and no Man can always write with Fire unless he is so far Master of his Time as to expect those Hours when his Spirits are warm and volatile. *Shakespeare* must therefore sometimes have Lines which are neither strong nor graceful. For who ever had Force or Grace that had not Spirit? There are in his *Coriolanus*, among a great many natural and admirable Beauties, three or four of those Ornaments which *Horace* would term ambitious, and which we in *English* are apt to call Fustian or Bombast. There are Lines in some Places which are very obscure and whole Scenes which ought to be alter'd.

I have, Sir, employ'd some Time and Pains and that little Judgment which I have acquir'd in these Matters by a long and a faithful reading both of Ancients and Moderns, in adding, retrenching and altering several Things in the *Coriolanus* of *Shakespeare*, but with what Success I must leave to be determin'd by you. I know very well that you will be surpriz'd to find that after all that I have said in the former Part of this Letter against *Shakespeare*'s introducing the Rabble into *Coriolanus* I

have not only retain'd in the second Act of the following Tragedy the
Rabble which is in the Original but deviated more from the *Roman*
Customs than *Shakespeare* had done before me. I desire you to look
upon it as a voluntary Fault and a Trespass against Conviction. 'Tis one
of those Things which are *ad Populum Phaleræ*,[1] and by no means inserted to please such Men as you.

Thus, Sir, have I laid before you a short but impartial Account of
the Beauties and Defects of *Shakespeare*, with an Intention to make these
Letters publick if they are approv'd by you; to teach some People to
distinguish between his Beauties and his Defects, that while they imitate
one, they may with Caution avoid the other. . . . (33-6)

*   *   *

To the SPECTATOR *upon his Paper on the 16th of April* [*1711*]

*   *   *

[Dennis quotes Addison's opening: above, p. 272]

. . . your Correspondent goes on: *This Error*, says he, with an insolent
and dogmatick Air, *they have been led into by a ridiculous Doctrine in
modern Criticism, that they are oblig'd to an equal Distribution of Rewards
and Punishments, and an impartial Execution of poetical Justice.*

But who were the first who establish'd this Rule he is not able to tell.
I take it for granted that a Man who is ingenuous enough to own his
Ignorance is willing to be instructed. Let me tell him then that the first
who establish'd this ridiculous Doctrine of modern Criticism was a
certain modern Critick who liv'd above two thousand Years ago,
and who tells us expresly in the thirteenth Chapter of his critical
Spectator, which Pedants call his *Poetick*, *That since a Tragedy, to have
all the Beauty of which it is capable, ought to be Implex and not Simple*
(by the way, Mr. *Spectator*, you must bear with this critical Cant, as
we do with your Speculations and Lucubrations), *and ought to move
Compassion and Terror, for we have already shewn that the exciting these
Passions is the proper Effect of a tragical Imitation, it follows necessarily, that
we must not choose a very good Man, to plunge him from a prosperous
Condition into Adversity, for instead of moving Compassion and Terrour,
that on the contrary would create Horrour, and be detested by all the World.*

And does not the same deluded Philosopher tell us in the very same

---

[1] Persius, 3.30: 'To the mob with your trappings'.

Chapter that the Fable to which he gives the second Preference is that which has a double Constitution and which ends by a double Catastrophe, a Catastrophe favourable to the Good and fatal to the Wicked? Is not here, Mr. *Spectator*, a very formal Recommendation of the impartial and exact Execution of poetical Justice? Thus *Aristotle* was the first who establish'd this ridiculous Doctrine of modern Criticism, but Mr. *Rymer* was the first who introduc'd it into our native Language; who, notwithstanding the Rage of all the Poetasters of the Times, whom he has exasperated by opening the Eyes of the Blind that they may see their Errors, will always pass with impartial Posterity for a most learned, a most judicious, and a most useful Critick. Now is not your Correspondent a profound and a learned Person? and ought he not to own himself oblig'd to me for this notable piece of Erudition?

But he goes on in his dictatorian way: *This Rule*, says he, *whoever establish'd it, has, I am sure, no Foundation in Nature, in Reason, and in the practice of the Ancients.* But what will this dogmatick Person say now, when we shew him that this contemptible Doctrine of poetical Justice is not only founded in Reason and Nature, but is it self the Foundation of all the Rules, and ev'n of Tragedy itself? For what Tragedy can there be without a Fable? or what Fable without a Moral? or what Moral without poetical Justice? What Moral, where the Good and the Bad are confounded by Destiny, and perish alike promiscuously? Thus we see this Doctrine of poetical Justice is more founded in Reason and Nature than all the rest of the poetical Rules together. For what can be more natural, and more highly reasonable, than to employ that Rule in Tragedy without which that Poem cannot exist? Well! but the Practice of the Ancients is against this poetical Justice! What, always, Mr. *Spectator*? will your Correspondent have the Assurance to affirm that? No, but sometimes. Why then, sometimes the Ancients offended against Reason and Nature. And who ever believ'd that the Ancients were without Fault, or brought Tragedy to its Perfection? But I shall take another Opportunity to shew that the Practice of the Ancients in all their Masterpieces is exactly according to this fundamental Rule. I have not time to do that in this short Letter because that would necessarily oblige me to shew that poetical Justice is of a much larger Extent than this profound Critick imagines, but yet I shall give the discerning Reader a hint of it in that which follows.

Poetical Justice, says your Correspondent, *has no Foundation in Nature and Reason, because we find that good and evil happen alike to all Men on this side the Grave.* In answer to which he must give me leave to tell him that this is not only a very false but a dangerous Assertion, that we neither know what Men really are, nor what they really suffer.

'Tis not always that we know Men's Crimes, but how seldom do we know their Passions, and especially their darling Passions? And as Passion is the Occasion of infinitely more Disorder in the World than Malice (for where one Man falls a Sacrifice to inveterate Malice a thousand become Victims to Revenge and Ambition, and whereas Malice has something that shocks human Nature Passion is pleasingly catching and contagious), can any thing be more just than that that Providence which governs the World should punish Men for indulging their Passions, as much as for obeying the Dictates of their most envenom'd Hatred and Malice?

Thus you see, for ought we know, Good and Evil does not happen alike to all Men on this side the Grave. Because 'tis for the most part by their Passions that Men offend, and 'tis by their Passions, for the most part, that they are punish'd. But this is certain, that the more Virtue a Man has the more he commands his Passions, but the Virtuous alone command them. The Wicked take the utmost Care to dissemble and conceal them, for which reason we neither know what our Neighbours are nor what they really suffer. Man is too finite, too shallow, and too empty a Creature to know another Man throughly, to know the Creature of an infinite Creator; but dramatical Persons are Creatures of which a Poet is himself the Creator. And tho' a Mortal is not able to know the Almighty's Creatures he may be allow'd to know his own; to know the utmost Extent of their Guilt, and what they ought to suffer; nay, he must be allow'd not only to know this himself, but to make it manifest and unquestionable to all his Readers and Hearers. The Creatures of a poetical Creator have no Dissimulation and no Reserve. We see their Passions in all their height, and in all their Deformity, and when they are unfortunate we are never to seek for the Cause.

But suppose I should grant that there is not always an equal Distribution of Affliction and Happiness here below? Man is a Creature who was created immortal, and a Creature consequently that will find a Compensation in Futurity for any seeming Inequality in his Dealing here. But the Creatures of a poetical Creator are imaginary and transitory. They have no longer Duration than the Representation of their respective Fables, and consequently, if they offend they must be punish'd during that Representation. And therefore we are very far from pretending that poetical Justice is an equal Representation of the Justice of the Almighty.

We freely confess that 'tis but a very narrow and a very imperfect Type of it; so very narrow, and so very imperfect, that 'tis forc'd by temporal to represent eternal Punishments; and therefore when we shew a Man unfortunate in Tragedy for not restraining his Passions we mean that every one will for such Neglect, unless he timely repents, be infallibly punish'd by infinite Justice either here or hereafter.

If upon this Foot we examine the Tragedies of *Sophocles* and *Euripides* we shall find that in their most beautiful Pieces they are impartial Executors of Poetick Justice. And 'tis upon this Foot that *Aristotle* requires that we should examine them. Your Correspondent, I must confess, is in the right when he says that that Philosopher declares for Tragedies whose Catastrophes are unhappy with relation to the principal Characters. But then what Instructions does he give us for the forming those principal Characters? We are neither to make them very vertuous Persons on the one side (that is, Persons who absolutely command their Passions), nor on the other side Villains who are actuated by inveterate Malice, but something between these two: that is to say, Persons who neglecting their Passions suffer them to grow outrageous, and to hurry them to Actions which they would otherwise abhor. And that Philosopher expressly declares, as we have shewn above, that to make a virtuous Man unhappy (that is, a Man who absolutely commands his Passions) would create Horror instead of Compassion, and would be detested by all the World. And thus we have shewn that *Aristotle* is for Poetical Justice, notwithstanding that he is for unhappy Catastrophes: and so one would think was your Correspondent. For when he enumerates and commends some *English* Tragedies which have unfortunate Catastrophes, there are not two of those which he commends whose principal Characters can be said to be innocent, and consequently there are not two of them where there is not a due Observance of poetical Justice.

Thus, Mr. *Spectator*, I have discussed the Business of poetical Justice, and shewn it to be the Foundation of all Tragedy; and therefore whatever Persons, whether ancient or modern, have writ Dialogues which they call Tragedies where this Justice is not observ'd, those Persons have entertain'd and amus'd the World with romantick lamentable Tales, instead of just Tragedies and of lawful Fables. (40–7)

57. Leonard Welsted, Longinus illustrated from Shakespeare

1712

From *Remarks on Longinus, In a Letter to a Friend*; added to Welsted's translation of *A Treatise on the Sublime* (1712); this text from 'The 3rd Edition, corrected' (Dublin, 1727).

Leonard Welsted (1688–1747), poet, friend of Steele and Theobald, attacked Pope and was attacked in turn (in *The Dunciad* and in the *Prologue to the Satires*).

There are numberless Instances of this kind of Sublime to be produced from our Poets: *Shakespeare* and *Milton* every where abound with them.... [Cites Hamlet's first speech to the Ghost.] (110)

*　　*　　*

[On the expression of 'great sentiments'.] One must attend very nicely to the Character of the Person who speaks these Things, and the occasion that brings them on; otherwise they appear I know not how, shocking. To use one Example more, I am never so much affected, never so much transported with the Spirit of any Thing as when I see *Othello* make his Exit with this noble Conclusion:

> —*Set you down This,*
> *And say besides, that in* Aleppo *once,*
> *Where a Malignant and a Turband-Turk*
> *Beat a* Venetian, *and traduc'd the State;*
> *I took by the Throat the Circumcised Dog,*
> *And smote him thus.—* [5.2.354 ff]

The Passion here is work'd up into an inimitable Sublimeness; as indeed most of the Sublime Passages in *Shakespeare* are interweaved with and raised by the Pathetick. (118)

*　　*　　*

Is there any thing Excellent in any Language, for which our Favourite *Shakespeare* will not furnish us with a Parallel? I will mention only those Lines where he introduces King *John* endeavouring to engage *Hubert* in the Murder of the young Prince, *Arthur*:

> *If this same were a Church-Yard where we stand,*
> *And thou possessed with a thousand Wrongs. . . .*
> *Then, in despight of brooded watchful Day,*
> *I would into thy Bosom pour, &c.* [3.3.40 ff]

I need not observe to you what a variety of fearful Circumstances the Poet here heaps together, what Images of Death and Horror he presents us with, and with what Solemnity he introduces them. . . . (122–3)

★   ★   ★

. . . *Fletcher* perpetually pleases me; but I am struck with Astonishment when I read *Shakespeare*. Can one read him without the utmost Emotion? Or would you not rather be Author of the Two wonderful scenes in *Julius Cæsar*, than all *Dryden*'s Plays put together; even tho' they were ten times as Voluminous as they are? (133)

58. John Hughes on *Othello*

April 1713

From the *Guardian*, 37 (23 April 1713); this text from the two-volume edition (1714).

John Hughes (1677–1720) was a poet and translator, who contributed to various periodicals: the *Tatler*, *Spectator*, *Guardian* and (with Sir Richard Blackmore) the *Lay Monk*. He edited Spenser's poems in 1715, and was responsible for an edition of *Hamlet* in 1718 (reprinted 1723).

No. 37 (23 April 1713)

★　　　★　　　★

It was with this agreeable Prepossession of Mind I went some time ago
to see the old Tragedy of *Othello*, and took my Female Wards with me,
having promised them a little before to carry them to the first Play of
Shakespeare's which should be acted. Mrs. *Cornelia*, who is a great
Reader and never fails to peruse the Play-Bills, which are brought to
her every Day, gave me Notice of it early in the Morning. When I
came to my Lady *Lizard*'s at Dinner I found the young Folks all drest,
and expecting the Performance of my Promise. I went with them at
the proper Time, placed them together in the Boxes and my self by
them in a Corner Seat. As I have the chief Scenes of the Play by Heart
I did not look much on the Stage but formed to my self a new Satisfaction in keeping an Eye on the Faces of my little Audience and
observing, as it were by Reflection, the different Passions of the Play
represented in their Countenances. Mrs. *Betty* told us the Names of
several Persons of Distinction as they took their Places in the Boxes, and
entertained us with the History of a new Marriage or two till the
Curtain drew up. I soon perceived that Mrs. *Jane* was touched with
the Love of *Desdemona*, and in a Concern to see how she would come
off with her Parents. *Annabella* had a rambling Eye, and for some time
was more taken up with observing what Gentlemen looked at her,
and with criticising the Dress of the Ladies, than with any thing that
pass'd on the Stage. Mrs. *Cornelia*, who I have often said is addicted to
the Study of Romances, commended that Speech in the Play in which
Othello mentions his *Hair-breadth Scapes in th' imminent deadly Breach*
and recites his Travels and Adventures with which he had captivated
the Heart of *Desdemona*. The *Sparkler* looked several times frighted,
and as the Distress of the Play was heightned, their different Attention
was collected and fix'd wholly on the Stage, till I saw them all, with a
secret Satisfaction, betray'd into Tears.

I have often considered this Play as a noble but irregular Production
of a Genius which had the Power of animating the Theatre beyond any
Writer we have ever known. The Touches of Nature in it are
strong and masterly, but the Oeconomy of the Fable, and in some
Particulars the Probability, are too much neglected. If I would speak
of it in the most severe Terms, I should say as *Waller* does of the
Maid's Tragedy,

> Great are its Faults, but glorious is its Flame.

BUT it would be a poor Employment in a Critick to observe upon the Faults and shew no Taste for the Beauties in a Work that has always struck the most sensible Part of our Audiences in a very forcible Manner.

THE chief Subject of this Piece is the Passion of *Jealousie*, which the Poet has represented at large in its Birth, its various Workings and Agonies, and its horrid Consequences. From this Passion, and the Innocence and Simplicity of the Person suspected, arises a very moving Distress.

IT is a Remark, as I remember, of a Modern Writer, who is thought to have penetrated deeply into the Nature of the Passions, that *the most extravagant Love is nearest to the strongest Hatred*. The Moor is furious in both these Extremes. His Love is tempestuous, and mingled with a Wildness peculiar to his Character which seems very artfully to prepare for the Change which is to follow.

HOW savage, yet how ardent is that Expression of the Raptures of his Heart when, looking after *Desdemona* as she withdraws, he breaks out,

> *Excellent Wretch! Perdition catch my Soul*
> *But I do love thee; and when I love thee not,*
> Chaos *is come again.* [3.3.91 ff]

THE deep and subtle Villany of *Iago*, in working this Change from Love to Jealousie in so tumultuous a Mind as that of *Othello*, prepossessed with a Confidence in the disinterested Affection of the Man who is leading him on insensibly to his Ruin, is likewise drawn with a Masterly Hand. *Iago*'s broken Hints, Questions, and seeming Care to hide the Reason of them; his obscure Suggestions to raise the Curiosity of the Moor; his personated Confusion and refusing to explain himself while *Othello* is drawn on and held in suspence till he grows impatient and angry, then his throwing in the Poyson, and naming to him in a Caution the Passion he would raise

> —*O beware of Jealousie!*— [3.3.169]

are inimitable Strokes of Art in that Scene which has always been justly esteemed one of the best which was ever represented on the Theatre.

TO return to the Character of *Othello*; his Strife of Passions, his Starts, his Returns of Love, and Threatnings to *Iago* who had put his Mind on the Rack; his Relapses afterwards to Jealousie, his Rage against his Wife, and his asking Pardon of *Iago*, whom he thinks he had abused for his Fidelity to him are Touches which no one can overlook that has the Sentiments of Human Nature, or has consider'd the Heart of Man in its Frailties, its Penances, and all the Variety of its Agitations. The Torments which the Moor suffers are so exquisitely drawn as to render him as much an Object of Compassion, even in the barbarous Action of murdering *Desdemona*, as the innocent Person her self who falls under his Hand.

BUT there is nothing in which the Poet has more shewn his Judgment in this Play, than in the Circumstances of the Handkerchief, which is employ'd as a Confirmation to the Jealousie of *Othello* already raised. What I would here observe is that the very slightness of this Circumstance is the Beauty of it. How finely has *Shakespeare* expressed the Nature of Jealousie in those Lines which on this occasion he puts into the Mouth of *Iago*:

> *Trifles light as Air*
> *Are to the Jealous Confirmations strong*
> *As Proofs of Holy Writ.* [3.3.326 ff]

IT would be easie for a tasteless Critick to turn any of the Beauties I have here mentioned into Ridicule; but such an one would only betray a Mechanical Judgment formed out of borrow'd Rules and Commonplace Reading, and not arising from any true Discernment in Human Nature and its Passions.

The Moral of this Tragedy is an admirable Caution against hasty Suspicions and the giving way to the first Transports of Rage and Jealousie, which may plunge a Man in a few Minutes in all the Horrors of Guilt, Distraction and Ruin. . . .

59. Lewis Theobald on *King Lear, Othello* and *Julius Caesar*

1715–17

From the *Censor*, 7, 10, 36, 70.

Lewis Theobald (1688–1744), poet, dramatist, translator, critic and scholar, issued his periodical the *Censor* (with contributions from others) in 1715 and 1717.

No. 7 (25 April 1715)

I consider *Tragedy* and *Comedy* as Two Opposite *Glasses*, in which Mankind may see the true Figures they make in every important or trifling Circumstance of Life. Indeed they must look with impartial Eyes to profit by the Reflections given, or they can never be Judges of the Charms or Inelegancies that make up their Composition. If they will be purposely blind or negligent their *Passions*, like their *Habits*, will hang undecently on them however often they may frequent the *Theatre*. The peculiar Province of *Tragedy* is to refine our Souls, to purge us of those Passions that hurry us into Misfortunes, and correct those Vices that make us incur the Wrath of Heaven and Condemnation of our Fellow-Creatures. The Influences of *Comedy* are of a lighter Nature, her Aim being only to divest us of Follies and Impertinences, which may sometimes make us obnoxious to *Odium* but often render us Objects of *Ridicule*. As the Task of the former is much the Nobler, as well as of most Consequence in Life, I shall for the Generality make my Observations on this Part of *practicable* Poetry.

My Purpose at *present* is the Examination of a *Tragedy* of *Shakespeare*'s which, with all its Defects and Irregularities, has still touch'd me with the strongest Compassion, as well in my Study as on the Stage: I mean that which bears the Stile of the True and Ancient *History* of *King Lear*. I intend not to charge it with those Errors which all this Author's Plays lie under thro' his being unacquainted with the *Rules* of *Aristotle* and the *Tragedies* of the *Ancients*, but to view it on the beautiful Side, to remark the Propriety of *Lear*'s Character, how well it is supported throughout all the Scenes, and what Spirit and Elegance reigns in the Language and Sentiments.

For the Satisfaction of my *Female* Readers, and that my *Criticisms* may descend to them with more Pleasure and Familiarity I will draw up an Abstract of the real Story of this *Tragedy* as it stands in our Old *British* History. [Summarises the plot.]

*　　*　　*

No. 10 (2 May 1715)

When I gave you an Abstract of the real History of *King Lear* in my Paper of last *Monday* I promis'd on this Day to make some Remarks on the Play; to shew how the Poet by natural Incidents has heighten'd the Distress of the History; wherein he has kept up to the Tenor of it; and how artfully preserv'd the *Character* and *Manners* of *Lear* throughout his Tragedy.

How far he has kept up to the Tenor of the History most properly comes first under Consideration, in which the Poet has been just to great Exactness. He has copied the *Annals* in the Partition of his King-dom, and discarding of *Cordelia*; in his alternate Monthly Residence with his two Eldest Daughters, and their ungrateful Returns of his Kindness; in *Cordelia*'s marrying into *France*, and her prevailing with her Lord for a sufficient Aid to restore her abus'd Father to his Domin-ions. Her Forces are successful over those of her two unnatural Sisters. But in some Particulars of the *Catastrophe* the Poet has given himself a Liberty to be Master of the Story. For *Lear* and *Cordelia* are taken Prisoners and, both lying under Sentence of Death, the latter is hang'd in the Prison, and the former breaks his Heart with the Affliction of it.

I come now to speak of those Incidents which are struck out of the Story, and introduc'd as subservient to the *Tragick* Action. To examine their Force and Propriety I must first consult the Poet's Aim in the Play. He introduces a fond Father who, almost worn out with Age and Infirmity, is for transferring his Cares on his Children, who disappoint the Trust of his Love and, possess'd of the Staff in their own Hands, contemn and abuse the Affection which bestow'd it. Hence arise two practical Morals: the first a Caution against Rash and Unwary Bounty, the second against the base Returns and Ingratitude of Children to an Aged Parent. The Error of the first is to be painted in such Colours as are adapted to Compassion, the Baseness of the latter set out in such a Light as is proper to Detestation. To impart a proper Distress to *Lear's* Sufferings *Shakespeare* has given him two Friends, *Kent* and *Gloucester*; the one is made a disguis'd Companion of his Afflictions, the other loses his Eyes by the Command of the Savage Sisters only for interceeding with them for a Father, and acting in his Favour. The good old King is, by the Barbarity of his Daughters, forc'd to relinquish their Roof at Night, and in a Storm. Never was a Description wrought up with a more Masterly Hand than the Poet has here done on the Inclemency of the Season. Nor could Pity be well mov'd from a better Incident than by introducing a poor injur'd old Monarch, bareheaded in the midst of the Tempest, and tortur'd even to Distraction with his Daughters Ingratitude. How exquisitely fine are his Expostulations with the Heavens that seem to take part against him with his Children, and how artful, yet natural, are his Sentiments on this Occasion!

> *I tax not you, ye Elements, with Unkindness;*
> *I never gave you Kingdoms, call'd you Children;*
> *You owe me no Subscription:—Then let fall*
> *Your horrible Pleasure.—Here I stand your Slave,*
> *A poor, infirm, weak, and despis'd Old Man;*
> *But yet I call you servile Ministers,*
> *That will with Two pernicious Daughters join*
> *Your high-engender'd Battles 'gainst a Head*
> *So Old and White as this. O! O! 'tis foul.* [3.2.16 ff]

What admirable Thoughts of Morality and Instruction has he put in *Lear's* Mouth on the Growling of the Thunder and Flashes of the Lightning!

> *—Let the Great Gods,*
> *That keep this dreadful Pother o'er our Heads,*
> *Find out their Enemies now. Tremble thou Wretch,*
> *Who hast within thee undivulged Crimes,*
> *Unwhip'd of Justice. Hide Thee, thou bloody Hand,*
> *Thou Perjur'd, and thou Simular of Virtue*
> *That art Incestuous, &c.* [3.2.49 ff]

And afterwards in the following Speech

> *Thou thinkest much that this Contentious Storm*
> *Invades us to the Skin so, &c.* [3.4.6 ff]

Now when the Poet has once work'd up the Minds of his Audience to a full Compassion of the King's Misfortunes, to give a finishing Stroke to that Passion he makes his Sorrows to have turn'd his Brain. In which Madness, I may venture to say, *Shakespeare* has wrought with such Spirit and so true a Knowledge of Nature that he has never yet nor ever will be equall'd in it by any succeeding Poet. It may be worth observing that there is one peculiar Beauty in this Play, which is, that throughout the whole the same Incidents which force us to pity *Lear* are Incentives to our Hatred against his Daughters.

The two Episodes of *Edgar* and *Edmund* are little dependant on the Fable (could we pretend to pin down *Shakespeare* to a Regularity of Plot), but that the Latter is made an Instrument of encreasing the Vicious Characters of the Daughters, and the Former is to punish him for the adulterous Passion as well as his Treachery and Misusage to *Gloucester*; and indeed in the last Instance the Moral has some Connection to the main Scope of the Play. That the Daughters are propos'd as Examples of Divine Vengeance against unnatural Children, and as Objects of *Odium*, we have the Poet's own Words to demonstrate; for when their dead Bodies are produc'd on the Stage *Albany* says

> *This Judgement of the Heav'ns, that makes us tremble,*
> *Touches us not with Pity.*— [5.3.231 f]

As to the General Absurdities of *Shakespeare* in this and all his other Tragedies, I have nothing to say. They were owing to his Ignorance of *Mechanical* Rules and the Constitution of his Story, so cannot come under the Lash of Criticism; yet if they did I could without Regret pardon a Number of them for being so admirably lost in Excellencies. Yet there is one which without the Knowledge of Rules he might have corrected, and that is in the *Catastrophe* of this Piece. *Cordelia* and *Lear* ought to have surviv'd, as Mr. *Tate* has made them in his Alteration of this Tragedy: Virtue ought to be rewarded as well as Vice punish'd; but in their Deaths this Moral is broke through. *Shakespeare* has done the same in his *Hamlet*, but permit me to make one Observation in his Defence there, that *Hamlet* having the Blood of his Uncle on his Hands *Blood will have Blood*, as the Poet has himself express'd it in *Macbeth*.

I must conclude with some short Remarks on the third thing propos'd, which is the Artful Preservation of *Lear*'s Character. Had *Shakespeare* read all that *Aristotle*, *Horace*, and the Criticks have wrote on this Score he could not have wrought more happily. He proposes to

represent an Old Man, o'er-gone with Infirmities as well as Years;
one who was fond of Flattery and being fair spoken, of a hot and
impetuous Temper, and impatient of Controul or Contradiction.

His Fondness of Flattery is sufficiently evidenc'd in the parcelling out
his Dominions, and immediate discarding of *Cordelia* for not striking
in with this Frailty of his. His Impatience of being contradicted appears
in his Wrath to *Kent*, who would have disswaded him from so rash
an Action.

> —*Peace*, Kent;
> *Come not between the Dragon and his Wrath:*
> *I lov'd her most, and thought to set my Rest*
> *On her kind Nursery. Hence, and avoid my Sight;*
> *So be my Grave my Peace, as here I give*
> *Her Father's Heart from her.*— [1.1.120 ff]

The same Artful Breaking out of his Temper is evident on *Goneril's*
first Affront to him in retrenching the Number of his Followers. There
is a Grace that cannot be conceiv'd in the sudden Starts of his Passion
on being controul'd, and which best shews it self in forcing Us to
admi re it.

> Lear. *What, Fifty of my Followers at a Clap?*
> *Within a Fortnight?*
> Alban.—*What's the Matter, Sir?*
> Lear. *I'll tell thee;—Life and Death! I am asham'd,*
> *That thou hast Pow'r to shake my Manhood thus;*
> *That these hot Tears, which break from me perforce,*
> *Should make Thee worth them: Blasts and Fogs upon thee!*
> *Th'untented Woundings of a Father's Curse*
> *Pierce ev'ry Sense about thee!* &c. [1.4.294 ff]

I cannot sufficiently admire his Struggles with his Testy Humour;
his seeming Desire of restraining it, and the Force with which it resists
his Endeavours and flies out into Rage and Imprecations. To quote
Instances of half these Beauties were to copy Speeches out of every
Scene where *Lear* either is with his Daughters or discoursing of them.
The Charms of the *Sentiments*, and *Diction*, are too numerous to come
under the Observation of a single Paper, and will better be commended
when introduc'd occasionally and least expected.

*   *   *

No. 36 (12 January 1717)

I have frequently perus'd with Satisfaction the *Othello* of *Shakespeare*, a Play most faulty and irregular in many Points but Excellent in one Particular. For the Crimes and Misfortunes of the *Moor* are owing to an impetuous Desire of having his Doubts clear'd, and a Jealousie and Rage, native to him, which he cannot controul and which push him on to Revenge. He is otherwise in his Character brave and open, generous and full of Love for *Desdemona*, but stung with the subtle Suggestions of *Iago* and impatient of a Wrong done to his Love and Honour. Passion at once o'erbears his Reason and gives him up to Thoughts of bloody Reparation. Yet after he has determin'd to murther his Wife his Sentiments of her suppos'd Injury and his Misfortune are so pathetick that we cannot but forget his barbarous Resolution, and pity the Agonies which he so strongly seems to feel.

> Oth.—*Had it pleas'd Heav'n*
> *To try me with Affliction, had it rain'd*
> *All kind of Sores and Shames on my bare Head. . . .*
> *But there, where I have treasur'd up my Heart,*
> *Where either I must live or bear no Life,*
> *The Fountain from the which my Current runs,*
> *Or else dries up—to be discarded thence!* [4.2.48 ff]

*   *   *

No. 70 (2 April 1717)

Of all the Plays, either Ancient or Modern, the Tragedy of *Julius Cæsar*, written by *Shakespeare*, has been held in the fairest Esteem and Admiration. I do not reckon from the Vulgar, tho' they, where their Passions are concern'd, are certainly no ill Judges, but from the establish'd Rules of Dramatic Poetry and the Opinion of the best Poets. As to particular Irregularities it is not to be expected that a Genius like *Shakespeare*'s should be judg'd by the Laws of *Aristotle* and the other Prescribers to the Stage. It will be sufficient to fix a Character of Excellence to his Performances if there are in them a Number of beautiful Incidents, true and exquisite Turns of Nature and Passion, fine and delicate Sentiments, uncommon Images, and great Boldnesses of Expression.

In this Play of our Countryman's I think I may affirm, tho' against the Opinion of untasting Criticks, that all these Beauties meet, and if I were to examine the Whole it would be no great Difficulty to prove the Truth of my Assertion. But I have singled out only one Scene to be the Subject of my present *Lucubration*. Omitting the incomparable Speeches of *Brutus* and *Mark Antony* (of which those of the latter were perhaps never equall'd in any Language) the Scene I have chose is the Quarrel and Reconciliation of *Brutus* and *Cassius*; and there being no better Way to shew the Excellency of it than by a Comparison with other similar celebrated Pieces I have therefore taken that Method.

The first Scene of this kind, in point of Time as well as Beauty, is the *Quarrel* between *Agamemnon* and *Menelaus* in the first *Iphigenia* of *Euripides*; this Scene, and that between *Amintor* and *Melantius* in *Fletcher* I shall compare together, and endeavour to shew that *Shakespeare* has excelled them both. In order to this I must quote the Remark which Mr. *Dryden* makes upon these three Pieces.[1] *The Occasion which* Shakespeare, Euripides, *and* Fletcher, *have all taken is the same, grounded upon Friendship: And the Quarrel of Two virtuous Men rais'd by natural Degrees to the Extremity of Passion, is conducted in all Three to the Declination of the same Passion, and concludes with the warm renewing of their Friendships. But the particular Groundwork, which* Shakespeare *has taken, is incomparably the best; because he has not only chosen Two of the greatest Heroes of their Age; but has likewise interested the Liberty of* Rome, *and their own Honour, who were the Redeemers of it, in the Debate.* In this Reflection Mr. *Dryden* does not seem to have fix'd upon the true Cause of the Superior Beauty in *Shakespeare*, for it is the same Thing if they had been imaginary Persons and the Poet had chose his Scene and his Names at Pleasure. *Amintor* and *Melantius* in *Fletcher* are a Proof that our being mov'd depends more on the Poet's touching our Passions nicely than our being acquainted with their Persons as they are recorded in History. It signifies nothing where a Man was born or who he is, the thing that touches depends upon the Character that the Poet gives of him at first, and his Name has no more Relation to the *Idea* than that the Audience know him by that Distinction. If the Spring of our Passions arose from what Mr. *Dryden* mentions we should neither be exalted nor depressed at many Scenes founded merely on the Imagination of the Writer, either in our Author or others. We will suppose, for Instance, that there never was any such Person as *Cato*. Yet if any Author, like Mr. *Addison*, should form to himself a Character of a great Man full of his Country, struggling for Liberty against the Tide of Ambition, and make him speak and act up to these Sentiments as He

[1] Dryden, Preface to *Troilus and Cressida*: see Volume I, p. 251.

has done 'tis no matter what Name he gave him, whether that of *Cato* or any other.

But I must confine my self to the Subject I propos'd. The Ground of the Dispute in *Euripides* is this. *Agamemnon*, who, with the Confederate Princes of *Greece*, had begun a War to revenge his Brother *Menelaus* and redeem his Wife, waits for a fair Wind at *Aulis*; and is told by the Augurs, that he must obtain it by the Sacrifice of his Daughter *Iphigenia*, which alone can appease the Resentments of *Diana*. *Agamemnon* generously consents to deliver her up to so great a Motive as the Vindication of his Brother's Honour, and sends for *Iphigenia* from her Mother on a Pretence of matching her with *Achilles*. But soon after the Father takes Place in his Soul, and he sends privately to countermand the Arrival of *Iphigenia*. *Menelaus* intercepts his Packet and reads it, upon which the other charges him with Boldness, as being his Superior. He replies in the Language of an Equal, mix'd with Threatenings. The Quarrel warms, till a Messenger comes to tell *Agamemnon* of the Arrival of his Daughter; and he then resumes his Design of Sacrificing her which his Brother as passionately contradicts as he before promoted. The Scene indeed is very pathetically work'd. The general good of our Country and the natural Love of our Children are the main Topicks which the Discourse turns on, and the Passions on each Side sink by soft Degrees.

In *Fletcher* the two Friends *Melantius* and *Amintor* grow warm hastily, are reconcil'd soon again, but when a Method is propos'd to ease them by Revenge of an Injury to both their Honours they quarrel anew and cannot be said to be justly reconcil'd, because the Business on which the Dispute happen'd is entirely left in the Hands of *Melantius*. Honour and Friendship, the Violation of each and the Desire of re-cementing them are the Topicks of this Action. The Passions are strong and vehement, but conducted more according to the luxuriant Fancy of the Poet than any Standard in Nature.

In *Shakespeare* there is a Beauty which is not in any of the Others, from the Original of the Quarrel. Which is, that Two Wise Men commence a Dispute about a Trifle, and in the Sequel of it a great many severe Truths which they never intended to tell one another are natur-ally introduc'd from the violent Working of their Passions. It may be objected that this is not a proper Ground for Men of their Characters to proceed to such indiscreet Violences: but what avail Objections when we see it every Day in Life and know what Lengths Warmth of Temper will carry the best of us all to? *Cassius*, unknowing of the

Occasion that the calm *Brutus* had to stir his Nature enters in a Heat, is receiv'd with a noble Resentment which is work'd mutually to a height by Aggravations easie and natural, till the Provoker submits, the Provok'd forgives, and each fondly excuse the Other of his Rashness. But there is another Beauty in *Shakespeare*'s Reconcilement, which is, that the Cause of *Brutus*'s giving way to his Choler does not appear till after they are reconcil'd, to which *Shakespeare* gives the most excellent Turn imaginable. For after they are cool enough to enquire into the Cause of each other's Resentments *Cassius* begins thus:

> Cas. *I did not think you could have been so angry.*
> Brut. *O Cassius, I am sick of many Griefs.*
> Cas. *Of your Philosophy you make no Use,*
> *If you give place to accidental Evils.*
> Brut. *No Man bears Sorrow better.* Portia *is dead.*
> Cas. *Ha!—Portia?—*
> Brut. *She is dead.*
> Cas. *How scap'd I killing, when I cross'd you so?*   [4.3.141 ff]

60. Thomas Killigrew the younger, suggestions for adapting *Julius Caesar*

c. 1715

From British Museum Add. MSS. 22629.

This letter was printed in the *Shakespeare Allusion-Book* and attributed to Thomas Killigrew the elder (1612–83); but G. B. Evans has argued that on the evidence of the handwriting and the reference to the Duke of Ormond, it ought to be assigned to his son (1657–1719), who wrote a successful comedy and some poetry: see the Introduction above, p. 14 and n. 25. The spacing-out of words in the drama text presumably represents either a rough form of verse-lineation or else some kind of punctuation.

> '*Act the Second. Brutus in his Orchard.*
>
> *Bru:* it must be by his death'

The rest of the Speech (tho beautifully poetical) shoud be left out, as a way of reasoning that will Justefie my killing any man, since there is no body so Inconsiderall as some how or other has it not in his power to hurt his fellow; & in the place of it I woud have Brutus conclud in this manner:

> if this Be wrong ye Immortal Gods who read the hearts of men
>   Judge not the Action, but the Intent.   Brutus might laugh
> whilst his sad country groaned, if Brutus was a Villain.   Yett I
> am strongly tempted by the repeated sharp complaints of Rome.
>   Brutus thou sleepst,   awake and see thy selfe.   Speak,
> strike, redress.   I will,   but first I'll prove this hauty man and
> try if he'll be mov'd by reason.   If not O Rome I make thee
> promise &c.

Here I would haue a Scene betwixt Caesar & Brutus, upon the Ill Success of which Brutus shoud take his resolutions.

Enter Brutus to Caesar and Calphurnia.

Caesar. Brutus thou'rt wellcome   Wrought on by *Calphurnia's*
fears I think this day I will not meet the Senat.   Dark dreams
have frighten'd her and she perswaded me. *Calphurnia*, say out
thy dream.
[*Caesar*.] Now Brutus tell me how should Caesar Act.
Brutus. A Roman Senator his Countrys friend   is by the gods
protected;   her dream portends no Ill but to the foe of Rome.
Caesar. Brutus thy words are dark as was Calphurnia's dream;
Lay by the Augur and assume the man.
Brutus. First tell me, are we Romans both, or must I Kneel, as
speaking to a God?
Caesar. I every where am Caesar.
Brutus. And I am Brutus whom Caesar once bid live.   Gods,
that you had then for the first time been Cruel,   for sure you
did not know, to give a Roman life   was to let Rome live free.
    If your Ambetion soars to Conquer all thats great, him who
non yett coud e'er subdue,   you must orecome yourselfe.
    The worlds a petty Victory.   Scylla or Catiline coud it
Inslave, and what thier little souls could Act Caesars superiour
genius shoud disdain.
Caesar. No more.   Remember Caesar once again gives Brutus
life.   Be wise and keep it.
                                                                    Exit Bru.
                    '*Act the Third florish.*'
Here I would have Brutus, after the rest have sued in vain for Mettelus's
being recalled, say thus.

Brutus. Peace, ye unworthy of the name of Romans,   how can
you meanly think on privat wrongs   whilst Rome's in Chains
and Murderd Liberty   call's loud for Justice?   Brutus
requiers of Caesar to recall the bannished Laws,   to sett his
country free by Laying down his power userp'd.
Caesar. Again dost tempt me?   Know, thou blind man, and
all the wandering herd that mutter Treasons in unwieldy Rome,
Caesar is fix'd as Jove, & with a nod can turn your murmers into
sighs and servil prayers to be forgiven.
Casca. Speake hands for me   [*Stabs.*
Brutus. Thus Brutus pleads again his Countrys Cause.   O twas
a dreadfull Conflict dreadfully decided.

'*Caesar.* Et tu Brute—*then fall Caesar*': this I woud have left out as it tends to reproach Brutus by the seeming tenderness of the Expressions, as if he coud not have fell without him, but that when he raisd his hand twas time for him to die. Besides, the words of a dying man make strongest Impressions & these last of Caesars blacken Brutus with Ingrati[tude], which excits pity for the tyrant & Horror for the Patriot, Contrary to the design of ye Author. Tho it is very possible many understand the beautys of Shakespeare better than me, yett I don't think it easie, Madam, for any body to admire 'em more.

This is by way of preface to the following difficultys. I can't account for hating the historical Caesar (and grieveing for the Poetical one) for my aversion to slavery, and yett following the Cause of the Tyrant with my best wishes thro all the fortunes of Antony & Octavius. This is a Contradiction I can solve no way but from disliking the Patriots (whom I comprehend all under Brutus, for without him I Question whether it woud ever have been attempted). Which at first sight seems to Justifie Brutus as finding himself the only man able to free his Country, but if I am not mistaken Brutus had no Country at all, was no longer a Roman but a Caesarian—that is, from a Citizen of Rome he became, by the mercy of the Conqueror, a Creature of Caesars. He shoud Either have refused his own life, as Cato did, or not taken Caesars. Since he coud not but see, after Pharsalia, what his benefactor aimd at, it was in my opinion a Tacit agreement ('thou shallt live Brutus'), but like the rest of the Vanquishd, in accepting life [he] was consenting to the Contract.

His Ingratitud is no where softend by Introduceing him moveing Caesar in behalfe of Rome. He expresses no reluctance (but in one word) to entering into the Conspiricy, nor shows the least sense of acknowledgment for life & fortune, both which he deriv'd from Caesar. For his first right, as I take it forfitted, it may be objected that touching Caesar upon so tender a point might have alarmd him & prevented the success without remidieng the Evil by discovering the Conjuration. But for my part I dont see why a friend Caesar lovd so dear—and a Brutus too—might not be suppos'd to say this thro an honnest open zeal for the Countrys good & honour and safety of his Patron, without being previously Ingag'd in a Conspiricy. I'm sure by the Charrecter of Brutus—loaded with obligations to Caesar—had he not appeard upon the Stage a Conspiritor I shoud never have suspected him from any discontent he utters till Cassius works him to his purpose. Nor Indeed is Caesar any where shown Jealouse of Brutus thro out as he is of Cassius, nor to my mind shown Vicious Enough (to Justefi thier putting him to death), no more than Brutus Vertuous Enough.

There is a goodnatured wellmeaning weakness not unlike the Duke of Ormond's. Brutus and Ormond were popular names, toolls that the Cassius's of all ages use to bring thier own Designs about with. Cassius's hate to Caesar for prefering Brutus to him—not his love to Rome—works that very Brutus up to distroy his friend, on the specious pretence of freeing his Country (who Else, good man, saw no Ills it sufferd). But of a sudden roused by the names of his Ancestors, without distinguishing the difference of their Cases or without ever, as I said before, trying his Master and his father (for Conquest and Kindness made Caesar both to Brutus), determins on a Plott with a sett of people whom he hardly knows but as Cassius declars em to him, most of which appear actueted by privat Peke, & even kill Caesar, interceeding for a perticular & a relation whom the Audience is no where told deserves the favour they beg. So that Caesar appears neither Cruel nor unjust in his refusal, as he woud have done if they had mentiond his restoreing liberty & Law, and stabd him upon his denying to Lay down his Power.

These are, as well as I coud degest my own thoughts, the Obstacls I allways find to Brutus; the help I propose in the short scene is no more than a ruled paper for others to write on. Brutus Certainly is a deffecttive Charrecter at best and therefore, I thought, wanted all the assistence poetical liberty woud allow him; very different from you, Madam, who need nothing but a faithfull historian to make you as much regreeted hereafter as you are Valued now, by

T. Killigrew.

61. Thomas Purney, Shakespeare and francophilia

1717

From the Preface to *Pastorals. Viz. The Bashful Swain: And Beauty and Simplicity* (1717).

Thomas Purney (1695–1728?) was educated at Cambridge, took Holy Orders in 1719 and was chaplain of Newgate from 1719 to 1727.

Upon the first Appearance of our other PIECES some took distast, I heard, at our passing over the *French Criticks* with so slender a Deference to their Opinions, seeing that Nation bears the Prize of Learning from those around it. Had I Abilities, this were a place improper, nor would time allow us to enter into the Merits of those numerous *Criticks*.

However, as I am desired not to expose these Pastorals so naked to the World as my Others, I'll give the time I should be talking in this Preface of my own Performance to the considering those of our Neighbours the *French*.

What Progress soever their *Criticks* have made in their Science it's evident enough the reputation of their Authors over EUROPE is owing to them. And had we as many such, to blaze our Writers Works and open their ordinary Beauties, sure I think they would make a different Figure in EUROPE from what they do. Our *Milton, Shakespeare, Otway,* and the rest would at least be known beyond the bounds of *Britain*. But a petty Enmity is held up between our Poets and our Criticks, which diverts the latter from their proper business and delight of dressing the Beauties of the former in engaging Colours. Whereas the *Criticks* of *France* are so kindly natured that they cannot see a Defect in their own Authors, nor a Beauty in those of another Nation.

Can any reason be, besides the *Criticks* putting the Writers in *France* on a certain mechanick regular Way, why their Authors are as well known to us as our own and no sooner in the *French* than the *English* Tongue? Can any reason be, besides, for our so valuing the *French* while they won't cast an Eye on us? If by chance they mention an Author of ours, which once or twice they do thro' all their Critiques, not satisfied to put him under theirs they will scarce allow it possible for our Nation to produce a perfect Piece. Yet methinks they should allow us ISLANDERS some little Sence, because 'tis else no Glory to surpass us. Nor do they think it much indeed, but would call it a Diminution to *Corneille* and to *Racine* to be put in compare with *Shakespeare* and with *Otway*, tho' the Preference at last should fall on the *French*.

What stops, I think, the general and universal Value for our Noblest Authors is Their Faults are Faults against the common known mechanick Rules of Poetry, as *Shakespeare*'s Blemishes and *Otway*'s are against the Unity of Place, and mixing Comedy throughout, and the like, which are obvious to every one; whereas how few can take the Beauties of *Shakespeare*, especially in the Sentiment, which is often indeed too clouded by the Language. The *French*, on the other hand, if they can't come up to our noblest Beauties, they learn from their *Criticks* to avoid our plainest Faults. And such Writings as are neither good nor bad acquire the widest and the easiest Characters for good. But yet give me a dozen faults if there's half as many noble Graces blended with 'em, before a Poem that's as regular as insipid.

'Twere too long to draw a full comparison of *Shakespeare*, and *Corneille* or *Racine*. But give me leave to appeal a little to the Judgment of the Reader.

Suppose *Shakespeare* had given *Corneille* the Character of a fierce Savage MOOR, such as *Othello*, then told him that to make his Temper chaufft and fermented by Jealousie would show such a Character in the finest Light; how think ye, even then, would *Corneille* have wrote the Play? We may guess from his own Performances. Would he have given us to see the Love between the Savage and the tender Lady as *Shakespeare* has done, or have drawn a charming Scene, where the honest old Love-Story would have been finely talkt over by 'em? How would the subtilness of *Iago* have been shewn in working up a furious *Warriour*? But worse yet, how would he have drawn the Strugglings of a great Soul between the fiercest Hatred and the tendrest Obligations to Love? I fear He must have told us *Othello* had such Contests in himself. How would he have described the roughest and most open Soul in the World biting in his Wrath, and dissembling before the tender *Desdemona*? I doubt a few Monologues would have supply'd the place of

*   317

that. In short, would not *Corneille* have shewn the Grief of the innocent, surpriz'd, and gentle *Desdemona* by a number of fine mournful Sentences between Her and a Confidant? Aye, and such a Scene would have raised a world of pity in a *French* Audience.

Such uncommon Characters as *Othello*'s, *Macbeth*'s, *Hamlet*'s, *Jaffeir*'s, *Monimia*'s, &c. are the only difficult ones to draw, the only Ones that shine on the Stage, and the only Ones I could never find in the *French* writers of Tragedy.

But there is a Species in Writing which seems natural to our Nation, and inconsistent with the *French* Vivacity. It has never yet been consider'd by any *Critick*, yet constitutes the Soul and Essence of Tragedy. I call this kind the GLOOMY, and it consists oftner in the general scene or view than in the Sentiment. For Instance, *Romeo* is wandring among the Trees, and anon espy's a glimering light at *Julia*'s Window; and in *King Lear* we see LEAR under a *Hovel* retired in the Night, while Thunder, Rain and Lightning were abroad.

All the Tragedys of *Shakespeare* which we call good abound with the *Gloomy*. And the want of it may be one great reason why *Corneille* and *Racine*, tho' they have so much Spirit in their Expressions, tho' their Thoughts are so rarely vitious and their Compositions agreeable to the common and easiest Rules, yet want the Life, what shall I call it, the VIS TRAGICA, which appears in the good Tragedies of *Shakespeare* and *Otway*.

The *English*, as I said, alone have Geniuses fitted for the *Gloomy*. But as we never abounded much with *Criticks*, never any has enter'd into the Nature of it, tho' sure it deserves an entire Discourse. And so sweetly amusing it is to the Soul that 'twill shine thro' Language, even ridiculous, and alone support a Sentiment. As here,

Put out the Light, and then put out the Light. [5.2.7]

The Language is a kind of *Pun*, and therefore to Minds that cannot take the Beauty of the Thought divested of it the line appears absurd.

But the chief use of the GLOOMY (in the Sentiment) is in *Soliloquies*, and would a Tragick-Writer be at pains to be Master of it he need never write, at least, a bad one. The *Soliloquies* of *Corneille* and *Racine* are only such because the Person that utters 'em is alone. The Thoughts are exactly of the same kind with those in the *Dialogue* part of the *Play*, without *Solemnity* or *Gloominess*. But what a solemn Awe do *Shakespeare*'s draw over the Mind. And some of *Otway*'s, as in *Venice Preserv'd*.

> *Jaffeir, on the Rialto.*
> *I'm here; and thus, the Shades of Night around me, &c.*
>
> Act 2.

But Instances were endless, especially out of *Shakespeare*. Yet 'twas the finesse, I believe, of his Imagination that fill'd his Tragedys with the GLOOMY, rather than his having e'er sate down and consider'd the *Pleasures of the Imagination*, and then the fittest Methods to excite those Pleasures. He felt his own Mind most agreeably amused whene'er the Gloomy overspread it, and most wrote (as was *Ovid* and *Spenser's* way) what most delighted him to write.

The *French* Writers have this to offer for their wanting the Soul and Essence of Tragedy: they generally observe the Mechanick Rules, especially Unity of Place, which *Shakespeare* alway break's thro'. Now the GLOOMY, as I said, is oftnest rais'd by the general Scene or View, by leading the Mind into secret Apartments and private Places; as PIERRE on the *Rialto every Night at twelve took his Evening's Walk of Meditation*. But if a Play-Writer would preserve the Unity of Place it must be by laying his Scene in a Thorough-Fare, in a Palace Yard, before the Door of an House, or in a publick Hall, as *Sophocles*, *Terence*, and the *French* Writers of Tragedy do. So that by cramping their Geniuses by the observation of this Rule (which yet is necessary in the Representation) they cut themselves off from the chief Opportunity of introduceing the Gloomy. And even in the Thought, the Gloomy cannot with advantage appear, unless held up and assisted by the Scene. How could this Thought have been supported in *Romeo and Juliet*

> *What light is that, which breaks from yonder Window,* &c. [2.2.2]

but by *Shakespeare's* leading us, with *Romeo*, into the Secret Retirement of an *Orchat*?

Or what could have furnish'd *Othello's* Soliloquy,

> *It is the Cause; It is the Cause, my Soul:*
> *Let me not name it to you, ye chast Stars,* &c. [5.2.1 f]

had not *Shakespeare* led us in into the Bed-Chamber of *Desdemona* in the Night-time?

In short, if 'tis otherwise introduced it must be out of the Action, as the Account of *Macbeth's* Lady walking in her Sleep, and *Hotspur's* Wife's relation of his talking in his Sleep, with the thoughts and contrivance of a Rebellion, and the like.

Here, then, give me leave to ask a Question of the free-thinking *English* Critick—one, I mean, who dares to take a view of Truth himself nor will like a Thought or Observation the worse because the *Greeks* or *Romans* have not touch'd it before. Such an one let me ask, Whether Tragedy must not be an imperfect Poem, either in the Reading or the Representation? Other reasons are for its being so, and there is, I think, but one Method of rendring it wholly compleat. But I have not Room or Time now either to pursue the Question Or to propose my Thoughts on the making the Poem compleat.

But there is another Question whose Answer is as easy, from what we have said. I have often heard it controverted, since I have apply'd my self to Letters in earnest, Whether a fine Genius is not crampt and deaden'd by the Rules? And if *Shakespeare*, &c, would have wrote so well had he been acquainted with *Aristotle* and the *Criticks*? This Question would resolve its self were it set in a true Light and the Distinctions in Poetry rightly made. But to make the Matter plain to the shallowest Thoughts Poetry must be divided into that of Reading and that of Representation. Under the first come all but Tragedy, Comedy, and the Unnatural Productions of Opera's, Masks, Farces, &c. 'Tis plain to me that some of the Rules are a Clog to Tragedy and Comedy. I shall say no more of Tragedy. Comedy has an equal Aversion to Unity of Place. For it bears hard upon its very Essence, an enlivening and diverting Joy. *Terence* tyed himself to the observance of this Rule, as the *French* have done in Tragedy; but as they quitted for it the Soul of Tragedy so he has let go the diverting part, which is the Soul of Comedy.

Suppose (tho' 'tis impossible) that the Poet could bring every delightful Scene which his Fancy is desirous of to his one single Spot of Ground (for our usual manner of confining the Scene to one Town or Country is no Unity: if I can fancy the Stage now the Tower, now the Court, &c. I can as well fancy it now in *London*, now at *Bath*, &c.). Supposing this, I say, yet by Unity of Place we lose the Pleasure of rambling into a Lady's Apartment, a Drawing-Room, a Chocolate-House, a delightful Grotto, &c. The Mind is always pleased in wildly roving unconfin'd, and to be tyed down to any one View or Prospect is almost as disagreable as *Spenser*'s long description of a Woman. All are disgusted and wearied by it, tho' 'tis diversified by his passing from her Shape to her Habit, from her Mien to her Face, &c. as the same general Object is still in sight. So 'tis in Comedies, where the Mind is still and still brought to the same general Place, tho' diversified by different Actions there. *Congreve* and our other Writers of Plays observe the other Rules, but cannot help being as diverting as their Fancies give 'em a Capacity of being.

In Tragedy then, and Comedy, the Immagination is restrain'd by Rule. In the Epick and Pastoral Poem, the Ode, Satyr, &c., 'tis not. Would *Ovid* and *Spenser* have took the pains of looking so far into *Criticism*, as to have compiled a regular and perfect Poem, the first might have introduced as many uncommon Descriptions (tho' not the same as we find in his *Metamorphoses*) and as many beautiful Surprizes into an Epick-Poem; and the latter might have found Opportunity of bringing into the same Poem all his Love and all his Pastoral Images which we find in that wild and romantick Piece his *Fairy Queen*, where the Scene is in *England* and *Ireland* and *Fairy Land*, and all in one Poem, and the Characters are Fairys, Hero's and *Briton's*, and all in the same Person. 'Tis true that in reducing their Storys and Descriptions to a regular Order, tending to one End and a moral Result, they must have bridled their Luxuriance of Fancy and not have wanton'd as they do; but this force they might have turn'd to what would really shine in Poetry, and 'twould be rather diverting the Stream of their rich Fancies into a proper Channel than any way restraining 'em.

The reason now of my advancing all this is to show that the *French* Writers of Tragedy are not superiour to our *Shakespeare* and *Otway* tho' they have observ'd the Rules of Time and Place, which the latter have not done, since there are Poems which won't admit of entire Regularity, and that the Drama stands in the number of those.

(Sig. A4ʳ–A8ʳ)

62. Charles Gildon, Shakespeare and the Rules

1718

From *The Complete Art of Poetry* (1718). The first of the two volumes includes a critical treatise in six parts (of which the present selection comes from the second dialogue, 'Of the Use and Necessity of Rules in Poetry') and specimens of 'Shakespeare's Beauties'. The treatise is largely derivative, as Gildon frankly explains in his preface: 'Whatever I found of use of my Design in Aristotle . . . Horace, Dionysius Halicarnassus, Boileau, Rapin, Dacier, Vossius, Buckingham's *Rehearsal*, Rymer, Buckingham's *Essay on Poetry*, Mr. Dennis, or any other, I have made bold with. . . .' (Sig. a₆ʳ)

[Laudon, Gildon's authority, speaks in defence of the rules.] 'It has, I confess, been an old Dispute whether *Art* or *Nature* made a *Poet*; but a Dispute I think, like many more grounded on the not well understanding the *Terms*. For *Art* entirely includes *Nature*, that being no more than *Nature reduc'd to Form*. However, *Horace*, near the end of his Art of *Poetry*, seems long since to have decided this Question with great *Clearness* and *Brevity*.

> *Some think that* Poets *may be form'd by* Art.
> *Others maintain, that* Nature *makes them so:*
> *I neither see what* Art *without a Vein,*
> *Nor* Wit *without the Help of* Art *can do;*
> *But mutually need each others Aid.*　　　　　Rosc.[1]

This is the Opinion of *Horace*, confirm'd by *Reason* and Experience. For without *Art*, there can be no Order, and without *Order Harmony* is sought in vain, where nothing but shocking *Confusion* can be found. Those scatter'd Sparks of a great *Genius*, which shou'd shine with united Glory, are in the huddle of Ignorance or want of *Art* so dissi-

---

[1] *A.P.*, 408 ff.

pated and divided, and so blended with Contraries, that they are extreamly obscur'd, if not entirely extinguish'd. Thus the Particles and Seeds of Light in the Primocal Chaos strugled in vain to exert their true Lustre, till Matter was by *Art Divine* brought into order, and this *noble Poem* of the *Universe* compleated in *Number* and *Figures* by the Almighty *Poet* or *Maker*.

But it has been the *Ignorance* of the Rules that has made the *Many* and their Advocates declaim with so much Vehemence against them, as Curbs to *Wit* and *Poetry*. For did they know them they wou'd plainly see that they do, in Reality, add to them the greatest Distinction and Honour they can hope for by setting up a *true Standard* by which the due Glory of *Wit* and *Poetry* may be paid to *Merit*, without so wretched a Fate as to be oblig'd to share with *Poetasters*, *Versifyers*, and *worthless Pretenders*; which certainly cannot be look'd on as an *ill-natur'd* Work, but the Effect of a *just* and *generous* Temper.

Thus (to instance in one sort of *Poetry*) the Enemies of *Art* wou'd fain persuade us that no Play in which the Rules of *Art* are observ'd will please; whereas, indeed, no Play did ever please for any Time but by those Parts of it which were conformed to the Rules, which cannot really be reduc'd to Practice but by a Person of the greatest *Capacity* and *Genius*. For can there be any Creature that pretends to the least Portion of a *rational Soul* who is pleas'd with the Conduct of *Shakespeare* (except in one or two Plays) in which there is nothing *curious*, nothing *great*, nothing *judicious*? No, it is the Excellence of that *Poet* in the *Expression* of the *Manners*, in the *Distinction* of the *Characters*, and some of his Draughts of the *Passions*—added to *Prescription* and the *Ignorance* of the Audience—that makes him please in those of his Plays which are fixt in the Esteem of the Town, to which the rest, though equally good, have often in vain endeavour'd to arise.

If some *Plays* have miss'd of Success, which were *call'd* regular by those who knew nothing of the *Rules*, I dare assert that they were *only* call'd but were not so in *Reality*. For it will be obvious to any Man who is acquainted with them that he who comes up to them must produce a *perfect Poem*, that must force itself with a *resistless Pleasure* on all that hear it. To keep still to the *Dramma*: he must perfectly *know*, and form his *Design*; he must *know*, *distinguish*, and *preserve* the *Manners*; he must be throughly acquainted with all the *Springs*, *Motions*, *Degrees*, *Mixtures*, *Accesses*, and *Recesses* of every *Passion*, with their *Opposition*, and *Consistence*. He must be perfect in the *Sentiments*, and know their Propriety and Agreeableness to the *Manners*, as those have to the

Action; he must be skill'd and practis'd in the *Diction*, which includes both *Numbers* and *Expression*. Who can do all this but a Man of a great *Capacity* of Soul (which we call *Genius*), a large and strong *Imagination* to receive and form the *Images* of Things, and a solid *Judgment* to reduce them to their *proper Order* and *Classes*? And this is writing *according to the Rules*.

But let the *Imagination* be never so strong, and fertile of *Ideas*, without the Assistance of Judgment (which can only be informed and directed by the Stated Rules) there can be nothing produc'd *entirely beautiful*. 'Tis all the rude Product of *uncultivated Wit*. There may be a great deal of rich Ore, but clogg'd with the dull and worthless *Sparr* and *indigested Earth*. But *Judgment*, like the Fire, can only separate the Parts and draw thence an uniform and valuable Mass of Metal.

The Rules are a great Help to many a Man of *Genius*; for it is so far from probable that it is scarce possible that unassisted Nature, tho' never so vigorous, can find out and practise all the Parts necessary to the forming a compleat Poem. For as in Architecture, Painting, and Musick no Man did give us any thing great and complete without knowing and long Practice of the Rules of those Arts; so in *Poetry* nothing truly excellent was ever yet seen without a Mastery in the *Poetic* Principles. . . .' (94-7)

*   *   *

'I do here allow that the *Drama*, on its first Appearance in *Athens* itself, was far from the Perfection it afterwards attain'd (tho' the Idea of Tragedy was certainly taken from the *Heroic Poem*), since we find it was in the Time of *Thespis* almost as rude and inconsistent as our *Stage* is in our Days, that first Raiser of the *Athenian Theatre* bringing nothing to Perfection. That was only effected by the *Magistrates'* Inspection of the Management, and the *gradual* Endeavours of *Æschylus*, *Sophocles*, *Euripides*, and others.'

'But my Friend' (interrupted I) 'you know that these Gentlemen urge that *Shakespeare* has appear'd in *England*, with the *highest Applause*, without the *Help of Art*.'

'But I must reply' (said *Laudon*) 'first, that so did *Thespis* and some others in *Athens*; but their *Absurdities* and *crude Entertainments* vanish'd on the Appearance of more *just* and *regular* Pieces. Next, that (as I have already observ'd) *Shakespeare* is great in nothing but *what is according to the Rules of Art*; and where his Ignorance of them is not supply'd by his *Genius* Men of *Judgment* and *good Sense* see such *monstrous Absurdities* in almost every Part of his Works that nothing but his *uncommon* Excellencies in the other cou'd ever prevail with us to suffer; and what he wou'd never have been guilty of had his Judgment been but well inform'd by *Art*. He had a *Genius*, indeed, capable of coming up to the *Rules* but not sufficient to find them out himself, tho' it be plain from his own Words he saw the *Absurdities* of his own conduct. And, I must confess, when I find that Sir *Philip Sidney* before him has discover'd these Faults of the *English* Stage, and that he himself has written one or two Plays very near a *Regularity*, I am the less apt to pardon his Errors— that seem of choice, as agreeable to his *Lazyness* or *easie Gain*—by what he committed to the *Theatre*.' (98–9)

★   ★   ★

[*Mrs Lamode*] '. . . dear *Laudon*, there's a Mode of *Wit* and *Poetry* as well as of *Cloaths*; and he or she that is out of the *Fashion* makes a very ridiculous Figure and is very *scandalous Company*. Wou'd it not be a very pretty Sight to have a young Lady come into the Drawing-Room in a *Ruff* and *Farthingal*? *London* and *Athens* are quite different Places, and the Modes and Manners of the People differ so much that what was bright, and pleasing in *Athens* must be dull, and insipid in *London*. . . .' (106)

★   ★   ★

[*Marisina*] 'As for your Ladyship's *Mode* and *Fashion* of *Wit* it may, perhaps, hold of the *Poems* of our Time, for we seldom find that they keep up their easily acquir'd Reputation more than one Season. But as the present Duke of *Buckingham* has it in his admirable *Essay on Poetry*,

True Wit is everlasting like the Sun.

And to shew your Ladyship that your Simile of *Ruffs* and *Farthingales* will be little Proof of what you urg'd it for, you must remember that *Shakespeare*'s Wit holds in Fashion still, though of the same Date with those Ornaments of Dress which wou'd now appear so very ridiculous. Time, that has so often chang'd our Modes of Apparel and made the same Things so often *modish* and *antiquated*, has only added Force, Respect, and Authority to the *true Wit* of One Hundred and Fifty Years standing. As we find this beyond Dispute in *Shakespeare*, so the same will hold good of those great Masters of *Poetry* among the Antients of *Rome* and *Athens*, who have in all Times, and all Nations (as soon as understood) kept up, nay encreas'd their Esteem and Value

325

whilst every thing else chang'd, Imperial Families, Kingdoms, whole Nations and People have perish'd or alter'd their *Modes, Forms,* and *Languages.*

And as for your Ladyship's *fine Things,* and *fine Language,* to prefer these to more charming and more essential Excellencies wou'd be as ridiculous as to prefer your Ladyship's *Dress* to your *Person*: a Compliment, I dare believe, that you wou'd not think so gallant as the *Mode* and *Fashion* require.' (107)

*   *   *

[*Laudon*] 'It is, as I have observed, urged against Criticism or the Rules of *Art* that a too regular Adherence to the Forms and Measures of them is a Restraint on a Writer's *Invention,* and does more Harm than Good in Composition, for that the Imagination cannot so freely diffuse and expand it self when it is oblig'd to any Bounds or Limits whatever. This Argument is sometimes illustrated and supported by that famous Example of an ungovernable Genius in *Heroic* Virtue; I mean *Alexander* the *Great,* whose vast Ambition never fail'd to hurry him beyond the due Measures of Conduct, upon which very Account, say they, his Exploits had always in them something wonderfully surprizing and astonishing. Whereas *Cæsar's* Actions, that were more cool, deliberate, and proportion'd to the Rules of Prudence and Policy, never give us such a sublime, exalted Idea of his Fortitude as we must necessarily entertain of the *Greek* Heroes. The Friends too of our great Dramatic Writer *Shakespeare* will not be perswaded but that even his monstrous Irregularities were conducive to those shining Beauties which abound in most of his Plays, and that if he had been more a Critic he had been less a Poet; that is, if he had known more of Nature (which only the Rules teach) he would have touch'd her less.' (123)

*   *   *

[*Gildon*] 'Why what is *Bad* often *pleases,* and that which is *Good* does not always do so, is not the fault of the Object but of him who judges. But what is *Good* will infallibly *please* those who can judge, and that is sufficient. By this we may see that a Play which shall bring those Things which are to be judged of by Reason within the *Rules,* as also what is to be judg'd of by the Sense, shall never fail to *please,* for that will please both the *Learned* and the *Ignorant.* Now this Conformity of Suffrages is the most sure and, according to *Aristotle,* the only Mark of the *Good* and the *Pleasant.* Now these Suffrages are not obtain'd but by the Observation of the *Rules*, and consequently these *Rules* are the only Cause of the *Good* and the *Pleasant*, whether they are follow'd methodically, or by Design, or by Accident only. For it is certain that there are many Persons who are entirely ignorant of these *Rules* who do not, however, fail of Success in some Particular. But this is far from destroying the *Rules*, since it serves only to shew their Beauty and proves how far they are conformable to *Nature*, since those often follow them who know nothing of them, as our *Shakespeare*.' (138)

63. George Sewell on the mangling of Shakespeare's plays

1719

The Epilogue to *Sir Walter Raleigh* (1719), pp. 67–8.

George Sewell (1690?–1726), poet, dramatist and pamphleteer, associated with Addison, Steele, Dennis and Aaron Hill.

What! Two new Plays! and those at once appear!
Sure, Authors fancy this a thriving Year!
Yet, to write Plays is easy, faith, enough;
As you have seen by *Cibber* in *Tartuffe*.
With how much Wit he did your Hearts engage!
He only Stole the *Play*,—he Writ the *Title-Page*.
  We dare not tread the Path our *Rivals* do;
We were resolv'd you should have something *New*.
'Tis double *Felony* (as I am told)
To pay Bad Money, and That clip'd and old:
And yet so partial are you in the Case,
We *suffer* still, but They have *Acts of Grace*.
Sure That *old* Theatre's your *Mistress* grown,
We are your *Wives*: You use us like your *own*.

Should SHAKESPEARE rise, and see (each murthering Day)
Scenes cut and alter'd, and mis-call'd his Play;
How would the reverend Bard regret the Shame?
Why thus: 'To rob my Urn, then stab my Fame,
Should be a Sin this Learned Generous Age
Ought to revenge upon the Guilty Stage.
But if, in vain, an honest Cause I plead,
Thus shall my Wish and Punishment succeed:
Flecknoe, the Sire of Dulness, shall inspire
His Sons to scribble, without Sense or Fire:
Players turn *Wits*, by Nonsense rise or fall,
Yet cry out boldly *'sBlood! We'll stand 'em all.'*
Thus far for SHAKESPEARE, and our Common Right:
Now for the *Author*'s Part, and then Good-night:
For I have a Request, before I go;
Speak plainly; Is our Poet damn'd, or—no?
If he is *Dull*, the Play perhaps may live;
For Wit's a Crime we know You can't forgive.
Wit cannot fall so fast, as *Folly* rises;
Witness the *Masquerade*—at *double Prices*.
Yet if you are not pleas'd with what *We've plaid*,
Go see old SHIRLEY drest in MASQUERADE.

64. John Dennis, from his adaptation of *Coriolanus*

1719

From *The Invader of his Country: or, the Fatal Resentment.*

First performed on 11 November 1719, Dennis's adaptation seems to have existed for some years prior to that: he refers to it in his *Essay on the Genius and Writings of Shakespeare* in 1711 (No. 56 above) while in 1713, in an attack on Dennis (*The Narrative of Dr. Robert Norris, concerning the strange and deplorable frenzy of Mr. John Denn—*), Pope said that it had been ready for the stage for four years: see *The Prose Works of Alexander Pope*, ed. N. Ault (Oxford, 1963, 1968), p. 167.

PROLOGUE

The Tragedy we represent to Day
Is but a Grafting upon *Shakespeare*'s Play,
In whose Original we may descry
Where Master-strokes in wild Confusion lye;
Here brought to as much Order as we can
Reduce those Beauties upon *Shakespeare*'s Plan.
And from his Plan we dar'd not to depart,
Lest Nature should be lost in Quest of Art:
And Art had been attain'd with too much Cost
Had *Shakespeare*'s Beauties in the Search been lost.
As *Philomel*, whom Heav'n and *Phœbus* teach,
Has Notes which Birds, that Man instructs, ne'er reach,
'So *Shakespeare*, Fancy's sweetest Child,
Warbles his Native Wood-Notes wild.'*
While ev'ry Note takes the rapt Heroe's Heart, ⎫
And ev'ry Note's victorious over Art. ⎬
Then what is ours, to Night, excuse for *Shakespeare*'s Part. ⎭

* Milton [cf. Volume I, p. 2]

You chiefly, who are truly *Britons* nam'd,
Whose Breasts are with your Country's Love inflam'd,
Whose martial Toils as long as Time shall live,
Whose Conquests Credit to old Fables give:
Conquests which more renown'd by Age shall grow,
To which ev'n late Posterity shall owe
The noblest History the World can show;
You in our just Defence must sure engage,
And shield us from the Storms of Factious Rage.
In the same Cause in which each Champion fights,
In the same noble Cause our daring Poet writes.
For as when *Britain*'s Rebel Sons of late
Combin'd with Foreign Foes t'invade the State,
She to your Valour and your Conduct owes
That she subdued and crush'd her num'rous Foes.
We shew, to Night, such Treasons to prevent,
That their Guilt's follow'd by their Punishment,
That Heav'n's the Guardian of our Rightful Cause,
And watches o'er our Sov'reign and our Laws.

*   *   *

[Act IV, Scene iii.]

SCENE *ROME*.

Enter the two Tribunes and Menenius.

  Bru. Then you hear nothing from him?
  Men. No, I hear nothing;
His Mother and his Wife hear nothing from him.
  Bru. In War this *Marcius* was a worthy Officer,
But insolent in Peace, o'ercome with Pride;
Ambitious even beyond Imagination,
And doating on himself.
  Sic. And aiming at perpetual Soveraignty.
  Men. Had *Caius Marcius* aim'd at Soveraignty
He would have been more popular,
For the *Patrician* who enslaves this People
Must do it by themselves.

Sic. We should, by this, have felt his Tyranny,
To all our Sorrows, had he gone forth Consul.

Bru. The Gods have well prevented it, and *Rome*
Sits safe and easy still without him.

Enter an Ædile.

Æd. Worthy Tribunes:
There is a Slave, whom we have thrown in Prison,
Reports the *Volscians*, with two several Powers,
Are entered in the *Roman* Territories,
And with the deepest Malice of the War
Destroy what lies before them.

Bru. Go see this Rumourer whipt for his bold Lie.
The *Volscians*, whom so lately we reduc'd,
Have not the Heart to break with us.

Enter Messenger.

Mess. The Fathers, in great Earnestness, are going
All to the Senate House; some News is come
That turns their Countenances.

Sic. 'Tis this Slave.
Whip him before the People's Eyes for daring
Thus to disturb the Town by his Invention.

Mess. But, worthy Sir,
The Slave's Report is seconded; and more,
More fearful is deliver'd.

Sic. What more fearful?

Mess. Sir, 'tis by many Mouths deliver'd freely,
How probably I cannot tell, that *Marcius*,
Join'd with *Aufidius*, marches against *Rome*,
And vows Revenge as ample as between
The youngest and the oldest of our *Romans*.

Sic. This is most likely!

Bru. Rais'd only, that the weaker sort may wish
Good *Marcius* home again.

Sic. The very Trick on't.

Men. This is improbable, and highly so;
He and *Aufidius* are no more compatible
Than the two Branches of a Contradiction.

Enter second Messenger.

331

2 Mess. You are sent for to the Senate:
A fearful Army, led by *Caius Marcius*,
Associated with fell *Aufidius*, rages
Upon our Territories, and already
Have mark'd their way with Fire, and Blood, and Ruin.

Enter Cominius.

 Com. Oh! you have made rare Work!
 Men. What News, what News?
 Com. Yes, you have helpt to ravish your own Daughters,
To see your Wives dishonour'd to your Noses!
 Men. What is the News, what is the News, *Cominius*?
If *Marcius* should be join'd with *Volscians*—
 Com. If *Marcius* should be join'd—
Why he's their God, he leads them like a Being
Made by some nobler *Artist* than meer Nature,
That forms Man perfecter, and shapes him better.
And under him they march with no less Confidence
Than Heroes when commanded by a God.
 Men. Oh! you have made good Work!
 Com. He'll shake your *Rome* about your Ears.
 Men. As *Hercules* the Pillars which he rais'd.
You have made fair Work.
 Bru. But is this true, Sir?
 Com. As sure as you'll look pale, and tremble too,
Before you find it other. All the Regions
With cheerfulness revolt, they who resist
Are mock'd for valiant Ignorance,
And perish constant Fools. And who can blame him?
Your Enemies and his find something in him,
Tho' you so much contemn'd him.
 Men. We are all undone, unless the Godlike Man
Have Mercy equal to forgiving Gods.
 Com. And who shall dare to ask it?
The Tribunes cannot do't for shame, the People
Deserve such Pity of him as the Wolf
Does of the Shepherd. Which of his best Friends
Has not deserted him and seem'd his Enemy?
 Men. True! Were he putting to my House the Brand
Which should consume it, I have not the Face

332

To say, I beg you cease. You have made fair Hands:
You and your Crafts-Men, you have crafted fair.
   Com. You have brought
A Trembling upon *Rome*, such as was never
So incapable of Help.
   Trib. Say not we brought it.
   Men. How! Was it we? We lov'd him.
But yet, like timerous Beasts, and dastard Nobles,
Submitted basely to your Noisy Clusters
And passively beheld him hooted from our Walls.
   Com. But they, I fear, who thus could hoot him out,
Will roar him in again. *Tullus Aufidius*,
The second Name of Men, obeys his Nod,
As if he were his Subaltern. Despair
Is all the Strength, Defence and Policy
That *Rome* can make against them.

Enter a Troop of Citizens.

   Men. Here come the Clusters!
And is *Aufidius* with him? You are they
That made the Air unwholsome, when you cast
Your stinking greasy Caps in nauseous hooting
At *Coriolanus'* Exile. Now he's coming,
And not a Hair upon a Soldier's Head
Which will not prove a Scorpion.
As many Coxcombs as you threw up Caps,
He'll tumble down, and pay you for your Voices.
Nay, 'tis no Matter.
If he could burn us all into one Coal,
We have deserv'd to be consum'd together.
   All Cit. Faith, we hear fearful News.
   1 *Cit.* For my own part,
When I said Banish him, I said 'twas pity.
   2 *Cit.* And so did I.
   3 *Cit.* And so did I. And, to say the Truth, so did very many of us;
nay, indeed, all of us.
   All Cit. Ay, all of us.
   Com. All of you say so! How came he banish'd then?
   1 *Cit.* What we did, we did for the best, and tho' we consented to
his Banishment, yet was it against our Wills.

333

Com. Against your Wills! You goodly things, you Voices!
Who urg'd you on to such a fatal Injury?

1 *Cit.* Why e'en our worthy Tribunes.

Com. Why then your worthy Tribunes are the Persons
Who have laid waste the *Roman* Territory,
Have brought their Country to the brink of Ruin,
Have to the Temples of our Gods set Fire,
Have fix'd the murthering Knife to all your Throats,
And, to the Arms of leud Licentious Ruffians,
Have given your Wives and Daughters. So farewell.

1 *Cit.* O terrible!

Com. Come on, *Menenius*, let us to the Capitol.

[*Exeunt* Com. *and* Men.

2 *Cit.* Have our Tribunes done all this?

3 *Cit.* The Furies break their Necks for it.

4 *Cit.* What need we trouble the damn'd Neighbours for what we can do ourselves? We are the Furies.

All Cit. Ay, we are the Furies, we are the Furies. To the Rock, to the Rock with them.

Bru. How!

Sic. What do I hear?

4 *Cit.* The Punishment they design'd for *Coriolanus*, let them feel themselves.

All Cit. To the Rock, to the Rock with them.

Bru. Hear me, my Masters.

1 *Cit.* No, no, you have prated us into Mischief enough already, a Plague o'your Rhetorical Throats for it.

Sic. Can you refuse to hear us then, my Masters?

2 *Cit.* No, by no Means, but you shall take a gentle leap first.

4 *Cit.* We shall see what a delicate Speech you'll make when your Neck's broke.

All Cit. To the Rock, to the Rock, away with 'em.

*   *   *

[Act V, Scene i.] Before Rome.

*   *   *

Cor. What is that Curt'sy worth? Or those Dove's Eyes,
Which can make Gods forsworn? I melt, and am not

334

Of stronger Earth than others. O for a Kiss
Long as my Exile, sweet as my Revenge!
Now, by the jealous Queen of Love, that Kiss
I carry'd from my Love, and my true Lip
Hath ever since preserv'd it like a Virgin.
But oh, ye Gods, while fondly thus I talk,
See, the most noble Mother of the World
Stands unsaluted; sink my Knee in Earth,
Of my deep Duty more Impression shew
Than that of common Sons.
    Vol. Have you forgot this Lady?
    Cor. The noble Sister of *Poplicola*,
The Moon of *Rome*, chaste as the Isicle
That's crudled by the Frost from purest Snow,
And hangs upon the Temple of *Diana*.
    Vol. This is a poor Epitome of yours,
Which by th' Interpretation of full Time
May shew like all your self.
    Cor. The God of Soldiers,
With the Consent of supreme *Jove*, inform
Thy Thoughts with Nobleness, that thou may'st prove
To Shame invulnerable, and shew in Battel
Like a great Sea Mark, standing ev'ry Flaw,
And saving those that eye thee.
    Vol. Ev'n he, your Wife, *Valeria*, and my self,
And all this Train of noble *Roman* Ladies,
Are Suitors to you.
    Cor. For any thing, except ungrateful *Rome*.
    Vol. Rome, tho' ungrateful, is your Country still.
    Cor. No; *Rome*, that cast me out, disown'd her Offspring;
And doubly I disown th' ungrateful City,
And *Volscian Antium* is my Country now.
'Tis *Antium* feeds, distinguishes, adores me,
Whereas *Rome* threw me out with basest Contumely.
    Vol. I never knew the Rabble yet was *Rome*;
Yet ev'n the Rabble have reveng'd thy Cause,
Have thrown their Tribunes from the Rock *Tarpeian*,
And voted thy Repeal.
    Cor. For that I thank my *Volscians*, and not them;
And I will laugh at their vile Fears, and use them

As my most deadly Foes; nay, my Revenge
Shall reach the very Walls that now protect them;
Yes, I'll destroy the very Walls that shelter them.

Vol. 'Tis a wild Vengeance,
That like an Earthquake, or a general Deluge,
Sweeps good and bad in a promiscuous Ruin:
Our noble Senators are all your Friends.

Cor. No Coward ever can be term'd a Friend,
A Coward loves himself too well to be a Friend;
And 'twas the abject Fear of the base Senate
That sacrific'd me to the Rabble's Rage.
For which, to *Volscian* Swords, and *Volscian* Fire,
I'll sacrifice their City and themselves.

Vol. Dar'st thou say this on this high Eminence,
From which thou now behold'st afflicted *Rome*,
Survey'st the awful Temples of our Gods,
That above all of *Capitoline Jove*?
Methinks I hear him from his sacred Hill
Speaking in Thunder thus: 'Have I decreed
That *Rome* should be my great Vicegerent here,
Should terminate its Empire with those bounds
That terminate the World; have I decreed this?
And *Marcius*, thou, dar'st thou attempt its Ruin?'
And as he utters this in dreadful Tone,
Methinks I see him o'er his sacred Temple
Lifting above the Clouds his awful Head,
And rolling in his Red Right Hand the Thunder.

Cor. That *Rome* should be the Mistress of the Universe
By Sovereign Justice ne'er could be decreed.
That Revelation's but a pious Fraud,
Invented first by *Rome*'s ambitious Chiefs
To sanctify their hourly Usurpations
And make Injustice wear Religion's Mask.

Vol. Oh impious!

Cor. The Wills of Gods eternal are, like them;
And nought by Gods to Men can be reveal'd
That contradicts their great Original Will,
That contradicts great Nature's sacred Laws,
Those sacred Laws of just, and right, and fit,
Which the informing Breath of *Jove* at first

Infus'd into our new-created Souls.

Vol. Yet still the Temples of our Gods are there,
Those Gods to whom thou hast so often sacrific'd,
The Gods of thy Fore-fathers. Can'st thou see them,
And impiously dar'st purpose to destroy them?

Cor. 'Tis true, indeed,
There are the Temples, but their Gods are Here:
Their Gods abandon'd *Rome*, when *Marcius* left it.
And above all the God they most adore,
Great *Mars*, the Father of their boasted Founder,
With me he went t' inhabit *Volscian* Land,
With me he marches all the toilsome Day,
With me he all the watchful Night encamps;
See where he marks his Way with Fire and Blood,
To scourge th' ungrateful *Romans*!

Vol. What hast thou said? Thy Voice has Daggers, *Marcius*,
And thou a cruel unrelenting Soul.
Ten thousand Widows, and as many Orphans
Already has thy dreadful Vengeance made;
Destroy'd their Substance all with Hostile Fire,
And now they wander helpless, friendless, comfortless,
And fill the Air with Cries and Lamentations,
Enough to pierce the Hearts of Gods and Men.

Cor. Thanks to their Tribunes, and their noble Senate.

Vol. From hence thou seest the Temples of our Gods:
Oh could thy Eyes but pierce the sacred Walls,
And shew thee the wild Horror that's within,
The dismal fight would break thy cruel Heart.
Prostrate before each unrelenting God,
Thou would'st behold old venerable Age,
And helpless Infancy, and holy Matrons,
And Virgins wither'd in their Bloom with Sorrow;
All fainting, swooning, dying with the fear
Of what may fall to-morrow.

Virg. Oh Gods, his Eyes their Firmness still maintain,
And we are lost for ever.

Vol. Yet hast thou made thy Mother and thy Wife
More wretched than the miserablest *Roman*,
As thou'rt the Cause of all this Desolation,
A Cause that we can neither hate nor curse,

Nor pray for thy Defeat; the rest can pray,
And they who cannot pray yet dare to hope,
And they who dare not hope yet dare to wish,
And still are happy in th' extreamest Line.
But we can neither pray, nor hope, nor wish;
What can we wish for? for our Country's Triumph?
That is, alas, to wish for thy Destruction:
Or for thy Victory? Oh that's our Country's Ruin!
    Cor. I cannot, must not any longer hear you.
    Vol. A little more, and I have done for ever:
Th' Ingratitude of *Rome* provokes thy Wrath
To such a height, that nought but its Destruction
Can satisfy thy thirst of dire Revenge;
And yet was e'er Ingratitude like thine?
    Cor. Ingratitude? To whom?
    Vol. To whom but me? to me, who gave thee Life,
By whom thou cam'st into the World a *Roman*,
Who took peculiar care t' instruct thy Childhood,
T'instruct thy Youth in every gen'rous Art;
Who form'd thy growing Limbs to Martial Strength,
And steel'd thy Breast with Fortitude Divine,
Contempt of Danger, and contempt of Death;
Inflam'd thy Breast with thy dear Country's Love,
Love of great Actions and eternal Fame;
And who distinguish'd thee from other *Romans*,
As much as they're distinguish'd by the Gods
From all th' inferior Nations who surround them.
Now in requital of these matchless Benefits,
Ungrateful *Marcius* murders me!
    Cor. What means my Mother?
    Vol. And can'st thou ask? And art thou then to know
That 'tis the Maxim of each *Roman* Matron,
That when she can no longer live with Honour,
Great *Jove* aloud calls out to her to die.
And can I longer live with Honour? No;
If thou go'st on with thy curs'd Enterprize,
Death or eternal Infamy's my choice.
For I must either live to see my Country
In its last Pangs, and hear its dying Groans,
While thou, my Child, art the detested Cause,

The Subject of its frightful Imprecations;
Or live to see thee dragg'd thro' *Roman* Streets,
A dreadful Spectacle to Gods and Men,
And doom'd to die the most accursed Death
Of Traytors and of Parricides.
Therefore thou either must desist, or kill me;
This very moment thou must kill me, *Marcius*;
Here, here's the Dagger, but thou giv'st the Blow.
Yes, thou must pass o'er Her who gave thee Life,
Before thou stir'st one Step t' assault thy Country.

   Cor. What would, at last, my Mother have me do?
Must I be banish'd by the *Volscians* too?
But justly banish'd, banish'd as a Traytor?
Must I betray my Benefactors then?
Must I betray th' important Trust repos'd in me?
And so become the Out-cast of all Nations?

   Vol. I would not have thee do a shameful thing,
But love thy Glory equal with my Life.
No; reconcile the jarring Nations only.

   Cor. That's to betray them: they resolve on Conquest,
And will be satisfy'd with nought but Empire,
At least with Restitution of the Lands
The *Romans* so unjustly have usurp'd from them;
That was the Treaty which *Menenius* sign'd,
And which *Rome* afterwards refus'd to ratify.
If without that Condition I desist,
How can I e'er behold *Aufidius* more?
Or with what Eyes regard the *Volscian* Lords?
Or from the *Volscian* People what expect
But Infamy and Ruin?

   Virg. The Gods forbid thou e'er should'st see them more!
No: *Rome*, repenting of its barb'rous Usage,
Has with one Voice repeal'd its cruel Sentence.
To *Rome* with me thou surely shalt return.

   Cor. And how can I behold afflicted *Rome*,
Or how can *Rome* behold me?
Me, who have laid its Territories waste,
Destroy'd its Cities with consuming Fire,
And made ten thousand of its bleeding Sons
Feel my remorseless Sword's devouring Edge.

If I was banish'd when I fought and conquer'd for them,
What can I now expect but certain Death
From its tumultous, feeble, faithless Tribunes?
Not only my Revenge, my Preservation
Requires that *Rome* should fall. Can you desire
Your Son should die to save his mortal Foes?
No: Perish, perish this ungrateful City!

　Vol. Dye then, *Volumnia*: But, before I die,
Thus, thus the Mother falls at the Son's Feet,
Not to ask any Pity for her self,
But Mercy, Mercy, for her sinking Country.
Down, Ladies, down.

　　Cor. Oh, the confusion of my tortur'd Soul!

　　Vol. Pronounce *Rome* safe, or I am fall'n for ever.

　　Cor. Ye Gods, ye Gods! live *Rome*, and *Marcius* die first!
Oh, rise, my Mother; you and *Rome* have conquer'd;
But your unhappy Son's for ever lost.
Hoa! Who waits there?
Give Orders that the Troops return tow'rds *Antium*,
And tell *Aufidius* I expect him here.
The Troops march back towards *Antium*, where must I go?

　Virg. Once more with us to *Rome* thou shalt return.
Thy Apprehensions to the Winds deliver:
Our *Romans* will regard thee as a God
For shewing Mercy to thy bleeding Country,
After such mortal Provocations giv'n
By black Ingratitude, and base Injustice.

　Vol. Thou hast done a Godlike Deed, and supream *Jove*,
And ev'ry God who sees it, will reward it.

　Virg. Thou'st rais'd up a whole miserable People,
All in a moment, from Despair to Rapture.

　Vol. Oh, the transporting Joy that we shall meet
At our Return in ev'ry Voice and Eye!

　Virg. Our greatest Conquerours were ne'er receiv'd
With half the Joy, with half the Acclamations!

　Vol. Then what must our tempestuous Raptures be!
Oh, we are happy as the Deathless Gods!
Nor shall our Triumph be confin'd to *Rome*,
Or the short Time we live.

　Virg. No: o'er the Universe its Fame shall spread.

Vol. Nations unborn, and Languages unform'd
Shall tell the blissful Tale, and bless the Actors.
Yes, with Immortal Bliss, Immortal Fame—
Virg. And everlasting Love we shall be crown'd.
Blest with the long Possession of my *Marcius*,
I ne'er till Death will part with him again.
    Cor. Here cease your Transports. See, *Aufidius* comes:
Please to retire to yonder Tent a while,
For I must take a long but fair Adieu.

                                       [Exit Women.

Enter Aufidius.

Tullus Aufidius.—Ha!
Why dost thou greet me with this alter'd Countenance,
This silent Wonder in thy wrathful Eyes?
    Auf. Just now a Slave brought Orders to the Troops
That they should backward turn their March to *Antium*;
And impudently said he came from you.
    Cor. 'Tis true, I sent him.
    Auf. Then, *Caius Marcius*, you have done much Wrong
To me, and all the *Volscians*.
    Cor. O *Tullus, Tullus*, hadst thou but been by
To hear the piercing things that mov'd my Soul,
Thou would'st have sworn they might engage even *Jove*
To change his high Decrees.
    Auf. Your Mother and your Wife we know have done this.
    Cor. The noblest Mother, and the tender'st Wife!
    Auf. Yes, they are dear Relations, I confess,
And 'tis for them you set at Scorn the Gods
By whom so solemnly you swore.
    Cor. Unlawful Oaths are in themselves invalid.
And is it lawful to destroy my Country?
    Auf. No, not your Country, but your mortal Foes;
And so the *Romans*, by their barb'rous Usage,
You said were grown. You said, and spoke the Truth;
And this is but a poor and mean Evasion,
And you must answer 't to th' Avenging Gods,
By whom you swore with bitter Imprecations.
    Cor. Then I will answer it; let that suffice;
And to the Gods alone I'll be accountable.

Auf. Yes, I dare trust them, soon they will revenge
The Wrong that's done to their Almighty Powers:
But you must answer your Offence to me.

   Cor. To you!

   Auf. To me, ungrateful Man.
Who took you in with open Arms but I,
A supplicating Exil and a Vagabond
Fallen below Pity, nay below Contempt?
Who gave his Honour to the *Volscian* Lords
That you inviolably should be theirs?
And rais'd you up to more than former Glory,
And even to envied Greatness, to the Power
Of taking a Revenge as ample as thy Wish?
Now what's the great Return you make for this?

   Cor. Such a Return as none but I could make;
Such a Return as, not ten Days ago,
Would have been Phrensy in the proudest *Volscian*
To hope or to expect.
I infus'd Spirit thro' your abject Troops,
Gave them a Taste of Deathless Victory,
First shew'd them that the *Romans* can be conquer'd:
Compell'd my Countrymen to sue for Peace,
And sign an ignominious Treaty with you,
The same Conditions which *Menenius* brought;
Shameful for them, but glorious to your Troops,
And advantagious to the *Volscian* State.

   Auf. Name not the faithless Treaty, that condemns you;
For to what serves it but to give *Rome* Breath
To recollect her self and pour Revenge
Into the very Heart of *Volscian* Land?
Doing no more, thou hast done less than nothing,
But rankled and envenom'd more a Foe
Too much provok'd by cursed Pride before.

   Cor. How selfish Men stalk under public Zeal
To their base Ends! Before this Peace was granted
Thou wert not satisfy'd, but to thy Followers
Thou breath'dst, in Corners, sullen Discontent.
Then I went on too fast, and too precipitate,
And left whole Fortresses and Towns behind me,
With an Intention to betray the *Volscians*,

By cutting off their Intercourse with *Antium*.
'Tis not too little but too much Success
That thus provokes the great *Aufidius'* Envy.

  Auf. Envy a Traytor and a Parricide!

  Cor. Thou say'st that I have Obligations to thee;
To them thou owest that thou speak'st this, and liv'st.
Yes, take thy Life; *Jove* gave it thee at first,
I give it now; and now I owe thee nothing.

  Auf. My Life from you! First have it in your Power.

  Cor. Thou know'st, *Aufidius*, 'tis much harder for me
To say I'll kill thee, than to strike the Blow.
Twelve times, thou know'st, when I advanc'd my Sword
The Destinies advanc'd their fatal Sheers,
And nought but ignominious Flight could save thee.

  Auf. And canst thou think thou art the Man thou wer't,
When thou retain'dst thy Honour and thy Virtue?

  Cor. Both Gods and Men with one Consent proclaim
That *Marcius* is the Man he always was;
His Honour and his Virtue still the same.
And therefore the Immortal Powers assist me,
And Fortune is my Friend and my Confed'rate,
And whatsoever Side I chuse, for that declares
Tis I that made my soaring Country stoop,
That never stoop'd before; and when they su'd
For Peace, to me they supplicating su'd,
And took no Notice of the Great *Aufidius*.
Now try the Voices of thy Countrymen;
I gave them Orders to march back to *Antium*,
See then if thou can'st lead them on to *Rome*.

  Auf. Too well I am convinc'd thou hast seduc'd,
By cursed Flattery, and by shameful Arts,
My Followers, my Soldiers, and my Friends.

  Cor. 'Tis likely I should stoop to flatter *Volscians*,
Who ne'er could bow my Nature to Compliance
Even with my Country's mean and abject Customs!
'Twas my Authority alone seduc'd them,
Authority from Deathless Actions drawn,
And from my Triumphs o'er their baffled Leader.

  Auf. Oh, they must needs admire the wondrous Man
Who for some certain Drops of Womens Rheum,

343

That are as cheap as Lies, betray'd and sold
The Labour of their Noble Enterprize,
Their Interest and their Glory.

Cor. Thus far I've struggling curb'd my impatient Nature,
But on thy Life no more; for, by great *Mars*—

Auf. Name not the God, thou Boy of Tears!

Cor. Nay then—

Auf. Upon this Spot retract thy injurious Order,
Or thou shalt seal it with thy Blood, or mine.

Cor. Then take thy Wish.
This Boy, that, like an Eagle in a Dove-Court,
Flutter'd a thousand *Volscians* in *Corioli*,
And did it without Second or Assistance,
Thus sends their mighty Chief to rail in Hell.

[*Fight.* Aufidius *falls.*

Auf. O *Marcius*! thou hast conquer'd, and *Aufidius*
Is now but Dust; but, with my flowing Blood,
My Frantic Passion cools; forgive me, *Marcius*,
That I thus far provok'd thy noble Nature:
And I, to merit thy Forgiveness, tell thee
That thou, like me, art in the Shades of Death,
And soon wilt follow me, unless thou—Oh!

[*Dies.*

Cor. Hail! and eternally Farewell, brave *Tullus*!
But what's the Caution Death thus interrupted?
Thou soon shalt follow me, unless thou—what?
Oh! here's the Explication of th' Ænigma.

Enter three of the Tribunes, with their Swords drawn.

1 *Trib.* Where is our General?

Cor. There.

1 *Trib.* What Wretch's Hand has done this cursed Deed?

Cor. A Wretch whose Hand's inur'd to *Volscian* Blood.
Then love thy self, and vanish. Go, be gone,
Provoke him not.

1 *Trib.* Provoke the Villain!
I come not only to provoke but kill him.

Cor. If thou hast Power to kill him, he'll engage

To own that he's a Villain. This to try.   [*Kills him.*
So, for all thee I still am very Honest.

   2 *Trib.* Our fourth Man either loyters, or betrays us.
Let us strike home, and let us strike together.
We will revenge our General and our Friend.
What, do you recoil?

   Cor. Yes, like a Martial Engine, to advance
With certain Execution. Lie thou there.

             [*Kills the second. Women shriek behind the Scenes.*

Enter fourth Tribune [*behind* Coriolanus' *back*]

   Vol. and Vir. Behind! Oh, look behind!
   Cor. The Women see and shriek. I must dispatch.
These two are Victims to my just Resentment,
Fall thou a Sacrifice to *Tullus'* Ghost

         [*Kills the 3d Trib. and the 4th runs him thro' the Back.*

   4 *Trib.* Now falls the Sacrifice which most will please him.

                       [*Loud Shriek.*

   Cor. No, treacherous Villain, I have Life remaining
To send thee to the under World before me,
And thou shalt be the Lacquey of my Fate.
Fly, Dog, and tell *Aufidius* that I come.   [*Kills him. Falls.*

Enter Volumnia, Virgilia, *and* Valeria.

   Vol. Alas, my Son, my Son!
   Vir. My dearest Lord!
Ah, Gods, the Blood runs streaming from his Wound!
He bleeds to Death! and is no Succour nigh?
Haste, fly for help!

   Cor. All Help is vain, for we must part, *Virgilia.*
   Vir. No, we must not; there's not a God in Heaven
So cruel to decree me quite so wretched.

   Cor. My Blood and Life are at the lowest Ebb.
   Vir. Ah, now I see a Sight that will distract me,
And dread the utmost Malice of my Fate;
For the first time my *Marcius* now turns pale.

   Vol. Yet looks undaunted still.
   Cor. Mother, farewell. Nay, if you weep!—

Vol. 'Tis I have only Cause, 'tis I have done this.
Thy filial Piety has been thy Fate;
And I have kill'd my Son.

    Cor. You have sav'd your Country.

    Vol. What's my Country now
To me, a Widow, helpless, childless, comfortless?

    Cor. My everlasting Fame be now your Son,
And your own Deathless Glory be your Husband.
Where-ever *Roman* Annals shall be read,
The Godlike Action you have done this Day
To endless Ages will transmit your Name,
And all the Good eternally will bless you.
Be it your Care to comfort poor *Virgilia*.

    Vir. Is this the Happiness that I expected?
Now first I hop'd to have thee mine entirely,
Inseparably mine, and now we part,
For ever part. And must we? No, we will not;
For when thou go'st *Virgilia* will not stay.

    Cor. Virgilia, let me die as I have liv'd,
And, like a *Roman*, view the Tyrant Death
With Scorn, as I have always done in Battle.
Thy Grief alone can make him formidable,
One parting Kiss; a long, a long Farewell.   [*Dies.*

    Vir. He's gone, he's gone, and I no more must see him!
No more must dwell upon his charming Tongue,
And hang on his enchanting Lips no more.
And thou prophetic Vision of the Night,
And ye the dire Forebodings of my Soul,
All, all is come to pass. See here he lies:
Ay, here he lies, surpriz'd, surrounded, murther'd.

    Vol. Yet in his Fall he still is *Coriolanus*,
Himself alone a Conqueror o'er Numbers;
Himself the dread Revenger of his Murther.
But the just Gods require an ampler Vengeance,
For their lov'd Heroe's Death. Even now the Years
Come crouding on, for so the Gods inspire me,
When *Rome* shall all the Land around possess,
And even the Name of *Volscian* be no more.   [*Shout.*

Enter Cominius, Menenius *and Attendants.*

My Lords *Cominius* and *Menenius* here!

Com. We came with fresh Instructions from the Senate,
And larger Offers still of shameful Peace,
But find the *Volscians* fled in wild Confusion,
And panic Fright, for so our Hinds inform us;
Upon what wondrous Accident they know not.

Vol. See there the Cause;
See where their mighty Chief, *Aufidius*, lies.

Men. And, Oh! see *Marcius* pale in Blood beside him.

Com. What provok'd Death to make this dismal Havock?

Vol. That Question must redouble all my Griefs:
I was the fatal, I the only Cause.

Com. You?

Vol. I, on my Son, prevail'd at length for Mercy;
Which caus'd *Aufidius* Rage, and all their Fates.

Com. O Death! thou hast a costly Conquest made,
And wasted all at once, like foolish Spendthrifts,
The Soil that would have brought thee many a plenteous Harvest.
Tho' *Marcius* fill'd his Country with Confusion,
Which still lies strugling in Convulsive Pangs,
He shall not pass unprais'd nor unlamented,
For 'twas thy Fate in Death, as in thy Life,
To be thy Country's Champion and Deliverer.

In solemn, slow Procession let us march,
And bear the sad Remains of him to *Rome*,
Where pompous Rites of Funeral shall be paid them.
Where, Ladies, you who have thus nobly sav'd
Your Country, shall receive immortal Honours.
But they who thro' Ambition, or Revenge,
Or impious Int'rest, join with foreign Foes,
T' invade or to betray their Native Country,
Shall find, like *Coriolanus*, soon or late,
From their perfidious Foreign Friends their Fate.

                                                    [*Exeunt Omnes.*

347

65. John Dennis, letters on Shakespeare

1719

From *Original Letters*, dated 1719, published 1721.

[Letter to Sir Richard Steele, 26 March 1719]

★   ★   ★

[On Dryden's *All for Love*] For was ever any thing so pernicious, so immoral, so criminal, as the Design of that Play? I have mention'd the Title of it, give me leave to set before you the two last Lines:

> *And Fame to late Posterity shall tell,*
> *No Lovers liv'd so great, or dy'd so well.*[1]

And this Encomium of the Conduct and the Death of *Antony* and *Cleopatra*, a Conduct so immoral, and a Self-murder so criminal, is, to give it more Force, put into the Mouth of the High-Priest of *Isis*. Tho' that Priest could not but know that what he thus commended would cause immediately the utter Destruction of his Country, and make it become a Conquer'd and a *Roman* Province. Certainly never could the Design of an Author square more exactly with the Design of *White-Hall* at the time when it was written, which was by debauching the People absolutely to enslave them.

For, pray Sir, what do the Title and the two last Lines of this Play amount to in plain *English*? Why to this, that if any Person of Quality or other shall turn away his Wife, his young, affectionate, virtuous, charming Wife (for all these *Octavia* was) to take to his Bed a loose abandon'd Prostitute, and shall in her Arms exhaust his Patrimony, destroy his Health, emasculate his Mind, and lose his Reputation and all his Friends, why all this is well and greatly done, his Ruine is his Commendation. And if afterwards, in Despair, he either hangs or drowns himself, or goes out of the World like a Rat, with a Dose of Arsenick or Sublimate, why 'tis a great and an envied Fate, he dies nobly and heroically. It is, Sir, with extream Reluctance that I have

[1] See Volume I, p. 185.

said all this. For I would not be thought to affront the Memory of Mr. *Dryden*, for whose extraordinary Qualities no Man has a greater Veneration than my self. But that all Considerations ought to give Place to the Publick Good is a Truth of which you, of all Men, I am sure, can never doubt.

And can you believe then, after having recommended Virtue and Publick Spirit for so many Years to the World, that you can give your Subalterns Authority to preach up Adultery to a Town, which stands so little in need of their Doctrine? Is not the Chastity of the Marriage Bed one of the chief Incendiaries of Publick Spirit, and the Frequency of Adulteries one of the chief Extinguishers of it[?] . . .

As I had infinitely the Advantage of *All for Love* in the Moral of *Coriolanus*, I had it by Consequence in the whole Tragedy. For the *Coriolanus* as I have alter'd it, having a just Moral and by Consequence at the Bottom a general and allegorical Action and universal and allegorical Characters, and for that very reason a Fable, is therefore a true Tragedy if it be not a just and a regular one; but 'tis as just and as regular as I could make it, upon so irregular a Plan as *Shakespeare*'s. Whereas *All for Love*, having no Moral and consequently no general and allegorical Action nor general and allegorical Characters, can for that Reason have no Fable and therefore can be no Tragedy. 'Tis indeed only a particular Account of what happen'd formerly to *Antony* and *Cleopatra*, and a most pernicious Amusement.

And as I had the Advantage in the Merit of *Coriolanus*, I had it likewise in the World's Opinion of the Merit and Reputation of *Shakespeare* in Tragedy above that of Mr. *Dryden*. For let Mr. *Dryden*'s Genius for Tragedy be what it will, he has more than once publickly own'd that it was much inferior to *Shakespeare*'s, and particularly in those two remarkable Lines in his Prologue to *Aurenge-Zebe*.

> *And when he hears his Godlike* Romans *rage,*
> *He in a just Despair would quit the Stage.*

And in the Verses to Sir *Godfrey Kneller*.

> Shakespeare, *thy Gift, I place before my Sight;*
> *With Awe, I ask his Blessing ere I write;*
> *With Reverence look on his majestick Face,*
> *Proud to be less, but of his Godlike Race.*[1]

And the same Mr. *Dryden* has more than once declar'd to me that there

[1] Cf. Volume I, p. 15.

was something in this very Tragedy of *Coriolanus*, as it was writ by *Shakespeare*, that is truly great and truly *Roman*; and I more than once answer'd him that it had always been my own Opinion. Now I appeal to you and your Managers, if it has lost any thing under my Hands.

But what is more considerable than all this, your Deputy Lieutenants for the Stage have ten times the Opinion of the Advantage which *Shakespeare* has over Mr. *Dryden* in Tragedy than either I or the rest of the World have. Ever since I was capable of reading *Shakespeare* I have always had and have always exprest that Veneration for him which is justly his due; of which I believe no one can doubt, who has read the Essay which I publish'd some Years ago upon his Genius and Writings. But what they express upon all Occasions is not Esteem, is not Admiration, but flat Idolatry. (105-9)

      ★   ★   ★

[From the Letter to Judas Iscariot, Esq.: 'On the Degeneracy of the Publick Taste', 25 May 1719]

      ★   ★   ★

A very great Part of those who pretend to be in Love with *Shakespeare*, if he were now living, and his most celebrated Plays were to be acted *De novo* without a Cabal, without Character or Prepossession, wou'd Hiss and Damn the very Things of which they are now the fashionable Admirers; which seems plain to me from this very Reason, because the modern Plays which they most approve of are the very Reverse of *Shakespeare*'s, with respect either to his Excellencies or his Faults.

Shakespeare is very justly celebrated for the Truth and Justness of his Characters, for the Beauty of his Sentiments, for the Simplicity and Dignity of his Dialogue, and for his moving the Passions powerfully by the meer force of Nature. But the present Spectators of Tragedies approve of those most in which the Passions are mov'd least. They will endure no Modern Tragedy in whose principal Character Love is not the predominant Quality. Now Love predominating in the principal Character too often falsifies and confounds those Characters, and by Consequence but too often destroys the Beauty of the Sentiments, because no Sentiment can be beautiful which is improper in him who speaks it. Besides, there are not three of our modern Tragedies which have any thing like those Sentiments which abound in *Shakespeare*— Sentiments which, at the same time that they shew Sagacity and Penetration, are easie, just, and natural.

The modern Readers and Spectators of Tragedies will endure no Tragedy which has the Simplicity and *naiveté* of *Shakespeare*'s Dialogue; a Simplicity, wherever the occasion requires it, attended with Force, and Dignity, and Pomp, and Solemnity. Instead of that noble and natural Dialogue they are for a flatulant Style, in which the Poet puts the Change upon himself and speaks almost always himself, instead of making his Characters speak.

But as the Readers and Spectators of Modern Tragedies approve of those most which are the very reverse of *Shakespeare*'s with respect to his Beauties and Excellencies, so they declare very loudly against his Faults. The Faults of *Shakespeare*, which are rather those of the Age in which he liv'd, are his perpetual Rambles, and his apparent Duplicity (in some of his Plays) or Triplicity of Action, and the frequent breaking the Continuity of the Scenes. The present Spectators declare against this in appearance, but at the same time approve of this Multiplicity of Action in some Modern Plays, concealed by a Jumble and a Confusion which is incomprehensible and altogether unintelligible. Another of *Shakespeare*'s Faults is the Length of Time employ'd in the carrying on his Dramatick Action. The present Spectators are extreamly shock'd at this in a modern Tragedy, but at the same time approve of those in which the Unity of Time is preserved by offending all Common Sense.

If a Modern Poet in one of his Tragedies should shew any Thing like *Shakespeare*'s Rambles, should introduce a Tragedy upon the Stage which should begin in *Europe* and end in *Asia*, like the Moor of *Venice*, that Play would be exploded and damn'd with very great Damnation. But the Modern Spectators of Tragedies greatly esteem and are fond of those in which the Unity of Place is preserv'd, sometimes by whimsical comick Absurdities, and sometimes by dreadful and pro-digious Extravagancies.

From all this I conclude, as I said before, that the Spectators of modern Tragedies, having the greatest Esteem for those which have least of *Shakespeare*'s Excellencies, and declaring loudly against his Faults, would damn *Shakespeare*, if living. (71-4)

66. Lewis Theobald, from his adaptation of *Richard II*

1719

From *The Tragedy of King Richard II . . . Altered from Shakespeare* (1720).

First performed on 10 December 1719, 'With new Scenes and Habits', Theobald's adaptation enjoyed a moderate success. The Preface includes an extremely detailed argument that Shakespeare knew both Greek and Latin, with citations of parallel passages from Aeschylus, Lucian and Plutarch. Few of the claims seem to have sufficient substance to be worth presenting here.

THE
PREFACE.

The Work of *Prefaces* to most Modern Plays has been either to accuse the Town of Unkindness, to complain of private Injuries from the Theatre, or to do Justice to the particular Merit of Some shining Actor. Remonstrances of the first kind are but once read, and sleep with the Reader. And as for Acknowledgments, tho' I have Some to make to the Performers, I must, like an honest Man, begin first with my largest Debts and make a Sort of Compensation for the Helps which I have borrowed from *Shakespeare*.

The many scatter'd Beauties which I have long admir'd in His *Life and Death of King Richard II* induced me to think they would have stronger Charms if they were interwoven in a regular Fable. For this Purpose, I have made some Innovations upon History and *Shakespeare*: as, in bringing *Richard* and *Bolingbroke* to meet first at the *Tower*; keeping *York* steady to the Interest of the King; heightening *Aumerle*'s Character in making him dye for the Cause; and in dispatching *Richard* at the Tower—who, indeed, was murther'd at *Pontefract* Castle. In these and such Instances I think there may be reserv'd a discretionary Power of Variation, either for maintaining the *Unity of Action*, or supporting the *Dignity* of the *Characters*. If the little Criticks will be angry at This I have Patience to weather their Ill Nature: I shall stand excus'd among the better Judges,

—*Dabiturque Licentia sumpta pudenter.*[1]

The Second Motive which I had for setting to Work on this Story was that it would afford me an Opportunity, in confessing my Obligations to *Shakespeare*, of doing him some Justice upon the Points of his *Learning*, and *Acquaintance with the Antients*, both which have not only been contested but even denied him in positive Terms. Perhaps, in robbing Him of these Secondary Aids, they might design a Compliment to the Force and Extensiveness of his Wit and Natural Parts.

Shakespeare is allowed by All to have had the most wonderful Genius and the warmest Imagination of any Poet since the Name of *Homer*. As these Qualities led him to say and express many Things sublimely, figuratively, and elegantly, so they often forc'd him out of his Way, upon false *Images*, hard *Metaphors*, and *Flights* where the Eye of Judgment cannot trace him. This Fault He has in common with All great Wits: *Homer* is accus'd of It by the Antients, there are many Instances of it in *Æschylus*, and *Sophocles* himself is not without these Transgressions of Fancy. This, indeed, is not a Point now to be contested; but whether *Shakespeare* had Them in a less or greater Degree than the Antients, or whether he offended by Imitation and their Authority, or by the irregular Force of his own Genius—*That is the Question.*

The Strength and Vigour of his Fancy have been confess'd and admir'd in the extravagant and supernatural Characters of his own Creation, such as his CALIBAN, *Witches*, &c. And give me Leave to take Notice of the *Delicacy* of his Spirit in One Instance, because the Observation has not, that I know of, ever yet been started by Anybody. No *Dramatic* Poet before *Shakespeare*, in any Language that I know or remember, has heighten'd his Distress from the Concurrence of the Heavens, as He has done in his *Lear*, by doubling the Compassion of the Audience for his Heroe when they behold a Storm, in which he is turn'd out, aggravate the Rigour of his Daughters Inhumanity. How beautifully is that rude and boisterous Night describ'd! And what Reflections on their Savage Treatment of a Father!

—*Things, that love Night,*
Love not such Nights as these: the wrathful Skies

[1] Horace, *A.P.*, 51: 'and licence will be granted, if used with modesty'.

Gallow the very Wanderers of the Dark,
And make them keep their Caves: Since I was Man,
Such Sheets of Fire, such Bursts of horrid Thunder,
Such Groans of roaring Wind, and Rain, I never
Remember to have heard.— [3.2.42 ff]

And again,

I tax not You, ye Elements, with Unkindness;
I never gave You Kingdom, call'd You Children;
You owe me no Subscription: then let fall
Your horrible Pleasure: Here I stand your Slave,
A poor, infirm, weak, and despis'd Old Man.
But yet I call you servile Ministers,
That will with Two pernicious Daughters join
Your high-engendred Battles, 'gainst a Head
So Old, and White, as This.—O! O! 'tis foul. [3.2.16 ff]

But This is a Digression, and 'tis Time now to come back to my Subject.

They who affirm that *Shakespeare* was wholly unacquainted with the Antients beg the Question, and perhaps have been unreasonably led into that Error by the false Opinion of Some of his Contemporaries, and the falser Interpretation of *their* Meaning by Some Moderns. *Ben Jonson* seems to be the Original from whence they copy One after Another; and the farther from Him, still the more erroneously. For my own Part I must declare concerning His Want of Understanding the Antients as Sir *John Denham* does concerning *Homer's* Want of Sight, in those beautiful Lines,

I can no more believe old Homer *blind,*
Than Those who say the Sun has never shin'd;
The Age was dark wherein He liv'd, but He
Could not want Sight, who taught the World to see.

The Application is easy: *Shakespeare*, who was the Father of the *British* Stage, who founded, rais'd, and modell'd it; who, tho' he vastly inrich'd the Theatre in his Life time, yet left such large Legacies to succeeding Poets; could never want those Aids of Learning which must be necessary for a Work of so extensive a Nature. He must know many Things from Others who went before Him, as well as observe many from his own Times, and invent, perhaps, many more from his own Fancy. If the Criticks will not allow This from the Reason of the

Thing we must come to Facts to prove it. We will first examine the Vulgar Error, deriv'd from *Ben. Jonson*. His Words are these, printed after *Shakespeare*'s Death, when we may be sure he hath spoke with the utmost Freedom of his Memory,

> *And tho' thou had'st small* LATIN, *and less* GREEK,
> *From thence to honour Thee*, &c.[1]

It is very evident that *Ben* allows him some Share of Knowledge in both these learned Languages, and it is not unlikely that He whose Pride lay in a greater Portion of Them might deliver himself with too partial a Contempt of *Shakespeare*'s less Acquirements. It is Natural for great Scholars so to do; and we see too many Examples of it every Day in their speaking of Others to justify the Opinion, and make it probable that *Ben*, who never was renown'd for his Humanity, might in these Verses stretch a Point in his own Favour and Commendation. Supposing Him then, even with *Ben*'s Abatements, but moderately furnish'd with these Materials of Science, the next Thing to be enquir'd is how far they might go toward the raising such a Superstructure as *Shakespeare* has rais'd upon them.

We know, by daily Experience, what a little Share of *French* or *Italian* will serve a Common Capacity to pick out the Meaning of most Authors in those Tongues, and make Him give no bad, if not the exactest, Account of his Reading. With This fair Allowance then of *Shakespeare*'s equal Knowledge in the learned Languages most, if not all, of his Fables, Histories, and particular Facts are easily accounted for, and he is put at least upon the Foot of a tolerable Scholar. But there is Something yet more peculiar in the Case of *Shakespeare*, consider'd as a *Poet reading a Poet*. Where there is a Similitude of *Genius* and *Spirit* the Application will be the greater, the Fancy will catch Fire, and with little Aid of Language find out a Meaning or make a better. I believe I could be able to prove that Mr *Dryden* has done This in a hundred Instances, and why should we deny That to *Shakespeare* which is so visible in One of his Greatest Successors? This I take to be a fair Proof of the general Point, unless any One can find a Way how He should come at the Knowledge of the *Greek* and *Roman* Stories any other Way than by understanding the Language of their Writers.

It is granted, I think, that we had few or no Translations from the Antients in *Shakespeare*'s Younger Years at least; the Time most proper to make himself Master of Languages, and in that Period in which

[1] Cf. Volume I, p. 24.

we are to look upon him as a Writer—for 'tis certain he left the Stage some Years before he dyed. However the Antiquaries may decide this Point I can't tell, but it seems to be allowed on all Hands that Dr. *Holland*, the laborious Translator and perhaps the First general One, began upon the *Greek* and *Latin* Authors long after *Shakespeare's* Decease.

As to particular Passages in his Works, to prove he was no inconsiderable Master of the *Greek* Story there are but Two Plays, his *Timon of Athens* and *Troilus and Cressida*, that can furnish me with Instances, but they are so numerous in These as to leave it without Dispute or Exception. But to prove that he owed several of his Thoughts and Sentiments to the Antients, whoever will take the Pains to dip into his Works with that View, I dare engage, will find evident Traces of Imitation where he could expect them neither from the Characters nor Fable.

* * *

PROLOGUE

The Tragick Muse aspires by various Ways
To catch the Soul, and to command your Praise;
Oft, breathing War, to generous Acts She warms,
And animates your Martial Breasts to Arms.
Then, as the *personated* Hero fights,
Your Bosoms kindle in your *Country's* Rights.
Our Author labours in an humbler Strain,
But hopes to sooth you with a pleasing Pain;
To move your Hearts, and force your Eyes to flow
With Tears, drawn from an ENGLISH *Monarch's* Woe.
Justly his Pen's mistaken Task he'll own,
If you can see a Prince, without a Groan,
Forc'd by his Subjects to renounce his Throne.
    If recent Times more fresh Examples bring,
How we can *murther*, or *depose* a King,
Fearful of Censure, and offended Law,
The Muse presumes no *Parallels* to draw;
Nor aims to make the sullen, factious Stage
Bellow with *Anti-Revolution* Rage.
From *Richard's* Ruin, only, she intends
To wound your Souls, and make you *Richard's* Friends.
    Immortal *Shakespeare* on this Tale began,
And wrote it in a rude, Historick Plan,

On his rich Fund our Author builds his Play,
Keeps all his Gold, and throws his Dross away;
Safe in this Aid, he can no *Thunder* dread,
Fenc'd with the God's *own* Laurel *round his Head.*

*   *   *

[Act I, Scene i.] London. Outside the Tower.

*   *   *

[Richard denounces Wiltshire, Bagot, Bushy and Green.]

King. O Villains! Vipers! damn'd without Redemption!
Dogs, easily won to fawn on any Man!
Snakes, in my Heart's-blood warm'd, that sting my Heart!
Wou'd They make Peace? Terrible Hell make War
Upon their spotted Souls for this Offence!
    Carl. Sweet Love, I see, changing his Property,
Turns to the sow'rest and most deadly Hate.
Again uncurse their Souls: their Peace is made
With Heads, and not with Hands. I learn'd but now
(But wou'd not grieve you with the heavy Tale),
They fell into the Snare of *Bolingbroke,*
And dy'd at *Bristol,* Victims to his Rage.
    King. O *Carlisle,* thou hast said enough, and brought me
Again into the Road of sweet Despair.
By Heav'n, I'll hate him everlastingly,
That bids me be of Comfort any more.
But, see! She comes, whose lovely Face has Pow'r
To charm Calamity, and sooth my Sorrows.

Enter Queen, *and Lady* Percy.

Welcome, my Queen! O welcome to my Arms,
Thou Rose of Beauty! Ha!—What mean these Tears,
That heaving Bosom, and this Burst of Sorrow?
    Queen. O *Richard!* These are but the Remnant Drops
Of that large Stock with which I've mourn'd thy Absence;
But my poor Heart, tho' yet I hold thee safe,
Sickens at the bad Contention of the Times
And, Prophet-like, shakes with approaching Horrors.
    King. O let not hateful Apprehension, Sweet,
With Giant Steps stride o'er thy peaceful Thoughts
And shock the Quiet of thy tender Soul.

357

Not all the Water in the rough rude Sea
Can wash the Balm from an anointed King:
The Breath of Worldly Men cannot depose
The Deputy and Substitute of Heav'n.
For ev'ry Man that *Bolingbroke* has prest
To lift the Sword against our sacred Crown,
Heav'n for his *Richard* hath in Heav'nly Pay
Myriads of Angels; and if Angels fight,
What Mortal Force can stand th' unequal Combat?

   Queen. But if the Pow'rs, that oft withhold the Scourge
Till we have fill'd the Measure of our Crimes,
Shou'd stretch the Hand of Indignation out
In fierce Revenge on the Licentious Land,
And suffer Usurpation to prevail,
Thou wou'dst not chide me for my loving Fears?
O let us arm against the worst, my Lord,
And better Fate will then be doubly welcome.

   King. But wilt Thou not despise me when I fall
And drag thee down to share my ruin'd Fortunes?
Wilt Thou not then, in bitterness of Anguish,
Reproach me that I drew thy helpless Youth
From the strong Sanctuary of paternal Love
To share the State of an unscepter'd King
And grow acquainted with the Bed of Sorrow?

   Queen. Tho' doubly I'm ally'd to Royalty,
Daughter of *France*, and Wife of *England*'s King,
I have a Soul that can look down on Pomp
And count it the Incumbrance of my Fortune.
Thy Virtues, not thy Scepter, make thee rich.
Let me enjoy the Blessing of thy Heart,
Tho' rude Ambition rob thee of the Crown,
In Privacy I shall be still the same,
Obey thee with the Duty of a Wife
And the Devotion of a Subject's Love.

   King. So young, and so resign'd! Thou chid'st me well
For getting up my Rest in giddy State
And Ostentation of despised Empire.
By Heav'n, I want no Kingdom having thee.
Let restless Spirits parcel out the Globe
And sweat for Limit and Prerogative,

Vexing the States, in which they Monarchize,
With Starts and Tumults of ungovern'd Pride.
I here disclaim all Thrones; nor will embroil
A Nation's Safety in my doubtful Quarrel.
All you that wou'd be safe fly from my Side;
Crowns shall no more from Love my Thoughts divide;
Discharge my Followers, let 'em hence, away,
From *Richard's* Night to *Bolingbroke's* fair Day.   [*Exeunt.*

*   *   *

[Act II, Scene ii.] The Outward Part of the Tower.

*   *   *

Bol. My gracious Lord, thus humbly at your Feet—
King. Fair Cousin, you debase your Princely Knee
To make the base Earth proud with kissing it.
I'd rather much my Heart might feel your Love
Than my unpleas'd Eye see your Courtesie.
Up, Cousin, up. Your Heart is up, I know:
Thus high at least, altho' your Knee be bent.
     Bol. My gracious Liege, I come but for my Own.
     King. Your Own is Yours, and I am Yours, and All.—
     Bol. So far be mine, my most redoubted Liege,
As my true Service shall deserve your Love.
     King. Well you deserve. They well deserve to have
Who know the strongest, surest, Way t'obtain!
     Bol. To your own Royal Justice I appeal
If Injuries, past the Suff'rance of a Man,
Have not been heap'd to spur me to Redress.
That I was banish'd, was your Highness' Will.
But when I was so, and my Father dy'd,
The Malice or the Avarice of Slaves
(Whose Sordid Minds hate all above themselves),
Seduc'd your Grace to seize upon my Lands,
Strip'd me of all the Rights of fair Succession,
From my own Seats tore down my Household-Coat,
Raz'd out my Impress, leaving me no Sign,
Save Men's Opinions and my Living Blood,
To shew the World I am a Gentleman.
     King. Enough, Complaints too harshly wound my Ears;

You must, and shall have Reparation done you.
Uncle of *York*, surrender up the Keys;
We to our Cousin's Charge resign our *Tow'r*,
And will be here henceforward as his Guest.

Aum. My gracious Liege, recall that hasty Grant
Or 'tis the last you will have Pow'r to make.

King. *Aumerle*, no more.—I am not to be mov'd.
The Die is cast that must decide my Fate.
Cover your Heads, and mock not Flesh and Blood
With solemn Rev'rence; throw away Respect,
Tradition, Form, and ceremonious Duty,
For you have but mistook me all this while.
I live with Bread like you, feel Want like you,
Taste Grief, need Friends, like you. Why then shou'd Pomp
Distinguish, whom Necessities make equal?

Bol. Permit us, gracious Sir, as Subjects ought,
To serve, and wait upon your Majesty.

King. Uncle, your Hand. Nay, do not weep, old Man;
Tears may shew Love but want their Remedies.—
Cousin, I am too young to be your Father,
Tho' You are old enough to be my Heir.
What you will have, I'll give; possess my Crown;
Let me but live till Nature lets me down.

As some fair Flow'r, that by the Sun Beams chear'd,
Has to the Spring its blushing Glories rear'd,
If once deserted by the Genial Ray,
Falls from its Pride, and sickens in Decay:
So I, that have enjoy'd my Fortune's Prime,
Too weak, to bear the Injuries of Time,
Blasted by Fate, shall soon my Honours shed,
Shrink up my Leaves, and drop my wither'd Head.   [*Exeunt.*

*   *   *

[Act V, Scene ii.] The Outward Part of the *Tower.*

*   *   *

North. My Lord, you now must instantly depart
And leave the Pris'ners to their Doom.

Aum. Farewel.
O *Carlisle*, I had treasur'd up a Hope

360

You might have seen us take the Stroke of Death,
And to old *York* reported that his Son
Fell not unworthy of his Birth or Cause.

Carl. Had I dy'd with You I had spar'd these Tears;
But these our Friendship and your Virtues claim.
My Lords, one last Embrace. Heav'n make you strong,
And arm your Breasts with Christian Fortitude
To stand the Terrors of the Scene before you.

[*Exit* Carlisle.

Sal. Come, let us meet this threat'ning Pomp of Death,
For we, my Lord, are like two desp'rate Men
That vow a long and weary Pilgrimage.
Let us not stand and count the Way with Sighs
But start with Hearts resolv'd, ere Fancy palls
And makes the Passage irksome to our Thoughts.

Aum. I paus'd not, *Salisbury*, to defer my Doom,
But mourn my suff'ring King and Country's Fate.
This Royal Throne of Kings, this little World,
This Earth of Majesty, this Seat of *Mars*,
This Fortress built by Nature for her self
Against Infection and the Hand of War;
This Land of Liberty, this dear, dear, Land,
Dear for her Reputation thro' the World,
This *England*, that was wont to conquer Others,
Has made a shameful Conquest of it self.
Our forfeit Lives how gladly should we pay
If that our Blood could wash its Stains away!

[*Exeunt.*

Northumberland (*Solus.*) So, now a little Interval of Time
Will, on that Quarter, set my Soul at Rest:
A Work of Consequence is still behind.
Let me confirm the yet unsettled Crown
To *Bolingbroke*, and Fortune then is mine.
The Means will be to move King *Richard* hence
And, by his Absence, cool the People's Love.

[*Exit* North.

[Act V, Scene iii.]

SCENE changes to an inner Apartment.

Enter King Richard, *and* Queen.

361

King. O *Isabella*! Fate cou'd ne'er intend
Those blooming Beauties for the Spoil of Grief
To waste in Tears and Health-impairing Woe.
Forsake this Wretch, whom Heav'n has quite thrown off
And Fortune is commission'd to destroy.
Think I am dead, or that ev'n now thou tak'st,
As from my Death-bed, my last living Leave.
If Thou wilt bear some Portion of Distress
Let it be from the Mem'ry of my Wrongs.
In Winter's tedious Nights sit by the Fire
With good old Folks, and let them tell Thee Tales
Of woful Ages distant far in Time.
Then, ere thou bid Good Night, to quit their Grief
Tell thou the lamentable Fall of Me,
And send the Hearers weeping to their Beds.

Queen. Alas, My Lord, you do distrust my Love!
You think my Heart was wedded to the State,
The Pomp of Courts, and Luxury of Empire,
And that my Soul is weaker than my Sex.
No, let Affliction rain upon our Heads,
Let angry Heav'n pour forth its Stores of Vengeance.
I am prepar'd t'encounter all its Fury,
Share the rough Visitation of the Storm
That breaks on You, and hush you into Comfort!

King. Exquisite Goodness! O thou more than Woman,
Thou Angel Form, link'd with an Angel's Mind!
By Heav'n, thy matchless Softness wounds me more
Than all the Rage of rude Calamity.
You righteous Pow'rs! do with Me what you please,
Heap Plagues upon me, let infectious Woe
Vary its Forms, and multiply my Tortures.
I am a Man, black with a Train of Crimes,
That have abus'd your sacred Trust of Pow'r
And made the Regal Office serve the Turns
Of Appetite and Arbitrary Will,
And therefore do deserve your just Correction.
But, oh! in Mercy spare her Innocence,
And Me the Pain of seeing her in Anguish.

Queen. Alas! Misfortunes fall too thick upon us,
For see, the stern *Northumberland*'s at hand.

Enter Northumberland.

North. My Lord, the Mind of *Bolingbroke* is chang'd.
The Council, careful for the Nation's Safety,
And to prevent Rebellion's busy Rage,
Have judg'd it meet that you shou'd leave the *Tow'r*,
And privately retire to *Pomfret* Castle.

King. Northumberland, thou Ladder by whose Steps
The mounting *Bolingbroke* ascends my Throne,
The Time shall not be many Hours of Age
More than it is ere foul Sin, gathering Head,
Shall break into Corruption. Thou shalt think,
Tho' he divide the Realm and give thee Half,
It is too little, helping him to All.
And He shall think, that Thou, who knew'st the way
To plant unrightful Kings wilt know again,
Being ne'er so little urg'd, another Way
To pluck him headlong from th' usurped Throne.

North. My Lord, I came not to discourse of This.
If I've done Ought unwarranted and ill
My Guilt be on my Head, and there's an End.
But, Madam, there is Order ta'en for You,
With all swift Speed you must away to *France*.

Queen. Has *Bolingbroke* the Law so much at Will
That he can abrogate Heav'n's eldest Law,
Step in betwixt the venerable Rites
Sacred even to the barbarous and rude,
And part whom strong Connubial Love has join'd?

North. Custom and Law must, where the Cause requires,
Give way to Time and strict Necessity.
'Tis fixt beyond Recall; therefore with Speed
Take Leave and part, for you must part forthwith.

King. Doubly divorc'd!—Bad Men, ye violate
A Two-fold Marriage: 'twixt My Crown and Me,
And then betwixt Me and my marry'd Wife!
Are there no Bolts of Vengeance for such Crimes?
Was it not Wrong enough to break your Faiths,
And strip me of my Crown, but must you too
Break the Possession of a Royal Bed
And stain the Beauty of a fair Queen's Cheeks

363

With Tears drawn from her Eyes by your foul Wrongs?
O *Isabella*!

Queen. Give thy Sorrows Vent,
And I will second them with equal Woe.
O, to what Purpose do'st thou hoard thy Words
And fix thy Eyes in dumb expressive Sadness?

King. I have no Words, no Utt'rance for my Thoughts,
When the Tongue's Office should be prodigal
To breath the Anguish of my breaking Heart.
Our Injuries press too hard upon my Soul
And, like unruly Children, make their Sire
Stoop with Oppression of their galling Weight.

Queen. But must we be divided? must we part?

King. Ay, Hand from Hand, my Love, and Heart from Heart.
Therefore in wooing Sorrow let's be brief,
For Woe's made wanton with this fond Delay.
Let me unkiss the Oath betwixt us, Love.
—And yet not so; for with a Kiss 'twas made.
O *Isabella*! I must towards the North,
Where shiv'ring Cold and Sickness pine the Clime,
And Thou to *France* from whence, set forth in Pomp,
You came to my Embrace, adorn'd like *May*,
Blooming in Sweets, and bright with springing Beauties,

North. My Lord, you do but aggravate your Pains
By length'ning out the Circumstance of Parting.

King. Insolent Man! how dar'st thou treat me thus,
Make pale our Cheek, and chase the Royal Blood
With Fury from its Native Residence?
The blackest Fiends take *Lancaster* and Thee!
Patience is stale, and I am weary of it.—
And now, We wo'not part.

North. —Nay then, a Guard!—

King. They shall not force thee from me.

> [Exton *and the Guard break in; part of them hurry away the Queen;
> the King snatches a Sword, kills two of them, and in the Scuffle is
> kill'd by* Exton.

Queen. Barbarous Men!—
Farewell, O *Richard*!

King. Villain, thy own Side

Yields thy Death's Instrument. O, I am slain!

  Exton. Let us away, lest Death, and not Reward
Pursue us for this hasty Deed of Slaughter.

                                    [*Exeunt* Exton *and* Guard.

Enter Bolingbroke, Northumberland, Ross, *and* Willoughby, *at several*
Doors.

  Bol. What Noise of Tumult did invade our Ears?
Ha! *Richard!* How came this?

  King. Question it not;
Content, that thy Fears with me ly bury'd:
Unrival'd, wear the Crown. O *Isabella!*   [*Dies.*

                 [*A Screaming within.*]

  Bol. What new Assault of Horror wounds us thus?

  Ross. The beauteous *Percy,* with a desp'rate Hand,
Hearing *Aumerle* was dead, a secret Dagger
Drew from her Side, and plung'd it in her Breast.

  North. My Daughter! Fate pursues my Guilt too fast.

                                [*Exit* North.

Enter York.

  York. Give way, bold Groom, I will not be repuls'd.
Where is my Son, thou Tyrant? Give him back.—

  Ross. My Lord,—

  Bol. To bed, old Man; I see, thou'rt ill.

  York. Now he that made me knows, I see Thee ill:
Thy Death-bed is no less than this wide Land,
Wherein Thou liest in Reputation sick,
Tainted with Murder.—Ha! Start Eyes, break Heart!
My Royal Master, welt'ring in his Blood?
Fate, thou art kind; This Blow was home, and sure.

                     [*Falls by the Body, and dies.*

  Bol. Support him;

  Will. 'Tis too late: he's dead at once.

  Bol. Lords, I protest, my Soul is full of Woe;
And to the Realm my Sorrow shall be known
That I on such Events should fix my Throne.
Tho' Vengeance may awhile withhold her Hand,
A King's Blood, unaton'd, must curse the Land.

67. John Dennis, Shakespeare and the Rules

1720

From *The Characters and Conduct of Sir John Edgar* (1720).

An attack on Steele and the managers of the Drury Lane theatre for their delays in presenting Dennis's *Coriolanus* in the winter of 1718–19. 'Sir John Edgar' was the pseudonym under which Steele issued his periodical *The Theatre* (January–April 1720).

[The second letter]

*   *   *

You should likewise have consider'd whether *Corneille*, who introduc'd the Rules among them, was acquainted with them when he first began to write? So far from it, that he himself owns that he did not so much as know that there were Rules. You should then have ask'd this Question, whether the Dramatick Poems which he wrote before he was acquainted with *Aristotle* are comparable to those which he wrote after he came to be convinc'd of the Necessity and Efficacy of his Rules? Any one who has read his Works could have told you that there is no manner of Comparison between them. It had then been Time to consider whether the Genius of *Shakespeare* himself would not have appear'd brighter and more glorious, if he had writ regularly.

This, Sir *John Edgar*, may be depended upon, that if you know anyone who calls himself a Poet and who is offended at Rules, that is, at Criticism, know, that that Aversion is a never-failing Mark of a very vile Scribbler. Know, that there never was in the World, nor ever will be, a Legitimate Epick or Dramatic Poet but he was fond of Criticism and of Rules; nay, he was himself a Critick, a just, a great, a severe Critick, and a Religious Observer of Rules.

The Rules of Poetry constitute the Art of it; which he who does not throughly understand can never be a great Poet. For how should any one perfectly practise an Art which he does not perfectly understand? Can any one believe that *Homer*, *Sophocles*, and *Euripides* did not write regularly and were not great Criticks, when one of the most penetrating of all the old Philosophers has taken the very Rules of the Art from his Observations of the Method which they took to succeed? The extravagant and absurd Aversion which we have shewn so long to Criticks and to Rules is one Cause at least that the very Species of Poets is shortly like to be extinguish'd in *Great Britain*.

'Tis now about a Century and a Half since the first Theatre was erected among us. Why have we since that Time improv'd in almost every Art, except Dramatick Poetry? Our Architecture is become quite another Thing. We are come to contemn our old *Gothick* and barbarous manner of Building, and are perfectly convinc'd that the ancient *Græcian* and *Roman* manner is not only more beautiful and more harmonious, but more useful and more convenient. We have since that Time made a very great Progress in Musick. Our National Painting is likewise vastly improv'd; so are likewise the Mechanick Arts. We have excell'd the very Nations from which we have taken them. And tho' we are esteem'd by our Neighbours to be but very indifferent Inventors we are very justly thought by them to be the greatest Improvers in the World.

For what Reason, then, have we made no Progress in our Dramatick Poetry? Why has the first who appear'd among us, ev'n in the Infancy of our Stage [Shakespeare], surpass'd all his Successors in Tragedy, by the Confession of those very Successors? Why has *Ben Jonson* excell'd all in Comedy who have attempted it after him? What Cause can be assign'd for this but that our Architects, Painters, and Masters of Musick have been humble and docile enough to study and follow the Rules of their Art, and to be corrected both by Foreign Examples and by domestick Remonstrances? Whereas the Persons whom we have call'd Poets, being very proud and very ignorant have rejected all these with Disdain. Which puts me in mind of the following Lines of my Lord *Roscommon* in his Translation of *Horace*'s *Art of Poetry*:

> *Why is he honour'd with a Poet's Name,*
> *Who neither knows, nor would observe a Rule;*
> *And chuses to be ignorant and proud,*
> *Rather than own his Ignorance, and learn?*

Which Lines, if they do not shew *Horace*'s Sense exactly, yet shew my Lord *Roscommon*'s; which is of no small weight.

Yet, after all, Sir *John*, to shew you that I am neither a Bigot nor a Slave to the Rules, my Opinion is that whereas the Rules are only

Directions to an Epick or Dramatick Poet for the Attainment of Sovereign Beauty, whenever it may happen, by very great Chance, that Sovereign Beauty can be better attain'd by suspending one of them for that Time than by a too rigid Observance of it, then by consequence the grand Rule is, resolutely to suspend it. And such a masterly Neglect of it for the Time shews a Poet to be both discreet and bold.

For as 'tis the Prerogative of a King to suspend the Execution of a Law when such a Suspension is, and appears to be, absolutely necessary for the Safety and Welfare of the Publick—which is the great Law, to which all other Laws ought to be subservient, and consequently for the procuring or promoting of which there is not one of them but what ought to be broken, as upon all other Occasions they ought to be kept inviolably; so 'tis the Prerogative of a Poet to set aside a Rule of his Art, or a Rule of an Art subservient to his own, whenever 'tis necessary for the Ennobling of his Art and the Enriching the Commonwealth of Learning.

However, this is a Law of eternal Obligation, That where-ever great Beauties can be shewn with the Rules as well as they can without them, there the Rules ought always to remain most sacred and inviolable. The Reason is plain: because when the Surprize and the Emotion is over which is caus'd by the Power of great Beauty the Reader, who comes to be cool and calm, is apt to look for Defects; and if he finds them—tho' not in the Part where the Beauties lye yet in the whole—he is apt to be shock'd. (30-3)

68. Charles Gildon on Shakespeare's faults

1721

From *The Laws of Poetry Explain'd and Illustrated* (1721).

This work is composed in the form of a commentary on Roscommon's 'Essay on translated verse', and 'borrows' much of its material from Rymer.

Tho' the favourers of the *English Tragedy* may pretend that these reflections reach only some few of obscure reputation, yet it is certain that no man who is acquainted with the taking *Tragedies* of the greatest part of the reign of King *Charles* the Second but does know that these reflections are grounded upon plays that were far from being obscure in those days; for a corroborating proof of which I shall instance the *Rehearsal,* which is wholly compos'd of the monstrous absurdities which then reign'd on the *English stage* and were applauded by the *vogue-makers* of that time as excellencies. To these I shall add Mr. *Rymer's* view of the *Tragedies* of the last age, where he proves, even according to Mr. *Dryden's* concession, what fantastical and ridiculous pieces those were which even to our days bear the name of the best *Tragic* performances in our language; I mean, *The Maid's Tragedy, King and no King, Rollo Duke of Normandy*, and the rest. Tho' Mr. *Dryden* owns that all or most of the faults Mr. *Rymer* has found are just, yet he adds this odd reflection (as I have elsewhere observ'd): *And yet,* says he, *Who minds the Critic, and who admires* Shakespeare *less?*[1] that was as much as to say, 'Mr. *Rymer* has indeed made good his charge, and yet the town admir'd the poet's errors still'. Which I take to be a greater proof of the folly and abandon'd taste of the town than of any imperfections in the critic, since the charge Mr. *Rymer* brings against these plays is that they have no *Fable,* and by consequence can give no instruction; that their *manners* and *sentiments,* to say nothing of the *diction,* are every where defective, nay unnatural, and therefore can give no rational or useful pleasure.

[1] Cf. No. 33 above, p. 86.

369

There is another sort of dramatic entertainments upon the *English* stage, call'd *Historical Plays*, in which tho' *Shakespeare* be the principal yet almost all the old *English* Plays are of the same kind; and indeed, tho' the title of Historical Plays be only given by the editors of his works to his lives of *King John*; *Richard II*; *Henry IV, V, and VI*; *Richard III*; and, *Henry VIII*, yet almost all his other Plays may properly be call'd Historical, for tho' they are not all the entire lives of particular persons yet they contain, generally speaking (for I think there is one or two exceptions), the historical transactions of several years—as the *Julius Cæsar* for example, in which we find not only the conspiracy against him but all that happen'd afterwards in the *Roman* state to the death of *Brutus* and *Cassius*; and indeed he might have continued it, with the same reason, down to the expiration of the *Roman* empire under *Augustulus*; nay, when his hand was in, he might have gone on to his own time.

In a conversation betwixt *Shakespeare* and *Ben Jonson*, Ben ask'd him the reason 'why he wrote those historical Plays.' He reply'd, 'That finding the people generally very ignorant of history, he writ them in order to instruct them in that particular.' A very poor and mean undertaking for a great poet, which not only afforded little or no improvement of the lives and manners of men but could by no means obtain the very end he propos'd, since the representing of a few events found in history could never make them historians, the writing the histories themselves being only capable of that which, when obtain'd, would make the general readers or hearers little the wiser, and not at all better men. Nay, he has in some particulars, if not falsify'd yet at least not justly represented the characters he has made use of as history represents them; particularly in *Richard II* who, as we find him in history, was the most abandon'd tyrant that ever sat upon the *English* throne, guilty of the most barbarous oppressions, most servilely fearful in adversity and most intolerably insolent when the danger was either remov'd or at some distance. And I can see no reason why he made choice of the most despicable character of all our kings, unless it was for the sake of two or three fine descriptions and some agreeable topics or common places, in which some of our modern *Play-wrights* have endeavour'd to imitate him; for having got together two or three descriptions, no matter of what, or whether to any purpose or not, these they tack together with some odd incoherent scenes, which are directed to no certain end and can therefore be of no use.

But, say the fautors of our stage, these pieces give pleasure, which is one considerable end of all poetry. But I must reply that the pleasure they give is but mean, poor, and lifeless, and infinitely short of that transporting delight which a just and regular *Tragedy*, written according to art, excites in the soul at the same time that it conveys lessons of the highest importance to human life. (156–9)

* * *

[Gildon quotes Roscommon's precept:

> *First then, soliloquies had need be few,*
> *Extremely short, and spoke in passion too.*]

The importance of this precept is plain from the offences committed against it by all our poets. *Shakespeare* has frequently *soliloquies* of threescore lines, and those very often—if not always—calm, without any emotion of the passions, or indeed conducive to the business of the play; I mean, where there is any business in the play peculiar to it. That famous *soliloquy* which has been so much cry'd up in *Hamlet* has no more to do there than a description of the grove and altar of *Diana*, mention'd by *Horace*.[1] *Hamlet* comes in talking to himself, and very sedately and exactly weighs the several reasons or considerations mention'd in that *soliloquy*,

> *To be, or not to be*, &c. [3.1.56 ff]

As soon as he has done talking to himself he sees *Ophelia*, and passes to a conversation with her entirely different to the subject he had been meditating on with that earnestness, which as it was produc'd by nothing before, so has it no manner of influence on what follows after and is therefore a perfectly detach'd piece, and has nothing to do in the play. The long and tedious *soliloquy* of the bastard *Falconbridge* in the play of *King John*, just after his being receiv'd as the natural son of *Cœur de Lion* [1.1.182 ff], is not only impertinent to the play but extremely ridiculous. To go through all the *soliloquies* of *Shakespeare* would be to make a volume on this single head. But this I can say in general that there is not one in all his *works* that can be excus'd by nature or reason.

Beaumont and *Fletcher* come under the same condemnation, without his other excellencies, to make amends for this and many other defects of much greater consequence.

[1] Horace, *A.P.*, 14–19: attacking 'purple patches'—such as a description of 'Diana's grove and altar'—which are unrelated to the context.

I am sensible that I shall raise the anger and indignation of many readers by what I have here said, what I have elsewhere observ'd, and what I shall hereafter add about the faults of *Shakespeare*; they will, like the *Romans* against *Horace*, cry out that I have lost all modesty.

Clamant periisse pudorem—[1]

For there were in his time, even in *Rome* itself, as well as in *England*, a sort of senseless bigots to what was lik'd and approv'd in their forefathers days, without examining into the merits of the cause. *Lucilius* was the incorrect idol of those times; *Shakespeare* of ours. Both gain'd their reputation from a people unacquainted with art; and that reputation was a sort of traditionary authority, look'd upon to be so sacred that *Horace* among the *Romans*, in a much more polite age than that in which *Lucilius* writ, could not escape their censure for attacking him; nor can Mr. *Rymer* or any other just *critic* who shall presume, tho' with the highest justice and reason, to find fault with *Shakespeare* escape the indignation of our modern traditionary admirers of that poet. (206-7)

*   *   *

[In dialogue] . . . there must be perpetually kept up that difference between the interlocutors, which their characters demand, to that degree that the hearer may easily distinguish between the persons speaking, tho' their names be not mention'd. In this I think there is no one excells *Shakespeare*, for we may without difficulty know whether it be *Brutus* or *Cassius* whom we hear, tho' the reader take no notice of their names. We every where find a hot impatience and choleric eagerness in all that Cassius says; but the anger of *Brutus*, as it proceeds from the highest sentiments of honour and honesty, so it always discovers a sort of unwillingness to exert itself. *Cassius* is voluntarily angry, *Brutus* always forc'd upon it. Nor is there anything in what either says but what is the natural and close consequence of these two states of anger. (233-4)

---

[1] *Epistles*, 2.1.80: 'cry out that modesty is dead'.

69. Aaron Hill, from his adaptation of *Henry V*

1723

From *King Henry V, Or, The Conquest of France by the English* (1723).

Although planned for production in 1721, this version by Hill (1685-1750) did not appear until 5 December 1723, and was billed as being 'On Shakespeare's Foundation'. In the Preface Hill writes: 'The inimitable and immortal *Shakespeare*, about a hundred and thirty Years since, wrote a Play on this Subject and call'd it, *The Life of King Henry V:* —Mine is a *New Fabrick*, yet I built on *His* Foundation; and the Reader, I am afraid, will too easily discover, without the Help of a Comparison, in what Places I am indebted to him' (Sig. A₃ʳ⁻ᵛ). Hill's major change is the addition of a love-plot-triangle, involving Henry with Katharine, Princess of France (who had fallen in love with the King earlier, under the name of Owen Tudor), and with Harriet (niece to Scroop), whom Henry had seduced but abandoned. To revenge herself Harriet, disguised as a boy, joins her uncle's plots with the French.

PROLOGUE

FROM Wit's old Ruins, shadow'd o'er with Bays,
We draw some rich Remains of *Shakespeare*'s Praise.
Shakespeare!—the Sound bids charm'd Attention wake,
And our aw'd Scenes, with conscious Reverence, *Shake*!
Arduous the Task, to mix with *Shakespeare*'s Muse!
Rash Game! where All who play are sure to lose.
Yet—what our Author *cou'd*, he dar'd to try,
And kept the fiery Pillar in his Eye.
Led by such Light as wou'd not *let* him *stray*,
He pick'd out *Stars* from *Shakespeare*'s milky Way.

Hid, in the Cloud of Battle, *Shakespeare's* Care,
Blind with the Dust of War, o'erlook'd the *Fair*:
Fond of *their* Fame, we shew their Influence here,
And place 'em, *twinkling* through War's smokey Sphere.
Without *their* Aid we lose *Love's* quick'ning Charms;
And sullen Virtue *mopes* in *steril Arms*.
Now rightly mix'd th' enliven'd Passions move:
Love *softens* War,—and War *invigorates* Love.

Oh!—cry'd that tow'ring *Genius* of the *Stage*,
When, first, *His Henry* charm'd a former Age:
  Oh! for a Muse of *Fire*, our Cause to friend,
  That might Invention's brightest Heav'n ascend!
  That, for a *Stage*, a *Kingdom* might be seen!   ⎫
  Princes to *act*, graced with their native Mien: ⎬
  And *Monarchs* to *behold* the swelling Scene!   ⎭
  Then *like Himself* shou'd warlike *Harry* rise:
  And fir'd with all his Fame blaze in your Eyes!
  Crouch'd at his Heels, and like fierce Hounds leash'd in,
  Sword, Fire, and Famine, with impatient Grin!
  Shou'd, fawning dreadful! but for *Orders*, stay:
  And, at *his* Nod,—*start*, horrible! away.

No barren Tale t' *amuse* our Scene imparts:
But points *Example* at your kindling *Hearts*.
Mark, in *their Dauphin* to *our King* oppos'd,
The different Genius of the *Realms* disclos'd:
There, the *French Levity*—vain,—boastful,—loud,
Dancing, in *Death*,—gay, wanton, fierce, and proud.
Here, with a *silent Fire*, a *temper'd* Heat!
Calmly resolv'd, our *English* Bosoms beat.

Art is too poor to raise the *Dead*, 'tis true:
But *Nature* does it by *their* Worth in *You*!
Your Blood that warm'd *their* Veins, still flows the *same*:
Still feeds *your Valour* and supports *their* Fame.

Oh! let it be waste no more in *Civil* Jarr:
But flow, for glorious Fame, in *foreign* War.

★　　★　　★

[Act I, Scene i.] The English Camp, before Harfleur.

*　　*　　*

Grey. I cannot love a Man who loves not me;
Thrice have I miss'd a Suit I stoop'd to kneel for,
And thrice seen Low-born Peasant Clowns supplant me;
Drudges in War! the brawny Works of Nature!
Sturdy-limb'd Ruffians fam'd for Fist and Football;
Broad-shoulder'd Rogues, strong-built to carry Armour,
The humane Sumpter-Mules of haughty *Harry*!
Fellows whose Souls seem'd seated in their Stomachs!
The Curse of Poverty involve my Fortune
If I forget the Scorn till I've reveng'd it.
　Scr. To Night, assembled in my Tent, we'll weigh
The fairest Means to reach the Point in View.
Meanwhile—a Secret This!—You Both remember
The lovely *Harriet*, my dead Brother's Daughter?
　Grey. Alas, poor *Harriet*! she, too, owes much to *Henry*!
The lawless Rover, ere his Father dy'd,
While the griev'd Nation rung with his Debauches,
Sullied your hapless Neice's Virgin Innocence.
　Scr. But, tir'd, like some mean Prostitute He left Her,
On poor Pretence that by his Father's Death
The Kingdom's Cares, reclining on his Breast,
Must banish Softness thence.—So turn'd Her off
Disgraceful, with the Cold Consideration
Of a vile Pension, which had she accepted
Had doubly punish'd Her in base Reward,
A sharp Memento, to remind her daily
That even her Pride was owing to her Shame!
　Cambr. Something like this Report brought scatter'd to Me.
I grieve to find it True—and hop'd it Slander.
Th' unhappy Lady, doubtless, feels much Woe.
　Scr. No Woe, my Lord! the Blood of *Scroop* disdains it;
Her Soul, too strong for Grief, boasts nobler Passions.
Stung with the pointed Sense of Shame and Scorn
She labours with Revenge, and aids my Plottings.
Shading her Charms beneath a Boy's Appearance
She baffles the keen Eye of watchful Policy,
And works out Wonders for the Cause we strive in.

375

Six Days are past since I dispatch'd her hence
To the *French* Camp, whence I expect Her hourly,
With Notices of more than vulgar Import.
My Lord, she comes—Perhaps 'twou'd be too sudden
At once to greet Her with confess'd Detection;
Please you a Moment to retire, and leave me
By gradual Preparation to instruct Her
How safely she may trust you with her Story.
    Cambr. The Caution is well weigh'd.
    Grey. Pursue your Purpose.

                           [*Exeunt* Cambridge, *and* Grey.

Enter Harriet.

    Scr. Welcome, Thou guardian Genius of thy Country!
Born to revenge thy own and All our Wrongs!
Welcome, as Peace to *Scroop*, or War to *Henry*.
    Har. O, Uncle! must this Man for ever flourish?
Harfleur, as I now pass'd, receiv'd him Conqueror.
How long will he escape the Woes he gives!
When will he fall, and the wrong'd World have Justice?
But down, big Heart—to-morrow from the *Dauphin*
Your Hopes, I think, will all find happy End.
    Scr. Saw you this peerless Pride of *France*, this *Katharine*?
Our Camp is fill'd with Rumours of her Beauty.
    Har. Beauty?—by Heaven, there's Meaning in that Question,
And not in vain these *French* Embassadors
Have urg'd the Match with *Katharine*—O! no sooner
They spread the Net than caught the willing Prey!
This Traitor King, This Ruiner of Woman,
Fir'd with her Praise, grows mad to have Her His;
More to undo me He wou'd blast Himself. . . .

                     ★   ★   ★

[Act II, Scene ii.] The French Camp.

SCENE *changes to the Princess's Pavilion.*

Enter The Princess [Katharine], *and* Charlot [*her confidant*].

    Prin. No, no, my *Charlot*! I disdain the Motive.
Love is a Flame too bright, too clear, to burn

As Interests bids it.—What imports it me
That coward *France* can shake at sudden Danger?
What are my Father's Fears to my Affections?
Shall I, because this hotbrain'd King of *England*
Sweeps o'er our Land with War and Devastation,
Shall I for That grow fond of the Destroyer?
Smile at the Waste of his unpunish'd Insolence,
Throw myself Headlong into hostile Arms,
And sell my Peace of Mind to save my Country?
Rather shall Death possess me than this *Harry*.
   Char. O! who can blame you for so just an Anger?
How could your Royal Father think such Ruin,
Such Blasts to nip your Joy?—what! cross the Ocean,
To waste your lovely Youth in a cold Island,
Cloudy, and dull! cut off from all Mankind,
Stormy and various as the People's Temper!
While the wide Continent is fill'd with Kings
Who court your Beauty and wou'd die to please you.
   Prin. Am I, because they call my Father Sovereign,
To be the Slave, the Property, of *France*?
Can nothing buy their Peace but my Undoing?
How nobler were it to quell Rage with Fury!
In Arms to check the bold Invader's Pride,
Meet Storm with Storm and buckle in a Whirlwind?
Then, if the dire Event swept me away,
My Ruin, tho' 'twere dreadful, would be glorious.
But to hold out a Proffer of my Person,
Poorly, and at a Distance! Hang me out
Like a shook Flagg of Truce!—oh! 'tis a Meanness
That shames Ambition and makes Pride look pale!
Where is the boasted Strength of Manhood now?
Sooner than stoop to This, were mine the Scepter,
I wou'd turn *Amazon*.—My Softness hid
In glittering Steel, and my plum'd Helmet nodding
With terrible Adornment, I wou'd meet
This *Henry* with a Flame more fierce than Love:

Enter Dauphin *and* Harriet.

   Dau. How's this, my Sister? Fir'd with Rage and Menace?
What hapless Object has inspir'd this Transport?

377

Prin. The Kingdom, Brother. Is it then a wonder,
That I, with due Disdain, receive the News,
That I am doom'd your Victim?

Dau. You have Reason;
'Tis on that Subject I would gladly speak,
And with your private Ear.

[*Exit* Charlot.

This gentle Youth,
Th' experienc'd Friend of *France*, brings some Discovery
Which, nearly touching your lov'd Interest, moves me
To hear th' important Message in your Presence.

Har. Oh! matchless Pattern of imperial Beauty!
That Heaven, that gave you Charms, protects 'em strongly.
Your Royal Father, the known Friend of Peace,
Still nobly anxious for his Country's Safety,
Sent a late Embassy and offer'd *You*.
You, fam'd for Beauty! You, much more a Princess
By your distinguish'd Charms than by your Birth.

Prin. 'Tis well, young Orator! Flattery, I find,
Is of your Island's Growth; so warm a Vice
Cou'd not, I thought, have brook'd so raw a Climate.

Dau. On with thy Tale;—if Flattery is a Sin
Her Mercy has been taught to give it Pardon.

Har. I need not tell you how our stubborn Monarch,
Safe in blind Distance, and a Stranger yet
To those all-conquering Eyes, refus'd the Offer;
Refus'd a Gem whose countless Value, known,
Will make Refusal its own Punishment:
Yet 'twas refus'd.—But when th' Ambassadors
Were with severe Defiance sent away
Henry a sudden Council call'd together,
In which, forgetful of his boasted Plainness,
That open, honest Heart he would lay Claim to.
He told his Lords, and gain'd their joint Concurrence,
That when advanc'd still farther into *France*,
When Fire and Sword shou'd spread his Fame before Him,
Means wou'd be found to close with courted Peace
And wed the Princess with improv'd Conditions.
'Tis true, he cry'd, I hate Her for her Race

But what has Love to do in Prince's Weddings?
The Match will serve to lull their Arms asleep;
And when that fair Occasion smiles upon me
I'll seize th' unguarded Kingdom—
   Dau. Why, 'tis well!
Forewarn'd by this Intelligence we'll match Him
With Treasons which become a Man's Designing.
He weaves the Web too coarse; not every Will
Is fram'd for Mischief—Policy requires
Spirit, and Thought! mere Blood and Bone can't reach it.
   Prin. You, Brother, may content yourself with That
But I not brook so well the Shame design'd me.
I am on Both Sides, then, the Toy of State!
One King's Condition and the other's Engine!
The Tool which *Harry*'s Treason is to work with!
Whence shall I borrow Rage to speak my Anger?
O! aid me, all ye Stings of Indignation!
Lend me thy Gall thou bitter-hearted Jealousy!
And every Fury that can *lash* assist me!
What will my Peacefull Father say to this?
Yes! He has chosen nobly for his Daughter!
Charles has a generous Son-in-Law in *Harry*.
O *France*! what lazy Frost has chill'd your Blood?
Where is that Pride of Arms, that boasted Courage,
Which your vain Tongues are swell'd with?—Where's the Soul
That in the warlike *Gauls*—your glorious Ancestors!—
Shook the proud World, and sham'd the *Roman Cæsars*?
If there remains the Shadow of past Glory,
If any Spark yet glimmers in your Breasts
Of your once furious Fire, Go, down upon Him!
Scatter his Army like the Wind-driven Sands,
Seize him alive and bring him me a Prisoner!
   Dauph. Prithee, no more of this vain Woman's Raving.
What we can do, we will.—But, for the Marriage:
Spite of this new-given Argument I fear
My Father's Love of Peace will force it forward.
   Prin. Sooner shall the two Kingdoms join their Cliffs
And, rushing with a sudden Bound together,
Dash the dividing Sea, to wash the Clouds!
   Har. What I have said Your Highnesses will hold

As a fair Proof, however else unwelcome,
That you have watchful Agents.—Well they know
The faithless *Henry's* Love of Change and Roving;
And when they thought with Pity on the Crowds,
The countless Crowds of Beautys He has ruin'd,
Then scorn'd, and left for new ones, they grew sad,
And, sighing, told each other 'twere a Shame
The lovely Princess shou'd be match'd so ill!

Enter Duke of Bourbon.

   Bour. Prince *Dauphin*! our Designs miscarry widely.
Your needful Presence only can support us.
The King, hem'd in with cringing Parasites,
Debates what Answer shou'd be sent to *Henry*:
And seems determin'd to propose an Interview
With *England's* King, a shameful Interview,
To urge this Match!
   Har. O, Madam, strive to cross it,
Or you are lost for ever!—*Henry's* Eye,
Shou'd he once see You, will reform his Will,
And he'll forego the Crown to conquer You.
   Dauph. Tarry, till I return with swift Instruction
What Answer you shall bear our *English* Friends.
                       [*Exeunt* Dauphin *and* Bourbon.
   Prin. —What! and no more than so? gone thus, and left me
Distracted, unassur'd, and torn with Terrors?
O! perish all the wily Aims of Policy!
These Statesmen's Craft confounds the tortur'd World,
And Truth and Innocence are hunted by them.
O! hard Condition ours! twin-born with Greatness!
What infinite Heart's Ease does high Birth lose, '
That the low World enjoys!—and what boast we,
Save Ceremony, which low Life has not too?
And what art Thou, thou Idol Ceremony?
What else but Place? Degree? and empty Form?
What drink'st thou of, instead of Homage sweet,
But poison'd Flattery?—O! be sick, vain Greatness,
And bid thy Ceremony give thee Cure!
Canst thou, when thou command'st the Beggar's Knee,
Command the Health of it?—No, thou proud Dream!

Laid in thy high-rais'd and majestick Bed,
Thou sleep'st less soundly than the wretched Slave
Who with full Body and a vacant Mind
Gets him to Rest, cram'd with distressful Bread,
Never sees horrid Night, that Child of Hell!
But sweats in the Sun's Eye from Rise to Set
And follows so the ever-rolling Year,
With profitable Labour to his Grave!
And, but for Ceremony, such a Wretch,
Winding up Days with Toil and Nights with Sleep,
Has greatly the Advantage of a King!
But I neglect the Stranger—Gentle Youth!
Forgive me, that my Sorrows, breaking o'er me,
Half drown'd Remembrance of the Thanks I owe You.
Why look you sad?—does any Grief oppress you?
   Har. Alas! great Princess! Grief and I have long,
Too long! been join'd.—Perhaps twou'd tire your Ear
To amuse you with a Tale of private Woe;
Else I cou'd melt your Pity into Tears
And force some Sighs to honour my Distresses.
I have a Sister—Ah! no—I *had* a sister!
Whom flattering Lovers call'd her Sex's Wonder!
Deceitfull *Henry* saw, and, seeing, lov'd Her.
He knelt—he swore—he pray'd—he sigh'd—he threatned—
Like Heaven, he promis'd Joys beyond expressing.
My Sister, long resisting, felt at last
The rising Passion swell her struggling Soul;
The kindled Fire grew stronger by Resistance,
And warm'd her slow Desire to yielding Ruin.
There broke the Charm—the fancied Treasure vanish'd,
And bitter Penitence and conscious Guilt
Became the gnawing Vultures of her Bosom.
The treacherous Prince no longer vow'd a Passion
But basely shun'd the Wretchedness he caus'd.
   Prin. See if the tender Creature does not weep!
Alas! thy mournful Story fills my Heart
With Grief almost as powerfull as thy own.
Trust me, 'twas base in *Henry* thus to leave Her.
   Har. O, Princess! He's a general, known Deceiver!
Far may your Fate divide you from his Wiles!

*   381

I cou'd swell Time and wear away the Sun
In dismal Stories of his perjur'd Loves.

Re-enter the Dauphin.

 Dau. Curses unnumber'd blast the cank'ry Breath
Of yon vile Sycophants!—I came too late;
The mean Resolve was past;—My Arts prevail'd not:
The two Kings meet, and all my Hopes are Air.
 Har. Something must be resolv'd that may prevent
This dangerous Treaty, or you're lost for ever.
 Dau. Fear not, I'll manage All to our Advantage.
But let us waste no Moments;—here within
I will instruct you further in my Purpose. [*Exeunt* Princess *and* Harriet.
 Now Fortune aid me, and inspire my Soul
With Force these peaceful Counsels to controul;
Meekness, tho' wise, sits tottering on a Throne,
And suffering Kingdoms King's false Steps attone;
In me let *France* her ancient Fire resume,
Or crush me nobly in my Country's Doom.   [*Exit.*

ACT III. SCENE I.

SCENE, *A* French *Pavilion.*

Enter Princess, *and* Charlot.

 Prin. O, *Charlot*! how will this new Tryal shake me!
What shall I do to arm my threaten'd Mind
Against th' Assaults of Madness? Tyrant Duty!
Why are thy Laws so binding? If Obedience
Must thus be blind, then sure Command shou'd see
With Eagle-Ey'd Discernment! Unkingly Father!
As if, to offer me, were Shame too gentle.
Curse on the blushful Thought!—I'll go to meet him!
Meanly obtrude my self upon his Scorn,
And hear the Bargain of my Price debated!
Is this to be a Princess? Perish Pride!
Oh let my base Example teach the Humble
How happy 'tis to stand below Ambition.
 Char. Were my poor Counsell worthy Your Attention
There's yet a Way, perhaps, to move the King:
His Tenderness is Equal to his Fear,

And may be mov'd to counterpoize Your Danger.
Disclose, with speaking Tears, the fatal Secret;
Tell him how All Your Heart, already fill'd,
Has Room for no new Comer.
 Prin. Art thou mad?
That were a dreadful Means to wound me deeper.
The Pride of State wou'd then new-fire his Anger;
And I, by Force driv'n on to wed this Monster,
This fighting Dæmon in the Dress of Royalty,
Shou'd lose all Hope once more to see the Stranger,
The lovely unknown Conqueror whose Addresses,
Whose—not to be describ'd—unnam'd Perfections,
Twelve long Months since first charm'd my list'ning Soul,
Spite of unequal Birth, to wish him mine,
And even tho' hated *England* gave him Being.
 Char. There I have something new to warm Your Hope with.
Led by kind Chance among the shining Train
Of *English* Youth who came with *Exeter*,
Occasion gave me Scope to form some Questions,
Which past as an unmeaning Love of Novelty.
I ask'd what Cavalier some twelve Months since,
Glitt'ring with Gems, outshone by his Behaviour,
Came with the Earl of *Westmorland* to *France*;
Was call'd his Nephew, thrice appear'd at Court,
Then vanish'd on Pretence of further Travel.
By this Description All at once, agreed
That *Owen Tudor* was the Person meant,
And lavish'd Hours of Rhetoric in his Praises.
 Prin. Alas! did I not know all This before?
England boasts no such Charmer but her *Tudor*!
This is not what I hop'd from thy Beginning.
 Char. I further learnt that *Tudor*'s Birth is such
As may entitle Him to Royal Love.
That fear'd Objection is of Force no longer,
When Your great Father shall perceive Your Flame
Burning, undimm'd, for an Imperial Off-spring,
Deriv'd from a long Line of *Britain*'s Kings.
 Prin. Ay! this indeed strikes Lustre thro' my Sorrows!
There's Promise in this Hope.—O gentle *Charlot*!
Secret as Death conceal the dear Intelligence,

As a last Prop to my endanger'd Passion.
Now will I boldly meet this Champion Lover,
This courtly Sir—who woo's in War and Thunder!

Enter Dauphin.

So, Brother, will the King consent to spare me?
Or must I stoop to see this shamefull Interview?
   Dau. You must excite Your Spirits to Your Aid,
And bid a bold Defyance to Your Blushes.
I've try'd all Arts in vain that Reason teaches.
Come!—I must guide You to the Lists of Love,
And You must teach Your Charms new Ways of Wounding.
The King will have Your Beauty take the Field
And does not fear, he says, but You can conquer!—
Him whom our Armies fly from You must face.
   Prin. Yes—I will go; but not as He expects me:
I'll face this Foe of *France* like *France*'s Daughter!
The Woes of Ruin overtake those Reptiles
Whose dronish Souls, bent under Age or Fear,
Have thus misled their Master!—Yes, my Eyes
Shall dart keen Glances—but the Wounds they give
Shall be of Shame, not Love—
                               [A Trumpet sounds.

   Dau. Hark! That shrill Trumpet's Notice summons Us!
Now, Sister! rouze your Gall and loose those Storms,
Those restless Tempests which, provok'd by Scorn,
Whirl with impatient Rage round Woman's Soul:
Fearless, defend the Freedom of Your Choice,
And with bold Innocence assert Your Hate;
I'll watch the rising Moments of Occasion,
And aid Your glorious Purpose all I can.
   Come—Let us dare the Brink of this rude Precipice
Which, cutting off our Way, must stop our Journey
Or, being bravely leapt, make Safety honourable.   *[Exeunt.*

[Act III, Scene ii.]

SCENE *changes to a Barrier, on a Bridge,*
Trumpets from Both Sides:

Enter, on one Part, the French *King, on the Bridge, attended by the Dukes of*
Orleans, *and* Bourbon, &c. *below:—On the other Side of the Bridge,*
King Henry, *with the Dukes of* Exeter, *and* York, Scroop, Cam-
bridge, *and* Grey, *below. The Kings Embrace over the Bar.*

Fr. King. The Peace we wish for smile upon this Meeting!
Health, and the Joys of a long happy Life
To our lov'd Brother *England*!—Right glad we are
Thus to behold Your Face. Bless'd be the Issue
Of this good Day! that these contending Kingdoms,
England, and neighb'ring *France* whose Chalky Shores
Look pale with Envy at Each other's Happiness,
May henceforth cease their Hate and plant Accord!
'Till War no more advance her bleeding Sword
To prey on Strife between them!
   K. Henry. To This, Amen!
   Fr. King. Since we thus meet You let it not disgrace me
If I demand th' Impediment why Peace,
Dear Nurse of Arts! shou'd not in this best Garden
Of the fair World lift up her lovely Visage?
Too plain, alas! the Marks of her short Absence!
Our Vine, the merry Chearer of the Heart,
Withers unprun'd;—Our Hedges, shooting wild,
Like careless Pris'ners overgrown with Hair,
Thrust forth disorder'd Twigs; Darnel and Hemlock
Root on our fallow Lays and, springing thick
Beneath their Shade, hide the neglected Culter.
   K. Hen. Not for Delight in Blood have we thus far
Advanc'd our Standard in the Eye of *France*;
Our deep-laid Purpose boasts a nobler Meaning.
The Eye of Kings shou'd watch their People's Safety;
And Ill shou'd I discharge the Trust Heaven leads me
If, sleeping o'er the Wrongs You do my Country,
I not demanded back the Power You hold,
And turn with threatning Point against our Bosom.
   Fr. King. Of this already we have let You know

385

Our Thoughts and Purpose. It remains to weigh
If, by wide-differing Means, we may not reach
The End we jointly aim at. Many Arrows
Come to one Mark; far distant Rivers flow
Ten thousand Ways yet meet in one main Sea!
How many Lines close in the Dial's Center!
So may our various Purposes at last
Meet in one fix'd Resolve and please us Both.

Enter the Dauphin *on the Bridge, leading the Princess in a Veil, attended by*
Charlot.

Our Son the *Dauphin* has, we hear, of late—
Fir'd with the first warm Flash of Provocation—
Return'd Defiance with too fierce a Throw.
Young Blood will boil; and You, so fam'd for Courage,
Will weigh That Error light. Receive Him, Brother,
As one who wishes Peace and seeks Your Love.

                              [*Presenting the* Dauphin.
   Dau. Sir! Kings and Fathers claim a double Right [*To King* Henry.
To tax our Duty, and *will* be obey'd.
I wou'd have met you with a warmer Grasp
Had *France* been held by me; but since His Will
Who governs mine holds back the Edge of War
And wou'd reach Peace by Roads less sharp and rugged,
I greet your Royal Presence, and submit
To Measures which I cannot yet approve.
   K. Hen. Approve is mine: I'm yet your Debtor, Sir,
But purpose to repay the Favour soon.
The Time is near when you perchance may feel
That wise Defiance should be arm'd with Safety,
And Fierceness, wanting Strength, but gnaws herself.
   Dau. When That wish'd Time—
   Fr. King. Our Son, reply no more;
Daughter! Your Hand.
   Prin. Your Pardon, Royal Sir, if I offend,
Or seem to wrong the Promise of my Duty!
I came in forc'd Obedience to Your Will
To attend this Interview. But if your Majesty
Permits me to declare my secret Thoughts
Of *England's* King, our publick Enemy,

Then let that Duty which I owe my Country
Inspire me to confess what fix'd Aversion,
What rooted Hatred, Nature bids me bear
To Him, of all Mankind the most abhorr'd;
Who brings Destruction on to mark his Way,
And woo's the Daughter with the Father's Ruin.

    Dau. Bravely declar'd, thou Sister of my Soul!   [*Aside.*

    K. Hen. Sorry we ought to be that War's Offences
Have made the Fair our Foe. You are an Enemy
Whom we, spite of Your being such, can fear!

    Prin. Oh my high beating Heart! 'tis *Tudor*'s Voice!   [*Aside.*

    K. Hen. In vain you shade Your Charms. That lovely Face,
Hid as it is, remains no Stranger to us;
We wear Your Image, Lady, on our Heart.

    Prin. 'Tis He!—'Tis *Tudor*!—O! amazing Chance!   [*Aside.*
Where slept my Soul, that at our first Approach
It flew not forth to meet him?—Support me, *Charlot*,   [*To* Charlot.
A sudden Mist dances before my Eyes.
O, *Charlot*! This is He! Whom we thought *Tudor*
Was Royal *Henry*! What a Chance is This!
Let me lean on Thee to devour his Accents,
And gaze him thro' at every word He speaks.

    K. Hen. Drawn by the soft Remembrance of Your Charms
Which, in my late-lost Father's Days, I saw
When at Your Court I was a Guest unknown;
In Honour, Madam, of your hostile Beauty,
I stopt th' impetuous Progress of my Arms!
Rein'd in the Vigour of impatient War,
And wasted Fortune's Smiles to gain this Meeting.
If I now listen to the Voice of Peace
Whence must it come, but from the Call of Love?
When You, fair Foe, shall try your wondrous Power,
I cannot promise Fame t'oppose Your Will.
The healing Sweetness of your soft Command,
Spread o'er your rescued Land, might quiet War;
Might, like sweet Musick's Influence, still Your Air;
Might bid loud Discord die away before it,
And drown th' inspiring Trumpet's shrill Alarms.

    Prin. Foe as you are to *France* there shines, methinks,
A kind of manly Merit in Your Meaning.

Something—I know not what—that Courage charms with
Wakes my Discernment to admire Your Worth,
And, spite of my Resentment, bids me greet You,
Bow to Your Virtues and confess Your Glory.
Cou'd my Desires incline Your Wills to Peace
The unbrac'd Drum shou'd sleep, and the glad Trumpet
Fall its fierce Hoarsness and inspire Delight;
All shou'd be calm, and while th' unruffled Kingdoms
Hush down the troubled Swell of dying Strife
France shou'd no more in her torn Bowels feel
The strong Convulsions which she shakes with now.

 Fr. King. Why, that's well said.—So speaks the Sex's Softness;
Your gentle Natures were not fram'd for Discord.

* * *

[Act IV, Scene i.] The English Pavilion.

* * *

 K. Hen. Uncle of *Exeter*!

Enter Exeter.

 Exe. What wills my Liege?
 K. Hen. Call me a chosen Guard.

[Exit Exeter.

 Charl. One thing I had forgot;
The Princess, fearful for her Person's Safety,
Claims Leave to pass your interposing Camp
And enter yon near Castle, *Agincourt*;
This was my only known and publick Errand.

 K. Hen. She shall have Royal and illustrious Welcome;
The Safety she bestows she must command.
We judge the Occasion happy, and we hope
The noble-minded Princess, passing near,
Will honour us with Licence to declare
What Thanks our Heart must owe Her, for our Words
Wou'd sully our Conceptions and deceive Her!

Re-enter Exeter, *with a Guard.*

Go with this Lady and observe Her Orders,
And whom she points you out seize and secure.

[Exeunt omnes, but the King.

388

My Soul with keen Impatience waits the Issue
Of this strange Notice—Treason?—'tis impossible!
Whom has my short Reign wrong'd?—what want a People,
Whom Wealth and Plenty smile upon at Home,
And whom abroad the Fame of Arms makes dreadful?
What wou'd Complaint have more?—Ill-judging Vulgar!
Were it not glorious to make Millions happy
Who that had Sense of Bliss wou'd be a King?
Th' unbusied Shepherd, stretch'd beneath the Hawthorn,
His careless Limbs thrown out in wanton Ease,
With thoughtless Gaze perusing the arch'd Heavens
And idly whistling while His Sheep feed round him
Enjoys a sweeter Shade than That of Canopies,
Hem'd in with Cares and shook by Storms of Treason!

Re-enter Exeter.

Now Uncle! what Discovery?
    Exe. Near Your Pavilion stood some *French* of Figure,
And with them a fair *English* Youth whom oft
I have observ'd, and wonder'd at his Beauty.
The Lady mark'd him out then took her Leave,
And as she left we seiz'd him—
    K. Hen. Let him come in alone.

        Exeter *goes out, and enter* Harriet *in Confusion.*

A very Boy!—Treason in Thee budds early!
Who art Thou? say to whom thou dost belong!
Silent?—Nay, then, there's Guilt! why art thou dumb?
Come farther this way—if thou shun'st the Light
Thy Deeds have Darkness in them.—Immortal Heaven!
What is it that I see?—Can'st Thou be *Harriet?*
    Har. Can'st Thou be *Henry*, and alive to ask it?
O! 'tis with Justice Fate thus overtakes me
For having meanly linger'd in my Vengeance!
High Heaven will reach Thee, Tyrant, tho' I cannot,
Since thy still-fortunate Deceits protect Thee,
Since perjur'd Love does not alone upbraid Thee
But thy Eternal Wiles win all alike,
And even thy Foes grow treacherous and assist Thee.
    K. Hen. But is it possible that Thou conspir'st,
That Thou can'st wish me dead?

Har. Insulting Tyrant!
Cool, frosty-hearted Monster!—Wish Thee dead?
Why, 'tis the only glorious Hope I live for!
Think on the Miseries Thou hast wrung my Soul with;
The biting Shame, the never-dying Anguish!
Think on the guilty Arts, the Oaths, the Subtleties,
The endless, inexpressible Deceits,
The Wiles and Perjuries which have undone me!
Think on the feign'd Endearments, studied Graces,
False Smiles, enticing Raptures, labour'd Flatteries,
And all that nameless Train of silent Treacheries
Which help'd thy tempting Tongue to make me wretched!
Look back on all this dreadfull Pile of Baseness
And then—Oh! Heaven!—if then Thou dar'st look farther,
If frighted Memory does not fly thy Soul,
Think, in the bitter Agonies of Conscience,
What follow'd all this Train of Preparation!
See me abandon'd to the Lash of Shame,
Turn'd out an Object for sharp-ey'd Derision,
By Friends forsaken and disown'd by Kindred,
Wild and distracted with unconquer'd Sorrow!
Expos'd to be the Mirth of wiser Hypocrites
And stand the Scorn-Mark of the hooting World.
Death!—Thou Destroyer, think of This, and then,
In the cool Insolence of Pride and Majesty
Ask me again if I can wish Thee dead?
   K. Hen. 'Tis true, fair Murderer, I have greatly wrong'd Thee!
And yet not I, but what I once was, wrong'd Thee.
'Tis a sad Theme, and Reason trembles at it:
Yet what *can* be—all that weak Words can give Thee,
And Grief, and Penitence, and Shame, and Love,
All this sit down and hear to calm thy Soul.

           [Takes her Hand,

   Har. Perish that treacherous Smoothness—
Unhand me, that my curdled Blood, all chill'd
As at a Serpent's Sting when thou com'st near me,
May flow in Freedom, and give Power to curse Thee.

           [Breaks from Him.

   K. Hen. Have You not Prudence? Are you mad?—Come hither!
I must by gentle Force compell thy Passion,

Since Reason cannot guide tempestuous Sorrow.
Calm thy loud Ravings.—If thy Shame offends thee.
Why wou'dst thou thus proclaim it? Be wiser, *Harriet*!
The quick-ear'd Camp will spread the Telltale Sorrow.
Nay 'tis in vain to struggle; sit and hear me.
                    [*He forces her into a Chair, and sits down by her.*
Sit and be patient, while Repentance pleads,
And Love's soft Sympathy condoles thy Woe.
As yet this Dress and its too bloody Purpose
Conceal Thee, and thou may'st be still conceal'd.
    Har. What wilt thou do? Why dost thou thus compell me,
Helpless, to listen to the Voice of Ruin?
                              [*Snatches at his Sword.*
Give me thy Sword—thy Words have lost all Power
To give me Comfort.—Is that too deny'd me?
Then I must hear Thee, hear thy base Upbraidings,
Friendless and destitute of all Assistance,
Must sit and tremble at my lost Condition.
Yet Thou art guiltier far than I can be!
O! Thou wert born to pull down Misery on me,
And Every Way to ruin and destroy me.
                                   [*Weeping.*

    K. Hen. If in this dreadfull Conflict of thy Soul
Distracted Judgment holds her ruffled Empire
Listen, and mark what my sad Heart shall utter.
Fatal our Course of Passion! Its Effect
Proves bitter, but the Cause was tend'rest Love!
Youth is unbridled, blind, and void of Fear,
Ever determin'd, deaf to Consequence,
And rolling forward upon Pleasure's Byas.
All Youth is thus—but mine was worse than All!
Wild and disorderly beyond Example!
Why did not thy discerning Reason tell thee,
A Wretch like me deserv'd no Pity from thee?
How cou'd a Madman's Hurry weigh thy Worth?
But Thou wilt say, my Oaths and Vows deceiv'd thee!
Ascribe that Guilt to thy own Power of Charming.
When the Blood boils, and Beauty fires the Soul,
What will the Tongue not swear? Discretion then
Does with a Peacock's Feather fan the Sun;

Yet in the midst of all those wild Desires
Which then divided my impatient Mind
Thou wert the warmest Wish my Soul persued!
My Love to Thee was permanent and strong;
Thy Beauties were my waking Theme, and Night
Grew charming by soft Dreams of thy Perfection.
Were I now what I was when *Harriet* bless'd me
Still were I Hers—My Love can never die!
And I think on thee, *Harriet*, with such Tenderness
As dying Fathers bless their weeping Sons with.
And were I not a King Thou still wert happy.

    Har. Can'st Thou then mourn the Sorrows thou hast caus'd me?
Am I still lov'd?—I thought thou hadst despis'd me.

    K. Hen. Still I regard Thee with the same Desires;
Gaze with the same transporting Pleasure on Thee
As when our bounding Souls first flew together
And mingled Raptures in consenting Softness.
But Kings must have no Wishes for Themselves!
We are our People's Properties! Our Cares
Must rise above our Passions! The public Eye
Shou'd mark no Fault on Monarchs, 'Tis contagious!
Else I to Death had borne the dear Delight
And, bless'd in mutual Transport, still liv'd Thine!
Call it not Guilt then, 'twas a dire Necessity!
And what remains is tenderest Penitence
And wish'd Atonement.—For the first, my Soul
In never ceasing Anguish mourns thy Misery.
Were the last possible my Love wou'd reach it;
But where the Ill's incurable, how vain
To rack the Sufferer with our useless Cordials!
What I cou'd do was done, but thy Disdain
Made frustrate all my Watchings o'er thy Fortune.
And now—

    Har. Enough! O Yet too lovely *Henry*!
My aking Heart, oppress'd twixt Joy and Pain,
Can bear no longer the fierce Pangs it feels.
Take now—but bless me yet once more, say, *Henry*
Once Mine, Dost thou with Pity think on *Harriet*?

    K. Hen. Pity's too mean a Word to reach my Woe.
The Grief it gives me to behold thee thus

Can but be *felt*! 'Tis not in Language, *Harriet*,
To cloath its mighty Bulk with due Description.

 Har. Take then these Letters, and be happy still.

             [Gives him Letters.

They will bring Safety to thee. Canst thou pardon me?
I shou'd Have been consenting to thy Murder!

 K. Hen. My sad Heart pardons thee and hopes it from thee.

 Har. Perhaps when I go hence we part for ever!
Pardon me, therefore, if I gaze upon thee,
My Eyes may never more behold thy Face!
The chilling Call of Death has warn'd me from thee,
And I shall be at Peace ere long and Happy.

 K. Hen. O! let me kiss away that mournful Sound.

 Har. Forbear.—My Soul, too sad to soften more,
Shrinks from the fatal Folly, much oblig'd
By this Forgiveness which has bless'd my Ruin.
By that kind Pity which you heal my Woes with
I have but one way left to thank Your Goodness.
I have one new Discovery yet to make You,

             [Feeling in her Pocket.

Containing the last Secret of my Soul.
I did not think so soon to have disclos'd it:
But since without it you can ne'er be happy
I send it, thus—directed to my Heart.

       [Draws a Dagger, and stabs herself.

 K. Hen. Rash Girl! What hast thou done?—Uncle of *Exeter*!
Help me! Who waits without? oh! help! support her!

Enter Exeter *and* York.

Harriet! the injur'd *Harriet*, dies!—O, Uncle!
Her catching Grasp by Fits strives hard to hold me!
Her straining Eyes half burst their watry Balls!
Vainly they glare to snatch a parting Look!
And Love, convulsive, shakes her struggling Bosom.
Care comes too late;—Her quivering Lips grow pale;
And frighted Beauty, loth to leave its Mansion,
Ebbs slow with the unwilling Blood away.
O! see the fatal Fruits of guilty Love!

 Exe. The sudden Wonder so confounds my Thoughts
I know not what Advice to give your Grief.

Poor *Harriet*! was it Thee I seiz'd for Treason?

 York. Who waits there?—Gently take away this Body,
Place it within till you have further Orders;
The mournful Object will but feed his Sorrow.

[They carry off the Body.
[K. Henry opens and reads the Letters.

 K. Hen. O Uncles! Here is Treason will surprize You!
Letters to some most near us from the *Dauphin*,
Concerning a large Sum of Gold, in Bribe
For our intended Murder, when the *French*
Shou'd first join Battle with us.

 Exe. Heaven forbid!

★   ★   ★

[Act V, Scene iv.] A large Champain, with the Castle of *Agincourt* at a Distance. On the one side the *English* Camp; on the other, the *French*.

★   ★   ★

Enter Orleans, *and* Bourbon.

 Orl. Well, Cousin *Bourbon*, is the Foe embattled?

 Bourb. When will the long'd-for Trumpet sound to Horse?
Do but behold yon poor and half-starv'd Band,
Our Show-dress'd War will suck away their Souls
And leave them but the Shells, the Husks, of Men!
There is not Work to busy half our Hands,
Scarce Blood enough in all their sickly Veins,
To give Each Sword a Stain. We need but blow on 'em,
The Vapour of our Valour will o'erturn 'em.

 Orl. 'Tis positive beyond Exception, Cousin,
That our superfluous Crowds who swarm unusefull
About our Squares of Battle were enough
To clear the Field of such a weakned Foe.

Enter the Dauphin.

 Dau. Sound out the Note to mount. Ha, ha, ha—Cousins!

[Sound to Horse.

Yon Island Carrions, desperate of their Bones,
Ill favour'dly become the Morning Field.
Their ragged Curtains poorly are let loose
And our Air shakes them, passing scornfully.

394

Big *Mars* seems Bankrupt in their beggar'd Host,
And faintly thro' a rusty Beaver peeps.
Their Horsemen sit unmov'd, and the poor Jades
Lob down their Heads, drooping the Hide and Hipps,
And in their pale dull Mouths the moldy Bitt
Lies foul with chew'd Grass, still and motionless;
And their Executors, the knavish Crows,
Fly o'er them all impatient for their Hour.
   Bour. They've said their Prayers, poor Rogues, and stay for Death.
   Orle. In mere Compassion we shou'd send them Dinners;
These *English* hate to die with empty Stomachs.
   Dau. See! my Guard waits me yonder!—On, to the Field!
Come, the Sun's high, and we outwear the Day.

                                            [Exeunt.

[Act V, Scene v.]

Sound of a Charge, with Drums, Trumpets, &c.

The Genius of England *rises, and sings.*

SONG.

   Earth of *Albion!* open wide:
   And give thy rising Genius way!
Swell with the Trumpet and triumph with Pride
   At the glorious Renown of this Day!
   Look! behold! the marching Lines!
   See! the dreadful Battle joins!
Hark! like two Seas the shouting Armies meet!
   Ecchoing Hills the Shock repeat!
And the Vale rings beneath their rushing Feet.

Now, hoarse and sullen, beats the dead, deep, Drum,
And mourns in sad, slow, sound the Overcome!
Now, thickning loud, insults the Ranks that yield,
And rolls a rumbling Thunder round the Field!
Now the Trumpet's shrill Clangor enlivens Despair,
And in Circles of Joy floats alarming in Air!
Till the Wind, become musical, charms as it blows,
   And enflames and awakens the Foes!
   Hark! Hark!—'tis done!
   The Day is won!

They bend! they break! the fainting *Gauls* give way!
And yield reluctant to their Victor's Sway!
   Happy *Albion*!—strong to gain!
Let Union teach Thee not to win in vain!

Enter in Confusion, Dauphin, Orleans, *and* Bourbon.

Dau. Death to my Hopes! All is confounded, All!

    ★   ★   ★

[Act V, Scene vii.]

    ★   ★   ★

Enter the Dauphin, *the Princess* Katharine, *and* Orleans.

   Dau. Once more, victorious and high-fated *Henry*,
We meet. Our Sister, anxious after Peace,
And our dread Sovereign and Imperial Father,
Committing to our Care the Publick Safety,
We come, with mighty tho' unwilling Wonder
To own the Hand of Heaven in Your Success.
Ten thousand *French* lye breathless on Yon Field,
Of whom but sixteen hundred Common Men!
On Your Side, if the strange Report not errs,
Besides the Duke of *York* and Earl of *Suffolk*,
None else of Name—and of all other Men
But five and twenty.—Heaven! thy Arm was here!
When, in plain Shock and even Play of Battle,
Was ever known so great, so little Loss?
But we've not lost to You—the Shame of Losing
Is overpaid by such a Victor's Glory.
Stand in my Place; Be Regent over *France*
Ev'n while my Father lives, and when his Days
Reach their nigh Period, Reign, and join the Kingdoms!
Take my lov'd Sister and be happy Ever!
For me, prophetic Hope foreshows me Comfort!
I shall not long survive my squander'd Fame.
Sister! farewell;— the Rest we leave to You.

                          [*Exit* Dauphin.
   K. Hen. The Prince, high-minded, swells with generous Sorrow,
And 'twere to injure him to urge him back.

Now, since I call these matchless Beauties mine,
Peace shall break out, and with enliv'ning Lustre
Chase moist Affliction from the Widow's Eye.
All shou'd be bless'd and gay when You thus smile;
Nature shou'd dance with Joy when Love and Peace
Thus twin'd together shade the shelter'd World.
   Prin. O! Noble *Henry*! spite of that Esteem
Thy glitt'ring Virtues strike my wond'ring Soul with,
Some Sighs must be allow'd to sad Reflection,
How dear our promis'd Joys have cost my Country.
   K. Hen. The tender Woe becomes thy gentle Nature;
Compassion is the humblest Claim of Misery,
And They who feel not Pity taste not Love.
Uncle of *Exeter*! send out to stop
Persuit, and stay the Hand of Desolation:
We must not waste a Country we have won.
Command that in their undissolv'd Array
Our Foot kneel humbly and our Horsemen bow,
And, ere they take their Rest, pay Heaven its Due.

   Thus have our Arms triumphant purchas'd Fame,
And warlike *England* boasts a dreadful Name;
O! that the bright Example might inspire!
And teach my Country not to waste her Fire!
But, shunning Faction and Domestic Hate,
Bend All her Vigour to advance her State.

70. The Duke of Wharton, in praise of Hill's *Henry V*

December 1723

From the *True Briton*, 56 (13 December 1723).

Philip, Duke of Wharton (1698–1731), was brought up by his father, learning by heart 'some of the principal Parts of the best *English* Tragedies . . . particularly those of the inimitable *Shakespeare*', in order 'to form him a complete Orator' ('Lewis Melville' [pseud. of Lewis S. Benjamin], *The Life and Writings of Philip Duke of Wharton* (1913), p. 17). He became a Whig peer in 1718, achieved notoriety as president of the 'Hell-Fire Club', and issued this opposition journal bi-weekly in 1723 and the following year.

To the *Author of the* TRUE BRITON.

SIR,

I THINK I may justly enough apply to the *Stage* in general what Mr. *Bays* in the *Rehearsal* is made to say of his *Play*: The Theatre is a Kind of Political *Touchstone*; for nothing sooner discovers a *sound* or *sickly* State than the *Taste* of its People at the Theatrical Assemblies, where no previous Arts of Preparation have been us'd, but the Audiences are left free to their own natural Impressions.

I HAVE been led into this Remark by the cold and unkind Reception which the new Tragedy of *Henry V* has met with in its Acting; and which appears, now the Play is publish'd, so shamefully disproportion'd to what ought to have been expected that one wou'd imagine nothing less than a general Depravity both of Morals and Reason cou'd have render'd it possible. The very *Subject* of this Play gave it no weak Pretence to the Favour of all *brave Englishmen*; but the *Moral* it was written for was so Generous and Seasonable that it ought to have made its Interest the Care of *Both Parties*.

> *Thus have our Arms triumphant purchas'd Fame,*
> *And Warlike* England *boasts a dreadful Name!*

Oh! that the bright Example might inspire,
And teach my Country not to waste her Fire!
But, shunning Faction and domestick Hate,
Bend all her Vigour to advance her State.

THE great and amiable Figure which King *Henry* makes throughout this Tragedy as a *Monarch*, a *Statesman*, a *Soldier*, and a *Lover*, ought no doubt to have endear'd Him in a very particular manner, to a *British* Audience; and the following Reflection of that Merciful and Noble Prince on the first Intelligence of a *Plot* against his *Life* deserves both Admiration and Applause. [Quotes from 'Treason!' to 'Storms of Treason!', above, p. 389.]

BUT when the Chief Agent of this Treason is deliver'd into his Hands and proves to be his late favourite *Mistress*, disguis'd like a *Boy*, the more securely to compass the Death of her Sovereign, what Prince but so Magnanimous and Heroick a one as *Henry* wou'd have drawn an Occasion from so bloody a Purpose to *punish* her with *Pardon*, to melt her Soul with his *Tenderness*, instead of resenting her Insults with the Frowns of provok'd Majesty. He considers his *own* Guilt as a softening of *hers*, and confesses, after a short Pause for Recollection of his Thoughts,

'Tis true, fair Murderer! I have greatly wrong'd *thee:*
And yet, not I, *but what I once* was, *wrongd thee!*
'Tis a sad Theme! and Reason trembles *at it,* &c.

IMAGINE a young Lady of high Birth, blooming Beauty, powerfully Allied of a violent and revengeful Spirit, urg'd and influenc'd by a Faction; remembring herself undone, and imagining she is not *only* forsaken but *scorn'd* and *hated* by the Man for whom she had sacrific'd both her Quiet and her Honour!—What *Power* of *Persuasion* must there be in Words and Sentiments adapted to a Scene where this ruin'd and inrag'd Revenger (not restor'd to the faintest *Hope* but, on the contrary, *convinc'd* that she is to be *abandon'd for ever*) is, notwithstanding, pleas'd and satisfy'd, and gradually charm'd into a Return of her Passion, till it produces a Discovery of her Accomplices in the Treason and her Death by her own Hands as an Atonement for her Purpose!

WHAT a Torrent of Applause must have distinguish'd such a Scene in any Country where the Audiences are accustom'd to be *awake*, and have a Relish of *Sentiments* or a Feeling of *Humanity*! And to what must we impute it that the Sex *most concerned* in this Incident of the

Play seem'd so little to be *touch'd* by it, while as if they join'd in a Confederacy (to lessen their own Value) they flock with Ecstacy to support some Tragedies and Comedies where their Modesty is shock'd, their Tenderness insulted, and their Last Favours rewarded with Insolence and Ingratitude?

ONE would scarce think it possible that the high and Publick Virtues express'd in the following Speech could be heard (from the Mouth of the *justest Actor* in the World) without *Praise*! without *Notice*! [Quotes from 'Still I regard Thee' to 'Thine'; above, p. 392.]

WHAT *Englishman*, not as tastless as the Bench he was sitting on, cou'd listen to that Description of *Mercy* which I am about to insert and not thankfully remember his own immediate Happiness, who lives in the glorious Reign of a Prince so noted for his *Clemency* that it always stands out, obvious, in the List of his Royal Attributes!

> *Oh! do not thus with Cruelty's keen Breath*
> *Blow off and scatter the sweet* Dew *of Mercy.*
> *When from the Heaven of Power that soft Rain falls,*
> *The thriving State looks fresh, Dominion prospers,*
> *And parch'd* Rebellion *shuts her drowthy Gapings.*
> Mercy *is the becoming* Smile *of* Justice.
> This *makes her* lovely, *as her Rigour* dreadful *!*
> *Either* alone *defective: But when* join'd,
> *Like Clay and Water in the Potter's Hand,*
> *They mingle Influence; and* together *rise*
> *In Forms which neither,* sep'rate, *cou'd bestow.*

BUT I had much ado, I must confess, to keep myself from laughing out when the King's *Prime Minister* in the Play, the chief Manager of his *Treasury*, a *Favourite*, and a *Traitor*, took upon him to counsel *Cruelty* for the *Benefit* of the *Government*! Hear the Wretch, and ask yourselves If it be possible to *match* him?

> —Mercy *is a Topick*
> *Copious and fair!—But Men who counsel* Monarchs
> *Must smile at simple Nature's moral Dreams,*
> *And skill'd in manly Rigour Cast off Pity.*
> Pity! *that* Waster *of a Prince's Safety!*
> *What!—shall a Villain* Hind *defy his* King,
> *Spurn at his Laws, and then cry—Help me,* Mercy!
> I wou'd have us'd my Sovereign like a Slave,
> And therefore must have *Mercy!—Out upon't!*

'Tis the Priest's Rattle!—Heaven's *ambrosial Diet!*
Too thin a Food for Mortals!—*Men wou'd* Starve *on't!*

THO' I laugh'd inwardly and despis'd him yet I felt my Indignation grow against him at every Word he spoke, and cou'd never bear the Sight of this Traitor Treasurer with Patience till they led him out to be *Executed*; and yet even then too the Audience, methought, sate as much in the *Spleen* as if *They* had been condemn'd to be hang'd with him.

I HAVE seen this Play *acted*!—I have *read* it over and over, and still with fresh Amazement at the Faintness it was received with! It seems the Author *made no Interest* (as the Phrase goes), that is to say, was so Civil to the Ladies and Gentlemen his Cotemporaries as to suppose they were qualify'd to *hear* and *see* for *themselves*, and had Courage to *avow* their Approbation of what pleas'd 'em without humbly waiting for the Opinion of their *Bell-Weathers*, that so they might be sure to move on with the Flock and wear their Understandings in the Dress *most in Fashion*.

I HAVE heard it asserted that what is fine in this Play is *Shakespeare's*, though the Men who object this can never have made that Comparison which should have gone before their Censure. Yet I am apt to believe that in an Age when People are so given to *plain Nature* the Writer of this Play would have succeeded a good deal better if, instead of supposing his King *Henry* to *love* like a *Gentleman*, he had push'd him *bluntly* upon his *Business*; as *Shakespeare* had done before him, in an extraordinary Scene of Gallantry, which I shall give you as a Specimen of the Justice of that Assertion above mention'd. And let it be judg'd by the fair *Representative* of Princess *Katharine* which of the *Two Harry's* a Modern Lady would be woo'd by? I flatter myself that no Exception will be taken against the Judge I have submitted it to; for every body must allow that she understands the nicest Difference betwixt one Thing and Another.

New *Harry* to the Princess.
From Honour's Lessons I have learnt to know
That He whose Life You sav'd should live for You:
I thought, when in your Father's Court I first
Fed my devouring Eye with Your Perfection,
I thought—fond Novice! and unlearn'd in Love!
I then felt Passion which could ne'er be heighten'd:
But now, inflam'd by rising Admiration,

As I come nearer *your amazing Excellence,*
Dazled with Lustre, I adore your Virtue,
Feel your whole *Influence, and am* lost *in* Love:

Old *Harry* to the Princess:

King. *Do you like me, Kate?*

Kate. Pardonnez moy, *I cannot tell, vat is* like *me.*

King. *Give me your Answer, —I 'faith, do: —and so clap Hands, and a Bargain: How say you, Lady? . . .*

Kate. *I cannot tell.*

King. *Can any of your Neighbours tell, Kate? Come, I know thou lovest me: And if ever thou beest mine, I get thee with* Scambling, *and thou must therefore, needs prove a good* Soldier-breeder. *—Shall not thou and I, between St.* Dennis, *and St.* George, *compound a Boy, half* French, *half* English, *that shall go to* Constantinople, *and take the* Turk *by the Beard? Shall we not? What say'st Thou, my fair* Flower de Luce?

Kate. *I do not know* dat.

King. *No, 'tis* hereafter, *to* know; *but now to* promise; *do but* You *promise, Kate, you will endeavour for your* French Part *of such a Boy; and, for my* English Moiety, *take the Word of a King, and a Batchelor—&c.—&c.*

MY Readers, I suppose, by this Time have enough of *Kate* and her Lover. But He whose Appetite is strong enough may find more in Abundance if he turns to the Original, in *Shakespeare*! The Flights of that prodigious Genius were unsteady, like the *Swallow*'s. He is sometimes as high as Heaven, and our Eyes ake with viewing Him! But he falls at once to the Ground, and skims along the *Ditches*, 'till we lose him in Dirt and Brambles.

I WILL end with this Remark, That I am glad I shall be past *Blushing* when our Posterity, inquiring an Age or two hence what *Dramatick* Performances were *their* Favourites who had not Taste for *Henry V?*, shall be answer'd with a Smile—*The Exploits of Harlequin!*—And *The Devil and Doctor Faustus!*

71. Alexander Pope, edition of Shakespeare

1725

From *The Works of Shakespeare, Collated and Corrected*, 6 vols (1725).

Most of Pope's critical opinions are conventional, and can be found in such predecessors as Dryden, Gildon, Farquhar, Rowe and Dennis. His claim that Shakespeare suffered through having been an actor is, however, original to him, and was severely criticized by an anonymous opponent (see No. 77 below).

It is not my design to enter into a Criticism upon this Author; tho' to do it effectually and not superficially would be the best occasion that any just Writer could take to form the judgment and taste of our nation. For of all *English* Poets *Shakespeare* must be confessed to be the fairest and fullest subject for Criticism, and to afford the most numerous as well as most conspicuous instances both of Beauties and Faults of all sorts. But this far exceeds the bounds of a Preface, the business of which is only to give an account of the fate of his Works and the disadvantages under which they have been transmitted to us. We shall hereby extenuate many faults which are his, and clear him from the imputation of many which are not: a design which, tho' it can be no guide to future Criticks to do him justice in one way, will at least be sufficient to prevent their doing him an injustice in the other.

I cannot however but mention some of his principal and characteristic Excellencies, for which (notwithstanding his defects) he is justly and universally elevated above all other Dramatic Writers. Not that this is the proper place of praising him, but because I would not omit any occasion of doing it.

If ever any Author deserved the name of an *Original*, it was *Shakespeare*. *Homer* himself drew not his art so immediately from the fountains of Nature: it proceeded thro' *Egyptian* strainers and channels, and came to him not without some tincture of the learning or some cast of the models of those before him. The Poetry of *Shakespeare* was Inspiration indeed: he is not so much an Imitator as an Instrument of Nature; and 'tis not so just to say that he speaks from her as that she speaks thro' him.

His *Characters* are so much Nature her self that 'tis a sort of injury to call them by so distant a name as Copies of her. Those of other Poets have a constant resemblance, which shews that they receiv'd them from one another and were but multiplyers of the same image: each picture like a mock-rainbow is but the reflexion of a reflexion. But every single character in *Shakespeare* is as much an Individual as those in Life itself; it is as impossible to find any two alike; and such as from their relation or affinity in any respect appear most to be Twins will upon comparison be found remarkably distinct. To this life and variety of Character we must add the wonderful Preservation of it; which is such throughout his plays that had all the Speeches been printed without the very names of the persons I believe one might have apply'd them with certainty to every speaker.

The *Power* over our *Passions* was never possess'd in a more eminent degree or display'd in so different instances. Yet all along there is seen no labour, no pains to raise them; no preparation to guide our guess to the effect or be perceiv'd to lead toward it: but the heart swells, and the tears burst out, just at the proper places. We are surpriz'd, the moment we weep; and yet upon reflection find the passion so just that we shou'd be surpriz'd if we had not wept, and wept at that very moment.

How astonishing is it again that the passions directly opposite to these, Laughter and Spleen, are no less at his command; that he is not more a master of the *Great* than of the *Ridiculous* in human nature; of our noblest tendernesses, than of our vainest foibles; of our strongest emotions, than of our idlest sensations!

Nor does he only excell in the Passions: in the coolness of Reflection and Reasoning he is full as admirable. His *Sentiments* are not only in general the most pertinent and judicious upon every subject, but by a talent very peculiar—something between Penetration and Felicity— he hits upon that particular point on which the bent of each argument turns, or the force of each motive depends. This is perfectly amazing from a man of no education or experience in those great and publick scenes of life which are usually the subject of his thoughts. So that he seems to have known the word by Intuition, to have look'd thro' humane nature at one glance and to be the only Author that gives ground for a very new opinion, that the Philosopher and even the Man of the world may be *Born*, as well as the Poet.

It must be own'd that with all these great excellencies he has almost as great defects; and that as he has certainly written better so he has perhaps written worse than any other. But I think I can in some measure account for these defects from several causes and accidents, without which it is hard to imagine that so large and so enlighten'd a mind could ever have been susceptible of them. That all these Contingencies should unite to his disadvantage seems to me almost as singularly unlucky, as that so many various (nay contrary) Talents should meet in one man, was happy and extraordinary.

It must be allowed that Stage-Poetry of all other is more particularly levell'd to please the *Populace*, and its success more immediately depending upon the *Common Suffrage*. One cannot therefore wonder if *Shakespeare*, having at his first appearance no other aim in his writings than to procure a subsistance, directed his endeavours solely to hit the taste and humour that then prevailed. The Audience was generally composed of the meaner sort of people, and therefore the Images of Life were to be drawn from those of their own rank. Accordingly we find that not our Author's only but almost all the old Comedies have their Scene among *Tradesmen* and *Mechanicks*, and even their Historical Plays strictly follow the common *Old Stories* or *Vulgar Traditions* of that kind of people. In Tragedy nothing was so sure to *Surprize* and cause *Admiration* as the most strange, unexpected, and consequently most unnatural Events and Incidents; the most exaggerated Thoughts; the most verbose and bombast Expression; the most pompous Rhymes, and thundering Versification. In Comedy nothing was so sure to *please*, as mean buffoonry, vile ribaldry, and unmannerly jests of fools and clowns. Yet even in these our Author's Wit buoys up, and is borne above his subject. His Genius in those low parts is like some Prince of a Romance in the disguise of a Shepherd or Peasant: a certain Greatness and Spirit now and then break out which manifest his higher extraction and qualities.

It may be added that not only the common Audience had no notion of the rules of writing but few even of the better sort piqu'd themselves upon any great degree of knowledge or nicety that way; till *Ben Jonson*, getting possession of the Stage, brought critical learning into vogue. And that this was not done without difficulty may appear from those frequent lessons (and indeed almost Declamations) which he was forced to prefix to his first plays, and put into the mouth of his Actors, the *Grex*, *Chorus*, &c. to remove the prejudices and inform the judgment of his hearers. Till then our Authors had no thoughts of writing on the model of the Ancients. Their Tragedies were only Histories in Dialogue, and their Comedies follow'd the thread of any Novel as they found it, no less implicitly than if it had been true History.

To judge therefore of *Shakespeare* by *Aristotle*'s rules is like trying a man by the Laws of one Country who acted under those of another. He writ to the *People*; and writ at first without patronage from the better sort, and therefore without aims of pleasing them; without assistance or advice from the Learned, as without the advantage of education or acquaintance among them; without that knowledge of the best models, the Ancients, to inspire him with an emulation of them; in a word, without any views of Reputation, and of what Poets are pleas'd to call Immortality: some or all of which have encourag'd the vanity or animated the ambition of other writers.

Yet it must be observ'd that when his performances had merited the protection of his Prince, and when the encouragement of the Court had succeeded to that of the Town, the works of his riper years are manifestly raised above those of his former. The Dates of his plays sufficiently evidence that his productions improved in proportion to the respect he had for his auditors. And I make no doubt this observation would be found true in every instance were but Editions extant from which we might learn the exact time when every piece was composed, and whether writ for the Town or the Court.

Another Cause (and no less strong than the former) may be deduced from our Author's being a *Player*, and forming himself first upon the judgments of that body of men whereof he was a member. They have ever had a Standard to themselves, upon other principles than those of *Aristotle*. As they live by the Majority they know no rule but that of pleasing the present humour and complying with the wit in fashion; a consideration which brings all their judgment to a short point. Players are just such judges of what is *right* as Taylors are of what is *graceful*. And in this view it will be but fair to allow that most of our Author's faults are less to be ascribed to his wrong judgment as a Poet than to his right judgment as a Player.

By these men it was thought a praise to *Shakespeare* that he scarce ever *blotted a line*. This they industriously propagated, as appears from what we are told by *Ben Jonson* in his *Discoveries*, and from the preface of *Heminge* and *Condell* to the first folio Edition.[1] But in reality (however it has prevailed) there never was a more groundless report, or to the contrary of which there are more undeniable evidences. As, the

---

[1] See Volume I, pp. I, 26.

Comedy of the *Merry Wives of Windsor*, which he entirely new writ; the *History of Henry VI*, which was first published under the Title of *The Contention of York and Lancaster*; and that of *Henry V*, extreamly improved; that of *Hamlet* enlarged to almost as much again as at first, and many others. I believe the common opinion of his want of Learning proceeded from no better ground. This too might be thought a Praise by some, and to this his Errors have as injudiciously been ascribed by others. For 'tis certain, were it true, it could concern but a small part of them; the most are such as are not properly Defects but Superfœtations, and arise not from want of learning or reading but from want of thinking or judging: or rather (to be more just to our Author) from a compliance to those wants in others. As to a wrong choice of the subject, a wrong conduct of the incidents, false thoughts, forc'd expressions, &c. if these are not to be ascrib'd to the foresaid accidental reasons they must be charg'd upon the Poet himself and there is no help for it. But I think the two Disadvantages which I have mentioned (to be obliged to please the lowest of people, and to keep the worst of company) if the consideration be extended as far as it reasonably may, will appear sufficient to mis-lead and depress the greatest Genius upon earth. Nay the more modesty with which such a one is endued the more he is in danger of submitting and conforming to others against his own better judgment.

But as to his *Want of Learning* it may be necessary to say something more: there is certainly a vast difference between *Learning* and *Languages*. How far he was ignorant of the latter I cannot determine; but 'tis plain he had much Reading at least, if they will not call it Learning. Nor is it any great matter, if a man has Knowledge, whether he has it from one language or from another. Nothing is more evident than that he had a taste of natural Philosophy, Mechanicks, ancient and modern History, Poetical learning and Mythology: we find him very knowing in the customs, rites, and manners of Antiquity. In *Coriolanus* and *Julius Cæsar* not only the Spirit but Manners of the *Romans* are exactly drawn; and still a nicer distinction is shown, between the manners of the *Romans* in the time of the former and of the latter. His reading in the ancient Historians is no less conspicuous in many references to particular passages; and the speeches copy'd from *Plutarch* in *Coriolanus* may, I think, as well be made an instance of his learning as those copy'd from *Cicero* in *Catiline* of *Ben Jonson*'s. The manners of other nations in general, the *Egyptians*, *Venetians*, *French*, &c. are drawn with equal propriety. Whatever object of nature or branch of science he either speaks of or describes it is always with competent if not extensive knowledge. His descriptions are still exact; all his metaphors appropriated, and remarkably drawn from the true nature and inherent qualities of each subject. When he treats of Ethic or Politic we may constantly observe a wonderful justness of distinction as well as extent of comprehension. No one is more a master of the Poetical story or has more frequent allusions to the various parts of it: Mr. *Waller* (who has been celebrated for this last particular) has not shown more learning this way than *Shakespeare*. We have Translations from *Ovid*[1] published in his name among those Poems which pass for his and for some of which we have undoubted authority (being published by himself, and dedicated to his noble Patron the Earl of *Southampton*). He appears also to have been conversant in *Plautus*, from whom he has taken the plot of one of his plays; he follows the *Greek* Authors, and particularly *Dares Phrygius*[2], in another (altho' I will not pretend to say in what language he read them). The modern *Italian* writers of Novels he was manifestly acquainted with, and we may conclude him to be no less conversant with the Ancients of his own country from the use he has made of *Chaucer* in *Troilus and Cressida*,[3] and in the *Two Noble Kinsmen*—if that Play be his, as there goes a Tradition it was (and indeed it has little resemblance of *Fletcher*, and more of our Author than some of those which have been received as genuine.)

I am inclined to think this opinion proceeded originally from the zeal of the Partizans of our Author and *Ben Jonson*, as they endeavoured to exalt the one at the expence of the other. It is ever the nature of Parties to be in extremes, and nothing is so probable as that because *Ben Jonson* had much the most learning it was said on the one hand that *Shakespeare* had none at all; and because *Shakespeare* had much the most wit and fancy it was retorted on the other that *Jonson* wanted both. Because *Shakespeare* borrowed nothing it was said that *Ben Jonson* borrowed every thing. Because *Jonson* did not write extempore he was reproached with being a year about every piece; and because *Shakespeare* wrote with ease and rapidity they cryed he never once made a blot. Nay the spirit of opposition ran so high that whatever those of the one side

[1] Cf. the note to p. 218 above.

[2] 'Dictys and Dares' were two of the apocryphal sources for the siege of Troy, often published together in the Middle Ages. Dares Phrygius is the priest of Hephaestus in the *Iliad*, and the ascription to him of a fifth century A.D. Latin work was uncritically accepted for many years.

[3] Dryden: Volume 1, p. 250.

objected to the other was taken at the rebound, and turned into Praises, as injudiciously as their antagonists before had made them Objections.

Poets are always afraid of Envy, but sure they have as much reason to be afraid of Admiration. They are the *Scylla* and *Charybdis* of Authors: those who escape one often fall by the other. *Pessimum genus inimicorum Laudantes*, says *Tacitus*;[1] and *Virgil* desires to wear a charm against those who praise a Poet without rule or reason.

> —*Si ultra placitum laudarit, baccare frontem*
> *Cingito, ne Vati noceat*—[2]

But however this contention might be carried on by the Partizans on either side I cannot help thinking these two great Poets were good friends, and lived on amicable terms and in offices of society with each other. It is an acknowledged fact that *Ben Jonson* was introduced upon the Stage, and his first works encouraged, by *Shakespeare*. And after his death that Author writes *To the memory of his beloved Mr.* William Shakespeare,[3] which shows as if the friendship had continued thro' life. I cannot for my own part find any thing *Invidious* or *Sparing* in those verses, but wonder Mr. *Dryden* was of that opinion. He exalts him not only above all his Contemporaries but above *Chaucer* and *Spenser*, whom he will not allow to be great enough to be rank'd with him; and challenges the names of *Sophocles*, *Euripides*, and *Æschylus*, nay all *Greece* and *Rome* at once, to equal him. And (which is very particular) expresly vindicates him from the imputation of wanting *Art*, not enduring that all his excellencies shou'd be attributed to *Nature*. It is remarkable, too, that the praise he gives him in his *Discoveries* seems to proceed from a *personal kindness*: he tells us that he lov'd the man as well as honoured his memory; celebrates the honesty, openness, and frankness of his temper; and only distinguishes, as he reasonably ought, between the real merit of the Author and the silly and derogatory applauses of the Players. *Ben Jonson* might indeed be sparing in his Commendations (tho' certainly he is not so in this instance) partly from his own nature and partly from judgment. For men of judgment think they do any man more service in praising him justly than lavishly. I say, I would fain believe they were Friends, tho' the violence and ill-breeding of their Followers and Flatterers were enough to give rise to

---

[1] *Agricola*, 41: 'that worst class of enemies—the men who praise'.

[2] Virgil, *Eclogues*, 7.27 f: 'If [Codrus] should praise me unduly, wreathe my brow with foxglove, lest his evil tongue harm the bard. . . .'

[3] See Volume I, No. I.

the contrary report. I would hope that it may be with *Parties*, both in Wit and State, as with those Monsters described by the Poets, and that their *Heads* at least may have something humane tho' their *Bodies* and *Tails* are wild beasts and serpents.

As I believe that what I have mentioned gave rise to the opinion of *Shakespeare*'s want of learning, so what has continued it down to us may have been the many blunders and illiteracies of the first Publishers of his works. In these Editions their ignorance shines almost in every page; nothing is more common than *Actus tertia, Exit Omnes, Enter three Witches solus*.[1] Their *French* is as bad as their *Latin*, both in construction and spelling; their very *Welsh* is false. Nothing is more likely than that those palpable blunders of *Hector*'s quoting *Aristotle*, with others of that gross kind, sprung from the same root, it not being at all credible that these could be the errors of any man who had the least tincture of a School, or the least conversation with such as had. *Ben Jonson* (whom they will not think partial to him) allows him at least to have had *some Latin*, which is utterly inconsistent with mistakes like these. Nay the constant blunders in proper names of persons and places are such as must have proceeded from a man who had not so much as read any history in any language: so could not be *Shakespeare*'s.

I shall now lay before the reader some of those almost innumerable Errors which have risen from one source, the ignorance of the Players, both as his actors and as his editors. When the nature and kinds of these are enumerated and considered I dare to say that not *Shakespeare* only but *Aristotle* or *Cicero*, had their works undergone the same fate, might have appear'd to want sense as well as learning.

It is not certain that any one of his Plays was published by himself. During the time of his employment in the Theatre several of his pieces were printed separately in Quarto. What makes me think that most of these were not publish'd by him is the excessive carelessness of the press. Every page is so scandalously false spelled, and almost all the learned or unusual words so intolerably mangled that it's plain there either was no Corrector to the press at all or one totally illiterate. If any were supervised by himself I should fancy the two parts of *Henry IV*, and *Midsummer-Night's Dream* might have been so, because I find no other printed with any exactness; and (contrary to the rest) there is very little variation in all the subsequent editions of them. There are extant two Prefaces, to the first quarto edition of *Troilus and Cressida* in 1609, and to that of *Othello*; by which it appears that the

---

[1] No such stage-direction occurs in the early texts of *Macbeth*.

first was publish'd without his knowledge or consent and even before it was acted, so late as seven or eight years before he died; and that the latter was not printed till after his death. The whole number of genuine plays which we have been able to find printed in his life-time amounts but to eleven. And of some of these we meet with two or more editions by different printers each of which has whole heaps of trash different from the other: which I should fancy was occasion'd by their being taken from different copies belonging to different Playhouses.

The folio edition (in which all the plays we now receive as his were first collected) was published by two Players, *Heminge* and *Condell*, in 1623, seven years after his decease. They declare that all the other editions were stolen and surreptitious, and affirm theirs to be purged from the errors of the former. This is true as to the literal errors and no other, for in all respects else it is far worse than the Quartos.

First, because the additions of trifling and bombast passages are in this edition far more numerous. For whatever had been added since those Quartos by the actors, or had stolen from their mouths into the written parts, were from thence conveyed into the printed text and all stand charged upon the Author. He himself complained of this usage in *Hamlet*, where he wishes that *those who play the Clowns wou'd speak no more than is set down for them* [3.2.37 ff]. But as a proof that he could not escape it, in the old editions of *Romeo and Juliet* there is no hint of a great number of the mean conceits and ribaldries now to be found there. In others the low scenes of Mobs, Plebeians and Clowns are vastly shorter than at present: and I have seen one in particular (which seems to have belonged to the playhouse, by having the parts divided with lines and the Actors' names in the margin) where several of those very passages were added in a written hand, which are since to be found in the folio.

In the next place, a number of beautiful passages which are extant in the first single editions are omitted in this. As it seems, without any other reason than their willingness to shorten some scenes: these men (as it was said of *Procrustes*) either lopping or stretching an Author to make him just fit for their Stage.

This edition is said to be printed from the *Original Copies*. I believe they meant those which had lain ever since the Author's days in the playhouse, and had from time to time been cut or added to arbitrarily. It appears that this edition, as well as the Quarto's, was printed (at least partly) from no better copies than the *Prompter's Book*, or *Piece-meal Parts* written out for the use of the actors: for in some places their very * names are thro' carelessness set down instead of the *Personæ Dramatis*, and in others the notes of direction to the *Property-men* for their *Moveables*, and to the *Players* for their *Entries*, † are inserted into the Text thro' the ignorance of the Transcribers.

The Plays not having been before so much as distinguish'd by *Acts* and *Scenes*, they are in this edition divided according as they play'd them, often where there is no pause in the action, or where they thought fit to make a breach in it for the sake of Musick, Masques, or Monsters.

Sometimes the scenes are transposed and shuffled backward and forward, a thing which could no otherwise happen but by their being taken from seperate and piece-meal-written parts.

Many verses are omitted intirely and others transposed, from whence invincible obscurities have arisen, past the guess of any Commentator to clear up, but just where the accidental glympse of an old edition enlightens us.

Some Characters were confounded and mix'd, or two put into one, for want of a competent number of actors. Thus in the Quarto edition of *Midsummer-Night's Dream*, Act. 5, *Shakespeare* introduces a kind of Master of the Revels called *Philostratus*, all whose part is given to another character (that of *Ægeus*) in the subsequent editions; so also in *Hamlet* and *King Lear*. This too makes it probable that the Prompter's Books were what they call'd the Original Copies.

From liberties of this kind many speeches also were put into the mouths of wrong persons, where the Author now seems chargeable with making them speak out of character; or sometimes perhaps for no better reason than that a governing Player, to have the mouthing of some favourite speech himself, would snatch it from the unworthy lips of an Underling.

Prose from verse they did not know, and they accordingly printed one for the other throughout the volume.

Having been forced to say so much of the Players I think I ought in justice to remark that the Judgment, as well as Condition, of that class of people was then far inferior to what it is in our days. As then the best Playhouses were Inns and Taverns (the *Globe*, the *Hope*, the *Red Bull*, the *Fortune*, &c.) so the top of the profession were then meer

---

* Much Ado about Nothing. *Act* 2. *Enter Prince* Leonato, Claudio, *and* Jack Wilson instead of Balthasar. *And in Act* 4. Cowley, *and* Kemp, *constantly thro' a whole Scene.* Edit. Fol. of 1623, and 1632.

† *Such as*

——My Queen is murder'd! *Ring the little Bell*——[This is not Shakespearian.]

——His nose grew as sharp as a pen, and *a table of Greenfield's*, &c. [*Henry V*, 2.3.18 ff]

Players, not Gentlemen of the stage. They were led into the Buttery by the Steward, not plac'd at the Lord's table or Lady's toilette; and consequently were intirely depriv'd of those advantages they now enjoy in the familiar conversation of our Nobility, and an intimacy (not to say dearness) with people of the first condition.

From what has been said there can be no question but had *Shakespeare* published his works himself (especially in his latter time, and after his retreat from the stage) we should not only be certain which are genuine but should find in those that are the errors lessened by some thousands. If I may judge from all the distinguishing marks of his style, and his manner of thinking and writing, I make no doubt to declare that those wretched plays, *Pericles, Locrine, Sir John Oldcastle, Yorkshire Tragedy, Lord Cromwell, The Puritan,* and *London Prodigal* cannot be admitted as his. And I should conjecture of some of the others (particularly *Love's Labour's Lost, The Winter's Tale,* and *Titus Andronicus*) that only some characters, single scenes, or perhaps a few particular passages were of his hand. It is very probable what occasion'd some Plays to be supposed *Shakespeare*'s was only this, that they were pieces produced by unknown authors or fitted up for the Theatre while it was under his administration; and no owner claiming them they were adjudged to him, as they give Strays to the Lord of the Manor. A mistake which (one may also observe), it was not for the interest of the House to remove. Yet the Players themselves, *Heminge* and *Condell,* afterwards did *Shakespeare* the justice to reject those eight plays in their edition, tho' they were then printed in his name, in every body's hands, and acted with some applause (as we learn from what *Ben Jonson* says of *Pericles* in his Ode on the *New Inn.*) That *Titus Andronicus* is one of this class I am the rather induced to believe by finding the same Author openly express his contempt of it in the *Induction* to *Bartholomew Fair* in the year 1614, when *Shakespeare* was yet living. And there is no better authority for these latter sort than for the former, which were equally published in his life-time.

If we give in to this opinion, how many low and vicious parts and passages might no longer reflect upon this great Genius, but appear unworthily charged upon him? And even in those which are really his how many faults may have been unjustly laid to his account from arbitrary Additions, Expunctions, Transpositions of scenes and lines, confusion of Characters and Persons, wrong application of Speeches, corruptions of innumerable Passages by the Ignorance, and wrong Corrections of 'em again by the Impertinence of his first Editors? From

*

413

one or other of these considerations I am verily perswaded that the greatest and the grossest part of what are thought his errors would vanish, and leave his character in a light very different from that disadvantageous one in which it now appears to us.

This is the state in which *Shakespeare*'s writings lye at present, for since the above-mentioned Folio Edition all the rest have implicitly followed it without having recourse to any of the former, or ever making the comparison between them. It is impossible to repair the Injuries already done him; too much time has elaps'd, and the materials are too few. In what I have done I have rather given a proof of my willingness and desire than of my ability to do him justice. I have discharg'd the dull duty of an Editor to my best judgment, with more labour than I expect thanks, with a religious abhorrence of all Innovation, and without any indulgence to my private sense or conjecture. The method taken in this Edition will show it self. The various Readings are fairly put in the margin so that every one may compare 'em, and those I have prefer'd into the Text are constantly *ex fide Codicum*, upon authority. The Alterations or Additions which *Shakespeare* himself made are taken notice of as they occur. Some suspected passages which are excessively bad (and which seem Interpolations by being so inserted that one can intirely omit them without any chasm or deficience in the context), are degraded to the bottom of the page, with an Asterisk referring to the places of their insertion. The Scenes are mark'd so distinctly that every removal of place is specify'd— which is more necessary in this Author than any other since he shifts them more frequently; and sometimes, without attending to this particular, the reader would have met with obscurities. The more obsolete or unusual words are explained. Some of the most shining passages are distinguish'd by comma's in the margin, and where the beauty lay not in particulars but in the whole a star is prefix'd to the scene. This seems to me a shorter and less ostentatious method of performing the better half of Criticism (namely the pointing out an Author's excellencies) than to fill a whole paper with citations of fine passages, with *general Applauses* or *empty Exclamations* at the tail of them. There is also subjoin'd a Catalogue of those first Editions by which the greater part of the various readings and of the corrected passages are authorised (most of which are such as carry their own evidence along with them). These Editions now hold the place of Originals, and are the only materials left to repair the deficiences or restore the corrupted sense of the Author. I can only wish that a greater number of them (if a greater were ever published) may yet be found, by a search more successful than mine, for the better accomplishment of this end.

I will conclude by saying of *Shakespeare* that, with all his faults, and with all the irregularity of his *Drama*, one may look upon his works, in comparison of those that are more finish'd and regular, as upon an ancient majestick piece of *Gothick* Architecture compar'd with a neat Modern building: the latter is more elegant and glaring, but the former is more strong and more solemn. It must be allow'd that in one of these there are materials enough to make many of the other. It has much the greater variety, and much the nobler apartments; tho' we are often conducted to them by dark, odd, and uncouth passages. Nor does the Whole fail to strike us with greater reverence, tho' many of the Parts are childish, ill-plac'd, and unequal to its grandeur. (I, i–xxiv)

[From the notes]

[On *The Tempest*, 2.1: the scene where Sebastian and Antonio mock Gonzalo]

All this that follows after the words, *Pr'ythee peace*—to the words *You cram these words*, &c. seems to have been interpolated (perhaps by the *Players*), the verses there beginning again; and all that is between in prose, not only being very impertinent stuff but most improper and ill plac'd Drollery in the mouths of unhappy shipwreckt people. There is more of the same sort interspers'd in the remaining part of the Scene. (I, 25)

*   *   *

[Head-note to *The Two Gentlemen of Verona*]

It is observable (I know not from what cause) that the Style of this Comedy is less figurative, and more natural and unaffected than the greater Part of this Author's, though suppos'd to be one of the first he wrote. (I, 155)

*   *   *

[On *The Two Gentlemen of Verona*, 1.2]

This whole Scene, like many others in these Plays (some of which I believe were written by *Shakespeare*, and others interpolated by the Players), is compos'd of the lowest and most trifling conceits, to be accounted for only from the gross taste of the age he liv'd in; *Populo ut*

415

placerent. I wish I had authority to have them out, but I have done all I could, set a mark of reprobation upon them; throughout this edition. ††† (I, 157)

* * *

[On *The Two Gentlemen of Verona*, 5.4.83: 'All that was mine in Silvia I give thee.']

It is (I think) very odd to give up his mistress thus at once, without any reason alledg'd. But our author probably followed the stories just as he found them, in his Novels, as well as in his Histories. (I, 226)

* * *

[On *King Lear*, 3.6.20 ff; the 'trial scene']

There follow in the old edition several speeches in the mad way, which probably were left out by the players, or by *Shakespeare* himself. I shall however insert them here, and leave 'em to the reader's mercy. (III i, 66)

* * *

[On *Richard II*, 1.1]

I must make one remark in general on the *Rhymes* throughout this whole Play: they are so much inferior to the rest of the writing that they appear to me to be of a different hand. What confirms this is that the context does every where exactly (and frequently much better) connect without the inserted Rhymes, except in a very few places; and just there, too, the rhyming verses are of a much better taste than all the others, which rather strengthens my conjecture (III ii, 96)

* * *

[On *Henry V*, 2.3.18 ff] . . . *his nose was as sharp as a pen, and a table of green fields.*]

These words *and a table of green fields* are not to be found in the old editions of 1600 and 1608. This nonsense got into all the following editions by a pleasant mistake of the Stage-editors, who printed from the common piecemeal-written Parts in the Play-house. A Table was here directed to be brought in (it being a scene in a tavern where they drink at parting), and this direction crept into the text from the margin. *Greenfield* was the name of the Property man in that time who furnish'd implements &c. for the actors. A *Table* of *Greenfield's.* (III ii, 422)

* * *

[On *Henry V*, 3.4: the French dialogue scene]

I have left this ridiculous scene as I found it; and am sorry to have no colour left from any of the editions to imagine it here interpolated. (III ii, 437)

*   *   *

[On *1 Henry VI*, 1.1.52 ff]

> *Henry* the Fifth! thy ghost I invocate;
> Prosper this realm.
> A far more glorious star thy soul will make
> Than *Julius Caesar*, or bright—

I can't guess the occasion of the Hemystic, and imperfect sense, in this place; 'tis not impossible it might have been fill'd up with '—*Francis Drake*—'. Tho' that were a terrible Anachronism (as bad as *Hector*'s quoting *Aristotle* in *Troilus and Cressida*) yet perhaps at the time that brave Englishman was in his glory to an *English*-hearted audience, and pronounced by some favourite Actor, the thing might be popular though not judicious; and therefore by some Critick, in favour of the author, afterwards struck out. But this is a mere slight conjecture. . . . (IV, 7)

*   *   *

[On *Julius Caesar*, 3.1.106 ff: the speech 'Stoop, Romans, stoop,' which Pope re-assigns to Casca]

In all the editions this speech is ascrib'd to *Brutus*, than which nothing is more inconsistent with his mild and philosophical character. But, as I often find speeches in the later editions put into wrong mouths, different from the first-publish'd by the author, I think this liberty not unreasonable. (V, 258)

*   *   *

[Head-note to *Troilus and Cressida*]

Before this Play of *Troilus and Cressida* printed in 1609 is a Bookseller's preface, showing that first impression to have been before the Play had been acted, and that it was published without *Shakespeare*'s knowledge from a copy that had fallen into the Bookseller's hands. Mr. *Dryden* thinks this one of the first of our Author's plays.[1] But on the contrary, it may be judg'd from the foremention'd Preface that it was one of his last; and the great number of observations, both moral and politick

[1] Cf. Volume 1, p. 250.

(with which this piece is crowded more than any other of his), seems to confirm my opinion. (VI, 7)

★   ★   ★

[On *Cymbeline*, 5.3.30 ff]

Here follows a *Vision*, a *Masque*, and a *Prophecy*, which interrupt the Fable without the least necessity and unmeasurably lengthen this Act. I think it plainly foisted in afterwards for meer show, and apparently not of *Shakespeare*. (VI, 219)

★   ★   ★

[On *Romeo and Juliet*, 1.3.79 ff]

In the common editions here follows a ridiculous speech, which is entirely added since the first. (VI, 259)

★   ★   ★

[On *Romeo and Juliet*, 3.3.117] *And slay thy lady too, that lives in thee?*

Here follows in the common books a great deal of nonsense, not one word of which is to be found in the first edition. (VI, 304)

★   ★   ★

[On *Romeo and Juliet*, 5.3]

Some lines are left out here and afterwards which are unworthy of *Shakespeare*, and no hint of them to be found in the old edition. (VI, 333)

★   ★   ★

[On *Othello*, 3.3.457 ff: 'Like to the Pontic sea . . .']

This simile is omitted in the first edition: I think it should be so, as an unnatural excursion in this place. (VI, 541)

★   ★   ★

[On *Othello*, 4.1.38 f]

Handkerchief—to confess, and be hang'd for his labour—First, to be hang'd, and then to confess—

No hint of this trash in the 1st edit. (VI, 551)

72. George Sewell on Shakespeare's poems

1725

From the Preface to 'Volume Seven' of Pope's edition.

Sewell seems to have taken upon himself to issue this additional volume, unsolicited by Pope. In effect it is a reissue of the spurious 'volume seven' of Rowe's edition, reprinting the *Poems* and the two long essays by Gildon (No. 50 above).

MEN of Learning and Leisure have usually busied themselves in reprinting the Works of the celebrated antient Authors in the *Greek* and *Latin* Languages. By which means it happens that of many of these we have more than we need, and Numbers of no Use at all; the *Editors* being so very inconsiderable as to drive Gentlemen of Taste back to the earliest Impressions of Books, where the genuine Sense appears in a truer Light than in the idle Comments of our modern Publishers. First Editions are rarely to be seen, but like Jewels in the Cabinets of the richly Curious; and many new ones bear little Value, either from their Commonness or Coarseness. What then has been done by the really Learned to the dead Languages, by treading backwards into the Paths of Antiquity and reviving and correcting good old Authors, we in Justice owe to our own great Writers, both in Prose and Poetry. They are in some degree our *Classics*; on their Foundation we must build, as the Formers and Refiners of our Language.

IN reforming old Palaces we find that Time and Carelesness have kept equal Pace in spreading Ruin; and so it fares with Authors, who carry with the Rust of Antiquity the Blemishes of Neglect and ill Usage. Of this SHAKESPEARE is a very remarkable Instance, who has been handed down from Age to Age very incorrect, his Errors increasing by Time and being almost constantly republish'd to his Disgrace. Whatever were the Faults of this great Poet the Printers have been hitherto as careful to multiply them as if they had been real Beauties; thinking perhaps with the *Indians* that the disfiguring a good

Face with Scars of artificial Brutes had improv'd the Form and Dignity of the Person. A fine Writer thus treated looks like *Deiphobus* among the Shades, so maim'd by his pretended Friend that the good *Æneas* hardly knew him again; and with him we may cry out,

Quis tam crudeles optavit sumere Pœnas?[1]

The Answer is easy, the Tribe of Editors, Correctors, and Printers, who have usually as little Pity for a *Helen* as she had for her *Husband*.

THESE Abominations of the Press, with several others, we shall no doubt find remov'd in the new Edition of his *Plays*. When a Genius of similar Fire and Fancy, temper'd with a learned Patience, sits down to consider what SHAKESPEARE would *Think*, as well as what he could *Write*, we may then expect to see his Works answer our Idea of the Man.

FAR be it from any Hopes of mine that this Edition of his Poems should equal his curious Correctness: a less faulty one than the former is all the Reader is to expect. A short History, and some few occasional Remarks will be added, to give Light to some Passages, as well of the Author, as of Mr. *Gildon*.[2]

THIS Gentleman republish'd these Poems from an old Impression in the Year 1710, at the same time with Mr. *Rowe*'s Publication of his Plays. He uses many Arguments to prove them genuine, but the best is the Style, Spirit, and Fancy of SHAKESPEARE, which are not to be mistaken by any tolerable Judge in these Matters. *Venus and Adonis, The Rape of Lucrece*, are out of Dispute, they being put to the Press, and dedicated by the Author himself to the Earl of *Southampton* his great Patron. So that Mr. *Rowe* is evidently mistaken when he says, *That his* Venus and Adonis *was the only Piece of Poetry he publish'd himself*; there being the same Authority for his *Rape of Lucrece*, as for the other.

IF we allow the rest of these Poems to be genuine (as I think Mr. *Gildon* has prov'd them) the Occasional ones will appear to be the first of his Works. A young Muse must have a Mistress to play off the beginnings of Fancy, nothing being so apt to raise and elevate the Soul to a pitch of Poetry as the Passion of Love. We find, to wander no farther, that *Spenser, Cowley*, and many others paid their First-fruits of Poetry to a real or an imaginary Lady. Upon this occasion I conjecture that SHAKESPEARE took fire on reading our admirable *Spenser*, who went but just before him in the Line of Life, and was in all probability

---

[1] *Aeneid*, 6.501: 'Who chose to wreak a penalty so cruel?'
[2] See No. 50 (b) above, p. 262.

the Poet most in Vogue at that time. To make this Argument the stronger, *Spenser* is taken notice of in one of these little Pieces as a Favourite of our Author's.[1] He alludes certainly to the *Faery Queen* when he mentions his *Deep Conceit*, that Poem being entirely Allegorical. It has been remark'd that more Poets have sprung from *Spenser* than all our other *English* Writers; to which let me add an Observation of the late Dr. *Garth*, that most of our late ones have been spoil'd by too early an Admiration of *Milton*. Be it to *Spenser* then that we owe SHAKESPEARE!

The Fairest Scyon of the Fairest Tree.

In Metaphor, Allusion, Description, and all the strongest and highest Colourings of Poetry they both are certainly without Equals. *Spenser* indeed trod more in the Paths of Learning, borrow'd, improv'd, and heighten'd all he imitated: But SHAKESPEARE's Field is *Nature*, and there he undoubtedly triumphs without a Rival. His Imagination is a perpetual Fountain of Delight, and all drawn from the same Source: even his Wildnesses are the Wildnesses of *Nature*. So that *Milton* seems to have hit his Character best when he says,

> —Shakespeare, *Fancy's sweetest Child,*
> *Warbles his native Wood-notes wild.*

The *Child of Fancy*, with the additional Epithet of *sweetest*, is an Expression perfectly fine, becoming both the Praiser and the Praised, and exactly after the manner of the antient Poets.

AND yet I cannot place his Learning so low as others have done, there being evident Marks thro all his Writings of his Knowledge in the *Latin* Language and the *Roman* History. The Translation of *Ovid*'s two Epistles, *Paris* to *Helen*, and her Answer, gives a sufficient Proof of his Acquaintance with that Poet.[2] Nor are these Letters so very easy for a common Translator, for there is a good deal of the Heathen Mythology and Poetical Fictions, of which SHAKESPEARE misses none but is ever faithful to the Original. How they may be receiv'd in these Days of flowing Versification I know not; but I have a Translation of the *Metamorphoses* of the same Age, far inferior to these Epistles.

BUT to return to Mr. *Gildon*, the Republisher of these Poems. He has prefix'd to them an *Essay* on the Rise and Progress of the Stage, and added Remarks on all his Plays in order to let the Reader into the Beauties and Defects of SHAKESPEARE. As to the Essay, tho there have

---

[1] There is no such allusion in the authentic poems of Shakespeare.
[2] Cf. the note to p. 218 above.

been many Things wrote in a loose unconnected manner on the same Subject yet I have seen nothing in our Tongue so regular, so fully explanatory, or so well supported by Instances from the antient Tragic Poets. One may safely say that this was the Study of his whole Life, the darling and over-ruling Passion of his Soul, which work'd off and shew'd it self on all Occasions both in Discourse and Composition. *Sophocles* and *Euripides* were his Idols, whom he look'd upon with a sort of religious Veneration, and took a Pride in making Converts to his Opinion by displaying their hidden Glories to the rest of Mankind. This intimate Acquaintance with these great Originals made him an excellent Judge of what deviated from their Standard. Great modern Names and Authorities were never his Guides, but a Conformity to the just Rules of the best antient Critics and the first Writers. For this Reason the Reader will find him in the Course of the Remarks bearing very hard on Mr. *Dryden*, tho at the same time that he condemn'd the Critic he admir'd the Poet.

THE same cannot be said of his Style as his Sense; his Expression being often dark, his Sentences long, unequal, and crouded with Words of the same Signification. A depression of Fortune, want of Health and Leisure allow'd him no Time for the Filings and Polishings of a correct Writer. And yet with all his Imperfections there is great Matter of Improvement to be pick'd out of his Essay and Remarks:

Cum flueret Lutulentus, erat quod tollere velles.[1]

I must not here leave Mr. *Gildon* without taking notice of an Argument he has brought to prove these Poems genuine, which is the Use of the Compound and Decompound Epithets, as if this was in a manner peculiar to SHAKESPEARE. Others have carried the matter further, and from thence argu'd SHAKESPEARE into an Understanding of the *Greek* Language, from whence they are deriv'd. Any one who is acquainted with old *English* Books may see they were in use before our Author's Time; and as for their being taken from the *Greeks* that will appear ridiculous when we consider how easily those Epithets are form'd. For allow but any Number adopted into our Tongue and a hundred may be coin'd in as many Minutes. For Instance, if I read *far-shooting* from the *Greek*, could not I presently compound *Fire-darting*, and twenty others? (vii–xii)

*   *   *

---

[1] Horace, *Satires*, 1.4.11: 'In his muddy stream there was much that you would like to remove.'

It is not my Province to speak of SHAKESPEARE's Plays; only I cannot
but observe that some of them do not answer their Titles. In *Julius
Cæsar* for Instance, there is little of the Man or his memorable Exploits,
unless what is said after his Death; and if any one were to form an
Idea of him from what SHAKESPEARE makes him speak he would make
but an indifferent Figure for the *Foremost of Mankind*.

★   ★   ★

I HAVE already run this Preface to a great length, otherwise I should
have taken notice of some beautiful Passages in the Poems; but a
Reader of Taste cannot miss them.

FOR my own part, as this Revisal of his Works obliged me to look
over SHAKESPEARE's Plays, I can't but think the Pains I have taken in
correcting well recompensed by the Pleasure I have receiv'd in reading.
And if after this I should attempt any thing *Dramatic* in his Vein and
Spirit, be it owing to the Flame borrow'd from his own Altar!
(xiii–xv)

73. Richard Savage on *The Rape of Lucrece*

May 1725

From the *Plain Dealer*, 116 (3 May 1725); this text from the
collected edition, 2 vols (1730).

This journal was produced by Aaron Hill and William Bond in
1724–5. The author of the essay signs himself 'R.S.': this would
seem to be Richard Savage (*c.* 1696–1724), poet and dramatist,
a protégé of Aaron Hill. Hill published an account of Savage's
miserable situation in the *Plain Dealer* on 26 June 1724, and
organised a subscription for Savage which resulted in the publication of his *Miscellaneous Poems*, 1726. On Savage's relationship
with Hill see Clarence Tracy, *The Artificial Bastard, a Biography of
Richard Savage* (Toronto, 1953).

To the *Author of the* PLAIN DEALER.

SIR,

TURNING over the Works of *Shakespeare* lately usher'd into the World by an extravagant Subscription, and finding the Six Volumes, tho' called *Shakespeare's* Works, contained not his *Venus and Adonis*, his *Rape of Lucrece*, and numberless other Miscellaneous Pieces which, for Richness of Fancy and the many beautiful Descriptions that adorn them are far from being inferior to some of his more celebrated Labours, I thought my self obliged to become a Purchaser of the Seventh Volume also, which appears to me to have no Demerit to occasion its Exclusion.

YOU, Mr. PLAIN DEALER, whose Lucubrations are so justly admir'd by all good Judges of Wit and Taste will indulge me the Transcription of a few of those numberless natural Beauties which shine every where thro' these charming Pieces; and the rather because I have been inform'd that this Volume, which is so necessary and essential a Part of the Works of that inimitable Author, has not, by some of the Wits in *Leading-Strings*, been look'd upon with equal Favour, because this Edition of it was not midwif'd into the World by the *great Names* that have condescended, for the *Emolument* of the *Publick*, to shine in the Title Page of the First Six Volumes. But as this may take up more Room than you will have to spare in one Paper, I shall now and then occasionally beg Leave, by your Means, to recommend to the *Implicite Witlings* of the Age those Beauties which might otherwise escape their Observation.

AND as it is impossible, where ever I open the Book, not to be surprized with the Beauties of this great Genius I will present your Readers with the first that offer'd it self, the Exclamation the violated *Lucrece* makes upon OPPORTUNITY and TIME for contributing to her Undoing:

O! Opportunity, thy guilt is great! [Quotes much of this speech, ll. 876 ff]

WITH this admirable Flow of Fancy, and lively Imagery does this unbounded Genius, forgetful indeed of her unfit Condition for Oratory, whom he represents as thus Copious while he is forcibly carried away by the Stream of his own charming Imagination. I shall only mention that the Description the Poet gives of her Rising to the Morn, her Last Will, her Parley with her Maid, the Maid's sympathizing

Behaviour, and his admirable Description of the Groom she sent to *Collatine* are Beauties, in their Way, that have no Equal but in the same Author. But I cannot forbear recommending his Description of the Picture he makes the unhappy Lady turn her Eyes to, of *Troy* beleagur'd by the *Greeks* to avenge the Rape of *Hellen*; which for Strength of Description surpasses any Thing of the like Kind, and shews the Excellency of the *Poet*'s Art above that of the *Painter* (as the *Soul* is to the *Body*), since 'tis impossible the Pencil of the latter can come up to what follows.

> A thousand lamentable Objects there,
> In *Scorn* of *Nature*, *Art* gave *lifeless Life*:

[Quotes ll. 1373–1435]

I SHOULD transcribe the whole Piece were I to give all the Beauties of this admirable Performance. I shall only add that the Description of HECUBA, and that of the deceitful SINON, and the different Passions and Reflections of LUCRECE on viewing the different Figures, are such Master-pieces that they leave us without Words to express the Wonder they inspire at the Force of that Genius whose Production and Glory they are. Your Paper, Mr. *Plain Dealer*, crowded as it generally is with Beauties, will not be disgrac'd by these Quotations; so that I have nothing by way of Apology to say but only to assure you That I am

Your constant Reader and Admirer,

R. S.

74. Lewis Theobald, from
Shakespeare Restored

1726

From *Shakespeare Restored: Or, a Specimen of the Many Errors, As well Committed, as Unamended, by Mr. Pope In His Late Edition of this Poet. Designed not only to correct the said Edition, but to restore the True Reading of Shakespeare in all the Editions ever yet publish'd* (1726).

The first systematic examination of Shakespeare's text, starting from an exposure of the 'epidemical Corruption' in Pope's edition.

[Introduction]
★ ★ ★

I CAN scarce suspect it will be thought, if I begin my Animadversions upon the Tragedy of *Hamlet*, that I have been partial to myself in picking out this Play as one more fertile in Errors than any of the rest. On the contrary, I chose it for Reasons quite opposite. It is, perhaps, the best known and one of the most favourite Plays of our Author; for these thirty Years last past, I believe, not a Season has elaps'd in which it has not been perform'd on the Stage more than once; and consequently we might presume it the most purg'd and free from Faults and Obscurity. Yet give me Leave to say what I am ready to prove, it is not without very gross Corruptions. Nor does it stand by itself for Faults in Mr. POPE's Edition: no, it is a Specimen only of the epidemical Corruption, if I may be allowed to use that Phrase, which runs thro' all the Work. And I cannot help saying of it as *Æneas* does of the *Greeks'*, Treachery upon the instance of *Sinon's*

— *Crimine ab uno*
Disce omnes:—[1]

IF *Hamlet* has its Faults so has every other of the Plays, and I therefore

---

[1] *Aeneid*, 2.65: 'and from one learn the wickedness of all'.

only offer it as a Precedent of the same Errors which, every body will be convinced before I have done, possess every Volume and every Play in this Impression.

BUT to proceed from Assertion to Experiment, in order to which I shall constantly be obliged—that the Emendations may stand in a fairer Light—to quote the Passages as they are read, with some part of their Context, in Mr. POPE's Edition; and likewise to prefix a short Account of the Business and Circumstances of the Scenes from which the faulty Passages are drawn; that the Readers may be inform'd at a single View, and judge of the Strength and Reason of the Emendation without a Reference to the Plays themselves for that purpose. But this will be in no kind necessary where Faults of the Press are only to be corrected. Where the Pointing is wrong, perhaps that may not be alone the Fault of the Printer, and therefore I may sometimes think myself obliged to assign a Reason for my altering it.

As every Author is best expounded and explain'd in *One* Place by his own Usage and Manner of Expression in *Others*, wherever our Poet receives an Alteration in his Text from any of my *Corrections* or *Conjectures* I have throughout endeavour'd to support what I offer by *parallel Passages*, and *Authorities* from himself. Which, as it will be my best Justification where my Attempts are seconded with the Concurrence of my Readers, so it will be my best Excuse for those *Innovations* in which I am not so happy to have them think with me.

I HAVE likewise all along, for the greater Ease and Pleasure of the Readers, distinguish'd the Nature of my Corrections by a short marginal Note to each of them: *viz. False Pointing, False Print, Various Reading, Passage omitted, Conjectural Emendation, Emendation* and the like, so that every body will at once be appriz'd what Subject-matter to expect from every respective Division. (vii–viii)

*   *   *

'The Examination and Correction of the Tragedy of *Hamlet*'

*   *   *

[Note 1. On *Hamlet*, 1.1.37]

. . . But may it not be objected that if we should read

> *Had made his Course* t'illumine *that Part of Heav'n, &c.*

this Additional *syllable* spoils the Scanning of the Verse? In a Word, too nice a Regard must not be had to the Numbers of SHAKESPEARE. Nor needs the Redundance of a *Syllable* here be any Objection, for nothing is more usual with our Poet than to make a *Dactyl*, or allow a supernumerary *Syllable* which is sunk and melted in the Pronunciation. It were most easy to produce above a thousand Instances of this Custom in him; but unnecessary, because they lie open to the Observation of every discerning Reader. (2)

★   ★   ★

It is a Licence in our Poet, of his own Authority to coin new *Verbs* both out of *Substantives* and *Adjectives*; and it is, as we may call it, one of the *Quidlibet audendi's* very familiar with him. I'll throw in a few Instances of the like kind, and it were very easy with little Pains to produce a Croud more. . . .

> And as Imagination* bodies *forth*
> The Forms of Things unknown, the *Poet's* Pen
> Turns them to Shape, &c.
>
> [*Midsummer-Night's Dream*, 5.1.14]

> Lord Angelo† dukes *it well in his* Absence, &c.
>
> [*Measure for Measure*, 3.2.88]
>
> (8)

★   ★   ★

[Note 11]

> But you must know, your father lost a father,
> That father [ ] his, &c.   [1.2.89]

All the Editions that I have met with, old and modern (and so I know the Players to this Day constantly repeat it), read

> But you must know, your Father lost a Father,
> That Father lost, lost *his;*—

The Reduplication of the Word *lost* here gives an Energy and an Elegance, which is much easier to be conceiv'd than explain'd in Terms. Every Reader of this Poet, however, must have observ'd how frequent it is with him to use this Figure (which the Rhetoricians have call'd *Anadiplosis*) where he intends either to *assert* or *deny, augment* or *diminish*, or add a Degree of *Vehemence* to his Expression. Of this Usage, were it necessary, I could bring a great Number of Examples, but the

---

* gives them bodies.

† acts, represents, the Duke.

Instances that I can at present remember in him which seem most to
resemble this before us are the following:

> —*The Duke does greet you, General,*
> *And he requires your* hast, post-hast *Appearance*
> *Ev'n on the Instant.*   [*Othello*, 1.2.37]

> *And That would* nothing *set my Teeth on Edge,*
> Nothing *so much as mincing Poetry.*   [1 *Henry IV*, 3.1.134]

> . . . *Who* dares, *who* dares
> *In Purity of Manhood, stand upright,*
> *And say, This Man's a Flatterer?* [*Timon of Athens*, 4.3.13 ff]
>   (13–14)

*   *   *

[Note 37]

> *You laying these slight* SALLIES *on my Son*
> *As 'twere a thing a little soil'd i'th'working,*   [2.1.39 f]

'Tis true, *Sallies* and *Flights* of Youth are very frequent Phrases, but
what Agreement is there betwixt the Metaphors of *Sallies* and a Thing
soil'd? Correct, as all the Editions that I have ever seen have it:

> *You laying these slight* SULLIES *on my Son*

Perhaps this *Substantive* may be of his own coining, from the *Verb*
to *sully*: but that, as I have already amply prov'd, is a Liberty which he
eternally assumes through his whole Works. (63)

*   *   *

[Note 39]

> *That He is mad 'tis true; 'tis true, 'tis pity;*
> *And pity, it is true:—*   [2.2.97 f]

Thus indeed several of the Editions read this Place, but they don't
seem to enter entirely into the Poet's Humour. *Polonius* (an officious,
impertinent old Courtier), priding himself in the Discovery which he
supposes he has made of the Cause of HAMLET's Madness, is so full of the
Merit of it that he can't content himself to deliver it in a plain and easy
Manner but falls into an affected jingling Sort of Oratory as he fancies,
and ringing the Chimes backwards and forwards upon the same
Words. No Body can read this Speech without observing that these
Figures and Flowers of Rhetorick are not only sprinkled but poured out

through the whole. They are Strokes of low Humour thrown in purposely *ad captandum populum*; or, to use the Poet's own Phrase, *to set on some Quantity of barren Spectators to laugh at*. I think, therefore, it should be wrote, as three of my Editions have it and as I know it is constantly pronounc'd on the Stage,

> That he is mad, *'tis* true; *'tis* true, *'tis* Pity;
> And Pity *'tis, 'tis* true.　　(64-5)

*　　*　　*

[Note 58]

> Haml. *Lady, shall I lie in your Lap?*
> Ophel. *No, my Lord.*
> Haml. *Do you think I meant Country matters!*　　[3.2.108 ff]

Certainly HAMLET's Answer is more natural, less abrupt, if we restore this Passage from the second *folio* Edition thus:

> Haml. *Lady, shall I lie in your Lap?*
> Ophel. *No my Lord.*
> *Haml.* I mean, my Head upon your Lap?
> *Ophel.* Ay, my Lord.
> Haml. *Do you think I meant Country Matters?*

But indeed if ever the Poet deserved Whipping for low and indecent Ribaldry it was for this Passage; ill-tim'd in all its Circumstances, and unbefitting the Dignity of his Characters as well as of his Audience.
(86-7)

*　　*　　*

[Note 76]

... There is an Addition in several of the Copies, which, tho' it has not the Sanction of any older Edition that I know of than the *Quarto* of 1637 yet has so much of the Style, Diction, and Cast of Thought peculiar to our Poet that I think we may warrant it to be his, and not an Interpolation of the Players without that Authority. Perhaps it was not written when he first finish'd the Play; or it was left out in the shortning the Play for the *Representation*, and so lost its Place in the *first* Editions, which were printed from the Players Copies. The Verses are these:

> —Ha! have you Eyes?
> You cannot call it Love; for at your Age
> The Hey-day of the Blood is tame, it's humble,

430

And waits upon the Judgment; and what Judgment
Would step from This—to This—? Sense sure you have,
Else could you not have Motion; but That Sense
Is apoplex'd: for Madness would not err;
Nor Sense to Ecstasie was ne'er so thrall'd,
But it reserv'd some Quantity of Choice
To serve in such a Difference. *What Devil was't,* &c.

[3.4.65 ff]

The same Book exhibits another small Addition, which is so much inferior to the former that I dare not so boldly vouch for it's being genuine.

. . . That thus hath cozen'd you at hoodman blind?
Eyes without Feeling, Feeling without Sight,
Ears without Hands or Eyes, Smelling sans all.
Or but a sickly Part of one true Sense,
Could not so mope.

[3.4.77 ff]
(103–4)

★   ★   ★

[The Appendix]

THE Examination of this single Play has drove out into such a Length that I am almost afraid to think of an *Appendix* to it. But I have tied my self down by express Engagement at my setting out, and I am satisfied, unless an Author acquits himself very badly, the Publick never care to bate him his Promises. I undertook, I think, boldly to prove That whatever Errors occurr'd in *Hamlet*, Errors of the same Sorts should be found in the other Plays throughout all the Volumes. 'Tis evident, the *Faults* of that Play have branched out into many *Classes*, and I have an ample Stock of Matter before Me to make good my Assertion upon every individual *Species*. As this is but a *Specimen*, I shall be excused from pointing out those innumerable *literal* Faults of the Press which every Reader can correct that does but throw his Eye over the Passages. As to the Faults of *Pointing* too, I shall confine my self to remark on Such only in which the Sense is palpably injured, in which the *Editor* has followed the old printed Copies, and in which he has either not seem'd to suspect a Fault or not understood how to rectify it.

The Design of this Work was an honest Endeavour to restore SHAKESPEARE from the Corruptions that have taken Place in all his Editions, and to this End I gave it as my Opinion that an *Editor* of Him

ought to be a *Critick* upon him too. The Want of *Originals* reduces us
to a Necessity of *guessing* in order to amend him, but these Guesses
change into Something of a more *substantial* Nature when they are
tolerably supported by *Reason* or *Authorities*. There is certainly a
Degree of Merit in a good Conjecture, tho' it be not so thoroughly
satisfactory and convincing as the Party who advances it flatters himself it must be. This calls to my Mind a Sentiment in an old *Latin*
Verse, though I do not remember at present to what Author we owe it:

> Bene qui *conjiciet, Vatem* hunc perhibebo *optimum*.[1]

I am far from entertaining so vain an Hope that every Conjecture
which I have ventur'd to make shall be followed with the Concurrence
and Applause of the Readers, but I may dare to assert Some of them are
so well-grounded and certain that They renew in Me a Wish that
Mr. POPE had proposed to himself to enter upon this Province. This
would naturally have led him to weigh every Line of his Author with
that Care and Judgment that, I believe, *Then* he would have *retracted*
some few of those Conjectures which he has made, and in which he
seems to have err'd either from Want of duly considering the Poet or
of a competent Knowledge of the Stage. The Cause of SHAKESPEARE is
here engaged, and the Restitution of Him concern'd; and therefore I
must beg Mr. POPE's Pardon for contradicting Some of his Conjectures
in which he has mistaken the Meaning of our Author. No other Cause
but This should provoke me to run so bold a Risque; and if I have the
ill Fortune to deceive my self in the Attempt I shall willingly submit to
own my self (as HAMLET says to LAERTES), *his Foil in my Ignorance*.

The exceptionable Conjectures of the *Editor*, I think, may be ranged
under these Heads: as, where he has *substituted a fresh Reading* and there
was no Occasion to depart from the Poet's Text; where he has *maim'd*
the Author by an unadvis'd *Degradation*; where he has made a *bad*
Choice in a *Various Reading* and degraded the better Word; and where
he, by *mistaking* the *Gloss* of any Word, has given a wrong Turn to the
Poet's Sense and Meaning.

Of the first Species of These I shall produce but a single Instance
because my Defence of the Poet will take up some Room. But I am in
hopes the Novelty of the Subject, and the Variety of the Matter, will
make it not appear too tedious. The Passage upon which I make my
Observation is This:

[1] Cicero, *De Divinatione*, II. v. 12: 'The best diviner I maintain to be the man who
guesses or conjectures best.'

I. *Troilus and Cressida* [2.2.163 ff]

> Paris *and* Troilus, *you have Both said well:*
> And *on the Cause and Question now in hand*
> *Have gloss'd but superficially, not much*
> *Unlike Young Men, whom* GRAVER SAGES *think*
> *Unfit to hear moral* Philosophy.

The EDITOR, I remember, in his Preface, speaking of the Method taken in his Edition, tells us that *the Various Readings are fairly put in the Margin, so that every one may compare them; and those he has preferr'd into the Text are* CONSTANTLY ex fide Codicum, *upon Authority*. I heartily beg the Pardon of this Gentleman if, thro' Ignorance, I shall assert a Falshood here, in being bold to say that This may be call'd an Exception to his Rule, that *Graver Sages* is preferr'd into the Text without *any* Authority, and that all the printed Copies read the Passage thus:

> —*not much*
> *Unlike Young Men, whom* ARISTOTLE *thought*
> *Unfit to hear moral* Philosophy.

'Tis certain indeed that *Aristotle* was at least 800 Years subsequent in Time to *Hector*, and therefore the Poet makes a remarkable Innovation upon Chronology. But Mr. POPE will have this to be One of those *palpable Blunders* which the Illiteracy of the first Publishers of his Works has father'd upon the Poet's Memory, and is of Opinion that it could not be of our Author's penning, *it not being at all credible, that these could be the Errors of any Man who had the least Tincture of a School, or the least Conversation with such as had*. 'Tis for this Reason, and to shelter our Author from such an Absurdity, that the *Editor* has ex- pung'd the Name of ARISTOTLE and substituted in its place *graver Sages*. But, with Submission, even herein he has made at best but half a Cure. If the Poet must be fetter'd down strictly to the Chronology of Things it is every whit as absurd for *Hector* to talk of PHILOSOPHY as for him to talk of *Aristotle*. We have sufficient Proofs that *Pythagoras* was the first who invented the Word *Philosophy* and call'd himself *Philosopher*: and he was near 600 Years after the Date of *Hector*, even from his beginning to flourish. 'Tis true, the Thing which we now understand by Philosophy was *then* known, but it was only *till then* call'd *Knowledge* and *Wisdom*. But to dismiss this Point, I believe this Anachronism of our Poet (and perhaps all the Others that he is guilty of), was the Effect of Poetick Licence in him rather than Ignorance.

It has been very familiar with the Poets, of the *Stage* especially, upon a Supposition that their Audience were not so exactly inform'd in Chronology to anticipate the Mention of Persons and Things before either the *first* were born or the *latter* thought of. SHAKESPEARE, again, in the same Play compares the Nerves of AJAX with those of *bull-bearing* MILO of *Crotona*, who was not in Being till 600 Years after that *Greek*, and was a Disciple of *Pythagoras*. Again, *Pandarus*, at the Conclusion of the Play talks of a *Winchester-Goose*: indeed, it is in an Address to the Audience, and then there may be an Allowance and greater Latitude for going out of Character. Again, in CORIOLANUS *Menenius* talks of *Galen*, who was not born till the second Century of the Christian Æra; and the very Hero of that Play talks of the Grievance that he must stoop to in begging Voices of *Dick* and *Hob*, names which I dare say the *Editor* does not imagine that SHAKESPEARE believ'd were ever heard of by that *Roman*. From his many Plays founded on our *English* Annals, and the many Points of History accurately transmitted down in them, I suppose it must be confess'd that he was intimately versed in that Part of Reading: yet in his *King Lear* he has ventur'd to make *Edgar* talk of the *Curfew*, a Thing not known in *Britain* till the *Norman* Invasion. In his *King John* he above fifty times mentions *Cannons*, tho *Gunpowder* was not invented till above a Century and an half after the Death of that Monarch; and what is yet more singular (as he could not be a Stranger to the Date of a remarkable Man who liv'd so near his own Time), twice in the Story of *Henry VI* he makes Mention of *Machiavelli* as a subtle Politician, tho' 'tis very well known He was chief Counsellor to the wicked *Cæsar Borgia*, and a Favourite to the Popes *Leo X* and *Clement VII*, the latter of whom did not come to the Papal Chair till the 15th Year of K. *Henry VIII*.

All these Transgressions in Time therefore, as I said before, are Liberties taken knowingly by the Poet and not Absurdities flowing from his Ignorance. There is one Passage I remember in our Author in which, if I am not mistaken, he may be presum'd to sneer at his own Licentiousness in these Points. It is in his *Lear*: the King's Fool pronounces a sort of Dogrel Prophecy, and as soon as he has finish'd it cries *This Prophecy* Merlin *shall make; for I do live* before his time. . . .

[Theobald gives other instances of poetic licence in anachronism from English and classical authors.]

If these Instances of Transgression in Time may go any Way towards acquitting our Poet for the like Inconsistencies I'll at any Time engage to strengthen them with ten Times the Number fetch'd from the

Writings of the best Poets, ancient and modern, foreign and domestick.

II. I come now to consider a *Degraded* Passage, by which I think we may safely affirm the Poet's Sense to be maim'd. It may be very justly said of SHAKESPEARE's *Style*, as He himself says of the Web of human Life, *it is of a mingled Yarn, good and ill together*. And therefore it must be own'd Mr. POPE has very often with great Judgment thrown out of the Text such low Trash as is unworthy of the Poet's Character and must disgust a Reader who is desirous to be pleased. But if unhappily some of his mean Conceits are so intermingled either with the Business or the Sense of the Context that they cannot be rejected without leaving an Imperfection there we must dispense with them, and content ourselves to be sorry for the *Levity* of the Author's *Pen*, or the *Vice* of the Times that forc'd him to bring in such *bald Witticisms*. (133–5)

*　　*　　*

IV. I'll now proceed to consider a Conjecture of the Editor's which I am very free to own is *ingeniously* urg'd: but there is Something more than *Ingenuity* requir'd, to guess for the *Stage* rightly. His Conjecture is grounded upon a marginal Interpolation that had crept into the Text of some later Editions in Dame *Quickly*'s admirable Description of the Manner in which *Falstaff* dy'd.

K. Henry V [2.3.18 ff] *For after I saw him fumble with the Sheets, and play with Flowers, and smile upon his Finger's End, I knew there was but one way; for *his nose was as sharp as a Pen.*

*His nose was as sharp as a pen, and a table of green fields.

These Words, and a table of green fields, *are not to be found in the old Editions of* 1600 *and* 1608. *This nonsence got into all the following Editions by a pleasant mistake of the Stage-Editors, who printed from the common piece-meal written Parts in the Play-house. A Table was here directed to be brought in* (*it being a scene in a tavern where they drink at parting*), *and this Direction crept into the text from the margin.* Greenfield *was the name of the Property-man in that time who furnish'd implements,* &c. *for the actors.* A Table *of* Greenfield's.

So far the Note of the EDITOR. Something more than *Ingenuity* is wanting, as I said before, to make these Conjectures pass current, and That is a *competent Knowledge* of the *Stage* and its *Customs*. As to the History of *Greenfield* being then Property-Man, whether it was really so or it be only a *gratis dictum* is a Point which I shall not contend about.

But allowing the marginal Direction, and supposing that a *Table* of *Greenfield*'s was wanting, I positively deny that it ever was customary (or that there can be any Occasion for it) either in the *Prompter*'s Book, or piece-meal Parts, where any such Directions are marginally inserted for the *Properties* or *Implements* wanted to add the *Property-Man*'s Name whose Business it was to provide them. The Stage-Necessaries are always furnish'd between the *Property-Man* and the *Scene-Keeper*; and as the Direction is for the *Prompter*'s Use and issued from him there can be no Occasion, as I said, for inserting the Names either of the one or the other.

But there is a stronger Objection yet against this Conjecture of the *Editor*'s in the Manner he supposes it, which he must have foreseen had he had that Acquaintance with Stage-Books which it has been my Fortune to have. Surely Mr. POPE cannot imagine that when Implements are wanted in any Scene the Direction for them is mark'd in the Middle of that Scene, tho' the Things are to be got ready against the Beginning of it. No; the Directions for *Entrances*, and *Properties* wanting, are always mark'd in the Book at about a Page in Quantity before the *Actors* quoted are to enter or the *Properties* be carried on. And therefore GREENFIELD's *Table* can be of no Use to us for this Scene.

I agree, indeed, with Mr. *Pope*, that these Words might be a *Stage-Direction* and so crept into the Text from the Margin, but I insist that they must be a Direction then for the *subsequent* Scene, and not for the Scene *in Action*. I don't care therefore if I venture my Conjecture too upon the Passage: I'll be sure, at least, if it be not altogether right it shall not be liable to the *Absurdity* of the *Objection* last struck at. I suppose, with the Editor, that over-against the Words of the Text there might be this Marginal Quotation so close to them that the Ignorance of the Stage-Editors might easily give them Admittance into the Text.

> —*his Nose was as sharp as a Pen.*
> *Chairs*, and a Table off. Green Fields.

The Scene in Action is part of Dame *Quickly* the Hostess her House, and Chairs and Table were here necessary: The following Scene carries us into the *French* Dominions. I therefore believe This was intended as a Direction to the *Scene-Keepers* to be ready to remove the *Chairs* and *Table* so soon as the *Actors* went off, and to shift the Scene from the *Tavern* to a Prospect of *green Fields*, representing Part of the *French* Territories.

But what if it should be thought proper to retract both Mr. POPE's and my own Conjecture and to allow that these Words, corrupt as they now are, might have belong'd to the Poet's Text? I have an Edition of *Shakespeare* by Me with some Marginal Conjectures of a Gentleman sometime deceas'd, and he is of the Mind to correct this Passage thus:

for his Nose was as sharp as a Pen, and a'talked of Green Fields.

It is certainly observable of People near Death when they are delirious by a Fever, that they talk of moving; as it is of Those in a Calenture that they have their Heads run on green Fields.[1] The Variation from *Table* to *talked* is not of a very great Latitude, tho' we may still come nearer to the Traces of the Letters by restoring it thus:

—for his Nose was as sharp as a Pen, and a' babled of green Fields.

To *bable*, or *babble*, is to mutter or speak indiscriminately, like Children that cannot yet talk, or dying Persons when they are losing the Use of Speech. (137–8)

*　　*　　*

[Note 55. *Merchant of Venice*, 4.1.121 ff]

Bass. *Why dost thou whet thy knife so earnestly?*
Shyl. *To cut the forfeit from that bankrupt there.*
Grat. *Not on thy* SOUL! *but on thy* SOUL, *harsh Jew,*
Thou mak'st thy knife keen;—

I don't know what Ideas the *Editor* had affix'd to himself of the Poet's Sense here; for my own Part I can find None as the Text stands now. I dare venture to restore Him from the Authority of some of the *Folio* Editions, tho' I am obliged at the same Time to restore such a Sort of Conceit and Jingle upon two Words, alike in Sound but differing in Sense, as our Author ought to have blush'd for. But be That upon his own Head. If I restore his Meaning and his Words he himself is account-able to the Judges for writing them.

Bass. *Why dost thou whet thy Knife so earnestly?*
Shyl. *To cut the Forfeit from That Bankrupt there.*
Grat. *Not on thy* SOLE, *but on thy* SOUL, *harsh Jew,*

---

[1] 'Calenture: A disease incident to sailors within the tropics, characterised by a delirium in which, it is said, they fancy the sea to be green fields and desire to leap into it' (*OED*).

Thou mak'st thy Knife keen;—

i. e. 'Tho' thou thinkest that thou art whetting thy Knife on the *Sole* of thy Shoe yet it is upon thy *Soul*, thy immortal Part, that Thou doest it, mistaken, inexorable Man! The bare Intention of thy Cruelty is so unpardonable that it must bring thy very *Soul* into Hazard.'

I dare affirm, this is the very *Antithesis* of our Author; and I am the more confident because it was so usual with him to play on Words in this manner, and because in another of his Plays he puts the very same Words in Opposition to one another, and That from the Mouth of one of his serious Characters. See *Romeo and Juliet* [1.4.13 ff]:

> Merc. *Nay, gentle* Romeo, *we must have you dance.*
> Rom. *Not I, believe me; You have dancing Shoes*
> *With nimble* SOLES, *I have a* SOUL *of Lead,*
> *That stakes me to the Ground, I cannot move.*

He is at it again within three Lines after, upon two other Words agreeing in Sound; as we find the Passage in the second *Folio* and several other Editions, tho' Mr. POPE has not inserted it.

> *I am too* SORE *enpierced with his Shaft,*
> *To* SOARE *with his light Feathers.—*   [1.4.19 f]

But, as I said, these Jingles are perpetual with Him.

(168–9)

★   ★   ★

[Note 84. *Coriolanus,* 5.3.47 ff]

> Coriol. — You Gods I PRAY,
> *And the most noble Mother of the World*
> *Leave unsaluted.*

I dare say an old Corruption has possess'd this Passage, for two Reasons. In the first Place, whoever consults this Speech will find that he is talking fondly to his Wife, and not praying to the Gods at all. *Secondly,* if he were employ'd in his Devotions no Apology would be wanting for leaving his Mother unsaluted. The Poet's Intention was certainly this: *Coriolanus,* having been lavish in his Tendernesses and Raptures to his Wife, bethinks himself on the sudden that his Fondness to her had made him guilty of ill Manners in the Neglect of his Mother. Restore, as it certainly ought to be:

—You Gods! *I* PRATE,
And the most noble Mother of the World
Leave unsaluted.

Mr. DENNIS (than whom in my Opinion no Man in *England* better understands SHAKESPEARE), in his Alteration of this Play, whether he made the same Correction which I now do, certainly understood the Passage exactly with me. An undeniable Proof of this is an Appeal to the Change in Expression which he has put upon it:

But Oh! ye Gods, while fondly thus I talk,
See, the most noble Mother of the World
Stands unsaluted.

I question not but his Reason for varying the Expression was because *prate* is a Term ill-sounding in it self and mean in its Acceptation. Our Language was not so refin'd, tho' more masculine, in *Shakespeare*'s Days; and therefore (notwithstanding the κακοφωνία) when he is most serious he frequently makes Use of the Word. . . . (181)

★   ★   ★

[Note 93. *Macbeth*, 3.2.13 f]

We have SCORCH'D *the Snake, not kill'd it.—*
She'll close, *and be herself;* —

This is a Passage which has all along pass'd current thro' the Editions, and likewise upon the Stage; and yet, I dare affirm, is not our Author's Reading. What has a Snake *closing* again to do with its being *scorch'd*? Scorching would never either *separate* or *dilate* its Parts, but rather make them instantly *contract* and *shrivel*. SHAKESPEARE, I am very well persuaded, had this Notion in his Head (which how true in Fact, I will not pretend to determine), that if you cut a Serpent or Worm asunder in several Pieces there is such an unctious Quality in their Blood that the dismember'd Parts, being only plac'd near enough to touch one another, will cement and become as whole as before the Injury receiv'd. The Application of this Thought is to *Duncan*, the murther'd King, and his surviving Sons: *Macbeth* considers them so much as Members of the Father that tho' he has cut off the old Man he would say, he has not entirely kill'd him; but he'll cement and close again in the Lives of his Sons, to the Danger of *Macbeth*. If I am not deceiv'd, therefore, our Poet certainly wrote thus:

We have SCOTCH'D *the Snake, not kill'd it.—*
She'll close, and be her self;—

To *scotch*, however the Generality of our *Dictionaries* happen to omit the Word, signifies to *notch*, *slash*, *cut* with Twigs, Sword, *&c*, and so SHAKESPEARE more than once has used it in his Works. So *Coriolanus* [4.5.185 ff]: *He was too hard for him directly, to say the Troth on't: Before* Corioli, *he* SCOTCH'D *him, and notch'd him, like a Carbonado.*

And so again, *Antony and Cleopatra*, [4.7.9 f]

> *We'll beat them into Bench-Holes, I have yet*
> *Room for six* SCOTCHES *more.*

To shew how little we ought to trust *implicitly to Dictionaries* for *Etymologies* we need no better Proof than from BAILY in his Explication of the Term SCOTCH-Collops; he tells us, that it means Slices of Veal fry'd after the *Scotch* Manner. But, besides that that Nation are not over-famous for the Elegance of their Cookery it is more natural, and I dare say more true, to allow that it ought to be wrote SCOTCHT-Collops, i.e. Collops, or Slices *slash'd* cross and cross before they are put on the Coals. (185–6)

★   ★   ★

[Note 107. *Othello*, 4.1.23 ff]

> *What if I said, I'ad seen him do you Wrong?*
> *Or heard him say, as Knaves be such abroad,*
> *Who having by their own importunate Suit,*
> *Or voluntary Dotage of some Mistress,*
> Convinced, *or* SUPPLIED *them, cannot chuse*
> *But they must blab.—*

I could not have wish'd to conclude with a more remarkable Instance of *Corruption* or One that fell more closely within the Method which I propos'd to my self of *amending*. All the Editions concur in the Reading, and yet I'll be bold to say 'tis neither *Sense*, nor *intelligible*, nor conveys our Author's *Sentiment* as it stands: so that it may fairly be look'd upon to have been one of his *Loci desperati*. His Meaning is undoubtedly this, that there are some such long-tongued Knaves in the World who, if they thro' the Force of Importunity obtain a Favour from their Mistress, or if thro' her own Fondness they make her pliant to their

Desires, cannot help boasting of their Success. Restore it, without the least Scruple, thus:

> *Who having by their own importunate Suit,*
> *Or voluntary Dotage of some Mistress,*
> Convinc'd, *or* SUPPLED *them, they cannot chuse*
> *But they must blab.*

I have already observ'd in the Course of these Sheets that it is usual with SHAKESPEARE, thro' Negligence or Licentiousness, to change his Numbers, as he does here: so no more need be said on that Head. To *supple*, 'tis well known, is to make *pliant* and *flexible*; and is particularly a Term in *Surgery* when any Part, swoln and stiff, is by *Fomentations*, &c. *reduced*, and made *soft* and *pliable*. To *convince*, here, is peculiar in its Sense; it is not, as in the common Acceptation, to make sensible of the Truth of any Thing by Reasons and Arguments, but to *overcome, get the better of*, &c. As the Usage of the Term in this Sort is one of the Author's Singularities, I'll produce two or three Passages in Support of This before us, where it bears the same Sense.

Macbeth, [4.3.141 ff]

> *Ay, Sir, there are a Crew of wretched Souls*
> *That stay his Cure; their Malady* convinces
> *The great Assay of Art.*

Love's Labour's Lost, [5.2.732 ff]

> *And tho' the mourning Brow of Progeny*
> *Forbid the smiling Courtesy of Love,*
> *The holy Suit which fain it would* convince, *&c.*

And so in *Cymbeline,* more aptly to the Place for which I bring these Authorities;

> *Your* Italy *containes None so accomplish'd a Courtier to* convince *the Honour of my Mistress.* [1.4.90 f]

[CONCLUSION]—I have endeavour'd to acquit my self of the Promises made in my *Introduction,* and produc'd and corrected *Errors* throughout the Poet, numerous when we consider This as a SPECIMEN only, of no Number when compar'd with that unequal Quantity which remain behind in Store to make our Author perfect. I may, indeed, say with Mr. POPE that I have gone thro' this Work *with more Labour than I can expect Thanks.* I have run a Risque, and must wait the Sentence of the *Publick* whether I have gone upon a mistaken View of Reputation or whether I have done any Thing to set SHAKESPEARE in a clearer Light than his *Editors* have hitherto done. It is upon this Issue I shall be determin'd whether I have already written too much on the Subject or whether I may promise my self Encouragement in prosecuting a Design that favours more of *publick Spirit* than *private Interest.*

I ought to be in some Pain for the Figure that these Sheets may make, this being the *first Essay* of *literal Criticism* upon any Author in the ENGLISH Tongue. The Alteration of a *Letter,* when it restores Sense to a corrupted Passage in a *learned Language,* is an Atchievement that brings Honour to the *Critick* who advances it: and Dr. BENTLEY will be remember'd to Posterity for his Performances of this Sort as long as the World shall have any Esteem for the Remains of *Menander* and *Philemon.* But I no more pretend to do Justice to that Great Man's Character than I would be thought to set my own poor Merit, or the Nature of *this* Work, in Competition with *his.* . . . (192–3)

75. Nicholas Amhurst(?) on Cardinal Wolsey

November 1727

From the *Country Journal or the Craftsman,* 72 (18 November 1727).

The *Craftsman,* a remarkably successful political journal, was founded on 5 December 1726 by Nicholas Amhurst (1697–1742), and received many contributions from Henry Saint-John, Viscount Bolingbroke (1678–1751), and William Pulteney, Earl of Bath (1684–1764). The main organ of the opposition to Walpole, the journal was packed with literary and historical exempla of political corruption, for which Shakespeare was frequently used.

To CALEB D'ANVERS, *Esq;*

SIR,

I went the other Night to the Play called *The Life of King Henry VIII*, written by *Shakespeare*, designing not only to treat my Eyes with a *Coronation* in Miniature and see away my *three Shillings*, but to improve my Understanding by beholding my Countrymen who have been near two Centuries in Ashes revive again, and act and talk in the same Manner as they then did. Such a Representation as This, given us by so great a Master, throws one's Eye back upon our Ancestors; and while I am present at the Action I cannot help believing my self a real Spectator and Contemporary with our old *Huff-bluff English* Monarch, *Henry VIII*, so much does the useful Delusion of a well-written Play delight and instruct us beyond the cold Narrations of a dry Historian. But the principal Figure, and that which stood fullest out to me, was the great *Minister*. There you see an ambitious, proud, bad Man of Parts, in the Possession of a wise and brave Prince, amassing Wealth, taxing the griev'd Commons, and abusing his Trust and Power to support his Vanity and Luxury. As it is usual with this Sort of *great Men*, all the Errors *He* commits are his *Master's* and every Thing that may be praise-worthy *his own*. We find a very remarkable Instance of This in the second Scene of this Play. Good Queen *Katharine* intercedes with the King that some *heavy Taxes* might be mitigated, which the People complained were levied upon them by the Order of this *wicked Minister*; and she particularly lays before the *King* an Account in what Manner his Subjects suffered for want of Encouragement in the *woollen Manufactures*, which *Trade*, tho' so beneficial to *England*, was *almost ruined*. The *King*, very justly alarmed and moved with the Recital of these Hardships which his People laboured under, commands the *Cardinal* to write into the several Counties forthwith, and gives his Orders that these *Taxes* should immediately cease, and free Pardon be granted to all who had denied the Payment of them; upon which the *Minister* turns to *Cromwell* and gives his Instructions in these Words:

> —*A Word with you.*
> *Let there be Letters writ to ev'ry Shire,*
> *Of the* King's *Grace and Pardon. The griev'd Commons*
> *Hardly conceive of Me. Let it be noised,*
> *That thro'* OUR INTERCESSION *this Revokement*
> *And Pardon comes.* [1.2.102 ff]

443

There cannot be an Instance of a more shocking Insolence. The *Minister* injures, and the *Minister* forgives. He wrongs the People, and is so gracious as to forgive the People whom he has wrong'd. What a Figure does a great and a brave Prince make under the Wing and Tutelage of such a Servant! A *Minister* like This *is a Spunge* (as the same excellent Author says in *Hamlet*) *who sucks up the King's Countenance, his Rewards, his Authorities.*

Shakespeare has chosen to bring this *Minister* upon the Stage in his full Lustre, when he was in high Favour and just after the *Peace* and *League* concluded with *France*; as we may observe in the first *Scene*, when the Duke of *Buckingham, Norfolk*, and the Lord *Abergavenny*, talking of the Transactions in *France* and the *Treaty* then lately finished by the *great Man*, the Duke of *Norfolk* says

> *The* Peace *between the* French *and us not values*
> *The* Cost, *that did conclude it.* [1.1.88 f]

Buckingham replies, the People then prophesied the sudden Breach of it; and *Norfolk* adds

> *Thus* France *hath flaw'd the League, and hath attach'd*
> *Our Merchants Goods.* [1.1.96 f]

And in the next Lines *Abergavenny* calls it

> *A* Title *only of* Peace, *and purchas'd too*
> *At a* superfluous Rate. [1.1.98 f]

In the next Scene *Buckingham* describes the *Minister* as partaking of the Natures of a *Fox* and a *Wolf* (equally ravenous and subtle, prone to Mischief and able to perform it) and compares this *Peace* to *a Glass that broke in rinsing*; and then he says

> *This cunning* Cardinal
> *Th' Articles of the* Combination *drew*
> *As himself pleased, and they were* ratify'd
> *As he cry'd, thus let be, to as much End*
> *As give a Crutch to the Dead.* [1.1.168 ff]

A little after This he says the *Emperor* grew jealous of this new Amity between *France* and us for that

> *From this League*
> *Harms peep'd that menac'd him. He privately*
> *Deals with our* Cardinal; *and, as I trow,*

Which I do well, for I am sure the Emperor
Paid ere he promised, whereby his Suit
Was granted ere 'twas ask'd; but when the Way was made
And paved with Gold; *the* Emperor *thus desired*
That he would alter the King's Course
And break the aforesaid Peace. Let the King know
(*As soon he shall by me*) *that thus the* Cardinal
Does buy and sell his Honour as he pleases,
And for his own Advantage. [1.1.182 ff]

At length we behold this *great Administrator* declining. The Favour of the King is gone, and the full Hunt is just ready to open when the Lord Chamberlain admonishes them to be cautious, lest they should not carry it against him; for, says He,

If you cannot
Bar his Access to the King, *never attempt*
Any thing on him; for he has a Witchcraft
Over the King in's Tongue. [3.2.16 ff]

But *Norfolk* replies

—*The King hath found*
Matter against him that for ever mars
The Honey of his Language. [3.2.20 ff]

The King, now satisfy'd that this *overgrown Servant* had acted unfaithfully, gives way to the Voice of his People and his own Interest and Honour, and dismisses him. He is accused on several Articles, *viz.* making *Treaties* without the King's Leave or Knowledge; squandering and embezzling the *publick Treasure,* &c. He is found guilty of a *Præmunire,* and all his Goods seized into the King's Hand. And now this Man, who made so very bad a Figure as a *Minister,* makes a very good one as a *Philosopher.* He became his Disgrace very well; and *Shakespeare* has put some Words into his Mouth which all *good Ministers* will read with Pleasure and *bad ones* with Pain. *Wolsey* says to *Cromwell,*

Mark thou my Fall, and That which ruin'd me.
Cromwell, *I charge thee fling away* Ambition.
By that Sin fell the Angels. How can Man then
(*The Image of his Maker*) *hope to win it?*
Love thyself last. Cherish those Hearts that hate thee.

* 445

Corruption *gains no more than* Honesty.
Still in thy right Hand carry gentle Peace,
To silence envious Tongues. Be just, and fear not.
Let all the Ends thou aim'st at be thy Country's;
Thy God's *and* Truth's.   [3.2.439 ff]

Thus, Sir, I have thrown together some of the Out-lines by which
the Character of this ambitious, wealthy, bad *Minister* is described in the
very Words of *Shakespeare*. Reflecting People may observe from this
Picture how like human Nature is in her Workings at all Times.

76. George Adams, Shakespeare and tragedy

1729

From the Preface to Volume I, *Sophocles' Tragedies, translated*
from the Greek, 2 vols, 1729.

George Adams (1698?–1768?), sometime Fellow of St John's
College, Cambridge, published various sermons and religious
works, and wrote the *Life of Socrates: an Historical Tragedy* (1746).

But here it must be understood, that I only by Tragedy mean those
of *Sophocles* and *Euripides*, and such as are built upon their Plan, not
such Stuff as ignorant Poetasters have imposed upon the World for
Tragedy since their Times. Who, studying more how to fill their
Pockets than improve their Hearers, chose to compose such Pieces as
would gratify Mens extravagant Humours, as better serving their
avaritious Purposes.

This Avarice is a Fault of which not Dossennus only was guilty, of
whom Horace gives this Character, *Epist. lib. 2.*

> *Gestit enim nummum in Loculos demittere; post hoc*
> *Securus cadat an recto stet Fabula talo.*[1]

---

[1] *Epistles*, 2.1.175 f: 'Yes, he is eager to drop a coin into his pocket and, that done, he
cares not whether his play fall or stand square on its feet.' This was Horace's judgment
of Plautus.

If the Praetor paid him well for his Pains in composing his Pieces, he was careless what Reputation they had afterwards in the World. I am afraid the celebrated *Shakespeare* cannot be intirely acquitted from having a Share in this Charge, which perhaps was the Occasion of so many gross Irregularities in that Poet, which nothing but his other Excellencies can excuse.

This Avarice of the Poets brought a Scandal upon the Art in general, and gave Ground to many Objections against it; which, abstracted from its Abuse, is one of the noblest Arts that ever was invented. (Sig a₂ʳ⁻ᵛ)

★   ★   ★

The other Objection against Tragick Poetry is that it is very much abused. This must certainly be granted; yet this Objection, however true, cannot lie against what I here contend for; since, as I said before, I would be here understood to mean only such Tragedies as are built upon the Plan of the Antients, *Sophocles* and *Euripides*, and according to those Rules down laid by *Aristotle* and *Horace*; not such abominable Stuff as our *English* Theatres have been crowded with since their Times, where the Spectators have been entertained with tedious Scenes of Courtship, abusive Language to the Clergy, ridiculous Contradictions, abominable Fustian; yea, we have Instances of their prophane Flights of Thought little better than Blasphemy. These were Faults which *Dryden* and *Lee* fell into, who have been followed herein by several other Poets since their Time, for which they are justly, though severely, scourged by the ingenious Mr. *Collier*. What an abominable Character doth *Dryden* give us of *Nourmahal*, in that Scene where she discovers her unnatural Love for *Aurengzebe*! How doth she talk, like a Woman lost to all Shame and Modesty! The Antients never ran into Errors of this Nature, for though *Phædra* in *Euripides* is in Love with *Hippolytus* yet her Honour throughout the whole Play so far prevails over her Love that it ties her Tongue from the least immodest Expression.

Shakespeare, however faulty in other Things, yet had none of this; we do not find his Plays stuffed with any such tender Sentiments between the different Sex before Marriage, which must be shocking and uneasie to the fair Sex, and offensive to that Modesty which is no less an Ornament to them than their Beauty. *Juliet* and *Desdemona* are both married before they make any Acknowledgments of their Love. (Sig. b₅ᵛ–b₇ʳ)

★   ★   ★

447

But to come to the Writers of our own Nation, the divine *Shakespeare* was the first who began this Art among us, and indeed who ended it too, for he has gain'd so much Praise in it that he hath scarce left any for those who come after him. And he is so much the more to be admir'd because he perform'd what he did without the Help of Learning; nor indeed did he need it, he could look within himself and there find all the Images of Nature perfectly painted. And *Ben Jonson* and *Fletcher*, who were his Contemporaries, tho' their Plots were generally more regular yet the Age in which they lived never esteemed them equal with him. As for Mr. *Dryden*, Dramatick Poetry was not his Talent, tho' in one of his Pieces, *viz. The World well lost*, he so well joins the Regularity of *Ben Jonson* with the Wit of *Shakespeare*, that I know not whether it be not the best of all his Writings of that kind. (Sig. c5^v–c6^r)

77. Unsigned essay, Shakespeare and the actors defended

1729

From *An Answer to Mr. Pope's Preface to Shakespeare. In a Letter to a Friend. Being a Vindication of the Old Actors who were the Publishers and Performers of that Author's Plays. Whereby The Errors of their Edition are Further Accounted for, and some Memoirs of Shakespeare and Stage-History of His Time are inserted, which were never before Collected and Publish'd. By a strolling player* (1729).

This pamphlet is signed 'Anti-Scriblerus Histrionicus' and is traditionally ascribed to one 'John Roberts', of whom nothing seems to be known. The textual arguments, however, especially the reconstruction of the ways in which the texts of the plays were affected by theatrical conditions, are so cogent that it is tempting to ascribe it to Lewis Theobald. Compare, for instance, his discussion of 'theatrical copy' in the preface to his edition, pp. 484 ff below. The awareness, too, of the increasingly high social status of the Elizabethan actor shows a historical sense extremely rare in this period, while a detailed acquaintance with the various editions of the Quartos is equally rare, and only matched by Theobald at this time.

. . . [I] therefore think it as utterly unreasonable to call *Shakespeare's* Judgment in Question as an Author, because he was an Actor, as to degrade Mr. *Pope's* Capacity as a Poet because he is *Pope* the Editor.

To reconcile what he calls here *Shakespeare's right* Judgment as a *Player* and his *wrong* Judgment as a *Poet* is far above my reach; I shall therefore refer it to those wiser Heads who can perfectly understand it. I always thought, in regard of Dramatick Poetry as well as every thing else, that Judgment was Judgment let who will be the Possessor of it, and when 'tis *Right* it can't be *Wrong*. But I find I was very much mistaken, for 'tis a Maxim, it seems, that when a Player has the *Impudence* to have any *Judgment* of Writing it must be *Wrong* of Course.

And therefore my differing in Opinion from this Gentleman in so material a Point must be ascrib'd to the general Calamity of wrong Judging that attends us all: that is to say, *to my right Judgment as a Player.* Poet and Player in his Thoughts are inconsistent, and 'tis impossible for any Person to have any Quantity of judicial Knowledge in Poetry if he ever engages on the Stage. Tho' he has the Advantage of Classick Education and the Politest Conversation, yet as being a Player it is not *rightly* Judgment in him; for all Judgment is engross'd into the Keeping of the Poets only, and if they are all of his Opinion they are resolv'd not to quit Possession or spare the Players the least Share.

I protest I am so dull of Apprehension I can't understand what it is he imputes to *Shakespeare's right Judgment as a Player.* For his complying with the Wit in Fashion and pleasing the reigning Humour certainly belongs to *his wrong Judgment as a poet,* as does every thing else, in my mind, that *Pope* has particularly laid to his Charge. And the chief Article against his wrong Judgment as a Poet consists of his *Super-fœtations,* and herein this Editor follows *Jonson* in his *Discoveries,* who shamefully brands *Shakespeare with falling into some things that cou'd not escape Laughter,* and very scandalously makes a false Quotation and mis-represents his Meaning.[1] But even these *Jonson* lays expressly on *Shakespeare,* and only charges the Players with *Mis-judgment in com-mending their Friend wherein he most faulted.* Yet our present Editor, still dissatisfied with this, wou'd fain acquit *Shakespeare* and load the poor Players with whatever proceeds from *his wrong Judgment as a Poet,* as is manifest by repeated Reflections dispers'd throughout the whole Work for that Purpose.

By these Men it was thought a Praise to *Shakespeare,* that he scarce ever blotted a Line. This they industriously propagated, as appears from what we are told by *Ben. Jonson* in his *Discoveries*— 'I remember (says *Jonson*) The Players have often mention'd it as an Honour to *Shakespeare, that he never blotted out a Line,* to which I answer'd, *Wou'd he had blotted out a Thousand!* Which they thought a malevolent Speech.'

That this shou'd be condemn'd by *Jonson* and *Pope* as a Fault first in *Shakespeare,* and next in the Players for commending it, is highly un-reasonable. According to the Nature of the Thing it ought to stand in his Favour as they intended it. For it is to be Understood in plain Terms no otherwise than their bare Account and Character (and I

[1] Cf. Volume 1, pp. 25 f.

believe was never used any otherwise) of his extensive Genius and
Exuberance of Fancy, that his Thoughts flow'd so swift upon him (*as
no Author ever had such a prodigious Compass*), he cou'd not spare Time to
correct at the Juncture of Penning them but always committed to
Paper what rude Ideas presented themselves in his vast Imagination, and
deferr'd their Improvement and Correction to his disengaged Hours
and a more leisure Recollection. And that this was his Practise is greatly
confirm'd by the improv'd Editions of those Pieces (as Mr. *Pope*
acknowledges) which were publish'd in his Life time, and yet this does
not destroy or gainsay the Character given of him by his Fellow-
Players, *That he never blotted out a Line*, at his Time of Writing and
Composing the Work. Notwithstanding Mr. *Pope* affirms, *there never
was a more groundless Report*. These Men no doubt were very well
acquainted with the Method and Custom of their Brother Comedian,
who was daily at Study for their Stage, and for the Course of Years of
his Writing for and belonging to the Theaters not Superior in Fortune
or Fame to the Rest, and of Consequence not so reserv'd but his
Companions well knew his Manner of Writing. And yet *Pope*'s contradicting this Report of the Players and affirming it to be groundless
still allows that *Shakespeare* did blot out and correct (and this he mainly
strengthens himself by several Instances, that is, he gives the Names of
some Plays, *The Merry Wives of Windsor, Henry V and VI*, and *Hamlet*,
which He *new Writ, extreamly improv'd*, and *enlarg'd to almost as much
again as at first*, so that you must needs be so good-natur'd to allow
Shakespeare's putting in some Thousands of Lines to be an unquestionable Proof of his putting out the same Quantity, or else Mr. *Pope* and I,
sic parvis componere, &c. will lose our Aim); and therefore Mr. *Jonson*
was to blame not to prove this False before, yet he grants it to be *Fact*
but *culpable!*

    In the end I don't find any Necessity for either of their Speeches;
either JONSON's *Wou'd he had blotted out a Thousand!* or POPE's *There
never was a more groundless Report!* The first I declare, with those *mis-
judging Players* was *a malevolent Speech*; and as to the latter I deny *the
undeniable Evidences to the Contrary*. They are both Malevolent enough
to the Actors, for *Jonson* inclines to say it as much in direct Opposition
of Opinion to the Players as in Detraction of *Shakespeare*; and *Pope*
pronounces his for no other View or Reason than to give the Players in
general the positive Lye. (6–9)

*   *   *

[Pope alleges that Shakespeare's actors] . . . were a Parcel of *Tavern-Haunters* and *Ale-Drinkers*, and were glad to get into the *Butteries*, poor Rogues, I warrant you, with the *Butlers*, as well as *the Stewards*! But how comes it they were in general so very Ignorant and Stupid? Why, because *The best Playhouses were then but Inns and Taverns, and the Top of the Profession were then meer Players, not Gentlemen of the Stage: they were led into the Buttery by the Steward, not placed at the Lord's Table, or the Lady's Toilette.*— Scandalously has he depriv'd this Old Set of Actors of all and every Qualification of Mind befitting a Player and requisite for the Business. He takes away their Education and Conversation, delivers them utterly void of Understanding, not Masters even of Common Sense or indu'd with any Natural or Acquir'd Parts, and in the End is very loath to afford them a competent Knowledge of their Mother-Tongue, much less of an other dead or living Language: *Their* French *is as bad as their* Latin, *their very* Welsh *is false; and Prose from Verse they did not know, but accordingly printed one for t'other.*— Why, what a Tribe of wretched Fellows must these be! And after all this, I wonder what they really did understand? They were *wrong Judges* of Poetry! They knew *Nothing* of Playing! They had no Comfort of polite Conversation! Nor had they any further *Taste of Life or Letters* than what they cou'd pick up over a Pot of Beer with their unthinking *Brethren* in the *Inns* where they play'd, or in taking a sparing Bottle of my Lord's Wine *in the Buttery with his* very learned *Steward.*— Oh, but this Invective against the Comedians of old conveys no Scandal to the Gentlemen of the later Stages, and worthier Followers of this Profession. For he pays a Compliment to their better Understandings and very generously allows them the Credit and Satisfaction (I won't say he's sorry for't) *of a Familiarity and Dearness with Persons of the first Rank of Nobility, and all other the superior Advantages they Enjoy, both in Education and Conversation.*— You may have forgot the Paragraph, and therefore I transcribe it at length. [Quotes 'Having been forc'd' to 'people of the first condition'; above pp. 412 f.]

But how comes all this Complaisance to the Modern Stagers? Only because in His very Edition of *Shakespeare* he is greatly indebted to the *Theatrical Improvements* which They (by being, according to his Confession, something better Judges of Men and Manners than the former) have redeem'd from Oblivion, either from *Antique* Editions or remnant *Manuscripts*, many of which (in what we call the Stock Plays) he has borrow'd and publish'd as his own. Tho' at the same Time he won't allow *these Gentlemen of the Stage* to be any Judges of what is *right*, and brings (for with a certain *Innuendo* he every where uses it in the *present Tense*) all their Judgment to that short Point, of pleasing the present Humour and complying with the Wit in Fashion. They may be—and he infers they are—better Judges as Players, but still it comes to the short Point above of being no better than *Taylors are of what is Graceful*, and their *right Judgment as Players* must be *wrong* in regard *of the Poets*. Besides there is no certain Grounds for taxing *These or Them* with such frequent *Interpolations*, tho' this calumnious Editor has so often charg'd *Both* with Innovations of this kind, *proceeding from one Source, The Ignorance of the Players*, both as his *Actors* and his *Editors*. And as to the Article of their *shortening* some *Scenes* as well as that of the *Additions* of Scenes, Speeches, Incidents, Words, &c., no doubt have been from the Poets own Choice or Consent, weigh'd with Judgment (be it *right* or *wrong*) as Poet and Player. For tho' his Plays were not all *publish'd* till after his Death we may conclude they were all *perform'd* in his Life; and thereupon 'tis reasonable to think that what ever Scenes are lopp'd off and neglected (even to this Day) in the Representation, were then, and are now serv'd so, from some traditional Foundation and Authority from *Shakespeare*. And whilst we can impute it to this in part, or intirely so, I can find no Reason substantial enough to charge it on the Ignorance, &c. of the Players. Especially since such Loppings pass with general Approbation of our Auditors, and much to the Advantage of our Author; which is evident from the Omissions of *Hamlet*, *Othello*, &c, and I can produce this *Editor's* Allowance of the same, tho' upon this Spot he can't be reconciled to their cutting out or putting in in any Degree.

In special Answer to the Articles alledged in general I shall shew what Foundation he had for all that he maintains against our Theatrical Predecessors, and Demonstrate how just he is in his History and Character of their Capacities and Condition by setting before you the most considerable and authentick MEMOIRS of those *Antique Players* who were of the same Stage, or at least of the same *Age*, with SHAKESPEARE and his *Original Editors*.

It is allow'd that, as the Reign of Queen *Elizabeth* is one of the most shining Parts of our History, and an Age of which *Englishmen* are accustom'd to speak with a particular Pride and Delight, it is also remarkable for having been Fruitful in Eminent *Geniuses* of very different Kinds. And among the rest flourish'd several of Great

Capacity in the Practice of Acting and Stage-Playing, whose Excellencies stand recorded in a particular Manner by the grave Author of the *Chronicle* of *England* among the Heroes and distinguish'd Men of that Age, and were likewise in so great Esteem with that Learned Man Sir *Francis Walsingham* that he procured *Her Majesty* to entertain *Twelve* of them as her *Comedians* and *Servants*, and establish'd them in *Sallaries* accordingly. (12-16)

[The author then gives biographies, with contemporary tributes, of Alleyne, Armin, Burbage, Field, Kempe and other actors.]

HEMINGE and CONDELL.

These two PLAYERS were *Shakespeare*'s EDITORS, and made considerable Figures according to their several Capacities in the Profession. There is scarce one *Drama* of those Days without their Names. They were of the chief Rank of Performers in *Jonson*'s, *Massinger*'s, and *Shakespeare*'s Plays; and, as I think, *Condell* was a *Comedian* and *Heminge* a *Tragedian*. The last in his later Years became Master or Manager of the Playhouse he belong'd to, as appears by a Speech in one of BEN's Plays. And besides their Acting they both follow'd Printing.

This is all I know historically of them, in relation of their Acting; but 'tis now requisite to say something in their particular Defence as *Printers* and *Publishers*.

'Tis true, they were the Persons who collected the Plays of *Shakespeare* and publish'd them together in a *Folio* Edition 1623, wherein it can't be deny'd but there are innumerable Mistakes; all which I believe may be indifferently accounted for without any Discredit to them or Shame to their Fraternity. 'Tis not to be depended upon that *Shakespeare* ever publish'd any one of his Plays himself, tho' he frequently revised and altered several of their Copies. But the Case was with him as with Mr. *Heywood* last mention'd, [who] declar'd in the Preface to one of his Plays *That he used to part with his Copies to the Players, and therefore suppos'd he had no further Right to print them without their Consent.* Nor could it be agreeable to his Inclination as a Player to make a Publication of them, for it seems it was then thought against the peculiar Profit of the *Houses* to have the Plays abroad in the World, and a main Point of Policy to preserve them from the Press. And indeed 'tis very possible that this was what chiefly contributed to the Support of so many *Stages* at a Time, the Town having no other Opportunity of enjoying the Writings of those *Dramatick* Poets but by paying the *Players* for the

Representations of them. And this I take to be the Reason that so few of *this* AUTHOR were printed in his Life-time. Our *Editor* can find but eleven, and some of them 'had two or more Editions by *different* Printers, with Heaps of Trash *different* from the other, which he fancies was occasion'd by their being taken from *different* Copies, belonging to *different* Play-houses.' And therefore I conclude that what Copies were exhibited from the Press must have been taken by the Ear, and absolutely printed without the Correction or Knowledge of the *Author*. This certainly was the Case, for 'tis granted that the several *Playhouses* did often act the self-same Plays at the same Time frequently, with Allowance of their Authors, tho' there were then no printed Copies of the same. Probably it might be thus, that when a Play had gone thro' it's *Run* (as we call it) at the Theatre where originally perform'd, the other Companies did purchase and procure a *written* Copy of the same from the *Poet* or the *Players* whose *Property* it was; and such *Right* was transferr'd and *assign'd* accordingly to such *Purchasers* for the Use of *their Stage*, with the same Privilege of performing as belong'd to the Original Company. Or sometimes, perhaps, the *contending Theatres* obtain'd, by indirect Methods, the *Transcripts* of *Plays* belonging to the *other* Stages. And from so frequent and double Representations it is rational to think that the meaner Class of Printers (who were not under such Restraints and Laws against Pyracies of the Press which are now in Force) did exhibit surreptitious Copies, taken by the Ear or by other fraudulent Means. And from hence it is that *all those first Editions of* SHAKESPEARE's *Plays are in every Page so scandalously false spelt, and the learned and unusual Words so intollerably mangled.* And notwithstanding some single Editions have *Shakespeare's* Name to them for the *Revisal* and *Corrections* in the *Title-pages,* that may be only the Artifice of those Booksellers, and perhaps as truly *grounded* as 'tis *continu'd.* Concerning which, take this singular Proof: the first Edition of *Henry IV* [Part I] (printed 1599) made Use of by Mr. *Pope* has the Words in the Title-page *Newly corrected by* WILLIAM SHAKESPEARE; and this same *Newly corrected by* WILLIAM SHAKESPEARE is convey'd down thro' all the Quarto Editions of that Play to the last printed (before the *Folio*) in 1622, six Years after his Death; and even this last (which I have by me) is without the Division of the Acts. So that it is as credible he corrected the *first* as he *Newly* did the *last,* after being dead so many Years. If they had the Impudence to steal the Copies they would hardly be afraid, or asham'd, to put out fresh Editions under the Title of his *New* Corrections, whenever there were any *Alterations* made by him in the

Original Copies lodg'd in the *Theatres* and made apparent by publick Performance. So that, according to this Observation and several other corroborating Circumstances, I infer that *Shakespeare* never publish'd any one Play himself, or even corrected it for the Press, or was any one *Edition* printed from his own original Manuscript. What then can be said for *Heminge* and *Condell*'s Collection? They declare theirs to be purg'd from the Errors of the former Editions, which were all stolen and surreptitious. Now Mr. *Pope* acknowledges this to be true as to the literal Errors, but in all other Respects 'tis far worse, he says, than the *Quarto's*. How then is this to be reconcil'd? Either their Plays must be printed from other pirated and corrupt Copies or else, if they had the Originals of *Shakespeare*, they must be guilty of all the Faults, by *arbitrary Additions, Expunctions, Transpositions of Scenes and Lines, Confusion of Characters and Persons, wrong Applications of Speeches,* and the monstrous Heap of Crimes drawn up by this EDITOR.

To clear this up a little I shall beg Leave to look upon these Men, for a while, only as *Printers* and *Publishers*, without any Regard of their *Playing*. In collecting these Plays they were under the Difficulty of gathering them from separate Theatres and different Possessors. For several of his Plays were compos'd for the Use of different Houses; and tho', as I observ'd before, that sometimes two or more Companies had on Purchase an equal Right of playing the same Pieces, or by other Ways did practise it, yet the sole Power of publishing every Tragedy and Comedy, &c, must be vested legally in the primitive Place of acting it. You may see by *Jonson*'s Folio that his Plays were acted by different Setts of People; and I think I can make it appear that the *List* of *Chief Actors* prefix'd to *Shakespeare*'s were never all of *One* Company. But I suppose it to be universally granted already that the original Performance of these Plays in Question were at separate Places, and by distinct Companies; if so, you will soon conceive the Trouble and Difficulty these two Men labour'd under in recovering SHAKESPEARE'S *Works* after his Decease. The Materials they had for it may be reckon'd under these Heads.

I. TRUE MANUSCRIPTS, belonging to their own Company (which was the very Body of Comedians this Author was a Member of) wherein perhaps were several *Places, Scenes, Speeches, Sentences, Lines,* and *Words,* &c. *shifted* and *chang'd, alter'd* and *corrected, obliterated, interlin'd,* and *interpolated,* of the Poet's own Work, as by repeated Representations he found Occasion to do himself or direct it to be done; besides being burden'd with *Marginal Quotations* for the *Entries* of the *Characters,* and

Directions for the *Property-Men's Moveables*, and other *Uses* of the *Prompter*; all which were troublesome to the Press, and caused several Absurdities.

2. FALSE TRANSCRIPTS of *other Company's*, either from the *Errors* of *Copyers* (occasion'd by *Alterations*) or *worn-out Originals* (where the Text was nigh illegible or very obscure); besides the Accidents above.

3. INCORRECT FIRST COPIES, of some *other of his Plays*, that were not in *general Acting* but only subsisted for the *Run*, and receiv'd not the Success to be the *Stock Plays*; which in *their Days*, perchance, were almost irrecoverable and very likely by *Fragments* only, and even those in the Hands of Persons remote from the Stage.

4. SOME PRINTED PLAYS (of which there were no Manuscripts existing), that they could by no other Means insert in their Volume than in making use of the *common Editions*, corrupt as they were, being highly necessary to make up the Collection.

After all this must be consider'd, too, the Inaccuracy and unpolish'd State of the Press in those Days, which is easily discover'd by the impure Impressions of other Plays (especially since we have this Gentleman's Opinion for it), *There being at that Time no Correctors of the Press, or such as were very illiterate*. These are the proper Considerations which, if justly weigh'd in their different Natures and Kinds, might have made *Aristotle* and *Cicero*, as well as *Shakespeare* (had their Works undergone the same Fate), appear to want Sense as well as Learning, and not the Reflections he has unjustly cast upon the Players as Actors and Editors. For I would fain be resolv'd of this Gentleman whether these Works might not have pass'd to us in as bad a Condition thro' Persons Hands of another Profession, who were to collect them thro' all the Disadvantages here sum'd up? 'Tis highly probable, I think, if the whole *Body*, or a *Committee* of the *Players* had apply'd themselves duely as *Editors* they could have produc'd a much perfecter Edition, and one that would not have disgrac'd their Judgments; and therefore it was negligent in them not to do it in Honour of their departed Brother, who had been the main Support of their Stages. But as they did not engage themselves in this Affair the Trash of these Plays cannot be imputed to them in gross for being his Actors; nor can we charge these *two Men* further than Tradesmen and *Publishers*, and as *Proprietors* only of these *purchas'd Copies*. (28–34)

78. Lewis Theobald on editing Shakespeare

1729-30

From letters to Warburton printed in *Illustrations of the Literary History of the Eighteenth Century*, ed. John Nichols, vol. II (1817).

[From a letter dated 8 April 1729] Your last most obliging Epistle is come to hand, together with the inclosed explanation of part of Edgar's madness. As you are so good to say I shall see the Book touching these Popish Impostures,[1] I shall with great impatience expect it remitted. . . .

I scarce need to observe to you, Sir, that *I ever labour to make the smallest deviations that I can possibly from the text; never to alter at all where I can by any means explain a passage into sense; nor ever by any emendations to make the Author better when it is probable the text came from his own hands.* (209-10)

* * *

[18 December 1729; on *The Taming of the Shrew*, 1.2.109 ff] 'An he begin once, he'll rail in his ROPE-tricks': From the terms following in the context, *throw a figure* and *disfigure*, I had once conjectured we should read, in his TROPE-tricks. But, I am afraid, the guess is not worth a farthing. (334)

* * *

[3 January 1730; on *King Lear*, 4.6.155 ff]

> *Lear.* Thou hast seen a farmer's dog bark at a beggar?
> *Clo.* Ay, Sir.
> *Lear.* And the creature run from the cur? there thou might'st behold the great image of authority: &c.

Thus is this charming piece of satire to be pointed, from the old books. But I have produced it likewise upon another account. This

---

[1] See Theobald's subsequent note on *King Lear*, 3.4.48 f, pp. 507 f below. In a later letter (2 December 1730; pp. 490 f) Theobald is able to inform Warburton who wrote this pamphlet.

figure, and method of imaging from absent circumstances, looks very like an imitation of the Antients. Minturnus, in his most accurate treatise *De Poeta*, speaking of these figures, I remember, subjoins this description of them:—*Quæ aut imaginem, aut quasi imaginem habet, aut collationem, &c.* and gives his opinion that they cannot but entertain.

Plautus has a good deal of this imagery. The following passage, to me, has a great resemblance to our Author's. Menæch. Act I. Scene 2, v. 34:

Men. DIC mihi, NUNQUAM TU VIDISTI tabulam pictam in Pariete, Ubi aquila catamitum raperet, aut ubi Venus Adoneum?

Pen. SÆPE. Sed quid istæ Picturæ ad me attinent?

Men. AGE, ME ASPICE.[1] (382)

★ ★ ★

[*Ibid.*; having completed *King Lear*] And now, dear Sir, I have done with this Play and Volume. I wish we were as well over the historical sett. The two *Henry IVs*, *Henry V*, and *Henry VIII* are full of entertainment and fine things. *John*, *Richard II* and *Richard III* are of the middling stamp: but the three parts of *Henry VI* scarce come up to that character. (386)

★ ★ ★

[20 January 1730; on *Henry V*, 3.4.47 ff] 'et le COUNT': 'I read COUN, a corrupt pronunciation of GOWN, by which Alice approaches the French word CON, cunnus: as *foot* does to *foutre*.' (427)

★ ★ ★

[29 January 1730] . . . on to *Richard III*, a Play that, unless Shakespeare's, would be as execrable to me as the character of its Hero. . . . I am sorry it was not of a better stamp and more worthy of observation, because I have so many old copies of this Play; Viz. both the folio editions, the following quartos, in 1597, 1598, 1602, 1612, 1629, and 1634. (453)

★ ★ ★

[5 February 1730] The next, *Coriolanus*, is much my favourite: though I had rather it sometimes wanted of the *sublime*, so it had more of the *pathos* in exchange. (477)

★ ★ ★

---

[1] *Menaechmi*, 143 ff: '*Men.* Tell me, have you ever seen a wall painting showing the eagle making off with Catameitus, or Venus with Adonis? *Pen.* Often. But what have such pictures got to do with me? *Men.* Come, cast your eye on me.'

[14 February 1730; on *Julius Cæsar*, 2.1.73]

No, Sir, their — are plucked about their ears.

Now, who would not suspect Mr. Pope, out of modesty, had shut out a word of bawdry here? The folios read,

No, Sir, their HATS are, &c.

But the Editor happened to know that the Romans wore *no hats*; and thence, no doubt, this hypercritical — hiatus.

Surely we should make mad work with this or any other of our Author's Plays did we attempt to try them so strictly by the touchstone of antiquity. (493)

*   *   *

[24 February 1730] I now proceed to *Titus Andronicus*, which, but for a few fine lines and descriptions, I could wish were not in the list of Shakespeare's acknowledged Plays. There is something so barbarous and unnatural in the fable, and so much trash in the diction, even beneath the three parts of *Henry VI*, that I am very much inclined to believe it was not one of our Author's own compositions but only introduced by him and honoured with some of his masterly touches. The story I suppose to be merely fictitious. Andronicus is a name of pure Greek derivation; Tamora I can find no where else mentioned; nor had Rome, in the time of her Emperors, any wars with the Goths that I know of; not till after the translation of the empire—I mean, to Byzantium. But, to take it with all its absurdities. (512)

*   *   *

[26 February 1730; on *Macbeth*, 2.3.111]

His *silver* skin LAC'D with his golden blood.

For *lac'd* you, Sir, proposed to read LAQU'D; but I am afraid *che c'est un peu plus recherchée*. By LAC'D I am apt to imagine our Poet meant to describe the blood running out, and diffusing itself into little winding streams which looked like the *work of lace*, upon the skin.

So *Cymbeline*:

—white and azure, LAC'D
With blue of heav'n's own tinct. [2.2.22 f]

And *Romeo and Juliet*:

Look, love, what envious streaks
Do LACE the sev'ring clouds in yonder East. [3.5.8]

Goary blood is most absurd. I know the vulgar say, *all of a gore-blood.*
But Shakespeare, I dare say, wrote GOLDEN.
So above:

— If he BLEED,
I'll GILD the faces of the grooms withal. [*Macbeth*, 2.2.55 f]

Besides, our Poet aimed at a contrast in the terms.
So Troilus:

I had as lieve Helen's GOLDEN tongue had commended Troilus for a
COPPER nose. [*Troilus and Cressida*, 1.2.99 f]

And again:

I'll hide my SILVER beard in a GOLD beaver.
[*Troilus and Cressida*, 1.3.296]

Et alibi passim. (523)

* * *

[2 March 1730; on Pistol's 'Have we not Hiren here' (2 *Henry IV*,
2.4.150). Theobald identifies Hiren as the sword of Amadis of Gaul, and
refers to Spanish dictionaries in order to explain the word's meaning.]
La Crusa explains *hiriendo* (the gerund from *hirir*) *en frappant, battendo,
percotendo*. From hence it seems probable that *hiren* may be derived;
and so signify a *swashing, cutting* sword. And admitting this to be the
eclaircissement of the passage what wonderful humour is there in the
good Hostess so innocently mistaking Pistol's drift, fancying that he
meant to fight for a strumpet in the house, and therefore telling him
On my word, Captain, there's none such here? (526-7)

* * *

[17 March 1730] I have now received the great pleasure of two of
yours (Nos. 28 and 29), dated the 12th and 15th instant. The very kind
regard you have for my character, which you are so partial to rate
much beyond my desert, is a proof of such friendship as I shall ever
highly esteem because it must be the offspring of a truly generous mind.
For which reason your most necessary caution against *inconsistency*,
with regard to my opinion of Shakespeare's *knowledge in languages*,
shall not fail to have all its weight with me. And therefore[1] the passages

1 The following paragraph is repeated almost verbatim in the Preface in both editions,
the first (1733) and second (1740), from which I have taken the emendation [than] below:
Nichols's text reads 'and'.

that I occasionally quote from the Classics shall not be brought as proofs that he imitated those originals, but to shew how happily he has expressed himself upon the same topics. Thus far, I think, I shall be safe, and should I venture to hint that the resemblance in thought and expression (which we should allow to be *imitation* in one whose learning was also questioned) may sometimes take its rise from strength of memory, and those impressions which he owed to the school. And if we may allow a possibility of this, considering that when he quitted the school he gave into his father's profession and way of living, and had, it is likely, but a slender Library of Classical Learning; and considering what a number of Translations, Romances, and Legends started in his time and a little before, most of which it is very evident he read; I think it may easily be reconciled why he rather schemed his plots and characters from these more latter informations [than] went back to those fountains for which he might entertain a sincere veneration but to which he could not have so ready a recourse. (564-5)

* * *

[11 April 1730] I could wish, if it be not too troublesome, you will at a leisure hour throw your eye over the Editor's Preface, and favour me with the remarks that occur to you upon it. (600)

* * *

[18 November 1731] I have likewise since received yours (marked II.) a reply to the contents of which shall engage a part of this. (I beg to premise, by the bye, that the confession I made in my last of my own difficulties had not the least glance, or aim, of trespassing on your friendship.) I agree with you perfectly as to such conjectures that bear the face of probability, and yet upon which I must not venture to tamper with the text, that they should however be submitted to judgment in a note. I mean to follow the form of Bentley's Amsterdam Horace, in subjoining the notes to the place controverted. As to the *three printed criticisms* with which you obliged me and the publick[1] it is a very reasonable caution that what is gleaned from them should come out anonymous; for I should be loth to have a valued friend subjected on my account to the outrages of Pope, virulent though impotent. I am extremely obliged for the tender concern you have for my reputation in

---

[1] These are probably the three letters by Warburton attacking Pope's textual competence, which were published anonymously in the *Daily Journal* on 22 March, 8 April and 18 April 1730, for most of the emendations proposed were adopted by Warburton in his edition: cf. Lounsbury, 353 ff.

what I am *to prefix to my Edition*; and this part, as it will come last in play, I shall certainly be so kind to myself to communicate in due time to your perusal. The whole affair of *Prolegomena* I have determined to soften into *Preface*. I am so very cool as to my sentiments of my Adversary's usage that I think the publick should not be too largely troubled with them. *Blockheadry* is the chief hinge of his satire upon me, and if my Edition do not wipe out that I ought to be content to let the charge be fixed: if it do, the reputation gained will be a greater triumph than resentment.—But, dear Sir, will you at your leisure hours think over for me upon the contents, topics, orders, &c. of this branch of my labour? You have a comprehensive memory, and a happiness of digesting the matter joined to it which my head is often too much embarrassed to perform; let that be the excuse for my inability. But how unreasonable is it to expect this labour, when it is the only part in which I shall not be able to be just to my friends! (For to confess assistance in a *Preface* will, I am afraid, make me appear too naked.) Rymer's extravagant rancour against our Author, under the umbrage of criticism, may, I presume, find a place here.

What you mention of your own negligence in expression during this correspondence, literally written *currente calamo*: wherever casually there be any such, if you dare trust me with the re-modeling be assured, in this office your reputation shall be as sacred to me as my own. (621–2)

79. Thomas Cooke on the morality of Tate's *King Lear*

1731

From *Considerations on the Stage, and on the Advantages which arise to a Nation from the Encouragement of Arts*, published originally in the weekly magazine, *The British Journal*, or *The Traveller*, 5 and 12 December 1730, then issued separately (this being the text used here) attached to Cooke's play *The Triumphs of Love and Honour* (1731).

Thomas Cooke (1703–56), poet, translator, dramatist, who also edited Marvell, issued a periodical *The Comedian: or Philosophical Enquirer* in 1732–3 and became editor of *The Country Journal: or The Craftsman* in 1741.

[Introduction]

*   *   *

THEY who are conversant with the antient *Greek* and *Roman* Authors know in what high Esteem Plays were supported by antient *Greece* and *Rome*, and at a Time when the Glory of those Nations had arrived to the full Meridian, at a Time when the *Greeks* and *Romans* were less tenacious of their Lives than of their Virtue, when they were so jealous of the latter that they would suffer Nothing to continue among them that could derogate from it or that could not add a Luster to the *Greek* and *Roman* Name. Such Representations doubtless had not been maintained among them, and at a public Expence, if the good Effect which they had on the Minds of the People was not visible. When the liberal Arts flourished with them *Greece* and *Rome* were the Admiration of the World; and when those ceased to be their Care they ceased to awe Mankind, and gradually lessened in the Eyes of the Kingdoms about them.

I SHALL not here pretend to answer any particular Person who has wrote against the Stage, for I do not remember one Work on that Side of the Question which is not entirely unworthy our particular Notice.

MOST of the Critics (as they are vulgarly and wrongly called) on both Sides seem in their Writings to mistake Pedantry for Learning and Cavilling for Argument, and by a dull and fruitless Prolixity tire their Readers before they have drudged Half thro their Works. I shall obviate the Objections which can be made to the Encouragement of dramatic Poetry by shewing the Advantages which arise from it.

[Quotes Horace, *Epistles*, 2.1.128 ff]

What *Horace* here says to *Augustus* of Poetry in General may, more properly than to any other Species, be applyed to dramatic Poetry in Particular: *that forms the Heart with Friendly Precepts; that is the Corrector of Severity, Envy, and Anger; that relates Facts as they are, and instructs each rising Age by known Examples; and that administers Comfort to the poor and the distressed.* The Task will not be difficult to prove that dramatic Poetry answers every End proposed in these Words of *Horace.* I shall examine three favourite dramatic Pieces, a Tragedy, a Comedy, and an Opera; and as I intend this as a moral Criticism on the Stage I shall confine my self chiefly to the Morality of those Pieces, and point out the Effect which they must naturally have in their Operation on the Minds of the Spectators. (48-9)

*   *   *

[Chapter II] On TRAGEDY. *A Criticism on* King LEAR.

THE Tragedy on which I choose to make my Remarks is *King Lear,* as altered from *Shakespeare* by *Tate*; because almost every Character in that Play is an Instance of Virtue being rewarded and Vice punished.

WHO can behold *Lear,* in the Beginning of the first Act, making that partial Disposition of his Dominions, investing the Husbands of *Goneril* and *Regan* with the Dower of *Cordelia* because she sayed she would love her Husband as well as her Father, without despising the choleric old King for so rash and unjust a Resolution? And what aggravates his Fault is his being deaf to the friendly Reprehensions of *Kent,* and banishing him for giving his Advice which, if regarded, would have prevented his committing so gross an Error. When we see *Goneril,* at the End of the first Act, depriving him of Half his Train we are scarcely inclined to pity him, so strong is his injustice to poor *Cordelia* imprinted in our Minds; but when he flys from *Goneril* to *Regan* for Comfort (who is for dismissing all his Train), the Ingratitude and Undutyfulness of the two Daughters raise our Detestation to such a Height that we lose the Remembrance of the Father's Offence to *Cordelia* in our Compassion for him. When he is turned out to the Inclemencys of the Storm, cast from a Throne to the lowest Degree of Misery, we view him as a Prince whose Weakness urged him on to an Act of Injustice, and whose Sufferings are the natural Consequences of his Rashness; yet we pity him, and are apt to think his Punishment too rigid. The sincere Repentance for, and the just Sense which he shews of the Wrongs which he had heaped on *Kent* and *Cordelia*, and the pathetic Manner in which he expresses himself, engage us to be Sharers in his Woes, and to wish him a speedy Relief from them.

O! KENT, CORDELIA,
You are the only Pair that I e'er wrong'd,
And the just Gods have made you Witnesses
Of my Disgrace, the very Shame of Fortune,
To see me chain'd and shackled at these Years!
Yet were you but Spectators of my Woes,
Not Fellow-sufferers, all were well.

[Tate's version; cf. Vol. I, p. 377]

WHEN he utters these Words he is in Expectation of Death from those whom he had raised to Empire; but he is soon freed from the Fears of it by being restored to his Throne, on which he places *Edgar* and *Cordelia* as a Reward due to their Virtue.

GLOUCESTER is more the Object of our Compassion than *Lear* because he has some Reason for treating his Son *Edgar* as he did. For tho *Edgar* was innocent *Gloucester* had Cause to think him guilty, being imposed upon by *Edmund*, who shewed him a Letter as from his Brother conspiring against the Life of his Father; which was so well counterfeited that *Gloucester* had no Reason to dispute it being wrote by *Edgar*. The filial Piety of *Edgar* and *Cordelia* to their Parents, and the Loyalty and Fidelity of *Kent* to his Prince, notwithstanding the Injurys which they had suffered from them, engage our Wishes in their Behalf. While they share their Fortune in the most miserable Part of it, eager to administer what Relief they can to the wretched, we approve of and admire their Virtue; and where we admire and approve we seldom want an Inclination to imitate.

WHILE *Lear* and the Companions of his Wretchedness are almost without Hopes, unerring Nature is pursuing her Course; the Vices of *Goneril*, *Regan*, and *Edmund* are working their own Ruin, and the

Uprising of those whom their Cruelty had reduced to the lowest State of Misery. Here is a Lesson *that administers Comfort to the poor and the distressed*. From the Fortunes of *Lear* and his Followers Wretches whose Wretchedness was accomplished by the Crimes of other Persons may learn to hope that the same Propensity to Evil that urged their Enemys wrongfully to effect their Fall will impel them to such Actions as shall render them unable to preserve what they have unjustly acquired, and thereby be the Cause of restoring the injured to their Right. Such is the Case betwixt *Lear* and his Daughters, and *Gloucester* and his Sons. While *Cordelia, Gloucester, Edgar* and *Kent* are in the most desperate Condition *Goneril, Regan, Edmund* and *Cornwall* are filling up the Measure of their Sins, which produce their own Punishment. *Goneril* and *Regan* are both false to the marriage Bed; both make *Edmund* the Object of their loose Desires; and he endeavours to gratify them both. Their Passion for *Edmund* is known to both; Jealousy is the Consequence of that Knowledge; and they are both poysoned, one by the other. Of the two Husbands of *Goneril* and *Regan, Cornwall* only assents to the Cruelty of his Wife, and he is killed by the Servant whom he wounded for crying out against the Barbarity of pulling out *Gloucester*'s Eyes. *Edmund* is not only guilty of Adultery with the two Sisters, and of Undutyfulness and Treachery to his Father and Falsehood to his Brother, but of Treason to *Albany* his Prince; and he falls by the Hands of his Brother *Edgar*, whose Challenge to *Edmund* is the Occasion of the Affair being set in a just Light to *Albany*, who from the Beginning shews a Dislike to the Proceedings of *Goneril* his Wife, and is Accessary to the Restoration of *Lear*. He therefore is successful in the Catastrophe.

NOW we have gone thro the Business of the Play let us sum up the moral Inferences which are to be made from it. *Edmund, Cornwall, Goneril*, and *Regan* are disloyal to their Prince, undutyful to their Parents, and every Way false to their Trust. Their Crimes are attended with so many horrid Circumstances that their Punishment is scarcely adequate to their Guilt. *Lear* and *Gloucester* had offended, but more to Appearance thro an Error of the Judgement than the Will; they are punished. They are made sensible of their Errors, and are placed in a State of Tranquility and Ease agreeable to their Age and Condition, with *Kent* (whose Loyalty remained unshocked to the last), rejoicing at the Felicity of *Edgar* and *Cordelia*, whom they had wronged, and who forsaked them not in the Hour of Distress, and who cherished a virtuous Love each for the other.

I HAVE read many Sermons, but remember no one that contains so fine a Lesson of Morality as this Play. Here is Loyalty to a Prince, Duty to a Parent, Perseverance in a chast Love, and almost every exalted Virtue of the Soul recommended in the lovelyest Colours; and the opposite Vices are placed in the strongest Light in which Horror and Detestation can place them. The Poet in this Play seems to labour at one Point which that great, that wise and good Man Archbishop *Tillotson* laboured at in most of his Sermons, which is to convince Mankind that, if we extend our Happyness no farther than the Grave, the Interest of all Mankind is to pursue Virtue and fly from Vice; that the first is in the Nature of itself productive of Joy, and the latter of Misery. The Poet has answered this End as much as he could in a Play; for had *Lear* been just to the Virtues of *Cordelia* he had not wanted a Refuge when he fled from the Disobedience of *Goneril* and *Regan*. I bring this Example, and leave the Reader to try every other Character of the Play and in every Circumstance to see if they will not justify the Truth of this Observation. The Poet shews in this Tragedy that the Vengeance of Heaven ⌈co-operates, as indeed it always does, with the natural Course of Things. And when Virtue meets her due Reward we may say, with *Cordelia, there are Gods, and Virtue is their Care* [Volume 1, p. 384]; for the all-wise Disposer of all Things has from the Beginning annexed Rewards to Virtue and Punishment to Vice; and in these we find Nature as consistent with herself as when we behold the Trees producing their proper Fruit. What more profitable Lesson can the People be taught than this? Virtue is the inexhaustible Fountain of Joy, and Vice of Misery; and this Lesson the Stage more effectually teaches than a Sermon because the Spectators have before their Eyes the Actions and the Causes of them. They see the Effects, and how they operate, and are convinced that they are the natural Consequences of such Causes; the Impression therefore that they must make in their Minds must certainly be in Favour of what seems lovely in their Eyes, and fruitful of Happyness. And we cannot suppose that they will soon enter on any Action like what they were just before instructed to behold with Horror and Detestation, and which is attended with inevitable Woe. (50-7)

80. William Levin on the decline in theatrical taste

1731

From the *Universal Spectator*, 131 (10 April 1731).

This journal was edited by Henry Baker (1698–1774) between 1728 and 1733, with contributions from John Kelly (1680?–1751), William Oldys (1696–1761), Defoe and others. The ascription of this piece to Levin is made in Baker's own copy, now in the Bodleian (Graham, *English Literary Periodicals*, pp. 105–6).

To Henry Stonecastle, Esq.

Sir, the Complaints against the Age in which we live are grown so numerous as to incline some of the best Judges to attribute many of them rather to a Desire of appearing singular than any real Intention of contributing towards an Amendment. . . .

The Subject then, both of my Complaint and of my Letter, shall be our present Want of Taste. . . . Taste is a metaphorical Term, and is taken for our Capacity in judging of such Pieces as we either read in the Closet or behold upon the Stage. The signs of a good Taste are our giving our Approbation to just and fine Sentiments cloathed in a corresponding Elegancy of Expression; as it is a certain Evidence of a bad one, our applauding vicious or improper Thoughts in any Diction whatever.

I shall forbear any Remarks on those Writers who meddle only with the severer Parts of Learning, and confine myself solely to the Poets, as the Authors more immediately under your Consideration; and whose Works, as they are more generally read, are consequently the best understood by the far greater Part of those who peruse your Papers.

Shakespeare and *Jonson* were the two first Writers who gave any Lustre to the Dramatick Performances of our Nation; and tho' we have since them had abundance of Authors in that Way yet I believe I shall hardly be contradicted in saying that there have been very few who can with any Justice be call'd their Equals, and not so much as one who can be said to have excell'd them.

Their distinguishing Talent consists in having always kept Nature in their View, from whence the Propriety of their Thoughts recommends them to those who read them with Judgment; and the entring into the Spirit of whatever Character they represent moves always the Passion of their Auditors, according to the excellent Observation of *Horace*

Si vis me flere, dolendum est
Primum ipsi tibi.[1]

The peculiar Excellencies of *Shakespeare* are the marvellous Boldness of his Invention and the admirable Energy of his Expression. *Jonson's* Perfections, on the other Hand, are his prodigious Art in weaving his Plots and that nice Distinction there is between all his Characters. This Difference lies in them merely thro' the one's Want of Knowledge in the *Antients* and the other's perfect Acquaintance and profound Respect for them; which is also the sole Occasion of their Mistakes, the former being often irregular and the latter sometimes too servile an Imitator.

However, their Beauties are a great Over-ballance for their Blemishes, and one may always pronounce in Favour of their Writings without Fear of being thought to have an ill *Taste*. In the Gross of the Dramatick Poets who succeed them the more exalted Characters met with a terrible Transformation: their Monarchs either thunder'd in tyrannical Bombast or whin'd forth their amorous Complaints with a Tenderness below their Rank. In *Comedy* the Alteration was also for the worse, the grand Parts being almost continually a Beau or Debauchee. In fine, the *Heroes* of that Sett of Writers were most of them *Almanzors*, and their fine Gentlemen *Dorimants*; the one a Character altogether out of Nature, the other a Disgrace to it.

This naturally leads me to the Mention of the Source of their Errors, which was plainly this, that the Poets of those Days, either thro' Force or Inclination, comply'd with the prevailing false Taste of Mankind rather than they would take any Pains to amend it. Mr *Dryden*, if I am not much mistaken, has almost own'd this in one of his Dedications; and whoever considers the present State of the *Drama* will readily observe the Consequence of such a Complaisance, *viz.* that the Town and its Authors both will grow daily worse and worse. 'Till instead of the manly Entertainments of a *Julius* and an *Othello*, the finish'd Work-

[1] Horace, *A.P.*, 102 f: 'If you would have me weep, you must first feel grief yourself.'

ings of a *Volpone* or an *Alchymist*, our Stages are polluted with the Conjurations of an *Harlequin Faustus*, or render'd yet more ridiculous from the Feats of a *Tom Thumb*.

Crito.

81. Lewis Theobald, 'On the text of Shakespeare's Poems'

1732

From *Miscellaneous Observations upon Authors*, ed. John Jortin (1731–2), ii, 242–50: a journal which appeared in two volumes only, consisting mostly of textual emendations of classical authors.

SIR,

UPON our casually talking together of SHAKESPEARE's *Poems* you ask'd me if they were in the same corrupt state as his Plays are found to be, and whether I had taken notice of any errors in them. I told you I had, and I now send you the correction of a few passages, from a cursory view, in which they have suffered injury from the Printer and not found redress from the editor. I'll begin with a few in which the breach of the rhyme evidently helps to point out the corruption.

In the Poem call'd *Venus and Adonis*, Stanz. 142:

> *For who hath she to spend the night withal*
> *But idle sounds, resembling parasites?*
> *Like shrill-tongued tapsters, answ'ring ev'ry call,*
> *Soothing the humour of fantastick Wits?*   [847 ff]

But the exercise of this fantastick humour is not so properly the character of Wits, but persons of a wild and jocular extravagance of temper. To suit this idea, as well as to close the rhyme more fully, I am persuaded the Poet wrote:

> *Soothing the humour of fantastick Wights.*

In the *same* POEM, Stanz. 153, the Poet is describing the plight in which *Venus* met the hounds who had ventur'd to attack the Boar:

> *And here she meets another sadly* scolding,
> *To whom she speaks, and he replies with howling.* [917 f]

Nothing is more certain than that we must read in the first line

> —*meets another sadly* scowling,

i.e. low'ring, and looking melancholly. . . . (242-3)

We'll now take a view of a few faults in which the sense is hurt exclusive of the rhymes. *Venus and Adonis*, Stanz. 169:

> *With death she humbly doth insinuate;*
> *Tells him of trophies, statues,* tombs, *and Stories,*
> *His victories, his triumphs, and his glories.* [1012 ff]

As *Venus* is here bribing *Death* with flatteries, to spare *Adonis*, the editors could not help thinking of pompous *tombs*. But *tombs* are no honours to *Death*, consider'd as a *Being*, but to the Parties buried. I much suspect our Author intended:

> *Tells him of trophies, statues,* domes,—

i.e. promises she will in gratitude erect trophies, statues, and *temples* to his *Deity*. The images seem to agree better thus; tho' I propose it but as a conjecture, and submit it to judgment. But how poorly does the verse go on! What a base *Anti-climax* does it fall into! What, after these pompous particularities, to tell Death of *Stories*? In short, the pointing is faulty; and the editors did not know that *stories* is a verb here, and means *rehearses over, gives the history of*. Take away the capital letter, and stop it thus, and we have the Poet's genuine sense:

> *Tells him of trophies, statues,* domes; *and stories*
> *His victories, his triumphs, and his glories.*

So again, in the sixteenth Stanza of his *Rape of Lucrece*, he employs this word as a verb:

> *He* stories *to her ears her husband's fame,*
> *Won in the fields of fruitful* Italy. [106 f]

Venus and Adonis, Stanz. 189.

> *Two Glasses, where herself herself beheld*
> *A thousand times, and* now, *no more reflect;* [1129 f]

Mr. *Sewell*, in his 4to edition of these Poems, alters the pointing thus:

> *—and now no more reflect;*

But how much will it improve the contrast of the thought, as well as restore our Author's manner of redoubling one and the same word, if we read

> *Two Glasses, where herself herself beheld*
> *A thousand times and more, no more reflect.*

Again, in the same POEM, Stanz. 198,

> *Here was thy father's bed, here is my breast,*   [1183]

As *Venus* sticks the flower to which *Adonis* is turn'd in her bosom, I think we must read, against all the copies, and with much more elegance:

> *Here was thy father's bed, here in my breast;*

For it was her breast which she would insinuate to have been *Adonis's* bed. The close of the preceding Stanza partly warrants this change:

> *—but know, it is as good*
> *To wither in my breast, as in his blood.*   [1181 f]

As the succeeding lines in this stanza likewise do:

> *Low in this hollow cradle take thy rest.*   [1185]

The Rape of Lucrece, Stanz. 5.

> *Or why is* Collatine *the publisher*
> *Of that rich jewel he should keep unknown*
> *From thievish* cares, *because it is his own?*   [33 ff]

Thievish Cares is certainly downright nonsense; and I once imagin'd it should be—*thievish* Carls, a word common enough with our Author; but upon considering the passage more narrowly I am persuaded he wrote it thus:

> *From thievish* ears, *because it is his own?*

This agrees with his calling *Collatine* the *publisher* of what he should keep unknown; and likewise with this sentiment in the succeeding stanza:

> *For by our* ears *our hearts oft tainted be.*   [38]

The Rape of Lucrece, Stanz. 90.

> Ha'st thou commanded? By him that gave it thee,
> From a pure heart command thy rebel will.   [624 f]

Not only the hobbling of the versification but the lameness of the sense point out a defect in the first line. Where is the substantive on which the relative *it* can depend? We must read:

> Hast thou command? By him that gave it thee, &c.

The Rape of Lucrece. Stanz. 152. *Lucrece*, bemoaning the injury of her rape in an *apostrophe* to her husband, professes that he shall not taste of her polluted body; neither shall *Tarquin* boast the deriving issue from her stain.

> This bastard grass shall never come to growth:
> He shall not boast, who did thy stock pollute,
> That thou art doating father of his fruit.   [1062 ff]

The words *stock* and *fruit* here are a demonstration that our Poet's metaphor is from the *inoculation* of trees. We must certainly therefore restore:

> This bastard graft shall never come to growth: (244–6)

*   *   *

[On Sonnet 77] '*Commit to these waste* Blacks'
. . . But what meaning or idea does *blacks* convey here?—Let us examine a few of the verses that precede these, and see if from thence we may borrow any instruction.

> Thy glass will shew thee how thy beauties wear;
> Thy Dial, how thy precious minutes waste:
> The vacant leaves thy mind's imprint will bear,
> And of this book this learning may'st thou taste:

I question not but you have observed by this time that our Poet must have wrote in the place first quoted
    Commit to these waste blanks,—
i.e. these *vacant leaves*, as he calls them in the other quotation. (247–8)

82. Lewis Theobald, edition of Shakespeare

1733

From *The Works of Shakespeare, Collated with the Oldest Copies, and Corrected, with Notes, Explanatory and Critical,* 7 vols (1733). On the allocation of parts of the text to Warburton see the Introduction above, p. 18.

[From the Preface.]

THEOBALD: THE Attempt to write upon SHAKESPEARE is like going into a large, a spacious, and a splendid Dome thro' the Conveyance of a narrow and obscure Entry. A Glare of Light suddenly breaks upon you beyond what the Avenue at first promis'd, and a thousand Beauties of Genius and Character, like so many gaudy Apartments pouring at once upon the Eye, diffuse and throw themselves out to the Mind. The Prospect is too wide to come within the Compass of a single View: 'tis a gay Confusion of pleasing Objects, too various to be enjoyed but in a general Admiration; and they must be separated and ey'd distinctly in order to give the proper Entertainment.

And, as in great Piles of Building, some Parts are often finish'd up to hit the Taste of the *Connoisseur*; others more negligently put together, to strike the Fancy of a common and unlearned Beholder; some Parts are made stupendiously magnificent and grand, to surprize with the vast Design and Execution of the Architect; others are contracted, to amuse you with his Neatness and Elegance in little; so, in *Shakespeare,* we may find *Traits* that will stand the Test of the severest Judgment; and Strokes as carelessly hit off, to the Level of the more ordinary Capacities; some Descriptions rais'd to that Pitch of Grandeur, as to astonish you with the Compass and Elevation of his Thought: and others copying Nature within so narrow, so confined a Circle, as if the Author's Talent lay only at drawing in Miniature.

In how many points of Light must we be obliged to gaze at this great Poet! In how many Branches of Excellence to consider, and admire him! Whether we view him on the Side of Art or Nature he ought equally to engage our Attention. Whether we respect the Force and

Greatness of his Genius, the Extent of his Knowledge and Reading, the Power and Address with which he throws out and applies either Nature, or Learning, there is ample scope both for our Wonder and Pleasure. If his Diction, and the cloathing of his Thoughts attract us, how much more must we be charm'd with the Richness, and Variety, of his Images and Ideas! If his Images and Ideas steal into our Souls, and strike upon our Fancy, how much are they improv'd in Price, when we come to reflect with what Propriety and Justness they are apply'd to Character! If we look into his Characters, and how they are furnish'd and proportion'd to the Employment he cuts out for them, how are we taken up with the Mastery of his Portraits! What Draughts of Nature! What Variety of Originals, and how differing each from the other! How are they dress'd from the Stores of his own luxurious Imagination; without being the Apes of Mode, or borrowing from any foreign Wardrobe! Each of Them are the Standards of Fashion for themselves: like Gentlemen that are above the Direction of their Tailors, and can adorn themselves without the Aid of Imitation. If other Poets draw more than one Fool or Coxcomb, there is the same Resemblance in them, as in that Painter's Draughts, who was happy only at forming a Rose: you find them all younger Brothers of the same Family, and all of them have a Pretence to give the same Crest. But *Shakespeare*'s Clowns and Fops come all of a different House: they are no farther allied to one another than as Man to Man, Members of the same Species: but as different in Features and Lineaments of Character, as we are from one another in Face, or Complexion. (I, i–iii).

*   *   *

No Age, perhaps, can produce an Author more various from himself, than *Shakespeare* has been universally acknowledg'd to be. The Diversity in Stile, and other Parts of Composition, so obvious in him, is as variously to be accounted for. His Education, we find, was at best but begun, and he started early into a Science from the Force of Genius, unequally assisted by acquir'd Improvements. His Fire, Spirit, and Exuberance of Imagination gave an impetuosity to his Pen; his Ideas flow'd from him in a stream rapid, but not turbulent, copious, but not ever over-bearing its Shores. The Ease and Sweetness of his Temper might not a little contribute to his Facility in Writing, as his Employment as a *Player* gave him an Advantage and Habit of fancying himself the very Character he meant to delineate. He used the Helps of his Function in forming himself to create and express that *Sublime* which

other Actors can only copy and throw out in Action and graceful
Attitude. But *Nullum sine Venia placuit Ingenium*, says *Seneca*.[1] The
Genius that gives us the greatest Pleasure sometimes stands in Need of
our Indulgence. Whenever this happens with regard to *Shakespeare* I
would willingly impute it to a Vice of *his Times*. We see Complaisance
enough, in our Days, paid to a *bad Taste*, so that his *Clinches, false Wit*,
and descending beneath himself may have proceeded from a Deference
paid to the then *reigning Barbarism*. He was a *Sampson* in Strength, but
he suffer'd some such *Dalilah* to give him up to the *Philistines*.

As I have mention'd the Sweetness of his Disposition, I am tempted
to make a Reflexion or two on a Sentiment of his which, I am persuaded, came from the Heart.

> *The Man, that hath no Musick in himself,*
> *Nor is not mov'd with Concord of Sweet sounds,*
> *Is fit for Treasons, Stratagems, and Spoils:*
> *The Motions of his Spirit are dull as Night,*
> *And his Affections dark as* Erebus:
> *Let no such Man be trusted.—*
> [Merchant of Venice, 5.1.83 ff]

Shakespeare was all Openness, Candour, and Complacence; and had
such a Share of Harmony in his Frame and Temperature, that we have
no Reason to doubt, from a Number of fine Passages, Allusions,
Similies, &c. fetch'd from *Musick*, but that He was a passionate Lover
of it. . . . (I, xv–xvii)

It has been remark'd in the Course of my Notes that Musick in our
Author's time had a very different Use from what it has now. At this
Time it is only employ'd to raise and inflame the Passions; it then was
apply'd to calm and allay all kinds of Perturbations. And, agreeable to
this Observation, throughout all *Shakespeare*'s Plays, where Musick is
either actually used or its Powers describ'd it is chiefly said to be for
these Ends. His *Twelfth Night*, particularly, begins with a fine Reflexion
that admirably marks its soothing Properties.

> *That Strain again;—It had a dying Fall.*
> *Oh, it came o'er my Ear like the sweet South,*
> *That breathes upon a Bank of Violets,*
> *Stealing and giving Odour!*   [Twelfth Night, 1.1.4 ff]

---

[1] *Epistles*, 114.12: 'No man's ability has ever been approved without something being
pardoned.'

[WARBURTON: This *similitude* is remarkable not only for the Beauty of the Image that it presents but likewise for the Exactness to the Thing compared. This is a way of Teaching peculiar to the Poets; that, when they would describe the Nature of any thing, they do it not by a direct Enumeration of its Attributes or Qualities but by bringing something into Comparison, and describing those Qualities of it that are of the Kind with those in the Thing compared. So here, for instance, the Poet willing to instruct in the Properties of Musick, in which the same Strains have a Power to excite Pleasure or Pain according to that State of Mind the Hearer is then in, does it by presenting the Image of a sweet South Wind blowing o'er a Violet-bank, which wafts away the Odour of the Violets and at the same time communicates to it its own Sweetness: by this insinuating that affecting Musick, tho' it takes away the natural sweet Tranquillity of the Mind, yet at the same time communicates a Pleasure the Mind felt not before. This Knowledge, of the same Objects being capable of raising two contrary Affections, is a Proof of no ordinary Progress in the Study of human Nature. The general Beauties of those two Poems of MILTON intitled *L'Allegro* and *Il Penseroso* are obvious to all Readers because the Descriptions are the most poetical in the World, yet there is a peculiar Beauty in those two excellent Pieces that will much enhance the Value of them to the more capable Readers, which has never, I think, been observ'd. The Images in each Poem which he raises to excite Mirth and Melancholy are exactly the same, only shewn in different Attitudes. Had a Writer less acquainted with Nature given us two Poems on these Subjects he would have been sure to have sought out the most contrary Images to raise these contrary Passions. And particularly as *Shakespeare*, in the Passage I am now commenting, speaks of these different Effects in Musick, so *Milton* has brought it into each Poem as the Exciter of each Affection. And lest we should mistake him as meaning that different Airs had this different Power (which every Fidler is proud to have you understand), he gives the Image of those self-same Strains that *Orpheus* used to regain *Eurydice* as proper both to excite Mirth and Melancholy. But *Milton* most industriously copied the Conduct of our *Shakespeare* in Passages that shew'd an intimate Acquaintance with Nature and Science.]

THEOBALD: I have not thought it out of my Province, whenever Occasion offer'd, to take notice of some of our Poet's grand Touches of Nature—some that do not appear superficially such but in which he seems the most deeply instructed, and to which, no doubt, he has so much ow'd that happy Preservation of his *Characters* for which he is justly celebrated. If he was not acquainted with the Rule as deliver'd by *Horace* his own admirable Genius pierc'd into the Necessity of such a Rule.

—Servetur ad imum
Qualis ab incoepto processerit, & sibi constet.[1]

[WARBURTON: For what can be more ridiculous than (in our modern Writers) to make a debauch'd young Man, immers'd in all the Vices of his Age and Time, in a few hours take up, confine himself in the way of Honour to one Woman, and moralize in good earnest on the Follies of his past Behaviour? Nor can that great Exemplar of *Comic* Writing, *Terence*, be altogether excused in this Regard, who in his *Adelphi* has left *Demea* in the last Scenes so unlike himself: whom, as *Shakespeare* expresses it, *he has turn'd with the seamy Side of his Wit outward.* This Conduct, as Errors are more readily imitated than Perfections, *Beaumont* and *Fletcher* seem to have follow'd in a Character in their *Scornful Lady.* It may be objected, perhaps, by some who do not go to the Bottom of our Poet's Conduct, that he has likewise transgress'd against the Rule himself by making Prince *Harry* at once, upon coming to the Crown, throw off his former Dissoluteness and take up the Practice of a sober Morality and all the kingly Virtues. But this would be a mistaken Objection. The Prince's Reformation is not so sudden as not to be prepar'd and expected by the Audience. He gives, indeed, a Loose to Vanity and a light unweigh'd Behaviour when he is trifling among his dissolute Companions, but the Sparks of innate Honour and true Nobleness break from him upon every proper Occasion where we would hope to see him awake to Sentiments suiting his Birth and Dignity. And our Poet has so well and artfully guarded his Character from the Suspicions of habitual and unreformable Profligateness that even from the first shewing him upon the Stage, in the first Part of *Henry IV*, when he made him consent to join with *Falstaff* in a Robbery on the Highway, he has taken care not to carry him off the Scene without an Intimation that he knows them all, and their unyok'd Humour; and that, like the Sun, he will permit them only for a while to obscure and cloud his Brightness, then break thro' the Mist when he pleases to be himself again, that his Lustre, when wanted, may be the more wonder'd at.]

[1] Horace, *A.P.*, 126 f: 'if you fashion a fresh character, have it kept to the end even as it came forth at the first, and have it self-consistent'.

THEOBALD: Another of *Shakespeare's* grand Touches of Nature, and which lies still deeper from the Ken of common Observation, has been taken notice of in a Note upon *The Tempest*, where *Prospero* at once interrupts the Masque of *Spirits* and starts into a sudden Passion and Disorder of Mind. As the latent Cause of his Emotion is there fully inquir'd into I shall no farther dwell upon it here.

Such a Conduct in a Poet (as *Shakespeare* has manifested on many like Occasions) where the Turn of *Action* arises from Reflexions of his *Characters*, where the Reason of it is not express'd in Words but drawn from the inmost Resources of Nature, shews him truly capable of that Art which is more in Rule than Practice: *Ars est celare Artem.* 'Tis the Foible of your worser Poets to make a Parade and Ostentation of that little Science they have, and to throw it out in the most ambitious Colours. And whenever a Writer of this Class shall attempt to copy these artful Concealments of our Author and shall either think them easy, or practised by a Writer for his Ease, he will soon be convinced of his Mistake by the Difficulty of reaching the Imitation of them.

> *Speret idem, sudet multùm, frustráque laboret,*
> *Ausus idem:—*[1]

Another grand Touch of Nature in our Author (not less difficult to imitate tho' more obvious to the Remark of a common Reader), is when he brings down at once any *Character* from the Ferment and Height of Passion, makes him correct himself for the unruly Disposition, and fall into Reflexions of a sober and moral Tenour. An exquisite fine Instance of this Kind occurs in *Lear*, where that old King, hasty and intemperate in his Passions, coming to his Son and Daughter *Cornwall* is told by the Earl of *Gloucester* that they are not to be spoken with, and thereupon throws himself into a Rage, supposing the Excuse of Sickness and Weariness in them to be a purpos'd Contempt. *Gloucester* begs him to think of the fiery and unremoveable Quality of the Duke: and this, which was design'd to qualify his Passion, serves to exaggerate the Transports of it.

As the Conduct of Prince *Henry* in the first Instance, the secret and mental Reflexions in the Case of *Prospero*, and the instant Detour of *Lear* from the Violence of Rage to a Temper of Reasoning, do so much Honour to that surprizing Knowledge of human Nature which is

[1] Horace, *A.P.*, 241 f: 'My aim shall be poetry, so moulded from the familiar that anybody may hope for the same success, may sweat much and yet toil in vain when attempting the same.'

certainly our Author's Masterpiece, I thought they could not be set in too good a Light. Indeed, to point out and exclaim upon all the Beauties of *Shakespeare*, as they come singly in Review, would be as insipid, as endless; as tedious, as unnecessary. But the Explanation of those Beauties that are less obvious to common Readers, and whose Illustration depends on the Rules of just Criticism and an exact Knowledge of human Life, should deservedly have a Share in a general Critic upon the Author. (I, xviii—xxiv)

* * *

THEOBALD: In touching on another Part of his Learning, as it related to the Knowledge of *History* and *Books*, I shall advance something that at first sight will very much wear the Appearance of a Paradox. [WARBURTON: For I shall find it no hard Matter to prove that from the grossest Blunders in History we are not to infer his real Ignorance of it, nor from a greater Use of *Latin* Words than ever any other *English* Author used must we infer his Knowledge of that Language.

A Reader of Taste may easily observe that tho' *Shakespeare*, almost in every Scene of his historical Plays, commits the grossest Offences against Chronology, History, and Antient Politicks, yet this was not thro' Ignorance, as is generally supposed, but thro' the too powerful Blaze of his Imagination; which, when once raised, made all acquired Knowledge vanish and disappear before it. For Instance, in his *Timon* he turns *Athens*, which was a perfect Democrasy, into an Aristocrasy, while he ridiculously gives a Senator the Power of banishing *Alcibiades*. On the contrary, in *Coriolanus* he makes *Rome*, which at that time was a perfect Aristocrasy, a Democrasy full as ridiculously by making the People choose *Coriolanus* Consul: whereas in Fact it was not till the Time of *Manlius Torquatus* that the People had a Right of choosing one Consul. But this Licence in him, as I have said, must not be imputed to Ignorance since as often we may find him, when Occasion serves, reasoning up to the Truth of History, and throwing out sentiments as justly adapted to the Circumstances of his Subject as to the Dignity of his Characters, or Dictates of Nature in general.

Then, to come to his Knowledge of the *Latin* Tongue, 'tis certain there is a surprising Effusion of *Latin* Words made *English*, far more than in any one *English* Author I have seen; but we must be cautious to imagine this was of his own doing. For the *English* Tongue, in his Age, began extremely to suffer by an Inundation of *Latin*; and to be overlaid, as it were, by its Nurse when it had just began to speak by her before-prudent Care and Assistance. And this, to be sure, was occa-sion'd by the Pedantry of those two Monarchs, *Elizabeth* and *James*, both great *Latinists*. For it is not to be wonder'd at if both the Court and Schools, equal Flatterers of Power, should adapt themselves to the Royal Taste. This, then, was the Condition of the *English* Tongue when *Shakespeare* took it up. Like a Beggar in a rich Wardrobe, he found the pure native *English* too cold and poor to second the Heat and Abundance of his Imagination and therefore was forc'd to dress it up in the Robes he saw provided for it: rich in themselves, but ill-shaped; cut out to an air of Magnificence, but disproportion'd and cumber-some. To the Costliness of Ornament he added all the Grace and Decorum of it. It may be said, this did not require or discover a Knowledge of the *Latin*. To the first, I think, it did not; to the second, it is so far from discovering it that I think it discovers the contrary. To make this more obvious by a modern Instance: the great MILTON like-wise labour'd under the like Inconvenience. When he first set upon adorning his own Tongue he likewise animated and enrich'd it with the *Latin*, but from his own Stock: and so, rather by bringing in the Phrases than the Words—and This was natural, and will, I believe, always be the Case in the same Circumstances. His Language, especially his Prose, is full of *Latin* Words indeed, but much fuller of *Latin* Phrases, and his Mastery in the Tongue made this unavoidable. On the contrary *Shakespeare*, who perhaps was not so intimately vers'd in the *Language*, abounds in the Words of it but has few or none of its Phrases; nor, indeed, if what I affirm be true, could He. This I take to be the truest *Criterion* to determine this long agitated Question.]

THEOBALD: It may be mention'd, tho' no certain Conclusion can be drawn from it, as a probable Argument of his having read the Antients that He perpetually expresses the Genius of *Homer*, and other great Poets of the Old World, in animating all the Parts of his Descriptions; and by bold and breathing Metaphors and Images giving the Properties of Life and Action to inanimate Things. He is a Copy, too, of those *Greek* Masters in the infinite use of *compound* and *de-compound Epithets*. I will not, indeed, aver but that One with *Shakespeare*'s exquisite Genius and Observation might have traced these glaring Character-istics of Antiquity by reading *Homer* in *Chapman*'s Version.

An additional Word or two naturally falls in here upon the Genius of our Author, as compared with that of *Jonson* his Contemporary. [WARBURTON: They are confessedly the greatest Writers our Nation could ever boast of in the *Drama*. The first, we say, owed all to his prodigious natural Genius, and the other a great deal to his Art and Learning. This, if attended to, will explain a very remarkable Appearance in their Writings. Besides those wonderful Masterpieces of Art and Genius which each has given us they are the Authors of other Works very unworthy of them. But with this Difference, that in *Jonson*'s bad Pieces we don't discover one single Trace of the Author of the *Fox* and *Alchemist*, but in the wild extravagant Notes of *Shakespeare* you every now and then encounter Strains that recognize the divine Composer. This Difference may be thus accounted for. *Jonson*, as we said before, owing all his Excellence to his Art, by which he sometimes strain'd himself to an uncommon Pitch: when at other times he unbent and play'd with his Subject, having nothing then to support him, it is no wonder he wrote so far beneath himself. But *Shakespeare*, indebted more largely to Nature than the Other to acquired Talents, in his most negligent Hours could never so totally divest himself of his Genius but that it would frequently break out with astonishing Force and Splendor.]

THEOBALD: As I have never propos'd to dilate farther on the Character of my Author than was necessary to explain the Nature and Use of this Edition, I shall proceed to consider him as a Genius in Possession of an Everlasting Name. [WARBURTON: And how great that Merit must be, which could gain it against all the Disadvantages of the horrid Condition in which he has hitherto appear'd! Had *Homer*, or any other admir'd Author, first started into Publick so maim'd and deform'd, we cannot determine whether they had not sunk for ever under the Ignominy of such an ill Appearance.] THEOBALD: The mangled Condition of *Shakespeare* has been acknowledg'd by Mr. *Rowe*, who publish'd him indeed, but neither corrected his Text nor collated the old Copies. This Gentleman had Abilities, and a sufficient Knowledge of his Author, had but his Industry been equal to his Talents. The same mangled Condition has been acknowledg'd too by Mr. *Pope*, who publish'd him likewise, pretended to have collated the old Copies, and yet seldom has corrected the Text but to its Injury. I congratulate with the *Manes* of our Poet that this Gentleman has been sparing in *indulging his private Sense*, as he phrases it; for He who tampers with an Author whom he does not understand must do it at the Expence of his Subject. I have made it evident throughout my Remarks that he has frequently inflicted a Wound where he intended a Cure. . . . He has attack'd him like an unhandy *Slaughterman*; and not lopp'd off the *Errors*, but the *Poet*.

When this is found to be Fact how absurd must appear the Praises of such an Editor!

[WARBURTON: It seems a moot Point whether Mr. *Pope* has done most Injury to *Shakespeare* as his Editor and Encomiast, or Mr. *Rymer* done him Service as his Rival and Censurer. Were it every where the true Text which That Editor in his late pompous Edition gave us, the Poet deserv'd not the large Encomiums bestow'd by him: nor, in that Case, is *Rymer's* Censure of the Barbarity of his Thoughts and the Impropriety of his Expressions groundless. They have Both shewn themselves in an equal *Impuissance* of suspecting or amending the corrupted Passages; and tho' it be neither Prudence to censure or commend what one does not understand yet if a Man must do one when he plays the Critick the latter is the more ridiculous Office. And by that *Shakespeare* suffers most. For the natural Veneration which we have for him makes us apt to swallow whatever is given us as *his*, and set off with Encomiums; and hence we quit all Suspicions of Depravity. On the contrary, the Censure of so divine an Author sets us upon his Defence; and this produces an exact Scrutiny and Examination, which ends in finding out and discriminating the true from the spurious.] (I, xxx–xxxvi)

*   *   *

THEOBALD: But, to return to my Subject, which now calls upon me to inquire into those Causes to which the Depravations of my Author originally may be assign'd. We are to consider him as a Writer of whom no authentic Manuscript was extant; as a Writer whose Pieces were dispersedly perform'd on the several *Stages* then in Being. And it was the Custom of those Days for the Poets to take a Price of the *Players* for the Pieces They from time to time furnish'd; and thereupon it was suppos'd they had no farther Right to print them without the Consent of the *Players*. As it was the Interest of the *Companies* to keep their Plays unpublish'd, when any one succeeded, there was a Contest betwixt the Curiosity of the Town, who demanded to see it in Print, and the Policy of the *Stagers*, who wish'd to secrete it within their own Walls. Hence, many Pieces were taken down in Short-hand and imperfectly copied by Ear from a *Representation*; others were printed from piece-meal Parts surreptitiously obtain'd from the Theatres, uncorrect, and without the Poet's Knowledge. To some of these Causes we owe the train of Blemishes that deform those Pieces which stole singly into the World in our Author's Life-time.

There are still other Reasons which may be suppos'd to have affected the whole Set. When the *Players* took upon them to publish his Works intire every Theatre was ransack'd to supply the Copy, and *Parts* collected which had gone thro' as many Changes as Performers, either from Mutilations or Additions made to them. Hence we derive many Chasms and Incoherences in the Sense and Matter. Scenes were frequently transposed, and shuffled out of their true Place to humour the Caprice or suppos'd Convenience of some particular Actor. Hence much Confusion and Impropriety has attended and embarras'd the Business and Fable. For there ever have been, and ever will be in Playhouses, a Set of assuming Directors who know better than the Poet himself the Connexion and Dependance of his Scenes; where Matter is defective, or Superfluities to be retrench'd; Persons that have the Fountain of *Inspiration* as peremptorily in them as Kings have That of *Honour*. To these obvious Causes of Corruption it must be added that our Author has lain under the Disadvantage of having his Errors propagated and multiplied by Time. Because, for near a Century, his Works were republish'd from the faulty Copies without the assistance of any intelligent Editor; which has been the Case likewise of many a *Classic* Writer.

The Nature of any Distemper, once found, has generally been the immediate Step to a Cure. *Shakespeare*'s Case has in a great Measure resembled That of a corrupt *Classic*; and consequently the Method of Cure was likewise to bear a Resemblance. By what Means, and with what Success, this Cure has been effected on ancient Writers is too well known and needs no formal Illustration. The Reputation consequent on Tasks of that Nature invited me to attempt the Method here, with this View, the Hopes of restoring to the Publick their greatest Poet in his Original Purity after having so long lain in a Condition that was a Disgrace to common Sense. To this End I have ventur'd on a Labour that is the first Assay of the kind on any modern Author whatsoever. [WARBURTON: For the late Edition of *Milton* by the Learned Dr. *Bentley* is, in the main, a Performance of another Species. It is plain, it was the Intention of that Great Man rather to correct and pare off the Excrescencies of the *Paradise Lost*, in the manner that *Tucca* and *Varius* were employ'd to criticize the *Æneid* of *Virgil*, than to restore corrupted Passages. Hence, therefore, may be seen either the Iniquity or Ignorance of his Censurers, who from some Expressions would make us believe the *Doctor* every where gives us his Corrections as the Original Text of the Author; whereas the chief Turn of his Criticism is plainly to shew the World that if *Milton* did not write as He would have him, he ought to have wrote so.]

THEOBALD: I thought proper to premise this Observation to the Readers, as it will shew that the Critic on *Shakespeare* is of a quite different Kind. His genuine Text is religiously adher'd to, and the numerous Faults and Blemishes, purely his own, are left as they were found. Nothing is alter'd but what by the clearest Reasoning can be proved a Corruption of the true Text, and the Alteration a real Restoration of the genuine Reading. Nay, so strictly have I strove to give the true Reading, tho' sometimes not to the Advantage of my Author, that I have been ridiculously ridicul'd for it by Those who either were iniquitously for turning every thing to my Disadvantage or else were totally ignorant of the true Duty of an Editor.[1]

[WARBURTON: The Science of Criticism, as far as it affects an Editor, seems to be reduced to these three Classes: the Emendation of corrupt Passages; the Explanation of obscure and difficult ones; and an Inquiry into the Beauties and Defects of Composition. This Work is principally confin'd to the two former Parts, tho' there are some Specimens interspers'd of the latter Kind, as several of the Emendations were best supported, and several of the Difficulties best explain'd, by taking notice of the Beauties and Defects of the Composition peculiar to this Immortal Poet. But This was but occasional and for the sake only of perfecting the two other Parts, which were the proper Objects of the Editor's Labour.] THEOBALD: The third lies open for every willing Undertaker, and I shall be pleas'd to see it the Employment of a masterly Pen.

It must necessarily happen, as I have formerly observ'd,[2] that where the Assistance of Manuscripts is wanting to set an Author's Meaning right, and rescue him from those Errors which have been transmitted down thro' a Series of incorrect Editions and a long Intervention of Time, many Passages must be desperate and past a Cure, and their true Sense irretrievable either to Care or the Sagacity of Conjecture. But is there any Reason therefore to say, That because All cannot be retriev'd, All ought to be left desperate? We should shew very little Honesty, or Wisdom, to play the Tyrants with an Author's Text; to raze, alter, innovate, and overturn at all Adventures, and to the

---

[1] A reference to Pope and his circle: cf. Pope's attack on Theobald in *The Dunciad* (1728) i.159 ff, where he is derided for restoring 'old puns' to Shakespeare's text, a charge repeated in cruder terms by Mallet in his poem 'Of Verbal Criticism'; see Volume 3, No. 84.

[2] In the Introduction to *Shakespeare Restored*.

utter Detriment of his Sense and Meaning. But to be so very reserved and cautious as to interpose no Relief or Conjecture where it manifestly labours and cries out for Assistance seems, on the other hand, an indolent Absurdity.

But because the Art of Criticism, both by Those who cannot form a true Judgment of its Effects, nor can penetrate into its Causes (which takes in a great Number besides the Ladies), is esteem'd only an arbitrary capricious Tyranny exercis'd on Books, I think proper to subjoin a Word or two about those Rules on which I have proceeded and by which I have regulated myself in this Edition. By This, I flatter myself, it will appear, my Emendations are so far from being arbitrary or capricious that They are establish'd with a very high Degree of moral Certainty.

As there are very few Pages in *Shakespeare* upon which some Suspicions of Depravity do not reasonably arise, I have thought it my Duty, in the first place, by a diligent and laborious Collation to take in the Assistances of all the older Copies.

In his *Historical Plays* whenever our *English* Chronicles, and in his Tragedies when *Greek* or *Roman* Story, could give any Light, no Pains have been omitted to set Passages right by comparing my Author with his Originals: for, as I have frequently observed, he was a close and accurate Copier where-ever his *Fable* was founded on *History*.

Where-ever the Author's Sense is clear and discoverable (tho', perchance, low and trivial), I have not by any Innovation tamper'd with his Text out of an Ostentation of endeavouring to make him speak better than the old Copies have done.

Where thro' all the former Editions a Passage has labour'd under flat Nonsense and invincible Darkness, if by the Addition or Alteration of a Letter or two I have restored to Him both Sense and Sentiment such Corrections, I am persuaded, will need no Indulgence.

And whenever I have taken a greater Latitude and Liberty in amending I have constantly endeavoured to support my Corrections and Conjectures by parallel Passages and Authorities from himself, the surest Means of expounding any Author whatsoever. *Cette voïe d'interpreter un Autheur par lui-même est plus sure que tous les Commentaires*, says a very learned *French* Critick.

As to my *Notes* (from which the common and learned Readers of our Author, I hope, will derive some Pleasure), I have endeavour'd to give them a Variety in some Proportion to their Number. Where-ever I have ventur'd at an Emendation a *Note* is constantly subjoin'd to justify and assert the Reason of it. Where I only offer a Conjecture, and do not disturb the Text, I fairly set forth my Grounds for such Conjecture and submit it to Judgment. Some Remarks are spent in explaining Passages where the Wit or Satire depends on an obscure Point of History; Others where Allusions are to Divinity, Philosophy, or other Branches of Science. Some are added to shew where there is a Suspicion of our Author having borrow'd from the Antients; others to shew where he is rallying his Contemporaries, or where He himself is rallied by them. And some are necessarily thrown in to explain an obscure and obsolete *Term*, *Phrase*, or *Idea*. I once intended to have added a complete and copious *Glossary*, but as I have been importun'd, and am prepar'd, to give a correct Edition of our Author's POEMS (in which many Terms occur that are not to be met with in his *Plays*) I thought a *Glossary* to all *Shakespeare*'s Works more proper to attend that Volume.[1]

In reforming an infinite Number of Passages in the *Pointing*, where the Sense was before quite lost, I have frequently subjoin'd Notes to shew the *deprav'd* and to prove the *reform'd* Pointing: a Part of Labour in this Work which I could very willingly have spared myself. May it not be objected, why then have you burthen'd us with these Notes? The Answer is obvious and, if I mistake not, very material. Without such Notes these Passages in subsequent Editions would be liable, thro' the Ignorance of Printers and Correctors, to fall into the old Confusion. Whereas a Note on every one hinders all possible Return to Depravity, and for ever secures them in a State of Purity and Integrity not to be lost or forfeited.

Again, as some Notes have been necessary to point out the Detection of the corrupted Text and establish the Restoration of the genuine Readings, some others have been as necessary for the Explanation of Passages obscure and difficult. To understand the Necessity and Use of this Part of my Task, some Particulars of my Author's Character are previously to be explain'd. [WARBURTON: There are *Obscurities* in him which are common to him with all Poets of the same Species; there are Others the Issue of the Times he liv'd in; and there are Others, again, peculiar to himself. The Nature of Comic Poetry being entirely satyrical, it busies itself more in exposing what we call Caprice and Humour than Vices cognizable to the Laws. The *English*, from the Happiness of a free Constitution and a Turn of Mind peculiarly speculative and inquisitive, are observ'd to produce more *Humourists* and a greater Variety of original *Characters* than any other People whatso-

---

[1] Such an edition never appeared; but cf. No. 81 above on the text of the poems.

ever. And These owing their immediate Birth to the peculiar Genius of each Age, an infinite Number of Things alluded to, glanced at, and expos'd must needs become obscure as the *Characters* themselves are antiquated and disused.] THEOBALD: An Editor therefore should be well vers'd in the History and Manners of his Author's Age, if he aims at doing him a Service in this Respect.

Besides, [WARBURTON: *Wit* lying mostly in the Assemblage of *Ideas*, and in the putting Those together with Quickness and Variety wherein can be found any Resemblance or Congruity to make up pleasant Pictures and agreeable Visions in the Fancy, the Writer who aims at Wit must of course range far and wide for Materials. Now the Age in which *Shakespeare* liv'd having, above all others, a wonderful Affection to appear Learned, they declined vulgar Images, such as are immediately fetch'd from Nature, and rang'd thro' the Circle of the Sciences to fetch their Ideas from thence. But as the Resemblances of such Ideas to the Subject must necessarily lie very much out of the common Way, and every Piece of Wit appear a Riddle to the Vulgar, this, that should have taught them the forced, quaint, unnatural Tract they were in (and induce them to follow a more natural One), was the very Thing that kept them attach'd to it. The ostentatious Affectation of abstruse Learning peculiar to that Time, the Love that Men naturally have to every Thing that looks like Mystery, fixed them down to this Habit of Obscurity. Thus became the Poetry of DONNE (tho' the wittiest Man of that Age) nothing but a continued Heap of Riddles. And our *Shakespeare*, with all his easy Nature about him, for want of the Knowledge of the true Rules of Art falls frequently into this vicious Manner.

The third Species of *Obscurities* which deform our Author as the Effects of his own Genius and Character, are Those that proceed from his peculiar Manner of *Thinking*, and as peculiar a Manner of *cloathing* those *Thoughts*. With regard to his *Thinking*, it is certain that he had a general Knowledge of all the Sciences, but his Acquaintance was rather That of a Traveller than a Native. Nothing in Philosophy was unknown to him but every Thing in it had the Grace and Force of Novelty. And as Novelty is one main Source of Admiration, we are not to wonder that He has perpetual Allusions to the most recondite Parts of the Sciences: and This was done not so much out of Affectation as the Effect of Admiration begot by Novelty. Then, as to his *Style* and *Diction*, we may much more justly apply to SHAKESPEARE what a celebrated Writer[1] has said of MILTON: *Our Language sunk under him, and*

_____
[1] Addison, *Spectator*, No. 297.

was unequal to that Greatness of Soul which furnish'd him with such glorious Conceptions. He therefore frequently uses old Words to give his Diction an Air of Solemnity, as he coins others to express the Novelty and Variety of his Ideas.]

THEOBALD: Upon every distinct Species of these *Obscurities* I have thought it my Province to employ a Note, for the Service of my Author and the Entertainment of my Readers. A few transient Remarks too I have not scrupled to intermix, upon the Poet's *Negligences* and *Omissions* in point of Art; but I have done it always in such a Manner as will testify my Deference and Veneration for the immortal Author. Some Censurers of *Shakespeare*, and particularly Mr. *Rymer*, have taught me to distinguish betwixt the *Railer* and *Critick*. The Outrage of his Quotations is so remarkably violent, so push'd beyond all bounds of Decency and Sober Reasoning that it quite carries over the Mark at which it was levell'd. Extravagant Abuse throws off the Edge of the intended Disparagement, and turns the Madman's Weapon into his own Bosom. In short, [WARBURTON: as to *Rymer*, This is my Opinion of him from his *Criticisms* on the *Tragedies* of the Last Age. He writes with great Vivacity, and appears to have been a Scholar; but as for his Knowledge of the Art of Poetry I can't perceive it was any deeper than his Acquaintance with *Bossu* and *Dacier*, from whom he has transcrib'd many of his best Reflexions.] THEOBALD: The late Mr. *Gildon* was one attached to *Rymer* by a similar way of Thinking and Studies. They were both of that Species of Criticks who are desirous of displaying their Powers rather in finding Faults than in consulting the Improvement of the World: the *hypercritical* Part of the Science of *Criticism*.

I had not mentioned the modest Liberty I have here and there taken of animadverting on my Author, but that I was willing to obviate in time the splenetick Exaggerations of my Adversaries on this Head. From past Experiments I have reason to be conscious in what Light this Attempt may be placed, and that what I call a *modest Liberty* will, by a little of their Dexterity, be inverted into downright *Impudence*. From a hundred mean and dishonest Artifices employ'd to discredit this Edition and to cry down its Editor I have all the Grounds in nature to beware of Attacks. But tho' the Malice of Wit, join'd to the Smoothness of Versification, may furnish some Ridicule, Fact, I hope, will be able to stand its Ground against Banter and Gaiety. (xlv–xlix)

★   ★   ★

[From the Notes]

[On *The Tempest*, 1.2.351 ff: 'Abhorred slave . . .']
In all the printed Editions this speech is given to *Miranda*; but I am
persuaded, the Author never design'd it for her. In the first place, 'tis
probable *Prospero* taught *Caliban* to speak, rather than left that Office
to his Daughter; in the next Place, as *Prospero* was here rating *Caliban*
it would be a great Impropriety for her to take the Discipline out of his
hands, and indeed in some sort an Indecency in her to reply to what
Caliban last was speaking of. Mr. *Dryden*, I observe, in his Alteration
of this Play, has judiciously placed this Speech to *Prospero*. I can easily
guess that the change was first deriv'd from the Players, who not
loving that any Character should stand too long silent on the stage, to
obviate that inconvenience with Regard to *Miranda* clap'd this Speech
to her Part. (I, 18)

★　　★　　★

[On *The Tempest*, 2.1.10 ff; rejected by Pope]
. . . For my part, tho' I allow the Matter of the Dialogue to be very
poor and trivial (of which, I am sorry to say, we don't want other
Instances in our Poet) I cannot be of this Gentleman's Opinion, that it
is interpolated. . . . Mr. *Pope*'s Criticism therefore is injudicious and
unweigh'd. Besides, poor and jejune as the Matter of the Dialogue is,
it was certainly design'd to be of a ridiculous Stamp, to divert and
unsettle the King's Thoughts from reflecting too deeply on his Son's
suppos'd Drowning. (I, 24)

★　　★　　★

[On *The Tempest*, 2.2.134: *I afraid of him? a very shallow monster.*—]
WARBURTON: It is to be observ'd, *Trinculo* is not charg'd with any Fear
of *Caliban*, and therefore This seems to come in abruptly: but in This
consists the true Humour. His own Consciousness that he had been
terribly afraid of him, after the Fright was over, drew out this Bragg.
This seems to be one of *Shakespeare*'s fine Touches of Nature, for that
Trinculo had been horribly frighten'd at the Monster, and shook with
Fear of him while he lay under his Gaberdine, is plain from What
Caliban says while he is lying there! *Thou dost me yet but little Harm;
thou wilt anon, I know by thy* trembling.] (I, 38)

★　　★　　★

[On *The Tempest*, 3.2]

The Part of *Caliban* has been esteem'd a signal Instance of the Copious-ness of *Shakespeare*'s Invention, and that he had shewn an Extent of Genius in creating a Person which was not in Nature. And for this, as well as his other *magical* and *ideal* Characters, a just Admiration has been paid him. . . . (I, 44)

*   *   *

[On *A Midsummer-Night's Dream*, 1.1.216 ff]

> *Emptying our Bosoms of their Counsels* swell'd;
> *There my* Lysander *and myself shall meet,*
> *And thence from* Athens *turn away our Eyes,*
> *To seek new Friends, and strange* Companions.

This whole Scene is strictly in Rhyme; and that it deviates in these two Couplets, I am persuaded, is owing to the Ignorance of the first and the Inaccuracy of the later Editors. I have therefore ventur'd to restore the Rhymes, as I make no Doubt but the Poet first gave them. *Sweet* was easily corrupted into *swell'd*, because That made an *Antithesis* to *Emptying*; and *strange Companions* our Editors thought was plain *English*, but *stranger Companies* a little quaint and unintelligible. It may be necessary, in Proof of my Emendation, to shew that our Author elsewhere uses the *Substantive* Stranger *adjectively*; and *Companies*, to signify *Companions*. . . . (I, 85–6)

*   *   *

[On *A Midsummer-Night's Dream*, 1.2.25 ff]

> *The raging Rocks*
> *And shivering Shocks*, &c.

I presume This to be either a Quotation from some fustian old Play, which I have not been able to trace; or if not a direct Quotation a Ridicule on some bombast Rants very near resembling it. (I, 88)

*   *   *

[On *A Midsummer-Night's Dream*, 3.2.329] *You* Minimus,—

This is no Term of Art that I can find; and I can scarce be willing to think that *Shakespeare* would use the Masculine of an Adjective to a Woman. He was not so deficient in Grammar. I have not ventur'd to disturb the Text; but the Author, perhaps, might have wrote;

> *You*, Minim, *you*,—

i.e.   You *Diminutive* of the Creation, you *Reptile*. (I, 120)

*   *   *

[On *A Midsummer-Night's Dream*, 5.1.113 ff; in Pope's edition]

> *We do not come as minding to content you,*
> *Our true intent is all for your delight,*
> *We are not here that you should here repent you,*
> *The actors are at hand; &c.*

Thus the late accurate Editor, deviating from all the Old Copies, has, by a certain peculiar Fatality, pointed this Passage. The whole Glee and Humour of the Prologue is in the Actor's making false Rests, and so turning every Member of the Sentences into flagrant Nonsense. . . . (I, 139)

* * *

[On *The Two Gentlemen of Verona*, 1.1.94]
   I, a lost Mutton, *gave your* Letter *to her, a* lac'd Mutton;
Launce calls himself a *lost Mutton* because he had lost his Master, and because *Proteus* had been proving him a *Sheep*. But why does he call the Lady a *Lac'd Mutton?* Your notable Wenchers are to this day call'd *Mutton-mongers*: and consequently the Object of their Passion must, by the Metaphor, be the *Mutton*. And *Cotgrave*, in his *English-French* Dictionary, explains *Lac'd* Mutton: *Une Garse, putain, fille de Joye*. And Mr. *Motteux* has render'd this Passage of *Rabelais*, in the Prologue of his fourth Book, *Cailles coiphées mignonnement chantans*, in this manner; *Coated Quails and* laced Mutton *waggishly singing*. So that *lac'd Mutton* has been a sort of standard Phrase for *Girls of Pleasure*. . . . That *lac'd Mutton* was a Term in Vogue before our Author appear'd in Writing I find from an old Play, printed in Black Letter in the Year 1578, call'd *Promos and Cassandra*; in which a Courtezan's Servant thus speaks to her:

> *Prying abroad for Playefellowes, and such,*
> *For you, Mistresse, I hearde of one Phallax,*
> *A Man esteemde of Promos verie much:*
> *Of whose Nature I was so bolde to axe,*
> *And I smealte, he lov'd lase mutton well.* (I, 156)

* * *

[On *The Two Gentlemen of Verona*, 1.3.84]
   Oh, how this Spring of Love resembleth well
This monosyllable was foisted in by Mr. *Pope* to support, as he thought, the Versification in the Close. But it was done for Want of observing *Shakespeare*'s Licences in his *Measures*, which 'tis proper, once for all, to take notice of. *Resembleth*, he design'd here should in pronunciation

make four Syllables; as *witnesse*, afterwards in this Play, and as *Fidler*, (in the *Taming a Shrew*) and *angry* (twice in *Timon of Athens*) are made *Trisyllables*; and as *fire* and *hour* are almost for ever protracted by him to two Syllables. (I, 165)

*   *   *

[On *The Two Gentlemen of Verona*, 3.1.278]
   With my Mastership? *why, it is at Sea.*
These poetical Editors are pleasant Gentlemen to let this pass without any Suspicion. For how does *Launce* mistake the Word? *Speed* asks him about his Mastership, and he replies to it *litteratim*. But then how was his Mastership at Sea, and on Shore too? The Addition of a Letter and a Note of *Apostrophe* ['my Master's ship!'] make *Launce* both mistake the Word, and sets the Pun right. It restores, indeed, but a mean Joke; but without it there is no Sense in the Passage. Besides, it is in Character with the rest of the Scene; and, I dare be confident, the Poet's own Conceit. (I, 192)

*   *   *

[On *The Merry Wives of Windsor*, 1.1.227]
   I hope, upon Familiarity will grow more Content.
Certainly, the Editors in their Sagacity have murther'd a Jest here. It is design'd, no Doubt, that *Slender* should say *decrease*, instead of *increase*; and *dissolved* and *dissolutely*, instead of *resolved* and *resolutely*; but to make him say on the present Occasion that upon Familiarity will grow more *Content*, instead of *Contempt*, is disarming the Sentiment of all its *Salt* and *Humour*, and disappointing the Audience of a reasonable Cause for Laughter. (I, 231)

*   *   *

[On *The Merry Wives of Windsor*, 3.1.15] *By shallow Rivers,*
The Stanza which Sir *Hugh* repeats here is part of a sweet little Sonnet of our Author's, and printed among his Poems, call'd *The Passionate Shepherd to his Love*. MILTON was so enamour'd with this Poem and the *Nymph's Reply* to it that he has borrow'd the Close of his *L'Allegro*, and *Il Penseroso* from them.—I don't know whether it has been generally observ'd, but it is with wonderful Humour, in his singing, that Sir *Hugh* intermixes with his Madrigal the first Line of the 137th singing *Psalm*. (I, 261)

*   *   *

[On *Measure for Measure*, 1.3.20]
    The needful Bits *and* Curbs *for headstrong* Weeds.
WARBURTON: There is no manner of Analogy or Consonance in the
Metaphors here; and, tho' the Copies agree, I do not think the Author
would have talk'd of *Bits* and *Curbs* for *Weeds*. On the other hand,
nothing can be more proper than to compare Persons of *unbridled Licentiousness* to headstrong *Steeds*; and in this View *bridling the Passions* has
been a Phrase adopted by our best Poets. . . .] (I, 321)

*   *   *

[On *Measure for Measure*, 5.1.36] *And she will speak most bitterly.*
Thus is the Verse left imperfect by Mr. *Rowe* and Mr. *Pope*; tho' the
old Copies of all fill it up, as I have done. I have restor'd an infinite
Number of such Passages *tacitly* from the first Impressions; but I
thought proper to take notice once for all, here, that as Mr. *Pope*
follows Mr. *Rowe's* Edition in his Errors and Omissions it gives great
Suspicion, notwithstanding the pretended Collation of Copies, that
Mr. *Pope* for the Generality took Mr. *Rowe's* Edition as his Guide.
(I, 384)

*   *   *

[On *Measure for Measure*, 5.1.467]
The introducing *Barnardine* here is seemingly a matter of no Consequence, as he is no Person concern'd in the Action of the Play nor
directly aiding to the *Dénouement*, as the *French* call it, of the Plot. But
to our Poet's Praise let me observe that it is not done without double
Art: it gives a Handle for the Discovery of *Claudio* being alive, and so
heightens the Surprize; and at the same time, by the Pardon of
Barnardine, gives a fine opportunity of making the *Duke's* Character
more amiable, both for Mercy, and Virtue. (I, 396–7)

*   *   *

[End-note to *Measure for Measure*]
I cannot help taking notice with how much Judgment *Shakespeare* has
given Turns to this Story from what he found it in *Cinthio Giraldi's*
Novel. In the first place the Brother, whom our Poet calls *Claudio*,
is there actually executed, and the ungrateful *Governor* sends his Head,
in a Bravado, to the Sister, after he had debauch'd her on Promise of
Marriage—a Circumstance of too much Horror and Villany for the
Stage. And in the next place this Sister afterwards is—to solder up her
Disgrace—marry'd to the Governor, and begs his Life of the Emperor,

tho' he had so unjustly been the Death of her Brother. Both which Absurdities our Poet has avoided by the Episode of *Mariana*, a Creature purely of his own Invention. The *Duke*'s remaining *incognito* at home, to supervise the Conduct of his *Deputy*, is also entirely our Author's Fiction.—This Story was attempted for the Scene by one *George Whetstone* (before our Author was fourteen Years old) in *Two Comical Discourses* (as they are call'd) *containing the right, excellent and famous History of Promos and Cassandra*: and printed in the old Black Letter, in 1578. Neither of these Discourses, I believe, were ever acted. The Author left them with his Friends, to publish, for He that very Year accompanied Sir *Humphry Gilbert*, Sir *Walter Raleigh*'s Brother, in his Voyage to *Norimbega* in the *West-Indies*. I could prove to Demonstration that *Shakespeare* had perus'd these Pieces; but whoever has seen, and knows what execrable mean Stuff they are I am sure will acquit him from all Suspicion of Plagiarism. (I, 398-9)

★   ★   ★

[On *The Merchant of Venice*, 2.9.47 ff]
> —*how much honour*
> Pick'd *from the* Chaff *and Ruin of the Times,*
> To be new *varnish'd.*

Mr. *Warburton* very justly observ'd to me upon the Confusion and Disagreement of the *Metaphors* here, and is of Opinion that *Shakespeare* might have wrote

> To be new *vanned.*—

i.e. winnow'd, purged: from the *French* Word *vanner*, which is deriv'd from the *Latin vannus, ventilabrum*, the *Fann* used for winnowing the Chaff from the Corn. This Alteration, as he observes, restores the Metaphor to its Integrity, and our Poet frequently uses the same Thought. So, in the 2d Part of *Henry IV*.

> *We shall be* winnow'd *with so rough a Wind,*
> *That ev'n our Corn shall seem as light as* Chaff.   [4.1.194 f]

And, again, in *K. Henry V*.

> *Such, and so finely* boulted *did'st thou seem,*   [2.2.137]

for *boulted* signifies *sifted, refin'd.* The Correction is truly ingenious, and probable; but as *Shakespeare* is so loose and licentious in the blending of different Metaphors I have not ventur'd to disturb the Text. (II, 37-8)

★   ★   ★

[On *The Merchant of Venice*, 3.2.239]
The Poet has shewn a singular Art here in his Conduct with Relation
to *Jessica*. As the Audience were already appriz'd of her Story, the
opening it here to *Portia* would have been a superfluous Repetition.
Nor could it be done properly while a Letter of such Haste and Consequence was to be deliver'd, and on which the main Action of the Play
depended. *Jessica* is therefore artfully complimented in *dumb Shew*,
and no Speech made to her, because the Scene is drawn out to a great
Length by more important Business. (II, 50–1)

*   *   *

[On *Love's Labour's Lost*, 2.1.180 ff]
I have made it a Rule throughout this Edition to replace all those
Passages which Mr. *Pope* in his Impressions thought fit to *degrade*. As
We have no Authority to call them in Question for not being genuine
I confess, as an Editor, I thought I had no Authority to displace them.
Tho, I must own freely at the same time, there are some Scenes
(particularly in this Play) so very mean and contemptible that One
would heartily wish for the Liberty of expunging them. Whether they
were really written by our Author, whether he penn'd them in his
boyish Age, or whether he purposely comply'd with the prevailing
Vice of the Times, when *Puns*, *Conundrum* and *quibbling* Conceits were
as much in Vogue as *Grimace* and *Arlequinades* are at this wise Period, I
dare not take upon me to determine. (II, 109–10)

*   *   *

[On *Love's Labour's Lost*, 5.2.570 ff]
 Your Lion that holds the poll-ax *sitting on a* Closestool,
Alexander the *Great*, as one of the Nine *Worthies*, bears *Gules*; a Lion,
Or, seiant in a Chair, holding a *Battle-axe* argent. *Vid.* Ger. Leigh's
Accidence of Armouries. . . .—But why, because *Nathaniel* had behav'd
ill as *Alexander*, was that Worthy's Lion and Poll-axe to be given to
Ajax? *Costard*, the Clown, has a Conceit in This very much of a Piece
with his Character. The Name of *Ajax* is equivocally us'd by him; and
he means, the *Insignia* of such a Conqueror as the Curate exhibited in
his wretched Representation ought to be given to *a Jakes*; — *sit Verbo
Reverentia!* The same sort of Conundrum is used by B. *Jonson* at the
Close of his Poem call'd the *famous Voyage*.
 And I could wish, for their eterniz'd sakes,
 My Muse had plow'd with his that sung A-jax. (II, 172)

*   *   *

[On *Love's Labour's Lost*, 5.2.866] *That's too long for a Play.*

Besides the exact Regularity to the Rules of Art which the Author has happen'd to preserve in some few of his Pieces this is Demonstration, I think, that tho' he has more frequently transgress'd the *Unity* of *Time* by cramming Years into the Compass of a Play, yet he knew the Absurdity of so doing, and was not unacquainted with the Rule to the contrary. (II, 181)

★   ★   ★

[On *All's Well that Ends Well*, 2.3.208] *Do not plunge thyself too far in anger, lest thou hasten thy trial; which* if—*Lord have mercy on thee for a hen;* . . . I have restor'd the Reading of the old *Folio*, and, by subjoining the Mark to shew a *Break* is necessary, have retriev'd the Poet's genuine Sense: [Quoted]. The sequel of the sentence is imply'd, not express'd: this Figure the Rhetoricians have call'd *Aposiopesis*. . . . (II, 395)

★   ★   ★

[On *All's Well that Ends Well*, 5.3.6]
    *Natural Rebellion, done i'th'*blade *of Youth,*
[WARBURTON: If this Reading be genuine the Metaphor must be from any Grain or Plant taking Fire: but I own it seems more in *Shakespeare's* way of Thinking to suppose He wrote:
    Natural Rebellion, done i'th' blaze of Youth,
i.e. in the Fervour, Flame, &c.] So He has express'd himself upon a like Occasion in *Hamlet*,   [1.3.115 ff]
        — *I do not know,*
    When the Blood burns, *how prodigal the Soul*
    Lends the Tongue Vows. These Blazes, O my Daughter, &c.
And so, again, in his *Troilus and Cressida*   [4.5.105 f]
    For Hector, *in his Blaze of Wrath, subscribes*
    To tender Objects.— (II, 444)

★   ★   ★

[On *Twelfth Night*, 1.3.89 ff]
    Sir And. — *O, had I but follow'd the Arts!*
    Sir To. Then had'st thou had an excellent head of Hair.
    Sir And. Why, would That have mended my Hair?
    Sir To. Past Question; for thou seest it will not cool *my Nature.*
Prodigious Sagacity! and yet thus it has pass'd down thro' all the printed Copies. We cannot enough admire that happy Indolence of Mr. *Pope*, which can acquiesce in transmitting to us such Stuff for

genuine Sense and Argument. The Dialogue is of a very light Strain, 'tis certain, betwixt two foolish Knights: but yet I would be very glad to know, methinks, what Sir *Andrew*'s following the *Arts* or his *Hair* being *mended* could have to do with the *cooling* or not *cooling* Sir *Toby*'s Nature. But my Emendation [*curl by Nature*] clears up all this Absurdity: and the Context is an unexceptionable Confirmation.

Sir And. *But it becomes me well enough, does't not?*
Sir To. *Excellent! It hangs like Flax on a Distaff, &c.*

I cannot pass over the remarkable Conundrum betwixt Sir *Andrew* wishing he had follow'd the *Arts* and Sir *Toby*'s Application of This to the using *Art* in improving his *Hair*, because I would observe what Variety and what a Contrast of Character the Poet has preserv'd in this Pair of ridiculous Knights. Sir *Toby* has moderate natural Parts, and a smattering of Education, which makes him always to be running his Wit, and gives him a Predominance over the other. Sir *Andrew* is a Blockhead by Nature, and unimprov'd by any Acquirements from Art, and so is made the very Anvil to Imposition and Ridicule. (II, 465–6)

*   *   *

[On *Twelfth Night*, 2.4.111 ff]
   — *She pined in Thought;*
   And, with a green and yellow Melancholy,
   She sate like Patience *on a Monument,*
   Smiling at Grief.

This very fine Image, which has been so universally applauded, it is not impossible but our Author might originally have borrow'd from CHAUCER in his *Assembly of Foules*.

   And her besidis wonder discretlie,
   Dame Pacience *ysitting there I fonde*
   With Face pale, *upon an hill of* sonde.[1]

If he was indebted, however, for the first rude Draught, how amply has he repaid that Debt in heightning the Picture! How much does the *green* and *yellow Melancholy* transcend the Old Bard's *Face pale*; the *Monument*, his *Hill of Sand*; and what an additional Beauty is *smiling at Grief*, for which there are no Ground nor Traces in the Original! Our Author has given us this fine Picture again in another Place, but, to shew the Power and Extent of his Genius, with Features and Lineaments varied:

[1] *Parliament of Fowls*, ll. 241 ff.

499

— *yet Thou*
Do'st look like Patience, gazing *on* Kings' Graves
And smiling [*harsh*] Extremity *out of Act.*

Pericles, Prince of Tyre [5.1.136 ff]

This absurd Old Play, I have elsewhere taken Notice, was not entirely of our Author's penning; but he has honour'd it with a Number of Master-Touches so peculiar to himself that a knowing Reader may with Ease and Certainty distinguish the Traces of his Pencil. (II, 490)

* * *

[On *Twelfth Night,* 5.1.111 ff]

Why should I not, had I the Heart to do it,
Like to th' Ægyptian Thief, at point of Death
Kill what I love!

In this *Simile* a particular Story is presuppos'd; which ought to be known, to shew the Justness and Propriety of the Comparison. I'll give the Synopsis of it from *Heliodorus's Æthiopics,* to which our Author was indebted for the Allusion. This *Egyptian* Thief was *Thyamis,* who was a Native of *Memphis,* and at the Head of a Band of Robbers. *Theagenes* and *Chariclea* falling into their Hands, *Thyamis* fell desperately in Love with the Lady, and would have married her. Soon after, a stronger Body of Robbers coming down upon *Thyamis's* Party, He was in such Fears for his Mistress that he had her shut into a Cave with his Treasure. It was customary with those Barbarians, *when they despair'd of their own Safety, first to make away with Those whom they held dear,* and desired for Companions in the next Life. *Thyamis,* therefore, benetted round with his Enemies, raging with Love, Jealousy, and Anger, went to his Cave; and calling aloud in the *Egyptian* Tongue, so soon as He heard himself answer'd towards the Cave's Mouth by a Grecian, making to the Person by the Direction of her Voice, he caught her by the Hair with his left Hand and (supposing her to be *Chariclea*) with his right Hand plung'd his Sword into her Breast. (II, 528)

* * *

[Head-note to *The Winter's Tale*] ARCHIDAMUS.

This is a Character of that Sort which the old Cruticks have call'd πρόσωπον προτατιχόν: one entirely out of the Action and Argument of the Play, and introduc'd only to open Something necessary to be known, previous to the Action of the *Fable. Donatus,* in his Preface to *Terence's Fair Andrian,* explains this Character thus. . . . 'By a *Protatick*

Character we are to understand such a One as is introduc'd in the Beginning, and never after appears in any Part of the Fable.' Such is *Sosia* in that Comedy of *Terence*, such, *Davus* in his *Phormio*, and *Philotis* and *Syra*, in his *Mother-in-law*. Such are the Servants of the *Capulets* and *Montagues* in our Author's *Romeo and Juliet*; the Two Gentlemen, who open his *Cymbeline*; the Sea-Captain, in the Second Scene of *Twelfth Night*; and (tho' thrown into the Middle of the Play) of the same Nature are the Gentlemen in *K. Henry VIII*, who are introduced only to make the Narratives of *Buckingham's* Arraignment, and *Anne Bullen's* Coronation. (III, 65–6)

★   ★   ★

[On *The Winter's Tale*, 3.1.1 f]
> *The Climate's delicate, the Air most sweet,*
> *Fertile the Isle—*

I must subjoin a very reasonable Conjecture of my Friend upon this Passage. — 'But the Temple of *Apollo* at *Delphi* was not in an *Island*, but in *Phocis* on the Continent. It's plain, the blundering Transcribers had their Heads running on *Delos*, an Island of the *Cyclades*. So that the true Reading is undoubtedly;

> *The Climate's delicate, the Air most sweet,*
> *Fertile the* Soil; —

Soil might with a very easy Transposition of the Letters be corrupted to *Isle*. But the true Reading manifests itself likewise on this Account, that in a Description the Sweetness of *Air*, and Fertility of *Soil*, is much more terse and elegant than *Air* and *Isle*.'   Mr. *Warburton*.

But, to confess the Truth, I am very suspicious that our Author, notwithstanding, wrote *Isle*, and for this Reason. The Groundwork and Incidents of his Play are taken from an old Story call'd *The pleasant and delectable History of Dorastus and Fawnia*; written by Mr. *Robert Greene*, a Master of Arts in *Cambridge*, in the Reign of Q. *Elizabeth*. And there the Queen begs of her Lord, in the Rage of his Jealousy, *That it would please his Majesty to send six of his Nobles, whom he best trusted, to the* Isle *of Delphos, there to enquire of the Oracle of Apollo*, &c. Another palpable Absurdity our Author has copied from the same *Tale* in making *Bohemia* a maritime Country, which is known to be Inland, and in the Heart of the Main Continent. (III, 98–9)

★   ★   ★

[Head-note to *Richard II*]

. . . Mr. *Gildon* acknowledges that *Shakespeare* has drawn K. *Richard's* Character according to the best Accounts of History; that is, insolent, proud, and thoughtless in Prosperity, dejected and desponding on the Appearance of Danger.—But whatever Blemishes he had either in Temper or Conduct, the Distresses of his latter Days, the Double Divorce from his Throne and Queen are painted in such strong Colours that those Blemishes are lost in the Shade of his Misfortunes, and our Compassion for Him wipes out the Memory of such Spots, *quas humana parum cavit Natura.*[1] (III, 255)

* * *

[On *Richard II*, 1.3.268 ff]

Boling. *Nay, rather, ev'ry tedious Stride I make,*
This and the six Verses which follow I have ventur'd to supply from the old *Quarto*. The Allusion, 'tis true, to an *Apprentice-ship* and becoming a *Journeyman* is not in sublime Taste, nor, as *Horace* has express'd it, *spirat Tragicum satis:*[2] however, as there is no Doubt of the Passage being genuine, the Lines are not so despicable as to deserve being quite lost. (III, 271)

* * *

[On *2 Henry IV*, 1.2.155]

You follow the young Prince up and down like his evil *angel.*
What a precious Collator has Mr. *Pope* approv'd himself in this Passage! Besides, if This were the true Reading, *Falstaff* could not have made the witty and humourous Evasion he has done in his Reply. I have restor'd the Reading of the oldest *Quarto*. The Lord Chief Justice calls *Falstaff* the Prince's *ill Angel*, or Genius: which *Falstaff* turns off by saying an *ill Angel* (meaning the Coin call'd an *Angel*) is *light*; but surely it can't be said that He wants *Weight*: ergo—the Inference is obvious. Now Money may be call'd *ill* or *bad*; but it is never call'd *evil* with Regard to its being under Weight. This Mr. *Pope* will facetiously call restoring *lost Puns*: but if the Author wrote a Pun, and it happens to be lost in an Editor's Indolence, I shall, in spite of his Grimace, venture at bringing it back to Light. (III, 452-3)

* * *

---

[1] Horace, *A.P.*, 352 f: 'faults which . . . human frailty has failed to avert'.
[2] Horace, *Epistles*, 2.1.166: 'for he has some tragic inspiration, and is happy in his ventures'.

[On *2 Henry IV*, 4.1.92] *Of forg'd Rebellion with a Seal divine?*
In one of my Old *Quartos* of 1600 (for I have Two of the self same
Edition, one of which, 'tis evident, was corrected in some Passages
during the working off the whole Impression) after the Line above
quoted I found this Verse:

> *And consecrate Commotion's civil* Edge.

I have thought the Verse worth preserving, and ventur'd to substitute
Page for *Edge*, with Regard to the Uniformity of Metaphor. Tho', I
confess, the Latter may very well do in this Sense: that the Sword of
Rebellion drawn by a Bishop may in some Sort be said to be conse-
crated by his Reverence; as the King, afterwards, talking of going to
the Holy Wars, says

> *We'll draw no Swords, but What are* sanctified. (III, 499–500)

★ ★ ★

[On *2 Henry IV*, 4.5.129] England *shall double* gild *his treble* Guilt
This line is in all the Editions in general, but Mr. *Pope's*, and he has
thought fit to cashier it. If he imagin'd the Conceit too mean, he ought
at least to have degraded it to the bottom of his Page, not absolutely
stifled it. But mean as the Conceit is, our Author has repeated it again
in his *K. Henry V.* [2 Prof. 26 ff]

> *Have for the Gilt of* France (O Guilt, *indeed!*)
> *Confirm'd Conspiracy with fearful* France. (III, 520)

★ ★ ★

[Head-note to *1 Henry VI*]
. . . I could point out many other Transgressions against History as
far as the Order of Time is concern'd. Indeed, tho there are several
Master-Strokes in these three Plays which incontestibly betray the
Workmanship of *Shakespeare*, yet I am almost doubtful whether they
were entirely of his Writing. And unless they were wrote by him very
early, I shou'd rather imagine them to have been brought to him as a
Director of the *Stage*, and so to have receiv'd some finishing Beauties
at his hand. An accurate Observer will easily see, the *Diction* of them
is more *obsolete* and the *Numbers* more *mean* and *prosaical* than in the
Generality of his genuine Compositions. (IV, 110)

★ ★ ★

[On *1 Henry VI*, 1.1.56; cf. Pope's suggestion, p. 417 above]
. . . I have only one further Remark to make upon the Topick in hand,
and 'tis this: that where the Authority of all the Books makes the Poet
commit a Blunder (whose general Character it is, not to be very exact)

'tis the Duty of an Editor to shew him as he is, and to detect all fraudulent tampering to make him better. But to fill up a Chasm by Conjecture, with an *Anachronism* that stares Sense out of Countenance: this with Submission to Mr. *Pope, Nec homines, nec Dii, nec concessere Columnae.*[1] (IV, 112)

*   *   *

[On *1 Henry VI*, 1.3.35] *Thou, that giv'st Whores*
The Brothel-houses, or *Stews*, which were of old licens'd on the *Bankside* at *Southwark* were within the District, and under the Jurisdiction, of the Bishop of *Winchester*. To this our Poet has again alluded in the last Speech of his *Troilus and Cressida:*

—but that my Fear is this,
Some galled Goose of Winchester would hiss.   [5.10.52 f]

For the Venereal Tumour, call'd a *Winchester-goose*, deriv'd its Name from that Bishop giving Dispensations to Strumpets. Nor were Harlots alone permitted to exercise their Function at the *Bankside*, but Male-Bauds were likewise indulg'd to keep publick Houses for the Reception of such Cattle. And these became so infamous that in the 11th Year of *Henry VI* we find a Statute was made, That none, who dwelt at the Stews in *Southwark*, should be impannell'd in Juries, nor keep any Inn, or Tavern, but there. These Stews in the 37th Year of King *Henry VIII* (*Anno* 1546) were, by Proclamation and Sound of Trumpet, suppress'd; and the Houses let to People of Reputation and honest Callings. (IV, 122)

*   *   *

[On *2 Henry VI*, 5.2.40 ff]

— Oh, let the vile World end,
And the premised Flames of the last day
Knit Earth and Heav'n together!

[WARBURTON: i.e. 'Let the vile World end now; and let those Flames, which are reserv'd for its Destruction hereafter, be *sent now*.'—*Shakespeare* is very peculiar in his *Adjectives*, and it is much in his Manner to use the Words borrow'd from the *Latine* closer to their original Signification than they were vulgarly used in. So here he uses *premised* in the Sense of the Word from which it is deriv'd, *praemissus*.] (IV, 295)

*   *   *

[On *3 Henry VI*, 1.3.48] *Dii faciant, laudis, &c.*
This is the 66th Verse of *Phillis* her Epistle to *Demophoon*, in *Ovid*.[2] It is

---

[1] Horace, *A.P.*, 373: 'neither men nor gods nor booksellers ever brooked.'
[2] Ovid, *Heroïdes*, 2.66.

a signal Instance, I think, that the Author knew perfectly well how to apply his *Latine*. (IV, 314)

*   *   *

[On *3 Henry VI*, 5.1.43 ff]
>   *But while he thought to steal the single ten,*
> *The King was slily finger'd from the* Deck.

Tho there may seem no Consonance of Metaphors betwixt a *single Ten* and a *Deck*, the latter Word being grown obsolete and not acknowledg'd by our Dictionaries in the Sense here required, yet *Deck*, in all our *Northern* Counties, is to this day used to signify a *Pack* or *Stock* of *Cards*.

The Allusion to *Cards*, every Reader must have observ'd, is very familiar with our Author; but I'll subjoin a few Instances in Proof, that occur to me at present. . . . (IV, 379)

*   *   *

[On *Henry VIII*, 2.4.181–2]
>   —*This Respite shook*
> *The Bosom of my Conscience,*

Tho this Reading be Sense, and therefore I have not ventur'd to displace it, yet I verily believe the Poet wrote:
> *The Bottom of my Conscience,*—

My Reason is this. *Shakespeare* in all his Historical Plays was a most diligent Observer of *Hollingshead*'s Chronicle, and had him always in Eye wherever he thought fit to borrow any Matter from him. Now *Hollingshead*, in the Speech which he has given to King *Henry* upon this Subject, makes him deliver himself thus: 'Which Words, once conceived within the secret *Bottom* of my *Conscience*, ingendred such a scrupulous Doubt, that my Conscience was incontinently accombred, vex'd, and disquieted.' *Vid. Life of Henry VIII*, p. 907. (V, 46)

*   *   *

[On *Henry VIII*, 3.2.47] *Marry this is but young,*
All the Old Copies read with me,
>   *Marry, this is yet but young;*

But the modern Editors have expung'd this harmless Monosyllable *yet*, supposing the Verse would *scan* more smoothly without it.
>   *Mār rȳ | thĭs ĭs | būt yŏŭng |*

I should not take Notice of so trifling a Variation were it not proper to observe that They herein advance a *false Nicety* of Ear against the Licence of SHAKESPEARE's *Numbers*: nay, indeed, against the Licence of all

English Versification, in common with that of other Languages. They do not seem to apprehend that *Mărrў thǐs* is in *Scansion* plainly an *Anapest*; and equal to a *Spondee*, or *Foot* of two Syllables. I shall take an Opportunity, when I come to *Hamlet*, to speak of the *Pes Proceleusmaticus*, so frequent in *Homer*, *Virgil*, and other the best *Classical* Poets. I'll only add here that I could produce at least two thousand of our Poet's Verses that would be disturb'd by this modern, unreasonable, Chastness of *Metre*. (V, 57)

          ★   ★   ★

[On *King Lear*, 2.1.119]
        —threading *dark-ey'd Night*.
I have not ventur'd to displace this Reading, tho I have great Suspicion that the Poet wrote
        —treading *dark-ey'd night*,
i.e. travelling in it. The other carries too obscure and mean an Allusion. It must either be borrow'd from the Cant-phrase of *threading of Alleys*, i.e. going thro bye-passages to avoid the high Streets; or to *threading* a *Needle* in the *dark*. (V, 137)

          ★   ★   ★

[On *King Lear*, 2.4.278-9]
    I will have such Revenges on you both
    That all the world shall—
This fine abrupt Breaking off, and Suppression of Passion in its very height (a Figure which the *Greek* Rhetoricians have call'd *aposiopesis*) is very familiar with our Author, as with other good Writers, and always gives an Energy to the Subject. That by *Neptune* in the first Book of the *Aeneid* is always quoted as a celebrated Instance of this Figure:
    Quos ego—Sed motos praestat componere fluctus[1]
What *Lear* immediately subjoins here, *I will do such Things—What they are, yet I know not*—seems to carry the visible Marks of Imitation.
    —Magnum est quodcunque paravi;
    Quid sit, adhoc; dubito. Ovid, *Metam.* l.6.[2]
    —Haud, quid sit, scio;
    Sed grande quiddam est. Senec. *in Thyest.*[3] (V, 154)

          ★   ★   ★

---

[1] 1.135: 'Whom I——! But better it is to calm troubled waves.'
[2] 6.619 f: 'I am prepared for some great deed; but what it shall be I am still in doubt.'
[3] 269 f: 'I know not what it is, but 'tis some mighty thing.'

[On *King Lear*, 3.4.48 f]

   Didst Thou give all to thy Daughters? and art thou come to this?

[WARBURTON: Here *Lear's* Madness first begins to break out. His Mind, long beating on his Afflictions, had laid a Preparation for his Frenzy, and nothing was wanting but such an Object as *Edgar* to set it on Work, as it were by Sympathy. In this our Author has shewn an exquisite Knowledge of Nature; as he has, with no less Propriety, distinguish'd the King's *real* from the other's *assum'd* Passion. What *Lear* says, for the most part, springs either from the Source and Fountain of his Disorder—the Injuries done him by his Daughters—or his Desire of being reveng'd on them. What *Edgar* says seems a fantastick Wildness, only extorted to disguise Sense and to blunt the Suspicion of his Concealment. This makes it that we are always most strongly affected with the King's Madness, as we know it to be a real Distress.] But tho what *Edgar* says seems Extravagance of Thought and the Coinage of the Poet's Brain only, to the End already mention'd, yet I'll venture to assure my Readers, his whole Frenzy is Satire levell'd at a modern Fact which made no little Noise at that Period of Time, and consequently must have been a rapturous Entertainment to the Spectators when it was first presented. The Secret is this: While the *Spaniards* were preparing their Armado against *England* the *Jesuits* were here busiely at Work to promote the Success by making Converts. One Method they used to do this was to dispossess pretended Demoniacks of their own Church; by which Artifice they made several hundred Converts among the common People, and grew so elate upon their Success as to publish an Account of their Exploits in this wonderful Talent of *exorcising.* A main Scene of their Business in this seeming-holy Discipline lay in the Family of one Mr. *Edmund Peckham*; where *Marwood*, a Servant of *Antony Babington's* (who was afterwards executed for Treason), *Trayford* (an Attendant upon Mr. *Peckham*), and *Sarah* and *Friswood Williams* and *Anne Smith* (three Chambermaids in that Family) were supposed to be possess'd by Devils, and came under the Hands of the Priests for their Cure. The Parties either so little lik'd the Discipline, or the Jesuits behav'd with such ill Address that the Consequence was, the Imposture was discover'd, the Demoniacks were examin'd, and their Confessions taken upon Oath before the Privy Council. The whole Matter being blown up, the Criminals brought to the Stake, and the Trick of *Devil-hunting* brought into Ridicule, Dr. *Harsenet* (who was Chaplain to Archbishop *Bancroft*, and himself afterwards Archbishop of *York*) wrote a smart Narrative of this whole Proceeding under the following Title: 'A Declaration of egregious Popish Impostures, to withdraw the Hearts of her Majesty's Subjects from their Allegiance, &c. under the pretence of casting out Devils, practis'd by *Edmunds*, alias *Weston*, a Jesuit; and divers *Romish* Priests, his wicked Associates, Whereunto are annex'd the Copies of the Confessions and Examinations of the Parties themselves, which were pretended to be possess'd and dispossess'd, etc. Printed by *James Roberts*, in 1603.'—This Transaction was so rife in every Body's Mouth, upon the Accession of King *James* the 1st to the Crown, that our Poet thought proper to make his Court by helping forward the Ridicule of it. I need only observe now that *Edgar* thro' all his Frenzy supposes himself possess'd by Fiends, and that the greatest Part of his dissembled Lunacy, the Names of his Devils, and the descriptive Circumstances he alludes to in his own Case are all drawn from this Pamphlet, and the Confessions of the poor deluded Wretches. The Address of our Author in this popular Piece of Satire, and that excentrick Madness he has built upon it, made me imagine the stating a Fact so little known might apologize for the Length of this Note on the Occasion. (V, 163-4)

*   *   *

[On *King Lear*, 3.6.97 ff] —*opprest Nature sleeps:*
These two concluding Speeches by *Kent* and *Edgar*, and which by no means ought to have been cut off, I have restored from the Old Quarto. The Soliloquy of *Edgar* is extreamly fine, and the Sentiments of it are drawn equally from Nature and the Subject. Besides, with Regard to the Stage it is absolutely necessary: for as *Edgar* is not design'd, in the Constitution of the Play, to attend the King to *Dover* how absurd would it look for a Character of his Importance to quit the Scene without one Word said, or the least Intimation what we are to expect from him? (V, 172)

*   *   *

[On *King Lear*, 3.7.98] *I'll never care what Wickedness I do,*
This short Dialogue I have inserted from the Old Quarto, because I think it full of Nature. Servants, in any House, could hardly see such a Barbarity committed on their Master without Reflections of Pity; and the Vengeance that they presume must overtake the Actors of it is a Sentiment and Doctrine well worthy of the Stage. (V, 176-7)

*   *   *

[On *King Lear*, 4.1.24] *Might I but live to see thee in my touch*
I cannot but take Notice that these fine *Boldnesses* of Expression are very

infrequent in our *English* Poetry, tho familiar with the *Greeks* and *Latins*. We have pass'd another signal one in this very Play

> Such *Sheets of Fire*, such Bursts of horried Thunder,
> Such Groans of roaring Wind and Rain, I never
> Remember to have *heard*. [3.2.46 ff]

For tho the verb *hear* properly answers to the *Thunder*, the *Wind*, and *Rain*, yet it does not so, but figuratively, to the *Sheets of Fire*. . . . (V, 178–9)

★   ★   ★

[On *King Lear*, 4.1.57 ff] *Five Fiends have been in poor* Tom *at once;* [WARBURTON: This Passage Mr. *Pope* first restor'd from the Old 4to; but miserably mangled, as it is there. I have set it right, as it came from our Author, by the Help of Bishop *Harsenet*'s Pamphlet, already quoted. We find there, all these Devils were in *Sarah* and *Friswood Williams*, Mrs. *Peckham*'s two Chambermaids, and particularly *Flibbertigibbet*, who made them *mop* and *mow* like Apes, says that Author. And to their suppos'd *Possession* our Poet is here satirically alluding.] (V, 180)

★   ★   ★

[On *King Lear*, 4.2.53–4]

>   *—that not know'st,*
> Fools *do these Villains pity,*

This I have retriev'd from the first *Quarto*. It seems first to have been retrench'd by the Players, for Brevity's sake; but, besides that the Lines are fine, they admirably display the taunting, termagant Disposition of *Goneril*, and paint out her Contempt of her Husband's mild pacifick Spirit. (V, 183)

★   ★   ★

[On *King Lear*, 4.6.87] *handles his Bow like a* Cowkeeper.
Thus Mr. *Pope* in his last Edition; but I am afraid I betray'd him into the Error by an absurd Conjecture of my own in my SHAKESPEARE *restored*. 'Tis certain we must read *Crowkeeper* here. . . . (V, 193)

★   ★   ★

[On *King Lear*, 5.3.510 f]

>   *Do you see this? Look on her, look on her Lips;*
> Look there, look there.—

Our Poet has taken the Liberty in the Catastrophe of this Play to depart from the *Chronicles*, in which *Lear* is said to be reinstated in his Throne

509

by *Cordelia*, and to have reign'd upwards of two Years after his Restoration. He might have done this for two Reasons. Either to heighten the Compassion towards the poor old King; or to vary from another, but most execrable, Dramatic Performance upon this Story, which I certainly believe to have preceded our Author's Piece, and which none of our Stage-Historians appear to have had any Knowledge of. The edition which I have of it bears this Title: *The true Chronicle History of King Leir, and his three Daughters, Gonorill, Ragan, and Cordella. As it hath bene divers and sundry times lately acted.* London; *Printed by Simon Stafford for* John Wright, *and are to be sold at his Shop at Christes Church dore next* Newgate *Market.* 1605. That *Shakespeare*, however, may stand acquitted from the least Suspicion of Plagiarism in the Opinion of his Readers, I'll subjoin a small Taste of this other anonymous Author's Abilities, both in Conduct and Diction. *Leir*, with one *Perillus* his Friend, embarks for *France* to try what Reception he should find from his Daughter *Cordella*. When they come ashore, neither of them has a Rag of Money, and they are forc'd to give their Cloaks to the Mariners to pay for their Passage. This, no doubt, our Playwright intended for a Mastery in Distress: as he must think it a notable Fetch of Invention to bring the King and Queen of *France* disguis'd like Rusticks, travelling a long way on Foot into the Woods with a Basket of Provisions, only that they may have the casual Opportunity of relieving *Leir* and *Perillus* from being starv'd. Now for a little Specimen of Style, and Dignity of Thinking. *Cordella*, now Queen of *France* and in her own Palace, comes in and makes this pathetick Soliloquy. . . .

> *I cannot wish the Thing that I do want;*
> *I cannot want the Thing, but I may have;*
> *Save only This which I shall ne're obtayne,*
> *My Father's Love; Oh, This I Ne're shall gayne. . . .*
> *And yet I know not how I him offended,*
> *Or wherein justly I've deserved Blame.*
> *Oh Sisters! You are much to blame in This;*
> *It was not He, but You, that did me Wrong.*
> *Yet, God forgive both Him, and You, and Me,*
> *Ev'n as I do in perfect Charity.*
> *I will to Church, and pray unto my Saviour,*
> *That, ere I dye, I may obtayne his Favour.*

This is, surely, such Poetry as one might hammer out, *Stans pede in uno*;[1] or, as our Author says, 'it is the right Butter-Woman's Rank to

---

[1] Horace, *Satires*, 1.4.10: 'while standing on one foot'.

Market: and a Man might versify you so eight years together, dinners, and suppers, and sleeping hours excepted.' [*As You Like It*, 3.2.86 ff]— Again, *Shakespeare* was too well vers'd in *Hollingshead* not to know that King *Lear* reign'd above 800 years before the Period of Christianity. The Gods his King talks of are *Jupiter, Juno, Apollo*, and not any Deities more modern than his own Time. Licentious as he was in Anachronisms he would have judg'd it an unpardonable Absurdity to have made a *Briton* of *Cordella*'s time talk of her *Saviour*. And his not being trapt into such ridiculous Slips of Ignorance seems a plain Proof to me that he stole neither from his Predecessors, nor Contemporaries of the *English* Theatre, both which abounded in them. (V, 217–18)

* * *

[On *Timon of Athens*, 4.3.12]
    It is the Pasture lards the Beggar's *Sides*,
'This, as the Editors have order'd it, is an idle Repetition at the best; supposing it did, indeed, contain the same Sentiment as the foregoing Lines. But *Shakespeare* meant a quite different Thing; and having, like a sensible Writer, made a smart Observation, he illustrates it by a Similitude thus:
    It is the Pasture lards the Weather's *Sides*,
    The Want that makes him lean.
And the Similitude is extremely beautiful, as conveying this Satirical Reflection, there is no more Difference between Man and Man in the Esteem of superficial or corrupt Judgments than between a fat Sheep and a lean one.'   Mr. *Warburton*.
    I cannot better praise the Sagacity of my Friend's Emendation than by producing the Reading of the first *folio* Edition (which I know he had not seen), where we find it thus exhibited:
    It is the Pasture lards the Brother's *Sides*, &c.
Every knowing Reader will agree that this Corruption might much more naturally be deriv'd from *Weather*'s than from *Beggar*'s, as far as the Traces of the Letters are concern'd, especially in the old Secretary Handwriting, the universal Character in our Author's Time. I will only add that our Poet, in his *As You Like It*, makes a Clown say the very same Thing in a more ludicrous manner.
    That the Property of Rain is to wet, and Fire to burn; that good Pasture *makes fat Sheep; &c.* [3.2.25 ff] (V, 272–3)

* * *

511

[On *Macbeth*, 1.3.83 ff]

> *Were such Things here, as we do speak about?*
> *Or have we eaten of the* insane Root,
> *That takes the Reason prisoner?*

. . . This Sentence, I conceive, is not so well understood as I would have every part of *Shakespeare* be by his Audience and Readers. So soon as the Witches vanish from the Sight of *Macbeth* and *Banquo*, and leave them in Doubt whether they had really *seen* such *Apparitions*, or whether their Eyes were not deceiv'd by some Illusion *Banquo* immediately starts the Question

> *Were such Things here*, &c.

I was sure, from a long Observation of *Shakespeare*'s Accuracy, that he alluded here to some particular Circumstance in the History, which, I hop'd, I should find explain'd in *Hollingshead*. But I found myself deceived in this Expectation. This furnishes a proper Occasion, therefore, to remark our Author's signal Diligence and Happiness at applying whatever he met with that could have any Relation to his Subject. *Hector Boethius*, who gives us an Account of *Sueno*'s Army being intoxicated by a Preparation put upon them by their subtle Enemy, informs us that there is a Plant which grows in great Quantity in *Scotland* call'd *Solatrum Amentiale*; that its Berries are purple, or rather black, when full ripe, and have a Quality of laying to Sleep or of *driving into Madness*, if a more than ordinary Quantity of them be taken. This Passage of *Boethius*, I dare say, our Poet had an Eye to. . . . (V, 395)

* * *

[On *Macbeth*, 1.7.6]

> *But here, upon this Bank and* School *of Time*

Bank and *School*—What a monstrous Couplement, as Don *Armado* says, is here of heterogeneous Ideas! I have ventur'd to amend, which restores a Consonance of Images,—

> on this Bank and *Shoal* of Time,

i.e. this *Shallow*, this *narrow Ford* of human Life, opposed to the *great Abyss* of Eternity. . . . (V, 405)

* * *

[On *Macbeth*, 3.2.46 f]

> —come, Sealing *Night*,
> *Skarf up the tender Eye of pitiful day;*

[WARBURTON: Mr. *Rowe* and Mr. *Pope* neither of them were aware of

the Poet's Metaphor here, and so have blunder'd the Text into Nonsense. I have restor'd from the old Copies,
—*come*, seeling *Night*,
i.e. *blinding*. It is a Term in *Falconry*, when they run a thread thro' the Eyelids of a Hawk first taken, so that she may see very little, or not at all, to make her the better endure the Hood. This they call *seeling* a Hawk.] (V, 427–8)

*　　*　　*

[On *Macbeth*, 5.5.23]
And all our yesterdays have lighted Fools
The way to study *death.*—
This Reading is as old as the 2d Edition in *folio*, but surely it is paying too great a Compliment to the Capacities of Fools. It would much better sort with the Character of wise Men to study how to die from the Experience of past Times. I have restor'd the Reading of the first *Folio*, which Mr. *Pope* has thrown out of his Text.
The way to dusty *Death.*
i.e. Death, which reduces us to Dust and Ashes.
Metonymia effecti pro efficiente. . . . (V, 466)

*　　*　　*

[On *Coriolanus*, 4.7.33 ff]
—*I think, he'll be to* Rome
As is the Aspray *to the Fish, who takes it*
By Sov'reignty of Nature.
Though one's Search might have been very vain to find any such Word as *Aspray*, as I easily imagin'd, something must be couch'd under the Corruption in its Nature destructive to Fish, and that made a Prey of Them. And this suspicion led me to the Discovery. The *Osprey* is a Species of the Eagle, of a strong Make, that haunts the Sea and Lakes for its Food, and altogether preys on Fish. . . . *Pliny* gives us this Description of its acute Sight, and Eagerness after its Prey. [Quotes *Natural History*, 10.3.8] It may not be disagreeable to go a little farther to explain the Propriety of the Poet's Allusion. Why will *Coriolanus* be to *Rome* as the *Osprey* to the Fish,
—*he'll take it*
By Sov'reignty of Nature?
Shakespeare, 'tis well known, has a Peculiarity in Thinking, and wherever he is acquainted with Nature is sure to allude to her most

uncommon Effects and Operations. I am very apt to imagine, therefore, that the Poet meant *Coriolanus* would take *Rome* by the very Opinion and Terror of his Name, as Fish are taken by the *Osprey*, thro' an instinctive Fear they have of him. 'The Fishermen (says our old Naturalist *William Turner*), are used to anoint their Baits with *Osprey's* Fat, thinking thereby to make them the more efficacious; because when That Bird is hovering in the Air all the Fish that are beneath him (the Nature of the Eagle, as it is believ'd, compelling them to it) turn up their Bellies and, as it were, give him his Choice which he will take of them'. *Gesner* goes a little farther in support of this odd Instinct, telling us 'that while this Bird flutters in the Air and sometimes, as it were, seems suspended there, he drops a certain Quantity of his Fat, by the Influence whereof the Fish are so affrighted and confounded that they immediately turn themselves Belly upwards; upon which he sowses down perpendicularly like a Stone, and seizes them in his Talons'.—To This, I dare say, *Shakespeare* alludes in this Expression of the *Sov'reignty of Nature*. . . . (VI, 100)

*　　*　　*

[On *Julius Cæsar*, 1.2.204 ff] —*he hears no Musick:*
This is not a trivial Observation, nor does our Poet mean barely by it that *Cassius* was not a merry, sprightly man: but that he had not a due Temperament of Harmony in his Composition, and that therefore Natures so uncorrected are dangerous. He has finely dilated on this Sentiment in his *Merchant of Venice. Act* 5 [1.83 ff]
> *The Man, that hath* no Musick *in himself,*
> *And is not mov'd with Concord of sweet Sounds,*
> *Is fit for* Treasons, Stratagems, and Spoils; . . . (VI, 133)

*　　*　　*

[On *Julius Cæsar*, 2.1.40] *Is not to morrow, Boy, the* first *of* March?
I dare pronounce a palpable Blunder here, which None of the Editors have ever been aware of. *Brutus* enquires whether the *first of March* be come, and the Boy brings him word 'tis wasted 15 Days. Allowing *Brutus* to be a most contemplative Man, and his Thoughts taken up with high Matters, yet I can never agree that he so little knew how Time went as to be mistaken a whole Fortnight in the Reckoning. I make no Scruple to assert, the Poet wrote *Ides*. But how could *Ides*, may it not be objected, be corrupted into *first?* What Similitude in the Traces of the Letters? This Difficulty may very easily be solv'd, by only supposing that the Word *Ides* in the Manuscript Copy happen'd

to be wrote contractedly thus, *j*ˢ. The Players knew the Word well
enough in the Contraction, but when the MSS came to the *Press* the
Compositors were not so well informed in it. They knew that jst
frequently stood for *first*, and blunderingly thought that jˢ: was meant
to do so too, and thence was deriv'd the Corruption of the Text.
But that the Poet wrote *Ides* we have This in Confirmation. *Brutus*
makes the Enquiry on the Dawn of the very Day in which *Caesar*
was kill'd in the Capitol. Now 'tis very well known that this was on
the 15th Day, which is the *Ides* of *March*. I ought to acknowledge that
my Friend Mr. *Warburton* likewise started this very Emendation, and
communicated it to Me by Letter. (VI, 143)

★   ★   ★

[On *Julius Cæsar*, 2.1.101] *Here lies the East:*
Mr. *Rymer*, in his Examination of the Tragedies of the last Age, has
left an invidious and paltry Remark on this Passage. [Quotes the
passage above, p. 57]—I cannot help having the utmost Contempt
for this poor ill-judg'd Sneer. It shews the Height of good Manners
and Politeness in the Conspirators, while *Brutus* and *Cassius* whisper,
to start any occasional Topick and talk *extempore* rather than seem to
listen to, or be desirous of overhearing, what *Cassius* draws *Brutus*
aside for. And if I am not mistaken there is a Piece of Art shewn in this
whisper which our *Caviller* either did not, or would not, see into.
The Audience are already apprized of the Subject on which the
Faction meet: and therefore this whisper is an Artifice to prevent the
Preliminaries of what they knew beforehand being formally repeated.
(VI, 146)

★   ★   ★

[On *Julius Cæsar*, 3.1.106 ff] *Stoop*, Romans, *stoop*;
Mr. *Pope* in both his Editions has, from these Words, arbitrarily taken
away the Remainder of this Speech from *Brutus* and placed it to *Casca*:
because, he thinks, nothing is more inconsistent with *Brutus*'s mild
and philosophical Character.[1] And as he often finds Speeches in the
later Editions, he says, put into wrong Mouths, he thinks this Liberty
is not unreasonable. 'Tis true, a diligent Editor may find many such
Errors committed even in the first printed Copies, but it has not often
been Mr. *Pope*'s good Fortune to hit upon them. I dare warrant the
Printers made no Blunder in this Instance, and therefore I have made

[1] See above, p. 417.

bold to restore the Speech to its right Owner. *Brutus* esteem'd the Death of *Cæsar* a Sacrifice to Liberty: and, as such, gloried in his heading the Enterprize. Besides, our Poet is strictly copying a Fact in History. *Plutarch*, in the Life of *Cæsar*, says, '*Brutus* and his Followers, *being yet hot with the Murther*, march'd in a Body from the Senate-house to the Capitol, with their *drawn Swords*, with an Air of Confidence and Assurance.' And, in the Life of *Brutus*,—'*Brutus* and his Party betook themselves to the *Capitol*, and in their way *shewing their Hands all bloody*, and their naked Swords, *proclaim'd Liberty* to the People.' (VI, 164)

* * *

[On *Antony and Cleopatra*, 1.4.46 f]
> *Goes to, and back*, lashing *the varying Tide*,
> *To rot itself with Motion.*

How can a Flag, or Rush, floating upon a Stream, and that has no Motion but what the Fluctuation of the Water gives it, be said to lash the Tide? This is making a scourge of a weak ineffective Thing, and giving it an active Violence in its own power. All the old Editions read *lacking*. 'Tis true, there is no Sense in that Reading; but the Addition of a single Letter will not only give us good Sense, but the genuine word of our Author into the Bargain—*Lackying* the varying Tide, i.e. floating backwards and forwards with the variation of the Tide like a Page, or *Lacquey*, at his Master's Heels. (VI, 227)

* * *

[On *Antony and Cleopatra*, 3.13.165].
> *By the* discattering *of this pelletted Storm.*

This Reading we owe first, I presume, to Mr. *Rowe*: and Mr. *Pope* has very faithfully fall'n into it. The old *Folios* read *discandering*: from which Corruption both Dr. *Thirlby* and I saw we must retrieve the Word with which I have reform'd the Text ['discandying']. *Cleopatra's* Wish is this: that the Gods would ingender Hail and poyson it; and that as it fell upon her and her Subjects and melted, their Lives might determine, as that dissolv'd and discandied. The congealing of the Water into Hail he metaphorically calls *candying*: and it is an Image he is fond of in several other Passages. . . . [Theobald cites examples from Act IV of this play, from *The Tempest*, *Timon*, *Hamlet*, and *1 Henry IV*.] (VI, 289-90)

* * *

[On *Antony and Cleopatra*, 5.2.310] [*Applying another Asp to her Arm.*
[*Cleopatra:*] O Antony! *nay* I will take thee too.

As there has been hitherto no Break in Verse, nor any marginal Direction, *Thee* necessarily must seem to refer to Antony. But 'tis certain *Cleopatra* is here design'd to apply One Aspick to her Arm, as she had before clap'd One to her Breast. And the last Speech of *Dolabella* in the Play is a Confirmation of This.

> *Here, on her* Breast,
> *There is a Vent of Blood, and something blown;*
> *The like is on her* Arm. [5.2.345 ff]

Dion Cassius, in the 51st Book of his *Roman* History, is express as to small Punctures of the Asp being discover'd only on her Arm. . . . And *Plutarch* says, towards the Conclusion of M. *Antony*'s Life, that she had two Marks imprinted by the Sting of the Asp, and that Caesar carried a Statue of her in Triumph with an Asp fix'd to her Arm. However, the Application of the Aspick to her Breast is not the Invention of our Poet. *Virgil*, who says nothing of the Locality of her Wounds, plainly intimates that she applied two of these venomous Creatures:

> *Necdum etiam* geminos *a tergo respicit* Angues. *Æneid*, VIII.[1]

Strabo, Velleius Paterculus, Eutropius, and *Lucius Florus* leave this Matter as much at large. But I remember to have seen Pictures of a *Cleopatra* (of what Age I can't say) with the Aspick on her Bosom, and her Breast bloody. Besides, *Leonardo Augustini*, among his antique Gemms, exhibits one of *Cleopatra* upon an Agot with an Aspick biting her right Breast. And *Strada*, the *Mantuan* Antiquary, who gives us a Medal of this Princess, says that she dy'd by Serpents apply'd to her Breasts. And *Domitius Calderinus*, upon the 59th Epigram of the IVth Book of *Martial*, says precisely that she procur'd her own Death by applying Asps to her Breast and Arm. . . . Had *Shakespeare* invented the Circumstance, Poetic Licence, and the Delicacy of his Imagery had been a sufficient Plea: but we find him true to Authority as well as to himself, in turning an occasional Hint into an unexpected Beauty.

> *Do'st thou not see my* Baby *at my* Breast,
> *That sucks the* Nurse *asleep?*   [5.2.307 f]

For this has a double Elegance, not only as it presents us with an amiable Picture but as it expresses too the benumning Effects of the Asp stealing fast upon her. (VI, 334–5)

*   *   *

[On *Troilus and Cressida*, 4.5.18]
> *Most dearly welcome to the* Greeks, *sweet Lady.*

---

[1] 8.697: 'nor as yet casts back a glance at the twin snakes behind'.

From this Line Mr. *Pope* has thought fit to degrade, or throw out of the Text, the Quantity of a whole Page. But is it not very absurd that *Diomede* should bring *Cressida* on where so many Princes are present, and preparing to give her a Welcome, and then lead her off abruptly, so soon as ever *Agamemnon* has said a single Line to her? *An ideò tantùm venerat, ut exiret?* as *Martial* says of *Cato*'s coming into the Theatre.[1] But is it not still more absurd for *Cressida* to be led off without uttering one single Syllable, and for *Nestor* and *Ulysses* to observe that she is a Woman of quick Sense, and glib of Tongue, as if she had said several witty Things? Methinks *Nestor*'s Character of her *Wit*, from her saying *Nothing*, is as extraordinary as the two Kings of *Brentford* hearing the *Whisper*, tho' they are not present, in the REHEARSAL. (VII, 88)

★ ★ ★

[On *Troilus and Cressida*, 5.2.120]
> *That doth invert that* Test *of Eyes and Ears.*

What Test? *Troilus* had been particularizing none in his foregoing Words, to govern or require the *Relative* here. I rather think, the Words are to be thus split:

> *That doth invert* th' Attest *of Eyes and Ears.*

i.e. That turns the very Testimony of Seeing and Hearing against themselves. (VII, 106)

★ ★ ★

[On *Troilus and Cressida*, 5.5.14 f]

> *The dreadful* Sagittary
> *Appals our Numbers.*

Mr. *Pope* will have it that by Sagittary is meant *Teucer*, because of his Skill in Archery. Were we to take this Interpretation for granted we might expect that upon this Line in *Othello*

> *Lead to the* Sagittary *the raised Search*,

Mr. *Pope* should tell us this meant to the Sign of *Teucer*'s Head: tho indeed it means only that Sign which the Poet, in his *Comedy of Errors*, calls by an equivalent Name the *Centaur*. Besides, when *Teucer* is not once mention'd by Name throught the whole Play would *Shakespeare* decypher him by so dark and precarious a Description? I dare be positive he had no Thought of that *Archer* here. To confess the Truth, this Passage contains a Piece of private History which perhaps Mr.

---

[1] I, *Pref.*: 'Why on our scene, stern Cato, enter here? Did you then enter only to go out?'

Pope never met with unless he consulted the old Chronicle containing the three Destructions of *Troy*, printed by *Caxton* in 1471, and *Wynkyn de Worde* in 1503, from which Book our Poet has borrow'd more Circumstances of this Play than from *Lollius* or *Chaucer*. I shall transcribe a Short Quotation from thence, which will fully explain *Shakespeare's* Meaning in this Passage. 'Beyonde the Royalme of *Amasonne* came an auncyent Kynge, wyse and dyscreete, named *Epystrophus*, and brought a M. knyghtes, and a mervayllouse Beste that was call'd *Sagittarye*, that behynde the myddes was an horse, and to fore a Man. This Beste was heery lyke an horse, and had his Eyen rede as a Cole, and shotte well with a bowe. This Beste made the *Grekes* sore *aferde, and slewe many of them with his Bowe*.' This directly answers to what our Poet says—

> —*The* dreadful *Sagittary*
> Appals *our* Numbers.

That our Author traded with the above quoted Book is demonstrable from certain Circumstances which he could pick up no where else and which he has thought fit to transplant into his Play: *viz.* the making *Neoptolemus* a distinct Hero from *Pyrrhus*, who was afterwards so call'd; the Corruption in the Names of the six Gates of *Troy*; *Galathe*, the Name of *Hector's* horse; the Bastard *Margarelon*; *Diomede* getting one of *Cressida's* Gloves; *Achilles* absenting from Battle on Account of his Love for *Polyxena*, and the Messages of Queen *Hecuba* to him; his taking *Hector* at a Disadvantage when he kill'd him; &c. (VII, 114–15)

⋆ ⋆ ⋆

[On *Romeo and Juliet*, 2.4.124 f]

> *I desire some* Confidence *with You.*
> Ben. *She will* invite *him to some Supper.*

Mr. *Rowe* first spoil'd the Joak of the Second Line in his Editions, and Mr. *Pope* is generally faithful to his Foot-steps. All the genuine Copies read, as I have restor'd to the Text,

> *She will* indite *him to some Supper.*

Benvolio, hearing the Nurse knock one Word out of joint, humorously is resolv'd he will corrupt another in Imitation of her. Both the Corruptions are used by our Author in other parts of his Works.

> Quick. —*and I will tell your Worship more of the Wart, the next Time we have* confidence, *and of other Wooers.*
> *Merry Wives of Windsor* [1.4.144]

Dogb. Marry, Sir, I would have some confidence *with You, that* decerns *you nearly.*   *Much Ado about Nothing* [3.5.3]

Quick.—*and he is* indited *to Dinner to the* Lubbar's *head,* &c.

           2 Henry IV [2.1.28]
           (VII, 164-5)

*   *   *

[Head-note to *Hamlet*]

. . . the Story is taken from *Saxo Grammaticus* in his *Danish* History. I'll subjoin a short Extract of the material Circumstances on which the Groundwork of the Plot is built; and how happily the Poet has adapted his Incidents I shall leave to the Observation of every Reader. The Historian calls our Poet's Hero, *Amlethus*; his Father, *Horwendillus*; his Uncle, *Fengo*; and his Mother, *Gerutha*. The Old King in single Combat slew *Collerus*, King of *Norway*; *Fengo* makes away with his Brother *Horwendillus*, and marries his Widow *Gerutha*. *Amlethus*, to avoid being suspected by his Uncle of Designs, assumes a Form of utter Madness. A fine Woman is planted upon him, to try if he would yield to the Impressions of Love. *Fengo* contrives that *Amlethus*, in order to sound him, should be closeted by his Mother. A Man is conceal'd in the Rushes to overhear their Discourse, whom *Amlethus* discovers and kills. When the Queen is frighted at this Behaviour of his he tasks her about her criminal Course of Life and incestuous Conversation with her former Husband's Murtherer; confesses, his Madness is but counterfeited to preserve himself and secure his Revenge for his Father, to which he injoyns the Queen's Silence. *Fengo* sends *Amlethus* to *Britaine*. Two of the King's Servants attend him, with Letters to the *British* King strictly pressing the Death of *Amlethus*; who, in the Nighttime, coming at their Commission o'er-reads it, forms a new one, and turns the Destruction design'd towards himself on the Bearers of the Letters. *Amlethus*, returning home, by a Wile surprizes and kills his Uncle. (VII, 226)

*   *   *

[On *Hamlet*, 1.4.17] *This heavy-headed Revel, east and west.*

This whole Speech of *Hamlet*, to the Entrance of the Ghost, I set right in my SHAKESPEARE *restor'd*, so shall not trouble the Readers again with a Repetition of those Corrections, or Justification of them. Mr. *Pope* admits I have given the Whole a *Glimmering* of *Sense*, but it is purely *conjectural* and founded on no *Authority* of *Copies*. But is this any Objection against Conjecture in *Shakespeare*'s Case, where no Original

Manuscript is subsisting, and the Printed Copies have successively blunder'd after one another? And is not even a Glimmering of Sense, so it be not arbitrarily impos'd, preferable to flat and glaring Nonsense? If not, there is a total End at least to this Branch of Criticism, and Nonsense may plead Title and Prescription from Time because there is no direct Authority for dispossessing it. (VII, 247)

*   *   *

[On *Hamlet*, 3.1.79 f]

> *That* undiscover'd Country, *from whose Bourne*
> No Traveller *returns.*

As some superficial Criticks have, without the least Scruple, accursed the Poet of *Forgetfulness* and *Self-Contradiction* from this Passage— seeing that in this very Play he introduces a Character from the other World, the *Ghost* of *Hamlet*'s Father—I have thought this Circumstance worthy of a Justification. 'Tis certain, to introduce a *Ghost*, a Being from the other World, and to say that no Traveller returns from those Confines is, literally taken, as absolute a Contradiction as can be suppos'd & *facto* & *terminis*. But we are to take Notice that *Shakespeare* brings his Ghost only from a *middle-State* or *local Purgatory*: a *Prison-house*, as he makes his Spirit call it, where he was doom'd for a Term only to expiate his Sins of Nature. By the *undiscover'd Country* here mention'd he may perhaps mean that *last* and *eternal* Residence of Souls in a State of full Bliss or Misery, which Spirits in a *middle* State could not be acquainted with or explain. So that if any Latitude of Sense may be allow'd to the Poet's Words, tho' he admits the Possibility of a Spirit returning from the Dead he yet holds that the State of the Dead cannot be communicated; and, with that Allowance, it remains still an *undiscovered Country*. We are to observe, too, that even his Ghost, who comes from Purgatory (or whatever has been signified under that Denomination) comes under Restrictions, and tho' he confesses himself subject to a Vicissitude of Torments yet he says at the same time that *he is forbid to tell the Secrets of his Prison-house*. . . . (VII, 287)

*   *   *

[On *Hamlet*, 3.2.245 f]

> [Oph.] *Still* worse *and* worse.
> Ham. *So you must take* your *Husbands.*

Surely this is the most uncomfortable Lesson that ever was preach'd to the poor Ladies: and I can't help wishing, for our own sakes too, it mayn't be true. 'Tis too foul a Blot upon our Reputations, that every Husband that a Woman takes must be worse than her former. The Poet, I am pretty certain, intended no such Scandal upon the Sex. But what a precious Collator of Copies is Mr. Pope! All the old *Quartos* and *Folios* read:

Ophel. *Still* better *and worse.*

Ham. *So you* mistake *Husbands.*

Hamlet is talking to her in such gross double *Entendres* that she is forc'd to parry them by indirect Answers, and remarks that tho' his Wit be *smarter* yet his Meaning is more *blunt.* This, I think, is the Sense of her— *Still* better *and worse.* This puts *Hamlet* in mind of the Words in the Church Service of Matrimony, and he replies *so you* mistake *Husbands,* i.e. So you *take* Husbands and find yourselves *mistaken* in them. (VII, 299)

★ ★ ★

[On *Hamlet*, 3.4.71 ff] —*Sense, sure, you have,* &c.

Mr. *Pope* has left out the Quantity of about eight Verses here which I have taken care to replace. They are not, indeed, to be found in the two elder *Folios* but they carry the Style, Expression, and Cast of Thought peculiar to our Author, and that they were not an Interpolation from another Hand needs no better Proof than that they are in all the oldest *Quartos.* The first Motive of their being left out, I am perswaded, was to shorten *Hamlet's* Speech, and consult the Ease of the Actor, and the Reason why they find no Place in the *Folio* Impressions is that they were printed from the *Playhouse* castrated Copies. But surely this can be no Authority for a modern Editor to conspire in mutilating his Author. Such *Omissions,* rather, must betray a Want of *Diligence* in *Collating,* or a Want of *Justice* in the *voluntary Stifling.* (VII, 313)

★ ★ ★

[On *Hamlet*, 4.7.117 f]

> For Goodness, growing to a Pleurisie,
> Dies in his own too much.

Mr. *Warburton* sagaciously observ'd to me that this is Nonsense, and untrue in Fact; and therefore thinks that *Shakespeare* must have wrote

> For Goodness, growing to a Plethory, &c.

For the *Pleurisy* is an Inflammation of the Membrane which covers the whole *Thorax,* and is generally occasion'd by a Stagnation of the Blood; but a *Plethora* is when the Vessels are fuller of Humours than is agreeable to a natural State, or Health: and too great a Fullness and Floridness of the Blood are frequently the Causes of sudden Death. But I have not disturb'd the Text because 'tis possible our Author himself might be out in his *Physics*; and I have the more Reason to suspect it because *Beaumont* and *Fletcher* have twice committed the self-same Blunder. . . .

If I may guess at the Accident which caus'd their Mistake, it seems this. They did not consider that *Pleurisie* was deriv'd from *Pleura*; but the Declination of *plus, pluris*, cross'd their Thoughts, and so they naturally suppos'd the Distemper to arise from some *Superfluity*. (VII, 341)

★   ★   ★

[On *Hamlet*, 5.2.94 ff]
Osr. *I thank your Lordship, 'tis very hot.*
Ham. *No, believe me, 'tis very cold; the Wind is northerly.*
Osr. *It is indifferent cold, my Lord, indeed.*
Ham. *But yet, methinks, it is very sultry and hot for my Complexion.*
Osr. *Exceedingly, my Lord, it is very sultry, as 'twere, I cannot tell how.*
The humourous Compliance of this fantastic Courtier to every thing that *Hamlet* says is so close a Copy from *Juvenal* (*Sat.* III.), that our Author must certainly have had that Picture in his Eye.
[Quotes 3.100 ff: 'If you smile, your Greek will split his sides with laughter; if he sees his friend drop a tear, he weeps, though without grieving; if you call for a bit of fire in winter-time, he puts on his cloak; if you say "I am hot", he breaks into a sweat.'] (VII, 357)

★   ★   ★

[On *Hamlet*, 5.2.107 ff] *Sir, here is newly come to Court Laertes.*
I have restor'd here several speeches from the elder *Quartos* which were omitted in the *Folio* Editions, and which Mr. *Pope* has likewise thought fit to sink upon us. They appear to me very well worthy not to be lost, as they thoroughly shew the Foppery and Affectation of *Osrick*, and the Humour and Address of *Hamlet* in accosting the other at once in his own Vein and Style. (VIII, 357).

★   ★   ★

[Head-note to *Othello*]
The Groundwork of this Play is built on a Novel of *Cinthio Giraldi* (Dec. 3. Nov. 7.), who seems to have design'd his Tale a Document to young Ladies against disproportion'd Marriages: . . . That they should

not link themselves to such against whom Nature, Providence, and a different way of Living have interpos'd a Bar. Our Poet inculcates no such Moral, but rather that a Woman may fall in Love with the Virtues and shining Qualities of a Man and therein overlook the Differences of Complexion and Colour. Mr. *Rymer* has run riot against the Conduct, Manners, Sentiments, and Diction of this Play: but in such a strain that one is mov'd rather to laugh at the Freedom and Coarseness of his Raillery than provok'd to be downright angry at his Censures. . . . [Quotes from the passage above, pp. 28 f]. Thus this *Critick* goes on, but such Reflexions require no serious Answer. This Tragedy will continue to have lasting Charms enough to make us blind to such Absurdities as the Poet thought were not worth his Care. (VII, 371-2)

*　　*　　*

[On *Othello*, 2.1.224 ff] *When the Blood is made dull with the Act of Sport, there should be a Game to inflame it, and to give Satiety a fresh Appetite; loveliness in Favour, Sympathy in Years, Manners, and Beauties.*

This, 'tis true, is the Reading of the Generality of the Copies: but methinks 'tis a very peculiar Experiment, when the Blood and Spirits are dull'd and exhausted with Sport, to raise and recruit them by Sport, for *Sport* and *Game* are but two Words for the same thing. I have retriev'd the Pointing and Reading of the elder *Quarto* ['againe to inflame it'], which certainly gives us the Poet's Sense, that when the Blood is dull'd with the Exercise of Pleasure there should be proper Incentives on each side to raise it again, as the Charms of Beauty, Equality of Years, and Agreement of Manners and Disposition: which were wanting in *Othello* to rekindle *Desdemona's* Passion. (VII, 411)

*　　*　　*

[On *Othello*, 3.4.55 ff]
Because this Episode of the *Handkerchief* has been attack'd by Snarlers and Buffoon-Criticks I am tempted to subjoin an observation or two in Justification of our Author's Conduct. The Poet seems to have been aware of the Levity of such Judges as should account the giving away an Hankerchief too slight a Ground for Jealousy. He therefore obviates this, upon the very Moment of the Handkerchief being lost, by making *Iago* say:

> *Trifles, light as Air,*
> *Are, to the Jealous, Confirmations strong*
> *As Proofs of holy Writ.* [3.3.326 ff]

Besides this, let us see how finely the Poet has made his Handkerchief of Significancy and Importance. *Cinthio Giraldi*, from whom he has borrowed the Incident, only says that it was the *Moor's* Gift, upon his Wedding to *Desdemona*; that it was most curiously wrought after the *Moorish* Fashion, and very dear both to him and his Wife; *il quel Pannicello era lavorato alla* Moresca *sottilissimamente, et era carissimo alla Donna & parimente al Moro*. But our Author, who wrote in a superstitious Age (when *Philtres* were in Vogue for procuring Love, and *Amulets* for preserving it), makes his Handkerchief deriv'd from an *Inchantress*; *Magick* and *Mystery* are in its *Materials* and *Workmanship*; its *Qualities* and *Attributes* are solemnly laid down; and the Gift recommended to be cherish'd by its Owners on the most inducing Terms imaginable, *viz.* the making the Party amiable to her Husband, and the keeping his Affections steady. Such Circumstances, if I know anything of the Matter, are the very Soul and Essence of *Poetry*. *Fancy* here exerts its great *creating* Power, and adds a Dignity that surprizes to its Subject. After this, let us hear the coarse Pleasantries of Mr. *Rymer*. [Quotes the passage above, p. 51] . . . Whether this be from the Spirit of a *true Critic* or from the Licence of a *Railer* I may be too much prejudiced to determine, so leave it to every indifferent Judgment. (VII, 447–8)

*   *   *

[On *Othello*, 4.1.232 ff]

> *For, as I think, they do command him home,*
> *Deputing* Cassio *in his Government.*

Had Mr. *Rymer* intended, or known how to make a serious and sensible Critic on this Play, methinks here is a fair Open given for Enquiry and Animadversion. *Othello* is, as it were, but just arriv'd at *Cyprus* upon an Emergency of defending it against the *Turks*; the Senate could hardly yet have heard of the *Ottoman* Fleet being scatter'd by Tempest; and *Othello* is at once remanded home, without any Imputation suggested on his Conduct, or any Hint of his being employ'd in a more urgent Commission. 'Tis true, the Deputation of *Cassio* in his Room seems design'd to heighten the Moor's Resentment: but some probable Reason should have been assign'd and thrown in to the Audience for his being recall'd. As to what *Iago* says afterwards, that *Othello* is to go to *Mauritania*, This is only a Lye of his own Invention to carry a

Point with *Roderigo*.—It is in little Omissions of this Sort that *Shakespeare's* Indolence, or Neglect of Art, is frequently to be censur'd. (VII, 461)

★　　★　　★

[On *Othello*, 5.1.27 ff] Cas. *I'm maim'd for ever.*

None of the Editions hitherto have by any marginal Direction accounted for what *Cassio* here says, and likewise for what he afterwards says, *My Leg is cut in Two.* We are not to suppose he receiv'd this violent Hurt in fencing with his Opposite; but as *Roderigo* and He are engaged, *Iago* with a broad Sword hacks at him behind. In this Incident our Author precisely copies his *Italian* Novelist. . . . 'The Captain (*Cassio*) coming one Night from the House of a Harlot (with whom he entertain'd himself), it being very dark, the *Antient* with his Sword ready drawn attack'd him, and let drive a Blow at his Legs with Design to cut him down. And he happen'd to cut him across the right Thigh in such a manner that with the Wound the miserable Gentleman fell to Earth.' (VII, 477)

★　　★　　★

[On *Othello*, 5.2.7] *Put out the light, and then put out the light.*

The *Players*, in all the Companies wherever I have seen this Tragedy perform'd, commit an Absurdity here in making *Othello* put out the Candle, which 'tis evident never was the Poet's Intention. *Desdemona* is discover'd in her Bed, in the dark; and *Othello* enters the Chamber with a single Taper. If there were any other Lights burning in the Room, where would be the Drift of putting out *his*? If there were no others, and that he puts *his* out, how absurd is it for *Desdemona* in the Dark to talk of his *Eyes rowling*, and his *gnawing his nether Lip*?—This I conceive to have been the Poet's Meaning: *Othello*, struck in part with Remorse at the Murther he's going to do, thinks it best to do it in the Dark; this compunction of Nature—in the hurry and perturbation of thought, and those Remains of Tenderness still combating in his Bosom—strikes him into an instant Reflexion that if he puts out the light he can rekindle it, but if he once puts out the Light of *her Life* that will be extinguish'd for ever. While he is busied in this Contemplation he throws his Eyes towards her; and then, sooth'd with her beauteous Appearance, sets down the Light to go and kiss her. Upon this *Desdemona* wakes; and they continue in Discourse together till he stifles her. (VII, 481)

★　　★　　★

[On *Othello*, 5.2.102 ff]
> *Methinks, it should be now a huge* Eclipse
> *Of Sun and Moon; and that th'* affrighted *Globe*
> *Should* yawn *at Alteration.*—

Mr. *Rymer* is so merry, as he thinks, upon this Passage that I can't help transcribing his wonderful Criticism. [Quotes the passage above, p. 52]—Such are the ludicrous Criticisms of your *Wits*! But is the Word *Eclipse* absolutely restrain'd to that natural *Phaenomenon* which we understand by it? If *Othello* thought his Deed so horrid that the Sun and Moon ought to start from their Spheres at it, and cease to enlighten this under-Globe, might not such a Defection be call'd an *Eclipse* with a Vengeance? Well; but then, can a Body be *frighted* till it *yawn*? Here again *yawn* is restrain'd to the *Oscitation* of a Man ready to fall asleep, and for the Joak's sake must mean no other kind of *gaping*. This Gentleman must have known, sure, that *yawn* (as well as χανδν, from which it is deriv'd) was oftner apply'd to the *gaping* of the *Earth* than employ'd to signify the δόμα κεχηνòς—the *yawning*, for instance, of a Critick *gaping* after a feeble Jeast. But I am afraid Mr. *Rymer* was not too diligent a Reader of the *Scriptures*. Let the Poet account for the Prophanation, if he has committed any, but it is very obvious to me his Allusion is grounded on a certain *solemn* Circumstance when *Darkness* is said to have *cover'd the whole Face of the Land*, when *Rocks* were *rent*, and *Graves open'd*. (VII, 484–5)

*   *   *

A
TABLE
OF
The several EDITIONS
OF
SHAKESPEARE'S PLAYS

Collated by the EDITOR.

EDITIONS *of Authority*.

MR. *William Shakespeare*'s Comedies, Histories, and Tragedies. Publish'd according to the true Original Copies. *London*, Printed by *Isaac Jaggard* and *Ed. Blount*, 1623. (*Folio.*)

Mr. *William Shakespeare*'s Comedies, Histories and Tragedies. Publish'd according to the true Original Copies. The *Second* Impression. *London*. Printed by *Thomas Cotes*, for *Robert Allott*, and are to be sold at the Signe of the Black-Beare in Paul's-Churchyard, 1632. (*Folio.*)

[Theobald lists the following Quarto editions]
A Midsummer Night's Dream, 1600
A Midsummer Night's Dream, 1600 [= 1619][1]
The Merry Wives of Windsor, 1602
The Merry Wives of Windsor, 1619
Much Ado About Nothing, 1600
The Merchant of Venice, 1600
The Merchant of Venice, 1600 [= 1619]
The Troublesome Reign of John King of England, Parts One and Two,
    1591; also 1611 and 1622 reprints.
Richard II, 1598
Henry IV, Part One, 1599
Henry IV, Part One, 1622
Henry IV, Part Two, 1600
Henry V, 1608 [= 1619]
The Whole Contention betweene the two Famous Houses, Lancaster and
    Yorke . . . [1619][2]
The First Part of the contention . . ., 1600
The True Tragedie of Richard Duke of Yorke, 1600
Richard III, 1597; also 1598 and 1602 reprints
King Lear, 1608 [= 1619]
Titus Andronicus, 1611
Romeo and Juliet, 1597
Romeo and Juliet, 1599
Hamlet, 1604; also 1611 reprint.
Othello, 1622

EDITIONS *of middle Authority*

THE Works of Mr. *William Shakespeare*, &c. The Third Impression,
1664. (*Folio.*)
[Theobald lists the following Quarto editions]
The Merry Wives of Windsor, 1630
The Merchant of Venice, 1637
Love's Labour's Lost, 1631
The Taming of the Shrew, 1631
Richard II, 1634

---

[1] In 1619 William Jaggard published ten Shakespearian Quartos with false imprints.

[2] This is an inferior text of *Henry VI*, Parts Two and Three; the next two items represent earlier issues of each part.

Henry IV, Part I, 1639
Richard III, 1624; also 1629 and 1634 reprints.
King Lear, 1655
Romeo and Juliet, 1637
Hamlet, 1637
Othello, 1630

EDITIONS *of no Authority.*

THE Works of Mr. *William Shakespeare*, in Six Volumes, adorn'd with Cuts. Revis'd and corrected, with an Account of the Life and Writings of the Author, by N. ROWE Esq.; *London*, printed for *Jacob Tonson* within *Grays*-Inn Gate, next *Grays*-Inn Lane, 1709. (*Octavo*.)
   The Same. (in 12*mo*.) 1714.
   The Works of *Shakespeare*, in Six Volumes. Collated and corrected by the former Editions, by Mr. POPE. *London*, printed for *Jacob Tonson* in the Strand, 1725. (*Quarto*.)
   The same. (in 12*mo*.) 1728. (VII, 495–503).

83. William Warburton on Shakespeare

1733

From notes contributed to Theobald's edition: see No. 78 above.

William Warburton (1698–1779), who became Bishop of Gloucester in January 1760, was a voluminous controversialist in philosophy, theology and literary criticism. Although he had attacked Pope anonymously he published a vindication of Pope's *Essay on Man* in 1738–9 and subsequently became friendly with him. He wrote notes for book 4 of the *Dunciad* (1742) and after Pope's death issued an edition of the *Dunciad* in 1744, and of Pope's works in 1751.

[On *A Midsummer-Night's Dream*, 2.2.45–6]
> O take the Sense, Sweet, of my Innocence;
> Love takes the Meaning in Love's conference.

'Tis plain here that the Players, for the sake of the jingle between *Sense* and *Innocence*, transpos'd the two last Words in the two Lines, and so made unintelligible Nonsense of them. Let us adjust them, and This will be the Meaning. When she interpreted his Words to an evil Meaning he says *O, take the Sense of my Conference*: i.e. judge of my Meaning by the Drift of the other part of my Discourse, and let That interpret This. A very proper Rule to be always observ'd when we would judge of any one's Meaning, the Want of which is the most common Cause of Misinterpretation. He goes on and says *Love takes the Meaning, in Love's Innocence*, i.e. the Innocence of your Love may teach you to discover mine. Another very fine Sentiment. So that these two most beautiful Lines were perfectly disfigur'd in the aukward Transposition. (I, 101)

★   ★   ★

[On *Much Ado about Nothing*, 5.1.295–6] *The Watch heard them talk of one* Deformed; *they say, he wears a Key in his Ear, and a Lock hanging by it, and borrows money in God's Name, &c.*
There could not be a more agreeable Ridicule upon the *Fashion* than the Constable's Descant upon his own Blunder. One of the most fantastical Modes of that Time was the indulging a *favourite Lock* of Hair, and suffering it to grow much longer than all its Fellows; which they always brought *before* (as we do the Knots of a Tye-Wig), ty'd with Ribbands or Jewels. King *Charles* the 1st wore One of those favourite Locks, as his Historians take Notice, and as his Pictures by *Vandike* prove; and whoever has been conversant with the Faces of that Painter must have observ'd a great many drawn in that Fashion. In Lord CLARENDON's *History compleated* (a Book in *Octavo*), being a Collection of Heads engrav'd from the Paintings of *Vandike*, we may see this Mode in the Prints of the Duke of *Buckingham*, Earl of *Dorset*, Lord *Goring*, &c., all great Courtiers.—As to the *Key* in the *Ear* and the *Lock* hanging by it, there may be a Joak in the Ambiguity of the Terms. But whether we think that *Shakespeare* meant to ridicule the *Fashion* in the abstracted Sense; or whether he sneer'd at the Courtiers, the Parents of it, we shall find the Description equally satirical. The *Key* in the *Ear* might be suppos'd literally: for they wore Rings, Lockets, and Ribbands in a Hole made in the Ear; and sometimes

Rings one within another. But it might be likewise allegorically understood, to signify the great Readiness the Courtiers had in giving Ear to or going into new Follies or Fashions. As for *borrowing Money* and *never paying*, that is an old *Common Place* against the Court and Followers of Fashions. (I, 476)

* * *

[On *Love's Labour's Lost*, 4.2.26 ff; Warburton reads: 'which we taste and feel, *ingradare* . . .'.] —*And such barren Plants are set before us, that we thankful should be; which we taste, and feeling are for those Parts that do fructify in us more than he.*
If this be not a stubborn Piece of Nonsense I'll never venture to judge of common Sense. That Editors should take such Passages upon Content is, surely, surprising. The Words, 'tis plain, have been ridiculously and stupidly transpos'd and corrupted. The Emendation I have offer'd, I hope, restores the Author; at least, I am sure, it gives him Sense and Grammar: and answers extremely well to his Metaphors taken from *planting.*—*Ingradare*, with the *Italians*, signifies to rise higher and higher; *andare di grado in grado*, to make a Progression; and so at length come to *fructify*, as the Poet expresses it. (II, 127)

* * *

[On *Love's Labour's Lost*, 5.2.331]
'This is the flow'r that smiles on everyone'
What the Criticks call the *broken, disjointed,* and *mixt* Metaphor are very great Faults in Writing. But then observe this Rule (which I think is of general and constant Use in Writing, and very necessary to direct one's Judgment in this part of Style) that when a Metaphor is grown so common as to desert, as 'twere, the *figurative* and to be receiv'd into the *simple* or *common* Style, then what may be affirm'd of the *Substance* may be affirm'd of the *Image*, i.e. the *Metaphor* (for a *Metaphor* is an *Image*). To illustrate this Rule by the Example before us. A very complaisant, finical, over-gracious Person was in our Author's time so commonly call'd a *Flower* (or, as he elsewhere styles it, the *Pink* of *Courtesie*) that in common Talk, or in the lowest Style, it might be well used without continuing the Discourse in the *Terms* of that Metaphor, but turning them on the *Person* so denominated. And now I will give the Reason of my Rule. In the less-used Metaphors our Mind is so turn'd upon the Image which the Metaphor conveys that it expects that the Image should be for a little time continued by Terms

proper to keep it up. But if, for want of these Terms, the Image be no sooner presented but dropt, the Mind suffers a kind of Violence by being call'd off unexpectedly and suddenly from its Contemplation: and from hence the *broken, disjointed,* and *mixt* Metaphor shocks us. But when the Metaphor is worn and hackney'd by common Use, even the first Mention of it does not raise in the Mind the *Image* of it self but immediately presents the Idea of the *Substance.* And then to endeavour to continue the Image, and keep it up in the Mind by proper adapted Terms would, on the other hand, have as ill an Effect because the Mind is already gone off from the metaphorical Image to the Substance. *Grammatical* Critics would do well to consider what has been here said when they set upon amending *Greek* and *Roman* Writings. For the much-used, hackney'd Metaphors in those Languages must now be very imperfectly known; and consequently, without great Caution, they will be subject to act temerariously. (II, 163-4)

* * *

[Head-note to *King John*]
Of all the *English* Princes that *Shakespeare* has taken into Tragedy King *John* was the fittest to have made a Hero for a Tragedy on the antient Plan. *Henry IV, V* and *VIII* had Qualities great enough for it, but were generally fortunate. *Richard II,* and *Henry VI* (*sit Verbo Venia*) were at times little better than Poltrons; and *Richard III* was so black a Villain that the Antients would have thought him fitter for a Gibbet than a Stage. But *John* had that Turbulence and Grandeur of the Passions, that Inconstancy of Temper, that equal Mixture of Good and Ill, and that Series of Misfortunes consequent thereto, as might make him very fit for a Hero in a just Composition. (III, 167)

* * *

[On *King John,* 3.3.9]
　　—the fat Ribs of Peace
　　Must by the hungry now be fed upon.
This Word *now* seems a very idle Term here, and conveys no satisfactory Idea. An Antithesis and Opposition of Terms, so perpetual with our Author, requires
　　Must by the hungry War *be fed upon.*
War, demanding a large Expence, is very poetically said to be *hungry,* and to prey on the Wealth and *Fat of Peace.* (III, 209)

* * *

[On 1 Henry IV, 2.4.125]
I would, I were a Weaver; *I could sing* Psalms, &c.

This is plainly a Fling at the *Puritanical* Sectaries of our Author's Time. And I have observ'd This, that when the Men of Wit of his Age, and since, would characterize an ignorant sanctified Zealot they have generally made him a *Weaver* by Profession; which shews that Spirit was most remarkable among those Mechanicks, and I believe I can account for its so happening. It is very well known that when *Philip* the 2d was for stifling the Birth of the *Reformation* in *Flanders* and the *Low Countries* by an inquisitional Restraint, many of the Inhabitants forsook their Country and sought Refuge amongst their Neighbours. Those who came into *England* brought over with them the *Woollen Manufactory* and the *Principles* of *Calvin*, and at the same time taught us to weave Cloth and ravel out the Contexture of Church-Government. So that *Puritanism* (a Word which then took its Rise) and *Weaving* were generally profess'd by one and the same Artist. Their Love for *Psalmody* was what then did, and still does, distinguish the Disciples of *John Calvin*. (III, 379)

* * *

[On 2 Henry IV, 2.4.96] Cheater *call you him? I will bar no honest man my House, nor no* Cheater.

The Humour of This consists in the Hostess's Mistake in the Signification of the Word *Cheater*. For the Officer who was concern'd in collecting the *Escheats* due to the *Crown* was call'd by the common People the '*Cheater*, i.e. the *Escheater*. And This was the honest Man the good Woman dreamt of. But as the publick Officers of the Revenue were always had in *Odium* I make no Doubt but the Poet meant here likewise to ridicule the Officer. (III, 474–5)

* * *

[On 2 Henry IV, 5.4.19] *Thou thin Man in a* Censer!

A *Censer*, 'tis well known, is a Vessel for burning Incense, a Perfume-pan. But what is this *thin Man* in it? I have seen several antique *Censers* exactly in the Shape of our Dishes for the Table, which, being of Brass, were beat out exceeding thin. In the Middle of the Bottom was rais'd up in imboss'd Work, with the Hammer, the Figure of some *Saint* in a kind of barbarous hollow *Bass-relief*, the whole Diameter of the Bottom. The Saint was generally He to whom the Church in which the Censer was us'd was dedicated (tho' I once saw one with an *Adam* and *Eve* at the Bottom.) Now this *thin Beadle* is compar'd, for his

Substance, to one of these *thin* hammer'd *Figures*, with the same kind of Humour that *Pistol* in the *Merry Wives* calls *Slender* a *laten* Bilboe. (III, 536)

* * *

[On *2 Henry IV*, 5.5.54 ff]
—Know, the Grave doth gape
For Thee thrice wider than for other Men

I cannot help observing on this Passage as one of *Shakespeare's* grand Touches of Nature. The *King*, having shaken off his Vanities, in this Scene reproves his old Companion Sir *John* for his Follies with great Severity. He assumes the Air of a Preacher; bids him fall to his Prayers, and consider how ill grey Hairs become a Buffoon; bids him seek after Grace, *&c.* and leave gourmandizing. But that Word, unluckily presenting him with a pleasant Idea, he can't forbear pursuing it in these Words, *—Know, the Grave doth gape for thee thrice wider, &c.* and is just falling back into *Hal* by an humourous Allusion to *Falstaff's* Bulk but He perceives it at once, is afraid Sir *John* should take the Advantage of it, so checks both himself and the Knight with

Reply not to me with a Fool-born jest;

and resumes the Thread of his Discourse, and moralizes on to the End of the Chapter. This, I think, is copying Nature with great Exactness, by shewing how apt Men are to fall back into old Customs when the Change is not made by degrees, as the Habit itself was, but determined of all at once, on the Motives of Honour, Interest, or Reason. And Nothing is more disgusting than that vicious Practice of *Dramatick Poets* of violating the *Unity of Character*, and giving the same Personage different Aims, Pursuits, Appetites, and Passions at the latter End of the Piece from what he set out with at the Beginning; that Rule of *Horace's* being much more general than He makes it:

Servetur *ad* imum
Qualis ab incœpto *processerit,* & sibi constet.[1] (III, 539)

* * *

[On *Henry V*, 4.1.300]
Since that my Penitence comes after all,
Imploring pardon.

We must observe that *Henry IV* had committed an Injustice, of which he and his *Son* reap'd the Fruits. But Justice and right Reason tell us

---

[1] Horace, *A.P.*, 126 f: 'If you fashion a fresh character, have it kept to the end even as it came forth at the first, and have it self-consistent.'

that they who share the Profits of Iniquity shall share likewise in the Punishment. Scripture again tells us that when Men have sinn'd the Grace of God gives frequent Invitations to Repentance, which in Scripture language are styled *Calls*. These, if they have been carelessly dallied with and neglected are at length irrevocably withdrawn, and then Repentance comes too late. This, I hope, will sufficiently vouch for my Emendation, and explain what the Poet would make the King say. (IV, 70–1)

*   *   *

[On *King Lear*, 2.4.189 f]
>   — *if your sweet sway*
>   Allow *Obedience*

Could any Man in his Senses, and *Lear* has 'em yet, make it a Question whether Heaven *allow'd* Obedience? Undoubtedly, the Poet wrote— Hallow *Obedience*,—i.e. if by your Ordinances you hold and pronounce it *sanctified*, and punish the Violators of it as sacrilegious Persons. (V, 150)

*   *   *

[On *King Lear*, 4.2.34] *She that herself will* shiver, *and disbranch,*
Shiver in this place should bear the Sense of *disbranch*; whereas it means to shake, to fly a-pieces into Splinters; in which Sense he afterwards uses the Word in this Act:
>   *Thou'd'st* shiver'd *like an Egg* [4.6.51]

So that we may be assured, he would not have used the Word in so contrary and false a Sense here, especially when there is a proper Word to express the Sense of *disbranching* so near this in Sound, and which eh uses in other places, and that is *sliver*: which, without doubt, is the true Reading here. So in *Macbeth*;
>   —*and Slips of Yew,*
>   Sliver'd *in the Moon's eclipse*; [4.1.28]

And, again, in *Hamlet*;
>   *There on the pendant Boughs, her Coronet Weeds*
>   *Clamb'ring to hang, an envious* Sliver *broke*; [4.7.174]
>   (V, 182)

*   *   *

[On *Macbeth*, 2.3.8 ff]
Here's an Equivocator—who committed Treason enough for God's sake, &c.
This Sarcasm is levell'd at the Jesuits, who were so mischievous in the

535

Reigns of Q. *Elizabeth* and K. *James* 1st and who then first broach'd
that damnable Doctrine. (V, 413)

* * *

[On *Macbeth*, 2.3.12]

Here's an English *Taylor come hither for stealing out of a* French *hose:*
The Archness of this Joak consists in this, that a *French* Hose being so
very short and strait a Taylor must be a perfect Master of his Art who
could steal any thing out of it. As to the Nature of the *French* hose, we
have seen that in *Henry VIII* our Poet calls them *short-bolster'd Breeches.*
(V, 413)

* * *

[On *Julius Caesar*, 1.2.87] *And I will look on* both *indifferently;*
What a Contradiction to this are the Lines immediately succeeding!
If He lov'd Honour more than he fear'd Death, how could they be
both indifferent to him? Honour thus is but in equal Balance to Death,
which is not speaking at all like *Brutus*: for in a Soldier of any ordinary
Pretension it should always *preponderate*. We must certainly read,
          And I will look on Death *indifferently.*
What occasion'd the Corruption, I presume, was the Transcribers
imagining the Adverb *indifferently* must be applied to Two things
oppos'd. But the Use of the Word does not demand it; nor does
Shakespeare always apply it so. In the present Passage it signifies
neglectingly, without *Fear* or *Concern*. And so *Casca* afterwards, again
in this Act, employs it.
          And Dangers are to me indifferent [1.3.115]
i.e. I weigh them not; am not deterr'd on the Score of Danger. (VI,
130)

* * *

[On *Julius Caesar*, 5.1.100] Bru. *Ev'n by the Rule*
This Speech from *Plutarch* our *Shakespeare* has extremely soften'd in all
the offensive parts of it, as any one may see who consults the Original,
and, with no less Caution, has omitted his famous Exclamation against
Virtue: O Virtue! *I have worship'd Thee as a real Good; but find thee only
an unsubstantial Name.* His great Judgment in this is very remarkable,
on two Accounts. First, in his Caution not to give Offence to a moral
Audience; and Secondly, as he has hereby avoided a Fault in drawing
his Hero's Character. For to have had *Brutus* gone off the Stage in the
manner *Plutarch* represents it would have suppress'd all that Pity
(especially in a Christian Audience) which it was the Poet's Business

to raise. So that as *Shakespeare* has manag'd this Character he is as perfect a one for the Stage as *Oedipus*, which the Criticks so much admire. (VI, 198)

* * *

[On *Antony and Cleopatra*, 1.1.11 ff]

A *Pillar* turn'd into a *Fool?* This is as odd a Transformation as any in all *Ovid!* But I am much inclin'd to think that *Shakespeare* wrote,

> The triple *Pillar* of the *World* transform'd
> Into a *Strumpet's* Stool.

Alluding to the common Custom of Strumpets sitting on the Laps of their Lovers. By this Correction the Metaphor is admirably well preserv'd (for both Stool and Pillar are Things for Support), and the Contrast in this Image is beautiful. The Supporter of the World turn'd to the Supporter of a Strumpet. And if we may suppose *Shakespeare* had Regard, in the Use of this Word, to the Etymology it will add a Quaintness to the Thought not unlike his Way, nor that of the Time he liv'd in; for *Stool* is deriv'd from Στύλθ, *Columna*, the *Base* or *Pedestal* of a *Pillar* having always been used for a *Seat* where it was broad enough for that Purpose. (VI, 212)

* * *

[On *Troilus and Cressida*, 1.2.4 f]

> —whose Patience
> Is as a Virtue fix'd,

What's the Meaning of *Hector's* Patience being fix'd *as a virtue?* Is not Patience a Virtue? What Room then for the Similitude? The Poet certainly wrote, as I have conjecturally reform'd the Text[1]; and this is giving a fine Character of it to say *His Patience is as stedfast as the Virtue of* Patience *itself;* or the *Goddess* so call'd: for the Poets have always personaliz'd the *Quality.* So we find *Troilus* a little before saying;

> Patience herself, *what* Goddess *ere she be,*
> Doth lesser blench at Sufferance than I do. [1.1.26 f] (VII, 12)

* * *

[On *Hamlet*, 1.3.107 ff]

> Tender your self more dearly;
> Or (not to crack the Wind of the poor Phrase)
> Wronging it thus, you'll tender me a Fool.

The *Parenthesis* is clos'd at the wrong place, and we must make likewise a slight Correction in the last Verse. *Polonius* is racking and playing on

---

[1] Warburton reads 'Is as *the* Virtue fix'd'.

the Word *Tender*, till he thinks proper to correct himself for the Licence; and then he would say '— not farther to crack the Wind of the Phrase by *twisting* and *contorting* it, as I have done'; &c. (VII, 244-5).

*　　*　　*

[On *Hamlet*, 2.2.86 ff] *My Liege, and Madam, to expostulate.*
There seem to me in this Speech most remarkable Strokes of Humour. I never read it without Astonishment at the Author's admirable Art of preserving the Unity of Character. It is so just a Satire on impertinent Oratory, especially of that then in Vogue—which was of the formal Cut, and proceeded by Definition, Division, and Subdivision—that I think every Body must be charm'd with it. Then, as to the *Jingles* and *Play* on Words, let us but look into the Sermons of Dr. *Donne* (the wittiest Man of that Age) and we shall find them full of this Vein: only, there they are to be admired, here to be laugh'd at. Then, with what Art is *Polonius* made to pride himself in his Wit:

A foolish Figure. —But, farewel it.

Again, how finely is he sneering the formal Oratory in Fashion when he makes this Reflection on *Hamlet's* Raving.

Tho this be Madness, *yet there's* Method *in it.*

As if Method in a Discourse (which the Wits of that Age thought the most essential part of good Writing) would make Amends for the Madness of it. This in the Mouth of *Polonius* is exceeding satirical. Tho' it was Madness, yet he could comfort himself with the Reflection that at least it was Method. (VII, 267)

*　　*　　*

[On *Hamlet*, 4.5.128 ff] *To Hell, allegiance! Vows, to the blackest Devil!*
Laertes is a good Character, but he is here in actual Rebellion. Lest, therefore, this Character should seem to sanctify Rebellion, instead of putting into his Mouth a reasonable Defence of his Proceedings (such as the Right the Subject has of shaking off Oppression, the Usurpation, and the Tyranny of the King, &c.) *Shakespeare* gives him Nothing but absurd and blasphemous Sentiments, such as tend only to inspire the Audience with Horror at the Action. This Conduct is exceeding nice. Where, in his *Plays*, a Circumstance of Rebellion is founded on History, or the Agents of it infamous in their Characters, there was no Danger in the Representation. But as here, where the Circumstance is fictitious, and the Agent honourable, he could not be too cautious. For the Jealousie of the Two Reigns he wrote in would not dispense with less Exactness. (VII, 332)

A Select Bibliography of
Shakespeare Criticism 1693–1733

Note. Items which cover a wider range, including this period, which were listed in Vol. 1 are not repeated here.

(A) COLLECTIONS OF CRITICISM

SMITH, D. N. (ed.) *Eighteenth Century Essays on Shakespeare* (Glasgow, 1903; Oxford, 1963: with a few corrections, and some notes by F. P. Wilson). One of the most valuable collections, albeit biased heavily in favour of Pope and Dryden and against Theobald.

DURHAM, W. H. (ed.) *Critical Essays of the Eighteenth Century* (New Haven, 1915).

ELLEDGE, E. S. (ed.) *Eighteenth-Century Critical Essays* (New York, 1961), 2 vols.

(B) INDIVIDUAL CRITICS: MODERN EDITIONS

HOOKER, E. N. (ed.), *The Critical Works of John Dennis* (Baltimore, 1939), 2 vols.

The *Spectator*, ed. D. F. Bond (Oxford, 1965), 5 vols.

(C) HISTORIES OF LITERARY CRITICISM

SMITH, D. N., *Shakespeare in the Eighteenth Century* (Oxford, 1928).

ROBINSON, H. S., *English Shakespearian Criticism in the Eighteenth Century* (New York, 1932).

(D) TEXTUAL STUDIES

MCKERROW, R. B., 'The Treatment of Shakespeare's Text by his Earlier Editors, 1706–1768', British Academy Shakespeare Lecture for 1933, repr. in *Studies in Shakespeare*, ed. P. Alexander (1964).

FORD, H. L., *Shakespeare, 1700–1740. A Collation of the Editions and Separate Plays* . . . (Oxford, 1935).

LOUNSBURY, T. R., *The First Editors of Shakespeare (Pope and Theobald)* (1906).

JONES, R. F., *Lewis Theobald. His Contribution to English Scholarship, With Some Unpublished Letters* (New York, 1919).

ISAACS, J., 'Shakespearian Scholarship', in *A Companion to Shakespeare Studies*, ed. H. Granville-Barker and G. B. Harrison (Cambridge, 1934).

(E) THEATRICAL HISTORY, ADAPTATIONS

The London Stage, 1660–1800. Part 2, 1700–1729, ed. E. L. Avery (Carbondale, Ill., 1960), 2 vols.

The London Stage, 1660–1800. Part 3, 1729–1747, ed. A. H. Scouten (1961), 2 vols.

HOGAN, C. B., *Shakespeare in the Theatre, 1701–1800* (Oxford, 1952), 2 vols.

BRANAM, G. C., *Eighteenth Century Adaptations of Shakespearian Tragedy* (Berkeley, Calif., 1956).

GRAY, C. H., *Theatrical Criticism in London to 1795* (New York, 1931, 1964).

SPRAGUE, A. C., *Shakespeare and the Actors* (Cambridge, Mass., 1940).

STONE, G. W., 'Shakespeare in the Periodicals, 1700–40', *Shakespeare Quarterly*, II (1951) and III (1952).

Index

The Index is arranged in three parts: I. Shakespeare's works; II. Shakespearian characters; III. General index. Adaptations are indexed under the adapter's name, in III below. References to individual characters are not repeated under the relevant plays.

I SHAKESPEARE'S WORKS

541

II SHAKESPEARIAN CHARACTERS

III GENERAL INDEX

Flecknoe, Richard, 67, 69
Fletcher, John, 3, 62, 94, 184, 230, 263, 266, 299, 309, 310, 408, 448; *Rollo Duke of Normandy*, 369

Galen, 434
Gammer Gurton's Needle, 235
Garrick, David, 12
Garth, Sir Samuel, 421
Gesner, Konrad von, 514
Gildon, Charles, 1–13 *passim*, 19, 63–85, 93, 281, 322–7, 369–72, 403, 419, 420, 421f, 490, 502; *Measure for Measure, or Beauty the Best Advocate*, 13, 130–44, 145; Shakespeare's life and works, 216–62
Graham, Walter, 469
Granville, George, Baron Lansdowne, 14, 161; *The Jew of Venice*, 13, 149–60, 196, 243
Gray, Charles Harold, 20
Greene, Robert, 501

Hales, John, 66f, 193, 217
Hanmer, Sir Thomas, 18
Harsenet, Samuel, 507f
Harte, Walter, 10
Heliodorus, 500
Heminge, John, 406, 411, 413, 454, 456
Heraclitus, 11
Heywood, Thomas, 218n, 254
Higgons, Bevill, Prologue to Granville's *The Jew of Venice*, 150f
Hill, Aaron, 327, 422; *King Henry V, Or, The Conquest of France by the English*, 14, 373–97, 398ff
Holinshed, Raphael, 505, 512
Holland, Philemon, 287n, 356
Homer, 65, 66, 77, 79, 82, 84, 177, 180, 217, 219, 224, 230, 250, 279, 281, 291, 353, 354, 366, 403, 482, 506
Hooker, Edward Niles, 5, 20
Horace, 26, 27, 28, 29, 69, 70, 74, 77, 81, 177, 191, 207, 217, 235n, 267n, 268n, 277, 291, 293, 306, 322, 353n, 367, 371, 372, 422, 446, 447,

462, 465, 470, 479, 480n, 502, 504n, 534n
Howard, James, 189
Hughes, John, 8, 9, 299–302

Jaggard, Isaac, 527, 528n
Johnson, Samuel, 1, 3, 9, 17
Jones, Richard Foster, 17
Jonson, Benjamin, 8, 23, 62, 63, 66, 88, 94, 184, 193f, 218, 263, 266, 291, 292, 354, 355, 367, 370, 406, 407, 408, 409f, 413, 448, 450, 451, 454, 456, 469, 470, 471, 482, 483, 497
Jortin, John, 471
Juvenal, 523

Kelly, John, 469
Killigrew the elder, Thomas, 188, 312
Killigrew the younger, Thomas, 14, 21, 312–15
Kneller, Sir Godfrey, 349

Langbaine, Gerard, 194n
La Rochefoucauld, François, duc de, 235
Lavater, Johann Kaspar, 230
Le Bossu, René, 490
Lebrun, Charles, 220f
Lee, Nathaniel, 447; *Lucius Junius Brutus*, 8; *Oedipus*, 68, 90, 224, 273; *The Rival Queens; or The Death of Alexander the Great*, 90, 185, 273; *Theodosius*, 273
Levin, William, 9, 12, 469–71
Livius Andronicus, 245
Livy, 286, 287
Locke, John, 189
Locrine, 413
Lollius, 250, 519
The London Prodigal, 413
The London Stage, 23
Lounsbury, Thomas Raynesford, 21
Lucan, 10
Lucian, 254, 352
Lucilius, 372
Lucius Florus, 517
Luther, Martin, 179

THE CRITICAL HERITAGE SERIES

GENERAL EDITOR: B. C. SOUTHAM

Continued